The Battles That Made
Abraham Lincoln

How Lincoln Mastered his Enemies to
Win the Civil War, Free the Slaves,
and Preserve the Union

Larry Tagg

SB

Savas Beatie
California

First edition, first printing

Tagg, Larry.
The Battles That Made Abraham Lincoln: How Lincoln Mastered his Enemies to Win the Civil War, Free the Slaves, and Preserve the Union / Larry Tagg. — 1st ed.
    p. cm.
Includes bibliographical references and index.
ISBN 978-1-61121-126-9
1. Lincoln, Abraham, 1809-1865. 2. Lincoln, Abraham, 1809-1865—Public opinion. 3. United States—Politics and government—1861-1865. 4. Public opinion—United States. 5. Presidents—United States—Biography. I. Title.
    E457.15.T15 2012
    973.7092—dc23
    2012039015

Previously published in hardcover as *The Unpopular Mr. Lincoln: The Story of America's Most Reviled President*, by Larry Tagg (ISBN: 978-1-932714-61-6 / 2009)

SB

Savas Beatie LLC
989 Governor Drive, Suite 102
P.O. Box 4527
El Dorado Hills, CA 95762
Phone: 916-941-6896
(E-mail) sales@savasbeatie.com

Savas Beatie titles are available at special discounts for bulk purchases in the United States by corporations, institutions, and other organizations. For more details, contact Savas Beatie Special Sales, P.O. Box 4527, El Dorado Hills, CA 95762, or you may e-mail us directly at sales@savasbeatie.com, or jump over to our informative website at www. savasbeatie.com for additional information.

To my dear wife Lori Jablonski
for her constant love and encouragement.

"To say that he is ugly is nothing, to add that his figure is grotesque is to convey no adequate impression."

— Edward Dicey, 1862

Contents

Contents (continued)

Illustrations are found throughout the book

Introduction to New Edition

It is the widely-held conviction of every election year that modern political campaigning is a creeping poison, more negative than ever. "Politics was never so mean!" is the common cry. The corrective for this view is a study of the campaigns against Abraham Lincoln.

From the moment of his election, Lincoln had to contend with the people's distrust of any authority. The Presidency, especially, was held in contempt by a public disgusted over the ravages of the Spoils System and rampant political corruption. The Founding Fathers—Washington, Adams, Jefferson, Madison, and Monroe—had given way to mediocrities—Taylor, Fillmore, Pierce, and Buchanan. For many, this recent string of watery presidents seemed to have its bitter culmination in "The Railsplitter," the anonymous man from the prairie who had never administrated anything larger than a two-person law office.

When he arrived in Washington, as a result of his awkward manners and his complete inattention to social convention and outward appearance, Lincoln had to battle the common prejudice concerning how a great man should look, act, and talk. Particularly among the elite, there was a shaking of heads after meeting Lincoln for the first time. The high-bred fastidious men of the East were aghast: How could anyone so ungentlemanly possibly be a statesman?

Even before he took office, president-elect Lincoln was at odds with those who regarded the states as sovereign powers, men who believed that every state had the right to dissolve the Union when the result of a national canvass did not serve its interests. Lincoln refused to concede this right, and maintained his conviction that the seceded states were not a separate nation but remained a part of the United States. And the war came.

From the war's outset, Lincoln became the foe of almost every member of Congress. That institution had enjoyed preeminence in government since the first days of the American democratic experiment, and Lincoln toppled it from its position of unrivaled power. From the start of the war, Lincoln made policy without consulting the lawmakers. The Union, with a third of its citizens in rebellion, faced an unprecedented threat, and to defend it Lincoln brandished emergency powers—some granted by the Constitution and some not. His most far-reaching policy, the freeing of the slaves, was made by proclamation—that is, by personal fiat—without Congressional approval. Two months after the Emancipation Proclamation, at the war's midpoint, only two congressmen could be counted as pro-Lincoln.

Lincoln battled during the entire war with the Democrats in the North—the "conservatives" of the time—who wanted to retain slavery and return the country to its prewar condition. The Democrats had held sway since Jefferson, and Lincoln's election to the presidency at the head of a regional party had interrupted their firm hold on power. As Lincoln's outrages against the precedents of the past continued, as casualties mounted in the Civil War and sorrow was piled on sorrow, Democrats' voices grew increasingly strident: He was the "despot" Lincoln, the "tyrant" whose insistence on war and emancipation would destroy their America.

Lincoln, however, did not need to look as far as the rival party for enemies. He was wounded even more deeply by those closest to him, the Radical Republicans—the "progressives" of the time, and the strongest wing of his own party—who were as much convinced of Lincoln's malignity as the conservative Democrats. Lincoln, the man in the middle, the man who waited, the man who heard all sides, could never be one of them. They reviled Lincoln as one whose heart was not in the holy work of freeing the slaves, and they sharpened their knives for him, even at the same time the Democrats were loudest in their woe.

Lincoln, too, fought his generals for most of the war. Some of them, like John Charles Fremont, were radical Republicans; some, like George McClellan, were conservative Democrats. All resented his interference. Lincoln's battle with the men in epaulettes would not turn decisively until the summer of 1864, when Lincoln placed Ulysses S. Grant at the head of the army in the East and William Sherman in the West.

Lincoln's response to his political enemies in the press, the Democratic newspaper editors, was unapologetic and fierce: He stopped their presses and put them in jail. They replied with acid-dipped pens, and daily published the most brutal vitriol in the history of American public discourse, even calling for his assassination.

The domestic battles in the North could not be fought by a man unfamiliar with, or squeamish about, the blunt use of political power. To preserve the nation Lincoln needed to be, and was, the ultimate politician; that is, a master of the art of the possible. His battles with his public foes were fought with hard-edged political weapons in a way that was possible only in mid-nineteenth century America in the rough-and-tumble heyday of bare-knuckled politics.

Larry Tagg
October 2012

Comic News, November 26, 1864

THE VAMPIRE.

Abe.—"COLUMBIA, THOU ART MINE; WITH THY BLOOD I WILL RENEW MY LEASE OF LIFE—AH! AH!"

Introduction

The Abraham Lincoln most Americans know today is a marble man, a mythic icon enshrined in a magnificent twenty-foot tall statue that looks down on visitors from beneath the dome of his Memorial, a Greek temple modeled after the Temple of Zeus.

One shibboleth of the Lincoln myth is the sentimental notion that he was the idol of the common people during his presidency. Unfortunately, the evidence for Lincoln's popular appeal is missing. Rather, he suffered from an almost unbroken series of failures to win the favor of the press, the public, and the nation's leading men.

The reasons for his unpopularity started with the wretched plight of the presidency itself as he took it up. Lincoln was inaugurated in an era when the presidency was tarnished by the string of poor presidents who preceded him, at a time when all authority was little regarded. The future of democratic government was itself in doubt, even by Americans. The torsions of the slavery debate and attacks by the rabid press routinely destroyed the reputations of public men.

Lincoln appeared on this stormy national scene virtually unknown except as a caricature, the Railsplitter. The people of the South saw the anonymous Illinoisan as a usurper, the illegitimate product of an electoral system that had betrayed the vision of the Founding Fathers. The people of the North feared the political machinery had lifted up a man woefully unequal to the national crisis. From his election by an absurdly low 40% of the electorate—lower than almost every *loser* of a presidential election in every two-party race in American history—his approval dropped to 25% by the time he took office, as state after Southern state showed its rejection of his legitimacy by leaving the Union, and nervous Northerners backed away from his uncompromising opposition to slavery's expansion. When he arrived in Washington in late February of 1861, he did so on a secret night train to avoid assassination; the scathing reaction of the national press to his undignified entrance mark the days before his inaugural as the historic low point of American presidential prestige.

From this poor start, Lincoln sank lower in the eyes of Washington leaders when they beheld at first hand his ungrammatical language, his Western diction, his uncouth ways, his awkward gait and posture, and his penchant for coarse humor. A certain manner was expected of earnest statesmen, and Lincoln disappointed those expectations completely. It was hard for men of the East to comprehend that such a man, with such vulgar habits, could ever be great.

His first proclamation six weeks after his inauguration, in which he called for 75,000 volunteers to suppress the uprising signaled by the firing on Fort Sumter, precipitated the loss of Virginia, Tennessee, North Carolina, and Arkansas, doubling the size and the population of the enemy Confederacy. During the first eighteen months of the Civil War that followed, his hesitant performance seemed to confirm the opinion of the many who saw him as an untutored rustic, hopelessly unequal to his task. As the dead piled up in unimaginable numbers and sorrow was added to sorrow, a nation that had known little of sacrifice blamed Lincoln for a dithering mismanagement of the war effort.

When, in September of 1862, he announced his intention to issue an Emancipation Proclamation one hundred days later, the Northern electorate showed its displeasure by rebuking him in a mid-term election so disastrous that a friend wrote, "I could not conceive it possible for Lincoln to successfully administer the government and prosecute the war with the six most important loyal States declaring against him at the polls."

When the issuance of the Emancipation Proclamation on January 1, 1863, resulted in the freedom of not one slave, its lack of efficacy discouraged the abolitionists at the same time its revolutionary spirit threatened to take the intensely Negrophobic states of the Old Northwest out of the Union. The revolt of the North's Lincoln-haters in the wake of the Emancipation Proclamation and the Federal Draft Law in March 1863 had its fiery culmination in the riot in New York City the following July, the largest civil insurrection in American history apart from the Civil War itself.

By 1864, Lincoln was so little regarded that the strongest elements in his own party tried to deny him another term. He engineered his renomination by stacking the Republican convention with appointees, a tactic possible only in the heyday of the Spoils System. As late as two months before the 1864 election, even Republican leaders wrote him off as a beaten man, and took steps to nominate a better candidate. Only by the combination of Democratic bungling and the miracle of last-minute Union victories on the battlefield was Lincoln reelected. As Ohio Republican Lewis D. Campbell observed, "Nothing but the undying attachment of our people to the Union has saved us from terrible disaster. Mr. Lincoln's popularity had nothing to do with it." Anti-Lincoln feelings hardened in the days after his reelection, as bitter Democrats and vanquished Southerners looked with dread on the prospect of another four years under "the despot Lincoln," a period that climaxed with Lincoln's assassination less than a week after the surrender of Lee's army.

The most sensational aspect of the criticism Lincoln endured was the unsurpassed venom of it. The press was unashamedly partisan, and in a historical era dominated by Democrats, most newspapers were Democratic, duty-bound to wound the Republican leader. There was much to criticize. During the Civil War's four years of unprecedented danger to the Union, they called Lincoln a "bloody tyrant" and a "dictator" for stretching the rules of the Constitution to allow arbitrary arrests, the suspension of *habeas corpus*, and the suppression of newspapers sympathetic to the Confederacy. Lincoln's greatest outrage, however, was that he took his place so resolutely at the center of American opinion during the bitterest time in the nation's history. As a man of caution and moderation, he was blasted from all sides by a Northern people whom the heat of battle had driven to political extremes.

If one considers politics as the art of the possible, Lincoln was the consummate politician. What he accomplished is all the more remarkable considering how limited his possibilities were as a result of his lack of esteem. The depth of Lincoln's travail is much of what ennobles him. To have a fuller knowledge of the bitterness of the opposition Lincoln faced is, in my view, necessary to a fuller appreciation of this most intriguing of presidents, whose humanity is, if anything, trivialized by being so bronzed over. While researching my book, I have been amazed that the story of Lincoln's unpopularity has remained so long untold at full length. It is better that it be so told, in order that we may better understand the man.

Larry Tagg
January 2009

Acknowledgments

Many people played roles large and small in helping me research this book. One man in particular was Harold Holzer, one of the world's leading Lincoln scholars. Mr. Holzer was generous with his time in sharing with me knowledge of Lincoln's humor and directing my searches in the large Lincoln bibliography. I am forever in his debt.

I am also deeply indebted to Captain Rob Ayer of the United States Coast Guard Academy for his superb developmental editing of my manuscript, his keen insights, and his confidence in my work.

It has been wonderful to work with my publisher Savas Beatie LLC. Managing Director Theodore P. Savas saw value in my manuscript early in its development. He provided constant support, demonstrated a painstaking attention to detail, and offered invaluable advice coupled with his tireless energy to help produce the book you are now reading. I had worked with Ted more than a decade ago on *The Generals of Gettysburg,* and it was good to work with him again. I am also indebted to Marketing Director Sarah Keeney for her continuing help in getting the word out about the book. Sarah understands marketing and publicity, and is always available for a phone call or email exchange. Veronica Kane and Tammy Hall have been working hard with Sarah to coordinate a book signing and speaking tour, and use all the new Internet technologies now available to authors to help promote books like mine. I am in very good hands.

I also owe a great debt to David Van Dusen for his technical expertise and artistic skill in creating the book's dust jacket, its accompanying website at www.larrytagg.com, and for producing the book trailer.

Hearty thanks are also due Brent Bourgeois and my wife Lori Jablonski for reading the manuscript and offering their invaluable comments during its long development.

Part One

Lincoln's Entrance

"What Brought Him Here So Suddenly?"

Chapter 1

Lincoln Comes to Washington

"We feel humiliated to the last degree by it."

On February 23, 1861, nine days before his inauguration, President-elect Abraham Lincoln sneaked into Washington on a secret night train, disguised in a soft felt hat, muffler, and short bobtail overcoat. Detective Allan Pinkerton, who traveled with him, provided the affair with a cloak-and-dagger coda when he telegraphed Lincoln's friends: "Plums arrived here with Nuts this morning—all right."

Lincoln had departed his home in Springfield, Illinois, twelve days earlier for a train tour across the northern states to Washington. The tour was a stately ceremonial procession, intended to introduce the new President-elect to the people. Bonfires, parades, cannon salutes, and noisy crowds greeted Lincoln's train at every stop. All the major cities through which he would pass had formally invited him to speak, except the last—no welcome had come from Baltimore.

Maryland's northern border marked the point where Lincoln would enter a slave state for the first time. Here he would go from a loyal region to one seething with rebellion. Baltimore's sullen silence was especially alarming since there the presidential cars would have to stop, uncouple, and be drawn by horses across a mile of city streets before being put back on the rails to Washington. The city's nickname was "Mobtown." Its political thugs, the "Blood Tubs" and "Plug Uglies," were notorious as the most vicious in the entire country, and if they rushed the train they were not likely to be stopped by police whose marshal, George P. Kane, was an open secessionist. A military escort couldn't be trusted, either—the local militia companies were drilling nightly for the moment when they would seize the city buildings and hoist the Confederate flag.

On February 21, two days before Lincoln's scheduled passage through Baltimore, the presidential train reached Philadelphia. That evening, as Lincoln shook hands with the crowd that packed the parlor of the Continental Hotel, his secretary tapped him on the shoulder and motioned him into a back room.

There he learned that Detective Pinkerton, working for the railroad whose line would take him to Washington, had uncovered a plot to assassinate him on his way through Baltimore. That same night, another messenger brought word that Charles Stone, the head of the loyal Washington militia, who had placed his own detectives in Baltimore, had also discovered a plot "for the destruction of Mr. Lincoln during his passage through the city." When Lincoln reached his hotel in the Pennsylvania capital of Harrisburg the next day, friends pleaded with him to dodge the Baltimore threat.

Lincoln was reluctant. "What would the nation think of its President stealing into its capital like a thief in the night?" he groaned. The nation, however, was at such a hair trigger that General-in-Chief Winfield Scott had warned, "a dog fight now might cause the gutters to run with blood." The stakes were too great for the risk to be ignored, and Lincoln's friends persuaded him to change his schedule and pass incognito on a secret midnight special through Baltimore.

Two hundred men, secretly armed and organized, were detailed to guard railway bridges and crossings along the route. To camouflage their purpose, they went to work whitewashing the bridges, which they did continuously for hours—five, six, seven coats. Telegraph wires were cut along the route to intercept hostile messages and maintain the illusion that Lincoln was remaining overnight in Pennsylvania.

After dark, Lincoln was smuggled out of his Harrisburg hotel in a closed, horse-drawn coach that sped to the railway depot by a winding route, and soon he was on a train plunging through the dark toward Philadelphia. There, Detective Pinkerton and the country's first female detective, Kate Warne, had arranged to hold the eleven o'clock train to Washington until Lincoln arrived, on the pretense of delivering an important package to the conductor, who was told the package had to be delivered to Washington by morning. For this last leg of the journey, Warne had reserved a seat for an invalid in the last car of the train.

The "important package," actually a bundle of old newspapers, was delivered to the unsuspecting conductor, and "the invalid"—Lincoln—was secreted into a berth in the rear car at the same time. Pinkerton gave the new passenger's ticket to the conductor, explaining that Warne's invalid friend must not be disturbed. Pinkerton rode most of the way on the rear platform of the train, watching for signals flashed by the guards at the bridges and crossings as they sped by. A second bodyguard, Lincoln's friend Ward Hill Lamon, sat inside with the contraband President-elect, his pockets bristling with two pistols, two small derringers, and two bowie knives. The trip went quietly, and Lincoln stepped onto the platform in Washington just before dawn, embarrassed by his undignified spy-thriller entry into the capital. He was greeted by a lone congressman and whisked to a closely guarded reception at Willard's Hotel.

Outside the small circle who greeted him at Willard's, the first to find out about Lincoln's secret disappearance were the ten thousand drawn up at Calvert Station in Baltimore later that day waiting to get a look at the new President-elect and hoot at him. An early train was mistaken for Lincoln's, and according to the report in the Baltimore *Sun*, "as soon as the train stopped, the crowd leaped upon the platforms, and mounted to the tops of the cars like so many monkeys, until like a hive of bees they swarmed upon them, shouting, hallooing and making all manner of noises."

After the train pulled out, the restless crowd swelled steadily until the real presidential cars finally pulled up. Then, when Mrs. Lincoln and the children stepped out alone, the crowd erupted. "The moment the train arrived, supposing Lincoln was aboard, the most terrific cheers ever heard were sent up, three for the Southern Confederacy, three for 'gallant Jeff Davis,' and three groans for the 'Rail Splitter,'" a witness wrote to a friend in Georgia. "Had Lincoln been there . . . he would have met with trouble." After this ugly scene, he reported, "The crowd retired quietly in disgust."

* * *

When news of Lincoln's disappearance spread, the Baltimore crowd's angry reaction was echoed in the press. Newspapermen everywhere shook their heads scornfully in editorials. A Northern editor deplored Lincoln's having "skulked off himself and left his family to come in the train which would be sure to carry them to destruction." The Southern press pitched their comments in the higher key of open contempt. The reaction in the next day's Baltimore *Sun* was typical:

> Had we any respect for Mr. Lincoln, official or personal, as a man, or as President-elect of the United States, his career and speeches on his way to the seat of government would have cruelly impaired it; but the final escapade by which he reached the capital would have utterly demolished it, and overwhelmed us with mortification. . . .

We do not believe the Presidency can ever be more degraded by any of his successors, than it has been by him, even before his inauguration; and so, for aught we care, he may go to the full extent of his wretched comicalities. We have only too much cause to fear that such a man, and such advisers as he has, may prove capable of infinitely more mischief than folly when invested with power.

A lunatic is only dangerous when armed and turned loose; but only imagine a lunatic invested with authority over a sane people and armed with weapons of offense or defense. What sort of a fate can we anticipate for a people so situated? And . . . what sort of a future can we anticipate under the presidency of Abraham Lincoln?

Things got worse. Joseph Howard, Jr., a writer for the *New York Times* already notorious as a hoaxer, awoke in Harrisburg on February 23 to find Lincoln gone, saw a chance for a prank, and imaginatively sketched Lincoln's disguise during his night ride as "a Scotch plaid cap and a very long military cloak." The *Times*, a Republican newspaper, printed it, and journals worldwide took it up as a good story. Everybody laughed. Cartoonists vied with each other to sketch "Washington's new arrival" in the most ridiculous strokes. *Harper's Weekly* sketched the journey showing Lincoln in the Scottish cap and long cloak, dashing for a waiting train. A *Vanity Fair* cartoon showed the president in Scottish kilts doing a high-stepping jig on a railway platform. Another showed a preposterously tall figure hidden completely in the cloak and topped with the plaid cap, wryly titled "From a Fugitive Sketch."

Political doggerel, a popular form of satire at the time, skewered Lincoln in papers across the nation. One Southern parody was set to the tune of "Dixie":

> *Abe Lincoln tore through Baltimore,*
> *In a baggage-car with fastened door;*
> *Fight away, fight away, fight away for Dixie's Land.*
> *And left his wife, Alas! Alack!*
> *To perish on the railroad track!*
> *Fight away, fight away, fight away for Dixie's Land.*

Elsewhere, thirteen new verses of "Yankee Doodle" were composed by the *Louisville Courier* and reprinted across the nation:

Harper's Weekly, March 9, 1861

"The MacLincoln Harrisburg Highland Fling"

They went and got a special train
At midnight's solemn hour,
And in a cloak and Scotch plaid shawl,
He dodged from the Slave-Power.

Lanky Lincoln came to town,
In night and wind and rain, sir,
Wrapped in a military cloak,
Upon a special train, sir.

The *Courier* continued: "[Lincoln] ran from the first whisperings of danger as fleetly as ever a naked-legged Highlander pursued a deer upon Scotia's hills. The men who made the Declaration of Independence did not make it good in that way. They fought for their rights; Lincoln runs for his . . . and leaves his wife. They ought to swap clothes. She is a true Kentuckian. . . . No

Harper's Weekly, March 9, 1861

"The Flight of Abraham: The Special Train"

Kentucky-born man would have run all the way from Harrisburg to Washington, with but the ghost of an enemy in sight."

The New Orleans *Daily Delta* was another voice in the overwhelming chorus of jeers from the South. Under the acid headline "Lo, the Conquering Hero Comes!" its comment began: "It is not pleasant to see even an enemy reduced to the state of degradation and humiliation into which our Black Republican foe has fallen." It shed crocodile tears for "that once proud Republic, so shamed and debased before the world by the ridiculous, vulgar and pusillanimous antics of the coarse and cowardly demagogue whom a corrupt and crazy faction has elevated to the chair, once filled by Washington, Jefferson and Jackson."

Even the Northern press winced at the President's undignified start. "'What brought him here so suddenly?' was on everybody's tongue," tut-tutted the editor of the Chicago *Tribune*. The New York *Weekly Journal of Commerce* mocked Lincoln's "Flight of the Imagination." *Vanity Fair* observed, "By the advice of weak men, who should straddle through life in petticoats instead of disgracing such manly garments as pantaloons and coats, the President-elect disguises himself after the manner of heroes in

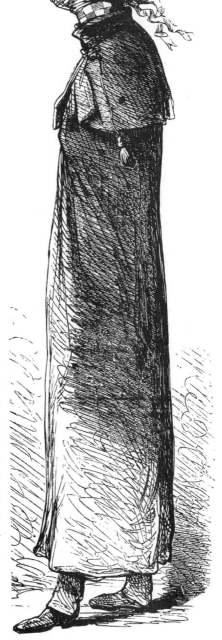

"The New President of the United States: From a Fugitive Sketch"

Vanity Fair, March 9, 1861

two-shilling novels, and rides secretly, in the deep night, from Harrisburg to Washington." The Brooklyn *Eagle*, in a column titled "Mr. Lincoln's Flight by Moonlight Alone," suggested the President and his advisors deserved "the deepest disgrace that the crushing indignation of a whole people can inflict." The New York *World* shouted, "How unwisely, how unfortunately, was Mr. Lincoln advised! How deplorably did he yield to his advisers!" The New York *Tribune* joked darkly, "Mr. Lincoln may live a hundred years without having so good a chance to die." To this morbid note the *New York Herald* added a sarcastic harmony: "What a misfortune to Abraham Lincoln and the Republican cause. We have no doubt the *Tribune* is sincerely sorry at his escape from martyrdom. Mr. Lincoln, with a most obtuse perception to the glory that awaited him, did not 'take fortune at the flood.'"

"We feel humiliated to the last degree by it," complained Republican Governor Blair of Michigan. "Never idol fell so suddenly or so far," mourned Massachusetts Republican Henry Dawes.

Lincoln himself, according to the testimony of his friends Ward Lamon and Alexander McClure, ever afterward regretted his night ride into Washington as one of the worst blunders of his political career, fully convinced in retrospect that "he had fled from a danger purely imaginary." "His friends reproached him, his enemies taunted him," wrote Lamon later; the President "was convinced that he had committed a grave mistake in listening to the solicitations of a professional spy and of friends too easily alarmed, and frequently upbraided me for having aided him to degrade himself at the very moment in all his life when he should have exhibited the utmost dignity and composure."

*   *   *

However much he may have blamed himself for the ridicule that greeted his arrival in Washington, Lincoln's secret approach to the capital was a prudent response to real dangers during some of the tensest weeks in the nation's history. Especially in view of the genuine danger, the contempt in the nation's reaction to Lincoln's unfortunate arrival was so widespread, so vicious, and so personal that it marks this episode as the historic nadir of presidential prestige in the United States. Though scandal and resignation would stain the terms of many presidents before and after Lincoln, presidential authority would never again sink to the low level it reached at Lincoln's arrival.

How could a man elected President in November be so reviled in February? The insults heaped on Lincoln after his undignified stumble into

Washington were not the result of anything he himself had done or left undone. He was a man without a history, a man almost no one knew. Because he was a blank slate, Americans, at the climax of a national crisis thirty years in coming, projected onto him everything they saw wrong with the country. To the opinion-makers in the cities of the East, he was a weakling, inadequate to the needs of the democracy. To the hostile masses in the South, he was an interloper, a Caesar who represented a deadly threat to the young republic. To millions on both sides of the Mason-Dixon line, he was not a statesman but merely a standard bearer for a vast, corrupt political system that had become unmoored from the bedrock of the Constitution and had conspired to rob them of "government by the people."

The political times had made the anonymous Railsplitter's presidency possible, and at the same time robbed it of esteem. His predicament was a legacy of the rowdy adolescence of American politics, the "Age of Jackson." Three broad historical trends in Jacksonian America combined to create this lowest ebb of the presidency as Lincoln took it up. The first was the notorious disrepair of the presidency that Lincoln inherited—weak from the beginning, further weakened by decades of shabby treatment, and stained by feeble performances from a string of the poorest Presidents in the nation's history. The second was the wave of corruption that had debauched the political system during the rise of political parties after Jackson and destroyed the public's respect for its elected officials. The third was the hostility produced by the slavery crisis, which withered the people's toleration for different points of view and resulted in the creation in the North of a sectional party—the Republicans—whose victory was unacceptable to the South, where Lincoln had not garnered so much as one vote. To appreciate the depth and breadth of the contempt that Lincoln faced during his four years in office, it is necessary to understand the savage times in which he so suddenly ascended.

Chapter 2

The Presidency

"Chief of very little and executive of even less."

A braham Lincoln was elected to preside over a federal government puny by design. The American system had been created as the political expression of a people who had fled the tyrants of Europe. Within memory of citizens still alive in Lincoln's time, the Founding Fathers had bent to the task of framing a government that would make impossible a home-grown version of the hated English monarchy. The resulting Constitution gave only a few specific powers to the central government, reserving all others to the states. The new central government's domestic functions were kept to a short list: it would provide internal improvements, it would set and collect customs duties, it would survey and sell the public lands in the West, and it would distribute the mails.

Besides being few, the powers granted the central government were weak. They were not "police" powers—they did not impose limitations on the behavior of citizens. Instead, Federal powers were carefully framed as "patronage" powers—they distributed grants of money, land, and jobs on a case-by-case basis. By this scheme, the framers allowed the infant central government to buy loyalty that would provide stability, and, just as important, avoid having to confront tough, divisive social issues that could tear it apart. The people of the new nation understood the Washington government to be a weak sister to the state governments. This was as it should be, they reckoned: state officials—closer to the people and thus wiser, safer, and more efficient—should retain control over the long and important list of powers which regulated the health, safety, and morals of the community.

America didn't need a strong central government. It had no powerful neighbors, no old society in need of reform, no needy millions to feed and educate. By the middle of the nineteenth century, America had achieved renown as the mighty mite of global wealth, and European correspondents were clogging the decks of Atlantic steamers to observe first-hand what, even into the Lincoln administration, was still called the American "democratic experiment." Edward Dicey, reporting for the British *Spectator*, wrote:

> Life, hitherto, has flowed very easily for the American people. The country is so large, that there is room for all and to spare; the battle of life is not an arduous one, compared to what it is in older countries. The morbid dread of poverty, which is the curse of English middle-class existence, is almost unknown in the New World. If the worst comes to the worst, and an American is ruined, the world lies open to him, and in a new state he can start afresh, with as fair prospects as when he set out in life.

It is little wonder that in such a land of plenty, any strong government action was resented as "interference," and the country developed what *Atlantic Monthly* editor James Lowell called "a happy-go-lucky style of getting along."

The government in Washington, then, was not supposed to do a great deal—and in the years before Lincoln, it didn't. The people's faith was in unfettered individualism. With their revolutionary-era belief in the evils of strong rule reinforced by spectacular success, Americans in 1860 lived under the weakest government in the world. Thomas Carlyle called America "the most favored of all lands that have no government." Even the few powers granted to the central government were exercised little. Tariffs were low. There was no national bank. There were few subsidies for internal improvements or state credit—the roaring engines of travel and transport were stoked by the muscle of private capital. Only Native Americans felt the Washington government's authority. The only time the central government touched the average citizen's life was when the mailman came. The government's work was so insignificant that U.S. congressmen commonly resigned their offices to run for election in the state legislatures, where the real issues were being argued.

Lack of respect for the feeble federal power was peaking as Lincoln took office, but the tradition of defying the national government was as old as the nation. On his first presidential trip to Boston in 1789, George Washington sat in a hotel room for two days fighting a battle of wills with Massachusetts governor John Hancock over who should call on whom. Since then, there had been a number of organized attempts to challenge the Washington government, by Northern as well as Southern states: Pennsylvania's Whiskey Rebellion in 1794, Virginia's and Kentucky's opposition to the Alien and Sedition Acts in 1798, the threat of secession in New England at the Hartford Convention in

1814, South Carolina's Ordinance of Nullification in 1833, and Northern personal liberty laws which flouted the federal Fugitive Slave Law in the 1850s.

*   *   *

Moreover, when Lincoln took office in 1861, he was twice removed from the focus of power. Not only was government power centered in the states rather than in Washington, but Washington power was centered in Congress rather than in the Presidency. During Lincoln's run for office, abolitionist orator Wendell Phillips mocked the power of the President, asking, "Did you ever see on Broadway a black figure grinding chocolate in the windows? He seems to turn the wheel, but in truth the wheel turns him." Lincoln lived in the golden age of legislature, where the President's task was to carry out the policies of the lawmakers who dispensed wisdom from beneath the alabaster dome of the Capitol. In Lincoln's century, all political parties, whatever else they proclaimed, adhered to one common principle: they all argued against a strong presidency. The times were dominated by those who believed the presidency was, in Patrick Henry's warning, an "awful squint toward the monarchy."

Americans focused their political interest on Congress through the entire first century of the nation's existence. In an era when the President almost never spoke in public once he had delivered his inaugural address, the real titans of the young nation's political arena—"The Great Compromiser" Henry Clay, the "Godlike Daniel" Webster, "The Champion of States' Rights" John C. Calhoun, "The Little Giant" Stephen A. Douglas—battled regularly beneath packed galleries in the chambers of the House and Senate. Every two years, newspaper readers nationwide followed the candidates for Speaker of the House almost as closely as they did presidential candidates, trying to discern which way the legislative winds were blowing. The President was not so much a force as a symbol: the nation's first citizen, the ceremonial head of state, receiver of distinguished visitors, signer of bills. As presidential observer Theodore Lowi put it: "In the nineteenth century, chief executives were chief of very little and executive of even less."

It is hard for us, in a time when the President is referred to routinely as "the most powerful man in the world," to imagine the presidency as the handmaiden to Congress as it existed in Lincoln's time. The intervening growth in the power and prestige of the Oval Office—the creation of a Presidency that has since overcome the caution of the Founders and put Congress in its shadow—has obscured the low expectations for it in Lincoln's century.

*   *   *

The role of the Washington government has been transformed since Lincoln by the astounding growth of the nation beyond what the Founders could foresee. Sweeping social changes and the rise of an industrial economy brought problems on a scale unimaginable in revolutionary times. Whereas in 1860 Americans still resented the national government for its "interference," they later turned more and more to the presidency as the only institution adequate to battle emergencies that came at ever-increasing speeds.

The result—government by a large professional bureaucracy, with the President at its head—has become known as the "institutional presidency," and marks a constitutional era entirely different from the congressional heyday in which Lincoln was elected. In the modern era, with scores of administrative agencies responsible only to the President, there has developed the exclusively modern notion that the President *is* the government.

It is difficult to remember that, compared to today's mighty ship of state, Lincoln steered a tiny skiff. Suffering from nearly three quarters of a century of penny-pinching, the apparatus that Lincoln worked in 1861 had grown little since George Washington's time. The central government did little more for its citizens in 1860 than it had done in 1800. Washington had established six executive departments; Lincoln inherited seven—the additional Interior Department had been carved out of the Treasury in 1849. All the departments were inadequately staffed, with overworked clerks toiling at low salaries in cramped quarters. The State Department of the 1850s, for example, handled foreign affairs with a staff of eighteen men.

At Lincoln's election, with the population of the United States at slightly more than 30 million, there were a mere 20,000 civilian federal employees, with another 16,000 soldiers on the payroll. By contrast, at the beginning of the 21st century, to serve a population ten times the 1860 population, the federal government now requires almost three million employees to run it—150 times the Lincoln-era figure—with another three million on the military payroll.

The change in the size of government is also reflected in the budget. The Federal budget Lincoln inherited in 1861 was sixty-three million dollars—or about one billion in today's dollars. A modern president flexes a Federal budget in the trillions.

The figure that speaks loudest about the public appreciation of the size of the President's job, however, and where we can best see the relative weakness of the presidency as Lincoln inherited it, is the size of the White House budget appropriated by Congress. In the first decade of the 21st century, the modern White House staff approaches 6,000 employees, in 125 offices, with an annual budget estimated at $730 million. In 1861, the White House staff consisted of a solitary secretary.

Until shortly before Lincoln arrived, in fact, there had been no budget at all for a staff for the president, commensurate with the people's low appraisal of the demands of his job. In those days, the people assumed that the president's seven cabinet members would provide him with all the information and advice he needed. For his daily business the Chief Executive was on his own. If he wanted to hire assistance, he usually paid sons or nephews out of his own salary. Only in 1857 was the post of "President's Private Secretary" established by Congress, at a salary of $2,500 per year. In addition, $1,200 was set aside for a steward to take charge of the White House, and $900 for a part-time messenger. There were still no adequate provisions for expenses. The yearly stationery budget, for example, had remained at $250 since the days of John Adams.

Lincoln's secretary, 28-year-old John G. Nicolay, who met Lincoln while working as clerk to the Illinois secretary of state, managed to wangle a second presidential assistant—his friend John Hay, a 22-year-old poet—by having him put on the payroll as a clerk in the Department of the Interior and detailed for special service at the White House. For much of Lincoln's tenure, these two stayed within the government budget by sleeping in a corner room on the second floor of the White House, across the hall from the Executive Offices.

Lack of an adequate staff had already tripped Lincoln on his unprotected approach to the capital and caused his pratfall into Washington. It had not occurred to President Buchanan to loan the President-elect a guard, nor were there any national police, nor anybody in the government whose job it was to see him from Springfield to Washington safely. Lincoln was shielded only by a few friends. If he had been attacked anywhere on the way, it would have been up to local police to investigate the crime and catch the guilty ones. A local court would have had the responsibility of trying, sentencing, and jailing them.

*   *   *

Any trappings of power—even so much as a bodyguard—were repulsive to Americans in 1860. They were still distrustful of their creation, the presidency. They did not seek great men. They knew the history of democracy in the world had been an unbroken series of failures. From Aristotle on, political philosophers agreed that democracy was unstable, and disintegrated into anarchy, then finally to despotism. The Roman republic had its Caesar. The brief republic of the Commonwealth of England had its Cromwell. The French Revolution had its Reign of Terror, and finally its Napoleon. As a fresh reminder, Louis Napoleon had overthrown the flimsy Second Republic of France as recently as 1852. Because early Americans were so acutely aware of the vulnerability of republics to conspiracies and plots, Americans in Lincoln's time had a strong distrust of men of genius. It was feared their talents would drive them to break free of the constraints of law by which ordinary men were bound.

The American habit of distrust was well marked. After his visit in 1842, novelist Charles Dickens wrote:

> One great blemish in the popular mind of America, and the prolific parent of an innumerable brood of evils, is Universal Distrust. Yet the American citizen plumes himself upon this spirit, even when he is sufficiently dispassionate to perceive the ruin it works; and will often adduce it . . . as an instance of the great sagacity and acuteness of the people, and their superior shrewdness and independence.

> "You carry," says the stranger, "this jealousy and distrust into every transaction of public life. By repelling worthy men from your legislative assemblies, it has bred up a class of candidates . . . who, in their very act, disgrace your Institutions and your people's choice. It has rendered you so fickle, and so given to change, that your inconstancy has passed into a proverb; for you no sooner set up an idol firmly, than you are sure to pull it down and dash it into fragments. . . . Any man who attains a high place among you, from the President downwards, may date his downfall from that moment; for any printed lie that any notorious villain pens, although it militate directly against the character and conduct of a life, appeals at once to your distrust, and is believed. . . . Is this well, think you, or likely to elevate the character of the governors or the governed, among you?"

> The answer is invariably the same: "There's freedom of opinion here, you know. Every man thinks for himself, and we are not to be easily overreached. That's how our people come to be suspicious."

If it was great men Americans feared, by the mid-nineteenth century Americans were getting exactly what they wanted.

Chapter 3

The Rise of Party Politics

"Deformed, mediocre, sniveling, unreliable, false-hearted men."

I n 1860, an apocryphal story made the rounds: the captain of a sailing vessel outbound from New York City was hailed by a ship homeward bound after a long voyage to China. The question came over, "Who is the President of the United States?"

The captain shouted back, "Abraham Lincoln."

A minute later, a second question came over: "Who the hell is Abraham Lincoln?"

Although much of Lincoln's initial lack of esteem could be attributed to the lack of regard for the institution of the presidency in the mid-nineteenth century, his problem was made worse by the fact that when he was elected President, Lincoln the man was unknown. The jeering mobs that rushed his train in Baltimore knew very little about him except that he had won the election as the nominee of the hated "Black Republican" party. Their knowledge of Lincoln himself was almost entirely limited to his nickname: "The Railsplitter."

Lincoln was well aware of his anonymity; he conceived his Springfield-to-Washington whistle-stop tour as a way to introduce himself to the people who had elected him. In one of his first utterances, at Indianapolis, he referred to himself disparagingly as "an accidental instrument of a great cause." James Lowell described him as "the unknown man whom a blind fortune, as it seemed, had lifted from the crowd." But in the weird political logic of his time, it was Lincoln's anonymity that had recommended him as a presidential candidate.

In the infancy of the Republic, while America was slow-moving and fragmented, while its many sections were governed locally and had little contact with each other, while any state's allegiance to Washington was loose and the government there did little, the President's role was small. But as the population grew and as the steamboat, the railroad, and the telegraph combined to bring the sections of the country into closer and closer contact, another political phenomenon developed to give the President a new kind of power never envisioned by the Framers. This phenomenon was the rise of American political parties, a development that, in the thirty years before Lincoln, sensationalized politics to an extent never seen in the world before and not approached since. In these "awkward years" of the republic, party politics became the national obsession. This new party system would pave the way for the nomination of Lincoln, but at a terrible price: Lincoln, the anonymous candidate, would find himself the leader of a nation as a stranger in the White House at a time when the country could least afford it. It was this gale wind of early party politics that blew the obscure Illinoisan into office in 1860, and fanned the flame of contempt for him at the same time.

An Abraham Lincoln could never have been chosen President in the political culture that existed in the infancy of the United States. The revolutionary nation builders who assembled in Philadelphia in 1787 had been squeamish about the idea of huge numbers of rank and file Americans choosing their own leaders. The thousands of years of tragic history of republican experiments in government had taught the delegates to the Constitutional Convention that the uninstructed teeming masses were "liable to yield their own opinions to the guidance of unprincipled leaders," as one put it. With this in mind, they drew up rules that restricted the vote to the "right people"—that is, landowners and taxpayers. These were the men who could be counted on to act responsibly by virtue of their economic stake in society. As added insurance that the selection of the President would be insulated from the "mobocracy" they dreaded, the voters would not choose the President. Instead, the Constitution required that, every four years, each state appoint electors, and the electors would choose the President.

The electors, as envisioned by the Founding Fathers, would be outstanding citizens, local notables with the confidence of the voters, whose vision would not be clouded by self-interest or party politics. They would elect the nation's most qualified man by congregating in sober reflection, smoking their pipes in thoughtful little puffs. After forging their choice, they would return to ordinary life, warm in the satisfaction of having selected the best man by an appeal to pure reason. In the first two elections, when George Washington was available, the electors only had to choose him to confirm the wisdom of the Founders' scheme. After Washington passed out of public life, however, the choice for the most qualified man inevitably muddied, and the presidential selection process descended quickly into something the Founders never foresaw: a tug-o'-war between political parties.

The Framers had detested political parties and had seen no place for them in America. They thought voters should be national in outlook; they should be above faction, and disagreements should be resolved solely on the issues. Yet before the echoes of Washington's Farewell Address had died away, political parties had formed over the fundamental issue of how strong the central government should be. This sudden scurry of the nation's leaders into two opposing camps had an immediate effect on presidential elections.

The Constitution, so clear about how the President would be elected, had been silent about how the candidates would be nominated. Taking advantage of this omission in the constitutional rules, both parties assembled informal congressional caucuses before presidential elections to determine their nominees behind closed doors, and privately narrowed what the Founding Fathers had hoped would be a teeming field of outstanding potential candidates to two—one for each party. Thus, by 1800, the decision of who would run for President had been taken away from the tiny group of eligible voters and seized by a much tinier group of congressmen. At election time, a state appointed its electors not as individuals of high character who could be counted on to vote their consciences, but as a slate of men pledged to one of the congressional caucus nominees.

The resulting concentration of power in Congress, called "King Caucus," was distilled further in the elections between 1800 and 1820 by the swift disappearance of the Federalist Party, which had contended for strong central government. Their rivals, Thomas Jefferson's Democratic-Republicans (or "Republicans," for short) inheritors of the belief that "that government is best which governs least," became virtually unopposed in Washington. This period has come down to us with the rosy moniker "The Era of Good Feelings," and it climaxed in the election of 1820, when President James Monroe was reelected by a vote of 231 to 1.

The Presidents sworn in during these formative years of the country could never have included a self-educated frontier character like Lincoln. Eligible voters—still only six percent of adult Americans—were too exclusive, too well-educated, too wealthy, too sophisticated. Because they were a like-minded elite, and because the central government was so small and so carefully limited by the Constitution that it little touched their daily lives, they applauded as the congressional gentlemen's club choreographed a stately parade of high-caliber aristocrats to their head: Washington, Adams, Jefferson, Madison, and Monroe. The system was embarrassingly undemocratic, but proponents of King Caucus could point to its triumphs—parties now seemed to be a thing of the past, the

Founders' vision of philosopher-patriot Presidents had been made real, and elected office was a place of honor, whose legitimacy no one argued.

* * *

In the run-up to the election of 1824, however, King Caucus collapsed. Property ownership had mushroomed as the population flooded into the land beyond the Appalachians, and as a result earlier restrictions on voting had become hard to enforce and were increasingly being thrown out. Tens of thousands of new white male voters, eager to be heard, blasted the old caucus system in angry resolutions and protests, and the Senate voted it out of existence. Without a new system of nominating candidates to take the place of the suddenly unfashionable caucuses, however, the ensuing 1824 election was the most chaotic in American history. Four candidates from the Democratic-Republican Party contended, none of whom could win an outright majority of electoral votes, and the election was thrown into the House of Representatives. John Quincy Adams won the election by backroom deal making, but the disgusted Andrew Jackson, who had gotten the most popular votes, was consumed for the next four years by the desire for revenge, convinced that the haughty, aristocratic Adams had thwarted the will of the people. The election was important for the history of American politics because of its chaos and the bitterness it caused. It pointed to the urgent want of some new machinery for selecting presidential nominees.

For the election of 1828, at least, no such machinery was needed. Two candidates rose into view by acclamation: President Adams would run again, and Jackson would seek his revenge. This time, the challenger had new help. Between 1824 and 1828 white manhood suffrage became the rule nationwide, and the number of voters tripled. "Old Hickory" clubs sprang up around the country. Speeches were spoken and parades were paraded in Jackson's honor. The hero of New Orleans appeared irresistible to the new masses of voters as the democratic ideal made real, the homespun man of the people. Jackson was a man without any known political principles, but he didn't need them. His military reputation and backwoods appeal were enough to vault him over Adams in 1828, and his election signaled America's lurch into genuine popular democracy.

Triggered by universal white manhood suffrage, "Old Hickory's" ascent as 7th President marked the emergence of a new prototype for the Chief Executive: a man born in humble circumstances, with experience on the frontier, boasting military exploits, without long apprenticeship in public life—a man whose stance on issues was fuzzy, but whose image was clear. His type would dominate American politics for the next thirty years and make possible the election of "The Railsplitter" in 1860. But Jackson's legacy for Lincoln would be mixed. While it spelled the end of the aristocrat Presidents and paved the way for the humble Illinoisan, it would also begin a moral slide in American politics that would, by Lincoln's time, undermine trust in the presidency and critically wound the public's belief in his legitimacy.

Jackson encouraged low expectations for government. Its operations should be minimal, he insisted, "like the dews of heaven, unseen and unfelt." He justified his policy as a Jeffersonian commitment to a strict constitutional interpretation—if the Constitution did not specifically grant a power, he would not exercise it. But Jackson also had a less lofty motive. He was a slave-owner, and since the Constitution granted no federal power over slavery, strict Constitutionalism made it easier to defend slave property. Alexis de Tocqueville, whose visit to America during Jackson's term produced the monumental *Democracy in America*, observed that "General Jackson's power is constantly increasing, but that of the president grows less. The federal government . . . will pass to his successor enfeebled." Tocqueville's prediction would be fulfilled. Jackson would be succeeded for thirty years by a string of mediocrities in the Oval Office who sustained his prejudices. They would be of two types: those who thought the President should be weak, and those who thought he should be weaker.

As Jackson was being lifted to the highest office on the power of his appeal to the masses, his handlers, led by Martin Van Buren, the greatest backroom schemer in American political history, sensed that a leader with the incandescence of Jackson could cast a light far beyond the end of his administration. But until now Jackson's following—which called itself the Democratic Party—was little more than a huge personality cult. There was no guarantee it would not be torn apart by rivalries and factions as soon as he left office. To turn what amounted to a glorified Scottish clan into a well-knit political party that could survive the end of its hero's term, Van Buren and the President's men groped for some machinery for presidential nominations—the loophole in the election process, ignored by the Framers and absent since the collapse of King Caucus—with which they could control their infant Democratic Party after Jackson stepped down.

A rival clique, the Anti-Masons, supplied the answer when they met in Baltimore in 1831 for the nation's first national party convention. This boisterous, banner-waving gang got national attention for their one-issue splinter group. It had the look of a democratic gathering of the people, delivering a party nominee in public. Van Buren and the rest of Jackson's handlers envied the high profile delivered on the cheap by the convention, and saw quickly how a few state bosses could manipulate such a gathering. They followed suit with their own Democratic Party convention in Baltimore in 1832 for the purpose of naming Van Buren as Jackson's running mate, which they rigged by pushing through rules which locked out insurgents.

Over the years, such rigging would become so commonplace in national party conventions that political patriarch John C. Calhoun later published a letter that declared conventions an undemocratic travesty: "I . . . contributed to put [the Congressional Caucus] down. . . . Far, however, was it from my intention in aiding to put that down, to substitute in its place what I regard as a hundred times more objectionable in every point of view." Americans grew to share Calhoun's disgust at the cynicism of party conventions, since Americans continued to be denied any influence in the nomination—a denial made doubly bitter by the pretense that the party bosses' nominees were "the choice of the people."

"That national conventions have already fallen into discredit with the people, there needs no ghost from the grave to reveal," the New York *Tribune* declared in 1854. The consistently poor quality of the presidential candidates that the conventions delivered—lowered by wires, *deus ex machina* style, onto the national stage—deepened voters' discontent. Their disillusionment would ultimately threaten to tear the nation apart in 1860, when, at the peak of the slavery crisis, the Republican Party bosses presided over a convention where nine states were not represented at all, and which produced a candidate almost unknown outside of his home state: Abraham Lincoln.

It was in the 1836 election that the new party system bared its muscles for the first time. Democratic Party hacks demonstrated that a small group could nominate a man at a convention and give him the aura of popular strength. They held a national convention to shout, parade, and wave banners over the orchestrated nomination of Martin Van Buren, their short, bald, bewhiskered, behind-the-scenes wheeler-dealer. He went on to win the presidential election that year over a fatally divided opposition. He was the first President elected by the party system, and, not coincidentally, the first President with little popular following. In 1860, Abraham Lincoln would fit much the same pattern, winning the election with less than 40% of the vote, at the worst possible time for the nation.

Old Hickory had become president by campaigning on his personal popularity rather than his policies. This emphasis on "the man, not the measures" was so potent with the new, unsophisticated masses of voters that the Democrats received the ultimate flattery in the form of a new party—the Whigs—who by 1840 had molded themselves in the Democrats' mirror image: that is, created primarily to beat Democrats, not to champion any particular set of ideas. Both parties wooed the teeming voters of an unphilosophical, optimistic, and unapologetically materialistic nation by running candidates who played down issues, who tried to be all things to all men, who avoided making enemies by refusing to be wedded to firm sets of principles. Such candidates possessed that most valuable of mid-nineteenth-century political assets: "availability." The crucial defect of this policy was that the men who made good candidates were rarely men who would make good presidents. This flaw did not go unnoticed by the people. They became increasingly cynical about the ability of the parties to nominate able men, particularly as they watched the nation drift, year after critical year, in the vacuum of leadership caused by the succession of mediocrities who found themselves president after Jackson. In 1860, there was no reason to believe that Lincoln would be any better. Indeed, he appeared to be the worst of the lot.

In 1840, after four years of Van Buren, the Democrats, discredited by a deep economic depression and high unemployment and crippled by Van Buren's lack of luster, faced almost certain defeat. The Whigs, now well organized by bosses of their own, had the luxury of knowing that whoever they nominated would probably win the presidency. At their party's first national convention, in 1839, Whig bosses ignored the one towering figure in the party, Henry Clay, whom most Whig voters wanted, and railroaded the nomination of the more pliable William Henry Harrison, a doddering general with one victory over the Indians in the Battle of Tippecanoe almost thirty years earlier.

* * *

The choice of Harrison reflected another cynical tendency in the era of rising parties: when victory was sure, the party bosses engineered the nomination of weak men, since they were easier to manipulate than great leaders with ideas of their own.

Popular cynicism skyrocketed once Harrison and Van Buren squared off against each other. The election of 1840, fabled for its superficiality, dirty tricks, and silliness, heralded a new age of elections as vulgar circuses, and ushered in the arrival of the Founding Fathers' worst nightmares. For the first time, vast sums of campaign money were raised and spent. Backing Harrison, a candidate with no ideas of his own, the Whigs decided to beguile the voters by substituting slogans, songs, and rallies for substance. When a Democratic newspaper sneered that the sixty-eight-year-old general would probably rather be back in his log cabin drinking hard cider, it was a godsend. The colorless Harrison now had an image that reminded the voters of Jackson's winning formula—a military hero with humble origins. Replicas of log cabins with coonskin caps nailed to the door appeared in town squares nationwide. At Whig rallies the kegs of spiked cider came out, and in the drunken romp that invariably ensued, songbooks were passed around and the revelers filled the night with the popular song:

> *Tippecanoe and Tyler too*
> *Tippecanoe and Tyler too*
> *And with them we'll beat little Van, Van, Van*
> *Oh! Van is a used up man.*

Harrison's victory at the polls vindicated the new approach to campaigning, where ideas and issues were not allowed to spoil the fun. Thoughtful citizens were repulsed, realizing that the entire arena of political discourse had been cheapened. When in 1860 a pile of wooden rails purportedly "split by the young Abe Lincoln himself" was dumped on the Illinois convention floor, Lincoln would gain an image which lent luster to his humble origins and give him a handy nickname—"The Railsplitter"—but he would lose credibility with a nation whose voters were looking for a man sober enough to calm a national hysteria, and thoughtful enough to find a way to turn aside a coming catastrophe.

But how could one expect a sober candidate when the whole nation was drunk with politics? As early as 1835 de Tocqueville had told the world, "the political activity which pervades the United States must be seen in order to be understood. No sooner do you set foot upon American ground, than you are stunned by a kind of tumult . . . almost the only pleasure which an American knows is to take a part in the government, and to discuss its measures." Other Europeans were similarly startled, even disgusted, at the sight of the American political free-for-all. Frances Trollope, writing in 1832, was appalled at the "election fever" she saw "constantly raging through the land." "It engrosses every conversation," she sniffed, "it irritates every temper, it substitutes party spirit for personal esteem; and, in fact, vitiates the whole system of society." Charles Dickens witnessed the same spectacle a decade later, and despaired, "I yet hope to hear of there being some other national amusement in the United States, besides newspaper politics." Every week, he saw "some new most paltry exhibition of that narrow-minded and injurious Party Spirit . . . sickening and blighting everything of wholesome life within its reach."

To account for the superheated atmosphere that ignited the explosion of partisan bitterness toward Lincoln, one must realize, paradoxically, how painfully boring life in America was in the mid-nineteenth century. Politics in the Age of Jackson was a brilliant, violent poison cultured in the featureless medium of drab American lives lived without ceremony in a landscape of mud and timber. The American Revolution had put an end to all the ancient pagan and religious festivals of the Old World, along with their color, pomp, and pageantry. Only one American vestige survived—the Mardi Gras in New Orleans. The religious holidays Americans observed were subdued occasions for prayer—even Christmas was only starting to shed the old Puritan ban on celebration. Also gone were the royal birthdays, the marriage celebrations for the nobility, and the historical festivals of Europe. Instead, America had one lone national holiday, the Fourth of July. Spectator sports, besides the occasional horse race or boxing match, were not yet thought of. Charles Dickens, touring in 1842, noted how lifeless American cities were compared to London: "How quiet the streets are. Are there no itinerant bands, no wind or stringed instruments? No, not one. By day there are no Punches, Fantoccini, dancing dogs, jugglers, conjurers, orchestrinas, or even barrel-organs." Dickens saw Americans too busy making money to have fun. "Healthful amusements, cheerful means of recreation, and wholesome fancies, must fade before the stern utilitarian joys of trade. . . . It would be well, if there were greater encouragement to lightness of heart and gaiety, and a wider cultivation of what is beautiful, without being eminently and directly useful," he sighed. As a remedy to the boredom of this dingy, cheerless world, there rose in America an unprecedented political delirium.

In the Age of Jackson, politics was the national pastime. In hotel lobbies, in bars, saloons, and taverns, on trains and steamboats, on street corners—wherever men gathered—they talked politics. Politics—with its fireworks, barbeques, torchlight parades with gaudy uniforms and floats, banners and badges, posters and prints, campaign songs, and delight in hours and hours of oratory—provided more than entertainment. It had the excitement and the emotion of battle. Every man belonged to a party and felt a part of the "team."

He voted for his party's candidate, even if he had taken no part in selecting him. And the politicking was continuous. The election calendar of that day was so fragmented and irregular, and so crowded—with three distinct spheres of activity: national, state, and local—that there was almost always an election going on somewhere, and the constant campaigning kept public emotions at a boil.

This was the golden age of American oratory. The spoken word educated and entertained the way radio, movies, and television would do a century later. Huge audiences would stand in the open air all afternoon to listen to a good stump speaker. Any man who expected a career in politics had to be able to deliver an address lasting from two to four hours, with pauses for crowds that cheered and yelled back, "Hit him again!" when he attacked his opponent. The all-male, hollering, half-sport-half-battle political style of the age was done best by political clubs crowded with "wild boys," gangs who frequently translated their enthusiasm into bloody melees at the polls. The result was a brutal and brutalizing brand of politics. In the years leading up to Lincoln's election, riots and battles were common at voting stations in New Orleans, Baltimore, Cincinnati, and New York.

*   *   *

This political delirium was stoked by a wildcat press, which was devoured by an American public as captivated by the printed as by the spoken word. In the Age of Jackson a forest of newspapers sprang up across the country, wherever a man felt like printing his version of the truth and could afford a press. By 1860, there were three thousand newspapers (twice as many as there are today) to distract, titillate, and inform a population of 30 million Americans. The teeming presses did not elevate the tone of the national discourse; they degraded it even further, turning out a weekly blizzard of sheets that were, on the whole, crude and scandalous. "The New York publications," wrote social observer George Combe, "are composed of the plunder of European novels and magazines; of reports of sermons by popular preachers; of stories, horrors, and mysteries; of police reports, in which crime and misery are concocted into melo-dramas now exciting sympathy, now laughter; with a large sprinkling of news and politics . . . they may be regarded as representing to some extent the general mind; and certainly they are not calculated to convey a very high opinion of it."

Dickens was less generous. He referred to the American press as a "monster of depravity," and despaired that, "While the newspaper press of America is in, or near, its present abject state, high moral improvement in that country is hopeless." He warned that "while that Press has its evil eye in every house and its black hand in every appointment in the state, from a president to a postman; while, with ribald slander for its only stock in trade, it is the standard literature of an enormous class, who must find their reading in a newspaper, or they will not read at all; so long must its odium be upon the country's head, and so long must the evil it works, be plainly visible in the Republic." In his novel *Martin Chuzzlewit*, Dickens satirized American newspapers by naming them the *Sewer*, the *Stabber*, the *Peeper*, and the *Rowdy Journal*.

No one expected newspapers to be fair or balanced in their political reports. The owner of a newspaper was many times its editor also, something like a present-day radio station owner doubling as its partisan talk show host. The country's editors were almost all in the pocket of a political party, and they hectored their readers into increasingly segregated, increasingly hostile political camps. The cost of doing business pushed the presses into bed with the parties. With the advent of the telegraph, the readers expected fresh news, but getting it was expensive. Since so many copies were mailed to distant subscribers, mailing costs were another financial drain. Squeezed by soaring costs, editors found a marketing strategy in appealing to a select audience—either Democrats, Whigs, merchants, or, later, Republicans. A newspaper's readers, in that unsophisticated day, looked to it for guidance on what a loyal party man should stand for and how he should vote, since they seldom read anything else.

Because the editors sustained the parties, the parties were obliged to sustain the editors, and their blessings flowed to those whose pages shouted the party line and ridiculed their opponents loudest and longest. This *quid pro quo* arrangement was no secret. An effective partisan editor could expect the government, if it were controlled by his party, to funnel public funds into his pockets in the form of immensely lucrative printing contracts for government documents—with no competition from lower bidders. Such tokens of the Administration's favor, moreover, conferred a sort of official rank on the preferred editor, inspiring the like-minded to subscribe to his paper over all others. In addition, pet editors were awarded public offices. They particularly prized postmasterships, since every postmaster could send material through the mail for free. Government advertising was another cash reward to editors for their devotion.

Since the party's blessings were bestowed on editors who proved themselves most loyal, editors outdid one another in praise of their party's men and damnation of their party's enemies. In stoking the boilers of the violent politics of the day, the newspaper business itself grew fraught with danger. The notorious and successful James Gordon Bennett, editor of the Democratic *New York Herald*, according to a horrified British observer, was "horse-whipped, kicked, trodden under foot, spat upon, and degraded in every possible way; but all this he courts because it brings him in money."

It was not surprising that in a violent nation, its editors were violent, on the page and off. Bloody duels were fought between rival editors, the most famous being an 1846 combat between the Whig and Democrat editors in Richmond, Virginia, who went at each other armed with pistols, rifles, broadswords and broadaxes, tomahawks, and bowie-knives, starting with gunshots and then closing and hacking away at each other with edged weapons. The badly mutilated Whig editor died; the Democrat returned to work. A touring Scottish minister, David Macrae, wrote that some Southern papers employed a man on their staff "to attend exclusively to the fighting part of the business. If the writing editor branded you before the public as a liar, and you went in Southern fashion to demand satisfaction, he handed you over politely to the fighting editor—the gentleman who managed the pistolling department." Also, it was not surprising that in a nation that had been ruled almost continuously by Democrats for decades, the hireling Democratic press ruled the nation's news. The abuse of this brutish, unashamedly biased party press was the longest and sharpest spike in the bed of nails Lincoln would endure after he appeared.

*   *   *

Another element introduced into politics in the two decades prior to Lincoln was the "dark horse" candidate. This gambit was the logical result of the policy of seeking the most "available," least controversial candidate. At the Democratic national convention in 1844, James K. Polk, a man whose name had rarely appeared in the Democratic newspapers, and who had not had one vote until the eighth ballot of the deadlocked gathering, won the nomination. There was an immediate outcry. People wondered what he had done to give him prominence over Buchanan, Van Buren, Douglas, Lewis Cass, and Calhoun. But the naysayers were ignored. It was precisely Polk's anonymity that translated into "availability" to delegates desperate for a candidate who would offend none of the party's factions. Polk subsequently defeated Clay in the 1844 election on the strength of the same negative asset. In diarist George Templeton Strong's opinion, Clay lost to Polk because Clay's long, distinguished career had inevitably produced enemies, while Polk "was impregnable from the fact that he had never done or said anything of importance to anybody . . . . Henceforth I think political wire-pullers will be careful how they nominate prominent and well-known men for the Presidency; they'll find it safer to pick up the first man they may find in the street."

Strong was right: two more dark horse candidates were elected in the next four elections. The first was in 1852, when the Democratic convention was hopelessly deadlocked over three strong candidates after three days of balloting. The party bosses produced Franklin Pierce, a man from New Hampshire whose views no one knew, and the newly anointed Pierce won the nomination on the 49th ballot. Strong wrote: "Nobody knows much of Franklin Pierce, except that he is a decent sort of man in private life. Very possibly he may run all the better, as Polk did, for his insignificance. Democracies are not over-partial to heroes and great men. A statesman who is too much glorified becomes a bore to them. . . . Democracy is secretly jealous of individual eminence of every sort, not merely that which grows out of wealth or station." Strong described Pierce as "a galvanized cypher, of whom nothing can be said but that he is a cypher." Pierce the Cypher won the election going away. Eight years later, in 1860, Abraham Lincoln became the most famous dark horse winner in the nation's history. His emergence from anonymity onto the doorstep of the White House at such a critical time would cause infinitely more woe than Polk's or Pierce's. Lincoln's victory at the polls was widely seen as the failure of a debauched political system, a system that had produced an illegitimate leader at a time of crisis.

*   *   *

All the features of the political "party game" in the Age of Jackson were well established by Lincoln's time: its domination by state party bosses, the vulgarity of its manic campaign hoopla aggravated by a scandalous hireling press, and its avoidance of hard issues and strong personalities. As the parties strengthened their grip over the political process, serious observers bemoaned the decline in moral tone that resulted. Southerners, especially, noticed the loss of dignity in government. The *Southern Quarterly Review* in 1844 complained that a party "blasts where it is excited, and virtue, withering, shrinks from its presence." A Carolina newspaper shouted about "The Dignity Departing," and reported that senators had become obsessed with "long details of personalities and party matters" and the scene in the House was "Buncombe speeches, and party squabbles." The Charleston *Mercury* in 1853 protested that "no one was safe, that men of sensitive and elevated character were being driven out of public life, leaving only the callous and unprincipled to possess public honors."

Out of their instinctive fear of great men, Americans had developed a genius for avoiding men of genius. This was aggravated by the torsions of the slavery issue at mid-century, and both parties avoided controversy by serving up a series of colorless placeholders for the nation's highest office. Between 1848 and 1860, despair was everywhere expressed over the weakest string of presidents in the country's history, before or since:

- Zachary Taylor, a Whig army general utterly without political experience, who campaigned on nothing but the promise never to "dictate" measures, and leaned on the Senator from New York, William Seward, to direct his administration;

- Millard Fillmore, thrust into the presidency by the death of Taylor, who presided over the Whigs' final, fatal division and disappearance as a national party;

- Franklin Pierce, a Democrat, too affable, too fond of liquor, who was controlled by his Cabinet and failed to be re-nominated after a four-year display of indecision;

- James Buchanan, also a Democrat at the mercy of his advisors, who presided over a corrupt administration, stood by as his party committed suicide on his watch, and proved feeble to the point of paralysis as the national moment of truth over slavery approached.

Walt Whitman wrote that the country's recent presidents had been "deformed, mediocre, sniveling, unreliable, false-hearted men." He was seconded in the pages of the *Springfield* (Mass.) *Republican*, who saw a pauper and idiot Government, the laughingstock of the world, "feeble-minded, *non compos*, worthy of guardianship by the strongest man." Large groups in all sections of the country felt that something was radically wrong with the Presidency at the moment Lincoln inherited it. As the campaign of 1860 approached, an unbroken line of watery Chief Executives had set expectations for the presidency at their lowest point.

Chapter 4

The Spoils System

"Stupidity which has excited the wonder of mankind."

The voters increasingly resented being shut out of the nomination process by the political kingmakers during the rise of the political parties in the Age of Jackson. They protested the poor quality of presidents produced by this unfair system, and they saw a disastrous culmination in the appearance of Lincoln. Nearly as harmful to Lincoln's legitimacy, though, was the fact that esteem for elected leaders had been slipping for a generation as a result of the corruption introduced by the spoils system.

Jackson and his handlers in 1829 had taken advantage of an attitude that had developed nationwide: public men were increasingly motivated by "the love of a snug office." Until Jackson's time, government jobs had been scarce, and seeking government jobs for profit had appeared unseemly among the original patriots who remembered the unselfish spirit of the Revolution. But these purists were dying off. At the same time, the number of government jobs was expanding along with the country, and so was the number of men seeking them.

Because business and industry in the new nation had not developed to the point where they could provide enough jobs, men who aspired to rise above manual labor were the most financially insecure. School teaching and the law were the only choices available to these increasing thousands of educated job seekers, but the former occupation was underpaid and the latter was overcrowded. Public office, then, became the principal hope of teeming, ambitious young men with families to support, and the competition for government jobs acquired the quality of desperation.

So when the clamor of Jackson's election subsided, instead of going home and resuming their lives after a public-minded job well done, the banner-wavers and the speechmakers who had elected him descended on Washington in a swarm, eager to get a job in his administration, beckoned to the public trough by the President himself.

Jackson, combative to the core, saw himself as "the trustee of the people," doing battle in their behalf with the aristocrats, the money men, the Congress, and the Court. Those battles, he figured, could best be won by an administration stacked with loyal men. After all, anybody could do the job of government. To a man like Jackson, whose own life was proof that a man could be many things—lawyer, general, farmer, politician—it stood to reason that the duties of government were plain and simple enough to be handled by ordinary citizens, who could—no, *should*—be hired and fired wholesale any time a new administration took office. One of his cronies, William L. Marcy of New York, put it most famously when he said defiantly of Jackson's men: "When they are contending for victory they avow their intention of enjoying the fruits of it. . . . They see nothing wrong in the rule that to the victor belong the spoils of the enemy." The "spoils system" cemented the loyalty of an army of mercenaries at thousands of desks in every government post, from postal clerks and city wards all the way up to the State Department. "You scratch my back, I'll scratch yours," became, without apology, the new way of doing the public's business. The nation's honored posts became places of profit.

And, to citizens appalled by the spoils system, those posts ceased to be honored. Jackson and his men had found the engine that would drive the new era of party politics, but it was one rotten with cynicism and self-seeking. There were some early Jeremiahs who foresaw the damage such a system would produce. James Madison wrote to a friend that wholesale rotation of offices "could not fail to degrade any Administration." New England religious leader and newspaper editor Horace Bushnell protested, "Such a system would corrupt a nation of angels."

But to the new mass of buckskin- and homespun-clad voters who had just turned their backs on aristocratic presidents and elected their man Jackson, such warnings from aristocrats were sour grapes, the deathbed curses of a bygone era. Spoils soon became accepted as part of the political game. There were few complaints at first, but when disillusionment with the party system itself arose, more and more worried observers began to see the spoils system as the adder whose bite could kill the republic. With increasing urgency, they prophesied the nation would fall into the hands of plunderers, corrupt spoilsmen whose only motivation was money and power. As early as 1842, a committee in Congress made a harsh pronouncement on the system's consequences:

The election ceases to be a fair and calm expression of the popular judgment on the principles and policy of Government, and becomes a tumultuous scramble for place and power. It is not merely a contest between the candidates . . . but between the incumbent of each subordinate office in the Government and all those who have fixed their eyes on his place. The distribution of the minor stations often excites more interest than the election itself. Who shall dispense the patronage? is the absorbing question . . . . When the election has ended, nothing is decided more than when it commenced, except that one set of men are to go out and another set are to come in. The victors practice the abuses for which they condemned the vanquished.

Then came boom times. The end of the Mexican War and the discovery of gold in California in 1848 added a million square miles of territory to the United States and millions of dollars to the Treasury. With more land and wealth in the national till, there was less restraint by ambitious men scheming to get part of it. In the 1850s, the blessing on the national treasury became a curse to public ethics. With the slavery crisis heating up at the same time, the Whig and the Democratic parties, in avoiding the hard question of slavery, slackened their commitment to the issues and became merely dispensers of spoils—"both have degenerated into mere faction, adhering together by the hope of public plunder," according to Georgia Senator Robert Toombs.

In the decade before Lincoln, corruption exploded. Daniel Lord, an eminent attorney, complained in 1849 that party patronage "has converted almost the whole body of ambitious young men into political hypocrites, and has resulted in filling the offices of the government with men who in every respect injure and disgrace the country." Even William Marcy, who had put a name to the spoils system in Jackson's day, was alarmed at what it had wrought. In 1851 he admitted to a friend, "The treasury doors have been so often opened that they appear to yield to the slightest pressure, & turn easily & smoothly on their hinges." His friend agreed that "demoralization is rapidly spreading over the whole country, and threatens to engulf the land in a sea of black and stagnant corruption."

The trend accelerated as the decade progressed, climaxing with Lincoln's predecessor, James Buchanan. Under Buchanan, offices across the land were bought and sold like commodities. In 1858, a newspaper editor visiting Washington was dismayed at seeing party leaders bartering public posts. He reported seeing office-brokers in the Senate, in the departments, even in the

White House, "and the actual sum of money to be paid for an office is as publicly named . . . as the prices of dry goods are named between a dealer . . . and his customers." Another disturbing practice demonstrated the zenith of the abuse of patronage as Lincoln approached. This was the use of Federal officeholders in a dual role as party delegates, which established an unholy union between the government and the party, and further estranged the people from the nomination process. Buchanan used federal appointees as bought-and-paid-for delegates in an attempt to secure his own renomination at the Democratic convention in 1860.

That same year, a British lord observed the debauchery in American democracy and listed its sins: "[H]onest men excluded from office, purchased state legislatures, government contracts awarded to incompetent in-laws of Cabinet members, a corrupted people embracing larcenous leaders." That year, too, Jackson's biographer, James Parton, warned, "The evil which he began remains, has grown more formidable, has now attained such dimensions that the prevailing feeling of the country, with regard to the corruptions and inefficiency of the government, is despair." Since Jackson, he charged, "the public affairs of the United States have been conducted with a stupidity which has excited the wonder of mankind."

By the time Lincoln appeared, the cancer of the spoils system had ravaged government so completely that *Harper's* magazine printed a jeremiad on its evils to the magazine's million readers: "Corruption is . . . perhaps more prevalent than . . . in any other first-class nation," it warned. "At every election many votes are bought." In Washington, bribery and the buying and selling of government favors "is an art. . . . On all sides one hears of nothing but the spoils. . . . Here and there the feeble voice of a philosopher or a greenhorn mutters something about principle, but his utterance is drowned in the hoarse croak of the practical men who clamor for spoils." In keeping with the peculiar terror of the times, *Harper's* feared the approach of a despot. Unless "the intelligent people" woke up, the country might soon fall into the hands of "Vigilance Committees or an Augustus or a Bonaparte." With each new scandal eagerly reported by a rabid partisan press, people read and watched in horror. Distrust replaced confidence in government.

* * *

Americans' fear of corruption in their elected leaders was heightened by their sense of the fragility of republics. Americans still harbored deep skepticism about their own "democratic experiment," and feared enslavement by government conspiracy. They were afflicted with a paranoid vision of a coming Caesar—a usurper, a president who would stack the government with his friends as a start toward tyranny. They remembered the colonies' subjugation to the venal "informal constitution" of Great Britain before the Revolution: the web of family connection, preferment, privilege, and patronage—even bribery—by which the British leaders had cemented their power. The Revolution, indeed, had been seen as a victory not only of liberty but also of virtue, and the price of freedom was eternal vigilance lest another corrupt tyranny take root in Washington. Now, with corruption so apparently triumphant, the situation was seen bathed in a lurid, apocalyptic glare—the Republic was tottering. Henry Dawes of Massachusetts told the House that if the system of patronage were extended, "one might despair of the Republic." An Illinois judge saw the same dark vision: "When official corruption can go unwhipt of Justice, . . . then organized society is ready to dissolve, and governments cease to exist." "Our foundations are crumbling," Reverend Henry Ward Beecher cried to his congregation. "The sills on which we are building are ready to break."

So said the Northerners. The real panic in 1860, however, was in the South. There was a real fear that spoilsmen appointed by the "Black Republican" Abraham Lincoln would establish a Southern abolition party and plunder their section. One religious leader in Charleston, William H. Barnwell, warned his congregation that Southern politicians would soon be turned by the offers of spoils. "The patronage of government," he cried, "has seduced but too many whose virtue seemed immaculate, and I tremble for our commonwealth lest she too may encounter the blighting smiles of Executive favor, and shame, burning shame—the shame of having sold herself for money." Another prominent South Carolinian, John Townsend, despaired that once Lincoln's spoilsmen came to power, "we shall be betrayed and weakened by desertion from all ranks, through the bribes which shall be held out to the ambitious or the needy." Southerners, believing that Lincoln's minions would soon corrupt their political virtue, used the imagery of purification to justify a final break with the North. "We cannot coalesce," preached another, "with men whose society will eventually corrupt our own, and bring down upon us the awful doom which awaits them."

* * *

The epidemic of corruption foreshadowed the end of republican government to many in the North, and provoked fear of Lincoln in the South. However, it could not by itself plunge an entire nation into civil war. For that, the American *bete noir* must be summoned. To accomplish the destruction of the Union, it was necessary to conjure slavery.

Chapter 5

The Slavery Debate

"You could not look upon the table but there were frogs."

That slavery was the cause of the Civil War has become a truism. But it is not obvious from the facts in 1860 why this should have been so. The South really had no vital grievances, no real cause for war. Placating slaveholders, in fact, had been a national tradition since before there was a nation. The history of the United States had been an unbroken series of triumphs for the proponents of the "peculiar institution" and surrenders by slavery's opponents.

The Founding Fathers had been sensitive to Southern feelings, and had left the treatment of the slavery question open ended. They had left the work on that issue "to be continued" rather than face it head on and risk the wreck of the Constitutional Convention. The word "slavery" never appeared in the Constitution, even though it was implicit in the "three-fifths compromise," in which slaves (referred to as "other persons") were counted to swell congressional power for the states where they lived, but discounted for any rights. The subject of slavery was thus banished from public discussion by the revered gathering of Washington, Franklin, Adams and Madison.

There seemed little danger in sweeping the problem under the rug. In the nation-building era there was unanimity among Americans North and South that slavery ran counter to the revolutionary spirit, counter to the "self evident truth" that all men are created equal. All the states, slave and free, were quieted in this period by a shared belief that slavery would wither away on its own. Post-revolutionary Southerners were awake to the fact that slavery violated republican values, and the consensus in the South was that slavery was a necessary evil, soon to die a natural death in the anti-slavery current of world opinion. It was seen as a temporary convenience, tolerated during the initial labors of clearing the land, after which free labor would be affordable. While Americans waited passively for the ultimate death of slavery, thirty years of complacency passed.

The Deep South was passive about slavery, however, only as long as slaves were limited to working rice, indigo, and black-seed cotton, none of which would grow outside the tropical coastal swamps of South Carolina and Georgia. By a twist of fate, the invention of the cotton gin in 1793 by Connecticut Yankee Eli Whitney made the hardier green-seed cotton a wildly profitable crop, and acreage leapfrogged across the Carolinas, Georgia, and the newly-created states of Alabama and Mississippi. By the time both Maine and Missouri applied for statehood in 1819, it was no longer clear that slavery would disappear.

Southern congressmen insisted that, since there were at that time eleven free and eleven slave states, and since there was no question but that Maine would enter as a free state, Missouri must be admitted as a slave state. The solution, dubbed the Missouri Compromise, continued the revolutionary-era tradition of appeasing the slaveholders. Missouri was enrolled as a slave state, and any future territorial acquisitions south of a line extending west along the latitude of Missouri's southern border was reserved for slavery.

Another decade passed, during which the nationwide indifference about the moral issue of slavery went undisturbed. Even after the abolition movement arrived in the 1830s, the federal "hands off slavery" policy continued, and national leaders sat mute on the subject for another decade. In 1844, a pro-slavery majority in Congress annexed Texas, entering its name on the roll of slave states and adding its millions of acres of virgin land to the production of cotton.

In 1848 the Mexican War—conjured out of nothing by slave-owning President James K. Polk, and pushed by the sturdy pro-slavery majority— added 1.2 million square miles of national territory, which renewed agitation over slavery in the new land and again brought the issue before the lawmakers. Pro-slavery men were again coddled, this time by the Compromise of 1850, which allowed the settlers in the new territories of Utah and New Mexico to decide for themselves whether the states made from them would be slave or free, and included the Fugitive Slave Law, which obligated the authorities in the northern states to return all escaped slaves to their Southern owners.

The Democratic presidents of the 1850s accelerated the Federal capitulation to the Southern slave-owners by pushing through the Kansas-Nebraska Act in 1854—which repealed the Missouri Compromise in favor of the South by declaring all United States territories open to slavery under the "popular sovereignty" principle—and by abetting the Supreme Court's Dred

Scott decision of 1857, which declared unconstitutional any federal law which prohibited slavery in any of the national territories.

* * *

At the time of Lincoln's arrival, the South had dominated the politics of the nation for as long as anyone could remember—by Jefferson and his successors, and then by Jackson and his. In 1861 the United States was seventy-two years old. During all those years every elected President had been a slave-owner or a pro-slavery Northerner, with the exception of the Adamses (and William Henry Harrison, the parenthetical President, who caught a cold at his inaugural and died one month later; his replacement was John Tyler, a slave owner). Twenty-three of the thirty-six Speakers of the House and twenty-four of the thirty-six Presidents Pro Tem of the Senate had been from the South. Twenty of the thirty-five Supreme Court justices had been Southerners, and the Court had never been without a Southern majority. The South enjoyed the cooperation of the most powerful party in America, the Democratic Party. By dominating the Democrats, the South had dominated Congress and won concessions so complete that by 1860 no territory was denied to slavery.

Then, with the election of Lincoln, Southern rule was interrupted. Even so, however, slavery was safe in the South. Lincoln had sworn never to interfere with slavery in the states where it existed—he was limited by the Constitution and could not, he said. Lincoln's only offense against slavery was his opposition to slavery's extension into the territories. And though this may have been an insult, it was not an injury. By 1860, there was nothing at stake. It was plain that slavery could not thrive in the territories; the natural barriers of climate and terrain had decided the issue. At the time of Lincoln's election, years after the vastness of the territories had been opened to slavery by the laws of 1850 and 1854, they contained a paltry forty-six slaves: two in Kansas, fifteen in Nebraska, twenty-nine in Utah, and none in New Mexico. Even Southerners realized that the whole controversy over the territories, as one man put it, "related to an imaginary Negro in an impossible place."

In fact, Southern fire-eaters could point to only one official transgression against slavery in the history of the Republic, and that was the personal liberty laws enacted by Northern states that flouted the Fugitive Slave Law of 1850 and aided the "underground railroad." However, here too they were beating a straw man, for only a handful of slaves, a few hundred out of a slave population of four million, escaped each year. Even the South's most radical newspaper, the

Charleston *Mercury*, wrote that Northern refusals to enforce the Fugitive Slave Law mattered only "in the insult they conveyed to the South, and the evidence they offered of Northern faithlessness." Nor were Republicans intransigent on this issue. Many, in fact, were willing to rescind the personal liberty laws to keep the peace and end Southern wrangling about unreturned runaways.

The two reasons given to justify secession in 1861, then—the Republicans' opposition to the extension of slavery into the West and the loss of runaway slaves—were entirely inadequate as causes of war. But the reasons for the violence of Southern feeling over the slavery question were visceral, not intellectual. After the bitter criminations and recriminations breathed into flame by extremists on both sides over the previous thirty years, there burned in the South a ferocious hatred of Northerners and a real desire to flee the Union. Southern fire-eaters relied on that ferocity when they precipitated the flight of seven states from the Union as a reaction to one purely political event—the election of Abraham Lincoln as President of the United States.

* * *

The slavery argument was so divisive because it was not counteracted by any binding sense of social responsibility. In the years between Jackson and Lincoln, the center could not hold. This roaring period from 1830 to 1860 was without any stabilizing institutions such as held nations together in the Old World. Paradoxically, the Old World powers of Europe—England, France, Spain, and Portugal, with their centuries-old systems of church, state, class, court, and finance—had used those hide-bound institutions to accomplish reform. All of the colonial European nations succeeded in abolishing slavery at home, slavery in their colonies, and the slave trade at sea before the middle of the nineteenth century.

America, however, was moving backward, against the tide of historical reform. Here, slavery was becoming more entrenched. Here, conservative institutions, which had made possible the wiping of the scourge of slavery from Europe, were under assault by the American "ideal of liberty." Liberty rested at the very center of the national character, and had given rise by the 1830s—after the cohesive power of the revolutionary spirit had died—to the celebration of the completely unfettered individual. The doctrine of the free individual became the most widely shared Jacksonian creed. Alexis de Tocqueville was so struck by Americans' faith that each man had the right, the power, even the duty "to sever himself from the mass of his fellows and to draw apart with his family and his friends . . . [leaving] society at large to itself," that he coined the term "individualism" to describe this thing at the core of the American character. The worship of the individual even trumped democracy. The great reformers of the era, the Boston Transcendentalists and the abolitionists, disdained the idea of rule by the muddy-booted many. "When were the good and brave ever in the majority?" asked Henry David Thoreau. "One, on God's side, is a majority," insisted Wendell Phillips.

There was nothing in the Age of Jackson to restrain liberty or the vigor of the individual man. It was a time of newness. It was a time of exuberance. It was a time of unprecedented plenty, of a limitless horizon of rich, untouched resources and vast lands begging to be developed. With the absence of threat from neighbors either to the north or to the south, there was no wasting of energy and wealth on defense, nothing to divert Americans from exploiting nature's abundance. Everyone was on the make—and on the move, since the mobile man could best seize opportunity.

In this milieu, all the recognized values of social order became eroded. Standards and traditions were forgotten, drowned out by the buzz and hum of a society disintegrating into a million tiny atoms. The high priest of intellectual culture, Ralph Waldo Emerson, gave voice to a new religion—the worship of novelty. "Let me admonish you, first of all, to go alone," he wrote, "to refuse the good models, even those which are sacred in the imagination of men . . . . Imitation cannot go above its model. The imitator dooms himself to hopeless mediocrity. . . . Yourself a newborn bard of the Holy Ghost, cast behind you all conformity."

Armored with this disregard for the wisdom of the past, the Jacksonian ethic begat a widespread hostility toward all authority. Tocqueville observed this American characteristic on his tour in 1831, when he wrote, "The citizen of the Southern states becomes a sort of domestic dictator from infancy; the first notion he acquires in life is that he was born to command, and the first habit he contracts is that of ruling without resistance. His education tends, then, to give him the character of a haughty and hasty man—irascible, violent, ardent in his desires, impatient of obstacles." In 1838, dismayed British visitor George Combe noticed the same unfortunate habits: "The people worship themselves as the fountains equally of wisdom and power. They bend all institutions in subserviency to their views and feelings. They are no longer led by, but they often dictate to, the wealthy and the highly educated." He observed "the great self-complacency of the mass of the people, who although very imperfectly educated, are persuaded by political orators that they know everything, and can decide wisely on every question; [there is a] general absence of reverence for authority or superior wisdom, displayed first in childhood and afterwards in the general progress of life."

Nowhere was this more obvious than in politics, where the Common Man was suddenly all-powerful. Writing of the effects of the universal voting franchise, Englishman Walter Bagehot observed:

> The steadily augmenting power of the lower orders in America has naturally augmented the dangers of the Federal Union . . . . [U]niversal suffrage . . . places the entire control over the political action of the whole State in the hands of common labourers, who are of all classes the least instructed—of all the most aggressive—of all the most likely to be influenced by local animosity—of all the most likely to exaggerate every momentary sentiment . . . . The unpleasantness of mob government has never before been exemplified so conspicuously, for it never before has worked upon so large a scene.

The rejection of authority was reflected in the sudden fade of prestige and power of the Chief Executive between 1789 and 1860, from the most revered Presidents—Washington-Adams-Jefferson-Madison-Monroe—to the most feeble—Taylor-Fillmore-Pierce-Buchanan.

Jacksonian society was so young, so little organized, so without stabilizing institutions, that it had no resistance to strain; it was at risk of shattering under the shock of an emotional convulsion such as slavery stirred. As Henry James noted:

> One might enumerate the items of high civilisation, as it exists in other countries, which are absent from the texture of American life, until it should become a wonder to know what was left. No State, in the European sense of the word, and indeed barely a specific national name. No sovereign, no court, no personal loyalty, no aristocracy, no church, no clergy, no army, no diplomatic service, no country gentlemen, no palaces, no castles, nor manors, nor old country houses, nor parsonages, nor thatched cottages, nor ivied ruins; no cathedrals, nor abbeys, nor little Norman churches; no great universities nor public schools . . . .

James' impressionistic sketch of American life was a list of missing conservative elements:

- There was "no sovereign, no court"—no royal power that could decree solutions and bind all parties.

- . . . "no personal loyalty." America was a land without personal allegiance. It was a country of provincials, people whose loyalty was to that which they could see at first hand—as expressed by the man who said, "I go first for Greenville, then for Greenville District, then for the up-country, then for South Carolina, then for the South, then for the United States."

- . . . "no church, no clergy." The most powerful engine for social cohesion in Western history was itself in atoms. In the aftermath of the Second Great Awakening of the 1820s and 1830s, religious enthusiasm was cresting, but its vitality was expressed in individual, personal rebirth. With camp meetings and new churches springing up everywhere, the churches themselves splintered into a thousand parts. Philosophers like Emerson and Thoreau were teaching that every man was his own minister.

- . . . "no army." The institution that worked hand-in-glove with the regimes of the Old World to translate policy into action was nowhere seen. American revolutionaries had preached the evils of the standing army, so there wasn't one. With no powerful enemies on its borders, there remained only the vestige of an army, a pigmy thing, a few thousand men idling in a hundred small outposts on the Western frontier.

- Neither was there a judicial system that carried authority. In Jacksonian America, there was no court esteemed enough to command a binding solution, such as the English Lord Chief Justice possessed in 1772, when he ruled that slavery was not supported by English law, and laid the legal basis for the freeing of England's 15,000 slaves. The courts in America, by contrast, were in wretchedly low repute, largely because there was no national bar to set and enforce professional standards. By the 1830s the democratic impulse in America had carried away all previous standards for admission to the law profession. If every man was the equal of every other, popular thinking went, no one should be prevented from practicing in any field. Indiana, for example, provided in its constitution that "every person of good moral character, being a voter, shall be entitled to admission to practice law in all courts of justice." In Illinois, Abraham Lincoln received a license to practice law in 1836 without any training; he had taught himself, reading books borrowed from friends. When he ran for election in 1860, only three years after the nadir of American jurisprudence—the Dred Scott decision, ignored by the majority of the people—there was a sneer explicit in referring to Lincoln as a "prairie lawyer." It was an epithet, one that drew its sting from a widespread contempt for lawyers and the profession of law. Anti-slavery intellectuals in New England developed the idea that there was no law they were bound to respect except a "higher law." Henry Thoreau's *Civil Disobedience* in 1849 exclaimed that breaking the written law was a duty in a society where the law protected slavery. William Lloyd Garrison went even further, shouting "To Hell with the Constitution" from the pages of the *Liberator*, and burning copies of the Constitution in public.

• And there was little national history. Public records weren't kept. Tocqueville himself had noticed, "no methodical system . . . pursued, no archives . . . formed, and no documents . . . brought together when it would be easy to do so." As a result, "the only historical remains in the United States are newspapers." Every new public official had to start from scratch, with no accumulated experience, no wisdom to draw upon. The bonds of nationhood were weak, sustained almost entirely by worship of the Founding Fathers. "We are so young a people," wrote George Templeton Strong in his diary, "that we feel the want of nationality, and delight in whatever asserts our national 'American' existence. We have not, like England and France, centuries of achievement and calamities to look back on; we have no *record* of Americanism and we feel its want. . . ."

All these were unavailable to Americans in the Age of Jackson. They had instead a lack of history, a worship of the individual, and a contempt for all authority—including the authority of their own democracy, which was still considered an "experiment." With no conservative institutions to provide cohesion, with nothing to which a statesman could appeal, demagogues dominated. With everything unsettled, power was seized by those most settled in their convictions, often the least responsible and the most extreme.

* * *

It was in this milieu of indiscipline and unbridled emotion that the abolitionists appeared in the early 1830s.

Abolition societies were a new phenomenon. In colonial America, the rare abolitionist had been an isolated zealot, possibly insane. Slavery was a system that had stood above criticism for three thousand years—*why would anyone oppose both the Old Testament and the natural order?* But the ancient rules trembled like the walls of Jericho before the terrible trumpets of the evangelical Christian movement of the 1820s. It begat thousands of reformers, men and women appalled at the wickedness of America, especially the sin of slavery. At the same time, Van Buren and the architects of the new Democratic Party understood that any national party—that is, one attracting both Northerners and Southerners—would be impossible if it took a stand on slavery, and avoidance of the issue became the rule during the rise of the national parties. Anti-slavery, thus ruled out of bounds in politics, sought and found other venues.

On January 31, 1831, the first issue of the *Liberator*, a Boston abolitionist newspaper edited by William Lloyd Garrison, marked the birth of the organized abolitionist movement in America. Garrison was a bomb thrower. He wrote to inflame, to shock, to incite. His sentences ended in exclamation points. He was a product of the 1820s evangelical explosion, and he took the spirit of Jesus overturning the tables of the money-changers in the Temple. In his first issue, he announced, "I *will be* as harsh as truth, and as uncompromising as justice. On this subject, I do not wish to think, or speak or write with moderation. No! No! Tell a man whose house is on fire, to give a moderate alarm; tell him to moderately rescue his wife from the hands of the ravisher; tell the mother to gradually extricate her babe from the fire into which it has fallen; — but urge me not to use moderation in a cause like the present. I am in earnest—I will not equivocate—I will not excuse—I will not retreat a single inch—AND I WILL BE HEARD."

The moral attack by abolitionists such as Garrison ended the "necessary evil" attitude of the South toward slavery, held since the Revolution. Abolitionists, many of whom were famous religious leaders, called slavery "sin," and all slaveholders, whether cruel or kind, "sinners." So now, to remove its terrible stain, the South increasingly defended slavery as a positive good. The violent and uncompromising attacks of Garrison and his followers produced for the first time a self-righteous defiance in the South. Attacks on slavery mobilized a new Southern patriotism, a new self-awareness in opposition to the abolitionists. And at the heart of this reaction was a new view of slavery as a blessing to both master and slave.

The new pro-slavery argument reaffirmed that slavery had God-given Biblical sanction, that science had established the biological inferiority of the

African race, and that history had proved slavery the best foundation for stability and progress. The personal odyssey of the champion of the South, Senator John C. Calhoun, provides an insight into the Southern mind at large. As a youth, Calhoun conceded that slavery was "a dark cloud that obscures half the luster of our free institutions." But after Northern attacks on it, he rushed to its support. "Many in the South," he explained, "once believed that it was a moral and political evil; that folly and delusion are gone; we see it now in its true light, and regard it as the most safe and stable basis for free institutions in the world."

The pro-slavery argument also claimed that slavery was the best way of life for the "irresponsible and childlike" Negro, giving him more protection than any other system. "The Negro slaves of the South are the happiest, and, in some sense, the freest people in the world," wrote one defender. "No fact is plainer than that the blacks have been elevated by their servitude in this country," wrote another; "We cannot possibly conceive, indeed, how Divine Providence could have placed them in a better school of correction." Another made the case for slavery in verse:

> *Instructed thus, and in the only school*
> *Barbarians ever know—a master's rule,*
> *The Negro learns each civilizing art*
> *That softens and subdues the savage heart,*
> *Assumes the tone of those with whom he lives,*
> *Acquires the habit that refinement gives,*
> *And slowly learns, but surely, while a slave*
> *The lessons that his country never gave.*

Buttressed by these supports, proponents of slavery went further, painting abolitionists as "criminal agitators," bent on destroying peace and order; as fanatics, heretics, the enemy of property rights and all other social controls.

Garrison's published rants would have had little effect in the North but for the sense of persecution and bitterness they provoked in the South. There, the Nat Turner Rebellion in 1831 intensified a sense of dread and insecurity. Believing abolitionists were bent on inciting more bloody insurrections, the defenders of slavery struck out wildly. Georgia offered a $5,000 reward for the trial and conviction of Garrison. Laws were passed forbidding teaching slaves to read. In defiance of Federal law, Southerners tampered with the mails. An abolitionist mailing campaign to distribute the *Liberator* and other anti-slavery publications to opinion-makers in the South was intercepted in post offices across the South in the 1830s, and the offensive tracts seized and burned. This censoring and burning of the U.S. mail outraged the North where Garrison could not.

Then, in 1837, a pro-slavery mob massed on the banks of the Mississippi River in Illinois to burn down the new printing press of the abolitionist preacher and publisher, Elijah Lovejoy. Mobs had already thrown three of Lovejoy's presses into the river, and when Lovejoy attempted to defend his fourth, the mob cut him down in a hail of bullets; he died shot five times. Lovejoy's murder gripped the nation's attention, and produced in the North a new wave of hostility to the defenders of slavery.

Beginning in the 1830s, the South was united by aristocrats who insisted that no frank discussion of slavery could safely be tolerated. "Freedom of speech is to be distinguished from licentiousness," they argued; "No man has a moral right to use the power of speech in defiance of reason and revelation." Under this repressive regime, the Southern pro-slavery consensus hardened in the years leading up to the Civil War. By 1859, Jefferson Davis could claim that ten years earlier there might have been men in the South who thought slavery wrong, but such had been the progress of "truth and sound philosophy," that "there is not probably an intelligent mind among our own citizens who doubts either the moral or the legal right of the institution of African slavery, as it exists in our country." Every Southern state except Kentucky passed laws controlling and limiting speech, press, and discussion of slavery. Virginia's law punished anyone who "by speaking or writing maintains that owners have no right of property in slaves" with up to a year in jail and a fine of up to $500. Louisiana punished conversation "having a tendency to promote discontent among free colored people, or insubordination among slaves" with a prison term of twenty-one years at hard labor to death.

But courts were slow. When something swifter and more effective was needed, the South turned to lynch mobs, called "vigilance committees," which were given quasi-legal status, as in South Carolina, where Governor Hammond believed that abolitionism could be "silenced in but one way—Terror—Death." According to the governor, a group of citizens who gathered to lynch abolitionists was "no more a mob than a rally of shepherds to chase a wolf out of their pastures."

Thus the combat was joined between Northerners, who grew up believing that life in the South was lived with chains, bloodhounds, auction blocks, and mobs; and Southerners, who were taught that evil slanderers in the North were anxious to stir up slaves to warfare to exterminate their white masters. Each side was able to demonize the other, since there was very little contact between the sections. The dispute over slavery became an entirely abstract moral struggle. Taking the form of "good" vs. "evil," of "the righteous" vs. "the wicked," the slavery argument was of the deadliest kind, and the least likely of solution.

With no conservative elements at work to bridge the divide, the slavery argument in America could only be a louder and louder shouting match, framed in moral absolutes. It became more and more venomous, as each side saw itself as divinely sanctioned, and the other side as an abomination in God's eyes. From the 1830s on, the oscillating pattern of claim and counter-claim, charge and counter-charge between Northern abolitionists and Southern "slavocrats" eventually spiraled into a dispute whose intensity produced a holocaust.

*   *   *

In the 1830s this bitter slavery battle was still being fought outside Washington. As long as the slavery controversy was fought in the abstract, it had little traction in the sphere of national politics. According to the Constitution, the only places where the Federal government had any jurisdiction over slavery were the Federal lands—the national territories and the District of Columbia. Only when there was new national territory could the slavery argument flare up in Congress, as it had over Missouri in 1820.

So after the war with Mexico ended in 1848, when the area of the United States was enlarged by more than a million square miles of western territory, the bitterness over slavery came into collision with "Manifest Destiny," the national obsession over land. In 1846, Pennsylvanian David Wilmot broke Congress' twenty-year-long code of silence on slavery and, from the floor of the House, urged a ban on slavery in the new territories. From then until Lincoln's election in 1860, arguments over slavery in the West overshadowed all other concerns in the nation's capital. At stake was the future of the continent. The Wilmot Proviso changed the political landscape forever—debates in Congress, which had up until this time been between national parties, were now between sections, North vs. South. Northern editors illumined the importance of the territories by pointing out that if slavery were allowed to go there, "the free labor of all the states will not," since free men did not want to compete with slave labor. If slavery were kept out, however, "The free labor of the states [will go] there . . . and in a few years the country will teem with an active and energetic population." To Southerners, it mattered little that the harsh, dry climate made an agrarian slave society impossible. The stakes were much bigger than profits. As one Georgia editor wrote, opening the territory to slavery would "secure to the South the balance of power in the [U.S.], and for all coming time . . . give to her the control in the operations of the Government."

Abuse from abolitionists had been one thing—after all, abolitionists were not popular in the North, either—but now the South found itself facing hostility in the very halls of Congress. Every issue, large and small, seemed to point back to the slavery issue. By 1848, the Senator from Missouri likened the omnipresence of the slavery argument to a plague of frogs: "You could not look upon the table but there were frogs, you could not sit down at the banquet but there were frogs, you could not go to the bridal couch and lift the sheets but there were frogs. We can see nothing, touch nothing, have no measures proposed, without having this pestilence thrust before us."

Once in Congress, the emotional temperature of the slavery debate soared. By 1860, practically every member of the House came to the floor armed with a knife or a gun. The South was still an aristocratic society where any gesture of inequality was an insult, and was properly met by a challenge to a duel. To accept such an insult was submission; it was surrender. Southerners had a violent reaction to being told by Northerners that they could not take their property into the West. It was a denial of Southern equality, and it was regarded as a damnable affront. As a Virginia Supreme Court justice saw it, the Wilmot Proviso "pretends to an insulting superiority on the one hand, and denounces a degrading inequality or inferiority on the other: which says in effect to the Southern man, Avaunt! You are not my equal, and hence are to be excluded as carrying a moral taint with you."

Moreover, there was a special acuteness in Southerners' sensitivity to any suggestion of inferiority—ironically, because of their constant exposure to the conditions of the black slaves themselves. Any loss of freedom, they felt, would put them on the road to a condition similar to these pitiful creatures. The editorials of the period are full of warnings alive with the imagery of chains, bonds, manacles, and fetters. The heady experience of being the master of other human beings bred a powerful devotion to freedom—their own. As a result, they saw their fight for slavery in the territories as a fight against despotism, a fight against their own enslavement. South Carolinian Lawrence M. Keitt said, "I would rather my state should be the graveyard of martyred patriots than the slave of northern abolitionists." Virginian George Fitzhugh complained that African slavery was "not half so humiliating and disgraceful as the slavery of the South to the North." An Alabama congressman: "It is clear that the power to dictate what sort of property the State may allow a citizen to own and work—whether oxen, horses, or negroes . . . is alike despotic and tyrannical." And another: "Southerners must refuse to be bridled and saddled and rode under whip and spur." Increasingly, they saw their duel with the North as being the extension of the battle against enslavement they had fought against King George III, except that, in 1861, Abraham Lincoln had taken the place of King George. The outgoing Secretary of War, Jacob Thompson, put the alternatives available to the South as "naked submission or secession"; "We are either slaves in the Union or freemen out of it."

*   *   *

Finally, the Southern exodus in reaction to Lincoln's election, so out of proportion to any threat he posed, was possible because fundamental principles of democracy had been violated for a generation. Civil liberties in the South were already in tatters, under assault by the logic of slavery. To buttress the pro-slavery argument, Southern opinion-makers tried to show that "the little experiment" of free society was a failure. "Modern free society, as at present organized," editorialized the New Orleans *Delta*, "is radically wrong and rotten. It is self-destroying, and can never exist happily and normally, until it is qualified by the introduction of some principle equivalent in its effect to the institution of slavery." The Richmond *Enquirer* agreed: "Free society in the long run is an impracticable form of society; it is everywhere starving, demoralized, and insurrectionary . . . cowardly, selfish, sensual, licentious, infidel, agrarian and revolutionary." Not only was free society a failure, the argument went, but workers within such a society were worse off: "the whole hireling class of manual laborers and 'operatives' as you call them are essentially slaves." The *Enquirer*'s solution? "Make the laboring man the slave of one man instead of the slave of society and he would be far better off." If one argued that a slave society was superior to a free one, it must mean that anybody could be a slave. The *Enquirer* boldly drew this conclusion in 1856:

> The South now maintains that slavery is right, natural, and necessary. It shows that all divine and almost all human authority justifies it. The South further charges, that the little experiment of free society has been, from the beginning, a cruel failure, and that symptoms of failure are abundant in our North. While it is far more obvious that Negroes be slaves than whites—for they are only fit to labor, not to direct—yet the principle of

slavery is in itself right, and does not depend on difference of complection.

Pointing out that Biblical slaves were not black, the *Enquirer* concluded that "confining the jurisdiction of slavery to that race would be to weaken its scriptural authority."

And while white men were not yet picking cotton in shackles, their liberties in the South were already violated. A Southerner could not teach a slave to read, nor could he hire one, or have one testify in court. He could not move or free his own slaves without permission. He could not speak against slavery, nor could he write, listen to, or read any opinions against slavery. An anonymous Virginian complained, "In Southern states the non-slave-holding whites are no longer free, a padlock has been placed on their mouths . . . , and they enjoy less liberty than the subjects of many European monarchs." He and anyone who agreed with him, however, found it wise to keep quiet.

The South claimed to be democratic, but the aristocrats there had no belief in democracy. A belief in true democracy would have demanded a free discussion. But from the 1830s on, Southern leaders had decided that slavery could not be safely discussed. By this systematic repression in the South, an entire generation had grown up hearing and reading little but the speeches and editorials of the extremists among them. They had been deluded by these men into believing that all Northerners were abolitionists, rabidly hostile to their institutions. In the grip of a hallucination shaped by the "fire-eaters," Southerners saw Abraham Lincoln as a deadlier John Brown, an avenger who would swoop down and destroy their society in an apocalypse of blood. It was only in a period that fostered a neglect of social duty that such a hallucination could become general. But this was such an age—the Age of Jackson, whose worship of the unfettered individual coincided fatally with the desperate striking-out of a Southern society that now dimly realized that its way of life was slouching toward oblivion.

Chapter 6

Lincoln's Nomination

"Who is this huckster in politics?"

The United States in 1860 was in need of a statesman of the stature of a Washington, someone who could overawe the devils of division in America long enough to allow time to free the slaves without a convulsion of violence. We have seen how the rules of society and politics in the Age of Jackson conspired against the ascent of a great national healer, both by creating the white-hot heat of the crisis, and at the same time making the election of a great man improbable. But how was it that a figure as unlikely as Abraham Lincoln was raised up to lead the country at this most explosive moment in its history?

He was the least qualified candidate for President ever elected—a private citizen, an obscure country lawyer in a provincial western state. His only brief appearance in Washington had been as a one-term congressman from 1847-1849, after winning the Seventh Congressional District of central Illinois by a vote of 6,340 to 4,829. By 1860 his distant, unremarkable two years in Congress had left no ripple on the pool of public memory.

He had never run anything larger than a two-partner law office.

In late November 1859, with only six months until the Republican national convention of May 1860, the Philadelphia *Press* listed forty-five men whose names were prominently mentioned as possible presidential nominees. Abraham Lincoln was not among them.

Outside his state, Lincoln was remembered only for his losing U.S. Senate race against Steven Douglas. Two years before, in 1858, Lincoln had entered the Senate campaign against the wishes of the party bosses back east. So little respect did the seaboard Republicans have for Lincoln and his frontier state party that they pressured the Illinois organization not to oppose Douglas for the Senate seat—in effect, telling the Illinois Republicans to drop dead. The Easterners were in the throes of a love affair with the Little Giant, charmed by the spectacle of his death-grapple with the pro-slavery President Buchanan for control of the Democratic Party. America's most famous Republican editor, the

New York *Tribune*'s Horace Greeley, lauded Douglas, saying, "no public man in our day has evinced a nobler fidelity and courage." Fellow anti-slavery editor William Cullen Bryant of the New York *Evening Post* called him a "good-enough Republican." They held out the belief that if Illinois Republicans made no contest against Douglas he would ultimately find a home in the Republican Party—and bring a hundred thousand Illinois Democrats with him. Illinoisans, however, knew Douglas better than that, and Lincoln's backers resented the interference. The Republican Chicago *Tribune* grumbled about "a considerable notion pervading the brains of the political wet nurses at the East, that the barbarians of Illinois cannot take care of themselves." A worried Lincoln wrote to a friend that "if the [New York] *Tribune* continues to din [Douglas'] praises into the ears of its five or ten thousand Republican readers in Illinois, it is more than can be hoped that all will stand firm." But Illinois Republicans did stand firm, and rebuffed the Easterners at their state convention by declaring Lincoln their nominee.

The credentials of the antagonists were unequal. Douglas, the Democratic incumbent, was a two-term Illinois Senator and had been a national figure for more than a decade, an acknowledged candidate for the presidency. Lincoln had meanwhile toiled in obscurity as a circuit court lawyer, riding in a buggy from town to town, arguing cases in crude county courts during the day, telling funny stories in the evening, and sleeping two-to-a-bed with other circuit lawyers at night. His political ambitions had become reanimated by the national uproar over the Kansas question in the mid-50s, and for the previous two years he had helped organize the infant Republican Party in the state without attracting outside attention. Lincoln himself was unsure. About the time Lincoln entered upon the campaign he wrote down these thoughts: "Twenty-two years ago Judge Douglas and I first became acquainted. We were both young men then—he a trifle younger than I. Even then we were both ambitious—I perhaps quite as much so as he. With me the race of ambition has been a failure—a flat failure; with him, it has been one of splendid success. His name fills the nation and is not unknown even in foreign lands. I affect no contempt for the high eminence he has reached . . .; I would rather stand on that eminence than wear the richest crown that ever pressed a monarch's brow."

Senator Douglas traveled the state in late summer of 1858 like the political star he was, in a private railroad car with a brass cannon on a flatcar in the rear. As the train approached a prairie town, a crew of two men in uniform would fire the cannon to boom the news ahead that the Little Giant was arriving. Conceding that Douglas' crowds would be bigger than any he could draw,

Lincoln shadowed Douglas on the first five towns on his tour, answering each of the Democrat's speeches with one of his own. He often traveled on the same train that drew Douglas' private car, riding as an ordinary passenger. Lincoln's men distributed handbills at the Douglas gatherings, notifying the people where and when the Republican candidate would reply. The Democratic Chicago *Times* scoffed: "Lincoln must do something, even if that something is mean, sneaking, and disreputable. The cringing, crawling creature is hanging at the outskirts of Douglas meetings, begging the people to come and hear him." Further,

> Mr. Lincoln . . . with a desperate attempt at looking pleasant, said that he would not take advantage of Judge Douglas' crowd, but would address 'sich' as liked to hear him in the evening at the courthouse . . . pleading his humility, and asking forgiveness of Heaven for his enemies, he stood washing his hands with invisible soap in imperceptible water, until his friends, seeing that his mind was wandering, took him in charge and bundled him off the grounds.

Lincoln responded to the newspaper abuse by changing tactics. He challenged Douglas to a series of debates. The Senator was understandably reluctant: as the heavy favorite, he would only be giving the obscure Lincoln a share of his publicity and prestige by appearing with him and confronting him head-to-head. Nevertheless, he could not afford to refuse. Douglas consented to seven debates.

Those debates have passed into lore, although they are now viewed in a circus-mirror lens that magnifies Lincoln and dwarfs Douglas according to the former's later achievements. Now famous as the Lincoln-Douglas debates, they were more properly the Douglas-Lincoln debates, according to the public standing of the two men at the time. Lincoln's sinewy logic and pungent expression of Republican principles got him noticed for the first time by the watchful back east. The debates failed to win him the election, however. Douglas emerged the hero of the contest, holding his state for the Democrats while most of the North went for the Republicans. The seaboard Republicans, who cared nothing for Lincoln, were glad of Douglas' triumph. They could trumpet the result as a rebuke to Douglas' Democratic Party enemies, the pro-slavery Democrats in Washington. A disappointed Lincoln wrote a letter to a personal friend as if chiseling his own political epitaph: "Though I now sink out of view, and shall be forgotten, I believe I have made some marks which will tell for the cause of civil liberty long after I am gone."

His friends refused to share his gloom. Encouraged by the notion that Douglas' certain presidential run in 1860 would buoy Lincoln's own career, since the debates had cast him in the public mind as Douglas' nemesis, they resolved to run him for the presidency. (Democratic papers, of course, reversed the argument to disparage Lincoln. As the Cincinnati *Enquirer* saw it, "Without Douglas Lincoln would be nothing, and this he virtually admits by being nothing but anti-Douglas. At once a parasite and enemy, he labors insanely to destroy that upon which depends his own existence.")

But the defeated Lincoln's campaigning spirit was missing in 1859. He did not share his friends' optimism—he said that he didn't lack the ambition, but had no confidence in success. "I must, in candor, say that I do not think myself fit for the Presidency," he wrote to a newspaper editor in April, and made the same disclaimer to another correspondent in July. Certainly his strengths were speech and debate, which would be at home in the Senate; he had none of the administrative talent or experience needed for the presidency. For the entire year, he played the role of the Republican soldier—practicing law, making occasional speeches in nearby states, and writing letters on high policy to influential Republicans. As late as November of 1859 Lincoln was still self-effacing: "For my single self, I have enlisted for the permanent success of the Republican cause, and for this object I shall labor faithfully in the ranks, unless, as I think not probable, the judgment of the party shall assign me a different position." As late as January 1860, he lacked support for a presidential try even in his home state. Many local politicians, especially in conservative southern Illinois, considered him too "liberal," a codeword for "anti-slavery." Others were put off by his lack of experience.

*   *   *

But there was an element of craft to Lincoln's self-imposed year in the wilderness after the debates. Maintaining, as he did during the whole of that year, that he was only looking toward another Senate try in 1864, he kept his name on the lips of the faithful while at the same time avoiding the brickbats of other presidential candidates. In fact, when he penned his November promise to "labor faithfully in the ranks," he had already made an appointment that revealed a craving for wider recognition. In October of 1859, he had agreed to lecture on politics in New York, at Henry Ward Beecher's famous Plymouth

Church in Brooklyn. The venue and sponsorship of the address were changed at the last minute, and on February 27, 1860, Lincoln delivered his speech at the downtown Cooper Union for the Young Men's Central Republican Union of New York City, with Republican kingmakers Horace Greeley and William Cullen Bryant giving silent benediction on the podium behind him and a large crowd of intellect and culture in front of him.

He made a shaky start. The New Yorkers whispered behind their hands when they saw his awkward manner and his ill-fitting clothes with suitcase creases still showing, and winced when they heard his shrill voice and his backwoods accent. ("Mr. *Cheer*man," he began.) But over the next two hours, his eccentricities were forgotten as the power of his ideas, the weight of his logic, the lucidity of his arguments, and the fascination of his gestures and expressions, which he had practiced for years in a thousand stump speeches given from wagon beds in prairie town squares, bound them by a spell. When he thundered the final words—"LET US HAVE FAITH THAT RIGHT MAKES MIGHT, AND IN THAT FAITH LET US, TO THE END, DARE TO DO OUR DUTY AS WE UNDERSTAND IT"—the fifteen hundred in attendance forgot themselves and jumped to their feet, shouted, waved their hats, and rushed the stage to shake his hand and praise him. (It was the only time New Yorkers would ever do so.) When he started the speech he had been what the New York *Times* called him: a lawyer of some local Illinois reputation. When he finished on that night only three months before the Republican nominating convention, Lincoln had become a presidential contender.

A poor performance at the Cooper Union so close to the convention would have killed Lincoln's chances for the nomination. Greeley advertised the event with the prediction, "It is not probable that Mr. Lincoln will be heard again in our City this year if ever." But, though it encouraged Lincoln and his friends in Illinois and spurred them to new efforts in the coming weeks, his spectacular showing did not have a commensurate power to vault him immediately to the prize—as witnessed by the next issue of the New York *Weekly Tribune*. It shuffled its account of Lincoln's Cooper Union speech back to pages two and three. The front page was devoted to a speech by "Mr. Republican"—William H. Seward.

On February 29, Seward had delivered his speech on the floor of the Senate to packed galleries, a phalanx of congressmen, and a full corps of scribbling reporters. His intended audience was much larger, however: thirty million countrymen were eagerly awaiting an address by the acknowledged spokesman for the Republican Party. This was the first full-dress pronouncement in two years by the man who figured to be the Republican candidate, pending his formal ratification by the delegates at the Republican convention two months away. Seward's speech was statesmanlike and eloquent. It was an olive branch to the South: a repudiation of the recent John Brown raid and a denial of any aggressive intent against slavery where it existed. Not only did the *Tribune* devote six first-page columns to the reprinting of Seward's entire speech, it had already printed two hundred and fifty thousand copies of it, and was preparing a pamphlet edition of a million within the month. What Seward said was front-page news.

Since joining the Republican Party in 1855, Seward's government experience, proven ability, political savvy, and long-time service to the free-soil cause had made him its distinguished leader. He and his partner Thurlow Weed, the New York party boss and editor of the Albany *Evening Journal*, were the most potent political combination since Andrew Jackson and Martin Van Buren. Together, they had made Seward governor of New York in 1838, elected him United States Senator from New York in 1849, reelected him in 1855, and lifted him into the highest echelons of national power. He had been President Zachary Taylor's most trusted advisor in 1850, and in 1856 had snubbed the Republican presidential nomination because he didn't think the brand-new party could win. Weed, the Stromboli who pulled the strings of a huge network of New York financial interests, had a proven record of raising slush funds. These "oceans of cash," Republicans were told, were funds they would need in the fall election; Seward men liked to bait opponents with the question, "If you don't nominate Seward, where will you get your money?" With the Republican convention looming in May, he was not only the first choice of his own delegate-rich New York, but also of New England and the upper tier of northern states: Michigan, Wisconsin, and Minnesota. All spring of 1860 Seward spoke confidently of the nomination, giving lavish parties and keeping in close touch with his powerful, rich friends in New York. When he left Washington to go home to Auburn to await the nomination in Chicago, he told friends that he expected to return to the nation's capital in a much higher capacity.

But the very things that made Seward strong made him weak. He had been a leading political figure for so long that he had made many enemies, and now they could be heard sharpening their knives. His strength was in the states that were probably won for the Republicans no matter who ran. The real battleground was in the lower tier of northern states that had voted Democratic four years ago: Illinois, Indiana, Pennsylvania, and New Jersey. If those states could be brought into the Republican column, the presidency would be theirs. And these were the states where Seward's radical reputation was a liability, where the voters were conservative on the slavery issue. They were disturbed by the memory of his 1852 speech wherein he had disparaged the Constitution in favor of a "higher law" which declared slavery a sin, and his 1858 "irrepressible conflict" speech, which had sounded like the blast of a battle trumpet. Many in these states blamed Seward's strident anti-slavery rhetoric for the impulse that had sent John Brown on the bloody-eyed Harpers Ferry raid that had inflamed the South the previous October. On the other hand, while Seward's moral fervor had made him a hero to the radicals in the North, he had betrayed them by his conciliatory speeches and soothing gestures toward the South as the election neared. Seward's coffers were swollen by shady financial deals made by his string-pulling partner, Thurlow Weed, and the stink of it offended many in the party, and would prevent them from pointing a self-righteous finger at the corrupt Buchanan administration. Also, Seward was the frontrunner, which pitted every other candidate against him.

Seward's rivals for the nomination appeared to be three. The first was Salmon P. Chase of Ohio, the darling of the radical anti-slavery wing of the party, courageous, of spotless character and commanding presence, handsome, cultivated, intelligent, and relentlessly ambitious for the presidency. His Republican credentials had been established long before any of the other contenders—he had been among the first national leaders to identify himself with the new party when doing so was a brave act of conscience. However, he was even more radical than Seward on slavery and thus shared Seward's difficulties in the key battleground states. He couldn't even command the full support of the delegates from his own state.

Perhaps more dangerous was Edward Bates of Missouri. Bates had the endorsement of the second most famous Republican, Horace Greeley, who was bitterly anti-Seward. Besides his personal antipathy to Seward, Greeley backed Bates because the latter was a Southern anti-slavery man, which made him popular in the Border States, not only the northern tier of Missouri, Kentucky, Maryland, and Delaware, but also the southern tier of Arkansas, Tennessee, Virginia, and North Carolina; he could get votes in the South as well as the North, and if he won the election, he would be the Republican most likely to keep the Deep South in the Union. But personally Bates was a cold fish. He excited no one. He had given all his recent years to legal work, he hadn't held office for twenty-five years, and he was little known in the East. He had supported the immigrant-bashing Know-Nothing Party in 1856, and was distrusted by the foreign elements in the party, particularly the Germans, who were needed to carry the Northwest. Bates' weaknesses were a mirror image of Seward's: he would run poorly in the most ardently Republican states, who saw him as a limp middle-of-the-roader. They pointed out that he had never even declared himself a Republican—Bates still called himself a Whig.

Neither could Simon Cameron of Pennsylvania be overlooked. He was a bare-knuckles machine boss, and he had the initial support of the immensely influential *New York Herald*, delegates from his own state, and tariff backers across the North. But his weakness was known to everybody: he had the morals of a pit viper. He summed up his ethics when he said, "An honest politician is one who, when he is bought, will stay bought."

So obscure was Lincoln as the convention approached that pundits still failed to include him on their lists of the top seven, or dozen, or twenty-one, or thirty-four hopeful candidates. Many Republican newspapers, including the *New York Times*, still misspelled his name "Abram" when they did mention him. An engraving of Republican nominees published in *Harper's* magazine in the days before the convention showed a large oval portrait of Seward in the center, pictured above the public buildings of Washington, D.C., where he would presumably soon be directing the government. Ten smaller portraits of the other hopefuls surrounded Seward's portrait, much like the court of the king. Inconspicuous among the ten, in the lower left, was Abraham Lincoln.

But in Lincoln's time, anything could happen at a convention. Although he was inconspicuous and unlikely, Lincoln's candidacy would be aided by the rules of the political game as it was practiced in the Age of Jackson.

* * *

It is interesting that in the drama of Lincoln's skyrocket rise from anonymous prairie lawyer to President of the United States in the six months between the conventions of May and the election of November of 1860, Lincoln himself was not on-stage. According to the campaign etiquette of the time, before the climax the hero must be snatched from view and hustled away into the wings. It is interesting that in an era of no-holds-barred political brawling, Americans were fastidious about this one item of decorum. They insisted that the candidates themselves strike a pose of disinterest during the maddest of the nationwide tumult and remain at home, sitting in their living rooms drinking tea quietly with little fingers extended, appearing not to seek the prize, but letting the honor come to them, if it did come, as if by surprise.

This being the fashion, the action during Lincoln's rise was taken up entirely by his friends, a brilliant group of Illinois jurists and newspapermen, all the more dangerous because they were overlooked and underrated by the smug eastern party bosses. They included Judge David Davis, the bull-necked, three-hundred pound leading figure of Lincoln's central Illinois eighth circuit; Norman B. Judd, a Chicago lawyer, railroad official, and Illinois Republican Chairman; and Charles H. Ray and Joseph Medill, the co-editors of the Chicago *Tribune*.

Lincoln's obscurity was essential to the first, crucial trick taken by his managers. In December of 1859, six months before the convention, the Republican National Committee met in New York to decide on the site for the party convention. Several cities were favored, most prominently St. Louis, home of rising candidate Edward Bates. Lincoln's man Norman Judd, who represented Illinois at the meeting, suggested Chicago, a city evocative of Republican fast-growing strength and go-ahead spirit. *In addition,* Judd said with the studied casualness of a veteran political poker player, *it would be neutral, since Illinois had no candidate of her own.* Heads nodded. In a show of hands, the Windy City was chosen as the convention site by one vote—Judd's own.

With just one week to go until the Chicago convention, Lincoln was still promised no votes at all. The next crucial coup, then, was for him to somehow gain the votes of all the Illinois delegates at the state Republican convention held in Decatur on May 9 and 10—a hard trick to pull off, since politically Illinois was two states: upstate Illinois, settled by emigrants from the northeast, anti-slavery in their views and pulling for Seward; and downstate Illinois—nicknamed "Egypt" for its political makeup so foreign to the northern counties, with Cairo its largest city—settled by Southerners, indifferent to slavery and leaning toward Bates. In February, Lincoln, still seeing himself as a candidate for the Senate in 1864, had penned a pessimistic letter to Judd concerning the Illinois delegation. Speaking of his senatorial chances, he wrote, "I am not in a position where it would hurt much for me not to be nominated on the national ticket, but I am where it would hurt some for me not to get the Illinois delegates." Judd's strategy was for Lincoln not to divide the already divided delegation by trying to cajole the delegates one by one, but rather to insist on a convention rule that all the delegates vote as a bloc, and trust state pride to compel the delegates to fall in behind it.

Lincoln was lucky in the location of the state convention. Decatur was in his base, the middle of the state. It had been his home, it was in the Eighth Circuit he had worn smooth in his many years as a lawyer, and the town was eager to cheer him. Lincoln's friends had their strategy well planned. On the first day of the convention, Lincoln called attention to himself with a late entrance, and received a tumultuous welcome by the three-thousand-strong hometown crowd, who hoisted him and propelled him over their heads, hand over hand, to a seat on the platform. As the shouting died down, his friend, Decatur politician Richard Oglesby, stood up and announced that he wished to offer Lincoln a contribution. The multitude, still on their feet, roared their approval, and, from the rear of the hall, down the center aisle came Lincoln's country cousin, bearded old John Hanks, carrying two weather-beaten fence rails festooned with American flags and a great banner that proclaimed:

> Abraham Lincoln. The Rail Candidate For President in 1860. Two Rails From a Lot of 3,000 Made in 1830 by Thos. Hanks and Abe Lincoln— Whose Father Was the First Pioneer of Macon County.

Seeing this, the crowd broke into pandemonium. Grown men made such a roar, surged forward in so irresistible a tide, and threw so many hats, canes, and newspapers into the air that part of the improvised canvas roof of the hall collapsed. After fifteen full minutes of barely controlled riot, the wreckage was cleared away and Lincoln rose slowly to speak. *These may or may not be his own rails*, he said, *but surely he had made many better ones!* The crowd roared again, and he sat down. Oglesby's and Hanks' two rough fence rails had conjured a vivid, stirring, homespun image of "the Railsplitter," one that would remind voters of frontier winners like "Old Hickory" and "Tippecanoe." (It was ironic that two country rails were the levers that would lift Lincoln into the White House. Lincoln himself had only distaste for his humble origins. He disliked manual labor and had left it behind as quickly as he could.) The next day, the three hundred local delegates—the Seward men and the Bates men—were compelled to vote "aye" when a Lincoln man introduced these instructions: "That Abraham Lincoln is the choice of the Republican party of Illinois for the Presidency, and the delegates from this State are instructed to use all honorable means to secure his nomination by the Chicago convention, and to vote as a unit for him." Thus did Lincoln's friends not only insure that he would be put in nomination on the floor at Chicago, but that the twenty-two Illinois delegates to Chicago would be solid for him.

* * *

Before the echoes of the cheers in Decatur had died away, crowds began gathering for the main event on the shore of Lake Michigan 150 miles to the north. Seward's managers arrived in Chicago on a special train, accompanied by thirteen carloads of convention delegates and boisterous revelers hand-picked for their booming voices. They brought along a brilliantly uniformed marching band with epaulets shimmering on their shoulders and white and scarlet feathers waving from their caps, and were joined by large contingents from Michigan and Wisconsin. Simon Cameron's handlers detrained with almost four hundred Pennsylvanian roustabouts, plus two bands for extra volume. St. Louis trains belched forth crowds of Bates' boosters.

But they were all dwarfed by the combined lung-power of the Lincoln enthusiasts. Norman Judd, the railroad man, had again proved the master of every contingency. Anticipating large imported cheering sections for the other candidates, his latest ploy would reduce their throatiest efforts to a seeming whisper. He had arranged for Illinois railroads to offer special discounts to the teeming thousands from all over the state who wished to come, to shout down the foreigners and to raise the roof for the Illinois man, the Railsplitter. Judd had gotten the word out, and it was estimated that forty thousand were surging around the convention hall as May 16, the first day of the convention, approached.

Now the Chicago newspapermen went to work. Two days before the convention, the gathered delegates woke up in their hotel rooms, opened Joseph Medill's Chicago *Tribune*, and read the headline: "The Winning Man, Abraham Lincoln," followed by a three-foot-long column of editorial superlatives, giving eight reasons why he should be named. (The first reason was that he had no record, and therefore "He will enter the contest with no clogs, no embarrassment.") The next day, the paper ran the same editorial again. The *Tribune* was capped on the morning of the third, decisive day of balloting by the headline "The Last Entreaty," summarizing once again the arguments for Lincoln.

Given that Lincoln's profile was hazy for most of the delegates, his strength lay in the fact that no one made "any positive objection" to him. He had no history, so nothing he had said or done had offended anybody—a rare asset among politicians after the bitterness and violence of the slavery-torn 1850s. The political map of the free states was not unlike the map of Illinois: anti-slavery men to the north, conservatives to the south. As before, Lincoln would stake out the middle, and be the man to whom all could finally come. If it would be triumph, it would be the triumph of "availability." He wrote his strategy to a friend in Ohio in March: "My name is new in the field; and I suppose I am not the *first* choice of a very great many. Our policy, then, is to give no offence to others—leave them in a mood to come to us, if they shall be compelled to give up their first love." His managers would concentrate on the delegates of the southern tier of free states, conservative states which had gone Democratic in 1856. These—Indiana, Pennsylvania, and New Jersey, along with Illinois—were the states everyone recognized as necessary to a Republican victory in November. One Iowa delegate, Fitz-Henry Warren, put the search for the "available" candidate memorably: "I am for the man who can carry Pennsylvania, New Jersey, and Indiana, with this reservation, that I will not go into cemetery or catacomb; the candidate must be alive, and able to walk at least from parlor to dining room."

Judge Davis, Norman Judd, and the rest of Lincoln's managers, fresh from Decatur, arrived in Chicago in the days before the convention and set up headquarters at the city's finest hotel, the Tremont House. Soon they were busy testing the wind in the chatter and the whisper of political secrets, raising toasts and laughing with the men in the doubtful delegations, and saying Lincoln's name in a hundred little groups and a thousand confidential conversations. Everything turned on whether Seward could win. By the morning of the convention's first day, Cincinnati *Commercial* reporter Murat Halstead reported that, among the stop-Seward forces, the celebrities were already shaken out: "The Bates movement, the McLean movement, the Cameron movement, the Banks movement, are all nowhere. They had gone down like lead in the mighty waters." All who had national reputations were victims of those reputations. The man who had none, who lacked enough prominence to be marked either as a conservative or a radical, the lawyer who had not set foot in Washington for more than a decade, was the coming man.

When the gavel came down on Wednesday, May 16, it silenced the expectant crackle and hum of the largest political gathering in the nation's history. The first day was prelude, given to the routine business of organization. Halstead wrote that the favorite word was "solemn"; "there is something every ten minutes found to be solemn." The oratory of the second day, devoted to the adoption of the party platform before a crowd even more tightly packed than the day before, sounded the crescendo to what was expected to be the climax in the evening: the nomination of William Seward as Republican candidate for president.

The Seward men were confident of a landslide. The auguries were all brilliant. Informal polls of passengers on trains converging on Chicago had indicated a lock for the front-runner: one train was 127 for Seward, 44 for all others combined; on another, it was 210 for Seward with 30 against; even the train from nearby Milwaukee had been 368 for Seward, 93 for Lincoln, 46 for all others. The delegates seemed ready to vote in the same proportions. A first-day motion by the stop-Seward men aimed at disadvantaging him with a voting rule had been easily defeated, 358 to 94. A straw poll that very afternoon indicated that Seward still had the votes.

The finished platform was adopted unanimously about six o'clock in the evening to "intense enthusiasm. . . . A herd of buffaloes or lions could not have made a more tremendous roaring," wrote Halstead. Seward's moment had arrived. Halstead reported, "So confident were the Seward men, when the platform was adopted, of their ability to nominate their great leader, that they urged an immediate ballot, and would have had it if the clerks had not reported that they were unable to proceed—they had no tally sheets. The cheering of the thousands of spectators during the day indicated that a very large share of the outside pressure was for Seward. There is something almost irresistible here in the prestige of his fame." But the tally sheets did not arrive. There was confusion. Some cried, "Ballot, ballot!" But it was the dinner hour, and a motion to adjourn was also heard. Above the hubbub, conventioneers saw the chairman bring down his gavel. The huge doors swung open, and the throng of ten thousand poured out into the Chicago streets. Thus, abruptly, was the second day ended.

For want of the tally sheets, the nomination was lost.

*   *   *

For on that night, as the popping corks of three hundred bottles of champagne punctuated the easy laughter in the rooms of the Seward men, the Lincoln men were sleeplessly at work, talking urgently with delegates, singly and in groups, going from hotel to hotel, floor to floor, room to room. The stop-Seward movement had been doomed without a consensus candidate, and as late as Thursday night there was none—the votes of the "battleground states" of the lower North were promised to a half dozen men. Just before midnight, in fact, Horace Greeley, Seward's bitterest foe, sent a telegram to his *Tribune* office: "My conclusion from all that I can gather to-night is that the opposition to Governor Seward cannot concentrate on any candidate and that he will be nominated!"

But the Lincoln men had captured an important prize: the delegation of Illinois' neighbor and political twin, Indiana. The Hoosier State's twenty-six delegates had not been promised to a native son. Moreover, the Republican candidate for governor in Indiana, Henry S. Lane, was convinced that he would go down to defeat if forced to ride Seward's radical anti-slavery coattails. That left either Lincoln or Bates. Huddling in caucus, the Hoosier delegates heard Gustave Koerner, a pro-Lincoln German, remind them that German voters had promised to bolt the party *en masse* if Bates, who had an anti-immigrant record, was chosen. He reminded them that the German immigrants were strongly anti-slavery, and a Bates nomination would seem to them a retreat from Republican principles. Needing the strong German vote, the Indiana delegates agreed to vote unanimously for Lincoln on the first ballot.

With Illinois and Indiana already for Lincoln, the Pennsylvania delegates, fifty-six strong, were suddenly ready to consider him. The Pennsylvanians were promised to their favorite son, Simon Cameron, on the first ballot. By now, however, it had become obvious that Cameron, with his lingering stain of corruption and no support outside his state, had no chance at the nomination. Andrew Curtin, the Republican candidate for governor in Pennsylvania, had the same objection to Seward as Lane of Indiana—with so many conservative Pennsylvania voters, Curtin would be defeated if Seward headed the ticket. The Pennsylvanians, like the Indianans, next considered Bates, and again Koerner spoke against Bates on behalf of the Germans, the "Pennsylvania Dutch," who were even more numerous in Pennsylvania than in Indiana. The Keystone State delegates now leaned toward the Illinoisan. Finally, word came back that Cameron would yield his delegates to Lincoln on the second ballot with a *quid pro quo*: Cameron must be promised the Treasury post in a Lincoln cabinet. The offer was telegraphed to Lincoln in Springfield. The stiff-backed Lincoln replied immediately with a rebuke: "I authorize no bargains and will be bound by none." But Judge Davis, the soldier with boots on the ground in Chicago, brushed off Lincoln's for-the-record wire. "Lincoln ain't here, and don't know what we have to meet, so we will go ahead as if we hadn't heard from him, and he must ratify it," he told the team. About midnight, Judge Davis tottered sleepily down the stairs of the Tremont House after meeting with the Pennsylvanians and told Joseph Medill, "Damned if we haven't got them." "How?" asked Medill. "By paying their price," Davis answered.

Now, in the wee hours of the morning, with the crucial states of Illinois, Indiana, and Pennsylvania promised, the stop-Seward movement took definite form and gathered momentum behind Lincoln. New Jersey came in next, then

Vermont and Virginia. Greeley, his ear to the ground, heard the rumble of falling dominoes, and went out again into the night to add his considerable weight to tumble a couple more. He instructed the Missouri delegates to switch from Bates to Lincoln at his signal, and pleaded with the New Hampshire and Maine delegations to fall in line for the nomination of the Illinois lawyer. With their work well started, the Lincoln men were content to wait for the balloting to see their plans mature.

The Illinoisans awoke on Friday, balloting day, determined to press every possible advantage for their candidate. An army of Chicago carpenters had wrought the biggest advantage of all: the "Wigwam," the city-block-sized Republican convention hall, built to order over the previous month. Holding ten thousand people, it was made entirely of pine boards that thrummed sympathetically with the slightest vibration. Murat Halstead called it an acoustic marvel, and wrote, "An ordinary voice can be heard through the whole structure with ease." With its wooden walls and curved roof resonating like the inside of a gigantic violin, it made ten thousand, shouting and stomping in unison, sound like a nation.

Lincoln's friends made sure they would shout and stomp for Lincoln. Jesse Fell and Ward Hill Lamon ordered a large supply of counterfeit tickets printed, kept a staff of young men busy all night forging official-looking signatures on them, and handed them out to husky-voiced Lincoln rooters, who were instructed to show up early. The Sewardites unknowingly assisted the plot by giving a parade Friday morning, led by their magnificently uniformed marching band. By the time they arrived at the Wigwam, their places had been taken by Lincoln men, who had been shoved through the doors until all the seats were occupied and the standing room was jammed. One Chicagoan reputed to be able to shout across the breadth of Lake Michigan was summoned to take a prominent position, and another equally leather-lunged galoot from Ottowa, Illinois, was imported to do the same in another quarter, both with instructions to lead a tempest of cheers whenever Lincoln's name was mentioned.

Their intended audience, the delegates on the broad platform, had been carefully seated under the direction of maestro Norman Judd. At one end of the platform he sat the Seward delegations of New York, Michigan, and Wisconsin, far removed from the prize delegations of the battleground states. At the other end, carefully sandwiched between Illinois and Indiana, was the fifty-six-delegate bonanza of Pennsylvania.

Seward was nominated first, and there were enough Seward men in the building to send up a tremendous shout. A few minutes later, Judd rose and said, "I desire, on behalf of the delegation from Illinois, to put in nomination, as a candidate for President of the United States, Abraham Lincoln of Illinois." The sudden wild roar, according to one witness, "made soft vesper breathings of all that had preceded. No language can describe it. A thousand steam whistles, ten acres of hotel gongs, a tribe of Comanches, headed by a choice vanguard from pandemonium, might have mingled in the scene unnoticed."

When the crowd quieted enough to continue, a Michigan delegate seconded Seward's nomination. Again, a deafening shout.

Then, Mr. Delano from Ohio seconded the nomination of Lincoln. Murat Halstead reported:

> The uproar was beyond description. Imagine all the hogs ever slaughtered in Cincinnati giving their death squeals together, a score of big steam whistles going . . . and you conceive something of the same nature. . . . The Lincoln boys . . . took deep breaths all around, and gave a concentrated shriek that was positively awful, accompanied it with stamping that made every plank and pillar in the building quiver.
>
> Henry S. Lane of Indiana leaped upon a table, and swinging hat and cane, performed like an acrobat. The presumption is he shrieked with the rest, as his mouth was desperately wide open, but no one will ever be able to testify that he has positive knowledge of the fact that he made a particle of noise. His individual voice was lost in the aggregate hurricane.

The New York, Michigan, and Wisconsin delegations sat together and were, in this tempest, very quiet. Many of their faces whitened as the Lincoln *yawp* swelled into a wild hosanna of victory.

Another reporter, from the *Daily Chicago Herald*, also noticed the delegates blanch in the face of the roaring crowd. "It was perfectly amazing to see the effect of 5,000 voices, yelling in made fury, upon the small band of delegates," he wrote. "They fairly quailed before the stentorian power of the people and the majesty of physical force."

And now, staring straight into the reddened, contorted faces of the frenzied multitude only a few feet away and with their ears still ringing, the delegates on the platform were asked to vote. From the outset, they demonstrated their reluctance to spit into such a wind. Starting with the New England states— Seward's base—it was clear that Seward had less strength than everyone had thought. The clerk first called the state of Maine. "Maine casts ten votes for Senator Seward, six votes for Lincoln of Illinois!" (A huge cheer from the convention crowd.) Then, "New Hampshire casts Seward one vote, Chase one vote, Frémont one vote, Lincoln seven votes!" (Another deafening cheer.) Then Vermont: "Ten votes for favorite son Jacob Collamer!" (Cheers again— ten more votes Seward would not get.)

With 233 needed to nominate, the first ballot yielded 173½ for Seward and 102 for Lincoln, with Cameron, Bates, and Chase receiving little more than the "native son" votes from their home states. "The division of the first vote caused a fall in Seward stock," reported Halstead.

Then, on the second ballot, the Pennsylvania bomb exploded. Forty-eight of its votes switched from Cameron to Lincoln, and, wrote Halstead, "the fate of the day was now determined." When the secretary announced the result of the second ballot, it was Seward 184½, Lincoln 181, with other votes scattered.

With the wind now so clearly blowing for Lincoln, the fatal defection from Seward on the third ballot began early in the New England states, and continued throughout. When the secretary reported the third vote, Lincoln stood at 231½—one vote and a half short of nomination. There was a pause of ten seconds, then a stuttering delegate from Ohio rose and cried, "I rise, M-M-Mr. Chairman, t-t-to announce the change of four v-votes of Ohio from Mr. Chase to Mr. Lincoln." According to Halstead, "there was a noise in the Wigwam like the rush of a great wind in the van of a storm—and in another breath, the storm was there. There were thousands cheering with the energy of insanity."

In a moment, the news was relayed to the twenty thousand crowding outside:

> And the roar, like the breaking up of the fountains of the great deep that was heard, gave a new impulse to the enthusiasm inside. Then the thunder of the salute rose above the din, and the shouting was repeated with such tremendous fury that some discharges of the cannon were absolutely not heard by those on the stage. Puffs of smoke, drifting by the open doors, and the smell of gunpowder, told what was going on.

*   *   *

Many, however, were disgusted by the frontier rowdiness of the hometown crowd, the stratagems of the managers, the din of the orchestrated cheers, and the boom of the cannon. "It is a damned shame," Republican stalwart Tom Corwin told a friend, "that no statesman can get nominated and elected, but they must nominate some man who can hardly read or write." Halstead, the sober Cincinnati reporter, shared Corwin's distaste. He thought Seward deserved the Republican nomination, and he pronounced a harsh judgment on what he had just seen:

> The fact of the Convention was the defeat of Seward rather than the nomination of Lincoln. It was the triumph of a presumption of availability over pre-eminence in intellect and unrivaled fame—a success of the ruder qualities of manhood and the more homely attributes of popularity over the arts of a consummate politician and the splendor of accomplished statesmanship.

When the startling news of Lincoln's ascension sped across the country, disappointed editors of a number of Republican newspapers echoed Corwin's and Halstead's verdict. The *New York Times* observed, "The main work of the Chicago Convention was the defeat of Gov. Seward; that was the only specific and distinct object toward which its conscious efforts were directed. The nomination which it finally made was purely an accident. . . ." The influential *Springfield* (Mass.) *Republican* called the result "the triumph of politically available mediocrity over the superior talents of the other candidates." The *Troy* (N.Y.) *Whig* predicted that "The nomination . . . will disappoint the country." The *St. Paul Pioneer* reported, "[C]urses both loud and deep were hurled at the Convention, for cowardly rejecting the great apostle of Republicanism, for a man whose political record consists in his defeat by Douglas for U.S. Senator." The *New York Evening Express* lamented, "Mr. Lincoln is a very respectable lawyer in Illinois, but with not the twentieth part of the education or talent that Mr. Seward has."

The Democratic papers, of course, were even less gracious. This was true even close to home. The hometown Springfield *Register* sneered, "The Republicans of Illinois, who, in urging the nomination of Mr. Lincoln as a candidate for the Presidency . . . intended only a little harmless pleasantry, now find that they were perpetrating a joke upon their party, that in its effect, is not likely to be proven 'all a joke.'" Another mid-state Illinois newspaper wondered, "What has Mr. Lincoln ever done for his country that he should ask the people of the United States to make him President? . . . In fact, his nomination, if it had not been done by the forms of a numerous and powerful party, would be considered a farce. . . . His nomination is an outrage on an intelligent people." A paper from downstate Illinois concurred: "That Wm. H. Seward, the very father of Republicanism, and the great representative man of the party, should be thrust aside for such a man as Abe Lincoln, of Springfield, the people were not prepared to believe. . . . We regard Lincoln as a man of decidedly ordinary parts, and this no doubt is the opinion of his party."

If Illinoisans—people familiar with Lincoln—were calling his nomination a joke, a farce, and an outrage, it followed that others more distant were even more contemptuous. The most widely read of them all, the *New York Herald*, said, "The conduct of the Republican Party in this nomination is a remarkable indication of small intellect, growing smaller. They pass over Seward, Chase, and Bates, who are statesmen and able men, and they take up a fourth-rate lecturer, who cannot speak good grammar." The same tone was taken by the Albany *Atlas and Argus*: "He . . . is not known except as a slang-whanging stump speaker . . . of which all parties are ashamed." And the *Boston Courier*: "The laboring mountains have truly produced a most ridiculous mouse!" The *Washington Constitution* called the nomination "A disgraceful burlesque." The *Baltimore American* dismissed Lincoln as a "third rate district politician." The Trenton *New American* affected disbelief: "By what process this selection was made it is hard to understand." As did the *Boston Post*: "The Chicago sectional Convention—a thorough geographical body—has crowned its work by nominating a mere local politician." The most encyclopedic disparagement of Lincoln, however, sprang from the presses of *The Philadelphia Evening Journal* under the headline "Why Should Lincoln Be President":

It is very evident that the "Republican" newspapers are hard put to it for something to say in favor of Mr. Lincoln. His record as a statesman is a blank. He has done nothing whatever in any executive, judicial, or legislative capacity, that should entitle him to public respect. There is not in all the history of his life any exhibition of intellectual ability and attainments fitting him for the high and responsible post in the Government for which he has been nominated. When in Congress, from 1847 to 1849, he was not only not distinguished by any display of parliamentary talent, or by any special service, but those who sat in the same Congress find it difficult to remember that any such person as Abraham Lincoln occupied a seat on the floor. His contest in 1858 with Mr. Douglas for the election as United States Senator from Illinois is the beginning of his fame, and . . . he exceeded even Seward in the extravagance of his views respecting the Slavery question, while his coarse language, his illiterate style, and his vulgar and vituperative personalities in debate, contrast very strongly the elegant and classical oratory of the eminent Senator from New-York. But the party organs think Lincoln is a capital man for a political canvass, because, forsooth, he was once a flat-boatman and a rail-splitter. . . . It does not by any means follow that because an individual who, beginning life as a flat-boatman and wood-chopper, raises himself to the position of a respectable County Court lawyer and a ready stump speaker, is therefore qualified to be President of the United States. . . . [I]t will not do to say that he is qualified to be and deserves to be President, because, as a boy, he split logs and steered a "broadhorn" on the Mississippi. . . . But we shall doubtless be asked to adopt it as a safe and judicious rule for the election of men to the highest posts in the Government. But will the people be cheated by such clap-trap? We think not.

In their lack of regard for the nominee, the defeated Republican candidates, to a man, agreed with the Democratic press. Edward Bates wrote in his diary entry for May 19, "The Chicago Republican Convention is over. That party, will henceforth, subside into weakness and then break into pieces. . . ." His praise for the nominee was faint almost to the vanishing point: he could bring himself only to write, "Mr. Lincoln personally is unexceptionable." William Seward, likewise, wrote a letter to Thurlow Weed fearing for the party's future. Nor did anyone else consider that Lincoln was a great man. Lincoln's friend, Ward Hill Lamon, later summed up the popular view of Lincoln in 1860:

Few men believed that Mr. Lincoln possessed a single qualification for his great office. His friends had indicated what they considered his chief merit, when they insisted that he was a very common, ordinary man, just like the rest of "the people"—"Old Abe," a railsplitter and a story-teller. They said he was good and honest and well-meaning; but they took care not to pretend that he was great. He was thoroughly convinced that there was too much truth in this view of his character. He felt deeply and keenly his lack of experience in the conduct of public affairs. . . . His most intimate friends feared that he possessed no administrative ability; and in this opinion he seems to have shared himself, at least in his calmer and more melancholy moments.

Party leaders speaking publicly in Iowa after the convention, according to one listener, "referred deprecatingly to the nominee, apologizing for having a 'rail splitter' for the Party's standard bearer—a man without the culture or experience and trained ability of [Seward]." Heading home from Chicago, Michigan convention delegates plastered their train with Lincoln portraits, but the crowds gathered at the railway stations sent up louder cheers for Austin Blair, Michigan's Republican candidate for Governor, than for Lincoln. One aboard that train would later remember "that the nomination of Lincoln . . . created at first, over a large portion of the North, more anxiety than enthusiasm."

Northerners were anxious about voting for a candidate they didn't know. The press couldn't get his name right—the "Wigwam Edition" biography of the new nominee was titled *The Life, Speeches, and Services of Abram Lincoln.* Only two members of the nominating committee that went to Lincoln's house after the convention had ever seen him before. Easterners, especially, were baffled. "I had never heard of him before," wrote prominent Philadelphian Sidney George Fisher. Fisher's friend William Meredith was also dismayed by Lincoln's nomination, as were many refined Easterners. In Meredith's view, said Fisher, Lincoln was "a Western 'screamer,' represents Western coarseness & violence. The papers say he was fond of horse racing, foot racing, etc. . . . Such is democracy. These very qualities, connecting him in sympathy with the masses, favor his success. Education, refinement, the birth & breeding of a gentleman would be against him." "I remember," wrote another Philadelphia Republican, "that when I first read the news on a bulletin board as I came down street in Philadelphia I experienced a moment of intense physical pain, it was as though some one had dealt me a heavy blow over the head, then my strength failed me. I believed our cause was doomed." In the intellectual capital of the nation, Ralph Waldo Emerson of Boston wrote, "we heard the result coldly and sadly. It seemed too rash, on a purely local reputation, to build so grave a trust in such anxious times."

"He is unknown here," echoed a dubious New Yorker, George Templeton Strong. "The *Tribune* and other papers commend him to popular favor as having had but six months' schooling in his whole life; and because he cut a great many rails, and worked on a flatboat in his early youth; all of which is somehow presumptive evidence of his statesmanship. The watchword of the campaign is already indicated. It is to be 'Honest Abe.' . . . But that monosyllable does not seem to me likely to prove a word of power." Strong had no enthusiasm for Lincoln's got-up rustic image. "I am tired of this shameless clap-trap," he wrote. "The log-cabin hard-cider craze of 1840 seemed spontaneous. This hurrah

New York, July, 1860

"A 'Rail' Old Western Gentleman"

about rails and rail-splitters seems a deliberate attempt to manufacture the same kind of furor by appealing to the shallowest prejudices of the lowest class."

*   *   *

"Honest Abe's" anonymity was even more complete in the South. There, the only knowledge of Lincoln came by way of the scurrilous screeds of secessionist newspaper editors. The Southern press universally called Lincoln's hated party the "Black Republican" party, to brand it with the mark of abolitionism and to distance it from the beloved Jefferson's earlier "Democratic-Republicans." Southern scribes lost all control in savaging the new candidate. Many descended to comments so primitive, so venomous, they were little more than name-calling. He was "a baboon," "a chimpanzee," "a rough, half-horse half-alligator character;" he was descended from "an African gorilla." Abe Lincoln became "that ape Lincoln." He was "a third-rate country lawyer"; he lived in "low Hoosier style"; he told "coarse and clumsy jokes." Secessionist firebrand Robert Barnwell Rhett of the radical Charleston *Mercury* called him a "relentless, dogged, free-soil border ruffian, . . . a vulgar mobocrat and a Southern hater . . . . an illiterate partisan." Day after day Rhett hammered away on the same tune: "A horrid looking wretch he is, sooty and scoundrelly in aspect, a cross between the nutmeg dealer, the horse swapper, and the night man, a creature 'fit evidently for petty treason, small stratagems and all sorts of spoils.' He is a lank-sided Yankee of the uncomeliest visage, and of the dirtiest complexion. Faugh! after him what decent white man would be President?" The cross-town Charleston *Courier* chimed in: Lincoln's portrait, it said, was "enough to scare one out of a night's rest."

Rhett and other slave state editors now decided Lincoln was more dangerous than Seward. Soon after Lincoln's candidacy was announced, the Louisville *Courier* pointed out that his doctrines were the "most subtle and dangerous form of anti-slaveryism" because they were so ambiguous. Southern opinion makers now argued that Seward's "irrepressible conflict" doctrine— the radical anti-slavery pronouncement that had cost him the nomination—had really been borrowed from Lincoln's "House Divided" speech from the 1858 Douglas senate race. The Richmond *Enquirer* called Lincoln's nomination a sign of "determined hostility" toward slavery by the Republicans, because they had chosen a man who, unlike Seward, was an "illiterate partisan . . . possessed only of his inveterate hatred of slavery," who exceeded Seward in the "bitterness of his prejudice and the insanity of his fanaticism." The *New York Herald* agreed, seeing Lincoln as the more dangerous man because he believed all of Seward's "revolutionary and destructive theories," but lacked Seward's "practical and experienced statesmanship."

Lincoln's Southern enemies must not have been listening to the abolitionists, because the abolitionists didn't trust him either. William Lloyd

Garrison called the Republicans "a cowardly party" for being unwilling to attack slavery where it already existed. Abolitionists ran their own candidate—Gerritt Smith, on a budget of fifty dollars—complaining that Lincoln ignored "all the principles of humanity in the colored race, both slave and free." Garrison's friend, the abolitionist orator Wendell Phillips, tore at Lincoln. "Who is this huckster in politics?" he asked his abolitionist listeners in a speech two weeks after Lincoln's nomination. "What is his recommendation? It is that nobody knows good or bad of him. His recommendation is, that out of the unknown things in his past life, journals may make for him what character they please." A few weeks later, after doing a little digging into Mr. Lincoln's past pronouncements, Phillips put a finer point on his attack, writing an article for the June issue of Garrison's *Liberator* entitled: "Abraham Lincoln, The Slave-Hound of Illinois."

*   *   *

The derision of Abraham Lincoln after his nomination in 1860 was more widespread and more openly contemptuous than of any other candidate in the nation's history. But Lincoln had the good fortune of running for president in the heyday of party politics, when people didn't vote for the candidate, but for the party. He was only the latest and most spectacularly unqualified example of a type that had been pawns in the party game since Jackson: the weak candidate nominated by a party sure of victory. For Lincoln had arrived accompanied by incredible luck. The Railsplitter was the torchbearer for a party that in 1860 had been given advantages over its opponents such as no other party had ever been given before.

Chapter 7

The 1860 Presidential Campaign

"Yesterday you were hanged in effigy in our town."

The Republican Party began like many other doomed splinter parties in the politically rambunctious Jacksonian period. The Antimasonic Party of 1832, the Liberty Party of 1844, the Free Soil Party of 1848 and 1852, and the American (or "Know Nothing") Party of 1856 were all born in an era when all a party needed to run a candidate for president was a printing press and volunteers to hand out ballots. The birth of the Republican Party was no more auspicious than the earlier failures. It had been conceived in 1854 as a reaction against Douglas' "Popular Sovereignty" doctrine, which had just been written into law as the Kansas-Nebraska Act. The Republicans managed to win in only two minor states that year, Wisconsin and Michigan. "Nobody believes that the Republican movement can prove the basis of a permanent party," observed the Albany *Argus* in 1855.

But in the next year dramatic events started a rush of voters toward this new party dedicated to breaking the political grip of the Slave Power:

- Northerners grew increasingly outraged at the continuing violence and murder in "Bleeding Kansas."
- In May of 1856 Southern congressman Preston Brooks, a Democrat, beat abolitionist Senator Charles Sumner over the head thirty times with a gold-headed gutta percha cane on the Senate floor, leaving him bloody and unconscious beneath his desk.
- In Central America that summer, Southern filibuster William Walker installed himself as president of Nicaragua, overthrew the government and legalized slavery. Despite the obvious illegality of his expedition, President Pierce, a Democrat, recognized Walker's regime as the legitimate government of Nicaragua, with a view to statehood. Emboldened, Walker recruited men for the conquest of Guatemala, El Salvador, Honduras, and Costa Rica.

Northerners expressed their reaction to the would-be Slave Kingdom-makers in the presidential election of November 1856, where, on a budget of just $50,000, the Republicans captured thirty-three percent of the national vote. Anti-Democratic, anti-Southern, and anti-slavery voters in that year had joined the party in a stampede. By the end of 1856 Republicans controlled most northern governorships and legislatures and had elected a large number of northern Congressmen.

In the four years from then until Lincoln's appearance, however, the news for the Republican Party only got better:

- In March of 1857 the Southern-dominated Supreme Court issued the Dred Scott decision, which ruled that Congress had no power to prohibit slavery in the territories. There was immediate resentment in the North, where state legislatures passed resolutions stating that the ruling was not binding. "Dred Scott" hardened Northerners' resolve to reconstitute the court after the election of 1860.

- During the Panic of 1857, after Southerners opposed efforts to stimulate the economy, many hard-hit Northern businessmen joined the Republicans. The Republican bosses cemented these new, wealthy voters into the party foundation by adding a protective tariff to their platform.

- In Congress, Southerners successively defeated a Northern Pacific railroad route, a homestead act, and land grants for colleges. Republicans promptly added provisions for all these to their platform, and welcomed millions of new voters into their ranks.

- A religious revival in 1857 and 1858 focused anti-liquor, anti-Catholic, and anti-slavery feeling, which was strong among rural Northern farmers. They, too, migrated to the Republican Party.

- The corruption under President Buchanan provided a windfall of anti-Democratic sentiment. In the year before the 1860 election, a House investigating committee published an exposé of massive fraud among Buchanan officials, disclosing graft and bribery in government contracts, in the civil service, even payoffs for votes in Congress itself. When the House report was made public in the middle of the summer campaign of 1860, Republicans made huge political capital of the scandal and printed a hundred thousand copies as campaign literature, playing on traditional

American fears of abuse of power in office as the gravest danger to liberty.

But the Republicans in the campaign of 1860 received a crowning gift—the suicide of the Democratic Party. The Democrats' most popular candidate, Stephen Douglas of Illinois, had committed sins unpardonable to Barnwell Rhett, William L. Yancey, and other Southern fire-eaters. Douglas' popular sovereignty doctrine, they said, was not aggressively pro-slavery enough (ironic, since Lincoln had criticized Douglas for just the opposite—being a tool of the Slave Power). Douglas' enemies in the Buchanan administration joined Rhett, Yancey, and the out-and-out secessionists. Together, at the May 1860 Democratic Convention, the anti-Douglas delegates walked out of the hall, leaving Douglas without enough votes for the nomination. The remaining delegates rescheduled the convention for June in Baltimore in the hopes of a rapprochement. There, however, the enemies of Douglas again rose and left. This time the remaining delegates nominated Douglas, and the anti-Douglas bolters nominated their own candidate, John C. Breckinridge of Kentucky. The tradition-rich Democratic Party—the country's only remaining national party—had thus split, leaving the infant Republican opposition, only in its second national election, guaranteed of a victory in the fall.

There was yet another party convention in May. In Baltimore, the conservative Constitutional Union Party convened for the first time in the shadow of the crisis over the nation's future, and named wealthy slaveholder John Bell of Tennessee its nominee. The party ignored the slavery issue and campaigned on the platform "the Constitution as it is, and the Union under it now and forever." Alluding to the failed "Know Nothing" Party of the 1850s, the Republicans called Bell's party the "Do Nothings." The lackluster Constitutional Unionists would splinter the opposition to Lincoln still further.

As the campaign summer wore on, Southerners were forced to look the prospect of a "Black Republican" victory in the fall square in the face, and, coming in the wake of the John Brown raid the previous October, the mood grew murderous. There was dread of a bloody revolt by slaves waiting only for the signal to be given by Yankee incendiaries—"untiring fanatics," "abolition fiends"—whom they feared had sneaked into their midst. Lurid tales came out of Texas of arson fires in a dozen towns, "kindled by the torches of abolitionists." One newspaper announced that a patrol had found four guns, a pistol, and a dagger in the hands of slaves. Another reported that Negroes were collecting hundreds of bottles of strychnine to poison the townspeople.

Though none of these stories were true, the terror swept across the South. In Georgia, thirty-six slaves were arrested and accused of planning to burn the town and annihilate the inhabitants. In an Alabama backwater, two whites and eight slaves were arrested, and one white man lynched. In Texas, a stranger—a Louisianan—was almost lynched when his appearance excited suspicion. A Mississippian wrote that within three weeks he had read of twenty-three abolitionist agents being lynched, and blamed "hellish" Northern organizations for their plots. Another Southern observer commented, "the minds of the people are aroused to a pitch of excitement probably unparalleled in the history of our country."

As mob violence boiled, Northerners in the South were ducked in ponds, marched to train depots at bayonet point, and pushed onto northbound cars. With the South in the throes of a paranoid hysteria, no one was foolhardy enough to contemplate working for the Republicans. In that day there was no such thing as a secret ballot. Voters picked up paper ballots at the polling place in temporary sheds emblazoned with party posters, then dropped the ballots, clearly marked with the voter's choice, into clear glass bowls. Both the ballots and the bowls had to be supplied by party volunteers. Since there were no Republican volunteers in the South, there was no way to collect Republican votes or protect Republican voters. Lincoln could look for no votes there.

That the Republicans were not allowed to contest the election in the South meant that Lincoln did not know the South and the South did not know Lincoln. The Republicans, however, could afford to be cavalier about their lack of votes in the South. They didn't need them. The election of 1856 showed them that if they held the Northern states they had won and added the Northern states they had lost—Illinois, Indiana, and Pennsylvania—they could gain a majority of electoral votes without getting one vote south of the Mason-Dixon line.

*   *   *

But the North did not know Lincoln either. With the election his to lose, he remained silent, whiling away the months of the campaign puttering in an office in the Illinois state capitol loaned by the governor. He received visitors affably, but made no speeches nor statements to the press, nor clarified his policies. What followed was what always happened in Jacksonian America when one party was sure of victory: Republicans mounted a safe campaign devoid of substance, a campaign of hoopla that would satisfy the public craving for pageantry and spectacle, a campaign that would leave Northern voters feeling bouncy but that bore little on the crisis in the South, and a campaign that would leave the public knowing almost nothing about the candidate himself.

The Republicans were united, organized, energetic, and well-funded. The campaign they mounted was a throwback to the victorious 1840 "log cabin and hard cider" campaign that had elected the little-regarded William Henry Harrison, heavy on barbecues and rallies, parades and banners, songs and mottoes. The most spectacular feature of the campaign was the "Wide Awakes," a quasi-military Republican organization that counted hundreds of thousands of enthusiastic young men in its colorful ranks. They paraded down streets across the North in disciplined zigzag formations, roaring cadenced cheers to the boom and crash of big brass bands while holding aloft oil-burning torches. They wore distinctive glazed caps and capes that protected them from the burning oil that rained down from the torches over their heads. (A pun on their garb was the source of their name: the fabric on their glazed gear had *no nap*—hence, the Wide Awakes.) Particularly memorable was one grand night march down Broadway in New York City that drew into its jaunty lines ninety thousand uniformed, shouting marchers, each a source of light, making the boulevard a river of fire. Rockets and roman candles shot starshells from behind each file, and, wrote George Templeton Strong, "the procession moved along under a galaxy of fire balls—white, red, and green. I have never seen so beautiful a spectacle on any political turnout." The cheering from the ecstatic crowds that jammed the streets was answered by the chants of the Wide Awakes and the fortissimo of the bands. The whole scene was climaxed by tens of thousands of voices singing "Ain't You Glad You Joined the Republicans?" to the tune of "The Old Gray Mare."

With Lincoln holed up and shut-mouthed in his office in Springfield, Northern voters who flocked to the picnics, parades, and rallies listened to Republican orators who had been recruited to fan out across the North on the party's behalf. In their speeches, the moral crusade against slavery was muted. Voters were counted on to vote their pocketbooks. "I know the country is not Anti-Slavery," observed Horace Greeley. "It will only swallow a little Anti-Slavery in a great deal of sweetening. An Anti-Slavery Man *per se* cannot be elected; but a Tariff, River and Harbor, Pacific Railroad, Free Homestead man may succeed although he is Anti-Slavery." So Republicans played instead on bread-and-butter themes, customizing the tune to local interests. The homestead issue—free land—was the subject of speeches in the Northwest, where the German and Scandinavian freesoilers saw it as necessary to their future prosperity. Support for the tariff was promised in Pennsylvania, New Jersey, and New England, which had been hard-hit by the recent economic panic. The Pacific Railroad was stressed in the Mississippi Valley, where businessmen were taut with concern about where the railhead would be. Internal improvements were pledged everywhere.

In the glare of the hoopla, in the din of the bands, the songs, and the blandishments to the voters in the estimated 50,000 Republican campaign speeches, Lincoln was obscured. To the voters he was little more than a caricature, a sketch—the Railsplitter. During the entire campaign from May to November he made not one public utterance, spoke only to well-wishers who dropped by his borrowed room, and wrote only privately to friends. Americans barely knew what he looked like. The first mass-produced print of Lincoln was made from a picture taken by Matthew Brady during his visit to New York for the Cooper Union speech in February 1860, and voters saw this same image—lithographed, engraved, printed, and reprinted—in every campaign pamphlet and illustrated magazine published in the East. (Looking at the likeness and shaking his head, one friend told him, "It's a good thing women can't vote.")

Americans had no way to get a sense of the man—whether he was conservative or radical, whether he was a man of no backbone like Franklin Pierce or of steely resolve like Andrew Jackson, whether he would be conciliatory or hostile toward the South—indeed, whether he was even capable of administering the government of a nation in crisis or whether those around him would have to direct it for him.

*   *   *

The uncertainty about Lincoln's intentions had immediate tragic consequences in the South. As the fall chill deepened and Election Day approached, the slave states were in a blaze. Muskets were being issued and military units organized in Alabama, South Carolina, and Georgia. Several Southern states were arranging to buy arms in Europe. No one dared speak publicly except to condemn the perfidy of the North. The highest public officials in the land, the Southerners in the Buchanan cabinet, openly threatened a revolutionary breakup of the Union. Buchanan's pro-Southern mouthpiece, the Washington *Constitution*, actually encouraged secession by predicting dire consequences of a Lincoln victory: "Let Lincoln be President, and how many months' purchase would the Union be worth?" The Knights of the Golden

Circle, a society formed to bring about a Southern slave kingdom that would encircle the Caribbean and include Mexico, Cuba, Central America, and the northern tier of South American states, became avowedly secessionist, falling in behind the extremists Rhett and Yancey. The ranks of the secessionists included the editors of several Southern newspapers, who now freely exulted in the prophesy of a new age of prosperity for the South after Lincoln was elected and the South broke away from the Union.

Election Day was November 6. Early the next morning, telegraph keys clicked out the news of Lincoln's victory. On November 8 this letter was posted from Pensacola, Florida:

To Abraham Lincoln

Yesterday you were hanged in effigy in our town.

a Citizen

Chapter 8

Lincoln's Election

"Let this low fellow rule?"

Polling places had been swamped by a record turnout: more than 81% of eligible voters cast ballots. Abraham Lincoln won the electoral college going away, with a total of 180 (with 152 needed to win) to Breckinridge's 72, Bell's 39, and Douglas' meager dozen. The numbers, however, were misleading. Lincoln's popular support was far short of the mandate needed to lead the nation out of the looming crisis. He was no "people's president." Nationwide, Lincoln polled only 39.8% of the popular vote—not only less than any other elected President in American history, but so low that only three *losers* of two-party contests have ever done worse: Herbert Hoover in 1932, Barry Goldwater in 1964, and George McGovern in 1972. All of Lincoln's electoral votes had come from the eighteen free states, and only 54% had voted for him even there. Not a single person voted for him in any of the ten Deep South states. In four Upper South states, his vote tally was a paltry 2%.

The 1860 election was an aberration. The electoral machine wrought by the Founding Fathers had been manipulated by the party system to produce an elected leader who embodied the Framers' worst nightmare: an unknown, sectional candidate whom half the country saw as illegitimate; an interloper, a usurper.

* * *

Southern fears at the prospect of a Lincoln presidency leaped from the pages of every newspaper. The alarm that rang loudest went to the Southerners' fear that their wealth would disappear. "The underground railroad will become an overground railroad," cried Barnwell Rhett from the pages of the Charleston *Mercury*. There would be a massive flight of slaves from the border states northward, he and others predicted, and a corresponding sell-off of slaves southward, with the result that the value of every slave would drop. After all, the ultimate purpose of Lincoln's party was to redefine property to exclude slaves, and slave property was the foundation of wealth in the South. One slave was worth a hundred, in some places a thousand, acres of land. The aggregate value of slaves in 1860 was more than the value of all the nation's factories, railroads, and livestock put together, or roughly one-half of the country's gross domestic product. Translated to a modern day sum, the figure would be a crushing five to six trillion dollars. Southern leaders were fairly foaming at the mouth with indignation. The stakes were indeed tremendous.

Property rights had always been at the top of the list of rights guaranteed by the Constitution. To have an idea of just how much was at stake, imagine a modern-day president whose election would cause one-half of the country's homeowners to risk losing the entire value of their homes. Southerners feared the foundations of their freedom would be gnawed away by conspirators. "Secret conspiracy, and its attendant horrors, will hover over every portion of the South," warned Rhett in the *Mercury*. "Slave property is the foundation of all property in the South. When security in this is shaken, all other property partakes of its instability. Banks, stocks, bonds, must be influenced. Timid men will sell out and leave the South. Confusion, distrust and pressure must reign."

The Washington *Constitution* predicted that Lincoln would appoint spoilsmen in the South—postmasters, customs house officers, federal marshals, and other positions of authority in every city and town, port and arsenal—who would be constantly, quietly at work for abolition, sowing discontent among the slaves. Everywhere in the Cotton States the most ruinous predictions were printed and shouted, read and heard:

- Lincoln would forever close the Western territories to slave labor. Slave populations, bottled up in the South, would mushroom and overwhelm their masters.

- Lincoln would fill vacancy after vacancy on the Supreme Court with abolitionists, and it and the other federal courts would become venues for anti-slavery activism. The Dred Scott decision would be reversed.

- Lincoln would wink at slave escapes and defiance of the Fugitive Slave Law. Once out of his shackles, no slave would ever be returned.

- "John Brown raids" would multiply and slave revolts would succeed unchecked by a smiling Abraham Lincoln, who as Commander-in-Chief would refuse to use the army to fight them.

- With the help of abolitionist postmasters in the South, anti-slavery propaganda would clog the mails, poisoning the minds of pliable citizens.

- Congress would plunder the South by passing a high protective tariff wholly in the interests of the North.

- The dream of the slave kingdom, the "Golden Circle," would die forever.

- A half million Wide Awakes—with their military drill, precision, and obedience to Lincoln, their leader—would execute his abolitionist projects.

- And finally, Lincoln would free more than four million Southern slaves, give them federal jobs, and urge them to copulate with and marry white women. "If you are tame enough to submit," preached one South Carolina Baptist, "abolition preachers will be at hand to consummate the marriage of your daughters to black husbands." The heated reply, from one Alabamian: "Submit to have our wives and daughters choose between death and gratifying the hellish lust of the Negro!! . . . Better ten thousand deaths than submission to Black Republicanism."

Seventy years before, James Madison had argued in *The Federalist* papers that the nation was so large and its interests so diverse that no one interest could ever gain control of the government. That argument had now failed. Southerners, in the fall of 1860, girded themselves to resist a future thrust on them by a Constitution that they felt had broken down; one that, when tested, did not sufficiently protect minority rights; one under which a Republican administration, using its Northern majority as a hammer and government jobs as a wedge, could turn the Constitution topsy-turvy, centralize power in Washington, and destroy the principle of state sovereignty. Their civilization shattered, their property worthless, the Southern states would be reduced to mere provinces of a consolidated despotism. "I shudder to contemplate it!" cried an Alabamian. "What social monstrosities, what desolated fields, what civil broils, what robberies, rapes, and murders of the poorer whites by the emancipated blacks would then disfigure the whole fair face of this prosperous, smiling, and happy Southern land." Atlanta's *Southern Confederacy* predicted apocalypse:

The South will never permit Abraham Lincoln to be inaugurated President of the United States, this is a settled and a sealed fact. It is the determination of all parties in the South. Let the consequences be what they may, whether the Potomac is crimsoned in human gore, and Pennsylvania Avenue is paved ten fathoms deep with mangled bodies, or whether the last vestige of liberty is swept from the face of the American continent, the South, the loyal South, the constitutional South, will never submit to such humiliation and degradation as the inauguration of Abraham Lincoln.

This editor, and others, spoke for the chivalry of the South. A highbred Carolinian correspondent wrote to a friend: "Did you think the people of the South, the Lords Proprietors of the Land, would let this low fellow rule for them? No. His vulgar facetiousness may suit the race of clock makers and wooden nutmeg venders—even Wall Street brokers may accept him, since they do not protest—but never will he receive the homage of southern gentlemen. . . ." Southerners, she said, would never submit to rule by a president who "exhibits himself at railway depots, bandies jokes with the populace, kisses bold women from promiscuous crowds."

While streets were thronged across the South with people talking of secession, Lincoln worked quietly in Springfield. There he received a basket of letters a day—the super-heated political atmosphere produced the most vile, venomous letters ever addressed to a president-elect, many from the Southern elite. They were "senseless fulminations, . . . disgraceful threats and indecent drawings," according to Henry Villard, the *New York Herald* correspondent. Lincoln's torture and execution were the most popular motifs—by stabbing, gunshot, and hanging. From South Carolina, addressed to Mrs. Lincoln, was a crude painting of him tarred and feathered with chains on his feet and a rope around his neck. Another letter contained a drawing of the Devil stabbing Lincoln with a three-pronged pitchfork, heaving him into the fires of Hell. Lincoln's friend Henry Clay Whitney wrote that during a visit to Lincoln after the election,

> . . . he showed me his recent contributions by mail, of the [Southern] chivalry: there were editorials, in pompous language, referring to him as the Illinois ape, a baboon, a satyr, a negro, a mulatto, a buffoon, a monster, an abortion, an idiot, etc. There were threats of hanging him, burning him, decapitating him, flogging him, etc. The most foul, disgusting and

obscene language was used in the press which were the organs of the Southern *elite par excellence*, of the nation, as they thought. Nor had the limner's art been neglected: in addition to several rude sketches of assassination, by various modes, a copy of *Harper's Weekly* was among the collection, with a full length portrait of the President-elect; but some cheerful pro-slavery wag had added a gallows, a noose and a black-cap.

*   *   *

Reactions were not limited to the elite. Soon after the election the following letter arrived from Louisiana, deeply expressive within a limited range:

Old Abe Lincoln

God damn your god damned old Hellfired god damned soul to hell god damn you and goddam your god damned family's god damned hellfired god damned soul to hell and god damnation god damn them and god damn your god damn friends to hell god damn their god damned souls to damnation god damn them and god damn their god damn families to eternal god damnation god damn souls to hell god damn them and God Almighty God damn Old Hamlin to to [sic] hell God damn his God damned soul all over everywhere double damn his God damned soul to hell

Now you God damned old Abolition son of a bitch God damn you I want you to send me God damn you about one dozen good offices Good God Almighty God damn your God damned soul and three or four pretty Gals God damn you

And by doing God damn you you

Will Oblige, Pete Muggins

Chapter 9

Lincoln in the Secession Winter

"He will totter into a dishonoured grave."

At noon on November 7, the day Lincoln's election was announced, the Charleston *Mercury* unfurled South Carolina's palmetto flag over its office to wild cheering from the crowd below. Diarist Mary Chesnut noted gaily in her diary that Federal Judge Andrew Magrath had resigned, and that pictures of the judge "were suspended . . . across various streets in Charleston. The happy moment seized by the painter to depict him was while Magrath was in the act of dramatically tearing off his robes of office in rage and disgust at Lincoln's election." The next day, the *Mercury* announced, "The tea has been thrown overboard—the revolution of 1860 has been initiated." Robert Barnwell Rhett knew that the revolutionary hammer must come down now, while the iron was hot, while the excitement favored the party of action. Movements for secession had swept these streets before in 1833 and 1850, and both times had come to nothing.

This time, though, fortune was with the secessionists. The South Carolina state legislature, heavy with wealthy slaveowners, was already convened—it was the only state whose legislators, not its voters, still chose the presidential electors. It was the last vestige of the Revolutionary aristocracy, and it was eager to forge a new chapter in history. Governor Gist, a wealthy planter and an ardent secessionist himself, had instructed the legislators, when they met on November 5 for the presidential vote, to remain in session in case Lincoln were elected, so that they might immediately consider their response. On Saturday, November 10, three days after Lincoln's election was announced, the reconvened South Carolina legislature called for a secession convention in mid-December. That same day, the United States senators from South Carolina resigned from Congress.

On Monday, November 12, the New York financial market plunged.

On Tuesday, November 13, the South Carolina legislature voted to raise a volunteer army of ten thousand men.

On Sunday, November 18, Georgia voted a million dollars for arms and troops, and scheduled a convention for mid-January to discuss secession.

It was not quite two weeks after Lincoln's election.

*   *   *

Lincoln himself was deplorably out of touch with the rage and dread that gave rise to the frenzy rippling from Charleston. The events that tumbled so quickly one after the other, from the curses at Lincoln's election in November to the cannon-roar at Fort Sumter the next April, occurred largely because the new President-elect was so slow in fathoming the temper of the times, because he so underestimated the intensity of feeling and so totally misperceived the extent of the crisis in the Deep South. Lincoln himself was unaware that he suffered from this blindness. He spoke with a Kentucky twang, after all. Because of his Kentucky birth, he thought of himself as a Southerner, a delusion that thrived only because he lived and worked among Northerners. He thought he understood Southerners, but he didn't. He had spent the 1850s in story-telling contests on the Illinois circuit, rather than broadening his views in the crucible of debate in Washington. Alone among the presidential candidates in 1860, Lincoln had stayed home in Springfield, Illinois, during the entire summer and fall campaign. From his two-story house on the Midwestern prairie, surrounded by well-wishers, friends, and gawkers, he had been completely insulated from the Southern people. He was a man who read little. Personal contacts were crucial to his understanding, and the last time he had spent any time among the people of the Cotton States was thirty years before, when in 1831, as a twenty-four-year-old, he had ridden on a flatboat to New Orleans. The last time he had spent any time in a slave-holding region had been during his stint in Washington, D.C., as a congressman a dozen years before. He had had no reason to spend time outside Illinois—his ambition, until very recently, was to be elected Senator from his state.

Lincoln had never taken the danger to the Union seriously. He had seen talk of war subside after the Compromise of 1850, after "Bleeding Kansas" in 1856, and after the John Brown raid in 1859. In 1856 Lincoln had said, "All this talk about the dissolution of the Union is humbug—nothing but folly." At the close of the Douglas debates in 1858, he had assured his audience that "this controversy will soon be settled, and it will be done peaceably too. There will be no war, no violence."

In the 1860 campaign, his success depended on Northern voters sharing his skepticism about the possibility of a war with the South. On August 15, he had written optimistically to a friend that he had received assurances that "in no probable event will there be any very formidable effort to break up the Union. The people of the South have too much of good sense, and good temper, to attempt the ruin of the government." On November 12—the same day on which South Carolina legislators called for a secession convention—the Chicago *Tribune* told readers that Mr. Lincoln "does not . . . believe that any of the States will . . . go off and organize a Confederacy." His calm in the face of the developing crisis was so complete that observers thought that he was either unaware of the situation or paralyzed by indecision.

On November 20, the Republicans of Illinois celebrated their Grand Jubilee in Springfield, but already the fizz had gone off the champagne—the crowds were smaller than before election time. Lincoln, according to newspaperman Donn Piatt, who spoke to him there, was confident the Southern fire-eaters could be brought around by dangling government jobs in front of them:

> [His] low estimate of humanity blinded him to the South. He could not understand that men would get up in their wrath and fight for an idea. He considered the movement South as a sort of political game of bluff, gotten up by politicians, and meant solely to frighten the North. He believed that when the leaders saw their efforts in that direction were unavailing, the tumult would subside. "They won't give up the offices," I remember he said, and added, "Were it believed that vacant places could be had at the North Pole, the road there would be lined with dead Virginians."

When Piatt repeated his warning that "the Southern people were in dead earnest, meant war," Lincoln laughed. A few days later, Lincoln showed the same cheer in a conversation with a Philadelphia reporter, saying, "I think, from all I can learn, that things have reached their worst point in the South, and they are likely to mend in the future."

What made Lincoln's complacency so dangerous to the nation was that, just now, when the South was in ferment, when his ways were still unknown, and when so much depended on the wisdom of his policies, the masses both North and South were desperately in need of soothing statements from him, their future leader, to defuse the crisis. He could have spoken—but he did not. Because his countrymen were listening so hard for Lincoln's voice, his silence thundered in their ears. Reporter Henry Villard was puzzled by Lincoln's attitude in the days after the election. "Stubborn facts of the most fearful portent," he wrote, were developing at an alarming rate. "He could not shut his eyes to their growing gravity. He could not block his mind to their serious logic. Every newspaper he opened was filled with clear indications of an impending national catastrophe. Every mail brought him written, and every hour verbal, entreaties to abandon his paralyzed silence, repress untimely feelings of delicacy, and pour the oil of conciliatory conservative assurances upon the turbulent waves of Southern excitement."

But "silence" had been the watchword of Lincoln's successful presidential run. He defended his continuing refusal to speak on the grounds that speaking "would do no good. I have already done this many—many, times; and it is in print, and open to all who will read. Those who will not read, or heed, what I have already publicly said, would not read, or heed, a repetition of it. 'If they hear not Moses and the prophets, neither will they be persuaded though one rose from the dead.'" But anyone wanting a statement of Lincoln's views would have to go back almost a year, to the Cooper Union speech in February, the last time he had spoken for the record. By now, during the months of November and December, when, according to Henry Adams, "the country was in a condition of utter disorganization," when in Washington there was "a strange and bewildering chaos, the fragments of broken parties and a tottering Government," the delirious rush of events in the Deep South brought tremendous pressure upon Lincoln to declare a policy. The shameless *New York Herald* did not even wait until Election Day to start turning the screws, falsely reporting on November 2 that Lincoln had a statement he would publish as soon as his presidency was assured. Then, on November 8, when the imaginary proclamation had failed to materialize, the *Herald* demanded one immediately, and did so again the next day, and again frequently thereafter. "There is only one man in the United States who has it in his power to restore the country to its former happy and prosperous condition," it declared, "and that man is the President elect. . . . If Mr. Lincoln will speak out in a manner calculated to reassure the conservative masses of all the States, the present cloud will pass away like a summer shower. . . ."

This and other demands from all sides for some word of good will drew no response from the President-elect, who still kept regular hours at the governor's office in the Illinois statehouse, oblivious to the fact that, from the moment of his election, the nation held him personally responsible for the secession movement. On the question of the disintegration of the nation, Lincoln's visitors found him eerily undisturbed. To friends and foes who wrote to him eager to learn his plans, he replied with a "Form Reply to Requests for Political Opinions" signed by his secretary John Nicolay, as follows:

> Your letter to Mr. Lincoln of [blank] and by which you seek to obtain his opinions on certain political points, has been received by him. He has received others of a similar character; but he also has a greater number of the exactly opposite character. The latter class beseech him to write nothing whatever upon any point of political doctrine. They say his positions were well known when he was nominated, and that he must not now embarrass the canvass by undertaking to shift or modify them. He regrets that he can not oblige all, but you perceive it is impossible for him to do so.

All his letters to friends were headed "Private," "Confidential," "Private and confidential," "Strictly confidential," or "For your eye only." He told them, "By the lessons of the past, and the united voice of all discreet friends, I am

Vanity Fair, December 29, 1860

"Badgering Him."
J[ames]. G[ordon]. B[ennett].—"Bow! Wow!Come out, Mr. Lincoln"

neither [to] write or speak a word for the public." He urged them to burn his correspondence, because, he said, "It is best not to be known that I write at all."

When he did share his thoughts privately with friends, his words were conciliatory and gentle; they spoke of restraint and common sense, exactly the affirmations the crisis demanded from the President-elect. Why, then, were his public pronouncements so guarded and rare? He touched on the reason in a letter to the editor of the Democratic Louisville *Journal.* After first chiding the Southern editor for "impressing your readers that you think I am the very worst man living," Lincoln explained that he abstained from comment "because of apprehension that it would do harm. . . . I have *bad* men to deal with, both North and South—men who are eager for something new upon which to base new misrepresentations—men who would like to frighten me, or, at least, to fix upon me the character of timidity and cowardice. They would seize upon almost any letter I could write, as being an *'awful coming down.'* I intend keeping my eye upon these gentlemen, and to not unnecessarily put any weapons in their hands." Here he referred not only to the extremists in the South who were hoping to goad him into an injudicious statement or something which they could twist, but also to the radicals in his own party who were scouring his every utterance for a hint of backsliding. He was explicit about the need to keep peace within his own party when he answered another man who begged him to say something to reassure merchants "honestly alarmed." "There are no such men," Lincoln maintained. "If I yielded to their entreaties I would go to Washington without the support of the men who now support me. I would be as powerless as a block of buckeye wood."

It is revealing that during this period he wrote and spoke so obsessively about "timidity" and "cowardice," about being left "powerless." His preoccupation bespoke an overriding concern about lack of stature—among the giants of his own party as well as those of the opposition. During this period, his natural good will was overridden by a nagging fear that to make it public would encourage "bold bad men to believe they are dealing with one who can be scared into anything." Where his anonymity had worked for him so recently as a candidate, it now worked against him as an elected leader. At a time when his views were not yet known, he was intimidated into concealing them until his Inaugural Address on the 4th of March.

*   *   *

To those who would know his policy sooner, his stock reply was: *My views are well known; you have only to read my speeches.* But he did not realize that in the South his views were not well known—or worse, known only in the distorted translations of hostile editors—and it had been a long, long time since he had given a speech. Worse yet, his two defining speeches—the Cooper Union speech of the year before, and the House Divided speech that opened his Senate run in 1858—were not written to calm anyone, but rather to exhort and inflame the enemies of slavery. The Philadelphia *Evening Journal*, for one, was not soothed by taking Lincoln's advice and reading them. "To expose Mr. Lincoln and to cover with shame the party that nominated him," scolded the *Journal*, "we need only to quote from these harangues (the house divided speech and others)."

Consider, as Southerners did, that speech. "A house divided against itself cannot stand," Lincoln had begun, paraphrasing the Bible scripture. Then, he portrayed an apocalyptic contest between two diametrically opposed sides:

> I believe this government cannot endure, permanently half slave and half free. I do not expect the Union to be dissolved—I do not expect the house to fall—but I do expect it will cease to be divided. It will become all one thing or all the other. Either the opponents of slavery will arrest the further spread of it, and place it where the public mind shall rest in the belief that it is in course of ultimate extinction; or its advocates will push it forward till it shall become alike lawful in all the States, old as well as new, North as well as South.

The speech that followed was a rallying cry for Republicans to put slavery on the path to extinction before the Democrats nationalized it. To destroy any doubt that such was the Democrats' goal, Lincoln went on to trace "the design," the conspiracy—always, in those days, a conspiracy—by 1850s pro-slavery Democrats to prepare the nation, step by step (or, in his house-building analogy, "plank by plank") for a future Supreme Court decision that would spread slavery nationwide. If he had known the Southern mood, Lincoln would have realized that, to Southern ears, the House Divided speech was the shrill call-to-arms of a paranoid Black Republican.

The Cooper Union speech had not been as incendiary as the House Divided speech, beginning instead as a carefully-researched, closely-reasoned argument that aimed to show that the Founding Fathers had never intended slavery to be extended. After his hour-long history lesson, however, Lincoln went on to turn the testimony of the Founders against the slaveholders, insisting that they, not the Republicans, were guilty of agitating the slavery question. Then, building to his climax, he proclaimed to Republicans—just as he had done earlier in the House Divided speech—that their duty was to stand firm in the belief that they were right and that slavery was wrong, and to "stand by our duty, fearlessly and effectively." The speech was anything but conciliatory, and Southerners could only see it as another utterance by an uncompromising, implacable foe.

As one editor put it, Lincoln's record, "brief as it is, is to his disadvantage." These were the only words Lincoln had for the citizens to ponder. He did not intend to make any further statement of his policy until he stood on the inaugural platform.

*   *   *

In waiting until then to unfold his views, however, he would have the problem of what to do in the meantime, during that agonizingly long interval in which he would be fiercely scrutinized—and still legally powerless. Here Lincoln was hamstrung by the antique American system which observed a wait of a full four months between a President's election on the first Tuesday in November and his inauguration the following March 4—unchanged since George Washington. In the national emergency brought on by Lincoln's election, the weeks and months between November and March were a deadly chasm. How would a man, not yet in power, work the machine under the dome of the Capitol from a frontier town 700 miles away?

Lincoln's silence, during these four crucial months, left a vacuum when leadership was urgently needed. In the weeks following the election, with everyone left to speculate on what the Cotton States would do and what stance Lincoln would take at his inaugural, the Republicans could adopt no uniform policy toward the South. Newspaper editors struck out in all directions, declaring their individual preferences—for compromise, for use of force, for peaceable separation. Concerned citizens heard a cacophony of voices, many irresponsible, some openly malignant, all now shouting as loudly as possible in an attempt to magnify their influence.

On November 9, two days after he trumpeted Lincoln's election, Horace Greeley, arch-Republican, brought the victory cheers to a confused hush with an eccentric proclamation from the pages of the New York *Tribune*: "If the Cotton States shall become satisfied that they can do better out of the Union than in it, we insist on letting them go. . . . We hope never to live in a republic whereof one section is pinned to the residue by bayonets." Greeley's "Go in peace" policy was a cagey gambit with a dual purpose: to deflect any thought of compromise in the North, and to affect with the South the same attitude as the man who says to his wife who is threatening to leave, *I'm not stopping you! Go ahead—there's the door!* Whatever Greeley's deep game, Lincoln undoubtedly read the provoking editorial with dismay.

On November 13, the Republican *New York Times* blithely reported, "Disunion sentiment is rapidly losing ground in the South. . . . There seems to be a great panic about disunion. We cannot, for the life of us, see the least foundation for it. Our Southern brethren talk loudly about secession,—but they have done little else for the last ten years." This smug skepticism had been a staple of the Republican Party, and Lincoln shared it. But on November 14, the *Times* did an abrupt about-face. It made a proposal for the settlement of the fugitive slave problem, in "a spirit of compromise and conciliation which, at the present moment, would be of incalculable value to the cause of Union." Thus, the *Times* signaled an awareness of the crisis.

On November 17, the Democratic *New York Herald* called on Lincoln to release his electors—in effect, to resign two weeks after his election. It warned, "If he persists in his present position, in the teeth of such results as his election must produce, he will totter into a dishonoured grave, driven there perhaps by the hands of an assassin, leaving behind him a memory more execrable than that of Arnold—more despised than that of the traitor Catiline."

Two weeks after his victory, already feeling extreme pressure to make some sort of reassuring statement, Lincoln made one awkward attempt at conciliation. He did not deliver it himself, however. He wrote two paragraphs and inserted them in the speech of Illinois Senator Lyman Trumbull at the Grand Republican Jubilee in Springfield on November 20. There, Trumbull spoke the words with Lincoln sitting behind him on the platform to signal his authority. "All of the States will be left in as complete control of their own affairs respectively, and at as perfect liberty to choose, and employ, their own means of protecting property, and preserving peace and order within their respective limits, as they have ever been under any administration," Trumbull began. He should have stopped there, but he plunged on, "Disunionists are now in hot haste to get out of the Union precisely because they perceive they can not, much longer, maintain apprehension among Southern people that their homes, . . . and lives, are to be endangered. . . . With such, 'Now or never' is the maxim." In Lincoln's script, these taunting remarks were followed by even more bitter sarcasm: "I am rather glad of this military preparation in the South. It will enable the people the more easily to suppress any uprisings there, which [the secessionists'] misrepresentations of purposes may have encouraged." Here, for all to hear, were Lincoln's fatal delusions made clear. He saw the secessionists as a small minority, frantic to push their program through before the Union-loving masses in the South threw them over, as he was sure they would soon do—and without any compromise by Republicans.

Just as Lincoln had predicted, Trumbull's speech satisfied no one. The Washington *Constitution* and other Southern critics denounced the speech as a declaration of hostility toward the South. The Boston *Courier* and others in the North rebuked it for weakness, thinking they saw in it a foreshadowing of the abandonment of Republican principles. After this failure, Lincoln swore off attempts at public statements, and quickly went back underground. With the prairie lawyer again hushed in Springfield, attention turned to the Thirty-sixth United States Congress, convening in Washington on December 3.

Chapter 10

The Flight Toward Compromise

"Prepare yourself for a complete disorganization of our party."

From June until November 1860, Republican congressmen had been campaigning in their districts—either for themselves, each other, or Abraham Lincoln. They had given speeches, shaken hands, kissed babies, raised money, given interviews for newspapers, written pamphlets, handed out literature, mixed with the voters at rallies and picnics, and waved from carriages in parades—but they always hewed closely to orders handed down by their state party bosses. The Republican strategy differed from state to state, but everywhere Republican candidates sounded the single note that stirred voters in every town, hamlet, and farm community from Minnesota to Maine: outrage at the wickedness of the Slave Power in the South, its corrupting influence, its long-term conspiracy to pervert the values of the American republic to its own selfish ends.

*   *   *

Once Congress was met on December 3, however, things changed. Now that the representatives from districts all over the North were talking face-to-face with their counterparts from the South, the hard-line speeches that had sounded so bold and righteous in front of the cheering crowds of autumn seemed strident and simplistic in the cold light of winter. The Republican fable that secession was a bluff, that the Cotton States had no real intention of leaving the Union, and that their threats were mere bluster meant to frighten timid voters and extort new concessions, was meeting hard reality in the noisy halls and chambers under the Capitol dome.

On the Hill, the word "compromise" had the aura of a hallowed tradition, not the stigma of weakness. It was not surprising, then, that in December, under these new circumstances, the harsh campaign rhetoric was forgotten and a new appreciation for the need for adjustment with the South grew up among the Republican congressmen. Within days after convening, both Houses hurried to form committees to hammer out a compromise acceptable to all sides. Many Republican leaders thought they discerned wisdom in dropping the anti-slavery Chicago platform.

But for Lincoln—still a private citizen, still in exile, still far removed in his borrowed office on the prairie and insulated from the pressures for compromise—the issue of slavery in the territories was etched in crystal, and his resolve remained diamond-hard. There must be no compromise. For him this was essential. The territories in the West had always represented the future of the nation, and he regarded the exclusion of slavery in the territories as the key issue over which the election had been fought. He saw his election as a signal that the nation had turned away from slavery—forever. In the territorial issue dual weighty themes were thus bound up: the foundation of the new society in the West, and the nation's first step in its journey toward the ultimate extinction of slavery.

Lincoln left no doubt that here he expected Republicans to stand firm. He also opposed any attempt to reestablish the Missouri Compromise line that would permit slavery in national territory below the latitude of 36°30'. It is hard for us to understand his sensitivity on this point, since there was no real danger of slavery taking root in the arid plateaus and deserts of the New Mexico Territory below that line. The southern border of the United States, however, which seems etched in granite to us, seemed a mere tissue to Americans in 1860. The people of Lincoln's time had seen the southern border change radically after the Mexican War, by the Treaty of Guadelupe-Hidalgo in 1848 and again by the Gadsden Purchase in 1853. In the 1850s there had been constant attempts by Southerners to move it further south by the formal purchase or outright seizure of Mexico, Cuba, and Nicaragua, in order to add more slave territory and eventually make a dozen more slave states. Lincoln realized that if slavery were permitted in national territory below any given latitude, it would only act as an incentive to grab more territory to the south. If Republicans surrender on the territorial question, he wrote, "it is the end of us, and of the government."

As warning shots across the bow of the growing movement toward compromise among the Republicans in Congress, Lincoln fired off letters, writing to three Illinois congressmen in four days. On December 10 he sent the first to Senator Lyman Trumbull, which began abruptly, "Let there be no compromise on the question of extending slavery. If there be, all our labor is lost, and, ere long, must be done again. . . . The tug has to come, and better now than at any time hereafter." He followed this with a similar letter the next day to

Congressman William Kellogg: "Entertain no proposition for a compromise in regard to the extension of slavery." A couple of days later, he wrote to Congressman Elihu Washburne, repeating the warning against compromise lest "immediately filibustering [as with William Walker in Nicaragua] and extending slavery recommences. On that point hold firm, as with a chain of steel." On December 17, he indirectly informed a conference of Republican governors of his resolve. "Should the . . . Governors . . . seem desirous to know my views," he wrote to his emissary, Thurlow Weed, "tell them you judge from my speeches that I will be inflexible on the territorial question."

Here Lincoln was at odds with the nation, even at odds with the North. With South Carolina hell-bent on leaving the Union, the masses now wanted compromise. As a result, Lincoln's support had already started shrinking in the first days after his election. Many of the 40% minority of voters who voted for Lincoln in November had voted for his homespun image as "The Railsplitter," or had voted Republican for the tariff, or homesteads, or against Democratic corruption—they had voted for Lincoln *in spite* of his stand on slavery, not because of it. These were the first to desert him. Even many anti-slavery Republicans were suddenly panicked, however, as a growing list of Deep South states prepared to secede. Seeing the republic threatened by Lincoln's intransigence on the issue of slavery in the territories, they too abandoned the party ranks.

"Iron-backed" Republicans were frantic at the mass defections. Norman Judd, meeting with Republicans in the Illinois legislature in December, reported "trouble holding them steady," even in the rah-rah Republican milieu of the Illinois state capital. New York millionaire Moses Grinnell warned Seward that "many of our Republican friends have strong sympathies with those who are ready to yield. . . ." Banker August Belmont of New York wrote of the thousands there who were repenting their votes for Lincoln, men he met every day "who confess the error, and almost with tears in their eyes wish they could undo what they helped to do." Now that committees in Congress were putting their heads together for a solution—which would necessarily demand compromise—the pro-slavery *New York Herald*, on December 9, confidently predicted that "better things will occur within a fortnight than the most ultra of either side anticipate." The 22-year-old Henry Adams, grandson and great-grandson of presidents, with his privileged view into the Republican heart from family's parlor in Washington, was in despair over the wavering lines in the Senate and House. It looked to him as though the old story would be retold: the anti-slavery legions would throw down their swords in the face of Southern

Harper's Weekly, April 13, 1861

"Consulting the Oracle." Columbia, standing for the people, gives Lincoln
a "Constitutional Amendment"; he has put the "Chicago Platform" behind him.

hostility. Adams wrote to his brother on December 9, listing "very fishy and weak-kneed" senators. A full third of Republicans were not to be trusted, he said. And the situation was only getting worse. On December 13, Adams wrote to his brother again, warning him to "prepare yourself for a complete disorganization of our party. . . . How many there will be faithful unto the end, I cannot say, but I fear me much, not a third of the House." By January 3 the *Herald* was crowing that many of the Republicans, victorious in November, now wanted adjustment, and that they were restrained from saying so only out of fear of the militant Republican press.

*   *   *

To show the incredible lengths to which the overwhelming majority of Northerners were willing to go to avoid the breakup of the Union in the Secession Winter, it is revealing to examine the most serious compromise proposal under consideration in the Senate in December: the Crittenden Compromise, so called after its sponsor, Senator John Crittenden of Kentucky. This document would have guaranteed for all eternity a hands-off policy toward slavery by the federal government. It contained a series of six unalterable constitutional amendments—amendments "no future amendment of the Constitution shall affect"—the most important of which recognized slavery of the African race "in all territory now held or hereafter acquired" south of the Missouri Compromise line. It also added that no future amendment should ever alter the three-fifths rule (for counting slaves for representation), nor abridge the right to recover fugitive slaves, nor give Congress power to encroach on slavery in the states where it already existed.

It is hard to imagine a proposal more at odds with the Chicago platform that Lincoln was dedicated to uphold. Yet converts to the new plan were streaming out of the Republican fold. Railway president John Brodhead of Philadelphia claimed that half of the Pennsylvanians who had voted for Lincoln now supported Crittenden; he was sure that "three fourths of the people of Pennsylvania and New Jersey warmly approve" the plan. Jay Gould, too, estimated "not less than a hundred thousand majority" in favor of compromise in Pennsylvania. New York insurance magnate James DePeyster Ogden wrote to Crittenden that conservatives were leaving the Republican Party, and that even moderates were pressing for compromise. Horatio Seymour predicted a New York majority of 150,000 in favor of the amendments—in New York City alone, 63,000 signed a petition endorsing the plan. In Massachusetts, a greater number signed petitions for Crittenden in December than had voted for Lincoln the month before. Crittenden himself was encouraged, he said, by "commendation . . . from high Republican sources." Others, such as John A. Dix of New York, looked ahead "with strong confidence that we could carry three-fourths of the States" needed to ratify the amendments. Governor Hicks of Maryland wrote to Crittenden on December 13 that millions were loyal to the cause of compromise, and the number was growing rapidly. Horace Greeley himself later admitted that, if it had been submitted to a popular vote, the Crittenden Compromise would have carried "by the hundreds of thousands."

The clamor for Crittenden's amendments mirrored the erosion of support for Abraham Lincoln in the first few weeks after his election. Starting with his absurdly low 40% election figure, and using as a guide Henry Adams' estimate of the December defections of his supporters in Congress—by one-third in the Senate, by perhaps two-thirds in the House—it is probable that, in the Secession Winter of 1860-1861, Lincoln's support—his "approval rating," in modern parlance—was no more than 25% nationwide, and that, even in the North, his support had dwindled to around 40%. This, indeed, was the estimate of the December 19, 1860, *New York Herald.* Half Lincoln's 1,800,000 votes had been Whigs and 315,000 party-jumping Democrats, the *Herald* claimed. Half those Whigs and all the Democrats, it surmised, were indifferent or hostile to his anti-slavery, leaving barely 1,000,000—less than one-fourth the 4.7 million who voted in 1860—to support Lincoln in his stand on slavery. Lincoln's woeful slide in popularity in the month after his election is further borne out by returns from Massachusetts, where, in the local elections of December, the Republicans' 51% November majority slid to a 40% minority.

But there would be no opportunity for the huge anti-Lincoln, pro-compromise majority to express itself. No compromise plan was ever submitted to the people. Extremists from both sides, over-represented in Congress, thwarted it. Congressmen from the Deep South would refuse to consider a compromise even if it had been offered—for their constituents, the word "compromise" connoted dishonor, as in the "compromise" of a woman's virtue. And in the North, there were enough stalwart Republicans to prevent any compromise from being offered in the first place. On December 22, the Crittenden Compromise was killed in committee. On January 16, Republican ultras defeated it again on the Senate floor, with the help of Deep South senators who refused to cast votes.

* * *

On the evening of December 20, South Carolina seceded, declaring, "The union is dissolved!" and citizens wild with delight lit every light in the city and poured into the streets to celebrate, with the sound of brass bands, clanging church bells, and one hundred roaring cannon ringing in their ears, amid bonfires, fireworks, and a military parade. Over the next six weeks, all six Deep South states, from Florida to Texas, followed South Carolina out of the Union. Overnight, the vital question became not whether a man was for or against slavery, but whether he was for or against secession. The sides were completely reshuffled. Extremists on both sides of the slavery question sought a separation; those in the middle wanted the Union preserved.

Lincoln was late to see the shift, tone deaf to the martial music that sounded in the angry Southern declarations. Lincoln in mid-December showed his inability to fathom the Southern sensitivity on the subject of slavery in a revealing letter to North Carolina congressman John A. Gilmer in which he said, "On the territorial question I am inflexible . . . . On that there is a difference between you and us; and it is the only substantial difference. You think slavery is right and ought to be extended; we think it is wrong and ought to be restricted. For this neither has any just occasion to be angry with the other." A week later Lincoln again discounted the explosiveness of this central question in a letter to Alex Stephens of Georgia: "You think slavery is right and ought to be extended, while we think is wrong and ought to be restricted. That, I suppose, is the rub. It certainly is the only substantial difference between us." Lincoln showed a failure of imagination when he thus dismissed a world of Southern feeling on this crucial subject. Was the difference, for him, merely abstract? Lincoln showed himself to have temporarily lost his sure sense for the workings of the heart of the common man.

From December to February, the country was thrown into an uproar as state after state left the Union and seized the Federal customs houses, forts, mints, and arsenals on their soil. Lincoln could only watch in despair as the paralyzed Buchanan government did nothing to block the exodus. In January, the Illinois state legislature convened, and Lincoln moved from the governor's office across the street to a dusty empty room over Smith's store, where he wrestled alone with the Republic's sins. *What was to be done with the seceding states? What was to be done with the federal property in those states? How would Federal authority be extended into a region that did not recognize that authority? Should he use the military to coerce the South into returning?* On these questions, as before, Lincoln kept silent.

During the weeks before his departure for Washington, while he grappled with these questions, he was assaulted by an army of office-seekers who descended in swarms and jammed every hotel room in Springfield, eager for spoils. It was a miserable and disgraceful invasion that so profoundly offended him that he was sick of office before he got into it, according to his law partner, William Herndon. At the same time, he had to meet for the first time with the leaders of his party and choose a Cabinet. All of this was necessary to unite a polyglot party that had years of practice in the role of The Opposition, but no experience in actually wielding power. Moreover, he had to write the most important inaugural address in the nation's history. Meanwhile, so many threats had been made, so many rumors were in the air, that party leaders feared Lincoln would never live to be inaugurated. He watched the nation disintegrate as a result of his election, an unknown President-elect with views so profoundly unpopular that he dared not utter them before he took office.

Under the combined weight of responsibilities and threats no American, certainly no private citizen, had ever known, Lincoln's soul passed into shadow. He began a "wilderness" period plagued by a melancholy so black and thick it would last through the rest of the Secession Winter. His friend W. H. L. Wallace wrote to his wife, "I have seen Mr. Lincoln two or three times since I have been here, but only for a moment & he is continually surrounded by a crowd of people. He has a world of responsibility & seems to feel it & to be oppressed by it. He looks care worn & more haggard & stooped than I ever saw him." Another friend who saw him then reported, "Not only was the old-time zest lacking, but in its place was a gloom and despondency." It was during this time that he saw a vision in a mirror of two Lincolns—one alive, one dead. He took it to mean that he would not survive his presidency.

Chapter 11

The Journey to Washington

"His speeches put to flight all notions of greatness."

With all the menacing rumors coming from the South, the timing of Lincoln's arrival in Washington was sensitive. Tradition had it that the incoming President should appear in the capital in mid-February, a couple of weeks before the inauguration. There had been so many threats of assassination, however, that the journey to Washington for the swearing-in had taken on an air of suspense. Lincoln's friend Ward Hill Lamon, who accompanied him as a bodyguard, wrote, "Some thought the cars might be thrown from the track; some thought he would be surrounded and stabbed in some great crowd; others thought he might be shot from a house-top as he rode up Pennsylvania Avenue on inauguration day; while others still were sure he would be quietly poisoned long before the 4th of March." Many of his friends had advised the President-elect to come as swiftly and as quietly as possible, avoiding all publicity. Medill of the Chicago *Tribune* wrote to Lincoln, as a "volunteer sentinel on the walls," that enemies planned to seize Washington with an army and that Lincoln should grab his "carpet sack" and hurry down. The cautious Lincoln, however, favored delay: "Our adversaries have us now clearly at disadvantage. On the second Wednesday of February, when the [electoral] votes should be officially counted, if the two Houses refuse to meet at all, or meet without a quorum of each, where shall we be? . . . In view of this, I think it best for me not to attempt appearing in Washington till the result of that ceremony is known."

With his approach to Washington thus closely gauged, Abraham Lincoln on February 11 gave a short address to the gathered townspeople of Springfield in a cold rain, disappeared into a train car, and headed east on his journey to Washington. So many towns and cities had invited him to visit that Lincoln felt obliged to schedule a long, slow, winding itinerary of 1,600 miles on eighteen different railroads. The train would travel at a sustained thirty miles an hour, guarded by flagmen stationed at every crossing and every half-mile along the track. There were some public objections to this "royal procession." *The Crisis* of Columbus, Ohio, objected to the holiday atmosphere of the procession, and chided, "So we shall have an 'ovation' before he reaches the capital of the nation. How little he seems to estimate the troubled times, the importance of his position, or the true theory of our system."

As he had said repeatedly for months, Lincoln was determined not to say anything that would anticipate his upcoming inaugural address. He thus plunged himself into a difficult situation. He was handicapped by the need to remain extremely guarded lest some careless utterance be taken as future government policy and ignite combustible public opinion in the slave states. He had nevertheless consented to speak at official welcomes in numerous major cities, as well as dozens of minor stops where he would show himself on the rear platform, bow, and deliver a few pleasant remarks along the route.

It would have been better if he had not spoken at all. Lincoln was not good at impromptu speeches. He tended to fumble with lame clichés when he had not prepared his thoughts and written them down beforehand. He had never been comfortable with appearing before crowds and saying high-sounding nothings. He was the opposite of the great orators of the day. When he had nothing to say, he could not cover the lack with pretty phrases. Without a vision, his gifts deserted him. His speeches on the twelve-day train journey were unfortunate. They were most often trite, and where they were not trite they were evasive, and where they were not evasive they were harmful. He left his listeners with off-the-cuff remarks that all too often gave the impression that a pitiably unfit man was about to take office.

On one of his very first stops, in Tolono, Illinois, he stepped onto the rear platform and delivered to the crowd only a maddeningly inadequate platitude: "Let us believe, as some poet has expressed it, 'Behind the cloud, the sun is still shining.'" He then disappeared into his car. Later that day, in Indianapolis, he made the homely observation that according to the secessionists' view, the Union "as a family relation, would not be anything like a regular marriage at all, but only . . . a sort of free-love arrangement to be maintained on what that sect calls passionate attraction." The Hoosiers on hand roared with laughter. But seeing the words in print, readers nationwide were appalled by what they considered his vulgar remarks. "Who would have supposed," clucked the New Orleans *Daily Crescent*, "that a man elevated to the Presidency of a nation would indulge in comparisons of this sort? Imagine George Washington or James Madison, on their way to the capital, making public speeches, destined to be read by the whole world, in which illustrations were drawn from such sources as these! . . . No wonder Seward . . . should hesitate to accept a position in the

Cabinet of one who has so poor an opinion of the popular intelligence, and so small an appreciation of the dignity of his office, as Mr. Lincoln displayed in his speech at Indianapolis."

In Indianapolis also, Lincoln broke his rule against saying anything of substance, and learned a bruising lesson. When he stepped off the train, Governor Oliver P. Morton had set the tone with a speech that was not an official welcome but rather a declaration of policy, exhorting Lincoln to stand firm for the Union. Lincoln, following Morton's lead, spoke that evening on the sensitive subject of whether asserting Federal authority could be fairly construed as "coercing" the Southern states. *What if the government simply held or recaptured its own forts, or enforced the laws by collecting duties, or stopped the mails where they were being violated?* "Would any or all of these things be coercion?" he asked rhetorically. For the next few days, newspapers all over the South twisted the speech to mean that Lincoln promised invasion and bloodshed, and was only waiting until he was in office to begin the war. The *Louisville Courier* cried, "It is a war proposition couched in language intended to conceal the enormity of the crime beneath pretexts too absurd to require exposure and fallacies too flimsy to deceive the most stupid." The Nashville *Patriot* attacked not the proposition but the man: "Whatever may have been the motive which suggested the Indianapolis harangues," it declared, "there can be no mistake as to one thing, and that is they prove him to be a narrow-minded Republican partisan incapable apparently of rising to the attitude of statesmanship necessary to a thorough comprehension of the national crisis, and the remedies demanded by patriotism to preserve the government he has been selected to administer."

In an attempt to avoid repeating his mistake, Lincoln performed even worse the next day, and the next. The age was not one in which humility was valued in its public men, especially just then, when Northern citizens were tense with the news that the Southern Confederacy was swearing in its own president, the venerable Jefferson Davis, in Montgomery, Alabama. Yet Lincoln confessed, "should my administration prove to be a very wicked one, or what is more probable, a very foolish one, if you, the people, are but true to yourselves and to the Constitution, there is little harm I can do, *thank God!*" He was self-conscious—almost apologetic—about the improbable fact of his election, calling himself "the humblest of all individuals that have ever been elected to the Presidency," a man "without a name, perhaps without a reason why . . . I should have a name." At Steubenville, Ohio, he confessed, "I fear that the great confidence placed in my ability is unfounded. Indeed, I am sure it is." Going on, he declared, "If anything goes wrong . . . and you find you have made a mistake, elect a better man next time. There are plenty of them." He told one crowd he had been elected President "by a mere accident, and not through any merit of mine"; he was "a mere instrument, an accidental instrument, perhaps I should say." Many, dismayed by such hand-wringing, were alarmed that the President-elect should have so much to be humble about.

In Columbus, Ohio, Lincoln took an even more unfortunate tack, dismissing the secession crisis with the canard, "there is nothing going wrong. It is a consoling circumstance that when we look out there is nothing that really hurts anybody. We entertain different views upon political questions, but nobody is suffering anything." Lincoln undoubtedly intended to calm his listeners, but he produced instead the alarming effect of a man who did not understand that the nation was in crisis. Here he revealed his dangerous underestimation of the intensity and depth of Southern feeling, and he struck this same note again and again as he approached Washington, at Pittsburgh—"In plain words, there is really no crisis except an artificial one"—and again at Cleveland: "I think that there is no occasion for excitement. The crisis, as it is called, is altogether an artificial crisis . . . . It has no foundation in facts." Such remarks baffled anybody who could read a newspaper, such as New York congressman Edwin Reynolds, who wondered aloud, "Have not our forts and vessels been seized, our arsenals invaded, our mints robbed, by men and States in arms? Has not our flag been fired into, our mails rifled and intercepted, our commerce on the Mississippi obstructed? Is not the public mind today, North and South, convulsed as never before?" The Saint Louis *Daily Missouri Republican* protested:

> At Columbus, Ohio, the President *improvised* a little—and certainly it is the most remarkable speech on record. The burden of it is that "nobody is hurt"—"nobody is suffering" from the present condition of affairs, pecuniary and political. Was the like of that ever heard? What could he have meant? With a perfect knowledge that the Union has been virtually dissolved—that six of the States have renounced this confederacy and formed a new government . . . he proceeds to tell us, that "nobody is hurt," and "nobody is suffering," from the present condition of the country.
>
> "Nobody hurt—nobody suffering"—what does this mean? We ask the people of St. Louis to respond to this inquiry. How has it happened that commerce is checked in every department; that our merchants are forced to curtail, and even to close their business; that hundreds and thousands

of worthy men are thrown out of employment, and left with their families
to starve—now is this the case if, according to Mr. Lincoln, there is "no
suffering?"

Politically and socially, did the United States ever present such an
aspect of complete wreck and abandonment, and yet Mr. Lincoln tells us
"nobody is hurt" and "nobody is suffering"!

The *New York Herald* accused Lincoln of "ignorance" of the danger to the
Union. He showed "no capacity to grapple manfully with the dangers of this
crisis," it said; "If Mr. Lincoln has nothing better to offer upon this fearful crisis
than the foolish consolations of his speech in Columbus, let him say nothing at
all." Serious people everywhere wondered if the new President was so deluded
as to be incompetent to lead the nation through such a time of decision.

Nor was Lincoln's longest treatment of a policy question to his credit. This
was the Pittsburgh speech in which he tackled the tariff, which in Pennsylvania
had been a more potent vote-getting issue than slavery. Here Lincoln was out of
his league. According to his law partner William Herndon, Lincoln had never
had a mind for figures. In Pittsburgh he admitted that he had no "thoroughly
matured judgment" on the subject and was "not posted" on the bill then under
consideration. He referred to the tariff in frontier style, calling it
"housekeeping" and "replenishing the mealtub." He stumbled on, expressing
the hope that every congressman would "post himself thoroughly" "so as to
contribute his part" in order to "be just and equal to all sections . . . and classes
of people," which, of course, was the opposite of what a tariff was intended to
do. Henry Villard rightly called the speech "crude, ignorant twaddle, without
point or meaning."

*   *   *

At other stops, Lincoln's homespun, Western-style attempts to provide a
light touch seemed to sensitive citizens to be inappropriate to the emergency of
the moment, as at Westfield, New York, where he hauled up the little girl who
had written him suggesting he grow a beard, and kissed her; and at Freedom,
Pennsylvania, where he invited a huge coal-heaver to clamber up onto the
platform with him and compare heights back-to-back. Such antics struck the
nation as undignified, certainly unpresidential. To Charles Francis Adams, Jr., it
was unseemly that the "absolutely unknown" Lincoln was "saying whatever

comes into his head," and "perambulating the country, kissing little girls and growing whiskers!"

Many sober-minded citizens, especially those reading accounts in newspapers, reacted to their first experience of the Washington-bound President-elect with similar dismay. The editor of the influential *Springfield* (Mass.) *Republican*, Samuel Bowles, despaired in a letter to a friend, "Lincoln is a 'Simple Susan.'" The most esteemed orator in America, Edward Everett, wrote in his diary: "These speeches thus far have been of the most ordinary kind, destitute of everything, not merely of felicity and grace, but of common pertinence. He is evidently a person of very inferior cast of character, wholly unequal to the crisis." From Washington, Congressman Charles Francis Adams wrote, "His speeches have fallen like a wet blanket here. They put to flight all notions of greatness." *Vanity Fair* joked slyly about Lincoln's poor performance, observing, "Abe is becoming more grave. He don't construct as many jokes as he did. He fears that he will get things mixed up if he don't look out." Even in Illinois, there were bitter public voices savaging his utterances during the journey:

> The illustrious Honest Old Abe has continued during the last week to make a fool of himself and to mortify and shame the intelligent people of this great nation. His speeches have demonstrated the fact that although originally a Herculean rail splitter and more lately a whimsical story teller and side splitter, he is no more capable of becoming a statesman, nay, even a moderate one, than the braying ass can become a noble lion. People now marvel how it came to pass that Mr. Lincoln should have been selected as the representative man of any party. His weak, wishy-washy, namby-pamby efforts, imbecile in matter, disgusting in manner, have made us the laughing stock of the whole world. The European powers will despise us because we have no better material out of which to make a President. The truth is, Lincoln is only a moderate lawyer and in the larger cities of the Union could pass for no more than a facetious pettifogger. Take him from his vocation and he loses even these small characteristics and indulges in simple twaddle which would disgrace a well bred school boy.

The Harrisburg *Daily Patriot and Union* published its dim view from the Pennsylvania capital:

The lack of good taste and proper dignity of deportment that has marked Mr. Lincoln's course since he left Springfield, Illinois, . . . is the subject of universal remark, as well as universal regret.

. . . Had he been the dignified statesman he ought to be, . . . it seems to us he would have proceeded from his home in Illinois to the Federal Capital by the most direct route, in a quiet way, avoiding all parade and ostentation, and thus save his friends and the nation at large the mortification of seeing the elected President of the country making the most puerile and disgusting displays of mountebankism that were ever given by any harlequin who ever strutted upon a stage or gamboled in a circus ring, to delight a gaping crowd, at twenty-five cents a head. . . .

We confess that we shudder as we contemplate the future in the person of this weak and ignorant man.

The Baltimore *Sun* affected hilarity: "There is that about his speechification which, if it were not for the gravity of the occasion, would be ludicrous to the destruction of buttons. Indeed we heard his Columbus speech read yesterday amidst irresistible bursts of laughter. . . . We begin to realize his qualifications as a barroom 'Phunny Phellow.'"

Further south, the reactions to Lincoln's speeches were improvisations on the theme of disgust. The Staunton (Virginia) *Vindicator*, wrote:

His speeches on his tour . . . have been a display of the most vulgar and ill-bred tastes, more alike to buffoonery of the clown than the logic of the statesman. Instead of rising to the dignity of his exalted position, he indulges in the disgusting and silly electioneering harangues, and exposes his ignorance both of the science of letters as well as the rules of rhetoric.

The Richmond *Examiner* called Lincoln "a beastly figure," and asserted, "No American of any section has read the oratory with which he has strewn his devious road to Washington, condensed lumps of imbecility, buffoonery, and vulgar malignity, without a blush of shame." The Charleston *Mercury* dismissed Lincoln's speeches as "fiddle-faddle," and Lincoln as a "weak compound of blockhead and blackguard." The *New Orleans Daily Crescent* told its readers, "If any one can read the speeches which Mr. Lincoln has made on his recent trip to Washington City without a feeling of intense disgust, we envy him not his disposition." The *Crescent*, however, was outdone by the crosstown New Orleans *Daily Delta*:

His silly speeches, his ill-timed jocularity, his pusillanimous evasion of responsibility, and vulgar pettyfoggery [sic], have no parallel in history . . . . We have repeatedly averred that the secession of the South was instigated by higher motives than a mere hostility to Lincoln; that the simple fact of his election was not the moving cause of that great movement. But his recent conduct will compel us to confess that the debasement of being ruled over by such a President—the disgust of having to look up to such a Chief Magistrate as the head of the Republic—is quite as powerful a justification for secession as could be presented. It is evident that the South has been quite as much deceived in its estimate of Lincoln as the North and his own party have been. His bearing in the debate with Douglas produced a general impression that he was a man of some ability, as a politician and a polemic. . . . But he is no sooner compelled to break [his] silence, and to exhibit himself in public, than this delusion vanishes, and the Hoosier lawyer dwindles into far smaller proportions than his bitterest enemies have ever assigned to him. . . . [H]e never opens his mouth but he puts his foot into it. In supreme silliness—in profound ignorance of the institutions of the Republic of which he has been chosen chief—in dishonest and cowardly efforts to dodge responsibility and play a double part—in disgusting levity on the most serious subjects, the speeches of Lincoln, on his way to the capital, have no equals in the history of any people, civilized or semi-civilized.

*   *   *

The newsprint blows that rained down on Lincoln transformed his jubilee procession into a painful run of the gauntlet on a continental scale. But he was only now approaching the most hazardous stretch in what had become, for the press at least, a hazing ritual. As he descended the Hudson River valley, one wag noted sarcastically, "Mr. Lincoln, having . . . brought his brilliant intellectual powers to bear upon the cultivation of luxuriant whiskers . . . has now . . . concentrated his mental energies upon the question—what hotel he shall stop at in New York."

Chapter 12

Lincoln and the Merchants

"The Undertaker of the Union."

For the first eight days of Lincoln's procession across the North, Lincoln's speeches drew jeers from the pens of distant partisans who scoured the text of Lincoln's remarks in cold print. Those on hand, however—the crowds who mobbed Lincoln at every stop, even in pouring rain and blowing snow—were not there to hear the final word on the nation's troubles, but merely to look at the Westerner who had come out of nowhere to lead the nation through the crisis, to hear the bands play and the cannon boom, and to show themselves for the Union.

The impression Lincoln made on the crowds on his eight-day progression from the Illinois prairie to the Hudson Valley was mixed. Villard discerned a letdown in the throng at seeing him in the flesh: "While he thus satisfied the public curiosity, he disappointed, by his appearance, most of those who saw him for the first time. I could see that impression clearly written on the faces of his rustic audiences. Nor was this surprising, for they saw the most unprepossessing features, the gawkiest figure, and the most awkward manners. Lincoln always had an embarrassed air, too, like a country clodhopper appearing in fashionable society, and was nearly always stiff and unhappy in his off-hand remarks."

One who agreed was a young Lexington, Kentucky, man who came to Cincinnati to see Lincoln. He wrote to his brother soon afterward, "Old Abe Lincoln was here this week. He looks, talks, & acts just as you may have seen some long, slab sided flat boat 'Capting,' who had sold his 'prodooce' at Memphis & invested 12$ at a slop shop tailor's in rigging himself out for Sunday. He is a disgrace as the headboss of any civilized nation." A friend who wrote to diarist Mary Chesnut in Charleston described Lincoln as "Awfully ugly, even grotesque in appearance, the kind who are always at the corner stores . . . whittling sticks, and telling stories as funny as they are vulgar."

Many in the small towns and farm communities, however, probably took away a more generous impression, like the Ohio lawyer and future president,

James A. Garfield, who, after seeing him for the first time, wrote, "He is distressingly homely. But through all his awkward homeliness, there is a look of transparent, genuine goodness which at once reaches your heart and makes you trust and love him." The Northern farmland through which Lincoln traveled was his base, the heart of his political strength. His friend Judge Davis thought it was not Lincoln himself, but the peril of the country that brought out the tumultuous crowds, but still, he marveled, "The whole trip . . . has been an Ovation such as never before been witnessed . . . It is simply astonishing."

Then, in the mid-afternoon of February 19, the Presidential train arrived in New York City, and the holiday mood changed.

* * *

New York City was a hostile pro-Southern enclave in the Republican North. In the November election, it had cast 62% of its votes for Lincoln's opponents. Here, his audience did not even approach the size of the crowd that had strained to see the visiting Prince of Wales three months before. The *New York Herald* observed, "the masses of people did not turn out." It reported a "crowd which cheered, and scoffed, and scowled him a doubtful welcome. He passed through almost unknown, and the crowd which followed his coach with cheers were actuated by curiosity as much as admiration." Walt Whitman, who was there, wrote that Lincoln

> possessed no personal popularity at all in New York City and not much political. But it was evidently tacitly agreed that if [his] few political supporters . . . present would entirely abstain from any demonstration on their side, the immense majority—who were anything but supporters— would abstain on their side also. The result was a sulky, unbroken silence, such as certainly never before characterized a New York crowd. . . . The crowd that hemmed around consisted . . . of thirty to forty thousand men, not a single one his personal friend, while, I have no doubt (so frenzied were the ferments of the time) many an assassin's knife and pistol lurked in hip- or breast-pocket there—ready, soon as break and riot came.

The sulky mood in New York City took its tone from the large Democratic immigrant population, which had a wait-and-see attitude toward the new man, but it also partook of the distrust of the big-time capitalists. The New York captains of commerce had a monetary stake in stability, in tranquility, in "business as usual." The present crisis threatened their empire. The merchants sanctified property rights, and they sympathized even with those whose property was black people. To them, it was the abolitionists who were the revolutionary troublemakers, the Republican platform that was the hostile program. The city's merchants owed a large share of their prosperity to shipping Southern cotton, an estimated two hundred million dollars a year. Surely, they thought, this was something Lincoln had to respect. One observer spoke of New York, with its financial dependence on the cotton trade, as "a prolongation of the South." The mayor, Democrat Fernando Wood, had in November floated the idea of New York itself seceding from the Union and becoming a "free city," the better to maintain its business with the departing Cotton States.

The merchants were for compromise. They had made themselves rich lending credit to Southern planters, and now had outstanding debts to the Southerners totaling $150 million to $200 million. A war would make those millions irrecoverable. Over the winter, they had organized to exert tremendous pressure to soften Republican policy. It was they who had spearheaded the strong demand for compromise in the North. In December, more than two thousand local New York businessmen had gathered to demand the redress of Southern grievances. They had written letters to parties in all sections begging for restraint from any rash action, organized mass meetings, drawn up compromise petitions that drew more than 100,000 signatures in the Eastern cities, and sent delegations to lobby congressmen.

Indeed, some stalwart Republicans were more alarmed about the merchants' threat to anti-slavery principles than the Southerners' threat. Radical Republican Zachariah Chandler had written Lyman Trumbull, "The mercantile world is in a ferment, even some good reliable Republicans are alarmed and wish something done. Now I have no fear that the senseless Southern howl will affect Mr. Lincoln in the least, but I do fear that this Republican alarm may extend even to Springfield." The merchants had certainly bent the ear of Thurlow Weed, who had published the first calls for compromise in the Albany *Evening Journal* in the weeks after the election. Big Money's man in Washington was Weed's partner William Seward.

Big Money's man would certainly not be Lincoln. In November and December, his election had touched off two panics on the New York Stock Exchange, whose merchants had clamored for concessions to the South to restore prices. Lincoln replied with a Western view of the wicked ways of Wall Street: "I am not insensible to any commercial or financial depression that may exist, but nothing is to be gained by fawning around the '*respectable scoundrels*' who got it up. Let them go to work to repair the mischief of their own making; and then perhaps they will be less greedy to do the like again." At work here was his prejudice against the Eastern elite, his frontier resentment at being looked down upon as raw and uncultured, his sense that the businessmen of the East were piling up fortunes from the plush leather chairs of their smoking rooms by manipulating markets and exploiting hard-working laborers of the West. "It annoyed me to hear that gang of men called respectable," he said.

The "respectable scoundrels," for their part, returned the feeling. The Eastern men resented the fact that so much political clout had shifted to the West. They were appalled at the boisterous energy of the Westerners, offended by their coarse, vulgar behavior. To them, the West was like a wild child now come of age. Abraham Lincoln—rangy, gawky, and socially awkward; the first president born west of the Appalachians—embodied everything about the frontier that made the merchants shudder.

And there was an even deeper dread at work among the Eastern aristocracy, something that had been noticed by Alexis de Tocqueville in his visit to America some thirty years before. Tocqueville discerned that, hidden beneath an "artificial enthusiasm" for democratic institutions, "it is easy to perceive that the rich have a hearty dislike of the democratic institutions of their country. The people form a power which at once they fear and despise." The diaries and letters of wealthy observers were rife with dismay at the power of the masses, with their persistent lawlessness and political corruption. British correspondent William Russell observed that among "the upper world of millionaire merchants, . . . Not a man there but resented the influence given by universal suffrage to the mob of the city, and complained of the intolerable effects of their ascendancy." The merchants viewed the election of Abraham Lincoln as the coarse culmination of the vulgar tendencies of what they called "the mob," or "the mobocracy."

The money men were delighted when, on the first morning of his visit to New York, Lincoln attended a breakfast with a hundred leading businessmen at the home of millionaire Moses H. Grinnell. The stock market rose at the news that the merchant princes finally had the President's ear. Lincoln disappointed them, however. When one remarked that he "would not meet so many millionaires together at any other table in New York," he provoked them with his response: "Oh, indeed, is that so? Well, that's quite right. I'm a millionaire myself. I got a minority of a million votes last November." Lincoln was reminding the fat cats that their bank accounts had to be balanced against the expressed wishes of millions of voters, but he gained some high-powered enemies by his flippancy. After an uncomfortable interval, the meeting broke up. The merchants emerged grim-faced.

(The intense pressure of the New York businessmen would be brought to bear again a week later, after Lincoln arrived in Washington. There, one of the merchants, William L. Dodge, visited Lincoln at his hotel and reminded him of the worry of the capitalists over the forthcoming inaugural address, insisting, "It is for you, sir, to say whether the whole nation shall be plunged into bankruptcy, whether the grass shall grow in the streets of our commercial cities."

Lincoln replied in his way—which was often, during this period, rather glib: "Then I shall say not. If it depends upon me, the grass will not grow anywhere except in the fields and the meadows."

Dodge persisted, "Then you will yield to the just demands of the South. You will leave her to control her own institutions. You will admit slave states into the Union on the same conditions as free states. You will not go to war on account of slavery."

Lincoln now set his teeth, and he replied slowly and steadily, "I do not know that I understand your meaning, Mr. Dodge, nor do I know what my acts or opinions may be in the future beyond this. I shall take an oath that I will, to the best of my ability, preserve, protect, and defend the Constitution of the United States. It is not the Constitution as I would like to have it, but as it *is*, that is to be defended. The Constitution will not be preserved and defended until it is enforced and obeyed in every part of every one of the United States. It must be so respected, obeyed, enforced, and defended, let the grass grow where it may." Dodge withdrew, muttering.)

Immediately after breakfast with the New York millionaires, Lincoln was hurried to City Hall, where he received a chilly reception from Mayor Fernando Wood. Facing Lincoln across George Washington's writing desk, he warned that New York was "sorely afflicted," with "all her material interests paralyzed," and "her commercial greatness endangered." Wood lectured Lincoln on his duty "to bring it back again to its former harmonious, consolidated and prosperous condition." In his reply, Lincoln turned the other cheek, graciously acknowledging the advice of the Mayor, and remained at City Hall for two hours to shake hands with citizens.

That evening the Lincolns attended a Verdi opera, *Un Ballo in Maschera*, at the sumptuous Academy of Music, where he unwittingly ran athwart the prevailing fashion that dictated that white gloves were in style for opera-going. Lincoln wore black gloves, and compounded his *faux pas* by dangling his huge hands over the railing of the red-velvet box. "I think we ought to send some flowers over the way to the Undertaker of the Union," laughed a Southerner in a box opposite. Everyone noticed. Newspapers said Lincoln had the manners of a gorilla. The Eastern elite despaired that a man who wore black gloves to the opera, and said "inaugeration," could ever be capable of statesmanship.

*   *   *

It must have been to Lincoln's immense relief when, the next morning, his train re-crossed the Hudson and rolled south across the farmland of New Jersey. He could not know that by that evening the jubilee procession would be over, forgotten amid urgent back-room talk of agents, spies, conspiracies, and assassination. For this was February 21, 1861, when the discovery of the Baltimore plot was revealed to Lincoln in his Philadelphia hotel room, when fate tapped him on the shoulder in the middle of his introduction to the American people and beckoned him into a smoky room full of friends who pleaded with him to make a secret ride through the Maryland capital and on, in the dark, to Washington.

The President-elect would go through the motions the next day, speaking at a flag-raising at Philadelphia's Independence Hall in the morning and making two more speeches in Harrisburg that afternoon. By the following day in Washington, in the wake of his secret night ride, after he was rushed to his suite at Willard's Hotel, all the omissions and failures of the last thirty years would settle onto the shoulders of the man still nine days short of taking office.

The poison pens of a hostile press would wound him.

A warlike new nation of seven states, just now forming in Montgomery, Alabama, would scoff at the imaginary danger he had faced in Baltimore, even while it recruited, trained, and fitted tens of thousands of very real soldiers to destroy his government.

Millions in the South who feared the coming of an American Caesar, and millions more in the North who dreaded the arrival of another inept chief like Pierce or Buchanan, would curse him.

And in Suite 6 at Willard's he would find on his desk a letter waiting for him. It read:

> if you don't Resign we are going to put a spider in your dumpling and play
> the Devil with you you god or mighty god dam sundde of a bith go to hell
> and buss my Ass suck my prick and call my Bolics your uncle Dick god
> dam a fool and goddam Abe Lincoln who would like you goddam you

excuse me for using such hard words with you but you need it you are nothing but a goddam Black nigger.

Part Two

Lincoln's First Eighteen Months

"No Man Living Needed so Much
Education as the New President."

Chapter 13

Lincoln's First Impression

"A cross between a sandhill crane and an Andalusian jackass."

While the weather in Washington in the last days of February veered from snow to sun to warm rain to choking dust, the nine days between Lincoln's arrival and his inauguration were a dizzying medley of consultations and receptions. An endless round of introductions occupied him—with the outgoing President and his Cabinet, congressmen, members of the Supreme Court, the mayor of Washington, office seekers, serenaders, and dozens of members of his own party who had come to look at the new man and press him with their views. In his parlor at Willard's Hotel, the press of humanity was tremendous.

All the men who met Lincoln were aware of the aching need for a great man, someone to do great deeds. The new President was needed to redeem a nation that, by late February, had divided into two nations, with two capitals, one in Washington and one in Montgomery. There was a basic conception of how a great man should look and act, especially among the many who considered themselves great men. They remembered the grand, august Daniel Webster as their model: the dark brow; the piercing, "lightning" eyes; the garments "unsurpassed"; the deep, powerful voice; the majestic oratory, delivered with Napoleonic bearing, with one hand thrust into the vest, the other hanging gracefully. Lincoln, by consensus, was far short of grand.

* * *

To begin with, high society had strict rules that governed who were gentlemen and who were not. A certain voice, manner, dress, style, and a kind of reserve were expected. Lincoln violated these rules completely. It was no great stretch for men bred in high society to conclude that a man so lacking in gentlemanly qualities could not be wise, could not be a statesman. As British journalist William Russell observed, "A person who met Mr. Lincoln in the street would not take him to be what is called a 'gentleman'; and, indeed, since I came to the United States, I have heard more disparaging allusions made by Americans to him on that account than I could have expected among simple republicans, where all should be equals." One evening in New York, Russell met several gentlemen, one of whom told him, "the majority of the people of New York, and all the respectable people, were disgusted at the election of such a fellow as Lincoln to be President and would back the Southern States, if it came to a split." After another two days in such company, Russell wrote further in his diary, "I was astonished to find little sympathy and no respect for the newly installed Government. They were regarded as obscure or undistinguished men. . . . One of the journals continued to speak of 'The President' in the most contemptuous manner and to designate him as the great 'Rail-Splitter.'"

In the eyes of many, Lincoln's most immediate problem was the subject of a letter he received two weeks after his election, postmarked Elgin, Illinois:

Deformed Sir,

The Ugly Club, in full meeting, have elected you an Honorary Member of the Hard-Favored Fraternity. –Prince Harry was lean, Falstaff was fat, Thersites was hunchbacked, and Slawkenbergus [sic] was renowned for the eminent miscalculation which nature had made in the length of his nose; but it remained for you to unite all species of deformity, and stand forth the Prince of Ugly Fellows.

In the bonds of Ugliness—Hinchaway Beeswax, President. Eagle-Eyed Carbuncle, Secretary of the Ugly Club.

Journalist Donn Piatt testified that "Mr. Lincoln was the homeliest man I ever saw." British journalist Edward Dicey insisted that "to say that he is ugly is nothing, to add that his figure is grotesque is to convey no adequate impression." He was the "homeliest and the awkwardest man in the Sucker State," according to fellow Illinoisan J. H. Burnham. New York correspondent Henry Villard said simply, "As far as all external conditions were concerned, there was nothing in favor of Lincoln." "His phiz is truly awful," agreed another observer. "Slouchy, ungraceful, round shouldered, leans forward (very much in his walk) is lean and ugly in every way," wrote still another. Carl Schurz confessed that at first, "I was somewhat startled by his appearance. . . . I had seen, in Washington and in the West, several public men of rough appearance; but none whose looks seemed quite so uncouth, not to say grotesque, as

Lincoln's." Diarist George Templeton Strong met the President in October of 1861, and even at that late date was not prepared for his first sight of Lincoln, reporting, "He is lank and hard-featured, among the ugliest white men I have seen. Decidedly plebian." Another friend, Pennsylvania politician Alexander McClure, admitted that, after coming face-to-face with Lincoln, "I doubt whether I wholly concealed my disappointment at meeting him. . . . I confess that my heart sank within me as I remembered that this was the man chosen by a great nation to become its ruler in the gravest period of its history."

That Lincoln was extremely odd—"grotesque" was the favorite term—was the universal reaction among men seeing him for the first time. The head itself was arresting, "coconut shaped and somewhat too small for such a stature," said Dicey, and he described the face that looked out from it as "furrowed, wrinkled, and indented, as though it had been scarred by vitriol." To William Herndon, Lincoln's law partner, his face was "long, sallow, and cadaverous, shrunk, shriveled, wrinkled, and dry, having here and there a hair on the surface." "His complexion was very dark, his skin yellow, shriveled, and 'leathery,'" according to his friend Ward Lamon. Dicey called attention to the "nose and ears, which have been taken by mistake from a head of twice the size." Russell saw the ears as comical, "flapping and wide-projecting," and the nose, "a prominent organ—stands out from the face, with an inquiring anxious air, as though it were sniffing for some good thing in the wind." Lincoln's "thatch of wild republican hair" was another source of amazement. The morning Lincoln was introduced to Nathaniel Hawthorne (who came away amazed that Lincoln had never heard of him), the novelist noticed his hair "had apparently been acquainted with neither brush nor comb that morning, after the disarrangement of the pillow." According to Herndon, it was "dark, almost black, and lay floating where his fingers or the winds left it, piled up at random"; "rough, uncombed and uncombable lank dark hair, that stands out in every direction at once," said Dicey; "bristling and compact like a ruff of mourning pins," noted Russell.

But it was Lincoln's "lean, lank, indescribably gawky figure" that inspired the most comment. In an age when men of substance were expected to look substantial—portly and well-upholstered—Lincoln was, according to Herndon, "a thin, tall, wiry, sinewy, grizzly, raw-boned man." Villard reported that by the time Lincoln reached Washington, "Always cadaverous, his appearance is now almost ghostly." To get the proper picture, Dicey suggested, "Fancy a man six-foot [actually six feet four inches], and thin out of proportion [he weighed only 180 pounds], with bony arms and legs, which, somehow, seem to be always in the way, with large rugged hands, which grasp you like a vise when shaking yours, with a long scraggy neck, and a chest too narrow for the great arms hanging by its side." Piatt sketched his impression of Lincoln as "a huge skeleton in clothes. Tall as he was, his hands and feet looked out of proportion, so long and clumsy were they. Every movement was awkward in the extreme."

McClure was prejudiced early on by Lincoln's "awkwardness that was uncommon among men of intelligence," and so were many. Hawthorne called him "loose-jointed"; "There is no describing his lengthy awkwardness, nor the uncouthness of his movement," he wrote. French journalist Duviergier de Hauranne marveled, "His posture was awkward and like nothing I've ever seen before—partly rigid and partly loose-jointed; he doesn't seem to know how to carry his great height." In the week before the inauguration, Russell described Lincoln's comic entrance to a room, "with a shambling, loose, irregular, almost unsteady gait, a tall, lank, lean man, considerably over six feet in height, with stooping shoulders, long pendulous arms, terminating in hands of extraordinary dimensions, which, however, were far exceeded in proportion by his feet." Herndon pictured him "thin through the breast to the back, and narrow across the shoulders; standing, he leaned forward—was what may be called stoop-shouldered, inclining to the consumptive by build. . . . The whole man, body and mind, worked slowly, creakingly, as if it needed oiling." Henry Clay Whitney, a fellow Illinois attorney, testified, "He was very awkward in all the little common-places of life . . . he was essentially uncouth; so in the company of ladies, or cultivated strangers. In such society—he would not know what to do with his hat, or his arms or legs. I have seen him, in company, put his arms behind his back; then bring them in front again, and then look around sheepishly, as much as to say, 'What can I do with them?'" One acquaintance swore that, partly because of Lincoln's stooped shoulders, his arms were longer than those of any man he had ever seen: "When standing Straight, and letting his arms fall down his Sides, the points of his fingers would touch a point lower on his legs by nearly three inches than was usual with other persons." So, too, with his legs. "The length of his legs [were] out of all proportion to that of his body," according to Ward Lamon. "When he sat down on a chair, he seemed no taller than an average man, measuring from the chair to the crown of his head; but his knees rose high in front, and a marble placed on the cap of one of them would roll down a steep descent to the hip." Lincoln's awkward, shambling walk, which struck everyone, was the result of a crane-like mismanagement of his gangling limbs, combined with his odd, flat-footed, clodhopper gait:

according to both William Herndon and Ward Lamon, he was slightly pigeon-toed, and when he walked, he set his whole foot flat on the ground, and then lifted it all at once, so that he lacked any spring or ease of motion. While walking, his long arms and hands hung like a giant's by his side, which magnified the grotesque effect.

Lincoln's opponents lampooned his odd appearance, as in this "mock biography":

> Mr. Lincoln stands six feet twelve in his socks, which he changes once every ten days. His anatomy is composed mostly of bones, and when walking he resembles the offspring of a happy marriage between a derrick and a windmill. . . . His head is shaped something like a rutabaga, and his complexion is that of a Saratoga trunk. His hands and feet are plenty large enough, and in society he has the air of having too many of them. The glove-makers have not yet had time to construct gloves that will fit him. In his habits he is by no means foppish, though he brushes his hair sometimes and is said to wash. He swears fluently. A strict temperance man himself, he does not object to another man's being pretty drunk, especially when he is about to make a bargain with him. . . . He can hardly be called handsome, though he is certainly much better looking since he had small-pox.

. . . and this, with more meanness than mockery, which was printed in the *Kentucky Statesman*:

> Abraham Lincoln is a man above the medium height. He passes the six foot mark by an inch or two. He is raw-boned, shamble-gaited, bow-legged, knock-kneed, pigeon-toed, slob-sided, a shapeless skeleton in a very tough, very dirty, unwholesome skin. His hair is or rather was black and shaggy; his eyes dark and fireless like a cold grate in winter time. His lips protrude beyond the natural level of the face, but are pale and smeared with tobacco juice. His teeth are filthy.
>
> In the next place his voice is untutored, coarse, harsh—the voice of one who has no intellect and less moral nature. His manners are low in the extreme and when his talk is not obscene it is senseless. In a word, Lincoln, born and bred a railsplitter, is a railsplitter still.

Lincoln's arrival in Washington was the target of three Sut Lovingood stories in the *Nashville Union & American,* a newspaper that had called Lincoln a "half-witted politician." The fictitious Sut was a rude, drunken hillbilly, who at one point offered a description of his new buddy, Abe Lincoln, whom Sut called "ole Windin' Blades" because his arms and legs were like the long blades used for winding yarn:

> If he aint a long wun an a narrow wun, I'm durned. His mouf, his paw, an his footsez am the principil feeturs, an his strikin pint is the way them ar laigs ove hizen gets inter his body. They goes in at each aidge sorter like the prongs goes intu a pitch fork. Ove all the durned skeery looking ole cusses for a president ever I seed, he am decidedly the durndest. He looks like a yaller ladder with half the rungs knocked out.
>
> I kotch a ole bull frog once an druv a nail thru his lips inter a post, tied two rocks to his hine toes an stuck a darnin needil inter his tail tu let out the misture, an lef him there tu dry. I seed him two weeks arter wurds, an when I seed ole Abe I thot hit were an orful retribution cum ontu me, an that hit were the same frog, only stretched a little longer, an had tuck to waring ove close tu keep me from knowin him, an ketchin him an nailin him up agin; an natral born durn'd fool es I is, I swar I seed the same watry skeery look in the eyes, an the same sorter knots on the 'back-bone.' I'm feard, George, sumthin's tu cum ove my nailin up that ar frog. I swar I am, ever since I seed ole Abe, same shape same color same feel (cold as ice) an I'm d——— ef hit aint the same smell.

The ludicrous effect of his long limbs was magnified by Lincoln's lifelong carelessness about clothes. "He probably had as little taste about dress and attire as anybody that ever was born: he simply wore clothes because it was needful and customary; whether they fitted or looked well was entirely above, or beneath, his comprehension," remembered Whitney. In 1855, a high-powered lawyer described Lincoln as "an ungainly back woodsman, with coarse, ill-fitting clothing, his trousers hardly reaching his ankles." At the time of the Douglas debates in 1858, he was still, according to a close acquaintance, "more or less careless of his personal attire, . . . he usually wore in his great canvass with Douglas a linen coat, generally without any vest, a hat much the worse for wear, and carried with him a faded cotton umbrella which became almost as famous in the canvass as Lincoln himself." The linen coat itself was memorable— Edwin Stanton recalled Lincoln "wearing a dirty linen duster for a coat, on the back of which the perspiration had splotched two wide stains that, emanating from each armpit, met at the centre, and resembled a dirty map of a continent." Carl Schurz, who met Lincoln during the debates, took away a vivid impression of his clothes: "On his head he wore a somewhat battered 'stove-pipe' hat. . . . His lank, ungainly body was clad in a rusty black dress coat with sleeves that should have been longer; but his arms appeared so long that the sleeves of a 'store' coat could hardly be expected to cover them all the way down to the wrists. His black trousers, too, permitted a very full view of his large feet."

As President-elect in 1861, his losing battles with his garments were a source of much head-shaking among those meeting him for the first time. William Russell first saw him then, "dressed in an ill-fitting, wrinkled suit of black, which put one in mind of an undertaker's uniform at a funeral." When Edward Dicey met Lincoln he was garbed "in a long, tight, badly fitting suit of black, creased, soiled, and puckered up at every salient point of the figure . . . [in] large, ill-fitting boots, gloves too long for the long bony fingers, and a fluffy hat, covered to the top with dusty, puffy crepe." When Hawthorne met him, "He was dressed in a rusty black frock-coat and pantaloons, unbrushed, and worn so faithfully that the suit had adapted itself to the curves and angularities of his figure, and had grown to be an outer skin of the man. He had shabby slippers on his feet." Lincoln had already come to grief over his black gloves at the New York opera, and now Mary Clemmer Ames, a Washington correspondent for the *Springfield* (Mass.) *Republican* noticed at a pre-inaugural reception, "Abraham Lincoln looks very awkward in white kid gloves and feels uncomfortable in new boots."

Miss Ames didn't know the half of it. Ward Hill Lamon testified to Lincoln's struggles with his accouterments:

> He had very defective taste in the choice of hats, the item of dress that does more than any other for the improvement of one's personal appearance. His hat for years served the double purpose of an ornamental headgear and a kind of office or receptacle for his private papers and memoranda.
>
> . . . I think Mr. Lincoln suffered much annoyance from the tyranny of fashion in the matter of gloves. The necessity to wear gloves he regarded as an affliction, a violation of the statute against "cruelty to animals." At about the time of his third reception [very possibly the one Ms. Ames attended] he had on a tight-fitting pair of white kids, which he had with difficulty got on. He saw approaching in the distance an old Illinois friend

named Simpson, whom he welcomed with a genuine Sangamon County shake, which resulted in bursting his white-kid glove with an audible sound. Then raising his brawny hand up before him, looking at it with an indescribable expression, he said, — while the whole procession was checked, witnessing this scene, — "Well, my old friend, this is a general bustification. You and I were never intended to wear these things. If they were stronger they might do well enough to keep out the cold, but they are a failure to shake hands with between old friends like us. Stand aside, Captain, and I'll see you shortly."

One of the most remarkable things about Lincoln's inattention to his appearance was that, during his years as the highest official in the land, it never improved. The well-heeled Captain Francis Donaldson met him in 1864, and he traced the same flaws as the men who met him when he got off the train from Illinois:

> He was, apparently, the tallest man I ever saw, and so thin too and so ugly. He had a long black double breasted frock coat which hung like a wrapper on his lean frame, and it was positively the dirtiest coat I ever beheld for a man having any pretentions to gentility, much less the President of the United States of America. Before he came into the room I was rather impressed by the occasion and honor of meeting the President. But when this homely, dirty, shabby, lean, lanky man appeared I lost all sense of the dignity of the surroundings and found myself filled with amazement that this was indeed Abraham Lincoln, President of the United States. . . . How can foreign nations, or indeed our own people, have respect for institutions when such a slovenly careless man is the *first gentleman of the land* . . . I never for a moment conceived him to be the uncouth, the common man I found him to be when face to face with him. I was the worst disappointed man conceivable.

Nor did Lincoln's speech redeem his appearance. "His grammar is weak," noted George Templeton Strong. The Cincinnati *Enquirer* grumbled that Lincoln pronounced "words in a manner that puzzles the ear sometimes to determine whether he is speaking his own or a foreign tongue." Lincoln had never lost his Kentucky twang, and his hillbilly mispronunciations marked him as a rube to Easterners' ears, uneducated and provincial. He might say, for instance, that he didn't *keer fer sich idees* as the secessionists espoused. Or that the *unly way he would ra-ally yearn respect was when people heerd his inaugeral—then they'd git the ra-al pitcher.* After meeting with Lincoln, George Templeton Strong ran back to his diary and tried to reproduce a story Lincoln told, the way he'd heard it come out of Lincoln's mouth:

> Wa-al that reminds me of a party of Methodist parsons that was traveling in Illinois when I was a boy thar, and had a branch to cross that was pretty bad-ugly to cross, ye know, because the waters was up. And they got considerin' and discussin' how they should git across it, and they talked about it for two hours, and one on 'em thought they had ought to cross one way when they got there, and another another way, and they got quarrelin' about it, till at last an old brother put in, and he says, says he, "Brethren, this here talk ain't no use. I never cross a river until I come to it."

Even this, Strong admitted, was a weak approximation, and that he despaired of capturing the story's "intense provincialism and rusticity." Lincoln's accent forever cemented the poor opinion of people such as Horace Greeley, who said of the President, "Here was an heir of poverty and insignificance, obscure, untaught, buried throughout his childhood in the primitive forests, with no transcendent, dazzling abilities." His speech appalled the well-bred General George McClellan, who, after a White House soiree, wrote to his wife that the most striking moment of the evening was when "the Magician asked the Presdt for his handkerchief—upon which [Lincoln] replied promptly, 'You've got me now, I ain't got any'!!!!"

Lincoln's tenor voice, too, was "high pitched and rather strident," "shrill, piping, and unpleasant"—"far from musical." Newspaperman Villard thought "His voice was naturally good, but he frequently raised it to an unnatural pitch." To editor Horace White, Lincoln's voice was "a thin tenor, or rather falsetto voice, almost as high pitched as a boatswain's whistle." It reminded nobody of the magnificence of Webster.

Many were put off by his lack of social graces—he had "a homeliness of manner that was unique in itself," in the generous phrase of his friend Alexander McClure. Though Lincoln's good-humored affability delighted many of his visitors, it also offended many. The New York smart set saw Lincoln as an oafish social failure. Society reporter Arabella Smith of the New York *Commercial Advertiser* wired back her impression of the latest Republican gathering:

I don't believe first class people in Washington go to President Lincoln's levees. Why, I've seen more intelligence in a small drawing room in New York than I could see in the reception and ante-rooms together that evening at the White House. . . . Between ourselves, if he were my husband and President, too, I shouldn't like him to be so good-natured and free-and-easy in his manners. I should want him to look and act the Chief Magistrate a little more. . . .

I'll tell you what I think. The President is Abraham Lincoln, as honest and upright a man as the world ever saw. But Abraham Lincoln, in one respect, is not yet a President. His speech, his bearing, and the society he seems most at home with show him to be still Mr. Lincoln only. He has not yet appreciated, socially, the position he has been called to occupy.

Sometimes Lincoln made a clumsy attempt at familiarity, as when he called Greeley "Horace" at first sight. His habit of straightaway asking tall men to "put backs," that is, stand back-to-back with him to see who was taller—from the coal-heaver in Freedom, Pennsylvania, who was delighted; to the pompous, sober, fastidious Senator Charles Sumner of Massachusetts, who was horrified—revealed a limited social repertoire. "Neither was Lincoln a good listener," said William Herndon. "Putting it a little strongly, he was often not even polite. In a conversation, he was rather abrupt, and in his anxiety to say something apt or to illustrate the subject under discussion, would burst in with a story." Carl Schurz, for one, thought little of it. He saw Lincoln as a kind of Western "noble savage," explaining poetically, "He is an overgrown nature-child and does not understand artifices of speech and attitude." But other high-minded leaders, such as Massachusetts Governor Andrew, never got over the feeling that Lincoln was a rowdy. Even to George Templeton Strong, who liked him, he was "a barbarian, a Scythian, a yahoo, or gorilla, in respect of outside polish."

What were serious men to make of a man who rarely read, and when he did, read out loud, like a schoolboy? A man who put on his stovepipe hat "country-style"—gripping it from behind his head, by the rear brim? In a reception line, Lincoln was comic. When he shook hands, he surrounded his partner's hand and went at it with gusto, pump-handle style, up and down. A surprised New York *Times* reporter wrote that he had never seen anyone go through the ritual with the "*abandon* of President Lincoln. He goes it with both hands, and hand over hand, very much as a sailor would climb a rope." He was "like a man pumping for life on a sinking vessel," according to another. Lincoln was uncouth, not only in receiving guests but in meetings. He discussed weighty matters of state with a slippered foot flung up on one corner of his desk. His favorite posture, even when conferring with great leaders on the most vital concerns, was to sit and slide far down in his chair, sticking both slippers so high above his head that they could rest on his mantelpiece; his secretaries called it "sitting on his shoulders." His official manner in these early days was unpracticed. It was sketched by William Russell, who was present when Lincoln received a diplomat:

> As he advanced through the room, he evidently controlled a desire to shake hands all round with everybody, and smiled good-humouredly till he was suddenly brought up by the staid deportment of Mr. Seward, and by the profound diplomatic bows of the Chevalier Bertinatti. Then, indeed, he suddenly jerked himself back, and stood in front of the two ministers, with his body slightly drooped forward, and his hands behind his back, his knees touching, and his feet apart. Mr. Seward formally presented the minister, whereupon the President made a prodigiously violent demonstration of his body in a bow which had almost the effect of a smack in its rapidity and abruptness, and, recovering himself, proceeded to give his utmost attention, whilst the Chevalier, with another bow, read from a paper a long address.

The United States was an earnest nation, in an earnest era, at a time when men were most earnestly seeking a way out of a national catastrophe. The tenor of the times can be seen in its portraits, in an ocean of photographs of faces with straight mouths, with lips pressed tight, projecting solemnity, purpose, determination. In these grimmest of times, Lincoln's most unforgivable sin for many, especially in the East, was that he told jokes. The anonymous diarist who called himself "Public Man" recorded the bias of outgoing Attorney General Edwin Stanton after a conversation in the first week after Lincoln's arrival: "It is impossible to be more bitter and malignant than he is," he wrote of Stanton. "Every word was a suppressed and a very-ill suppressed sneer, and it cost me something to keep my temper in talking with him even for a few moments. When he found that I had only met Mr. Lincoln once, to my recollection, he launched out into a downright tirade about him, saying that he 'had met him at the bar, and found him a low, cunning clown.'" Lincoln similarly offended a diplomat from Holland, who complained, "His conversation consists of vulgar anecdotes at which he himself laughs uproariously." Strong added that "his laugh was the laugh of a yahoo." The painter Francis Carpenter called his laugh "the 'neigh' of a wild horse on his native prairie." Solemn congressman George Julian observed, "When he told a particularly good story, and the time came to laugh, he would sometimes throw his left foot across his right knee, and clenching his foot with both hands and bending forward, his whole frame seemed to be convulsed with the effort to give expression to his sensations." Henry Villard described Lincoln's storytelling manner and matter that struck so many as unpresidential:

> His body shook all over with gleeful emotion, and when he felt particularly good over his performance, he followed his habit of drawing up his knees, with his arms around them, up to his very face. I am sorry to state that he often allowed himself altogether too much license in the concoction of the stories. He seemed to be bent upon making his hit by fair means or foul.
>
> In other words, he never hesitated to tell a coarse or even outright nasty story, if it served his purpose. All his personal friends could bear testimony on this point. It was a notorious fact that this fondness for low talk clung to him even in the White House. More than once I heard him "with malice aforethought" get off purposely some repulsive fiction in order to rid himself of an uncomfortable caller. Again and again I felt disgust and humiliation that such a person should have been called upon to direct the destinies of a great nation in the direst period of its history. . . . At the time of which I speak, I could not have persuaded myself that the man might possibly possess true greatness of mind and nobility of heart.

Henry E. Dummer, a lawyer who spent time with the future President in Illinois, said that he was a man of "purity" but had an "insane love" for dirty stories. He remembered an occasion in 1859 when someone asked Lincoln why he did not assemble his stories into a book. Lincoln laughed, "Such a book would stink like a thousand privies." Lincoln's secretary, John Hay, played on words in calling him "the *riskiest* of story tellers." As late as 1864, George Templeton Strong protested, "I do wish Abraham would tell fewer dirty stories." Close friend Ward Lamon explained it this way:

> Although Mr. Lincoln's walk among men was remarkably pure, the same cannot be said of his conversation. He was endowed by nature with a keen sense of humor, and he found great delight in indulging it. But his

humor was not of a delicate quality; it was chiefly exercised in hearing and telling stories of the grosser sort. In this tendency he was restrained by no presence and no occasion. It was his opinion that the finest wit and humor, the best jokes and anecdotes, emanated from the lower orders of the country people. It was from this source that he had acquired his peculiar tastes and his store of materials.

An example of Lincoln's low-brow bent was the story his law partner, William Herndon, said he heard the future President tell "often and often." Herndon explained that Lincoln was a diffident man, rather shy in society, especially in a crowd of ladies and gentlemen at a party. For that reason, he admired audacious men, quick-witted, cheeky, and self-possessed. Lincoln loved to tell this story to illustrate the power of audacity:

Well, there was a party once, not far from here, which was composed of ladies and gentlemen. A fine table was set and the people were greatly enjoying themselves. Among the crowd was one of those men who had audacity—was quick-witted—cheeky and self possessed—never off his guard on any occasion. After the men & women had enjoyed themselves by dancing, promenading, flirting, and so on, they were told that the supper was set. The man of audacity—quick-witted—self-possessed and equal to all occasions—was put at the head of the table to carve the turkeys, chickens, and pigs. The men and women surrounded the table and the audacious man, being chosen carver, whetted his great carving knife with the steel and got down to business, and commenced carving the turkey, but he expended too much force and let a fart—a loud fart so that all the people heard it distinctly. Of course it shocked all terribly. A deep silence reigned. However, the audacious man was cool and entirely self-possessed; he was curiously and keenly watched by those who knew him well, they suspecting that he would recover in the end and acquit himself with glory. The man, with a kind of sublime audacity, pulled off his coat—rolled up his sleeves—put his coat deliberately on a chair—spat on his hands—took his position at the head of the table—picked up the carving knife and whetted it again, never cracking a smile nor moving a muscle of his face. It now became a wonder in the minds of all the men and women how the fellow was to get out of his dilemma. He squared himself and said loudly and distinctly—"Now, by God, I'll see if I can't cut up this turkey without farting."

Then, according to Herndon, Lincoln would add, "I worshipped the fellow."

Many of Lincoln's first Eastern auditors were left open-mouthed by such stories, lacking the insight of journalist Donn Piatt, who, perhaps because he was a Westerner, could see through to the purpose in their telling. He described after-dinner conversations back in Springfield:

> We had gatherings at which men only formed the company, and before those good honest citizens . . . Mr. Lincoln gave way to his natural bent for fun, and told very amusing stories, always in quaint illustration of the subject under discussion, no one of which will bear printing. They were coarse, and were saved from vulgarity only by being so strangely in point, and told not for the sake of the telling as if he enjoyed the stories themselves, but that they were, as I have said, so quaintly illustrative.

Carl Schurz was another one of the few who discerned the point of Lincoln's tales. "He interspersed our conversation with all sorts of quaint stories," he wrote, "each of which had a witty point applicable to the subject in hand, and not seldom concluding an argument in such a manner that nothing more was to be said." Throughout his presidency, Lincoln would call on this ability to apply a frontier story to clinch an argument. Countless opponents found themselves laughing, not only at a story but in wonder at the brand of genius that could effortlessly produce something so homely yet so *apropos*; whereupon Lincoln could gracefully turn away, leaving his adversary with the sudden realization that the last word had been said and the point won by the uneducated, disheveled man from the prairie.

Men with delicate aristocratic sensibilities, though, were horror-struck, such as the Georgia poet and musician Sidney Lanier, who, after meeting Lincoln in the days before the inauguration, wrote to his father, "What a *disgusting* Scene was the Lincoln *hand*-Shaking affair! I think the disgrace of the United States had its fit culmination therein: the scene ought to go into History under the title of 'The Great Apotheosis of the Great Hog.'" Lanier's view was jaundiced by his love for the South, but Missouri's Colonel Alexander Doniphan and West Virginia's Sherrard Clemens, both of whom met Lincoln in the days before the inauguration, were Unionists, and neither was as kind as Lanier. Doniphan wrote home that Lincoln was "a man of no intelligence, no enlargement of views, as ridiculously vain and fantastic as a country boy with his first red morocco hat." Clemens was even more disappointed, describing the Illinoisan as "a cross between a sandhill crane and an Andalusian jackass. He is,

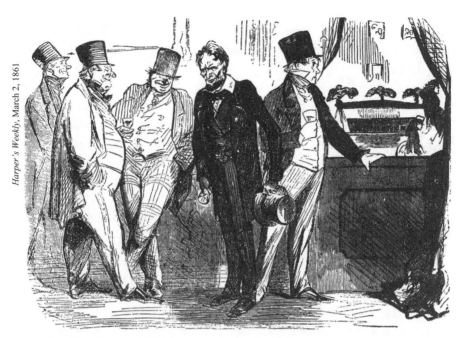

Harper's Weekly, March 2, 1861

"Our Presidential Merryman." Lincoln tells jokes while a hearse
bearing the Constitution passes outside.

by all odds, the weakest man who has ever been elected . . . vain, weak, puerile,
hypocritical, without manners, without social grace, and as he talks to you,
punches his fists under your ribs. He swears equal to Uncle Toby, and in every
particular, morally and mentally, I have lost all respect for him. He is
surrounded by a set of toad eaters and bottle holders."

There was another provocation to those proud men in the East for whom
Lincoln's greatest crime was his self-esteem. These men despised Lincoln for
being an uneducated Westerner with the presumption to dictate to his betters.
The high-bred George Templeton Strong called him "superficially vulgar and a
snob." Don Piatt noted that a "sense of superiority possessed President Lincoln
at all times." As his secretary John Hay observed, "Lincoln's intellectual
self-confidence was galling to vastly better educated men, learned men, like
Sumner and Chase. It would be absurd to call him a modest man. No great man
is ever modest. It was his intellectual arrogance and unconscious assumption of
superiority that men like Chase and Sumner could never forgive." An example
of the breathtaking way in which Lincoln was capable of dismissing the great
and powerful was provided when Lincoln had the only meeting he was ever
destined to have with Charles Francis Adams—American royalty, son and

grandson of Presidents, Boston Brahmin, status-conscious, cool and aloof. Lincoln had just appointed Adams ambassador to Great Britain. As Adams' son told the story:

> [Charles Francis Adams] had been summoned to Washington by the secretary of state [Seward] to receive his verbal instructions. The country was in the midst of the most dangerous crisis in its history; a crisis in which the action of foreign governments, especially of England, might well be decisive of results. The policy to be pursued was under consideration. It was a grave topic, worthy of thoughtful consideration. Deeply impressed with the responsibility devolved upon him Mr. Adams went with the new secretary to the State Department, whence, at the suggestion of the latter, they presently walked over to the White House, and were ushered into the room which more than thirty years before Mr. Adams associated most closely with his father [John Quincy Adams], and his father's trained bearing and methodical habits. Presently a door opened, and a tall, large-featured, shabbily dressed man, of uncouth appearance, slouched into the room. His much-kneed, ill-fitting trousers, coarse stockings, and worn slippers at once caught the eye. He seemed generally ill at ease,—in manner, constrained and shy. [Seward] introduced [Adams] to the President, and [Adams] proceeded to make the usual conventional remarks, expressive of obligation, and his hope that the confidence implied in the appointment he had received might not prove to have been misplaced. They had all by this time taken chairs; and the tall man listened in silent abstraction. When Mr. Adams had finished, — and he did not take long, — the tall man remarked in an indifferent careless way that the appointment in question had not been his, but was due to the secretary of state, and that it was to "Governor Seward" rather than to himself that Mr. Adams should express any sense of obligation he might feel; then, stretching out his legs before him he said, with an air of great relief as he swung his long arms to his head: — "Well, governor [Lincoln's way of addressing Seward], I've this morning decided that Chicago post-office appointment." Mr. Adams and the nation's foreign policy were dismissed together! Not another reference was made to them. Mr. Lincoln seemed to think that the occasion called for nothing further; as to Mr. Adams, it was a good while before he recovered from his dismay; — he never recovered from his astonishment, nor did the impression then made ever wholly fade from his mind.

Most prominent men thought Lincoln merely simple. After all, they only knew him by his campaign image as "The Railsplitter," the humble embodiment of rustic simplicity. Men thought him well-intentioned, honest, and entertaining—but, especially so soon after his sneaking entry into Washington, they could see no sign of power. Alexander McClure later wrote:

> Few, very few, of the Republican leaders of national fame had faith in Lincoln's ability for the trust assigned to him. I could name a dozen men, now idols of the nation, whose open distrust of Lincoln not only seriously embarrassed, but grievously pained and humiliated, him. They felt that the wrong man had been elected to the Presidency, and only their modesty prevented them, in each case, from naming the man who should have been chosen in his stead.

One without regard for the new President was British diplomat Lord Lyons, who, on the eve of the inaugural, said, "Mr. Lincoln has not hitherto given proof of his possessing any natural talents to compensate for his ignorance of everything but Illinois village politics. He seems to be well meaning and conscientious, . . . but not much more." Another was vice-president-elect Hannibal Hamlin, who visited Lincoln on his very first day in Washington and left filled with uneasiness about Lincoln's "honest simplicity and want of necessary knowledge of men." The Public Man wrote in his diary what many suspected: "He is not a great man, certainly, and, but for something almost woman-like in the look of his eyes, I should say the most ill-favored son of Adam that I ever saw. . . . Half an hour with Mr. Lincoln confirmed my worst fears." Henry Villard, after months of experience shadowing the President-elect, wrote, "I doubt Mr. Lincoln's capacity for the task of bringing light and peace out of the chaos that will surround him. A man of good heart and good intention, he is not firm. The times demand a Jackson."

The Public Man assumed what most intellectuals who met Lincoln assumed: that he could not direct his own administration, that he would delegate the task of directing the nation to other, abler hands. The Washington correspondent of the *New York Herald*, for instance, had written on Lincoln's approach, "He is unequal to the crisis, and will feel it so sensibly when he arrives here that it is inferred he will rush for safety into the arms of some man of strong will, who will keep his conscience and manage the government." Chicago *Tribune* editor C. H. Ray thought that getting Salmon Chase into the Cabinet was necessary, since that man's "great ability in affairs will give the force to Mr. Lincoln which nature has denied him." In the week before the inauguration, Horace Greeley confessed his worries: "Old Abe is honest as the sun, and means to be true and faithful; but he is in the web of very cunning spiders and cannot work out if he would." The *Louisville Daily Courier* put into print similar fears of many in the South who saw in Lincoln low ability, no education, and no experience—"simply, we believe, an honest man, he will be the tool of a fanaticism which he represents, and the instrument of the able, unscrupulous, and daring men whom he will call around him." Many among the elite in the North simply threw up their hands, such as Henry Adams, who wrote after seeing him at the Inaugural Ball that Lincoln looked as though "no man living needed so much education as the new President but all the education he could get would not be enough."

* * *

Lincoln would never completely shed this image—the uneducated, well-intentioned bumbler, the weak, pliable, vacillating tool of those around him—during his lifetime. It prejudiced those in the South, who were already tilted against him; it prejudiced people in the Border States, who were hanging in the balance in the crucial first days of his presidency; it prejudiced people in the Democratic Party in the North, who were already skeptical of his administration; and it prejudiced the men of every faction in his own party, who could never get over the conviction that Lincoln was being used by their enemies to thwart them. Because Lincoln was so easy to approach, yet so naturally reticent and so innately secretive, and because he always sought the ideas of others while delaying his own decisions until the last possible moment before they must be rendered, he seemed indecisive, and remained easy to underestimate during the course of the coming war and the presidential term that would end with his death. This gave him an advantage—he could remain opaque while those around him became transparent—but at a great cost: in the most divisive period in the nation's history, powerful men on all sides—the Cabinet, the generals, the opinion-makers, the Congress, the editors—would discount his sagacity, even when he was most wise; they would sneer at his weakness, even when he was most resilient. The image of the homely ditherer, at the mercy of events, would persist until his assassination forced a mournful reappraisal four years later.

Chapter 14

The First Inaugural

"It is the knell and requiem of the Union, and the death of hope."

F our years earlier, President Buchanan in his inaugural had paraded gaily between two elaborate floats, the Goddess of Liberty on her pedestal and a full-rigged ship, manned by smiling and waving sailors from the Navy Yard. On March 4, 1861, Abraham Lincoln took office at the center of a tense military maneuver. For weeks, General in Chief Winfield Scott had been building a small army in Washington—653 professional soldiers, along with 925 nervous, unready District of Columbia militiamen—for the test of Inauguration Day. He had been meeting daily with his officers, planning and drafting orders for a ceremony many secessionists were oath-bound to prevent. Dozens of threats lent urgency to his arrangements, including this, sent to Lincoln:

> Dear Sir,
>
> Caesar had his Brutus, Charles the First his Cromwell. And the President may profit by their example. From one of a sworn band of 10, who have resolved to shoot you in the inaugural procession on the 4th of March, 1861.
>
> Vindex

The state of uncertainty in the days approaching the ceremony was underlined on its eve, when Scott's own secretary, after he wrote out the general's instructions for the troops, resigned his commission and crossed the Potomac to join the Confederate army.

Crowds assembling along Pennsylvania Avenue on the raw, wind-whipped morning of Inauguration Monday looked up and down a broad street adorned with few decorations. Many of the residents of the houses along the parade route had shuttered their windows in scorn for the proceedings. On commanding housetops, spectators were elbowed aside by squads of riflemen who dipped their barrels over the roof edges and kept eagle eyes on the windows opposite. At street level, platoons of soldiers were stationed every hundred yards. Secret police mingled with the crowds.

About noon, as the wind blew the clouds away and a bright sun dried the muddy streets, President Buchanan arrived in his barouche at Willard's Hotel to call upon the President-elect. A few minutes later a band struck up "Hail to the Chief" as the pair emerged, and the loaded coach started toward the Capitol building between double files of District of Columbia cavalry. Their colonel, Charles Stone, rode alongside the carriage, occasionally digging his horse with his spurs to keep the cavalry horses uneasy, making it harder for anyone to get a good shot at Lincoln between the prancing, skittish mounts. In front of Lincoln's carriage marched the elite Sappers and Miners company, brought in for the occasion from West Point. Stone's newly organized militia infantry, marching behind, completed the armed phalanx around the carriage. On the side streets rode flanking squadrons of regular cavalry, synchronizing their progress with the presidential party to intercept any assassins who might hurtle down the intersecting streets toward the President-elect.

The carriage approached the Capitol from the west, and Buchanan and Lincoln entered its north door through a protective 50-foot-long passageway enclosed by a high, boarded fence guarded by Marines. A reporter who saw Lincoln as he entered the building noted that he looked pale, fatigued, and anxious. A few minutes later the official party emerged from the east side of the Capitol onto the inaugural platform, and came under the gaze of dozens more of Stone's riflemen, scanning the crowd in pairs from every window on that side of the building. Stone had received a warning the night before that there would be an attempt to blow up the platform, so directly beneath the boards under Lincoln's feet were militiamen who had been there all night guarding the structure. They had been joined at daybreak by another battalion of Stone's District volunteers, who formed a solid semicircular wall in front of the President between the platform and the gathering spectators. Finally, as Lincoln stepped forward to address the crowd and the nation, he could look to his left and see two batteries of artillery, ready and manned, their bronze muzzles lowered on the multitude from the brow of Capitol Hill, with the figure of Winfield Scott, in full plumed regalia, drooping in his buggy alongside.

Thus, with the glints from hundreds of gun barrels playing over the somber crowd, Abraham Lincoln delivered his half-hour address, then took the oath of office from Chief Justice Taney. The passing of power was saluted by the booming of General Scott's guns. That evening, a company of Virginia horsemen that, it was rumored, would dash across the Long Bridge and take Lincoln captive at the Inaugural Ball, failed to materialize. Clara Barton was able to write in her diary that night, "The 4th of March has come and gone, and we have a *live*, *Republican* President, and, what is perhaps singular, during the whole day we saw no one who appeared to manifest the least dislike to his living."

That much, at least, was true. But Southerners heaped contempt on a ceremony that saw, "for the first time in the history of this Country, the Chief Magistrate, in abject terror of his life, inaugurated into his high office under the countenance and protection of shining bayonets, gleaming swords and loaded cannon." President Lincoln himself must have come away from the day's ceremonies deeply disturbed by the sight of the grim army that had been assembled for a bodyguard—proof, visible at every hand, that his was an administration conceived in a crucible and installed under siege.

* * *

Lincoln's First Inaugural Address was the most anxiously awaited official pronouncement in the history of the United States. Citizens North and South were eager to know what the incoming President would do to save the nation, and their eagerness was multiplied by the suspense of the year-long silence—it would be his first public utterance since his Cooper Union speech in February of 1860. The new president, painfully aware of the nation's feverish expectations, had crafted the address for weeks to show jut-jawed firmness to mirror the mood in the North, precisely balanced by dulcet words of forbearance to pacify the South. He fully expected his remarks to act like a soothing oil poured over the troubled waters of the nation. Horace Greeley, who sat behind him on the inaugural platform, testified that Lincoln expected the speech to "dissolve the Confederacy as frost is dissipated by the vernal sun."

Lincoln fully expected the Union to be saved, and peace preserved, by holding the iron rod in one hand and extending the olive branch with the other. To satisfy the North and encourage Unionists everywhere, he affirmed at length that the Union was permanent and indissoluble: "I . . . consider that . . . the Union is unbroken; and to the extent of my ability I shall take care . . . that the laws of the Union be faithfully executed in all the States. . . . The power confided in me will be used to hold, occupy, and possess the property and places belonging to the government, and to collect the duties and imposts." Having demonstrated his resolve, however, he immediately waived all Federal jurisdiction in the South: "But beyond what may be necessary for these objects,

Harper's Weekly, March 2, 1861

"A President-elect's Uncomfortable Seat." Old Abe: "Oh, it's all well
enough to say, that I must support the dignity of my high office
by Force, but it's darned uncomfortable, I can tell you."

there will be no invasion, no using of force against or among the people
anywhere. . . . While the strict legal right may exist in the government to enforce
the exercise of [Federal] offices, the attempt to do so would be so irritating . . .

that I deem it better to forego for the time the uses of such offices." His policy, thus stated, faced both ways. He would perform his Constitutional duty of seeing that the laws be observed, but only "so far as practicable," and "unless my rightful masters, the American people, shall withhold the . . . means, or . . . direct the contrary." He would vigorously assert the Federal authority, but he would not exercise it.

It soon became evident, to Lincoln's dismay, that his Inaugural Address had changed nothing and moved no one. Attempting to be all things to all people, it met the same fate as other attempts at conciliation during the previous months. Perhaps secessionist fire-eater T. R. R. Cobb in Montgomery, Alabama, got closest to the truth when he wrote: "We are receiving Lincoln's inaugural by telegraph, it will not affect one man here, it matters not what it contains." At the moment Lincoln was sworn into office, there were determined men in both North and South whose passions were already at such a fanatical pitch that the ghost of George Washington himself descending to the platform could not have made them put away the knives they had for each other.

Even among those on hand to hear Lincoln's address, those who were predisposed to like it liked it; those who weren't didn't. Senator Wigfall of Texas lounged in a Capitol doorway and pantomimed his contempt for Lincoln's words in full view of the crowd. Charles Francis Adams, Jr., dismissed the affair as "A tall, ungainly man addressing a motley gathering . . . with a voice elevated to its highest pitch. . . . a somewhat noticeable absence of pomp, state, ceremony." The Public Man commented:

> Mr. Lincoln was pale and very nervous, and did not read his address very well. His spectacles troubled him, his position was crowded and uncomfortable, and, in short, nothing had been done to render the performance of this great duty either dignified in effect or, physically speaking, easy for the President. The great crowd in the grounds behaved very well, but manifested little or no enthusiasm, and at one point in the speech Mr. Lincoln was thrown completely off his balance for a moment by a crash not far in front of him, followed by something which for an instant looked like a struggle . . . a spectator falling out of a tree.

Henry Adams concluded, "The address has disappointed every one, I think." The next day, Wall Street rendered its verdict: stock prices fell.

Response from afar was strictly along party lines. The Republican papers—the Chicago *Tribune*, the St. Louis *Democrat*, the New York *Evening Post* and *Tribune*, the *Springfield* (Mass.) *Republican*—all applauded politely, but Henry Villard noticed that the inaugural message "was received with nothing like enthusiasm even by the Republicans." Their opposites, the papers from the already-seceded states, all denounced Lincoln's address as "just what was expected from him, stupid, ambiguous, vulgar and insolent, and is everywhere considered as a virtual declaration of war." The voice of the Charleston *Mercury* was the shrillest of this choir, hearing in the address the "tocsin of battle" from "King LINCOLN—Rail Splitter ABRAHAM—Imperator!" the "Ourang-Outang at the White House," who "staggers to and fro like a drunken man under the intoxication of his new position."

Democrats in the North also hissed the inaugural: "It would have been almost as instructive if President Lincoln had contented himself with telling his audience yesterday a funny story and letting them go," shrugged the *New York Herald*. Under the headline "The Country No Wiser than it was Before," it called the speech "weak, vacillating, unsatisfactory and contradictory." The Philadelphia *Morning Pennsylvanian* called it a spectacle "to terrify the heart of every patriot," with the President "surrounded and guarded not by the honest hearts of a happy people, but safely esconced [sic] out of the people's reach, within a military cordon bristling with bayonets." It was "a sad disappointment to the country," according to one Pittsburgh journal. "A wretchedly botched and unstatesmanlike paper," agreed the *Hartford Times*. The Chicago *Times* concluded that the Union was now "lost beyond hope." New York City's Democratic mayor Fernando Wood signaled his reaction by refusing to fly the national flag over City Hall.

Much depended on how the speech was received in the eight key Border States, the slave states whose loyalties were still hanging in the balance between their departed sister states to the south and the loyal Union members to the north. Privately, there was new confidence. Virginia Governor John Letcher thought Lincoln's address strengthened the resolve of conservatives to remain calm. Jubal Early of Virginia and John A. Gilmer of North Carolina were similarly encouraged by its assurances.

Their optimism, however, was expressed privately in letters to friends. More widely heard were the fiery blasts of the Border State editors. The Baltimore *Exchange* discerned in Lincoln's message a promise of bloodshed: "If it means what it says, it is the knell and requiem of the Union, and the death of hope." The *Arkansas True Democrat* announced, "If declaring the Union perpetual means coercion, then LINCOLN'S INAUGURAL MEANS WAR!" A North Carolina editor damned it as "deceptive. It coats with the semblance of peace and friendship what smells of gore and hate." The Richmond *Enquirer* heard in it "the cool, unimpassioned, deliberate language of the fanatic. . . . Sectional war awaits only the signal gun. . . . The question, 'Where shall Virginia go?' is answered by Mr. Lincoln. She must go *to war*."

Since every reader was by now familiar with Lincoln's lack of formal education, it was smart and fashionable to deride Lincoln's perceived lack of literary style. The Jersey City *American Standard* found the address "involved, coarse, colloquial, devoid of ease and grace, and bristling with obscurities and outrages against the simplest rules of syntax." The Davenport *Democrat* also graded it down: "a wishy-washy, unscholarly affair—unworthy of an undergraduate, to say nothing of a statesman." The *Philadelphia Evening Journal* called it "one of the most awkwardly constructed official documents we have ever inspected. It abounds in platitudes, incoherencies, solecisms, illogical deductions, and is pitiably apologetical for the uprising of the Republican party." Another Philadelphia paper presumed to rank it historically: "A lame, unsatisfactory and discreditable production inferior in every respect to anything that has ever emanated from any former President." A New Orleans editor sneered at it as "mean, involved and inconclusive, evidently such as only persons of very imperfect education would employ." "A loose, disjointed, rambling affair," pronounced the Chicago *Times*. The Toronto *Leader* heard a "tawdry and corrupt schoolboy style." Even ex-President John Tyler criticized Lincoln's grammar in a letter to a friend.

*   *   *

Among those who did not criticize the language of the First Inaugural, most concluded that it must be the work of someone else. William Russell of the London *Times* told his readers that the President's message "is generally attributed to Mr. Seward." In fact, most informed onlookers, North and South, thought Abraham Lincoln was not the man in charge. They assumed the raw, inexperienced new Chief Executive was in the pocket of his smarter, abler Secretary of State-designate, New York Senator William Seward. They expected what savvy *Springfield Republican* editor Samuel Bowles expected: government by "the New Yorker with his Illinois attachment."

Chapter 15

The Struggle with Seward, Then Sumter

"A blindness and stolidity without a parallel in the
history of intelligent statesmanship."

I n December, William H. Seward had been uncharacteristically subdued.
His lack of vigor was due mostly to his lingering disappointment at having
been refused his party's nomination and replaced by an unknown. Wallowing in
self-pity, on November 18 he had moped, "I am without schemes or plans,
hopes, desires, or fears for the future that need trouble anybody, as far as I am
concerned." But Seward was also restrained by caution. As disconsolate as he
was, he still had an eye to the future, and so was reluctant to take any step that
might jeopardize a high post in the coming administration.

The President-elect, for his part, had always considered Seward the obvious
choice for first place in his Cabinet by virtue of his long history of leadership
and ability. On December 8, 1860, Lincoln mailed his offer of the State
Department to Seward, writing warmly, "It has been my purpose, from the day
of the nomination . . . to assign you, by your leave, this place in the
administration." In so doing, Lincoln's aim was to deputize Seward—"Mr.
Republican"—to keep party ranks straight and facing front on the political
battlefields of Washington. Seward would carry the fight against compromise
into the Senate chamber and House floor, into smoky hotel lobbies, parlors,
and dining rooms, even the Buchanan White House, until Lincoln himself
arrived for the swearing-in. What Lincoln could not know was how faithfully
Seward would follow orders.

*   *   *

For, in the weeks following Lincoln's election, as South Carolina hurtled
toward secession and bitterness over slavery threatened to tear the nation in
two, Seward saw political opportunity in a new national majority that was
alarmed by the extremists on both sides and eager for compromise. This new
majority needed a statesman to lead them and give them a voice. William

Seward was the nation's most intelligent, most seasoned, and most talented statesman-at-large. Nor were his talents bridled by any reluctance to switch his position when it was to his advantage. He was the canniest of politicians, always alert to the main chance, and he was especially alert now, so soon after seeing his presidential hopes smashed on the third ballot of the Republican convention.

Seward did not say yes to Lincoln's offer of the State Department immediately. Before he responded, he sped to Albany to huddle with his partner Thurlow Weed, just before Weed entrained to meet Lincoln for a consultation in Springfield. Looking for a way to gauge Lincoln's susceptibility to a moderating influence, Seward and Weed collaborated over the weekend of December 15 and 16 on an editorial that appeared in the December 17 issue of Weed's Albany *Evening Journal,* one that favored compromise with the South. They knew a copy of the article would reach Lincoln by the time he met with Weed three days later.

When he read the editorial on December 20, an irritated Lincoln expressed his disapproval to Weed face to face. Lincoln didn't see the need for compromise. Even on that historic day—the very day that South Carolina announced it had seceded from the Union, with its national Palmetto Flag raised and all of Charleston surging, drunken with delight, into the streets— Lincoln dismissed the secession movement, telling Weed it was just "some loud threats and much muttering." The President-elect quickly changed the subject, sounded out Weed on Cabinet appointments, and apparently put the ugly business in the South out of his mind.

But, if he had thought longer on the timing and the temper of the *Evening Journal* editorial, Lincoln would have realized that here was a window to the soul of William Seward. Seward's appraisal of the situation differed from Lincoln's. Seward was a man whose temperament fitted him for the give-and-take of the Senate. He was a student of the possible, distrustful of extremists, always willing to modify his position if it was necessary to buy action. Seward embraced only causes he thought could win. His unwillingness to tilt at windmills, his absence of idealism, and his lack of self-righteousness allowed him to have friends on both sides of the slavery issue, among abolitionists as well as slave-holders. Now, his keen vision—unclouded by strong feeling, in contrast to Lincoln's— and his place at the center of the Washington scene allowed him to realize, before Lincoln did, that the fundamental problem that faced the government was no longer slavery, it was secession. As Northerners slowly became aware of the gravity of the threat to the nation, they would have time to wonder at the

Vanity Fair, March 2, 1861

"The Inside Track." Thurlow Weed to President Elect—"Trust to my friend Seward—trust to us. We'll compromise this little difficulty for you. But trust to us. Gentlemen from the country are often egregiously swindled by unprincipled sharpers. (Impressively) *Trust to us*."

irony of the Republicans' choice of a nominee. They had rejected, for his extremism, Seward, the man who now embraced compromise; and chosen instead, for his moderation, Lincoln, the man who would never yield an inch.

Many, perhaps most, Republicans at this time expected Seward to assume his rightful ascendancy over Lincoln in the new government. The lives of the two men, on a balance, weighed heavily in favor of Seward. He was eight years older than Lincoln. When Lincoln was still a boy attending irregular "blab schools" in log cabins, Seward was studying at stately Union College in Schenectady. When young Lincoln was wrestling, telling yarns and keeping store in New Salem, Seward was leader of the New York Senate. When Lincoln was a self-taught lawyer starting his Springfield practice, Seward was the thirty-three-year-old governor of New York. When Lincoln was quitting Washington after one term in the House, Seward was the New York senator guiding the hand of President Zachary Taylor. Since then, for the last dozen years, Seward had been senator from the most populous state in the Union, the man synonymous with the Free Soil movement and the Republican Party, while Lincoln plied his law practice in obscurity on the Illinois Eighth Circuit. It is no wonder that many Americans believed the fate of the nation rested, not with Abraham Lincoln, but with William Seward. And it is no wonder that Seward himself heartily agreed with them.

After being passed over for the nomination, Seward had campaigned in the summer and fall as the Oracle of the party, but remained condescending toward Lincoln, hardly ever mentioning the candidate in his speeches. Many agreed with the *New York Herald* that Lincoln, in his unfitness, would require someone to run the government for him. Seward certainly thought so. He clung to a notion, as he confided to a German diplomat, "that there was no great difference between an elected president of the United States and an hereditary monarch"—that is, neither was really in charge. "The actual direction of public affairs belongs to the leader of the ruling party," he insisted. Seward gave his support for the ticket, but only with a view to keeping a place open for himself as the "Premier," the President in fact if not in name, the man who would hover behind Lincoln and dominate the inferior man's mind.

By mid-December the waiting was over. Lincoln had promised him the State Department, and Seward, rejuvenated, threw off his malaise. The dignity and status of the new office revived him. That Lincoln was a man so unqualified for the coming task, his ability so doubtful, inspired Seward still more. Lincoln's absence from Washington until just before his inaugural gave Seward the opportunity to take up the reins in the meantime, and he felt the intoxication of new power.

The stiffening influence of Lincoln's "chain of steel" instructions to Republicans in December had doomed compromise over the extension of slavery, but with that, Lincoln's influence ended until his inauguration. He had achieved the negative goal of defeating the Crittenden amendments in

Congress, but he had shown no positive star to steer by. With the question of slavery extension answered with a firm "No," the issue was secession, and on this question Lincoln remained mute. This was the moment Seward stepped forward and took up the Republican standard. Seward now saw himself as the indispensable man in the hour of crisis. He welcomed the role of savior of the democracy, even while he affected a duty-bound weariness under the yoke of responsibility. "I will try to save freedom and my country," he wrote to his wife. "I have assumed a sort of dictatorship for the defense, and am laboring night and day with the cities and States."

Seward's firm belief that the country's future depended on the maturing of his own plans was sure to force a collision with Lincoln after the inauguration. It is important, then, to trace the comet-streak of Seward's career during January and February of 1861 in order to appreciate the titanic struggle that the little-regarded Lincoln faced in March and April for the soul of his own party and the control of his own administration. More, the dissonance between Lincoln's program and Seward's in those critical months would result in an explosion of hostility toward Lincoln by four previously loyal slave states— Virginia, North Carolina, Tennessee, and Arkansas—and convert their three million citizens into enemies at the start of the Civil War in April.

With Lincoln's offer of State in his pocket, Seward felt at liberty to make his views known. On his return trip to Washington after his mid-month conference with Weed in Albany, he gave an off-the-cuff after-dinner talk to the New England Society at the Astor House in New York City on December 22. The wealthy diners were panicked by the news, received the day before, that South Carolina had gone out of the Union. He told them, "If you will only give it time, sixty days' more suns will give you a much brighter and more cheerful atmosphere." Give *him* time, he meant. All winter, those who talked to Seward heard him repeat the same cheery refrain: *Sixty days, and everything will come right.*

Schooled by a dozen years' worth of jousts with Southern leaders on the floor of the Senate, Seward parted ways early on with Republicans who thought the Southern fire-eaters were bluffing; he took seriously the prospect of the secession of the Cotton States in the near future. In fact, he regarded the loss of those states as a *fait accompli*. They were in thrall to the fire-eaters, and would be impossible to conciliate no matter what was pledged or promised, he knew. Seward refused to be preoccupied with them. Instead he concentrated on the decision of the Border States whether to join their departing sisters. He would bend his efforts—by conciliation, forbearance, and patience—to win the trust of the still-loyal multitudes of these northernmost slave states still undecided.

For it was Seward's view that any confederacy confined only to the seven Cotton States, though it stretched from the islands of South Carolina to the Rio Grande, would be a failure. It could never be more than an obscure republic, he reckoned, lacking factories and straining under twin burdens: keeping two and a half million slaves under guard by a roughly equal number of whites, and sealing its several thousand miles of border against the flight of slaves to territory from which they could never be reclaimed. The cherished Slave Power dream of a Caribbean empire—the "Golden Circle"—would, Seward thought, be crushed under the weight of the massive debt piled up trying to raise an army and build a navy strong enough to wrest the lands to the south from the mighty European powers. Confined within its narrow space, a pariah in the world community, the very slaves that made it rich would make it poor.

The impossibility of a Cotton State empire was the first principle of the strategy that would animate Seward's efforts from the beginning of January until the fall of Sumter in mid-April. To cement the failure of secession, Seward was convinced, it was only necessary to prevent the remaining eight slave states from being drawn into the confederacy with them. The key was to keep the loyalty not only of the upper tier of Border States—Missouri, Kentucky, Maryland, and Delaware—but also the lower tier—Arkansas, Tennessee, North Carolina, and, most important of all, Virginia. To keep these, Seward's strategy would be to be the lamb and not the lion, to appease, to conciliate, to stall for time. When the Cotton States realized their sisters could not be tempted away from the Union, they would return.

Seward watched with special interest the rise of a new Union Party in the Border States, made up of Unionists of all political stripes. "All *old* party platforms are now either breaking down or being swallowed up in the universal desire of the people to save the republic from dissolution," one admirer wrote to Seward, "and a new one, constructed upon Union principles per se will inevitably spring up after the 4th of next March. *It is for you take the lead or not in the movement.*" Seward met secretly with Union Party leaders who seduced him with promises, such as James Barbour of Virginia, who said, "Come forward promptly with liberal concessions. . . . You may lose a portion of your own party North. But you place yourself and the new administration at the head of a national conservative party which will domineer over all other party organizations North and South for many years to come. You above all men have it in your power to bring the really conservative elements North and South into an organization the most useful and the most powerful yet seen in this country." This emerging opportunity—to lead a new Union Party that would sweep everything before it—was heady wine to the man whose hopes of being the national standard bearer had so recently been laid to rest.

According to the young Henry Adams, Seward looked ahead to the Virginia Congressional elections in May as the decisive point where, if only a collision could be avoided until then, Union-loving Virginians would throw out the fire-eaters at the polls, elect Union Party leaders, and thus sound the death knell of the secession movement there, after which the Cotton States would come back like so many prodigal sons. But the fullness of Seward's design was even more splendiferous than that—it included his ascension to power. According to his friend, the English diplomat Lord Lyons:

> Mr. Seward's real view of the state of the country appears to be that if bloodshed can be avoided until the new government is installed, the seceding States will in no long time return to the [Union]. He seems to think that in a few months the evils and hardships produced by secession will become intolerably grievous to the Southern States, that they will be completely reassured as the intentions of the Administration [which Seward would presumably direct], and that the Conservative element which is now kept under the surface by violent pressure of the Secessionists will emerge with irresistible force. From all these causes he confidently expects that when elections are held in the Southern States in November next, the Union party will have a clear majority and will bring the seceding States back into the [Union]. He then hopes to place himself at the head of a strong Union party, having extensive ramifications both in the North and in the South, and to make "Union" or "Disunion" not "Freedom" or "Slavery" the watchword of political parties.

Seward was not alone in his expectations that the new Union Party—binding Northern Democrats and conservative Republicans with the Unionists of the Border States—would overwhelm and supersede the extreme Republicans. The *New York Herald* predicted that "the two or three hundred thousand voices in the North, in favor of coercion and involving the nation in the horrors of civil war"—that is, Lincoln's constituency—"shall henceforth be disregarded," and "over a million Union loving citizens in the States of Virginia, Kentucky, Tennessee, Missouri, Maryland, and Delaware, will rally in their places, to the support of the government." The statesman who would anchor this "great Union party," according to the *Herald*, was none other than the incoming Secretary of State, William Henry Seward. Seward thus envisioned himself lifted up on the shoulders of a nascent Union movement, acclaimed as the architect of a powerful new Union Party, under whose banner patriotic multitudes North and South would rejoice— minus the discredited extremists, the enemies of compromise on both sides, including Lincoln. As the hero of a grateful republic, would not he, Seward, ascend, as the nation-saver, to a place alongside George Washington, the nation-builder?

*   *   *

For Seward's grand plan to bear fruit, he needed to ensure that the government was transmitted safely to Lincoln on March 4. And in early January, there was widespread alarm that the government would not survive until then. President Buchanan was heard to say in despair that he would be the last President of the United States. There was talk that treason was alive in the highest echelons of the Buchanan government, that the traitors would hand over Southern forts and arsenals—perhaps even Washington itself—to the secessionists before Lincoln arrived. There were rumors that armies of Southern riders would soon descend on Washington, seize it with the help of thousands of sympathetic Washingtonians, and make it the capital of the new slave nation. Seward had also to guard well against what Lincoln feared most: that secessionists would prevent his legal election to the presidency by obstructing the counting of the electoral vote in February.

Seward acted against these dangers with promptness and efficiency, by a thousand schemes, plied with unstinting energy. He took steps to keep informed of any sinister goings-on in the Buchanan government by cultivating a clandestine relationship with Buchanan's new Attorney General, Edwin Stanton, maintained in theatrical style by secret messages. Rumors that Washington would be captured by an army of thousands of Southern horsemen evaporated by mid-January, but Seward helped form a House committee to seek out any future disloyal plots.

February 13, 1861, the day for the counting of the electoral vote in Congress, approached on the crest of a new swell of rumors of a powerful conspiracy to seize the government buildings to prevent Lincoln's formal election. Seward responded by renewing a decades-old intimacy with General-in-Chief Winfield Scott and enlisting him to insure against an obstruction of the vote. When crowds began moving toward the Capitol that morning they found armed guards at every entrance—no one could go in except senators, representatives, and people with written tickets of admission signed by the

Speaker of the House or the Vice President. Sprinkled through the multitude were loyal colonels of militia in civilian clothes. They were joined by a hundred plainclothes policemen from Philadelphia and New York, ready with revolvers and clubs hidden beneath their coats. Horses attended nearby cannon loaded with canister—cans of musket balls that made a shotgun of each piece— enough to make a red mist of any mob foolish enough to attack. Scott had accumulated Regular soldiers from all over the East, and before the sun rose he had positioned them, with more cannon, in front of the White House, Treasury, General Post Office, Patent Office, and all the bridges on the Potomac. Even the Congressmen were overawed by all the military hardware. "The quietest joint Assembly of the two houses that I have ever known," was how Senator Ben Wade described it. The electoral vote went ahead without incident.

*   *   *

Even harder than maintaining the national authority and insuring the orderly transfer of power to Lincoln, however, and a thousand times more baffling and labyrinthine in its execution, was the responsibility of steering the nation on the cautious course that would seduce the Border States away from the departing Cotton States, insure the election of Union Party men, and achieve the ruin of secession. Here again, while Lincoln paced and pondered in the solitude of his statehouse room in Springfield, Seward was the main actor on the national scene. He immediately mounted the rostrum to broadcast his vision.

William Seward understood the dramatic power of making only rare addresses in the Senate. He had held the nation spellbound in February 1860 after his return from Europe, when he addressed the Upper House as the presumptive Republican candidate. On January 12, 1861, he achieved a similar sensation with his first speech since the election. The situation was grave. Mississippi, Florida, and Alabama had all seceded from the Union in the previous week. Federal forts, arsenals, and navy yards were being seized all over the South. Speaking as the future Secretary of State, with Lincoln still mum, he was the man everyone expected to enunciate the Republican solution to the national crisis. Crowds gathered more than two hours before Seward took the floor, and when the Senate galleries filled, listeners overflowed into the halls, the cloakrooms, even into the galleries in the House.

Seward began on a statesmanlike note by declaring that cutting geographical and historical ties was a practical impossibility. He followed by recommending a list of concessions. By the time Seward ended his two-hour oration, with a pledge to "meet prejudice with conciliation, exaction with concession . . . and violence with the right hand of peace," listeners were in tears. The tone had been heartfelt, patriotic, soothing. As policy, however, it was incomprehensible. The most common reaction to his address was bafflement—crusty old Thaddeus Stevens of Pennsylvania muttered to a friend, "I listened to every word and by the living God I have heard nothing." Seward, however, had reestablished his preeminence. By mid-January it was apparent to all that he was the Republican man of the hour. Henry Adams wrote to his brother on January 17 that Seward "is now . . . virtual ruler of this country."

Seward certainly thought so. He was convinced that he was the Pole Star around which all revolved. "Mad men North and mad men South are working to produce a dissolution of the Union by civil war," he wrote to his wife around this time. "The present administration [Buchanan's] and the incoming [Lincoln's] are united in devolving on me the responsibility of diverting these disasters." He could not come home now, he told her. "It seems to me that if I am absent only three days, this Administration, the Congress and the District would fall into consternation and despair. I am the only hopeful, calm, conciliatory person here."

The New Yorker drew into his orbit powerful allies. One was Charles Francis Adams with his presidential pedigree, a prominent Representative from Massachusetts. Adams had been a zealous anti-slavery man, but throughout the winter Seward made himself at home in the Adams household, and under Seward's influence Adams bent publicly toward compromise.

Seward also drew close arch-Democrat Stephen Douglas. Douglas gave a ceremonial dinner on January 24, where Seward cast off his Republicanism like a dirty shirt when he rose to give the toast, "Away with all parties, all platforms of previous committals, and whatever else will stand in the way of the restoration of the American Union." In the same compromising spirit, he told anyone who would listen what he told the Russian Minister to Washington: that Lincoln should cut loose from the Republican radicals and save the country by appealing to conservatives of all parties.

Seward also took pains to maintain his correspondence with Union Party leaders in the crucial state of Virginia, to whom he twice confided that he favored the substance of the Crittenden Compromise, recently defeated. When on January 19 the Virginia legislators called for a Peace Conference to meet in Washington in "an earnest effort to adjust the present unhappy controversies,"

Seward was exultant. While the Peace Conference was in session, whatever fate befell conciliation in Congress, Seward could point to the Conference, insist that attempts at compromise were not exhausted, and thus continue to stall for time with the South.

By the time Lincoln left Springfield for his approach to Washington, Seward had pulled so hard on the Republican tiller to steer it by the star of conciliation that the party's course had been skewed entirely from the basic antislavery principle it had fought for in the election. His new policy of appeasement received its culminating expression a few days before Lincoln's inauguration when, in organizing the new territories of Colorado, Nevada, and Dakota, the Republican majorities in both houses of Congress declined to demand that slavery be excluded there. That at this critical hour they had renounced their bedrock principle—exclusion of slavery from the territories— was not lost on Douglas. He rose in the Senate to crow, "They have abandoned the doctrine of the President elect. . . . Not one of his followers this year voted [to exclude slavery in the territories] once. The Senator from New York, the embodiment of the party, . . . did not propose it. . . . Practically, . . . the whole doctrine for which the Republican party contended as to the territories is abandoned, surrendered, given up; non-interference is substituted in its place." A disgusted Republican stalwart admitted: "Mr. Seward waived the anti-slavery guaranty on behalf of the Republicans."

Events, however, seemed to confirm the wisdom of Seward's patient policy. On February 4, Seward was rewarded with his first victory in the biggest prize of all—Virginia. Voters there showed their attachment to the Union by overwhelmingly electing Unionist delegates to their secession convention. A friend exulted to Seward, "The Gulf Confederacy can count Virginia out of their little family arrangement." Henry Adams wrote hosannas to Seward in a letter to the Boston *Advertiser*, saying, "For more than two months the Seward republicans have been watching, hoping, praying for the signs of a break in the storm. Governor Seward's reputation as a political prophet, his influence as a statesman . . . depended and was pledged on this result. He has gone on the principle that this was only a temporary fever, and now it has reached the climax and favorably passed it." The tide, it seemed, had turned. For the next month, right up to the time of Lincoln's inauguration, victories for Unionism in the Border States were as consistent as defeats had been in the Cotton States the two previous months. With Lincoln about to take office, seven slave states had left the Union, but the northernmost eight were still safely in.

The young Adams sketched Seward in the glow of these triumphs: "The ancient Seward is in high spirits and chuckles himself hoarse with his stories. He says it's all right. We shall keep the border states, and in three months or thereabouts, if we hold off, the Unionists and Disunionists will have their hands on each other's throats in the cotton states." The man who regarded himself as the guiding light of the coming administration had reason to boast. He had shepherded the national authority safely through dangerous days into the hands of the President-elect, and at the same time had not only avoided any aggression or hostility which would have wrecked his program of returning the Cotton States, but had held the majority of the slave states in the Union, and kept alive the hope that they would lure the departed states back into the Union. "Those who saw and followed Mr. Seward during all the anxieties and cares of this long struggle," wrote Adams, would not forget his example. "Cheerful where everyone else was in despair; cool and steady where everyone else was panic-struck; clear-sighted where other men were blind; grand in resource where every resource seemed exhausted; guiding by quiet and unseen influences those who seemed to act independently on their own ground." With this "armory of weapons, [Seward] fought, during these three months of chaos, a fight which might go down in history as one of the wonders of statesmanship."

The nation's political chiefs would now weigh Seward's triumph of statecraft against the tentative, halting steps of the anonymous President-elect, who "crept into Washington," "cowardly and disgraceful."

*   *   *

Seward made sure he was the first man to greet Lincoln when the buggy from the train station deposited the President-elect at the side door of Willard's Hotel on the morning of February 23. From the hour of Lincoln's arrival in Washington, Seward took pains to be seen always at his side. On that first morning, Seward took breakfast with Lincoln, then squired him around the places of government. The first evening, Lincoln ate dinner at Seward's house. The next morning Lincoln appeared on Seward's arm again, for services at St. John's Church. In the week before the inauguration, wherever Lincoln went— to meet with President Buchanan and his Cabinet, to meet with Congress, to meet with the Supreme Court—Seward was always there to introduce him, leaving the general impression that he controlled Lincoln's schedule. "Seward has had Old Abe under his thumb every moment since his arrival," grumbled one observer. Vice President-elect Hamlin, alarmed, asked Lincoln frankly what many were asking: *was his administration to be a Seward Administration or a Lincoln Administration?* Lincoln assured him he would be his own man, but Hamlin went away unconvinced.

The first important test of wills between Lincoln and Seward was fought that week behind closed doors at Suite No. 6 at Willard's over the makeup of the Cabinet. Seward insisted, as the "Premier," on being consulted in the choice of members. He invoked Andrew Jackson, who had always maintained that the Cabinet should be a unit, and pointed to the fact that all recent Cabinets had been collections of like minds. Seward—an ex-Whig, a moderate, favoring compromise—wanted the Cabinet made in his image: men like Charles Francis Adams of New England, Simon Cameron of Pennsylvania, Henry Winter Davis of Maryland, plus any of a number of Border State Unionists. Lincoln, however, wanted to cast the net wider, to have a "ministry of all the talents." He wanted to include Salmon Chase of Ohio, Gideon Welles of New England, and Montgomery Blair of Maryland—all ex-Democrats, all "iron-backed," uncompromising Republicans. The stakes of the Cabinet battle were enormous, and the campaign for the Cabinet's soul was appropriately ferocious. For the next several days, for hours on end, dozens of business and political leaders from every faction came to Suite No. 6 pleading, wheedling, storming, and demanding. When, by March 2, two days before the inauguration, no dent had been made in Lincoln's resolve to stand by his own choices, Seward took pen in hand and wrote out his resignation.

The morning of Inauguration Day, before the parade to the Capitol for the swearing-in, Lincoln wrote his reply to Seward, the man who considered himself the leader of the Republican Party, the man without whom neither the party nor the nation could be saved. Lincoln's was a blunt request that Seward take back his resignation—by nine o'clock the following morning. He handed it to his secretary to be copied, with the comment, "I can't afford to let Seward take the first trick."

Lincoln had called Seward's bluff, and the New Yorker yielded. His plan, he knew, could not be worked—he could not heal the nation—if he were cast into the outer darkness. In a letter to his wife, Seward wrapped himself in the flag. "A distracted country appeared before me," he explained. "I did not dare to go home, or to England, and leave the country to chance." The letter revealed a man who still regarded himself as the savior of the republic, and still was dismissive of Lincoln.

For even at the moment of his capitulation on the Cabinet, Seward had more reason than ever to believe that he molded national policy. Seward had just heard Lincoln deliver an Inaugural Address that his own hand had guided. The Lincoln of the First Inaugural was much more conciliatory than the Lincoln of Springfield, and this had been due largely to changes written into the speech by Seward. After church at St. John's on the day after his arrival, Lincoln had handed him a draft of the speech, and Seward had remained in his library for the better part of the day, going over the document word by word. He made scores of small changes, removing any hint of threat, rounding off any hard edges that would ruin his own program of appeasement of the Border States. Seward insisted on a softer stance, schooling Lincoln with the claim, "Only the soothing words which I have spoken have saved us and carried us along thus far. Every loyal man and indeed, every disloyal man in the South, will tell you this."

Besides crowding each page with softening phrases, Seward made a major change in Lincoln's inaugural: he deleted the President's promise to abide by the Republican antislavery platform. If Lincoln ignored his advice, Seward warned, the speech would "give such advantage to the Disunionists that Virginia and Maryland will secede, and we shall within ninety, perhaps within sixty days, be obliged to fight the South for this capital, with a divided North for our reliance." Lincoln conceded. He removed any mention of the Republican platform.

And Seward re-wrote Lincoln's ending. The inaugural, which had until now been a well-reasoned, logical, lawyerly dissertation like all Lincoln's earlier speeches, was transformed by Seward's addition of a noble and poetic finish. Lincoln reworked it into the powerful conclusion:

> I am loath to close. We are not enemies, but friends. We must not be enemies. Though passion may have strained, it must not break our bonds of affection. The mystic chords of memory, stretching from every battle-field, and patriot grave, to every living heart and hearthstone, all over this broad land, will yet swell the chorus of the Union, when again touched, as surely they will be, by the better angels of our nature.

Personally, too, the New Yorker had found a place in Lincoln's heart. For in Seward Lincoln had met his "man of audacity": quick-witted—cheeky and self possessed—never off his guard on any occasion. Seward was a man who had the nerve to lecture Edwin Booth on how to improve his acting, the temerity to hold forth on the art of dress to the meticulous Adamses. Lincoln was drawn to this man who shared his own lack of malice and added to it a boldness, a fearlessness, an ability to laugh while others' teeth chattered. But, as Gideon Welles later wrote regretfully, "It was this almost implicit trust in Mr. Seward at the commencement which for a time caused serious embarrassment, and almost forfeited the confidence of the country in the ability and integrity of the President to administer the government."

*   *   *

Lincoln's "hands-off" inaugural policy was only possible in the era of weak government. It was the very feebleness of Federal power that allowed Lincoln to think that he could avoid a clash with the South. Here again, it is important to realize the immense difference between the bulk of the Federal government today—which, if withdrawn, would completely collapse any state, both socially and economically—and the tiny government Lincoln headed. At the time, Federal presence in the South was felt in only four ways: U.S. marshals and judges administered the few Federal laws; postmen delivered the mail; customs officers collected duties in Southern ports; and a handful of soldiers maintained forts and arsenals. If these meager agents suspended their activities, Federal authority would become an abstraction. Lincoln thought he could continue this limbo government indefinitely in the seceded states without sparking a conflict.

In order to give the impression of authority but avoid a clash, he only needed to "hold, occupy, and possess" the four Southern forts that were still in Federal hands. They were Forts Jefferson and Taylor, two insignificant and isolated forts in the Florida Keys; Fort Pickens in Pensacola Bay, out of range of rebel shore guns and not in danger; and Fort Sumter, nestled in Charleston Harbor, within easy cannon range and holding enormous emotional significance. It was Sumter to which all eyes were turned. As a loyal Union bastion nestled in the "Cradle of the Rebellion," it was certain to become a symbol, a naked test of wills, a lightning rod that could spark revolt into war. Even so, Lincoln reckoned that Sumter and the others could be quietly held, as promised, with the *status quo* undisturbed.

But in his first morning as president, Lincoln learned that his reckoning had been based on a false premise. For when he arrived at his office on March 5, he found on his desk an urgent message from Major Anderson, the commander at Fort Sumter. It told him that the fort, unless it was resupplied, must be surrendered by mid-April; there was only bread enough for twenty-eight more days, salt pork for slightly longer. The news meant that, on the first morning of its existence, the most eagerly awaited policy in the nation's history—Lincoln's exhaustively considered rule of action, shaped in his mind through four months of agonized thought and consultation and proclaimed in his Inaugural Address—had to be abandoned. Now, he must do one of two things: surrender the fort, the symbol of national authority, or supply the fort by force, breaking his vow of passivity and knocking the chip off South Carolina's shoulder. This dilemma, trying to steer between the Scylla of national disgrace and the Charybdis of civil war, would consume him in the coming weeks.

Vanity Fair, March 23, 1861

"Prof. Lincoln in His Great Feat of Balancing."

This knottiest of problems, however, came at a time when Lincoln was besieged at all hours by the inevitable horde of spoils-seekers. He was charged with the most sweeping removal of federal officials in the nation's history—a complete turnover of appointees, from clerks' assistants to foreign diplomats. He told Villard, "It was bad enough in Springfield, but it was child's play compared with this tussle here. I hardly have a chance to eat or sleep. I am fair game for everybody of that hungry lot." He had to reward the men who had "made" him, and still take care to distribute spoils to every side. He had to satisfy each geographical area and all men of eminence, while balancing the hazards of offending any of the squabbling factions in the Republican ranks. He had to consult with the Cabinet officers, bargain with the Congressional delegations, haggle with the editors. With all the rivalries, intrigues, and perplexities in the young party, pressure came from every direction, and everyone spoke in imperatives and pressed their favorites.

Like a plague of locusts they came, forty thousand eager hopefuls, crowding into Washington from all over the North. Every man who had tacked up a banner at a rally or hired a hall for a meeting was convinced he had elected the President, and he came to claim his just reward—as a diplomat, a paymaster, a port collector, a marshal, a superintendent, a postmaster, an agent, a deputy, an assistant, a clerk. At Willard's, two blocks from the Executive Mansion, one correspondent saw the hotel bulging with "more scheming, plotting heads, more aching and joyful hearts, than any building of the same size ever held in the world." Office-seekers crowded the main corridors and overflowed the staircases and landings into the halls, reading-room, and barbershop, the writing-room, onto the porch and down the steps. A hotel clerk told the reporter that "two thousand and five hundred patriots" had recently dined in the main dining room. "Everybody wants a place and it must be found, or he'll know the reason he's not in Abraham's bosom," he quipped. Seward wrote to his wife, "Solicitants for offices besiege the President . . . . The grounds, halls, stairways, closets, are filled with applicants." The crush was so bad, he told her, that it was difficult to get in and out of Lincoln's office. Senator Fessenden of Maine wrote home, "I have been to see him two or three times, but stayed but a few moments each time, as I was pained and disgusted with the ill-bred, ravenous crowd that was around him." In early April, Edwin Stanton wrote to James Buchanan, "Mr. Lincoln I have not seen. He is said to be very much broken down with the pressure that is upon him in respect to appointments."

The exhausted President was making things worse for himself by his own clumsiness at administration. He was a stranger to routine, an enemy of rules.

He adopted no hours for business, but opened his doors to this solid press of bodies from nine in the morning until dark. Lincoln himself later admitted to a friend that when he entered office, "he was entirely ignorant not only of the duties, but of the manner of doing the business." According to close friend Henry Whitney, "Mr. Lincoln had no method, system or order in his exterior affairs; he had no library, no clerk, no stenographer; he had no commonplace book, no index *rerum*, no diary. Even when he was President and wanted to preserve a memorandum of anything he noted it down on a card and stuck it in a drawer or in his vest pocket." Those around him noticed his lack of system, and they shook their heads and complained to friends. Seward confided to Charles Francis Adams that Lincoln had "much absorption in the details of office dispensation, but little application to great ideas." Senator Charles Sumner told Adams, "The difficulty with Mr Lincoln is that he has no conception of his situation. And having no system in his composition he has undertaken to manage the whole thing as if he knew all about it." Agreed Adams, "He is ignorant, and must have help." So too thought Senator Fessenden: "Our poor President is having a hard time of it. He came here tall, strong and vigorous, but has worked himself almost to death. The good fellow thinks it is his duty to see to everything, and to do everything himself, and consequently does many things foolishly."

The press, witnessing the spectacle of a historic stampede of pigs to the national trough, grew caustic at the alarming incongruity of a President preoccupied with presiding over this unseemly shoving match while showing no sign of a policy toward the growing national emergency in Charleston Harbor. In the *New York Herald*, Lincoln appeared as a Nero, fiddling while the nation tottered toward catastrophe. By mid-March, the *Herald* was publishing fresh insults in every edition, calling Lincoln "unconciliatory," "ignorant," "vicious," "fanatical," "mean," "cowardly," "fatal," and "imbecile" (a favorite epithet of the time, used in its former meaning of "weak," or "impotent"). Even the usually supportive *New York Times* rebuked Lincoln, declaring that he "owes a higher duty to the country . . . than to fritter away the priceless opportunities of the Presidency in listening to the appeals of competing office-hunters." Lincoln confessed to *Times* editor Henry J. Raymond, "I am like a man so busy in letting rooms in one end of his house, that he can't stop to put out the fire that is burning in the other."

* * *

And he did not see how high the flames were rising. The new seven-state republic in the South pulsed with drumbeats and the rhythmic tread of thousands of recruits drilling. On March 6, two days after Lincoln took office, the Confederate Congress authorized President Davis to accept 100,000 soldiers. Southern state governors raised regiments and hurried them off to join the new army, aided by a ready militia that had been drilling intently for eighteen months, ever since the John Brown raid had raised the boogeyman of armed slave revolt. Galvanized by a combination of revolutionary zeal and the instinct to protect their homes, Southern men rushed into national service. By the beginning of April, the Confederate army was 45,000 strong, already three times the size of the United States army, which was spread out in tiny outposts watching Indians in the West. Five thousand Confederate troops poured into Charleston alone, which bristled each day with new artillery emplacements sighting their guns on Sumter.

Lincoln's almost mystical belief in the Union would be a powerful blessing to the nation in the coming war, but in March of 1861, his delusion that most Southerners shared his belief endangered the republic. While he waited in vain for loyal Southerners to rise, Confederate armies prepared for battle. It was a military advantage that would last deep into the second year of the coming war. Lincoln's mistake was clearest to those who had been in the South, who had witnessed first-hand the unanimity and military excitement there, and then, coming north, found confusion and complacency. When they went to warn him, Lincoln had a too-easy way of talking about the national predicament, particularly a maddening habit of giving the glib reply, "I guess we'll keep house." Soon-to-be-General William Sherman was introduced to him during this time, and remembered later:

> I must have reached Washington about the 10th of March. I found my brother there, just appointed Senator, in place of Mr. Chase. My feelings, wrought up by the events in Louisiana, seemed to him gloomy and extravagant. About Washington I saw but few signs of preparation, though the Southern Senators and Representatives were daily sounding their threats on the floors of Congress, and were publicly withdrawing to join the Confederate Congress at Montgomery.
>
> One day, [my brother] John Sherman took me with him to see Mr. Lincoln. . . . John said, "Mr. President, this is my brother, Colonel Sherman, who is just up from Louisiana, he may give you some information you want."

"Ah!" said Mr. Lincoln, "how are they getting along down there?"

I said, "They think they are getting along swimmingly—they are preparing for war."

"Oh well!" said he. "I guess we'll manage to keep house."

I was silent, said no more to him, and we soon left. I was sadly disappointed, and remember that I broke out on John, damning the politicians generally, saying, "You have got things in a hell of a fix, and you may get them out as you best can."

Lincoln was whistling past the graveyard, and William Sherman and other clear-eyed observers knew it. One was a fifty-five-year-old Polish émigré now living in Washington, Count Adam Gurowski, who summed up the alarm of many when he wrote a March 1861 entry in his diary:

Through patronage and offices everybody is to serve his friends and his party, and to secure his political position. Some of the party leaders seem to me similar to children enjoying a long-expected and ardently wished-for toy. . . . They, the leaders, look to create engines for their own political security, but no one seems to look over Mason and Dixon's line to the terrible and with lightning-like velocity spreading fire of hellish treason. . . .

I am told that the President is wholly absorbed in adjusting, harmonizing the amount of various salaries bestowed on various States through its office-holders and office-seekers.

It were better if the President would devote his time to calculate the forces and resources needed to quench the fire. Over in Montgomery the slave-drivers proceed with the terrible, unrelenting, fearless earnestness of the most unflinching criminals. . . .

Nothing about reorganizing the army, the navy, refitting the arsenals. No foresight, no foresight! either statesmanlike or administrative. Curious to see these men at work. The whole efforts visible to me and to others, and the only signs given by the administration in concert, are the paltry preparations to send provisions to Fort Sumpter [sic]. What is the matter? What are they about?

Seward's aura of authority now glowed even brighter in contrast with Lincoln, who appeared distracted and uncertain. As men in Charleston aimed their cannon at Sumter, as United States army and navy officers deserted daily and migrated south, as Southern leaders bade farewell to friends in Congress, as clerks in Washington offices boldly pinned on their lapels the blue cockades that were badges of secession, Lincoln appeared to be dithering, spending his daylight hours tending to the self-serving mob of wire-pullers lined up outside his office.

*   *   *

But in fact, although his tussle with the tar-baby of practical politics tarnished the image of "Honest Abe," his weeks of attention to patronage were vital, not only to make a government, but to make a party to support it. His infant Republican Party was patched together from miscellaneous elements which had until now been held together only by their opposition to the Democrats. Most Republicans were ex-Whigs, whose party had disappeared in the mid-1850s. But the party also included their adversaries, the ex-Democrats, stout anti-slavery men whose consciences had compelled them to risk their careers by deserting the party in power, and who regarded the ex-Whigs as mere opportunists. There were ex-Know Nothings, and also their foreign-born enemies. There were abolitionists, and men who hated abolitionists. There were those for saving the Union, and those for dividing it. There were conservatives and radicals, ideologues and money men, reformers and spoilsmen. Every Republican who had held office in the last decade was the enemy of some Republican faction, every man offensive to some other man. Until now, the Republicans could submerge all their internal rivalries in a common hostility to the Democratic administration. Now that the party had assumed responsibility for government, all the conflicting interests and objectives, all the dissensions between the different types of men, came to the surface.

These differences were distilled in Lincoln's Cabinet. For his closest advisors, Lincoln had selected men representing as many different Republican factions as he could. The high council included his three rivals for the nomination—Seward, Edward Bates, and Salmon Chase; two more to redeem promises his managers made at the convention to buy their states' delegates— Caleb Smith of Indiana and Simon Cameron of Pennsylvania; and two regional choices—Gideon Welles from New England and Montgomery Blair from the Border State of Maryland. This official family roiled with loathing. Among its members was not one personal or political friend of the new President. The lack of harmony was no secret. Democrat Edwin Stanton, writing from Washington, gloated in a letter to Buchanan, "Every day affords proof of the absence of any settled policy, or harmonious . . . action, in the administration. Seward, Bates, and Cameron, form one wing, Chase, Welles, and Blair the opposite wing. Smith is on both sides, and Lincoln sometimes on one, sometimes on the other. There has been agreement on nothing."

The Cabinet's only common coin was distrust, and in this it mirrored the party that Lincoln sought to bind together. Its deep divisions foreshadowed the hostility he would face for the next four years whenever he proposed any broad national policy. From this seven-man Cabinet, no less than four Judases would rise in the months ahead to betray their chief. But the lines along which party opinion had fractured in the past, and would fracture in the future, had in March of 1861 suddenly disappeared. In Lincoln's first month in office, the crucible of events unfolding in Charleston Harbor had boiled all differences down to one: whether to abandon Fort Sumter or resupply it.

With the sides on this vital question so sharply drawn, Lincoln's allergy to routine had results in the Cabinet far more dangerous than the unseemly pushing and shoving in the swarming halls of the White House. His easy-going approach to leadership was an invitation for Seward, with his fully developed agenda, to step up and seize the scepter. While he treated the President, as Welles observed, "with a familiarity that sometimes borders on disrespect," Seward took it upon himself to direct the heads of the other departments as if they were his clerks. Seward declared an end to regular twice-a-week "Cabinet days," an institution observed since Washington's time. He decided instead that the Cabinet would convene only by his invitation. When Seward did summon the Secretaries, Lincoln, having no idea how to conduct a Cabinet meeting, presided over formless sessions without dignity and without content. No seats were assigned, with one exception: Seward always sat at the President's immediate right. Welles' diary provides a view inside:

> There was very little concerted action. At the earlier meetings there was little or no formality; the cabinet meetings were a sort of privy council or gathering of equals, much like a senatorial caucus, where there was no recognized leader and the Secretary of State put himself in advance of the President. The Secretary of State . . . from his former position as the chief executive of the largest state in the Union, as well as from his recent place as a senator, and from his admitted experience and familiarity with affairs, assumed, and was allowed, as was proper, to take the lead in consultations and also to give tone and direction to the manner and mode of proceedings. The President, if he did not actually wish, readily acquiesced in this.

Instead of convening Cabinet meetings he considered irrelevant, however, Seward preferred to spend his days alone at the President's side. He moved into a house across Lafayette Park from the Executive Mansion, where he and Lincoln spent long hours chatting and trading stories in his private office. In public their heads were seen bent together in conversation, walking, driving, and taking meals. Seward made it his business to know every detail of the workings of the other Departments, while always keeping State Department business behind a veil. This overbearing behavior aroused the deep resentment of the other Secretaries, but it also had the effect intended by Seward—it reinforced his popular image as the government's master spirit.

That Seward had a definite program conferred an advantage over Lincoln, who during March was still searching for a policy. It allowed Seward to march straight to his goal, which in the urgent circumstances of March 1861 was to surrender Fort Sumter as soon as possible. The Secretary of State had been straining for months, through back channels and personal appeals, to accomplish the surrender of the fort, which was crucial to his program of avoiding a shooting war long enough to allow his Union Party constituents in Virginia to win their state elections in May.

Here again Seward enlisted the help of his doddering old ally Winfield Scott. On the day before Lincoln's inauguration, Scott had delivered written views on the new government's options, not to Lincoln, but to his old crony William Seward, as if to indicate that he expected the Secretary of State to decide policy. Scott was notorious for being weak with a pen and for having his most important papers written for him by others. In this case, his choice of words and phrasing were remarkably like those of William Seward himself. Certainly Scott's views coincided exactly with Seward's, strongly opposed to the horror of a civil war and preferring a "hands-off" policy, even to the point of saying, "Erring Sisters, depart in Peace." Seward made the most of the document, waving the paper all over Washington in the next few days to show his influence over General Scott and reinforce his claim as the new government's prime mover.

On March 5, Lincoln's first morning in office, Major Anderson's revelation of the exhausted supplies at Sumter was followed by an endorsement by General Scott exactly in step with Seward's design: "I now see no alternative but a surrender." On March 9, Lincoln asked Scott for a more thoughtful reexamination of the military situation, and Scott replied two days later in the same pessimistic vein, insisting that evacuation was "almost inevitable," and that holding it would take "a fleet of war vessels & transports, 5,000 additional regular troops & 20,000 volunteers"—a call for volunteers that would exceed the size of the entire U.S. army, require new acts of Congress to recruit, and take from six to eight months to train. As he read the note, Lincoln, perplexed, did not yet realize that he was reading the mind of William Seward in the hand of Winfield Scott.

On March 14 an anxious Cabinet held two three-hour meetings to discuss General Scott's written opinion that evacuation of Fort Sumter was a "military necessity." Each member was asked to answer the question: *Was it wise to try to provision the fort?* Seward's reply was, of course, an emphatic "no." Four more Secretaries—Caleb Smith, Gideon Welles, Simon Cameron, Edward Bates—fell into line behind Seward. Chase equivocated. Postmaster General Montgomery Blair stood alone against surrender. He insisted that giving up the fort would demoralize the North, and that firm action would do more than appeasement to end the rebellion and avoid bloodshed. But the sheer bulk of opinion against holding Sumter, from the highest military officers to a heavy majority of his experienced advisors, swayed the new President. It appeared in mid-March that Lincoln was willing to evacuate the fort. On March 18, he prepared a summary of his advisors' opinions, writing that the weight was heavily "in favor of withdrawing the Troops from Fort Sumpter [sic]."

Once again, it seemed, William Seward had triumphed. Following on his victories through the Secession Winter and his recent success as ghostwriter of the Inaugural Address, his sweeping victory in the Cabinet vote on Sumter cemented his belief that he was directing affairs, especially in view of the public criticism of Lincoln's balky start. Seward's mail was crowded with letters from Unionists telling him as much. One from North Carolina reported that everyone there considered him "the Hector or Atlas of not only his Cabinet, but the giant intellect of the whole north," while they dismissed Lincoln as "a 3rd rate man." Prominent Washingtonian Benjamin Ogle Taylor told him, "Unionists look to yourself, and only to you Sir, as a member of the Cabinet—*to save the country.*"

Seward took this sense of himself as the Premier—the power, the man without limits—into the arena of negotiation, with tragic results. As Lincoln was being sworn in, a trio of commissioners from the new Confederate States of America had arrived in Washington. Martin J. Crawford, A. B. Roman, and John Forsyth had been sent from Montgomery as "ambassadors," to bring about "the speedy adjustment of all the questions growing out of separation . . . of two nations," starting, of course, with the transfer of Fort Sumter. They regarded Seward as the only leader with enough sway to manage a surrender.

After all, Seward had told them so. Crawford and Forsyth reported that "a talk with Seward convinced them that he was to rule the new administration."

The arrival of the commissioners, however, complicated Seward's attempts to give up the fort. They warned him at the outset that if he failed to treat with them, Fort Sumter would be attacked and war would commence. If that happened, Seward's grand design would be shattered. On the other hand, any official meeting with the ministers would imply recognition of the Confederacy as a sovereign nation. This would also be disaster, since recognition by the European powers could be expected to follow, and the permanent separation of the Cotton States would be more certain than ever.

Here Lincoln's lax administrative style had its most damaging effect. His *laissez-faire* manner resulted in an official free-for-all where policy and rumor were indistinguishable, an imbroglio where Seward could make commitments without Lincoln's knowledge. For the next few weeks, Seward, a man supremely at home in this murky world of backstairs negotiation, played a high-stakes diplomatic game with the rebel envoys through a coterie of go-betweens. For almost two weeks after his arrival in office, Seward dodged the attempts of the commissioners to parley, while at the same time confiding through third parties that, with the influence of himself and General Scott, Fort Sumter would be evacuated.

Simultaneously, Seward carried his whispering campaign to the Washington newspapers. On March 11, the *National Intelligencer*, a Seward mouthpiece, carried a passionate editorial pleading for withdrawal from Sumter. Even more startling was the announcement by the *National Republican*, another journal with close ties to Seward, that the Cabinet had decided to evacuate not only Sumter, but Pickens. The news rang like gospel to all corners of the continent. On March 12, two Charleston newspapers, the *Courier* and the *Mercury*, gleefully announced that Sumter would soon be turned over without a shot being fired. On March 13, the *New York Herald's* Washington correspondent declared in its pages that "I am able to state positively that the abandonment of Fort Sumter has been determined upon by the President and his Cabinet."

As Seward signaled evacuation, scores of prominent men across the North joined him, Scott, the Cabinet majority, and the millions who advocated a withdrawal. Democratic leader Stephen Douglas rose in the Senate to declare that Fort Sumter belonged to South Carolina and that "Anderson and his gallant band should be instantly withdrawn." Neal Dow of Maine wrote that a Sumter evacuation would be "approved by the entire body of Republicans in this state" because it was "undoubtedly a Military *necessity*." The national mood seemed changed. Even the New York *Times* reported "growing sentiment throughout the North *in favor of letting the Gulf States go*." On March 19 the Associated Press reported that Sumter would be surrendered the following day. Seward sent secret runners to the Union Party in Virginia with the news that the evacuation of Sumter was imminent. George Summers, a leading Virginia Unionist, wrote to Seward that the news "acted like a charm" to Unionists there, and "gave us great strength. . . . A reaction is now going on in the State. . . . We are masters of our position here, and can maintain it if left alone."

*   *   *

While the South cheered the news of Sumter's imminent surrender, iron-backs in the North damned Lincoln. *Even the pathetic Buchanan had not dared to surrender the Gibraltar of Charleston Harbor! It was nothing less than a folding of the tent, an admission that the Union was dissolved!* The Columbus *Daily Capital City Fact* aired "a burning sentiment of contempt. . . . Shame upon the subterfuge, that would clothe cowardice in the unfitting garments of 'military necessity'!" The Cincinnati *Daily Times* charged Lincoln with "stepping directly into the footsteps of his predecessor," with "the same supineness, cowardice, imbecility, or whatever else it may be termed, which marked and damned the Administration of Buchanan. . . . Why, every honest Republican blushed at the infamous hypocricy [*sic*]."

Privately, too, there was bitter resentment at the humiliation. Henry Villard wrote that "Washington was full of indignant Northern men, in and out of Congress, giving vent to their wrath at the supposed blindness, incompetency, or cowardice . . . of Lincoln and his Cabinet." A Springfield friend wondered, "Is it possible that Mr. Lincoln is getting scared?" Charles Francis Adams despaired of Lincoln: "The President is drifting the country into war, by [his] want of decision. Everywhere at this place is discouragement. . . . I see nothing but incompetency . . . the man is not equal to the hour." The nib of George Templeton Strong's pen bit the page of his diary where he wrote, "The bird of our country is a debilitated chicken, disguised in eagle feathers. We have never been a nation; we are only an aggregate of communities, ready to fall apart at the first serious shock and without a centre of vigorous national life to keep us together." Republican hardliners wrote to their man in the Cabinet, Salmon Chase, that Lincoln's plan to evacuate was "submission to a band of traitors"; Lincoln's would be "a blacker and more infamous name" than Buchanan's; "the new administration is done forever"; "The South will proclaim [Lincoln] a Damned fool, and the North a damned Rascal." Lincoln himself received letters like this blistering curse from New York:

> Dear Sir I voted for you thinking that *in* you the country would find a defender of its rights & honor. I am totally disappointed. You are as destitute of policy, as weak, and vassalating as was your predecessor . . . . Do you imagine your course is meeting the favor of republicans—even in New York? No Sir! Democrats rejoice over it, knowing that it will demoralize & overthrow the party, Give up Sumpter, Sir, & you are as dead politically as John Brown is physically. . . . You have got to do this thing Sir, else the country will do it without you. . . . As a republican I am sorry to have to *say* these things. But *facts vindicate* this statement, Either *act, immediately* & *decisively* or resign & go home.

. . . and this plea from Cincinnati:

> Thirty days more of *"Peace Policy"* at Washington—and not only the Republican party, but the Government itself will be gone to destruction or placed beyond remedy! We have been beaten in our City election—the same in St. Louis—Cleveland—Rhode Island—Brooklyn—and lost two Members of Congress in Connecticut—all from the demoralization and discouraging effect produced by the apparent *inaction* and *temporizing* policy of the new Administration, and the impression that *Fort Pickens* was going to be given up also to the rebels!
>
> . . . The most fatal infatuation that ever did or can possess a statesman is the idea of a *Peace Policy* in the present emergency! It only encourages and strengthens the enemy, while it disheartens the friends of the Union in the seceded States, as well as the *real* friends of the Union every where!
>
> . . . *Give not an inch*—and *dont* be afraid of *war*! Do *what you will*—*War*, (to some extent) *is inevitable*!

In the Senate, an enraged Lyman Trumbull turned up the heat on Lincoln, introducing a resolution that "the true way to preserve the Union is to enforce the laws of the Union," and "it is the duty of the President to use all the means in his power to hold and protect the public property of the United States"—a hint at impeachment. The influential New York merchants, until now strong proponents of Seward's "hands-off" line, finally saw the Confederate threat to

New York trade and reversed themselves, printing a belligerent call for Lincoln to "shut up every Southern port, destroy its commerce, and bring utter ruin on the Confederate states." Indeed, the worst thing for business, they agreed, was this damned uncertainty, and the *Times* reflected their mood, declaring, "A state of war would almost be preferable."

In the torture created by the drift of the administration, the exasperated New York papers indeed reached a rare note of unison. "Come to the Point!" demanded the *Tribune*—"If we are to fight, so be it; if we are to have peace, so much the better. . . . At all events, let this intolerable suspense and uncertainty cease!" Lincoln's vacillation was no better than "the disgraceful policy of his predecessor," howled the New York *Evening Post*. "Wanted—A Policy" shouted the *Times*, and devoted two columns to a broadside: "It is idle to conceal the fact that the Administration thus far has not met public expectations," it scolded. "The Union is weaker now than it was a month ago. Its foes have gained courage, and its friends have lost heart." Lincoln's administration had exhibited "a blindness and stolidity without a parallel in the history of intelligent statesmanship." Lincoln himself had "spent time and strength in feeding rapacious and selfish partisans, which should have been bestowed upon saving the Union," and "we tell him . . . that he must go up to a higher level than he has yet reached." Lincoln's influential German friend, Carl Schurz, sent a warning from the Northwest:

> There is a general discontent pervading all classes of society. Everybody asks: what is the policy of the Administration? And everybody replies: Any distinct line of policy, be it war or a recognition of the Southern Confederacy, would be better than this uncertain state of things. Our defeat at the recent elections has taught us a lesson which can hardly be misunderstood. The Republicans are disheartened, groping in the dark, not knowing whether to support or oppose the Administration.

* * *

Seward, of course, had leaked his own Sumter policy to the press in the hope of bullying Lincoln's into line. But while Seward waited for his will to be done—for the troublesome garrison at Sumter to file solemnly out and sail home—he still had the problem of what to do with the Confederate commissioners. By mid-March, he could stall a meeting with the rebel trio no longer. He knew he must reject their request for a meeting and that soon they must withdraw, that the signal would be given for the lanyards to be yanked on the Charleston guns, the shells would fly, the masonry of Sumter would be blasted into powder, the war cry would go up from a million throats, and his policy would end in failure. So, with a new recklessness born of desperation, Seward improvised yet again.

On March 15, during a conversation with Alabamian Supreme Court Justice John A. Campbell, Seward let fall that the reason he couldn't meet with the commissioners was "because the evacuation of Sumter was as much as the administration could bear at one time." Startled by this statement and realizing its implications, Campbell probed further. He was going to write a letter to Jefferson Davis, he said. "What shall I say on the subject of Fort Sumter?"

Seward replied, "You may say to him that before that letter reaches him . . . how far is it to Montgomery?"

"Three days," answered Campbell.

"You may say to him," continued Seward—the man of audacity—quick-witted—self-possessed and equal to all occasions—"that before that letter reaches him, the telegraph will have informed him that Sumter will have been evacuated."

Campbell immediately rushed to see the commissioners, as Seward knew he would, and assured them in writing that Sumter would be evacuated in five days. After the five days passed and Sumter had not been surrendered as promised, Seward appeared unruffled. When the suspicious commissioners sent Campbell back for an explanation, Seward chided the judge in his most cheerful and buoyant manner—"after all, these things can't be expected to move with 'bank accuracy'!"—and pledged again that the fort would be given up. In Charleston, each successive day was now being named "Evacuation Day."

The President of the United States, Abraham Lincoln, had been forgotten in all of this. He knew nothing of these conversations. Seward, in assuming Lincoln had been convinced by the Cabinet vote to surrender Fort Sumter, had erred. Even in the din of the shouting during the tense weeks of the Sumter dilemma, Lincoln was listening only to his most deep-seated political instinct. As his friend Alexander McClure put it, "In all political or administrative movements Lincoln played the waiting game. When he did not know what to do, he was the safest man in the world to trust to do nothing." The President privately told his secretary, John Hay, "My policy is to have no policy." He remained undecided and kept his own counsel. Running up the white flag was a conclusion he was not ready to accept.

Instead, on March 21, he dispatched two trusted friends, Stephen A. Hurlbut and Ward Lamon, to Charleston by train to find out first-hand how much Union sentiment remained in the Deep South. Once there, Lamon, who had been Lincoln's closest companion on the February train procession to Washington, played his part poorly. He met with all the principals, and convinced everyone, from the Governor of South Carolina to the loyal soldiers in the fort, that Sumter would be surrendered. While he was in Charleston he corresponded, not with the President, but with Seward. His message—"I am satisfied of the policy and propriety of immediately evacuating fort Sumter" —left no doubt that even Lamon had dismissed Lincoln and now swerved to the Premier. Hurlbut, fortunately, did his job quietly and ably. Once back in Washington on March 27, he handed Lincoln a decisive sixteen-page report: "Unquestionably separate nationality is a fixed fact," it said. "They expect a golden era, when Charleston shall be a great commercial emporium." He saw there "an unanimity of sentiment which is to my mind astonishing." There was "no attachment to the Union." At least five Cotton States were "irrevocably gone. . . . There is positively nothing to appeal to." Reading this, the scales fell from Lincoln's eyes. He saw clearly the stark scene before him. The Deep South would never come back peacefully. Forbearance and appeasement would never bring reunion.

The next day, March 28, matters came to a head. On that day General Scott sent Lincoln a message advising him to abandon *both* forts—Fort Pickens as well as Fort Sumter—since "the evacuation of both the forts would instantly soothe and give confidence to the eight remaining slave-holding states, and render their cordial adherence to the Union perpetual." These were too obviously Seward's words. This time the Premier had overplayed his hand. Sumter could reasonably be given up on the basis of "military necessity," but Pickens never. Lincoln's disillusionment with General Scott was complete. The military master on whom he had relied was unmasked as Seward's shill. Lincoln called the Cabinet hurriedly into session that evening, and there told them, with strong emotion, Scott's new advice. After a moment of amazed silence, there were curses against the now-obvious partisanship of Scott. A new vote was taken on Sumter, and the majority, which two weeks before had voted for surrender, switched sides. All but Seward and Smith now voted to send provisions and hold the fort. Lincoln had already made up his mind, however. If he had ever seriously considered evacuating Sumter, he had repented. He now prepared decisively to aid the fort. He had read a second opinion, prepared by naval officer Gustavus Fox, which said that small, fast tugboats, backed by warships, could run past the rebel guns under cover of darkness and land supplies at Sumter's gate. On March 29, after pacing in his office through an entire sleepless night, Lincoln wrote a request that Fox go to New York and prepare his expedition.

Seward saw immediately that, in order to remain the author of events, he would have to move boldly and fast. With only a few days to retrieve the situation before the Sumter expedition sailed, the Secretary of State improvised new schemes with frantic energy.

First, in an eleventh-hour effort to prompt a withdrawal from Sumter, he put forward a new plan to reinforce Fort Pickens in Pensacola Harbor as a public show that, at the same time that Sumter was being evacuated by military necessity, "the possessions and authority of the United States" would be strictly maintained in the Gulf. On the 29th, the same day Lincoln's orders for Fox's expedition went out, Seward organized his own expedition—kept secret, even from the Secretaries of War and the Navy—to reinforce Pickens.

In addition, Seward—now more than ever the man of audacity—prepared an amazing document, one that, in one stroke, would relieve the bumbling Lincoln from control of the administration and put himself in charge. He headed his fantastic paper "Some Thoughts for the President's Consideration," and laid it before President Lincoln on April 1. It began with a harsh indictment: "We are at the end of a month's administration, and yet without a policy either domestic or foreign." It then provided a solution: "CHANGE THE QUESTION BEFORE THE PUBLIC FROM ONE UPON SLAVERY" to a question of "UNION OR DISUNION." To accomplish this, Seward repeated his proposal to evacuate Fort Sumter, since it was associated with the slavery question, and substitute the defense of Pickens. Seward then recommended that Lincoln declare war on France and Spain, reasoning that the Cotton States would rush to join a trumped-up war rather than be left out of the long-sought land grab for the slave-rich Caribbean islands. Seward climaxed his startling "Thoughts" with nothing less than a quiet *coup* attempt, the culmination of his struggle with Lincoln for control of the government. He coolly suggested that Lincoln abdicate his constitutional authority and delegate him, Seward, to pursue and direct policy:

> Whatever policy we adopt there must be an energetic prosecution of it.
> For this purpose it must be somebody's business to pursue it and direct it incessantly.

Either the President must do it himself, and be all the while active in it,
or
Devolve it on some member of the cabinet. Once adopted, debates on
it must end, and all agree and abide.
It is not my especial province.
But I neither seek to evade nor assume responsibility.

If Lincoln was taken aback by Seward's lunge for power, he never lost his temper, nor, even in the crucible of those fateful days, his equilibrium. To Seward's suggestion of a transfer of authority, Lincoln replied in person, with elegant restraint and a simplicity that allowed no argument: "If this must be done, I must do it."

Even now, however, Seward could not bear to relax his grip on the shreds of his program. He summoned to Washington John B. Baldwin, a leading Unionist from Virginia, whose all-important state now teetered on the brink of secession, to sway Lincoln toward a surrender. Lincoln, however, would not be bent. His first words in his meeting with the Virginian were, "I am afraid you have come too late."

Meanwhile, Seward doggedly persisted in his elaborate minuet with the Confederate commissioners. On March 30, Judge Campbell arrived again at Seward's door to inquire about the delay in evacuating Sumter. Seward put him off until April 1, when he wrote a note stating, "I am satisfied the Government will not undertake to supply Fort Sumter without giving notice to Governor Pickens."

"What does this mean?" Campbell asked. "Does the President design to attempt to supply Sumter?"

Seward lied. "No, I think not. It is a very irksome thing for him to surrender it. His ears are open to everyone, and they fill his head with schemes for supply. I do not think he will adopt any of them. There is no design to reinforce it."

Campbell wrote to Jefferson Davis laying blame for the delay on Lincoln: "the President is light, inconstant, and variable. His ear is open to every one—and his resolutions are easily bent." Over the next few days, Southern suspicions were raised by the bustle of activity in New York harbor. To Campbell's new inquiry about the ships being prepared, Seward gave his last false assurance on April 7, when he scribbled off an enigmatic note without signature or date: "Faith as to Sumter fully kept. Wait and see."

The false pledges coming from Seward's desk would have their terrible consequences in the days ahead. Meanwhile, as newspapers printed reports of "a large military expedition . . . fitting out in the Northern ports," the nation held its breath. The *New York Herald* condemned Lincoln as a bringer of war, predicting, "the Lincoln administration will be compelled to succumb in disgrace amidst the execrations of the people and the curses of mankind." As the Sumter-bound fleet left port on April 8 and 9, the *Herald* slashed at the "vicious, imbecile, demoralized Administration," and called for Lincoln's head, declaring, "Our only hope now against civil war of an indefinite duration seems to lie in the over-throw of the demoralizing, disorganizing, and destructive [Republican] party, of which 'Honest Abe Lincoln' is the pliant instrument." Edwin Stanton wrote to Buchanan on April 11:

> The feeling of loyalty to the government has greatly diminished in this city. . . . The administration has not acquired the respect and confidence of the people here. Not one of the cabinet or principal officers has taken a house or brought his family here. Seward rented a home "while he should continue in the cabinet," but has not opened it, nor has his family come. They all act as though they meant to be ready to "cut and run" at a minute's notice. Their tenure is like that of a Bedouin on the sands of the desert. This is sensibly felt and talked about by the people in the city, and they feel no confidence in an administration that betrays so much insecurity. And besides, a strong feeling of distrust in the candor and sincerity of Lincoln personally and of his cabinet has sprung up. If they had been merely silent and secret there might have been no grounds of complaint. But assurances are said to have been given and declarations made in conflict with the facts now transpiring in respect to the South, so that no one speaks of Lincoln or any member of his cabinet with respect and regard.

Shortly before dawn on April 12, as Lincoln's relief expedition tacked into its final approach to Fort Sumter, rebel cannoneers opened fire on the fort with the forty-three guns ringing Charleston harbor. A day and a half later, after the boom, whistle, and crash of four thousand rounds of pounding shot and exploding shell, with its barracks on fire, with flames licking at its magazine, with choking smoke and cinders filling the casements, the exhausted defenders of the crumbling fort lowered their flag and sent up a white bed sheet.

Southerners' predictions that Virginia would rush to secede as soon as the first blow was struck at Fort Sumter, however, proved wrong. Although pro-Confederate mobs ran and shouted in the streets of Richmond, Union

Party leaders there remained optimistic, and still expected the sitting Virginia secession convention to call a Border State conference on the crisis. Union Party men kept cool heads, according to letters written by several leaders shortly after Sumter, one of whom reasoned that it was "more incumbent than ever" for "Virginia and the other border slave states to maintain their mediatorial position." By assembling promptly, insisted another, "they could yet command the peace between the two warring sections." This was not a forlorn hope—only three months before, in January, Charleston guns had fired on the U.S. Navy ship *Star of the West* when it attempted to ferry supplies to Fort Sumter, and the incident had not sparked a wider war. Even Horace Greeley had then spoken of the hostile shots merely as "highhanded." The forbearance of Major Anderson in not returning fire with the guns from the fort at that time had been applauded, and calm had prevailed.

*   *   *

In the tense early weeks of his administration, however, Lincoln had closeted himself with Postmaster General Montgomery Blair's hawkish father, Francis P. Blair, Sr. "Old Man Blair," one of the elder statesmen of the nation, had become famous thirty years earlier as part of Andrew Jackson's influential "Kitchen Cabinet" and editor of the Democratic Party organ, the Washington *Globe*. He had wielded influence ever since, and had founded the Republican Party in the 1850s.

Lincoln's friends William Herndon and Ward Lamon testified that Lincoln believed that "far less evil & bloodshed would result from an effort to maintain the Union and Constitution" than from allowing the South to go. Now, Old Man Blair pressed him with the wisdom of a quick, crushing stroke such as Jackson would have delivered, believing, as Lincoln did, that a war would be avoided by bravely confronting what they saw as a handful of fire-eaters who held a Union-loving Southern population momentarily in thrall.

Recent history indicated that long, costly wars were obsolete. Napoleon had won many of his campaigns with one great victory. Mexico had been subdued with the loss of fewer than two thousand lives. The recent Swiss civil war had lasted three weeks and killed just over a hundred. Lincoln revealed his idea of the scope of conflict in 1859 when he told an audience that "if . . . you undertake to destroy the Union, it will be our duty to deal with you as old John Brown has been dealt with. . . . We hope and believe that in no section will a majority so act as to render such extreme measures necessary." The "extreme measures" against John Brown that Lincoln referred to took a total of seventeen lives. As a worst-case example, back in 1856, Lincoln had seen the proto-civil war in Kansas die down after a loss of just two hundred.

So now Border State Unionists were thunderstruck when, on April 15, newspapers nationwide carried the text of a proclamation by President Lincoln:

> I, Abraham Lincoln, President of the United States, in virtue of the power in me vested by the Constitution, and the laws, have thought fit to call forth, and hereby do call forth, the militia of the several States of the Union, to the aggregate number of seventy-five thousand, in order to suppress combinations too powerful to be suppressed by the ordinary course of judicial proceedings, and to cause the laws to be duly executed.

Southern Unionists who had stayed calm after the firing at Sumter now panicked. They called Lincoln's proclamation summoning a hostile army of 75,000 men "villainous" and "disastrous." North Carolina's Jonathan Worth cried that, with the April 15 call for troops, "Lincoln prostrated us. He could have devised no scheme more effectual than the one he has pursued, to overthrow the friends of the Union here."

Worth's friend John A. Gilmer, whom Lincoln had recently considered for a Cabinet post, told Seward, "The fight at Charleston had done us no harm." A Virginia Unionist agreed, "the conflict at Charleston could not have carried us out," as did a North Carolina congressman who thought that "Union feeling was strong up to the recent proclamation." Now they were undone. Virginia Unionist John Botts called Lincoln's call for troops "in many respects the most unfortunate state paper that ever issued from any executive since the establishment of the government."

Unionists throughout Virginia, Tennessee, and North Carolina pointed over and over to the proclamation as the crucial outrage. Tennessee Congressman Horace Maynard reported that in his state "the President's extraordinary proclamation" unleashed "a tornado of excitement that seems likely to sweep us all away." Men who had "heretofore been cool, firm and Union loving" had become "perfectly wild" and were "aroused to a phrenzy of passion." In his opinion, Lincoln's proclamation "has done more to promote disunion than any and all other causes combined." William Holden, Unionist editor of the *North Carolina Standard*, wrote, "If Mr. Lincoln had only insisted on holding the federal property, and had called in good faith for troops to defend Washington City, the Union men of the border states could have sustained him.

But he 'crossed the Rubicon' when he called for troops to subdue the Confederate States. This was a proclamation of war, and as such will be resisted." *Louisville Daily Journal* editor George Prentiss, who had condemned the "revolutionists" in Charleston for attacking Fort Sumter and predicted that no "widespread fighting" would result from the Charleston incident, was incensed at Lincoln's "hare-brained and ruinous" response. "We are struck with mingled amazement and indignation. The policy announced in the Proclamation deserves the unqualified condemnation of every American citizen," he wrote, concluding that Lincoln was unfit to govern. Some Border State men even suspected that Lincoln, fearing that their Union Party attempts might be successful at keeping the peace, decided to "drive us all into rebellion" so he could carry out "the old John Brown business of freeing our slaves and punishing us for the sin of having held them."

Border State Unionists felt betrayed. Since the inaugural and throughout March, the Lincoln administration, through its spokesman Seward, had consistently signaled a peace policy toward the seceded states. The mid-April attempt to resupply Sumter now appeared to be a double cross, and the April 15 call for troops was seen as a blindside blow against the South. Judge Campbell, who had acted in good faith as Seward's intermediary in March, wrote bitterly, "I think no candid man, who will read over what I have written and consider for a moment what is going on at Sumter, but will agree that the equivocating conduct of the administration . . . is the proximate cause of this great calamity." Lincoln "allowed it to go forth to the world that Fort Sumter was to be evacuated," was the charge. Seward's assurances had been taken as pledges, and Lincoln had "basely falsified" those pledges. "This, to our apprehension, is *rank usurpation*, and as freemen, we cannot submit to it," proclaimed one Carolina journal. "Toward the Union men of the border states this conduct is infamous. To the South as a whole it is a gross and intolerable wrong—to the Union Party, in particular, it is *treachery and fraud*." The *Alexandria* (Va.) *Gazette* cried, "It is against the friends of the Union at the South, that the Administration has struck its hardest blows." According to Worth in North Carolina, "Union men feel that just as they had got so they could stand on their legs, Lincoln had heartlessly turned them over to the mercy of their enemies."

In the Confederate view, the Lincoln government had begun with a fatal breach of faith. It was now widely believed in the Deep South that Lincoln had pursued a duplicitous course since he had taken the oath, that he had schemed since his inaugural to deceive the commissioners and lull the South with sweet lies while he prepared for war. The *New Orleans Daily Delta* on April 18 cursed "the disgusting baseness of the pitiable creature, this burlesque of a President."

But it was the assault on Lincoln by the Border States that was most devastating, coming from states that were still in the Union. The *Louisville Journal* judged harshly, "If Mr. Lincoln contemplated this policy in the inaugural address, he is a guilty dissembler; if he has conceived it under the excitement raised in the seizure of Fort Sumter, he is a guilty hotspur. In either case, he is miserably unfit for the exalted position in which the enemies of the country have placed him." Revered Kentuckian compromiser John J. Crittenden felt "deceived by false assurances of a peaceful policy." A loyal North Carolina editor complained that the Unionists had been "cheated, imposed upon, and deceived" by Lincoln and that "secessionists were right in their conjectures concerning him." One Virginian hoped "the God of battles" would "crush to the earth and consign to eternal perdition, Mr. Lincoln, his cabinet, and all 'aiders and abettors,' in this cruel, needless, corrupt betrayal of the conservative men in the South." Another warned that having "knocked away the props that have upheld the Union party in this county," Lincoln would find "as sturdy a set of rebels" there as in any other part of the South. William W. Blackford, a Virginian who would ride with Jeb Stuart, wrote with the sorrow and sense of tragedy that was felt across the Border States: "I was opposed to secession. . . . I thought that Lincoln, though a sectional candidate, was constitutionally elected and that we ought to have waited to see what he would do. But when he called for troops from Virginia and we had to take one side or the other, then of course I was for going with the South in her mad scheme, right or wrong." The perfidy of the Lincoln government had given the Confederate cause a new moral strength equal to any number of military divisions. It now saw itself as a virtuous revolution, one necessary to save liberties from a scheming despot.

The wires that carried the text of Lincoln's call for troops soon carried telegrams to the governors of all the states notifying them of the number of troops each would be expected to furnish. The Border State governors' replies to President Lincoln were scathing:

Beriah Magoffin of Kentucky wired on April 15, the same day the request was received: "I say emphatically Kentucky will furnish no troops for the wicked purposes of subduing her sister Southern States."

John W. Ellis of North Carolina also wired that day: "I regard the levy of troops made by the Administration for the purpose of subjugating the States of the South as in violation of the Constitution and a gross usurpation of power. I can be no party to this wicked violation of the laws of the country and to this war upon the liberties of a free people. You can get no troops from North Carolina."

John Letcher of Virginia wired on April 16: "The militia of Virginia will not be furnished to the powers at Washington for any such use or purpose as they have in view. Your object is to subjugate the Southern States, and a requisition made upon me for such an object . . . will not be complied with. You have chosen to inaugurate civil war, and having done so, we will meet it in a spirit as determined as the Administration has exhibited toward the South."

Isham G. Harris of Tennessee, on April 17: "Tennessee will not furnish a single man for purpose of coercion, but 50,000, if necessary, for the defense of our rights and those of our Southern brethren."

Claiborne Fox Jackson of Missouri, also on April 17: "Your requisition, in my judgment, is illegal, unconstitutional, and revolutionary in its object, inhuman and diabolical, and cannot be complied with. Not one man will the State of Missouri furnish to carry on any such unholy crusade."

. . . and Henry M. Rector of Arkansas, on April 22: "The demand is only adding insult to injury. The people of this Commonwealth are freemen, not slaves, and will defend to the last extremity their honor, lives, and property against Northern mendacity and usurpation."

Two days after Lincoln's proclamation came one of the most critical moments in American history. On April 17, 1861, the Virginia Convention in Richmond voted 88 to 55 to secede. Virginia, the "Mother of Presidents," stretching from the Atlantic Ocean to the Ohio River, whose Arlington Heights looked down from across the Potomac River upon the public buildings of Washington, left the United States. The Virginian *Staunton Spectator*, until now a Unionist newspaper, recalled the crucial moment in verse the next New Year's Day:

> *I told you last spring of old Abe's "Proclamation,"*
> *That insulted the South, and united our nation:*
> *Virginia declared, tho' opposed to secession,*
> *She'd never submit to a tyrant's oppression.*
> *Since war is declared, no longer she waits,*
> *But hastens to join the Confederate States.*

Seizing the opportunity to emphasize the new loyalty of their sudden sister, the Cotton State rebels moved the capital of the Confederacy from Montgomery to Richmond. In the coming weeks, Tennessee, North Carolina, and Arkansas followed Virginia out of the Union, and the number of stars on the Confederate flag grew to eleven.

*   *   *

"It appears, we confess, to complete the character of Mr. Lincoln's policy as including every known kind of blunder," observed Britain's *Manchester Guardian*. After six weeks of multiplying confusion by failing to provide a controlling will and a unified voice in his administration, the new President, with one stroke of the pen, had provoked the doubling of the size and population of the enemy nation. The four newly-seceded Border States' foundries would roll heavy iron plate and cast cannon, and they would provide powder works and major factories to rival the Union where the Cotton States had had none. Material advantages were not the only ones transferred to the Confederacy: Lincoln had also multiplied the South's hostility. It was now a nation that carried on its banners the fresh spirit of a crusade against the Usurper, the Tyrant: Abraham Lincoln, the "destroyer of peace."

Chapter 16

The Capital Surrounded

"Wanted—A Leader"

Lincoln's April 15 call to arms, at the same time it branded him a despot in the South, unified the entire North in a wild spasm of flag-waving zeal. There, the Babel of political tongues that had proliferated over decades of bitter debate was drowned out in an instant by the patriotic hurrah from twenty million loyal throats. Northern cities and towns rang with rallies. Militiamen paraded, fifes and drums evoked the Minute Men, prominent men speechified, and huge crowds frothed and cheered. Everywhere it was the same. "Fort Sumter is temporarily lost, but the country is saved. Long live the Republic!" cried the New York *Tribune*. On the day of the proclamation the *New York Times* reported that "On every corner, yesterday, in every car, on board every ferry-boat, in every hotel, in the vestibule of every church, could be heard the remark: 'I am a Democrat, dyed in the wool; I voted against Lincoln, but I will stand by the Government of my country when assailed, as it now is, by traitors.'" An Illinois man wrote, "Secession, disunion, and even fault finding is done with in this City. We shall all stand firmly by the administration and fight it out."

The name "Abraham Lincoln," however, had little magic for the people. It was missing from the speeches, letters, and articles that poured out during those explosive few days of patriotism known as the Uprising of the North. The people spoke instead against treason, or for the supremacy of law, or about religious righteousness, or the revenge of Sumter, or love of the old Union, or the flag. *Duty* was the impulse, not love of Lincoln.

Even as the masses surged into town squares to show themselves for the flag, loyalty to Lincoln was tendered only on condition of a quick victory. The *New York Herald* adopted the view of the New York merchants: "The business community demand that the war shall be short; and the more vigorously it is prosecuted the more speedily will it be closed. Business men can stand a temporary reverse. They can easily make arrangements for six months or a year. But they cannot endure a long, uncertain and tedious contest."

Few worried. Prophecies for the war were that it would be brief. Many who applauded Lincoln's call for 75,000 volunteers, and perhaps Lincoln himself, believed the troops would bring the rebellion to an end merely by appearing, armed and ready. Seward was still sure the trouble would be over in ninety days. The *New York Times* and the Philadelphia *Press* predicted the "local commotion" in Dixie would be ended "effectually in thirty days." The Chicago *Tribune* boasted that "Illinois can whip the South by herself," and foresaw victory "within two or three months at the furthest." The New York *Tribune* told its readers that "Jeff. Davis & Co. will be swinging from the battlements at Washington . . . by the 4th of July."

While the North entertained its romantic idea of a short, glorious war, Lincoln was well aware that, if the war became drawn out, disappointment—and criticism—would be sharp. Within days of Sumter, *Harper's Weekly* put the responsibility for a short war squarely on him, declaring,

> [I]f ABRAHAM LINCOLN is equal to the position he fills, the war will be over by January, 1862. . . . The whole Northern people are of one mind on the subject, party divisions are obliterated, twenty millions of people place at the service of the Administration their lives and their money. With such support, and such resources, if this war be not brought to a speedy close, and the supremacy of the Government forcibly asserted throughout the country, it will be the fault of ABRAHAM LINCOLN.

The *Weekly* ended with a finger-wagging: "We do not propose to reecho the censure which the Administration has already incurred at the hands of its friends for its want of energy. We hope that in the future it will be energetic enough to satisfy everybody. But Mr. Lincoln must remember that this is no time for trifling. The rebels have appealed to the sword, and by the sword they must be punished."

The first glorious impulse of the Northern rush to the colors climaxed on Saturday, April 20, with a rally by 100,000 people in staunchly Democratic New York City. George Templeton Strong jotted down his impressions in his diary:

> Broadway crowded and more crowded as one approached Union Square.
> Large companies of recruits in citizens' dress parading up and down,
> cheered and cheering. Small mobs round the headquarters of the

regiments that are going to Washington, starting at the sentinel on duty. Every other man, woman, and child bearing a flag or decorated with a cockade. Flags from almost every building. The city seems to have gone suddenly wild and crazy.

*   *   *

Lincoln, however, did not hear the news. Already, in the four days after his call for troops, the flame of the rebellion that blazed across North Carolina and Virginia had overleaped the nation's capital and spread to Baltimore. There, on April 19, the day before the New York rally, the train bearing the 800-strong Sixth Massachusetts militia, the first armed Northern regiment moving through Baltimore to the defense of Washington, was intercepted on the city streets by a howling secessionist mob whose members tore up the tracks and attacked the soldiers with paving stones when they climbed down from the cars. The terrified Bay State militiamen leveled their muskets and opened fire, and the mob responded with a hail of rocks and pistol fire. When the melee was over and the Sixth Massachusetts hurried onto the cars toward Washington, twelve Baltimoreans and four Massachusetts men lay dead or dying, with thirty-one soldiers and dozens of civilians wounded.

That evening, Baltimore militiamen destroyed all the railroad bridges and cut the telegraph lines from the north. Washington, now ringed by rebellion in Maryland and Virginia, was completely cut off from communication with the rest of the loyal states.

Word of the Baltimore uprising electrified the South. Southerners had predicted a war made short by a quick capture of the national capital, believing that such a *coup* would give the Confederacy a halo of prestige that would bring immediate recognition by foreign powers. The *Richmond Examiner* sounded a bugle:

> There is one wild shout of fierce resolve to capture Washington City, at all and every human hazard. The filthy cage of unclean birds must and will be purified by fire. . . . Our people can take it, and Scott the arch-traitor, and Lincoln the Beast, combined, cannot prevent it. The just indignation of an outraged and deeply injured people will teach the Illinois Ape to retrace his journey across the borders of the Free negro States still more rapidly than he came.

The *Richmond Whig* predicted Jefferson Davis would soon dine in the White House, warning Lincoln he could save himself some trouble if he were "in readiness to dislodge at a moment's notice!" The *New Orleans Picayune* prophesied "the removal of Lincoln and his Cabinet, and whatever he can carry away, to the safer neighborhood of Harrisburg or Cincinnati—perhaps to Buffalo or Cleveland."

A Southern railroad superintendent wrote to inform the Confederate Secretary of War that railroads could carry 5000 to 7000 men daily at the rate of 350 miles per day, and urged instant action: "Lincoln is in a trap. . . . One dash, and Lincoln is taken, the country saved, and the leader who does it will be immortalized." Visible Southern sympathy among the residents of Washington, hundreds of whom wore secessionist badges pinned to their lapels even while they worked in the Federal offices, increased the certainty that the capital was in imminent danger of capture. Edwin Stanton wrote to Buchanan, "The impression here is held by many that in less than thirty days Davis will be in possession of Washington."

It was no secret that Virginia had close to 15,000 active militiamen organized, uniformed, equipped, and drilled. And now militiamen all over Maryland were flocking to Baltimore to reinforce the rebels there. Washington, surrounded on all sides, had no one to defend it. Townspeople had little faith in the new-minted District of Columbia militia, a few hundred locals who agreed to patrol the public buildings on the condition that they be home for supper. William Russell of the London *Times*, who was in Washington, sketched them as "starved, washed-out creatures, most of them, interpolated with Irish and stumpy Germans."

And there were no reinforcements. The day of Lincoln's proclamation had passed without a single soldier from the North arriving. The next day had passed, and another, and still no troops had appeared. On April 17 came the alarm that the rebels had seized the arsenal at Harper's Ferry, a short march up the Potomac. On the heels of that came word that the rebels had taken the United States Navy Yard at Norfolk, Virginia, and that $30 million in guns, ships, and munitions had gone up in flames.

On Thursday, April 18, two swashbuckling types—Cassius Clay of Kentucky and Senator Jim Lane of Kansas—strode into Willard's Hotel and divided the boarders loyal to the North into two groups, while Southerners stood aside and looked on. Clay was soon drilling his so-called "Clay Battalion" in the ballroom, while Jim Lane marched his new "Frontier Guards" two blocks to the White House and passed out muskets. That evening, under the glow of the chandeliers in the East Room, the men who had been hotel guests a few hours earlier opened ammunition boxes, distributed cartridges, and went to sleep on the velvet carpets clutching their weapons, with Lincoln and his family upstairs.

The Lincolns were instructed that, when the rebels came rushing into the city, they were to run across the lawn to the sturdy Treasury building, which was being fortified by General Scott as a citadel for a last-ditch defense. Every window there was being barricaded, every door fitted with iron bars, every portico filled with sandbags. Its basement was stocked with a supply of water and two thousand barrels of flour in preparation for a siege, and troops occupied the State Department building and the Riggs Bank building on its flanks. At the other end of Pennsylvania Avenue, the Capitol was also made ready to repulse an assault. Its doors and windows were boarded up and blocked by stones and casks of cement, and the iron plating intended for the construction of the new dome was hauled onto the porticoes to make breastworks.

On Friday, April 19, the evening of the Sixth Massachusetts Baltimore massacre, Lincoln was shaken by word that stretcher-bearers were meeting their train, and that dozens of soldiers with handkerchiefs pressed to their wounds were being taken to the E Street Infirmary, while the dirty, exhausted remainder bedded down in the Senate chamber of the Capitol. Over the coming hours, as the Baltimore bridges were burned and telegraph lines went dead, Washington citizens realized they were cut off from the North, and the growing anxiety for the safety of the Federal City gave way to terror such as it had not known since the British burned it in 1814.

That weekend, northbound trains were packed, as thousands of hotel guests—most of whom had been office seekers only days before—scurried for safety. They jostled for places with thousands of women and children piling on board to flee the capital. The price of vehicles skyrocketed as families seized every conveyance—carriages, wagons, carts, even wheelbarrows and baby buggies—and loaded them with children and belongings. They pushed and shoved their way in long lines of traffic along the streets pointing out of town to the north. Stanton wrote to Buchanan "no description could convey . . . the panic that prevailed here for several days after the Baltimore riot . . . ."

More thousands fled south over the bridges across the Potomac to join the rebellion, including scores of army and navy officers, and hundreds of government clerks and their families. They spread tales of helplessness and panic in the White House that soon reached the ears of gleeful Southern editors.

The *Richmond Whig* on April 20 had "reliable information" that "Old Abe had been beastly intoxicated for the previous thirty-six consecutive hours, and that eighty Border Ruffians, from Kansas, occupied the East Room to guard His Majesty's slumbers. It is broadly hinted in a Washington paper, that his guard exerts a despotic control over the Presidential inmate—that all his decrees are of its inspiration." This news was soon followed by another report:

> A gentleman arrived here this morning, who, with several others, was arrested while passing through Washington, for being Southerners, and taken into the presence of the august Baboon. He declares that Lincoln was so drunk that he could scarcely maintain his seat in the chair; and it was notorious in Washington that he had been in a state of intoxication for more than thirty-six hours. The man is scared nearly to death and few people in that city are in any better condition.

The *Whig* story that the cowardly Lincoln was a prisoner of his White House guards took on a life of its own. The *New Orleans Delta* printed a letter from a Southern woman in Washington that revealed "Old Lincoln sleeps with a hundred men in the east room to protect him from the Southern army. He is expecting them to attack the city every night; he keeps a sentinel walking in front of his bed-room all night, and often gets so frightened that he leaves the White House, and sleeps out, no one knows where. These are facts." Later, in the *Petersburg Express*, a story ran that "He has not passed a night in the White House for two weeks, but goes into the barracks to sleep with his armed hirelings all around him. He does not so much as take off his boots, that he may be ready to run on a second's warning." One story had it that Lincoln locked himself up in an iron cage out of fear of assassination, and another that he woke up every night screaming "Jeff Davis is after me! Jeff Davis is after me!"

With no mail and no word—not so much as a newspaper—coming from the North, loyal Washingtonians heard the same rumors. "[The panic in Washington] was increased by reports of the trepidation of Lincoln that were circulated through the streets," Stanton informed Buchanan. The townspeople fell prey to their imaginations. "The town is full tonight of feverish rumours about a meditated assault upon this town," wrote John Hay in his room in the White House. Locals refused to fill desks left empty by the exodus of the Southern clerks out of fear that the coming Confederate regime would take reprisals. There was word that rebel scouts were already at the bridges, and that a rebel mortar battery was on the Arlington Heights. Confederates ships were reported on their way up from Norfolk to bombard the city. Another rumor had it that forty thousand Virginia volunteers armed with bowie knives would attack across the Long Bridge. Mobs were feared to be converging to sack the capital from Richmond, from Baltimore, and from Harper's Ferry. The Prussian embassy hung a sign in German script over its entrance in hopes that it would be spared by the coming Southern horde. Word passed that secessionists would start fires all over Washington to aid the invasion, and that mines were being laid under the Treasury building, where Scott's workers were busy preparing for a last stand.

Along with panic came the conviction that the weak hand of the countrified Railsplitter—so unqualified, so new in office, so unequal to the emergency—was to blame. That conviction increased after a visit to the White House on Sunday, April 21, by Mayor Brown and three prominent citizens from Baltimore, where the secessionist mob still held sway. Mayor Brown told Lincoln that Baltimore citizens protested his proclamation calling for 75,000 troops and considered it a declaration of war and a violation of their constitutional rights. Lincoln's response demonstrated that, six weeks after his inauguration, he was still playing the part of the Untutored Westerner. According to Brown, he leaped up and protested with great feeling, "Mr. Brown, I am not a learned man! I am not a learned man!" telling Brown that his proclamation had been misunderstood, that he had no intention of bringing on war, but that he only wanted to defend the capital. Lincoln concluded the meeting by promising Mayor Brown that, rather than disturb their city, he would march Northern troops around it.

Lincoln's truckling to the Baltimoreans was magnified in the lens of the national emergency. Now, added to the spectacle of a Commander-in-Chief unable to protect his own capital, here he was capitulating to the Mayor of Baltimore. Anger among the Cabinet was immediate. A few minutes later, in fact, when Secretary of the Navy Gideon Welles arrived and heard of Lincoln's weak show, he "Jumped up, swung his hat under his arm and hastily walked out, telling them that if that was their policy he would have no responsibility in the matter," according to a friend. Edward Bates burned with shame in his diary:

> They think and in fact find it perfectly safe to defy the Government, And why? Because we hurt nobody; we frighten nobody; and do our utmost to offend nobody. *They* cut off *our* mails; *we* furnish theirs gratis. *They* block our communications, *We* are careful to preserve theirs—*They* assail and obstruct our troops in their lawful and honest march to the defense of this

Capitol [sic] while *we* as yet have done nothing to resist or retort the outrage.

They every day are winding their toils around us, while we make no bold effort to cut the cord that is soon to bind us in pitiable impotence. They warm up their friends and allies, by bold daring, and by the prestige of continued success—While we freeze the spirits of our friends every where, by our inaction and the gloomy prestage [sic] of defeat.

Secretary of the Treasury Chase complained that Lincoln had no policy besides "merely the general notion of drifting, the Micawber policy of waiting for something to turn up." He sent Lincoln a letter scolding that "the disunionists have anticipated us in everything, and that as yet we have accomplished nothing but the destruction of our own property. . . . What next? Do not, I pray you, let this new success of treason be inaugurated in the presence of American troops. Save us from this new humiliation."

News of the episode with Mayor Brown reached the North, portraying Lincoln as paralyzed and helpless. The New York *Tribune* dripped sarcasm, saying, "If good Uncle Abe wants to read the secessionists another essay proving that he never meant them any harm, or Gov. Seward has another oration to deliver to them on the glories and blessing of the Union, let the performances come off by all means, but this will have to be before Jeff. Davis and Wise capture Washington."

*　*　*

The city was a desert. Wind blew dust onto shuttered shops and vacated houses. Offices and all theaters and saloons were closed. There was silence in the empty halls of the large hotels. At Willard's, a thousand guests had dwindled to forty. Lincoln's secretaries later remembered, "An indescribable gloom . . . hung over Washington . . . , paralyzing its traffic and crushing out its life." Henry Villard said he could count the people on Pennsylvania Avenue on his fingers. "Business was at a standstill," wrote Frederick Seward. "The railway station was silent, the wharves deserted. Groups of people gathered at street corners exchanging, in low tones, their forebodings of disaster, or their hopes of relief." Nothing was in motion besides carts loaded with flour barrels, tottering toward the basements of Scott's forts at the Treasury and the Capitol. Townspeople trickled into the train depot to wait for the soldiers, but none came.

Lincoln himself—stepping over the Frontier Guards in the East Room, hearing the hammers pounding at the Treasury Building across the yard, and seeing the District militia drilling awkwardly under his windows—was in an agony of doubt. Henry Villard recalled the "impatience, gloom, and depression" that settled over the capital in that week, and added: "No one felt it more than the President. I saw him repeatedly, and he fairly groaned at the inexplicable delay in the advent of help from the loyal States." John Hay overheard Lincoln mutter to himself as he looked out his window, "Why don't they come? Why don't they come?" On his desk were warnings, such as the Southern newspaper clipping that offered $100,000 for his "miserable traitorous head," and this letter:

> To Abe Lincon Esqr
>
> *Dear Friend* I take this method of informing you that you better prepair yourself for an asailing mob that is organizing in Baltimore as far as I can inform myself is about 12000 m. strong they intend to seize the Capitol and yourself and as they say that they will tar & put cotton on your head and ride you and Gen Scot on a rail this secret organization is about 70000 members in Maryland and Virgina and thay can be all brought to gether in five days, the person that rits this was a member and is bound by a strong oath which if they now who I was I wold not be suffer to live but justis to you and my country make me do this.

According to Alexander McClure, Lincoln knew that Beauregard's Charleston army could be transported to Washington by rail within three or four days, and McClure heard the President say to General Scott, "It does seem to me, General, that if I were Beauregard I would take Washington."

In the eerie, trancelike mood of the empty capital city, under the immense pressure of expecting momentary capture, Lincoln's imagination began to play tricks on him. He later told Carl Schurz that, one afternoon alone in his room,

> a feeling came over him as if he were utterly deserted and helpless. He thought any moderately strong body of secessionist troops, if there were any in the neighborhood, might come over the 'long bridge' across the Potomac, and just take him and the members of the Cabinet—the whole lot of them. Then he suddenly heard a sound like the boom of a cannon. "There they are!" he said to himself. He expected every moment

somebody would rush in with the report of an attack. But nobody came, and all remained still.

Then he thought he would look after the thing himself. So he walked out, and walked, and walked, until he got to the Arsenal [two and a half miles to the southeast, a 45-minute walk]. There he found the doors all open, and not a soul to guard them. Anybody might have gone in and helped himself to the arms. There was perfect solitude and stillness all around. Then he walked back to the White House without noticing the slightest sign of disturbance. He met a few persons on the way, some of whom he asked whether they had not heard something like the boom of a cannon. Nobody had heard anything, and so he supposed it must have been a freak of his imagination.

April 24, a day wounded soldiers of the Sixth Massachusetts regiment visited him at the White House, was, according to Hay's diary, "a day of gloom and doubt. Everybody seems filled with a vague distrust and recklessness." Lincoln told the soldiers, "I don't believe there is any North. The Seventh Regiment [New York militia, reported approaching] is a myth. Rhode Island [also reported sending a regiment] is not known in our geography any longer. *You* are the only Northern realities."

The silent terror and anguished watching and waiting continued for six days. On April 25, spirits were at lowest ebb. Winfield Scott was composing his "General Order No. 4," which began, "From the known assemblage near this city of numerous hostile bodies of troops it is evident that an attack upon it may be expected at any moment." Then, at noon, the Sixth Massachusetts men on Capitol Hill were set cheering by the sight of a train approaching from the north, covered with soldiers. Crowds of citizens came running pell-mell to the depot, where the shriek of the locomotive whistle heralded the arrival of the Seventh New York Militia regiment, whose mechanics and tracklayers had repaired a railroad route around Baltimore by way of Annapolis. The wild shouts of the townspeople were heard all the way to the Executive Mansion. In the bright sunlight, the New York militiamen in their spotless gray uniforms climbed off the train and formed ranks. According to Lincoln's secretaries,

The Seventh marched up Pennsylvania Avenue to the White House. As they passed up the magnificent street, with their well-formed ranks, their exact military step, their soldierly bearing, their gaily floating flags, and the inspiring music of their splendid regimental band, they seemed to sweep all thought of danger and all taint of treason out of that great national thoroughfare and out of every human heart in the Federal City. The presence of this single regiment seemed to turn the scales of fate. Cheer upon cheer greeted them; windows were thrown up; houses opened; the population came forth upon the streets as for a holiday. It was an epoch in American history. For the first time, the combined spirit and power of liberty entered the nation's Capital.

After the Seventh New York, regiments came in an unbroken stream. In a few days Washington was crowded with the camps of 10,000 militiamen from the North.

*   *   *

The near loss of the nation's capital at the war's outset reinforced the opinion of the press that Lincoln was feeble and overmatched by the crisis. Lincoln's standing with the opinion-makers, already abysmally low, sank. Patience with Lincoln had run out even in the stalwart *New York Times*, as shown in three columns that Lincoln clipped from it, tied together with ribbon and saved, labeled "Villainous articles." The first, headlined "Clear the Track!" praised a would-be dictator named George Law, a two-bit New York City demagogue the *Times* liked for his get-tough stance with the Maryland rebels:

> George Law only speaks the universal sentiment of the whole community, without reference to party or to class, when he tells President Lincoln that the Government must clear the path to Washington, *or the people will do it for them*. There is a perfect unanimity among the people on this subject.

The second column, reacting to Lincoln's appeasement of the Baltimore mob by detouring troops around the city, was headlined "A Startling Report," and was even clearer in its threat to Lincoln:

> We will simply remark that the President runs no small risk of being *superseded* in his office, if he undertakes to thwart the clear and manifest determination of the people to maintain the authority of the Government of the United States, and to protect its honor. We are in the midst of a Revolution, and in such emergencies the people are very apt to find some *representative* leader, if the forms of law do not happen to have given them

one. It would be well for Mr. Lincoln to bear in mind the possibility of such an event.

The depth of contempt for Lincoln in the third *Times* article, dated April 25, is plain in its title: "Wanted—A Leader":

> In every great crisis, the human heart demands a leader that incarnates its ideas, its emotions, and its aims. Till such a leader appears, everything is disorder, disaster, and defeat. The moment he takes the helm, order, promptitude and confidence follow as the necessary result. When we see such results we know that a hero leads. No such hero at present directs affairs. The experience of our Government for months past has been a series of defeats. It has been one continued retreat. Its path is marked by the wrecks of property destroyed. It has thus far only urged war upon itself. It confidingly enters into compacts with traitors who seek them merely to gain time better to strike a fatal blow. Stung to the quick by the disgraces we have suffered, by the disasters sustained, by the treachery which threatens the annihilation of all order, law, and property, and by the insults heaped upon our National banner, the people have sprung to arms, and demand satisfaction for wounded honor and for violation of laws, which must be vindicated, or well may at once bid farewell to society, to government, and to property, and sink into barbarism.
>
> Where is the leader of this sublime passion? Can the Administration furnish him? . . . From a dream of profound peace we awake with our enemy at our throat. Who shall grapple with this foe?

The same sentiments were heard in Washington. As soon as the mails were restored, men close to the President received letters such as the one sent to Treasury Secretary Chase: "For God's sake get Mr Lincoln to quit telling anecdotes—and to go to work in earnest. Richmond, Va. should be in possession of the Government by 1st June at the farthest!" Count Gurowski wrote to Charles Sumner, "Neither pighead Lincoln nor the whole Cabinet have been elected with the view of crushing a civil war." The count told his diary his disappointment at "the undecided conduct of the administration; at its want of foresight; its eternal parleying with Baltimoreans, Virginians, Missourians, etc., and no step to tread down the head of the young snake. No one among them seems to have the seer's eye."

Nor had Lincoln's patience with the Baltimoreans done him any good there. On April 27, Baltimore *Sun* declared that, under Lincoln, the government had "become a vast consolidated despotism." Even Reverend R. Fuller, one of a Baltimore delegation who had visited the White House in April, wrote to Chase his ungrateful opinion that "From Mr. Lincoln nothing is to be hoped, except as you can influence him. . . . I marked the President closely. Genial and jovial, he is wholly inaccessible to Christian appeals, and his egotism will forever prevent his comprehending what patriotism means."

Another Maryland native, James Ryder Randall, after his friend was wounded in the April 19 Baltimore melee with the Sixth Massachusetts, scribbled down the words that would become the Maryland state song, "Maryland, My Maryland." His lines were printed in the New Orleans *Sunday Delta* on April 26, put to the tune of "O Christmas Tree," and soon became one of the marching songs of the new Confederacy:

> *The despot's heel is on thy shore,*
> *Maryland, My Maryland!*
> *His torch is at thy temple door,*
> *Maryland, My Maryland!*
> *Avenge the patriotic gore*
> *That flecked the streets of Baltimore,*
> *And be the battle queen of yore,*
> *Maryland! My Maryland!*

The "despot" of the song's first line was Abraham Lincoln.

Chapter 17

The Hundred Days to Bull Run

"The imbecility of the Administration culminated in that catastrophe."

Lincoln, in fact, had accomplished the failure of secession in Maryland. When the Maryland legislature met on April 26, it stormed and fumed, it protested solemnly against the war and gave its "cordial assent" to the independence of the Southern states, but it did not secede. Within a week, the Baltimore merchants realized their trade with the North was gone, and by the next week rebellion there was ended. On May 4, Hay wrote in his diary, "The Maryland Disunionists . . . called today upon the President. Their roaring was exquisitely modulated. It had lost the ferocious timbre of the April days. They roared as gently as twere any nightingale." Baltimoreans hurried to restring the telegraph lines and rebuild the burned bridges, and normal traffic was restored by the middle of May.

When Lincoln drafted his proclamation of April 15, there had been the question of when to convene the Congress. In this decision he was influenced by Seward, who advised him not to hurry, saying, "History tells us that kings who call extra parliaments lose their heads." A confusion of voices among the leaders now could be deadly to the Union. Border State delegates might block urgent action. Radicals from the Northeast might alarm conservatives everywhere. Lincoln put the emergency session off until July 4, eighty days away.

* * *

In the meantime, he took unto himself the powers of a dictator:

- On April 19, the same day as the Baltimore massacre, he ordered a blockade on Southern ports—an act of war—without consent of Congress.

- On April 20, he ordered the raid of every telegraph office in the North to seize copies of every telegram sent and received in the previous twelve months.

- On the evening of April 21, Lincoln held a meeting of the Cabinet in one of the Navy offices—away from any White House spies—where he asked for and received a free hand to use illegal means if they became necessary in the emergency. Seward later referred to this as the Cabinet's most thrilling meeting. It was there, he said, that Lincoln and his advisors "put in force the war power of the government, and issued papers and did acts that might have brought them all to the scaffold."

- Thus given *carte blanche* by his advisers, Lincoln signed war measures in a rush. He selected private citizens to purchase warships, and gave $2 million to three trusted New York merchants to buy arms and form new regiments, ignoring the legal requirement to seek approval of Congress when dipping into the Treasury.

- He closed the mail to "disloyal" publications.

- He called for an additional 42,000 volunteers to serve for three years, and augmented the regular army by 22,000 men and the navy by 18,000. Here again, Lincoln ignored the constitutional requirement that Congress "raise and support armies."

None of these measures was much criticized. The nation, after all, was still at a high pitch of patriotism, and Northern editors were daily encouraging high officials to use any means necessary to put down the rebellion. The phenomenal power Lincoln seized during these weeks was a source of wonder to European onlookers. After all, this was a country so suspicious of central power that, for fear of it, a civil war had just broken out. A German diplomat marveled, "One of the interesting features of the present state of things is the illimited power exercised by the government. Mr. Lincoln is, in that respect, the equal, if not the superior, of Louis Napoleon."

The only measure that aroused controversy in these first weeks—and continues to do so today—was Lincoln's suspension of the safeguard of civil liberties written into the Constitution: the writ of *habeas corpus*. It was this rule that, since Anglo-Saxon times, had prevented arbitrary imprisonment. Without it, the military could arrest anyone suspected of aiding the enemy and hold him indefinitely without bothering to bring charges. On April 27, Lincoln suspended *habeas corpus* on the military line between Philadelphia and Washington. It was a secret, however, and drew no outcry from Lincoln's critics until, in the early morning of May 25, John Merryman, a wealthy secessionist and lieutenant in the Maryland militia who had had a hand in burning the bridges after the Baltimore riot, was dragged from his bed and thrown into prison at Fort McHenry.

Merryman sent a petition for a writ of *habeas corpus* to the United States district court in Baltimore, which, as it happened, was on the circuit of the eighty-four-year-old Chief Justice of the United States, Roger Taney—the proslavery justice who had written the Dred Scott decision in 1857. Taney solemnly issued the writ, which was disobeyed by the commander at Fort McHenry, who produced, not the prisoner, but a short reply that he was under "instructions from the President." The stage was set for a showdown, not only between Taney and Lincoln, but between the judicial and executive branches of the government. On May 28, 1861, in one of the greatest moments of drama in American judicial history, the ancient, dignified Taney approached the courthouse in Baltimore on the arm of his grandson as an admiring crowd opened a path before him. Inside, he slowly read an opinion known as *Ex parte Merryman*, which would serve for the rest of the war as the source document for all who opposed Lincoln's repression of civil liberties. In it, he cited many precedents to argue that the President had usurped the power to suspend the writ of *habeas corpus* from Congress, and usurped "judicial power also by arresting and imprisoning a person without due process of law." Lincoln was taking, he said, "more regal and absolute power over the liberty of the citizen than the people of England have thought it safe to intrust to the Crown—a power which the Queen of England cannot exercise at this day and which could not have been lawfully exercised by the sovereign even in the reign of Charles the First."

In speaking out, Taney worried that he himself might be imprisoned. Lincoln did not arrest Taney, but he felt he could not give in to the Chief Justice on this question, and he ignored Taney's opinion—Merryman continued to languish in his cell in Fort McHenry. Taney's opinion, however, was quickly published in newspapers and pamphlets in Baltimore and across the Confederacy. A few members of the Northern Democratic press also took up the issue. The *Cincinnati Daily Enquirer*, for example, protested that the Constitution "is an instrument whose powers can not be enlarged or abridged to meet supposed exigencies at the caprice or will of the officers under it. . . . Exigencies and necessities will always arise in the minds of ambitious men, anxious to usurp power—they are the tyrants' pleas, by which liberty and constitutional law, in all ages, have been overthrown." Complaining about Lincoln's unconstitutional enactments and his suspension of *habeas corpus*, *The*

Crisis borrowed Thomas Jefferson's phrase for King George III from the Declaration of Independence, crying, "Is he not a President, 'whose character is thus marked by every act which may define a tyrant, unfit to be the ruler of a free people?'"

In these early months of the rebellion, however, with distrust widespread and fear of traitors rife, the protest lacked heat. In fact, Lincoln was so emboldened by the low political price he paid for this first repression of civil liberties in Maryland that, one month later, on July 2, he stretched the area of suspension of *habeas corpus* to "the vicinity of any military line . . . between the City of New York and the City of Washington," and in October he stretched it all the way to Bangor, Maine. Along the line, due process of law was voided and military power ruled. And this new "line" was ill defined. It ran between places far apart on the map, and included a large percentage of the population.

It was only later in the war that the opposition press would voice sustained outrage over the loss of freedoms. For now, Lincoln's most important critics on this issue were in Congress. They ratified Lincoln's emergency orders grudgingly, on the last day of the special July 4 session of Congress. Even then, the ratifying provision had to be sugar-coated by tucking it away as a "rider" in a popular bill increasing soldier pay. Also, there was an important exception to Congress' late show of support: despite a whopping two-thirds Republican majority in both Houses, Lincoln's suspension of the writ of *habeas corpus* was not mentioned in the approval. Opposition had come, not only from all the Democrats and Border State congressmen, but also from Republicans unwilling to concede Lincoln's encroachment on what had always been a Congressional power. Senator Trumbull, from Lincoln's own state of Illinois, spoke for many: "I am not disposed to say that the Administration has unlimited power and can do what it pleases, after Congress meets."

* * *

The controversy was muted, however, because while Congress debated, huge armies were gathering for battle—despite the fact that, in mid-July, when the three-months troops Lincoln had called up on April 15 were ready to go home, they were still little more than an armed rabble, woefully unready to attack.

From the beginning, Lincoln had been the Commander-in-Chief of a halting, creaking war machine. The unmilitary chief of an unmilitary nation, he had privately sworn on April 21—after the national humiliation of promising

Mayor Brown he would detour troops around Baltimore—that it was the last time he would interfere in military concerns. He gave over army matters entirely to General Scott. Lincoln was open about his martial naiveté. At an early meeting with his generals, when Seward admitted that he and Lincoln didn't understand the technical terms for fortifications, Lincoln piped up, "That's so, but we understand that the *rare* rank goes right behind the front!"

Without leadership from Lincoln, military matters immediately became confused. On April 22, Hay overheard Chase telling Lincoln, "All these failures are for want of a strong young head. Everything goes in confused disorder. General Scott gives an order, Mr. Cameron gives another. Half of both are executed, neutralizing each other." Indeed, Cameron was an unfortunate choice for Secretary of War. He was a weak reed—a poor administrator, easily overwhelmed. Visitors to the Secretary found him evasive, his office aimless and cluttered. General-in-Chief Winfield Scott was unsteady as well, immobilized by vertigo, gout, and chronic fatigue and edema from what was probably congestive heart failure—the inroads of age and gluttony on his six-foot-four, three-hundred-pound body. He frequently dozed off at meetings, and could no longer mount a horse. When the old general rode to the White House for a conference, Lincoln frequently came down to the driveway and stood beside his buggy to spare him the pain of climbing the stairs.

Lincoln's situation was further complicated by the poor financial condition of the national government. The treasury was empty. There was no national bank, no national currency. The sprawling economy, with its myriad local banks, was not suited for huge national projects. There had been no Federal taxes for thirty-five years. Americans were not used to paying them, and a new tax would have crippled the war spirit. Lincoln, without a treasury, without an army, and without laws adequate to create them, was forced to fall back on the vigor of the individual states to raise, officer, and equip the 75,000 troops he had called up.

The troops that answered the emergency call of April 15 could, by an antique law, serve for only three months. Those months—May, June, and July—saw a jumbled, uncoordinated effort by the Northern governors to improvise an army many times larger than had ever been fielded in the nation's history. They labored in the face of chronic shortages, waste, and delay, and with little help from Secretary Cameron and his miniscule staff. Soon-to-be-general Oliver Otis Howard complained that during June and July "no one seemed to know what was to be done or what could be done." Lincoln, in fact, made matters worse by authorizing, willy-nilly, new regiments pressed by ambitious men, with no thought for the War Department's losing battle with logistics. James Wadsworth, a wealthy New Yorker who had come to Washington to seek an officer's commission, bemoaned the confusion Lincoln wrought: "[T]he Government is weak, miserably weak at the head. The President gets into at least one serious scrape *per diem* by hasty, inconsiderate action. While I was there he accepted X_____'s regiment and regretted it an hour later."

The federal government was exposed for the poor power it was. Muskets, uniforms, blankets, tents, and medical equipment were in short supply. Even when orders had been written and contracts signed, arms and provisions were slow to arrive. Recruits were ill-fed, ill-clothed, and ill-housed. Camps were improvised. There was a lack of facilities, equipment, weapons, kitchens, even military plans. Out of a desire not to provoke Southerners and Border State men, no warlike preparations had been made, not even for the security of the capital. Some recruits were installed in public buildings, others in camps located without regard for defense or drill.

When, by the middle of May, Washington was secure, Lincoln was pressed with the problem of what to do next. His April 15 call for troops had announced that "the first service assigned to the forces hereby called forth will probably be to re-possess the forts, places, and property which have been seized from the Union," and on the afternoon of April 25, after the arrival of the 7th New York regiment, Lincoln repeated to Hay that his plans were to "provide for the entire safety of the Capital . . . and then go down to Charleston and pay her the little debt we are owing her." But this pipe dream soon evaporated.

Instead, General Scott, meaning to avoid a long, bitter struggle by limiting the horrors of war, revealed on May 3 a plan that would "envelop the insurgent States and bring them to terms with less bloodshed than by any other plan." Instead of an invasion, Scott proposed to rely on "the sure operation of a complete blockade of the Atlantic and Gulf ports," along with "a powerful movement down the Mississippi to the ocean" with a fleet of gunboats supported by soldiers, undertaken in November, when the weather was cool and the troops were trained. Thus surrounded, the rebel government would suffocate and finally surrender. This method would take a long time to work, and the thrust would be in the West, while the eastern army stood on defense. Scott saw that this last piece would not be popular in the teeming East, and that his plan's greatest obstacle would be "the impatience of our patriotic and loyal Union friends. They will urge instant and vigorous action, regardless, I fear, of consequences."

In this, Scott proved a great prophet. Newspapers scoffed at the slowness of his scheme, calling it the "Anaconda Plan." In fact, Lincoln had already heard the first note of impatience as soon as troops started stepping off the trains at the Washington depot. Almost before the first arrivals could throw down their bedrolls in the Capitol building, the popular view was that Lincoln was not doing enough to subdue the rebellion. On May 1, two eminent Massachusetts abolitionists, Senator Henry Wilson and Judge Rockwood Hoar, called on Lincoln and every member of the Cabinet, urging aggressive fighting. On their heels, radicals Ben Wade and Zachary Chandler assailed Lincoln, "hot for war," according to a witness. They spoke for millions in the North who, out of jingoism, impatience, and military ignorance, were weary of "drift" and infatuated with the fantasy of crushing treason with a single blow.

To the war lovers in Congress and the millions at home cheering their boys off at train stations across the North, Lincoln seemed to be dragging his feet. *Hostile campfires flickering every night on the Arlington Heights? Well, go get the traitors and hang them!* The prickly Count Gurowski grumbled in his diary:

> Instead of boldly crushing . . . instead of striking at the traitors, the administration is continually on the lookout where the blows come from, scarcely having courage to ward them off. The deputations pouring from the North urge prompt, decided, crushing action. This thunder-voice of the twenty millions of freemen ought to nerve this senile administration. The Southern leaders do not lose one minute's time; they spread the fire, arm, and attack with all the fury of traitors and criminals.
>
> The Northern merchants roar for the offensive; the administration is undecided.

To many, Lincoln was yet again proving himself hopelessly unready. New York Senator Preston King thought him "not only unequal to the present crisis, but to the position he now holds at any time." Consul to Paris John Bigelow, after listening to Lincoln discuss military matters for half an hour, came away struck by

> *a certain lack of sovereignty.* He seemed to me . . . like a man utterly unconscious of the space which the President of the United States occupied that day in the history of the human race, and of the vast power for the exercise of which he had become personally responsible. This impression was strengthened by Mr. Lincoln's modest habit of

disclaiming knowledge of affairs and familiarity with duties, and frequent avowals of ignorance, which, even where it exists, it is as well for a captain as far as possible to conceal from the public.

Edwin Stanton was in harmony with King and Bigelow, blasting "the painful imbecility of Lincoln" in a letter to General John Dix in New York.

The impatient multitude who demanded immediate action, however, had to wait—no move could be made against Virginia, after all, until its people voted to ratify its leaving the Union. And indeed, on May 23, the day the citizens of Virginia voted to secede, the Lincoln administration struck a blow. That night, under a full moon, Union troops ran across two bridges on the Potomac and fanned out over Arlington Heights and Alexandria. They seized a thin swath of Confederate soil against no opposition, with the loss of only one soldier, who, after racing to the roof of an Alexandria hotel to cut down a Confederate flag, was shotgunned by the owner.

That soldier, however, was the young, impetuous Elmer Ellsworth, colonel of New York's colorful Fire Zouaves and a dear friend of the President. News of his loss plunged the nation into mourning. Alexander McClure explained, "public sentiment had at that time no conception of the cruel sacrifices of war. The fall of a single soldier, Colonel Ellsworth, at Alexandria cast a profound gloom over the entire country." Ellsworth's lone sacrifice instantly blew new wind into the sails of the North's ardor for battle. On May 27, New York lieutenant Francis Barlow wrote that the popular impatience for a crushing blow on the rebellion was so great that if Lincoln did not attack immediately, a military dictatorship might replace him. "Already the murmurs of discontent are ocean-loud against the slow and cautious courses of the war," said Barlow.

As the July 4 special session of Congress approached, Lincoln became absorbed in writing his Opening Message, and he depended more and more on General Scott to oversee military preparations. After June 19 he refused visitors so that he could devote himself to the Message entirely. His absence from the military hum caused the many who already considered him a puppet to further discount his influence in affairs. The *New York Herald* flew the headline "Something Wrong in High Quarters," and warned that his "feeble" measures would weaken the Union cause in Europe. At the same time, Horace Greeley was fuming that instead of "energy, vigor, promptness, daring, decision," there was "weakness, irresolution, hesitation, and delay." The troops, he said, were "being demoralized by weeks of idleness."

Greeley's frustration soon boiled over into print. On June 21, the editorial in his New York *Tribune* had a sarcastic bite: "Our soldiers have been requested to fire blank cartridges in all engagements with Southern forces . . . there is no intention to press this suppression of the rebellion . . . we are to run after the old harlot of a compromise." Then, on June 24, a banner flared across the top of its editorial page:

THE NATION'S WAR CRY

Forward to Richmond! Forward to Richmond! The Rebel Congress must not be allowed to meet there on the 20th of July! BY THAT DATE THE PLACE MUST BE HELD BY THE NATIONAL ARMY!"

The banner was reprinted day after day through early July, and the "Forward to Richmond!" cry was taken up in the Northern press, including the *New York Times*. "By no government in the wide world other than this of ours," it ranted, "is treason treated so kindly or rebellion sprinkled with so much rosewater." Even the faithful New York *Evening Post* had finally grown restless, observing, "The whole administration has been marked by a certain tone of languor. . . . We have been sluggish in our preparation and timid in our execution."

Greeley, the editors, the congressmen, and the millions knew nothing of war. William Russell of the London *Times* mocked "the arrogant tone with which writers of stupendous ignorance on military matters write of the operation which they think the generals should undertake." Armies were not made from scratch in a week, or even a season. Winfield Scott, already dead set against an invasion, distrusted the fighting ability of the green volunteers gathering in Washington and continued to counsel delay at least until the soldiers could learn the basic elements of drill and maneuver.

Gurowski scribbled the rebuttal to military men like Scott into his diary: "Strategy—strategy repeats now every imbecile, and military fuss covers its ignorance by that sacramental word. . . . The people's strategy is best: to rush in masses on Richmond." At this early point in Lincoln's presidency, when he lacked the stature to lead, the voice of the people was not something he could ignore. Northern morale must be sustained—by fighting, if necessary.

Everyone knew the Confederate army was busy. Southern recruits were massing in Virginia at Harpers Ferry and the Norfolk naval yard. At Manassas Junction—only thirty miles from Washington—a small army assembled to defend the direct route to Richmond. This rebel mob so near the capital acted on the Northern public like a red flag to a bull. As one general ruefully recalled soon afterward, "The country could not understand, ignorant as it was of war and war's requirements, how it could possibly be true that, after three months of preparation and of parade, an army of thirty thousand men should be still utterly unfit to move thirty miles against a series of earthworks held by no more than an equal number of men." *After all, Andrew Jackson had merely waved his hat, and his rude pioneers had beaten the British at New Orleans!*

*   *   *

So on June 29, Lincoln convened a Cabinet meeting in his library to hear a plan of attack presented by Brigadier General Irvin McDowell, a protégé of Secretary Chase and a favorite of Radical Republicans. Unsurprisingly, it was the Radicals' plan: a quick march to hit the rebels where they were. Lincoln approved it.

The jump-off was scheduled for July 9, but was delayed because of a lack of horses and mules to pull the wagons. When McDowell's army of some 30,000 finally lurched into motion on July 16, there were only enough wagons for ammunition and ambulances. There was no cavalry to scout ahead, no staff to provide information, and no good maps to guide the officers through the dense woods. The men, unused to discipline, treated the march like a lark, halting to fill their canteens when they crossed a stream and deserting their columns to pick blackberries whenever they got hungry.

Once McDowell's men arrived in front of the rebels on July 18, it took three days before the real fighting started. On the day of the battle, July 21, Washingtonians hurried down to the battlefield—either in their carriages and buggies or on horseback—and spread out their blankets and baskets to enjoy a Sunday picnic while they watched the stirring spectacle of Union victory. When the cannon roared, one lady with an opera glass within earshot of William Russell exclaimed, "That is splendid. Oh, my! Is not that first-rate? I guess we will be in Richmond this time tomorrow."

Things did not remain splendid. The thousands of Union soldiers who had been up all night marching around the enemy left flank were exhausted by the time the fighting began. The combat was prolonged, confusing, and often waged at very close quarters. The afternoon was waning when late-appearing rebel reinforcements reached the field. A rout ensued as the tired, panic-stricken Union soldiers pushed their way through the debris of battle amid the heat, dust, noise, and confusion. Then it started to rain, and the mob of refugees surged back toward the capital like the rush of a great river, soaked and streaked with the clay of the roads, throwing away knapsacks, belts, canteens, blankets, coats, and muskets. By the next morning, the residents of Washington awoke to find the beaten, footsore, mud-caked soldiers sleeping in the dripping rain—on the steps of houses, by basements or fences, on sidewalks, and in vacant lots.

As the wires carried news of the casualties from the battle of Bull Run across the North, citizens were horrified as the figures rose to 5,000 killed, wounded, and missing for both sides. Americans had never lost so many men in any battle in its history—this was closer to the losses in the entire War of 1812 or the entire Mexican War. Recriminations after the bloody debacle were many and fierce. The Richmond *Enquirer*, of course, knew right where to put the blame: "Of these men Abraham Lincoln is the murderer. We charge their blood upon him. May the Heavens, which have rebuked his madness thus far, still battle his demon designs."

From Washington, Stanton wrote to Buchanan:

> The imbecility of the Administration culminated in that catastrophe—an irretrievable misfortune and national disgrace never to be forgotten are to be added to the ruin of all peaceful pursuits and national bankruptcy as the result of Lincoln's "running the machine" for five months. . . . The capture of Washington seems now inevitable . . . . While Lincoln, Scott, and the Cabinet are disputing who is to blame, the city is unguarded and the enemy at hand.

Stanton guessed that it would not be long "until Jeff Davis turns out the whole concern."

Radical Senator Ben Wade of Ohio, too, sneered at Lincoln's haplessness, saying, "I do not wonder that people desert to Jefferson Davis, as he shows brains; I may desert myself." Illinois Senator Lyman Trumbull judged that Lincoln was "not equal to the occasion"; he lacked "positive action." The *New York Herald* blamed the loss on the abolitionists, but rebuked Lincoln for weakness and for trusting "everything to his Cabinet, to his party and to Providence." He must, insisted the *Herald*, "cease to be the politician, and perform the duties of the statesman." Among those who blamed Lincoln for pushing the recruits prematurely into battle was General Scott, albeit in a backhanded way. "Sir," Scott said to Lincoln, "I am the greatest coward in America. . . . I deserve removal because I did not stand up, when my army was not in condition for fighting, and resist it to the last." Lincoln immediately perceived the slight, saying, "Your conversation seems to imply that I forced you to fight this battle." Scott declined to pursue the subject further.

Greeley, wracked by guilt for his heavy hand in ordering the advance from the pages of the *Tribune* and fearing the Union irrevocably gone, sobbed

Privately distributed, July or August, 1861

"Comedy of Death." Lincoln is a harlequin onstage with generals as toys.

mightily to Lincoln in a letter dated "Midnight" for dramatic effect: "You are not considered a great man, and I am a hopelessly broken one."

*   *   *

For most, a grim new realism dawned. As the three-months men went back to their homes, a new dedication grew up in the North, a new resolve to take firmer steps to crush the rebellion. The Chicago *Tribune,* which earlier had predicted a short war, blew a new trumpet: "If this is to be a war of years instead of months, so let it be." The debacle at Bull Run, however, signaled the end of the solidarity brought on by the war fever, and the end of the gala period that Lincoln had enjoyed before the defeat. One editor foreshadowed a new peace movement when he wrote to Seward on August 9, after making a tour of the North: "There is no longer observable that feeling of unanimity in support of the Administration . . . or that confidence in the war and its ultimate issue, which pervaded the popular heart a few weeks ago. . . . There is an anti-war party slowly but surely forming all over the North."

There was a different group in the North, however, whose members were glad of a good blood-letting. Indeed, they believed that the defeat at Bull Run had helped their cause, since if the war became drawn out and bitter, either the United States must be destroyed or slavery must die. Massachusetts Senator Charles Sumner wrote to abolitionist Wendell Phillips that "our defeat was the worst event & the best event in our history; the worst, as it was the greatest present calamity & shame,—the best, as it made the extinction of Slavery inevitable. Be hopeful. I am. Never so much so."

Chapter 18

The Rise of the Radical Republicans

"Thus Mr. Lincoln is deserted by his party."

Presidents in Abraham Lincoln's time were seldom heard from. After a President's inaugural address, his statements usually came only once a year—in the Annual Message to Congress, the precursor of the State of the Union address, delivered on the first Monday of December at the opening of the congressional session. The bombs bursting in April of 1861, however, compelled Lincoln to call a special session of Congress for July 4, and his eighty-day dictatorship in the interim obliged him to formally ask Congress to authorize his unconstitutional acts.

More than that, though, Lincoln's July Message to Congress was needed to define the nation's war aims. Outrage over Fort Sumter was universal, but many in the North were like Nathaniel Hawthorne, who wrote to a friend in May, "Though I approve the war as much as any man, I don't quite understand what we are fighting for, or what definite result can be expected." Northern loyalty was fragmented. It was a time when a man's patriotism rested with his own state, or, at farthest, his own section. In the South, the defense of slave property and the dread of invasion had submerged state rivalries and quickly made that section a unified nation with the single aim of self-preservation. In the North, however, there were a variety of war aims in the several sections, and there was danger that the national good might be obscured by local prejudices. The Yankees of New England would fight to free the slaves and to maintain the mercantile system that had worked so strongly to their advantage as the manufacturing center of the country. The frontiersmen of the Far Northwest, however, cared little for the preservation of New England's mercantile power, and even less for the freedom of black men who would compete with them as settlers; but they would fight to expand their influence into the territories of the West. The farmers of Illinois, Indiana, and Ohio, where neither abolitionism, nor mercantilism, nor freedom of the West had any strong appeal, would fight for the Union tradition. The men in the Border States would fight only for the

Union with slavery intact. The immigrant wage slaves in the teeming cities of the Eastern seaboard would fight only for pay.

Lincoln's Message was needed to cement the Northern war purpose, but also to cement his party. Now that the exodus of southern Democrats had left the Republicans in charge, the business of governing exposed a chasm between the two wings of the Republican Party: the conservatives, who prized the Union above all; and the Radicals, who pressed for ending slavery and punishing the rebels.

*   *   *

The Radicals despised Lincoln. The easy-going, joke-telling, live-and-let-live man in the White House could never be one of them.

The Radical Republicans in these early war months must have pinched themselves in disbelief over their good fortune. Before Fort Sumter, they had been a small splinter group, scorned as shrill abolitionists. They had been easily pushed aside by the big men, the Southern Democrats. Then the outbreak of the war had vaulted them into the vanguard of a nation that was suddenly at war with slaveholders, and the vacant desks of the Southern Democrats in Congress had left them—as the most unified and passionate bloc—in control of both Houses.

The Radicals in Congress were battlers, happy only when they were storming a castle. They were stern, imposing, impatient, intolerant, unyielding, and utterly humorless. They were provincials—almost all were born and raised in New England, or descended from New Englanders—and they took strength from their ignorance of the wider world. Although never a majority, they derived power beyond their numbers from their talent and their devotion to a solid front. In the Senate, they were led by men who headed the powerful committees that shaped war legislation:

- Ben Wade of Ohio was the chairman of the Committee on Territories. It is a clue to his temper that he had kept a squirrel rifle at his desk on the Senate floor during the previous Secession Winter. "Bluff" Ben's square-jawed, clean-shaven face showed his combativeness. He had a voice that thundered and little black eyes that blazed. Fellow Republican and former law partner Joshua Giddings wrote that Wade "denounced the President as a *failure* from the moment of his election and began to lay his plans for his own advancement."

- Michigan's hero, Zachary Chandler, chairman of the Committee on Commerce, was as brawny and fierce as Ben Wade, and he too wielded power like a blunt instrument. He subscribed to Thomas Jefferson's notion that the "tree of liberty must be refreshed from time to time with the blood of patriots and tyrants." Before Sumter, Chandler had welcomed the beckon of war, saying, "Without a little blood-letting this Union will not be worth a rush." Gideon Welles sketched him as "steeped and steamed in whisky— coarse, vulgar, and reckless."

- If Wade and Chandler were the war horses of the Senate Radicals, Charles Sumner, chairman of Foreign Relations, was the show horse. He was the most elegantly tailored man in the Capitol, both in his clothes and in his ideas. Six feet two inches tall, handsome and broad-shouldered, born to Boston money, he typically wore a cape over a maroon vest, with a blue-violet necktie and high silk hat, checkered trousers, and fawn-colored English gaiters. So conscious of his manners that he would not allow himself to slouch even in private, he was as pompous and fastidious in his speech as he was in his appearance.

- The Radicals in the Senate were matched in the House by leaders like the club-footed, knit-browed, "despotic ruler of the House" Thaddeus Stevens, chairman of Ways and Means, who ached to loosen the purse strings of the nation for a war of extermination. Lincoln had provoked Stevens' resentment in March by naming Simon Cameron to sit for Pennsylvania in the Cabinet rather than him, and Stevens was never cordial with Lincoln thereafter.

At first, their differences with Lincoln were not so profound and heated as they would later become. But the day after Lincoln's April 15 call for troops they were already criticizing Lincoln for half-measures, even as they were just beginning to feel their new muscle. Horace Greeley of the New York *Tribune*, the Radical mouthpiece, said that 75,000 troops were not enough—500,000 should have been called. A few days later, after Baltimore's Mayor Brown forced Lincoln to detour troops around his city, the disgusted Ben Wade complained bitterly about the new President's surrender in a letter to a friend, ending ominously, "the stern demand for justice of a united people cannot and must not be baffled by the imbecility or perverseness of one man though he be the President of the United States."

Another rift appeared after Lincoln issued a proclamation on April 19 calling for the blockade on the ports of the South. Thad Stevens ran to the White House to point out that, by international law, Lincoln's call for a "blockade" signaled recognition of the Confederacy as a belligerent nation, not just an insurgency. (The proper legal phrase in case of an insurgency would have been to "close the ports.") Stevens later recalled Lincoln's response:

"Well, that is a fact. I see the point now, but I don't know anything about the law of nations and I thought it was all right."

"As a lawyer, Mr. Lincoln, I should have supposed you would have seen the difficulty at once."

"Oh, well, I'm a good enough lawyer in a western law court but we don't practice the law of nations up there, and I supposed Seward knew all about it, and I left it to him. But it's done now and can't be helped, so we must get along as well as we can."

From then on, whenever Lincoln would call the war an internal "conflict" against insurgents who still deserved the protection of the Constitution, Stevens would point to the blockade, insisting that legally Lincoln had acknowledged the Confederacy as a nation at war, without any protection by the Constitution and therefore subject to the law of nations, which declared *inter arma silent leges*: "in war, anything goes"—just the kind of fight to the death he and the Radicals demanded.

Thus, Lincoln was forced to campaign in May and June on two fronts, as he would throughout the war. While he struggled to build an army and win battles on Confederate soil, he had to work to unify the will of the political leaders in Washington at the same time. As he summoned the Army of the Potomac from the hamlets of the North and faced them toward Bull Run, he labored alone to handwrite the forty-odd foolscap pages of his Message to Congress.

*   *   *

In that era Presidents still adhered to the example set by Thomas Jefferson, who had refused to stand in front of Congress, considering such appearances a vestige of English rule, where kings opened Parliament. So, in the Jeffersonian tradition, on July 5 Lincoln sent his secretary to the Capitol with his Message, and a clerk read it before Congress in a monotone. Lincoln's language was characteristically clear and lawyerly. After reviewing the events of secession and justifying his response, he whittled away at the issues until the vital nub of the conflict was in view:

> [It] embraces more than the fate of these United States. It presents to the
> whole family of man, the question, whether a constitutional republic, or a
> democracy—a government of the people, by the same people—can, or

cannot, maintain its territorial integrity, against its own domestic foes. It presents the question, whether discontented individuals, too few in numbers to control administration . . . can always . . . break up their Government, and thus practically put an end to free government upon the earth. It forces us to ask: "Is there, in all republics, this inherent, and fatal weakness?" "Must a government, of necessity, be too strong for the liberties of its own people, or too weak to maintain its own existence?"

A few found fault with Lincoln's Message. The London *Spectator*'s gun was double-barreled: "Mr. Lincoln writes like a half-educated lawyer, and thinks like a European sovereign." The London *Herald* sang a familiar tune:

We lay down the President's message with a strong feeling of disappointment. It is far from equal to the occasion. Mere awkwardness of style and form we take no account of. The age of cultivated American statesmanship has long passed away. The refined intellect of the United States now shuns political life. It would have been absurd to expect from a man who has passed the best part of his life in the backwoods and the wooden capital of a new State the elegance and lucidity which distinguish the State papers of the first fifty years of the Union.

Closer to home, the *The Crisis* of Ohio charged that the Address' "partisan tone, and sectional principles . . . merit the instant notice and condemnation of every lover of the old constitutional rights of the States, and of all who still hope yet to preserve, and finally restore the old Union, upon the principles of justice, conciliation and peace."

Ohio's arch-Democrat Clement Vallandigham, giddy in his first chance to denounce Lincoln on the floor of the House, was ready with a laundry list of reproaches. He called Lincoln's April 15 call for troops an exercise in "wicked and most desperate cunning." Andrew Jackson, he said, had acted with the authority of Congress, unlike "our Jackson of today, the little Jackson at the other end of the avenue, and the mimic Jacksons around him." Lincoln the usurper, he said, had struck down personal liberty and free speech, and for these "shameless peculations and frauds . . . the avenging hour . . . will come hereafter." Vallandigham was echoed in the Senate by Lazarus Powell of Kentucky, who rose to condemn Lincoln, roaring, "There never was a king, potentate or sovereign, when he was assuming powers that did not belong to him for the purpose of crushing the liberties of his people, who did not do it under the plea of necessity."

But these critics were out of step with the martial tread of the North. Any criticism of Lincoln's Message was damped by the North's new military zeal and the suspense over the army's impending march toward Richmond. Few patriots had the heart to quibble with the President's Address while the thunderheads of the battle at Bull Run approached.

There was also genuine enthusiasm for Lincoln's speech. Gone was the cautious, forbearing tone of the Inaugural. People heard for the first time the clank of metal in Lincoln. His ability to illuminate the fundamental issues of secession, and his forceful account of the events surrounding Sumter and his response to them impressed many, including the recently critical *New York Times* correspondent, who couldn't resist opening with a jab at Lincoln's "obvious faults in style," but went on to praise the Message, saying, "it is evidently the production of an honest, clear-headed and straightforward man," and he credited "its direct and forcible logic and quaint style of illustration." The editor of *Harper's Weekly*, too, signaled a revised view of the rustic Illinoisan: "I can forgive the jokes and the big hands, and the inability to make a bow. Some of us who doubted were wrong."

Radical Republicans, though, scowled in their desks. Why, they asked, on the grand occasion of the first Republican Congress in the history of the nation, was there no mention at all of slavery? Frederick Douglass complained, "Any one reading that document, with no previous knowledge of the United States, would never dream from anything there written that we have a slaveholding war waged upon the Government . . . while all here know that *that* is the vital and animating motive of the rebellion."

For the Message's failure to mention slavery, it was still fashionable to blame the evil influence of Seward, Lincoln's most conspicuous advisor. A disappointed Wendell Phillips told a crowd, "We have an honest President, but, distrusting the strength of the popular feeling behind him, he listens overmuch to Seward." Count Gurowski had complained as early as the previous spring, "Lincoln is under the t[h]umb of Seward; to a degree almost ridiculous, Seward brings him out to take airing as were he Lincoln's nurse." Now, Gurowski voiced the Radical view in his diary entry for August: "Mr. Lincoln in some way has a slender historical resemblance to Louis XVI—similar goodness, honesty, good intentions; but the size of events seems to be too much for him."

*   *   *

Another reason for the sulking among many Republican legislators was wounded pride over the loss of their historical prerogatives. The superiority of Congress over the President was a hallowed tradition, polished by the recent string of lumpish Presidents. The Chief Executive's job had always been to do the will of the legislators, but now suddenly the worm had turned. As Lincoln's Message pointed out, he had already taken all the important emergency measures in the spring; they were by now *faits accomplis*. Congress, not summoned until after war was decided, was now expected to rubber stamp the decrees of this least presidential of Presidents.

The Radicals' first job, as they saw it, was to get back their right to direct the war. From the first gavel on Independence Day, they labored to recapture the war power from the little-regarded President and push their agenda to end slavery and punish the traitors. They began by proposing a Confiscation Act, aimed at taking away the property of anyone who had held office under the Confederacy, or who had taken up arms against the government, or who had aided treason in any way. Little was decided, however, while the nation held its breath for the impending battle in Virginia.

Then, the day after the battle ended in disaster at Bull Run, Kentucky Unionist John J. Crittenden introduced a resolution that stated the war's purpose in bedrock conservative terms: "to preserve the Union with all the dignity, equality, and rights of the several States unimpaired"—that is, to restore the Union, and slavery, as it was. Most Radicals (or "Jacobins," as Lincoln's secretaries liked to call them, after the extreme revolutionary club of the French Reign of Terror) swallowed hard and voted for Crittenden's resolution even though it directly opposed everything they stood for, believing that to object now would divide popular support for the all-out war that they wanted so badly. Old Thad Stevens did take the floor to blister Crittenden's proposal, declaring, "A rebel has sacrificed all his rights. He has no right to life, liberty, or the pursuit of happiness. . . . If their whole country is to be laid waste, and made a desert, in order to save the Union from destruction, so let it be!" Crittenden's conservative resolution, however, was approved almost unanimously.

From this low point the Radicals rekindled their opposition to what they saw as Lincoln's weak and vacillating prosecution of the war. The beacon of the Radicals' ascendancy would be the Confiscation Act. Lincoln had a traditional American horror of any bill that would take private property, but despite that and his distaste for Thad Stevens' ugly threat to make the South "a desert," he did not oppose the act. Lincoln was hands-off with Congress, and would remain so. He had lived his political life in the Whig Party, traditional foes of presidential meddling. Also, Lincoln was still a novice at the presidency and knew it and didn't mind admitting it. His "frequent avowals of ignorance" were what had disgusted John Bigelow in May. (Lincoln had recently provided another example when he remarked to German diplomat Rudolph Schleiden, "I don't know anything about diplomacy. I will be very apt to make blunders.") He was learning the ropes. He was unfamiliar with Wade, Chandler, Sumner, Stevens, and the rest, and didn't want to try a test of wills with those mighty Washington insiders. For their part, each of them thought he was smarter than Lincoln, who still seemed like a good-natured, well-meaning joker. With Lincoln silent, on July 26, the Radicals pushed through their punitive Confiscation Act of 1861, by which the courts could seize any property used for "insurrectionary purposes."

* * *

After Bull Run, the war on the Potomac went quiet and the scene of action passed to the West. There, in Missouri, continued, writ large, the battle that had recently risen in Congress—between conservatives and radicals, between a program of restoring the old Union and a program of abolition and punishment. This dispute would torment Lincoln's entire presidency. In its many forms it would distress him almost as much as the armies of the Confederacy. The furious debate would rise again and again—over the hiring and firing of generals, over military strategy, over emancipation, over the makeup of the Cabinet, and finally over the reconstruction of the nation. The argument would not die down, and the war of words would outlast both the Civil War and Lincoln.

In the summer of 1861, after losing Virginia and saving Maryland, Lincoln saw the necessity of keeping the other Border States, Missouri and Kentucky. This time Lincoln read the feeling in Kentucky rightly. Lincoln knew that conservatism and compromise, the lifelong teachings of Henry Clay, still claimed the heart of opinion there. True, Governor Magoffin was anti-Lincoln: he had rebuffed the President's April 15 call for troops with a vow to "furnish no troops for the wicked purpose of subduing her sister Southern States." But he was not anti-Union: a week later he refused a similar call from Jefferson Davis. Lincoln in April wrote to Kentucky Senator Garrett Davis his friendly assurances "that if Kentucky made no demonstration of force against the United States he would not molest her." He listened patiently to deputations of Kentuckians, kept in touch with Union men by word of mouth, and was careful to confer secretly so his enemies couldn't hang him by a written pledge. When Kentucky officially declared a policy of "neutrality" in mid-May, Lincoln calmly accepted this attitude in the face of fierce resentment from Northern editors who clamored, *Who is not for us is against us!* and *Better an honest traitor than a hypocrite!* Opinion-makers in the North attacked Lincoln for his tenderness with Kentucky. Sabers rattled along the length of the Ohio River as the governors of contiguous Illinois, Indiana, and Ohio all hinted darkly at an invasion. New England's opinion was that of James Lowell, who gnashed his teeth at Lincoln's "Little Bo-Peep Policy" ("let them alone and they'll come home"). Time, however, would bear out Lincoln's wisdom. In mid-September, a Confederate army violated Kentucky's neutrality, and the Bluegrass placed itself shakily under the Union banner.

Lincoln's hand was not as sure in Missouri. In the spring, when all eyes were on the East, when Washington was threatened and when the cry was "Forward to Richmond," Lincoln had been too distracted to concentrate for long on the war on the frontier. Missouri's secessionist Governor Claiborne Jackson was vehemently anti-Lincoln; he had declared the President's call for troops "inhuman and diabolical." Meaning to take the state into the Confederacy, he gathered the state militia just outside St. Louis at "Camp Jackson," and armed them with cannon smuggled upriver from Baton Rouge.

To counter the menace, Lincoln handed off matters there to the scion of one of Missouri's most prominent families, the Blairs. Lincoln was still under the spell of Old Man Blair in Washington, whom he consulted in almost every important decision. It was one of Blair's sons, Montgomery, Lincoln's Postmaster General, whose iron-backed stance had prevailed on Sumter. Now, Lincoln left the defense of Missouri to the other son, Frank Blair, Jr., at forty-one the youngest of the clan and the idol of Missouri Republicans.

It was a bad choice at a bad moment. Frank was a hard drinker, arrogant, headstrong, and excitable, and he chose an equally overzealous military man, the fiery-haired Captain Nathaniel Lyon, to recruit, drill, and lead an army of loyalists based in St. Louis. Neither was one for the patient waiting that was producing slow success in Kentucky. Blair and Lyon struck immediately at Camp Jackson. They succeeded in chasing the secessionists into the woods.

But their rash attack set the state ablaze. Missouri descended into the worst kind of warfare, where neighbor hunted neighbor. By mid-June murderous guerrilla bands roamed across Missouri, leaving behind victims stiffening in the sun with bullets in their heads.

Lincoln knew that to bring order out of the fierce turmoil in the state, he needed a military commander of stature, a man adept in politics as well as in arms. His choice was the favorite of both the Blairs and the Radical Republicans: John Charles Frémont. "The Pathfinder," as he was known, was an erratic, energetic explorer of international renown who had been the first Republican presidential candidate in 1856. Although Frémont was a novice at soldiering, Lincoln was eager to put the illustrious folk hero to use, and eager also for some applause from the Radicals. He made Frémont major general on July 3 and assigned him to command the vast, newly-created Department of the West, which stretched from the Mississippi to the Rockies. Lincoln gave his only instructions to Frémont in the time it took him to walk the general down the White House steps: "I have given you *carte blanche*. You must use your own judgment, and do the best you can." Frémont took Lincoln at his word. No sooner did the new generalissimo arrive in St. Louis on July 25 than he installed himself in an elegant mansion surrounded by Hungarian guards in gaudy uniforms, and began wiring Washington with demands for more men, money, and arms. Within a month he was tangled in a destructive feud with Frank Blair.

Meanwhile, the military situation deteriorated. In late August, threatened by 10,000 rebels reported to be gathering in northern Missouri, overwhelmed by what he called "the tide of rebellion, rapine, and plunder which has literally swept over the State," flouted by Blair and neglected by Washington, Frémont determined on a startling move. Through the night of August 29 and into the morning of August 30, 1861, Frémont composed a proclamation that would bring terror to his foes in Missouri. In the morning, when light broke, he read it proudly to his wife and her friend, who assured him that it was genius and would light his name down through the ages. Frémont issued the proclamation immediately, before any second thoughts could cloud his judgment.

Frémont's proclamation—which reached Lincoln by newspaper—broadcast that all of Missouri was now under martial law, and that Frémont had assumed the powers of the governor. All civilians caught with weapons in their hands would be tried by court-martial and shot if disloyal. Rebels' property in the state would be confiscated—and their slaves would be freed.

Of course! rhapsodized the jubilant Radicals in a common shout. They had been demanding exactly this since April. Many Republican moderates, when they read Frémont's resolve to punish the rebels and free the slaves, admired it too. Frémont instantly became the Republican hero, eclipsing the tardy, indecisive Abraham Lincoln as the standard-bearer of the Republican war effort.

The President was stunned. He knew Frémont's edict was unauthorized by the Confiscation Law passed only the month before, which required that a rebel's loss of property be decided in a civilian court. He wrote the gentlest of letters to Frémont, pointing out that freeing the slaves was certain to undo all his hard work in Kentucky, turning that crucial slave state against the Union, and asked the general kindly to modify the last paragraph. He purred a final soft note: "This letter is written in a spirit of caution, and not of censure."

Lincoln's sweet-tempered nuance got nowhere with Frémont. The general replied that if Lincoln wanted the order reversed, he would have to do it himself—and take the consequences.

*   *   *

Lincoln did. On September 11 he sent a letter to Frémont ordering him to revoke the orders to shoot captured rebels and emancipate slaves.

Radical Congressman George W. Julian of Indiana wrote later that Frémont's proclamation stirred and united the people of the North during its ten days of life far more than any other event of the war. When Lincoln yanked them back to political reality after the heady elation of Frémont's liberation of the slaves, Republicans everywhere were furious. Already tired of the war and alert for a smart stroke that would bring it to a quick end, Frémont had lifted their hopes. Lincoln dashed them. A tempest of revolt shook the party in contempt of his moral authority. Lincoln's own mail was three to one in favor of Frémont. There were widespread prophecies that Frémont, not Lincoln, would be the nominee in 1864. A Cincinnatian wrote to Horace Greeley that if a cheer were hip-hipped for Lincoln there, the response would be a groan. The Germans of St. Louis, fervently antislavery, rallied *en masse* for Frémont.

Elsewhere across the North, Republicans addressed outraged letters to Washington. "It would have been difficult to have devised a plan to more effectually dispirit the People of this section than your order," a Wisconsin man wrote to Lincoln. An Iowan wrote to Seward that Frémont's fate was causing "*extreme* dissatisfaction" there, and predicted volunteering would end in the Northwest. A Connecticut man who had polled friends from four Midwest states told Gideon Welles, "They unanimously condemn the President's letter [overruling Frémont] & as unanimously approve of Frémont's Proclamation." Another spoke for many Radicals: "It is said that we must consult the border states. . . . Now with all due respect . . . , permit me to say damn the border states. . . . A thousand Lincolns and Sewards cannot stop the people from fighting slavery." Cincinnati Judge George Hoadly wrote to Chase:

> My wife expressed the common feeling about Lincoln's letter to Frémont, by saying it seems to her to be the old conflict of Mr. Feeble-Mind and Mr. Ready-to-Halt [Lincoln and Seward] with Mr. Greatheart [Frémont]. I have heard men of sense, such as are called conservative, advocate the wildest steps, such as the impeachment of Mr. Lincoln, the formation of a party to carry on the war irrespective of the President and under Frémont, etc. For myself, I must say that if the letters of Mr. Lincoln to Magoffin and Frémont are any fair indication of his character and policy, I pray God to forgive my vote for him. General Frémont is thus far the favorite of the Northwest, because he has come up to the standard. And if the election were next fall, to displace him would be to make him President.

Even Lincoln's old law partner William Herndon voiced disgust. "Does [Lincoln] suppose he can crush—squelch out this huge rebellion by pop guns filled with rose water?" he grumbled. "He ought to hang somebody and get up a name for will or decision—for character. Let him hang some Child or woman, if he has not Courage to hang a *man.*"

From pulpits in every Northern town poured alleluias for Frémont and tirades against Lincoln. Horace Greeley scolded the President like a schoolchild in the pages of the New York *Tribune*: "Mr. Lincoln and his advisers may not yet be aware of the fact; but there is war in Missouri. A desperate, unscrupulous, bloodthirsty foe is over-running the State . . . Gen. Frémont's policy was simply a matter of military necessity." The editors of Chicago's *Tribune* also hated Lincoln's annulment: "My own indignation is too deep for words," stormed its editor Horace White; "Our Pres has broken his own neck if he has not destroyed his country." Joseph Medill, one of the original engineers of Lincoln's nomination in Chicago, thought this breach of faith was worse than another Bull Run disaster because it took away the penalty for rebellion and left the war "a mere scheme for mutual assassination." "The President's letter to Gen. Frémont has caused a funeral gloom over our patriotic city," Medill wrote to Salmon Chase. Medill would thereafter look to Chase for right-thinking Republican leadership.

The Democratic journals that usually flayed Lincoln after any pronouncement happily laid low during the Frémont imbroglio, savoring the spectacle of the attack on Lincoln by the Radical wing of the Republican Party.

When the *Anti-Slavery Standard* angrily called Lincoln "the unlooked-for assistant of Beauregard and Davis," the Democratic Chicago *Times* editors printed the article without comment.

Most of the high-placed criticism of Lincoln came from Republican leaders who felt betrayed by Lincoln's about-face on slavery. Ben Wade could be counted on to weigh in—and he did, in a philippic to Zack Chandler:

> What do you think of Old Abe's overruling Frémont's proclamation? So far as I can see, it is universally condemned and execrated in the North, and I have no doubt that by it he has done more injury to the cause of the Union by receding from the ground taken by Frémont than McDowell did by retreating from Bull Run. I shall expect to find in his first annual

Frank Leslie's Budget of Fun, November 1, 1861

"Union and Fremont Proclamation." Lincoln—"I'm sorry to have to drop you, Sambo, but this concern won't carry us both!"

message a recommendation to Congress to give each rebel who shall serve during the war a hundred and sixty acres of land. Unless the President shall divest himself of such squeamishness, all the mighty exertions of the North to subdue this rebellion will be paralyzed. . . . The President don't object to Genl Frémont's taking the life of the owners of slaves, when found in rebellion, but to confiscate their property and emancipate their slaves he thinks monstrous. . . . Such ethics could come only of one born of "poor white trash" and educated in a slave State.

Likewise Charles Sumner, in a letter to Francis Lieber:

To me the Presdt's letter [to rescind Frémont's proclamation] is full—too full of meaning. It means that Slavery shall only be touched by Act of Congress *& not through Martial Law*. This weakens all our armies.

The London *Times* is right. We cannot conquer the rebels as the War is now conducted. There will be a vain masquerade of battles,—a flux of blood & treasure & nothing done!

Never has there been a moment of history when so much was all compressed into a little time & brought directly under a single mind. Our Presdt is now dictator, Imperator—what you will; but how vain to have the power of a God if not to use it God-like.

"He is not a genius," said Wendell Phillips of Lincoln. "He is not a man like Frémont, to stamp the lava mass of the nation with an idea." William Lloyd Garrison called Lincoln's action "timid, depressing, suicidal" and accused him of "dereliction" for prolonging the war and subverting the government, an impeachable offense. Lincoln may be 6 feet 4 inches tall, cried Garrison, but he was "only a dwarf in mind." Schuyler Colfax of Indiana predicted that Lincoln's policy would lose the party thousands of votes in the West. When the Pennsylvania Anti-Slavery Society met in late October, Lincoln was compared to Pharaoh.

It was the letter of his Illinois friend, Senator Orville Browning—a man so conservative that he had supported Bates over Lincoln at the convention—that provoked Lincoln's best defense of his part in the Frémont affair. "Mr. President," began Browning,

It is in no spirit of fault finding that I say I greatly regret the order modifying Genl Frémont's proclamation.

That proclamation had the unqualified approval of every true friend of the Government within my knowledge. I do not know of an exception. . . . Its revocation disheartens our friends, and represses their ardor. . . . I am very sorry [your] order was made. It has produced a great deal of excitement, and is really filling the hearts of our friends with despondency. . . . [Frémont] has a very firm hold upon the confidence of the people. . . .

There has been too much tenderness towards traitors and rebels.

We must strike them terrible blows, and strike them hard and quick, or the government will go hopelessly to pieces.

Lincoln's reply was a model of patience, lucidity, and good sense. "Coming from you, I confess it astonishes me," he began, "[t]hat you should object to my adhering to a law [the Confiscation Act], which you had assisted in making, and presenting to me, less than a month before . . . ." As usual, Lincoln cut to the heart of the issue: these matters, he insisted, "must be settled according to laws made by law-makers, and not by military proclamations." Frémont's proclamation, he said, "is simply 'dictatorship.' . . . Can it be pretended that it is any longer the government of the U.S.—any government of Constitution and laws,—wherein a General, or a President, may make permanent rules of property by proclamation?" (On this point, Lincoln would famously change his mind. Exactly one year later, on September 22, 1862, he would make just such a proclamation, known to posterity as the Emancipation Proclamation.) From property, Lincoln turned to policy. To free Missouri slaves would be to lose Kentucky, which, he was convinced, would be fatal. "I think to lose Kentucky is nearly the same as to lose the whole game," he wrote to Browning. "Kentucky gone, we can not hold Missouri, nor, as I think, Maryland. These all against us, and the job on our hands is too large for us. We would as well consent to separation at once, including the surrender of this capitol [sic]."

During the following weeks of September and October, Frémont imprisoned himself in the palace of his empire in Missouri. With *carte blanche* from Lincoln, the Pathfinder surrounded himself with cronies who got rich off contracts granted like boons from a prince. Rumors of scandal became commonplace. It was whispered he was planning to establish a "Northwest Confederacy." The Blairs hardened their opposition to him. At the same time, a mountain of details crushed him. Envoys from Lincoln returned to Washington and shook their heads as they reported his towering ineptitude.

When, on November 2, Lincoln replaced Frémont with General Henry Halleck, a Democrat, he had to weather a new gale of protest. In fact, there was some question at first whether his letter of dismissal would even be obeyed. "The german people have talked about making [Frémont] Dictator," Lincoln's friend Leonard Swett warned from Missouri. "Some of his officers in quite high standing have talked so too." When Frémont did step down, William Cullen Bryant's New York *Evening Post* lamented that Lincoln's decision "smote the community like a loss in battle." New Yorkers massed at the Cooper Union to hear Massachusetts Senator Sumner praise Frémont, and to adopt a resolution glorifying the general and his antislavery stand. The *Cincinnati Gazette* reported that citizens there were pulling portraits of Lincoln from their walls and trampling the face of the President underfoot. A Treasury agent, returning from a tour of the Midwest as far as Iowa, wrote, "I have never seen such excitement, such deep indignant feeling everywhere I have traveled." The Democratic Chicago *Times* laughed and pointed from the sidelines. "[The Republicans'] attitude towards [Lincoln]," it told its readers, "is that of absolute abandonment of his administration . . . . We cannot now count more than two or three republican journals of any prominence which support him cordially . . . . Thus Mr. Lincoln is deserted by his party before he has been a year in office."

*   *   *

In his hundred days in command, Frémont had made himself a champion of the enemies of slavery in the North. He had proclaimed the slaves free in Missouri. Even though that freedom had been only on paper, and even though it had been short-lived, his heroic gesture had heartened crusaders everywhere. It had also accomplished something even more important, and more long-lasting: it had recast the image of the abolitionists and their friends in government, the Radical Republicans. No longer were they perceived as merely a lunatic fringe, a fanatical splinter led by Puritan preachers from New England. The events of the summer and fall of 1861, climaxed by Frémont's short tenure in Missouri, had solidified the antislavery leaders as legitimate patriots. For this to be accomplished, Lincoln—the man of moderation, the man who waited, the man who had to consider all sides, the man who was sworn to uphold the Constitution—had to take a beating in the Republican press and in the halls of power in Washington, the two places where Radicals dominated. The Jacobins were now no longer looked on merely as martyrs and zealots, but full partners in the War of the Rebellion—and they were fully arrayed against the Lincoln government.

Chapter 19

The Phony War of 1861

"We want the President to kill somebody."

I n the fall of 1861, while Lincoln endured the wrath of Frémont's supporters, Northerners began to mutter at the lack of news from the Eastern army. All eyes were again drawn to the banks of the Potomac.

At Bull Run, Northerners had learned that the war could not be won in a rush by an armed gang pushed into battle by headlines in New York. Bull Run taught the country that success would only come by patient attention to strict military principles—and at a high price. So when April's three-month volunteers went home in the days after the battle, they were replaced and exceeded by new men signed up for three years. The hillsides around Washington were bleached with their tents, and the glow of their campfires could be seen from the White House every evening, spangling the twilight. Because the unlucky General McDowell was tainted by the rout at Bull Run, the new army would fight under a new commander.

*   *   *

There was no controversy over who that man would be. By late July 1861, only one Union general had won any battles. These lone victories—small ones, against outnumbered foes, but yet victories—had been won earlier in July in the mountains of western Virginia by Major General George McClellan. McClellan had heralded his tiny triumphs in Napoleonic style, and the Northern press, desperate for any good news and without any reporters on the scene, had printed McClellan's puffed-up versions. The day after the Bull Run battle, Lincoln sent a telegram to McClellan: "Circumstances make your presence here necessary. Charge some other general with your present department and come hither without delay." McClellan was thus summoned to Washington as a savior.

George Brinton McClellan could look back on a life fit for a savior-in-training. He was the son of a prosperous Philadelphia physician, reared in the aristocratic circles of that conservative city, and educated at elite private schools that prepared him for entry into West Point, by special permission, at age fifteen—two years under the minimum age. There he excelled, graduating second out of the fifty-nine members of the Class of 1846. Two months after his graduation, McClellan sailed to the Rio Grande and into the Mexican War. There, at the age of twenty, he sparkled on the engineering staff of General Scott and won renown for his bravery in a battle during which two horses were shot out from under him and a grapeshot broke his sword hilt. In 1855, he was hand-picked by Secretary of War Jefferson Davis to study European armies at first hand. He went to the Continent to study fortifications in the Crimean War, and afterward consulted with high officials, including the emperors of France and Austria. Returning to the United States, he introduced the "McClellan saddle" and saw it adopted by the U.S. Army. In January of 1857, impatient with the slow advancement of an army career, he resigned to become chief engineer of the Illinois Central Railroad. He was hired as president of the Ohio and Mississippi Railroad two years later, and moved to Cincinnati, where he lived when the Civil War began. Within two weeks of the fall of Fort Sumter, he accepted the Ohio governor's offer of the command of the Department of the Ohio, which included the states of Ohio, Indiana, and Illinois, as well as parts of western Virginia and Pennsylvania. In May 1861, he entered the service as a major general, second in rank only to General-in-Chief Scott. After his short campaign in western Virginia in June and July, he received Lincoln's telegram, arrived in Washington on July 26 to a conqueror's welcome, and immediately took command of the nation's supreme field army. He was thirty-four years old.

The Union needed a hero. The new general installed himself at the head of the Washington army amid "one continuous ovation," as he himself described it. McClellan was a Democrat, but even the Radical Republicans were breathless in admiration of his ability and charisma. They adopted him as one of their own. Zack Chandler squired the new general around town as if he had discovered him. Washington, D.C., the nervous little outpost, bowed and curtsied. "I find myself in a new & strange position here," he wrote to his wife the day after he arrived. "I seem to have become *the* power of the land. I almost think that were I to win some small success now I could become Dictator or anything else that might please me . . . ."

McClellan did not disappoint. With his arrival, the ravening and drunken soldiers disappeared from the city streets and were back in their camps. Even that great grumbler, Count Gurowski, noted, "For the first time since the armaments, I enjoyed a genuine military view. McClellan, surrounded as a general ought to be, went to see the army. It looks martial. The city, likewise, has a more martial look. . . . It seems that a young, strong hand holds the ribbons." On August 1 the New York *Tribune* ran the headline "Confidence Renewed" over an article that praised the young general and "the admirable system of discipline that he has put in force."

McClellan's days were a blur of energetic attention to every detail. He held staff conferences after breakfast, then saw visitors and conducted business. In the afternoon he rode out to review troops, inspect camps, and survey the terrain for fortifications, rarely returning before nine or ten at night; then, after another staff conference, he did paperwork until the early morning hours. Often he was in the saddle twelve hours a day, his blouse so sweated through that it bled blue onto his linen shirt.

Always he remained conspicuous. Rather than sleep in a tent among the troops, he rented a house in town across Lafayette Park from the White House. He was a magnificent horseman, and when he rode off to the camps, he galloped through the city streets at the head of a flying column of orderlies and a squadron of cavalry, whose horses' hooves thundered as they kicked up clouds of dust, choking the open-mouthed spectators who poured onto the sidewalks to gape at the pageantry of the daily spectacle. Once arrived in the camps, he rode pell-mell down their length, from the Chain Bridge to Alexandria, holding his cap high in one hand to greet the ovations of the cheering soldiers, who shouted themselves hoarse in fanatical devotion to their "Little Mac."

McClellan oozed ability. His first impression charmed the Washington set in a way that Lincoln never could. Men noticed his grace of movement, his leopard suppleness. "His manner," wrote one who saw him then, "is self-possessed, unaffected, though remarkably self-complacent, with natural dignity and frankness. His talk, to the point, earnest, honest, and intelligent. . . . [T]here is an indefinable air of success about him and something of the 'man of destiny.' He looked like one who always had succeeded and always will succeed." What a contrast to the man in the White House! William Russell remarked on the serenity of his dark blue eye, the firmness of his mouth, the animation of his features. "His voice is sweet, his address affectionate, his manner winning," wrote another who saw him then. McClellan looked every inch the man born to command. His full head of dark hair topped handsome, regular features. Dr. Oliver Wendell Holmes wrote that his perfectly modeled head balanced on "a neck such as not one man in ten thousand possesses," and this on a body "muscular as a prize-fighter's." Even Lincoln's secretaries wrote later, "[I]n everyone, from the President of the United States to the humblest orderly who waited at his door, he inspired a remarkable affection and regard." He was the "idol of Washington drawing-rooms," they said. Already there was frank talk that he would be the next President.

*   *   *

The worship went instantly to McClellan's head, with terrible consequences for the nation. For what was not apparent was that a life of too-easy success and abundant natural gifts had spoiled something at the core of George McClellan. His rearing in an aristocratic family in the conservative upper crust of Philadelphia society had made him caste conscious, always with a sense of his own superiority. At West Point, he had noticed that "In almost every class, those who are gentlemen associate together, and have nothing whatever to do with those forward impudent fellows who never can be gentlemen." "Some how or other," young cadet McClellan admitted, "I take to the Southerners. I am sorry to say the manners, feeling, and opinions of the Southerners are far, far preferable to those of the majority of the Northerners at this place." He shared with the plantation aristocrats their arrogance, their sense of entitlement to command, their contempt for common folk, their tantrums with superiors—attitudes that would be tragically out of place at the head of a great democratic army.

His inbred aristocracy and his sudden idolization by the important men in Washington were pernicious: he refused to consider himself subordinate to either his civilian chief, President Lincoln, or his military one, General-in-Chief Scott. During the fall months of 1861, while he organized and trained his Army of the Potomac, and while he enjoyed a period entirely free from prodding politicians, his combative spirit was turned entirely against his two superiors.

General Scott felt McClellan's jealousy of his authority at once. In his first week, the young general got in the habit of dealing directly with President Lincoln, ignoring Scott in the chain of command. McClellan neglected to consult Scott in making his plans. His letters to his wife Ellen are a chronicle of galloping resentments. Week after week his letters were full of his "war" with his senior. For three months the proud old warrior suffered McClellan's petulant refusal to hear his opinions. Then, finally, on November 1, Winfield Scott, the greatest soldier in the history of the nation between the Revolutionary and Civil Wars, graciously passed the baton to his tormenter and announced his retirement "for reasons of health." Lincoln gave McClellan Scott's title of

General-in-Chief of all the nation's armies, and put him in charge of overall Union strategy. "I can do it all," was McClellan's reply.

Lincoln would quickly learn the painful lesson that it was folly to appease McClellan, who grew more conceited with every accumulation of power. Now that Scott was disposed of, the new General-in-Chief proceeded to cultivate an intense dislike of the President himself. Lincoln was unaware of just how vulgar he seemed to a snob such as McClellan, and how much malignity there was in that snobbery. McClellan was still very much the gentleman from Philadelphia, and his abhorrence of Lincoln's informal manners and country habits was visceral. Among his notes for his memoirs, McClellan wrote that the President "was not a man of very strong character, & as he was destitute of refinement—certainly in no sense a gentleman—he is easily wrought upon by the coarse associates whose style of conversation agreed so well with his own."

Lincoln made the problem worse by deferring to the young general. According to McClellan, Lincoln "liked me personally, and certainly he was always much influenced by me when we were together." He said Lincoln even implied that he, McClellan, was more important to the Union war effort, telling him "they would probably give more for my scalp at Richmond than for his." Lincoln erred in affecting an easy familiarity with the haughty, extremely proper general, calling him "George"—"Is George in?" he would ask, when he came across Lafayette Park to McClellan's headquarters.

Lincoln's habit of coming over unannounced to talk strategy at all hours was an exasperating annoyance to McClellan, who showed his disdain for the President by keeping him waiting. Lincoln arrived one evening when the London *Times'* William Russell was there, and Russell noted his entrance: "a tall man with a navvy's cap, and an ill-made shooting suit, from the pockets of which protruded paper and bundles." Lincoln was told the general was resting, but that he would be informed the President was there to see him. "'Oh, no; I can wait. I think I'll take supper with him,'" Lincoln said, and sat down to wait with the others in the room. "This poor President!" was Russell's reaction. "Trying with all his might to understand strategy . . . . He runs from one house to another, armed with plans, papers, reports, recommendations, sometimes good-humoured, never angry, occasionally dejected, and always a little fussy." Lincoln was sweet-tempered enough to bear the wait with equanimity, but the aides with him steamed at the insult. "A minute passes," remembered one, "then another, and then another, and with every tick of the clock upon the mantel your blood warms nearer and nearer its boiling-point. Your face feels hot and your fingers tingle, as you look at the man [Lincoln], sitting so patiently over there . . . and you try to master your rebellious consciousness."

Perhaps Lincoln would have been less patient if he had been aware of McClellan's sense of superiority, or the fact that the Young Napoleon, in his arrogance, took Lincoln's humility for weakness. McClellan's commentary on the events of these weeks survives in letters to his wife. The letters have the sound of a man who already expected to succeed Lincoln in the presidency, a man who was writing for posterity, saying, in effect, "See what I had to put up with?" McClellan's letters to Ellen, written between his arrival in Washington in late July and hers in December, brimmed with malice and petty conceit:

- "The Presdt is an idiot." (August 16)
- "I am becoming daily more disgusted with this administration—perfectly sick of it. If I could with honor resign I would quit the whole concern tomorrow." (October 2)
- "I can't tell you how disgusted I am becoming with these wretched politicians . . . . The Presdt is nothing more than a well meaning baboon." (October 11)
- "I have not been home for some 3 hrs, but am 'concealed' at Stanton's to dodge all enemies in shape of 'browsing' Presdt etc. . . . I have a set of scamps to deal with—-unscrupulous & false . . . . It is perfectly sickening to have to work with such people & see the fate of the nation in such hands. . . . [I]t is terrible to stand by & see the cowardice of the Presdt, the vileness of Seward, & the rascality of Cameron—Welles is an old woman—Bates an old fool. . . . I am thwarted & deceived by these incapables at every turn." (October 31)
- "It is sickening in the extreme & makes me feel heavy at heart when I see the weakness & unfitness of the poor beings who control the destinies of this great country. . . . I went to the White House shortly after tea where I found 'the original *gorilla*,' about as intelligent as ever. What a specimen to be at the head of our affairs now! . . . I went to Seward's, where I found the 'Gorilla' again, & was of course much edified by his anecdotes—ever apropos & ever unworthy of one holding his high position. . . . I suppose our country has richly merited some great punishment, else we should not now have such wretched triflers at the head of affairs." (November 17)

The tragic flaw of callow America—its worship of the individual, its distrust of authority—was made flesh and played out on an epic scale in the antagonism between the Union's main actors, Abraham Lincoln and the fiercely insubordinate George McClellan. For a while, McClellan patronized his Commander-in-Chief. His sneering attitude at first expressed itself in amusement at the unmilitary Lincoln's quaint presumption. General Samuel Heintzelman described a strategy meeting in McClellan's map room during which Lincoln pointed to a map and made "remarks, not remarkably profound, but McClellan listened as if much edified." Heintzelman said that afterward McClellan saw the President out, "& as he pushed the door to, looking back said, 'Isn't he a rare bird?'"

Two days later, however, McClellan's amusement had turned to disdain. On the evening of November 13, Lincoln, Seward, and Hay went to McClellan's, and, finding him absent, decided to wait in the parlor. About an hour later, McClellan returned home from a wedding, and was told the President was waiting to see him, whereupon, according to Hay, McClellan "went up stairs, passing the door of the room where the president and Secretary of State were seated. They waited about half-an-hour, and sent once more a servant to tell the General they were there, and the answer coolly came that the General had gone to bed." Hay resented this blatant snub as "the unparalleled insolence of epaulettes," and warned, "It is the first indication I have yet seen of the threatened supremacy of the military authorities."

No issue was bigger, in this era of violent suspicions, than supremacy of the military authorities. It hinted at a military coup. The politicians distrusted the generals, and the generals distrusted the politicians. The hopes and fears of both groups hinged on control of Lincoln—vested by the Constitution with authority over each, in his twin capacities as Commander-in-Chief and Chief Executive—and, because the Railsplitter was perceived by both sides as weak and indecisive, each side badgered him mercilessly with pleas and threats. Lincoln was particularly easy to criticize. He was a man of moderation, impenetrable in his thinking and at the same time open to suggestion. No matter which side his policy favored, the other would accuse him of a shameful surrender. The Radical Republicans, as the group most eager to see the rebels scattered and punished, were the most vehement politicians, and so the battle for supremacy—and the tug-of-war over Lincoln—was most desperate when the commanding general was a Democrat, as McClellan was.

McClellan hated the Radical Republicans. "The Radicals had only the negro in view, & not the Union," he wrote later. "They cared not for the results, knew little or nothing of the subject to be dealt with, & merely wished to accomplish a political move for party profit, or from sentimental motives." McClellan was adamant that the war's purpose should remain the Democrats' purpose: the restoration of the Union as it was, with slavery intact. He had been educated at West Point, an institution that emphasized the science of military engineering and fortifications. He was well read in the strategic theories of Baron Henri Jomini, the Swiss interpreter of the Napoleonic military art. To such men, war was an elaborate game of vectors and concentrations, best left to professionals; interference by politicians led to holocausts like the French Revolution. McClellan's profound contempt for politicians only deepened during the months he made his headquarters in Washington, which he came to refer to as "that sink of iniquity." Certainly he liked the Radicals, those craven lurkers in the halls of power, less than his aristocratic friends at the gentleman's club at West Point, many of whom were now leading Confederate troops.

Other West Point-educated officers felt the same. Because the military academy required that each new student be appointed by a congressman, in an era when Democrats dominated, West Pointers were overwhelmingly conservative Democrats like McClellan. They were distrustful of any Republican administration, especially one whose departments were shot through with disloyal personnel. They were disgusted by the orgy of greed, corruption, and waste in the War Department, and contemptuous of Lincoln's free way of handing out general's stars to politicians—amateurs, such as John C. Frémont—whom the militarily naïve President had lifted directly from civilian life into high rank, and who were now barking orders to the West Pointers, men with a lifetime of training and service.

The West Point men had another cause to resent Lincoln. He had insulted their patriotism in his July 5th Message to Congress, wherein he had pointed out, "Not one common soldier or common sailor is known to have deserted his flag," but, in contrast, "in this, the government's hour of trial, large numbers" of army and navy officers "have resigned and proved false to the hand which had pampered them . . . ." *Yes*, thought the West Pointers, *one third of the U.S. Army's 1,108 officers had deserted to the South—they had gone with their states, as any gentleman would do. And why no praise for those that remained?* The officers felt that Lincoln's insult was the cheap appeal of a demagogue for popular approval, and that by impugning their patriotism he had undercut their authority and damaged the army's discipline.

The Radicals cheered Lincoln's stab at the officers. For them, the Democratic gentleman's club at West Point was too chummy. This was at the heart of Republicans' distrust of McClellan and the other West Pointers at the tip of the Union spear. The Radicals doubted that such men had the desire to fight their high-bred mess hall pals at the head of the Confederate armies. Ben

Wade went on record as saying that West Point turned out false, ungrateful men; it was "aristocratical" and "exclusive." Zack Chandler swore that West Point had recently hatched more traitors than in all history since Judas Iscariot, and not all of them had gone South. Republicans were especially nervous about officers' talk of making McClellan dictator.

* * *

Now, as the weeks grew chill and the forests went gold and red, the army still squatted in its camps. McClellan's genius for organization and training had wrought the most splendid army the continent had ever seen. It had grown to 150,000 men, and had been drilling non-stop for three months. But, as Attorney General Bates had confided to his journal as early as September 30, "We absolutely need some dashing expeditions. The public spirit is beginning to quail under the depressing influence of our inaction." People expected the army to deliver quick, hard blows against the rebels, and here were the Confederate Stars and Bars still fluttering from Virginia hilltops maddeningly close to the capital city.

McClellan would not move because, by a trick in his psyche, at the same time he thought he was superior to the President, he thought he was inferior to the enemy. The second conviction depended on the first: on October 31, the same day that he complained to his wife about the "incapables" in the government and "the cowardice of the President," he wrote to the Secretary of War that the rebels facing him were 150,000 men "well drilled and equipped"—which was three times their actual number. His thinking seems to have been the same as Count Gurowski's, who had earlier grumbled into his diary, "They do it differently on the other side of the Potomac. There the leaders are in earnest." McClellan, like Gurowski, was convinced that the South was always one step ahead of the North, and his belief was built on his fixed faith in the aristocracy. The plantation aristocrats—the gentlemen—would always be better equipped, better drilled, better disciplined. They would naturally be better prepared for war than the "gorilla" in the Oval Office.

Men of McClellan's breeding had only scorn for the vulgar crowd in Washington who had been lifted into power by the muddy-booted democracy. A hundred times better was the South, where Jefferson Davis had been named President by the acclamation of his elite peers, as George Washington had been. A comparison between Davis and Lincoln was an embarrassment to the latter. Davis had been educated at West Point. Davis had been a hero in the Mexican

War. Davis had been Secretary of War under Franklin Pierce. Surely *he* knew how to raise an army and win a war. Even the arch-Republican New York *Tribune* admitted that Davis was "commonly presumed the abler of the two; he is certainly the better grammarian." The little children in Virginia sang the song:

> *Jeff Davis rides a snow-white horse;*
> *Abe Lincoln rides a mule.*
> *Jeff Davis is a gentleman;*
> *Abe Lincoln is a fool.*

Haunted by the feeling that his own Commander-in-Chief was too inept to provide him with resources that the vastly superior enemy certainly enjoyed, McClellan persisted in thinking he was outnumbered throughout his career at the head of the Army of the Potomac. There was no one to argue with him—in the Civil War, all intelligence was gathered by the army, none by the tiny government in Washington.

By October the Radicals were chafing at McClellan's delay. The weather was fine and cool, the roads hard and dry. Why was there no advance, no battle? Horace Greeley forgot the lessons of the summer and began to reprise his cry of "On to Richmond!" in the columns of the *Tribune*. By mid-October Zack Chandler had lost faith in McClellan, growling, "He seems to be devoting himself to parades & military shows instead of cleaning the country of rebels." McClellan had foreseen their impatience, and in a meeting with Lincoln on October 10 had extracted a promise. "I intend to be careful and do as well as possible," the general said. "Don't let them hurry me, is all I ask."

Lincoln replied, "You shall have your own way in the matter, I assure you."

While McClellan dashed along his lines and enjoyed the display of his troops, the Confederates went to work building batteries on the banks of the lower Potomac, which scared off sea traffic and effectively blockaded the capital. It was an embarrassment to the nation, and the complaints of the Radicals grew to a wail, especially after the bloody calamity at the Battle of Ball's Bluff on October 21. The battle was a nasty, mismanaged affair on the Virginia bank of the upper Potomac thirty miles above the capital, and it cost the life of Lincoln's dear friend Colonel Edward Baker, who was cut down along with scores of his men, many of them shot in the back as they frantically tried to swim across the river to safety. The bodies washed against the pilings of the Washington bridges for days, and the Radicals, who had started to gather for the opening of the December session of Congress, seethed. Chandler despaired of the "timid, vacil[l]ating and inefficient" Lincoln government. Wade called Lincoln a "fool," and snorted, "You could not inspire Old Abe . . . with courage, decision and enterprise, with a galvanic battery." Even inside the Cabinet there was concern. Attorney General Bates lamented, "It is now evident that the Adm[inistratio]n has no system—no unity—no accountability—no subordination." Secretary of War Cameron was throwing up his hands, asking, "What shall we do? Neither the President nor I know anything about military matters."

Five days after Ball's Bluff, the Radicals descended on Lincoln. "This evening the Jacobin Club, represented by Trumbull, Chandler, and Wade, came up to worry the administration into a battle," wrote John Hay in his diary; "The wild howl of the summer is to be renewed." Complaining that the war was bogging down, they demanded an advance—*a defeat could be no worse than a delay!* Lincoln put them off, and a frustrated Chandler explained the country's paralysis to a friend: "Lincoln means well but has no force of character. He is surrounded by Old Fogy Army officers more than half of whom are downright traitors and the other one half sympathize with the South." Lincoln antagonized the Jacobins by remaining steadfastly on the side of McClellan. He met with the general to warn him that he must consider the rising tide of restlessness, but ended by telling him, "You must not fight until you are ready."

So more weeks passed. By November 20, when McClellan staged a giant review of 70,000 troops—the grandest yet—on a vast Virginia field, reports of the neat regiments arrayed in their straight rows no longer delighted the Northern people. Now, they snickered at the daily bulletin from the capital: "All quiet on the Potomac." Belief in McClellan was beginning to slip away.

*   *   *

People's confidence in the government as a whole dwindled as well. In late November a group of distinguished Bostonian visitors who called at the White House came away saddened, one saying of Lincoln, "We have seen it in his face: hopeless honesty; that is all." His companion was Julia Ward Howe, who had just days before written the lyrics to "The Battle Hymn of the Republic" in her hotel room. She wrote how Lincoln told them he had "heerd" a good story, and she observed that with the war dragging on, few had faith in their President: "The most charitable held that he meant well." British author Anthony Trollope, visiting Washington at the time, described a scene of melancholy, a city of downcast faces, "with that sort of indifference which arises from a break down of faith in anything." Even Lincoln himself, attending a concert in the White House by the popular abolitionist Hutchinson family singers, looked worn-out and dejected. Twice during the performance he closed his eyes in exhaustion.

Then came more bad news for Lincoln. On November 25, Secretary of War Simon Cameron released his annual report to Congress. Already widely distrusted for his corruption, Cameron's stunning inadequacy at the War Department had made him the most despised member of the cabinet. With his practiced eye on the political weather vane, he had recognized the coming strength of the Radicals, and he attempted to save his job by joining them. He included a paragraph in his report urging that captured slaves be used as soldiers, which went far beyond the Confiscation Act passed in the summer session. He sent a copy of his report to Lincoln on November 30, but Lincoln, with characteristic inattention to the business of the Cabinet, didn't look at it. Taking Lincoln's silence for approval, Cameron mailed his report to postmasters for release to newspapers with Lincoln's forthcoming Annual Message to Congress. Too late, Lincoln discovered his slip. He immediately ordered that all copies of Cameron's report be seized, with a new paragraph to replace the inflammatory one. Some copies of the original had already reached the press, however, and were widely reprinted. Lincoln was forced to publicly repudiate Cameron's provocative idea, and Radicals were incensed at the President for blocking another blow at slavery. One of Lincoln's earliest supporters, editor C. H. Ray of the Chicago *Tribune*, voiced the depth of outrage at this newest betrayal, writing, "Old Abe is now unmasked, and we are sold out."

On the heels of this came even more bad news. In November, two Confederate diplomats, Mason and Slidell, had run the sea blockade and were on their way to Europe on a British ship, the *Trent*, when it was overtaken and boarded by a zealous Union naval officer, who forcibly dragged the two diplomats off the ship and imprisoned them in Boston harbor. At the news, every super-patriot went wild with joy. The British ambassador in Washington, Lord Lyons, spoiled the celebration when he presented a formal demand that the United States apologize to Britain and release the prisoners or prepare for war. Lincoln, with no military successes to his credit and with the Radicals still fuming over the Frémont debacle, was faced with an international crisis that threatened war with the mighty British at the same time as the rebellion. In the end, the Lincoln government prudently backed down and released the two Confederate envoys.

The international embarrassment of a retreat before the British ultimatum, however, added fuel to the Radicals' ire. As Congress convened, the Radicals were in a high fever, spoiling for a fight with the President. Everywhere there was anxiety and discouragement. Lincoln, the nominee of a party that had been founded on antislavery, had twice denied slaves the blessings of freedom in the first fall of the war. Pro-slavery Democrats, McClellan and Halleck, were at the head of the two Union armies East and West, and neither appeared anxious to strike a blow against the enemies of the Union. It had been almost eight months since rebels had fired on Fort Sumter, and five months since Bull Run, and neither defeat had been avenged, even though the manhood of the North had leaped to the standard and the governors of the states had stretched every sinew to arm and equip them. Not only was there no action, there was no plan of action. The mood in Congress was represented by Senator Grimes of Iowa, who wrote to his wife, "I reached Washington last night, weary with the journey, and disgusted with . . . the course of the Administration. If the other Northwestern members feel as I do, there will be something more during the coming session than growling and showing our teeth. And, from what I hear, they do feel excited and incensed." In the whispers and murmurings in the corridors of the Capitol were hints that the Radicals were grimly whetting their blades. By bold enactments they would gain control of the war and force emancipation.

* * *

On December 3, 1861, a congressional clerk strode down the aisle of the convened members of both Houses to read Lincoln's First Annual Message to Congress. Those who hoped for a ringing statement of purpose and decision were disappointed. The Message was a loose, rambling laundry list, drifting from topic to topic—the London *Times* called it "ill arranged and worse expressed." Lincoln seemed to want to show that things were business-as-usual with the United States, but his Message succeeded only in advertising a distracted president caught up in mundane details. It had no phrases that would reach across years or inspire multitudes. Nowhere in it was there a signal of energy in winning the war. The *Cincinnati Commercial*'s verdict was typical: "It is not a great State paper. As for its style—enough is said when we observe that Mr. Lincoln certainly wrote it himself. . . . [H]e brings to the aid of the country no such aid as first rate Executive ability." London's *Saturday Review* said the

Message gave "a fair picture of the man—illiterate, narrow-minded, technical, without any definite aim or policy."

In the Message, Lincoln ignored the Radicals; he included not one word to please them. His only mention of emancipation came in a proposal to colonize confiscated slaves abroad. Instead of embracing any part of their ultra-Republican program, he warned against making the war a "violent and remorseless revolutionary struggle," and he told the nation, "We should not be in haste to determine that radical and extreme measures, which may reach the loyal as well as the disloyal, are indispensable."

Thaddeus Stevens reacted violently, sputtering that Lincoln was an untrue and unsound Republican whom the conservative Northwest had foisted on the party. Enraged opposition spread as telegraph wires relayed the Message to the newspapers. Three men who had worked hardest for Lincoln's nomination in Chicago now signaled their loss of faith in him. In New York, Horace Greeley criticized the President's faint-hearted conservatism in the pages of the *Tribune*; the Chicago *Tribune*'s C. H. Ray called Lincoln "reactionary and feeble," adding, "when the time comes, we are ready to oppose Lincoln, the cabinet, McClellan or anybody else"; and Judge Davis washed his hands of his former friend in a letter to his wife, "There is no greatness about him. He is simply a stump speaker."

Other prominent Illinoisans derided Lincoln's Annual Message in letters to their senator, Lyman Trumbull. "Not one single manly, bold, dignified position taken," wrote one, "but a . . . timid, timeserving, commonplace sort of an abortion of a message, cold enough . . . to freeze h-ll over." Another rued of Lincoln, "No man . . . ever threw away so completely, an opportunity . . . to make himself revered, and loved by millions, and to secure to himself a place and a name in history . . . ." "Let the administration continue thus," wrote another, "and the Republican Party would be forever broken and Lincoln 'the most unpopular man in the nation.'" Even more ominous was one that said, "Every one is . . . disappointed at the Presidents course . . . . The first man I met . . . this morning in a rage declared that if a speedy change . . . did not soon occur, he hoped some Brutus would arise and love his country more than he did the President." Trumbull did not contradict them. He had reached the conclusion that Lincoln "lacks confidence in himself and the will necessary in this great emergency."

Abolitionists abused the Annual Message and its author. "What a wishy-washy message from the President," wrote William Lloyd Garrison. "It is . . . evident that he is a man of very small caliber, and had better be at his old business of splitting rails . . . . He has evidently not a drop of anti-slavery blood in his veins." Wendell Phillips denounced Lincoln's failure to mention emancipation as a shameful evasion, crying, "I demand of the government a policy!" to the roar of an Anti-Slavery Society crowd. He belittled Lincoln's honesty by pointing out that "as a pint-pot may be full, and yet not so full as a quart, so there is a vast difference between the honesty of a small man and the honesty of a statesman." In the same vein, the Anti-Slavery Society published a claim that Lincoln was a hypocrite, good for nothing more than a lesson in the danger of half measures. The Society indicted the President with wit and at length:

> A sort of bland, respectable middle-man, between a very modest Right and the most arrogant and exacting Wrong; a convenient hook whereon to hang appeals at once to a moderate anti-slavery feeling and to a timid conservatism practically pro-slavery . . . . He thinks slavery wrong, but opposes the immediate abolition of it; believes it ought to be kept out of the Territories, but would admit it to the Union in new States; asserts the power of Congress to abolish it in the District of Columbia, but would have leave asked of the slave-holders for the exercise of that power; considers slave-catching as a "distasteful" business, but would enforce it by Congressional enactments, not only under but beyond the Constitution's warrant for it; dislikes the slave trade, but is not ready to forbid it between the States; affirms the equality of white men and black in natural rights, but is "not in favor of negro citizenship"; in short, if we rightly understand him, regards impartial justice as a most excellent thing, but as somewhat too fine and costly for everyday wear.

Among the Radicals, Lincoln's respect for moderate sentiments was seen as kowtowing to the Border States. "For the last three months K[entuck]y has been the government," wrote one exasperated critic to Senator Trumbull. "We are paying to[o] much for Kentucky. . . . I hope Mr. Lincoln can leave Washington without making Buchanan's administration respectable." Exasperated, James Lowell demanded, "How many times are we to save Kentucky and lose our self-respect?"

Now that they were again convened in Congress, the Radicals could show their muscle. Gone was the tentativeness of the previous summer, a fact they made clear at once. On December 4, one day after hearing of the President's Annual Message, the House refused to re-adopt the conservative Crittenden

Resolution of July—a sharp denial of Lincoln's go-slow appeal. Notice was served that Congress would make the end of slavery an object of the war. Horace Greeley exhorted the Radicals from his pulpit at the New York *Tribune*: "It is high time that we had either war or peace," he thundered, "and a contest in which we guard and protect our enemies on their most exposed and critical point is not war. It is at best one of those sham fights so current of late on the Potomac."

The army might have been Lincoln's saving grace in these dark days. It carried the fortunes of Lincoln's government on the points of its bayonets. As would be the case throughout the war, a victory in battle, a strategic point captured, even so much as an energetic advance, would more than anything else inspire the Northern people and boost confidence in Lincoln.

McClellan had talked since September of a blow against the Confederate army still camped at Manassas. On his tours of the front lines in the autumn, he would halt his generals, point, and say, "We will strike them there." The grand advance was scheduled for late November. The nation expected it, and the men in Washington, already impatient, demanded it—Zack Chandler told Lincoln that if the army didn't fight a battle before going into winter quarters, he "was in favor of sending for Jeff Davis *at once*." But as the jump-off date for the strike at Manassas approached, McClellan's natural caution crept over him—he was outnumbered, he insisted—and in early December he hatched a new plan. Although the Young Napoleon would not reveal the details of it to Lincoln for many weeks, by his new scheme the army would board ships, sail 120 miles down Chesapeake Bay, and land east of Richmond at Urbanna on the Virginia shore, bypassing the rebel army. From there, by quick marches, he could reach Richmond before the enemy could arrive to defend it. Besides promising a flashy victory, this new movement, by avoiding a bloody battle at Manassas, would be brilliant strategy. It would be the splendid maneuver that would prove the superiority of the West Pointers and lift McClellan himself into the presidency. It would be so much more fitting for the savior of the Republic to take the enemy capital by sheer strategy, with no loss of life. A grateful nation, quickly reunified after the bloodless capture of the rebel seat of power, would light his way to the White House in 1864, perhaps sooner.

With December, however, came the winter rains. Day after day it poured, and Virginia roads turned into bottomless rivers of liquid mud, making campaigning impossible. McClellan was forced to put off his masterstroke until the spring. On December 12, the New York *Tribune* reported that the army was settling in for the winter in the comfort of its snug log huts.

*   *   *

Outraged Radicals rent their garments in frustration. They conceived a potent solution, one that would restore their lost Congressional ascension over the President as well as propel the army forward. The December session had barely begun before Zachary Chandler mounted the podium to propose an investigation to "lay the blame where it belongs" for the disasters at Bull Run and Ball's Bluff. Within five days both Houses had overwhelmingly approved the formation of a "Joint Committee on the Conduct of the War," giving it broad powers to investigate the war's men and events. The Committee, composed of three senators and four congressmen, had Ben Wade at the head and Chandler at his right hand, and from the beginning it was an Inquisition. For the next three years, it would remain a persistent challenge to Lincoln's direction of the war effort, and one of the Radicals' most formidable weapons in their crusade to make the war revolutionary.

Since none of its members had any military experience, the Committee's political purpose was painfully apparent to Lincoln, but Wade and Chandler were unfazed. Lincoln needed to know that if he had war powers, Congress had them too, and he would have to consult with them more closely from now on. Besides, Wade and Chandler pooh-poohed the very idea of military expertise. They rejected the West Pointers' claim that military leadership was some specialized science, knowable only after years of rigorous Academy instruction. They held that the average American could learn all there was to learn in a few weeks. They snorted at the word "strategy"—wars, they believed, were won by hard fighting, by attacks followed by more attacks.

The Committee's first target, of course, was Lincoln's man, "Tardy George" McClellan. They were prepared to believe any treachery of this insolent, aristocratic, overcautious Democratic general. McClellan's plan, according to Wade, was to prolong the war until both sides became so war-weary that they would call back the Democrats—the only party that still existed both North and South—to make a peace. On December 21 the Committee called McClellan himself in for an interview, but he had just taken to his sickbed, stricken with typhoid, and was too ill to rise.

The Committee, not to be deterred, turned its attention to the President. Countrymen everywhere were attacking Lincoln. The Chicago *Tribune* published demands for "an active war" and drastic measures against slavery. A new round of letters circulated denouncing the President and his Cabinet. "We want the President to kill somebody," began one, summing up the general

Radical feeling. "I greatly fear that the President is not up to the task and to the demands of the time," went another from Boston. From Illinois came a warning: " . . . I find that nearly a majority of the men who voted for Uncle Abe are beginning to come out against him . . . . They curse Lincoln and call him a *Damed* [sic] old *traitor . . . .*" Another Illinoisan complained that Republicans there were "nearly paralyzed by the imbecility of President Lincoln in the management of the war," adding, "Nothing is more common than to hear men who did all in their power for the election of Abe Lincoln . . . say that Lincoln has done more to aid Secessia, than Jefferson Davis has done. Were the trial made to-day, Mr. Lincoln would not receive one in ten of the votes given him in Illinois at the late presidential election." Thaddeus Stevens rose in the House to bellow that Congress, not the President, would run the war, and they would run it their own way.

Especially embarrassing to Lincoln was a lecture by Horace Greeley to a packed hall at the Smithsonian Institution in Washington, where the President sat onstage with members of the Cabinet. To Lincoln's discomfort, Greeley launched into fervent praise of Frémont's recent efforts to free slaves in Missouri, and partisans in the crowd began jeering at Lincoln. Using the moment to full advantage, Greeley turned around and glared at Lincoln as he exclaimed that freeing slaves should be the war's guiding purpose. The audience roared its approval, and Lincoln, the villain, was forced to sit and suffer the righteous indignation of the thousand people in the room.

To this public humiliation was added the Committee's private one. On New Year's Eve a wary Lincoln met with the Committee on the Conduct of the War for ninety minutes, during which Wade bitterly accused the President of betraying the nation, saying, "You are murdering your country by inches in consequence of the inactivity of the military and want of a distinct policy in regard to slavery." The balance of supremacy was shifting unmistakably toward the Capitol end of Pennsylvania Avenue. The Committee had demonstrated its ability to rouse fear and suspicion. "I am confident that Mr. Lincoln and Gen. McClelland [sic] are both afraid of it," one Radical wrote confidently shortly afterward.

*   *   *

Lincoln's dressing-down by a hostile committee was a fitting way to see out the last hours of the Old Year. As 1861 drew to a close, there were no triumphs Lincoln could celebrate, and none he could foresee. Now that McClellan was down with typhoid fever, the Army of the Potomac was paralyzed. More, because McClellan was General-in-Chief, his silence meant that military operations everywhere were frozen. Meanwhile, the costs of raising, transporting, training, feeding, clothing, and sheltering the 700,000 men who had come into the Union ranks were bleeding the Treasury white. There had been nothing to cheer on the battlefield. Lincoln had not proven himself by dramatic actions or inspiring words. He presided over a party that had split into warring factions. His only success had been a retreat from a war with Britain. To millions across the North, the administration seemed to be drifting, and moderates shared the Radicals' distrust of a President who seemed powerless to put things right. Neither he nor McClellan had been able to explain why the Army of the Potomac had not moved, and Lincoln himself did not know why. Ben Wade called the government "blundering, cowardly, and inefficient." Count Gurowski's summing-up at years' end was, "If the new year shall be only the continuation of the faults, the mistakes, and the incapacities prevailing during 1861, then the worst is to be expected."

Doubt was a virus that spread across the North and sapped its strength of purpose. It even infected the Cabinet. Edward Bates thought Lincoln was unequal to his duties, and in his diary entry for December 31st he described a Cabinet meeting during which he had lectured the President:

> Many of the deficiencies ought before now, to have been corrected. . . . [T]he dangerous fact exists, that the Sec of War and the Prest. are ignorant of the condition of the army and its intended operations!
>
> If I were President, I *would* command *in chief*—not *in detail*, certainly—and I *would* know what army I had, and what the high generals (my Lieutenants) were doing with that army.
>
> . . . It seemed as if all military operations were to stop, just because Genl McClellan is sick! . . . I . . . told the President that *he* was commander in chief, and that it was not his *privilege* but his *duty* to command; and *that* implied the necessity to *know* the true condition of things.
>
> That if I were in his place, I *would know*; and if things were not done to my liking, I would order them otherwise. That I believed he could get along easier and much better by the free use of his power, than by this injurious deference to his subordinates[.]

Bates closed the year on a note of despair over Lincoln: "But I fear that I spoke in vain. The Prest. is an excellent man, and, in the main wise; but he lacks *will* and *purpose*, and, I greatly fear he has not the *power to command.*"

Lincoln's despair was deeper than all the others'. After a melancholy conversation with John Dahlgren at the Navy Yard soon after the New Year, Dahlgren reported that "For the first time I heard the President speak of the bare possibility of our being two nations." On January 10, at rock-bottom, Lincoln sought out Quartermaster General Montgomery Meigs and moaned, "General, what shall I do? The people are impatient; Chase has no money and he tells me he can raise no more; the General of the Army has typhoid fever. The bottom is out of the tub. What shall I do?"

Chapter 20

Democrats Disappear

"All who do not shout hosannas to Abe Lincoln are denounced."

The most remarkable thing about the crescendo of criticism of Lincoln in the last months of 1861 was that so little of it came from the Democratic press. With so much fault to be found with the administration's prosecution of what many Democrats called "the present unholy war," the silence of the anti-Lincoln editors was eerie.

The reason was fear. The Democratic press had gone to earth, driven underground by a season of violent repression. Lincoln—fearful for the fragility of what was still called "the democratic experiment," breathing the atmosphere of suspicion that was thick across the whole of the North, and still suffering the special spike of terror from being surrounded in Washington the previous spring—had reacted in the summer and fall by presiding over a trampling of civil liberties.

In the beginning, even during the Uprising of the North after Lincoln's call for troops, the Democratic editors had attacked Lincoln out of sheer force of habit. Some drew him in simple strokes as a bloodthirsty tyrant. The *New York Evening Day Book* declared, "Mr. Lincoln is evidently a believer in the savageries of old Europe, and thinks that the only way to 'save the Union' is to resort to the bayonet, just as Louis Napoleon 'saves' society in France!" The Bedford (Pa.) *Gazette* was another: "The so-called 'peace policy' of the Lincoln Administration," it proclaimed, "has all at once been turned into one of blood and horror. . . . Mr. Lincoln and his partisans may learn to pray that the curse placed upon their political sins may be removed." Maine's Bangor *Democrat* protested that Lincoln "has undertaken to convert [the] Government into an instrument of tyranny," and compared him to the hated Tories of 1776. "Abraham Lincoln," it said, "a Tory from his birth, is putting forth all the powers of Government to crush out the spirit of American liberty. Surrounded by the gleaming swords and glistening bayonets at Washington, he sends forth fleets and armies to overawe and subdue that gallant little State [South Carolina] which was the first to raise its voice against British oppression."

* * *

The Democratic press, however, was soon quieted by the example of the *New York Herald,* the lion of the pro-slavery Democratic journals in the North. On April 12, the *Herald* had made its sympathies visible by blazoning the new Confederate flag over its coverage of the Sumter battle. Three days later, on the afternoon of Lincoln's call for troops, an angry mob gathered outside the *Herald* office, threatening to destroy the building and everyone inside unless it made a patriotic show. Panicked *Herald* employees sent an office boy running to buy a Union flag, and only after editor James Gordon Bennett himself unfurled it from an upper-story window and bowed repeatedly to the crowd below did the mob disperse. Bennett had made his fortune with a talent for telling which way the wind was blowing, and the experience instantaneously converted him. He was now a devoted defender of the Union, proclaiming the next day, "there will now be but one party, one question, one issue, one purpose in the Northern States—that of sustaining the government."

In the spread-eagled fervor of these early days of the war, Northern mobs imposed their own ironclad censorship not only on the press but on free speech. One private citizen wrote that in New York it was not safe "for a man to express . . . doubt of the duty of northern men to march in obedience to Lincoln's call," and another, after twice being threatened for criticizing Lincoln, resolved to be more "prudent."

The official crackdown followed within a month of Sumter on the evening of May 13, 1861, when Major General Benjamin Butler marched back into Baltimore with the same thousand men of the Sixth Massachusetts who had been stoned and shot at on their way through town three weeks earlier, and declared martial law. In the next few days, the first civilian prisoners—including John Merryman—were dragged off without charges to Fort McHenry. The treachery of Baltimore remained a popular theme in the Republican press in the coming weeks, and in June, Worthington G. Snethen, a columnist for the New York *Tribune* who had fed his readers a steady diet of "secessionist Baltimore" stories and was convinced of further plots there, arranged a private meeting with Secretary of War Simon Cameron. A few days later, Cameron gave a secret order to "seize at once and securely hold the four members of the Baltimore police board . . . together with their chief of police," and at midnight on June 27, one thousand blue-coated soldiers marched out of Fort McHenry and, silent except for the crunch of their boots on the paving stones, marched through the darkened streets of Baltimore, picking up any policemen along the way who might spread word of their approach. When they reached police chief George Kane's house at three in the morning, they rousted Kane out of bed, marched him back to the fort, and threw him in a cell with Merryman. Four days later the other members of the Baltimore police board joined him in prison, arrested on suspicion of disloyalty.

The incident was reported closely, with healthy outrage, by the Democratic press. The August 1, 1861, issue of the Democratic Brooklyn *Eagle* shone a harsh light on the removal of the "State Prisoners" from Fort McHenry to Fort Hamilton in New York—eleven men "against whom no charges have been preferred." This item was followed by a righteous attack on Lincoln reprinted from the *Cincinnati Enquirer*:

> The Old Constitution has been superseded by a new one, and . . . we are now under the new Republican Constitution. The Old Constitution was a noble, liberty protecting instrument—a shield to the citizen against arbitrary and unwarrantable searches and seizures.
>
> It contains no provision authorizing the President to suspend the privilege of the writ of *habeas corpus*;
>
> No provision authorizing the President to proclaim martial law when and where he pleases;
>
> No provision empowering the President to increase the standing army at his pleasure;
>
> No provision to authorize the President to violate the right of the people to be secure in their persons, papers and effects against unreasonable searches and seizures;
>
> No authority to arrest the citizen for circulation petitions relating to the peace and welfare of the country;
>
> No license to military officers to stop the publication of Newspapers at their will and pleasure.
>
> All *that* was reserved for the new Republican Constitution, under which the President is acting. It is under this new Constitution the propositions are made in Congress by Republicans . . . . This fact will be a sufficient explanation in the future for a great many other curious and startling things it may see performed by Republican officials.

The fury over the presidential excesses of the spring and early summer deepened in the discouragement after the defeat at Bull Run, which inspired new blasts at Lincoln from Democratic journals demanding peace and an end to the "effusion of blood." By the middle of August 1861, a peace movement was in full flower, and peace meetings were held all over the North. They were thronged by Democrats stirred by sympathy for their Southern brothers, resentment of Lincoln and his party for starting the war, and belief that the South could be won back by appeal to the time-honored principles of the party of Jefferson and Jackson, with "the Constitution as it is, and the Union as it was."

These anti-war Democrats, however, felt keenly the flimsiness of their civil rights in such days of distrust. A meeting of the Association of the Democratic Editors of the State of New York on June 27 was a grim war council. The editors published a warning against any "attempt to muzzle the Democratic press by mobs and terrorism, to prevent citizens from expressing their honest opinions."

The monster the Democratic editors feared was soon shocked into life by the passage of the Confiscation Act on August 6. It stated that any person supporting the rebellion was liable to the seizure of any property used for that aim. Zealots could now contend that any anti-Lincoln newspaper in the North was a tool of the rebellion, and its type, press, office, and paper could therefore be seized or destroyed. Within days of the passage of the Confiscation Act, the anti-Lincoln *New York Daily News* published a list of 154 papers opposed to "this unholy war." It was a defiant roll call of the ranks of "peace" papers in anticipation of the coming storm against them.

That storm broke immediately, spearheaded by bad-tempered ninety-day Union soldiers just then returning home from service after Bull Run. On August 8 a mob of newly-returned soldiers demolished the office of the anti-war *Democratic Standard* of Concord, New Hampshire, and threw the type, desks, and papers out the window and onto the sidewalk, where they set the whole pile on fire. On August 12, a mob in Bangor, Maine, pried open the offices of the Bangor *Democrat* with a crowbar, rushed in, threw the contents out the window, and made a bonfire of them in the town square. A week later, in Haverhill, Massachusetts, a crowd of angry ex-soldiers and their friends seized the editor of the *Essex County Democrat*, tarred and feathered him, and rode him out of town on a rail. In Easton, Pennsylvania, a rabble gutted the offices of the anti-war *Sentinel.* In West Chester, Pennsylvania, a mob destroyed the *Jeffersonian*'s subscription lists, threw the printing type out the window, and damaged the press. In the next week, the Stark County, Ohio, *Democrat* was burned, and the Bridgeport, Connecticut, *Farmer* was smashed. By the end of August, the anti-war movement was in retreat, and many of the planned Peace meetings were being cancelled. The fury against the anti-war presses threatened to spread from the small towns to the cities. In New York City, police were detailed to guard the entrances to the *Daily News*.

There, however, the rage against the anti-war Democratic papers conjured no mobs. Instead, it percolated through the courts. On August 16, a New York grand jury asked formally whether "certain newspapers"—specifically the *New York Daily News*, *Journal of Commerce*, *Day Book*, *Freeman's Journal*, and the Brooklyn *Eagle*—could be charged with a crime for their opposition to the war. Postmaster General Montgomery Blair twisted the grand jury's question into an indictment, and on August 22 issued an order to bar the five newspapers from the mails. In the days when the better part of these big-city newspapers' circulation was distributed by the mails to readers across the country, Blair's order was a death sentence.

On August 28, the *New York Herald* led with the headline "AN ACCOUNTING," and listed the names of eighteen casualties in the Democratic press in the previous month: seven "Northern papers destroyed by mob," two "Northern secession papers suppressed by civil authority," two more "Northern secession papers died," four "Northern secession papers denied transportation in the mails," and three "Secession papers changed to Union." A Cincinnati editor complained privately to Simon Cameron, "All who do not shout hosannas to Abe Lincoln and endorse his unconstitutional and unholy war upon the people of the South are denounced as tories. . . . The people behind Lincoln know perfectly well that it is not and never has been unlawful to discuss or to denounce the measures of the government in times of peace or war."

But the casualty list grew. On August 29, the New York *Day Book* closed. On August 31, the rural Pennsylvania *Carbon Democrat* was destroyed. On September 7, a Westchester, New York, grand jury named the local Yonkers *Herald*, the Highland *Democrat*, the *Eastern State Journal*, and the German language *Staats Zeitung* and *National Zeitung* as "disseminators of doctrines which, in the existing state of things, tend to give aid and comfort to the enemies of the Government." Postmaster General Blair barred the Baltimore *Exchange* from the mails on September 10. Its editor, F. Key Howard, struck back in print the next day, crying, "The course which a despotic and foresworn administration has pursued towards us will not in the slightest degree influence our conduct. . . . As we have violated no law we can afford to despise Mr. Lincoln's warnings or menaces." By the time he wrote this, however, Howard was nearly alone in defying the Lincoln administration. By September, most Democratic editors feared for their livelihood, if they didn't fear for their lives.

Out of that fear, criticism of Lincoln's administration went below ground in the States. The *Toronto Globe* commented on the crackdown, "This is not only an exceedingly foolish way of proceeding—it not only insures its own punishment by encouraging a race of journalists who will never speak the truth except when likely to please, but it does more than almost anything else to lower the American people in the estimation of all civilized nations." Southern newspapers trumpeted the suppression of the Northern Democratic press as new evidence of Lincoln's "reign of terror," reporting that "journals are suppressed for denouncing the actions of the Government," and that truthful Northern papers "are gutted and destroyed by Northern mobs, or suppressed by Northern officials, and their editors arrested or imprisoned without the privilege of a hearing or the hope of redress." Here was proof that "no Neapolitan despotism or Spanish Inquisition ever exceeded in the measure of its cruelty, the present Dictatorship at Washington."

The foreign press could throw brickbats from a safe distance; but, as the serpent of suspicion coiled around the North, few there dared to oppose the mob violence that Lincoln silently endorsed, and few dared to question Lincoln's grim doctrine that, since without the government there could be no freedoms, citizens now must give up their freedom to oppose the government.

*   *   *

During the gagging of the Democratic press and the earlier political arrests, Lincoln himself had remained completely in shadow. The active part was always taken by mobs, by local officials, or by Cabinet members. Lincoln was obscured, too, by the chaos of the crackdown, with orders flying in all directions from Federal marshals, district attorneys, city police, even private citizens. In September, however, there was a fresh, very ugly, very public slew of political arrests in Maryland, and in that episode Lincoln was briefly glimpsed.

As the summer of 1861 had waned, fears for the safety of Washington had waxed. General McClellan, newly installed, was convinced that waves of rebels would overwhelm Washington at any moment. In this atmosphere of dread, a sensational document surfaced and made the rounds of high offices in early September—a copy of what was purported to be Jeff Davis' personal plan to "cross two columns over the Potomac" and invade Maryland. According to this document, the signal for the attack would be the passage of an ordinance of secession by the Maryland legislature, scheduled to convene on September 17. Secretary Seward's son Frederick described a carriage ride he took about this time with his father, Lincoln, and McClellan. The official purpose of the ride was to inspect the military camps in Georgetown, but young Seward reported that the party's carriage rattled ten miles past Georgetown to General Banks' headquarters in Rockville. There the President and his small party withdrew to an isolated grove of trees, where they made plans to intercept the Maryland lawmakers' approach to the legislative session on the 17th and have secessionist members "quietly turned back toward their homes." Since each legislator's views were already well known, Seward remembered Lincoln remarking that there would be little difficulty "separating the sheep from the goats."

Lincoln then faded from view, and in the following days, the plan to "quietly turn back" the secessionist legislators grew harsher. On September 11, Secretary of War Cameron sent two orders. One was to General Banks to arrest any or all of the members of the Maryland legislature to prevent an act of secession. The second was to General Dix in Baltimore to arrest conspicuous secessionists there.

At midnight the next night, police fanned out across Baltimore and dragged fifteen men from their beds and locked them up in Fort McHenry, including Mayor Brown, Congressman Henry May, ten members of the Maryland legislature, and three newspaper editors, including the defiant F. Key Howard. Less than a week later, when the legislature convened in Frederick, Maryland, twenty-one more state legislators, secretaries, clerks, and printers were rounded up and thrown in jail.

The teeming prisoners were all Democrats. They were all held without charges in Federal prisons. If ever there were a time for protest by the press, this was it. Instead, Democratic editors applauded politely in editorials like this one from the Chicago *Times*:

> The action of the government in the matter of the arrests in Maryland is right, and that it has been taken will reanimate the courage of loyal citizens everywhere. It indicates that the day of trifling is past, and that rebels wherever found, and whatever their position, are to be treated as rebels. No doubt the Legislature of Maryland were bent on mischief. . . . The action of the government has nipped the scheme in the bud, and proclaimed to all other Maryland rebels what sort of a rod is in pickle for them. The government *should* continue to go forward after this same

fashion. It is the only right thing to do wherever the Federal power is omnipotent.

What was at work was something more than a survival instinct on the part of the Democratic editors. They had heard rumors of Lincoln's distaste for the Confiscation Act on August 6, and they had read with glee Lincoln's repudiation of Frémont's emancipation proclamation in Missouri. They were seduced by the illusion that Lincoln might be one of them after all. There was, for a time, the strange sound of wooing from the Democratic press. On November 22, the Chicago *Times* dropped to a knee and blurted out a proposal:

> Mr. Lincoln will, before the lapse of much more time, have to choose between political parties, and depend upon the party which he shall choose for the support of his administration. And the parties between which he will have to choose are the democratic and abolition parties. . . .
> If Mr. Lincoln has not already chosen, he will choose the democratic party. . . . He may rely on its support, and it is a reliance that has never failed any President.

*   *   *

Lincoln would disappoint them, of course. His first duty had been to uphold the Constitution, and to that end he had courted the support of Northern conservatives—the Democrats, the Border State men, and the conservative Republicans. But the conservatives could only prevail, and the old institutions could only remain intact, if the war were short.

When victory receded over the coming months, Lincoln would cast them off and embrace a hard, relentless war. Then the Democratic editors would see Lincoln in a harsh, new light, and they would be twice as loud in denouncing political arrests, which by the end of the war would total at least 14,400. (Translated into the population of the present day, the number of arrests would be nearly 150,000 citizens.) The Democrats would anoint themselves the "*habeas corpus* party," and in the elections of 1862 and 1864 the outcry over the loss of civil liberties would harden into one of their bitterest and most persistent indictments of Lincoln's term.

Chapter 21

A Military House Divided

"Heaven save a country governed by such counsels!"

It has been said that one bad general is better than two good ones; and the saying is true, if taken to mean no more than that an army is better directed by a single mind, though inferior, than by two superior ones, at variance, and cross-purposes with each other.

S o said Lincoln in his Message to Congress in December of 1861. It proved he knew something important about leadership. In the first six months of 1862, however, he showed that he had not learned it. He fashioned an army that was hydra-headed—commanded by not one, nor even two, but by one or two dozen generals and bureau chiefs. This was Lincoln's most meddlesome period of the war as a Commander-in-Chief, and at its culmination in July, the mighty Union drive to win the war—the Peninsula Campaign—collapsed.

The story of the ruin of the war's most controversial campaign began on the winter evening of January 6, 1862. The Committee on the Conduct of the War had called Lincoln to appear before them that evening, and they were bristling. In the course of the meeting, the committee was stunned by the revelation that Lincoln did not know McClellan's plans for the army. Indeed, wrote committee member George Julian, "We were greatly surprised to learn that Mr. Lincoln himself did not think he had the *right* to know." Lincoln said he simply trusted McClellan's judgment and didn't intend to interfere, provoking Wade into a long, vicious tirade (Julian, a witness, euphemistically termed it "remarkably bold and vigorous," with "undiplomatic plainness of speech") against McClellan and Lincoln's do-nothing administration. The President was stung. Coming on the heels of the December 31 Cabinet meeting during which Edward Bates had lectured him on his duties, and the Committee meeting that evening when Wade had accused Lincoln of betraying the nation, this was the third time in a week that Lincoln had been blistered face-to-face for his military neglect.

He was still subdued two days later when, at a ceremonial dinner, he was uncharacteristically silent. One man at the table noted of the conversation, "Mr. Lincoln took no part in it. Neither the lively sallies of [author and poet] N. P. Willis nor the inciting remarks of some of the ladies could distract him from his inner reflections, or lighten the moral or physical fatigue to which he visibly yielded."

Lincoln could not have learned McClellan's plans even if he had wanted to. The general had been sick in bed with typhoid for three weeks. Lincoln was worried that he might die while his plans were still unknown and that the war effort might be paralyzed for months. The President went to McClellan's house, but he was sent away. Lincoln's depression worsened until he sought out Montgomery Meigs on January 10, sat at his fireplace, and moaned, "The bottom is out of the tub."

At Meigs' suggestion, Lincoln summoned two of McClellan's subordinates, Generals Irwin McDowell and William Franklin, to the White House, along with Secretaries Seward and Chase and Assistant Secretary of War Thomas Scott. At this meeting, Lincoln gave the first indication that he was breaking the hands-off rule that he had followed toward the military since just after the Baltimore uprising the previous April. He had recently checked out *The Science of War* from the Library of Congress and was attempting to learn strategy. Now, he told McDowell and Franklin that "if General McClellan did not want to use the army, he would like to *'borrow it.'*" When Lincoln asked for their opinions on what should be done, McDowell put forward the favorite plan of his Radical backers, which was the same as it had been in June: hit the Rebel army where they were, at Manassas. Franklin, being a protégé of McClellan, hinted at McClellan's still-undisclosed strategy: a descent by water to the Virginia coast east of Richmond, behind the rebel army and close to their capital. Balked by lack of a consensus, Lincoln adjourned the meeting. The same group held inconclusive meetings again the next day and the next.

*   *   *

Conspicuously missing from these war councils was Secretary of War Simon Cameron. The Cabinet had always been a prime target of Lincoln's critics. Instead of attacking the President, who was proof against removal until the next election and who was assumed to be dependent for his policies on the counsels of his betters, Lincoln's foes attacked his Cabinet, hoping to install new advisers who more nearly shared their views. For months now, politicians and the press had been demanding the shakeup of the incompetent administration that had presided over such a spectacular mismanagement of the war. Confidence in Lincoln's main advisor, William Seward, was at low ebb—the only good thing anyone could say for Seward was that he was not as bad as Simon Cameron.

Cameron's very presence in the Cabinet was owing to a backroom deal made at the nominating convention. When war came, the War Secretary suddenly became the most crucial member of the Cabinet, and swiftly proved his incompetence. Cameron kept no apparent records, and according to one Representative, "in any official matter he would ask you to give its status and what he had last said about it." After being reminded, "he would look about, find a scrap of paper, borrow your pencil, make a note, put the paper in one pocket of his trousers and your pencil in the other." This bungling style had resulted in army contracts so wasteful—and so profitable to his friends—that by the end of 1861 Cameron was the despair of patriots of every stripe. At the same time, he was "openly discourteous to the President," according to the notes of Lincoln's secretary John Nicolay. The final straw had been Cameron's official War Department report in late November, a public break with Lincoln's policy against arming the slaves, which had embarrassed Lincoln just as he was about to deliver his Annual Message to Congress.

Now, on January 11, 1862, in the middle of his series of conferences with the generals, Lincoln reassigned Cameron, naming him Minister to Russia—or, as a *Vanity Fair* cartoon lampooned the President's backwoods mispronunciations, to "the Court of the Kezzar." Cameron left for St. Petersburg with a final slap at Lincoln: "We want a great man and have not got him—but I ought not to have said that."

For his replacement as Secretary of War, one candidate stood out. Edwin McMasters Stanton had achieved the impossible. Not only had William Seward recommended him, but also Seward's opposite, Salmon Chase. Not only did George McClellan approve him, but also McClellan's enemies, Ben Wade and Zack Chandler. Stanton's approval by both extremes of the political spectrum was a testament to his reputation, his ability, and his forked tongue.

As Attorney General during the previous Secession Winter, Stanton had secretly reported the doings in the Buchanan Cabinet to Seward, their Republican foe. Turning about, he remained in Washington during the first months of the Lincoln administration and wrote private letters to Buchanan telling him of Lincoln's "imbecility" at every new development. When McClellan became the new power in August 1861, Stanton "did his best to ingratiate himself with me, and professed the warmest friendship and devotion," McClellan wrote later, and continued,

> The most disagreeable thing about [Stanton] was the extreme virulence with which he abused the President, the administration, and the Republican party. He carried this to such an extent that I was often shocked by it. He never spoke of the President in any other way than as the "original gorilla," and often said that Du Chaillu [famous as the first white man to have seen a gorilla] was a fool to wander all the way to Africa in search of what he could so easily have found at Springfield, Illinois. . . .
> He often advocated the propriety of my seizing the government and taking affairs into my own hands.

Stanton had formed his poor opinion of Lincoln during the McCormick Reaper patent case in 1855. Lincoln had been hired by McCormick's rival, the Manny Company, when the case was expected to be tried in Chicago. When the venue was changed to Cincinnati, Lincoln was not informed that he had become superfluous to the case, and, after making elaborate preparations, he came to Cincinnati only to be rudely snubbed by the more recently hired—and more professionally prominent—Edwin Stanton of Pittsburgh. Stanton, after seeing the gawky, poorly-dressed Illinoisan, wanted nothing to do with "that damned long-armed Ape," and, according to one account, declared, "If that giraffe appeared in the case I would throw up my brief and leave." Lincoln was of course deeply hurt, but he stayed on and watched with interest as the high-powered Eastern lawyers argued the case. Now, in his selection of a new Secretary of War, Lincoln remembered the sting of the incident, but he considered only Stanton's expert performance in court.

Stanton brought order and urgency to the War Department, but also contempt for his elected superior. A.K. McClure wrote that he himself heard Stanton scores of times speak of, and several times even speak to, Lincoln with "a withering sneer." McClure continued:

> [Stanton] loved antagonism, and there was hardly a period during his remarkable service as a War Minister in which he was not, on some more or less important point, in positive antagonism with the President. In his antagonisms he was, as a rule, offensively despotic, and often pressed them upon Lincoln to the very utmost point of Lincoln's forbearance . . . .
> He respected Lincoln's authority because it was greater than his own, but

he had little respect for Lincoln's fitness for the responsible duties of the Presidency.

The week Simon Cameron was dismissed, Stanton courted the Radicals' support for his nomination by privately criticizing McClellan's idleness. Characteristically, Stanton was at the same time snuggling up to the generalissimo himself, whispering warnings to McClellan of the President's secret meetings with McDowell and Franklin. "My first inkling of [the meetings]," wrote McClellan, "came through Mr. Stanton, not yet Secretary of War, who said to me: 'They are counting on your death, and are already dividing among themselves your military goods and chattels.'"

Thus alerted, McClellan rose shakily from his sickbed on January 13 and slumped into a carriage that took him to the White House, where he made a dramatic entrance at a crowded war council that included President Lincoln, Secretaries Seward, Chase, and Blair, and Generals McDowell, Franklin, and Meigs. The overheated air of the room crackled with jealousies and resentments. McClellan was convinced that McDowell "was at the bottom of the affair . . . hoping to succeed me in command," and that the purpose of the meeting was to "'dispose of the military goods and chattels' of the sick man so inopportunely restored to life."

When McClellan sat down, there was "a good deal of whispering among the others," he remembered later, "especially between the President and Secretary Chase." Lincoln rose and broke the ice by pointing to a map and asking McDowell and Franklin to explain again the plans in view. McClellan sat sullenly with his head down, mute. Meigs moved his chair next to the general and whispered, "The President evidently expects you to speak; can you not promise some movement towards Manassas? You are strong." McClellan muttered that the rebels were strong also. Meigs persisted, "The President expects something from you." McClellan whispered in reply, "If I tell him my plans they will be in the *New York Herald* tomorrow morning. He can't keep a secret, he will tell them to [his eight-year-old son] Tad."

Chase finally brought the meeting to a head by asking McClellan—with "uncalled-for irritation," and "in a very excited tone and manner," according to the general's memoir—exactly what he intended doing with his army, and when he intended doing it.

McClellan allowed a long pause before answering. "No General fit to command an army will ever submit his plans to the judgment of such an assembly. There are many here entirely incompetent to pass judgment on them; . . . no plan made known to so many persons can be kept secret an hour. . . ."

There was another uncomfortable pause while Lincoln and Chase whispered together. Finally Lincoln rose and asked, "Have you fixed upon a particular time for your advance?"

McClellan replied yes, he had.

"Well, on this assurance I will be satisfied, and I will adjourn this Council," said the President, and everyone hurried gratefully for the door.

The January 13 gathering was a watershed in the relations between Lincoln and McClellan. It was the unsure President's first break with his top general and with his own rule against divided counsels, and it begat McClellan's break with him. McClellan saw the episode as a conspiracy against him, and he would never again fully trust the President. Further, as the breach widened, and as McClellan grew more openly distrustful, his entourage of young, conservative, upper-class Democratic officers would become an anti-Lincoln cabal, convinced that the President was in league with the abolitionists in the Committee on the Conduct of the War, and that Lincoln and the abolitionists were determined to undo their plans. After the awkward war council of January 13, McClellan's relations with Lincoln would become more and more strained at the most unfortunate time—just as he was readying the war-winning campaign the North had awaited ever since Bull Run.

McClellan's distrust of Lincoln, however, was exceeded by the Radicals'. For, during these months of indecision, while Lincoln sometimes acted under the sway of their Committee, he also continued to back his General-in-Chief. So fixed were the Radicals in their purpose to destroy McClellan that Lincoln's faithfulness to him was gall and wormwood to them. Wade called Lincoln's administration "weak and wicked." Count Gurowski was convinced that McClellan's men inside the Cabinet were Seward and Blair—"And Lincoln is in their clutches," he hissed.

As McClellan sulked and kept his plans secret from Lincoln following the January 13 council, Stanton and the Radicals met day after day for hours, making savage rumblings aimed at McClellan's undoing. On January 24, Lincoln had his first meeting with Secretary Stanton, and both men were pleased to find that, though each had been counted a friend of McClellan, they were in full agreement that his army must move—that, in Stanton's phrase, "the champagne and oysters on the Potomac must be stopped." So, finally, on the strong urging of Stanton, McClellan met with the President in late January and sketched his scheme to float the army to the Virginia coast and march into

Richmond before the rebel army could arrive from Manassas. Lincoln disapproved it, for two reasons. First, it would take too long to prepare. And, more importantly, it removed the Army of the Potomac from its protective position between the rebels and Washington.

*   *   *

Lincoln by now had taught himself just enough military theory to be dangerous. His intellectual arrogance was a habit, and, not surprisingly in a time when people thought anybody could be a general, he wanted to try his hand at being one. He had told Orville Browning on January 12 that "he was thinking of taking the field himself," and on January 26 he told Navy Assistant Secretary Gustavus Fox that he believed "he must take these army matters into his own hands." His new resolve was crowned on January 27, when he issued "President's General War Order No. 1," which directed a general movement of land and sea forces go forward on February 22—a date chosen for no other reasons than that it was soon and it was Washington's Birthday.

Lincoln appeared to be taking on the role of the active Commander-in-Chief as Bates had suggested; yet, as Lincoln himself admitted later to Ulysses Grant, the War Order was a mistake. It brought nothing but new ridicule upon him. It had never been the business of Presidents to order armies into motion, and no general took it seriously—in fact, no movement was ever started in obedience to General War Order No. 1. The military men saw the absurdity of scheduling an advance so soon and without any thought to the weather, logistics, or the movements of the enemy.

On January 31, four days after General War Order No. 1, Lincoln put a finer point on it by issuing Special War Order No. 1, which specified an attack on the enemy at Manassas, which was the only attack that could be mounted before Washington's Birthday. McClellan immediately wrote to Lincoln and asked if he might write his objections to the President's plan and reasons for preferring his own. Here Lincoln's War Orders had their reward: McClellan finally revealed his own plans in full detail. On February 3, McClellan placed on Stanton's desk a complete report, page after page on his plan to descend the Potomac and the Chesapeake by a fleet of transports and land the army on the Virginia coast east of Richmond at Urbanna, at the mouth of the Rappahannock River, then move southwest by rapid marches to Richmond.

Lincoln was not convinced that McClellan's plan was better than his own, yet he yielded. It would prove to be one of Lincoln's most far-reaching blunders of the war. For he still mistakenly supposed that the next battle would end the war, and his own plan to attack the rebels at Manassas brought that battle sooner and closer to the Army of the Potomac's Washington base than some future battle around Richmond. Fewer things could go wrong. It would have been better by far if he had either insisted on his own plan and fired McClellan if he had been unwilling to follow it faithfully, or given McClellan full rein and supported the general's sea-going plan. Instead, in an outward show of the division within himself about what strategy to pursue, Lincoln proceeded to divide his support for his general, divide the army, and divide military responsibility, with disastrous consequences for the country.

Even in his social life, Lincoln was not immune from widespread resentment over the listless war effort. On February 6, the Lincolns hosted a gala ball to show off Mary's newly-restored White House, an affair which many considered unseemly in view of the country's calamity. Eighty notes of regret came in response to the Lincolns' invitations. Ben Wade and his wife, for example, responded, "Are the President and Mrs. Lincoln aware that there is a civil war? If they are not, Mr. and Mrs. Wade are, and for that reason decline to participate in feasting and dancing." Far worse, the White House ball marked the beginning of a terrible personal tragedy for the Lincolns. During the festivities, they slipped away frequently to go upstairs and hold the hand of their gentle, animated, intelligent eleven-year-old son Willie, who was stricken with a fever. It turned out to be typhoid. Willie lingered for two weeks, then died on February 20, staggering Lincoln with the unsurpassed grief of a father for his favorite son.

While Lincoln anguished at Willie's bedside, the Radicals of the Committee on the Conduct of the War fulminated in private meetings with Secretary Stanton. They respected the President's privacy until Willie's funeral on February 24, but they were back at him the next day.

The Radicals pointed out that Washington's Birthday had come and gone, and still the army had not stirred. To establish a lodgment inside the army command, they wanted the Army of the Potomac divided into four corps, each under a general who would report directly to the War Department. At this, Lincoln stalled. He had not thought about it, he said, and he was sure McClellan would oppose it, perhaps even resign. The Committee persisted, returning to the White House on March 3 with fresh demands for the army corps. This time the meeting collapsed into an argument between Lincoln and Wade, who wanted McClellan removed. *If McClellan were removed*, Lincoln asked, *who would command the army?* "Well, anybody!" Wade exploded. "Wade," Lincoln replied, "anybody will do for you but I must have somebody." He concluded, "I must use the tool I have."

Lincoln went from offending the Radicals to offending McClellan. On the morning of March 8, Lincoln met with the general and broached the subject of treason. There was "an ugly matter" they had to discuss, he said. He confronted McClellan with the charge that the general's design in removing the army from Washington was so the enemy could seize it. The general jumped up and roughly demanded that Lincoln take it back, whereupon the President backpedaled, saying he was merely repeating what others had said. McClellan told Lincoln he had called a meeting of his twelve division commanders for later that day, and that he would put them to a vote between Lincoln's overland plan and his own sea-borne scheme. This satisfied the President, who was grateful for yet another war council to deliver him from the responsibility of a decision.

Lincoln was naïve in thinking the army's council of generals would decide the issue on its merits. McClellan certainly knew better. The Army of the Potomac was the most politicized army in the world, and McClellan was keenly aware that personal jealousies and party politics had divided the twelve division commanders into two factions. The senior generals—McDowell, Sumner, Heintzelman, Keyes, and Chief Engineer Barnard—were Republicans. They had spent their lives in the army, and resented McClellan's sudden vault from civilian life to army command. They also resented the other seven generals, McClellan's "pets," the young Democrats who owed their positions to McClellan, the men he kept around him and consulted in all things. These young generals were conservative like their commander and patron, and they detested the elder generals for their liberal leanings.

It was no surprise to McClellan, then, that later that day, by a vote of eight to four, the generals agreed with his own plan. Lincoln was forced to go along with the decision, for he saw the madness in disregarding the judgment of a panel of generals—if he insisted on his attack on Manassas and things went wrong, he would be crucified. Instead, he countered with a blunt use of his power as Commander-in-Chief later the same day. Observing that the senior generals agreed with his own plan, he issued President's General War Order No. 2, which divided the Army of the Potomac into four corps, with the older, Republican generals commanding them—accomplishing the Radical scheme. General War Order No. 2 also delighted the Radicals by putting General James Wadsworth, an abolitionist Republican, in command of the Washington defenses. On the same day, Lincoln added President's General War Order No. 3, which insisted that McClellan's proposed change of base from Washington to the Virginia coast could not be made without providing enough troops for the defense of the capital, and that the newly-named corps commanders would be consulted in deciding the size of "such force as . . . shall leave [Washington] entirely secure." The Republican generals responded that a force of 40,000 to 50,000 defenders would be enough to keep the capital safe.

The next day, however, events intervened. The rebel army at Manassas suddenly retreated thirty miles south to the Rappahannock River. Lincoln saw the rebel move as proof that his plan to strike them at Manassas had been the right one—*hadn't the rebels seen their mortal danger, and withdrawn before the fatal blow could fall?* Immediately came another, more bitter, confirmation. When McClellan marched his army to Manassas, he discovered that the Confederate earthworks had been occupied by a fraction of what he had supposed. Even the rebel cannon were mere stagecraft—logs painted black and stuck through crude embrasures. Lincoln, gripped by the idea that the war could have been ended in Napoleonic style by one climactic battle, was tortured, convinced that he had been right all along about the correct strategy and that he had squandered the chance to annihilate the rebels while they were both exposed and close at hand.

The revelations in the abandoned enemy camps at Manassas worked a mighty change in the normally tender-hearted Lincoln. His despair turned to rage—"He surprised and delighted the committee by completely losing his temper," according to member George Julian—and on March 11 he issued another War Order, relieving McClellan of command as General-in-Chief of all the nation's armies, and limiting him to command of the Army of the Potomac. From now on, all army commanders would report, not to McClellan, but to the War Department, where Lincoln and Secretary Stanton would direct operations from the telegraph room.

The clumsiness of the War Order had evil consequences. At the moment when McClellan was finally ready to meet the enemy, when all the Union armies in Virginia were most in need of a single guiding hand, Lincoln's new order had the effect of splintering command among a handful of generals at the head of a half-dozen armies dotting the landscape. The generals would now answer to Lincoln and Stanton, two lawyers with no knowledge of how to write a military order, much less conceive or carry out complicated military plans.

In his reply to Lincoln, McClellan acquiesced graciously—for the record. Privately, he seethed. He saw Lincoln as a man in league with his enemies, the Republicans who were unwilling to let him, McClellan, win the war because they realized he would reunite the old Union—with its Democratic majority and slavery intact—and be elected its next President. As McClellan saw it, the purpose of the War Order removing him from overall command was "to tie my hands in order to secure the failure of the approaching campaign."

Little Mac had a bad habit of exaggerating enemy strength, but his estimate of his political enemies in Washington was right on. He wrote to his wife, "The rascals are after me again. . . . If I can get out of this scrape you will never catch me in the power of such a set again." He then dodged the furor by disappearing into his work. With the Urbanna landing rendered obsolete by the rebels' retreat from Manassas, he now prepared to sail his army farther south, to Fort Monroe at the tip of the Yorktown Peninsula, a thumb of land jutting southeast into Chesapeake Bay with Richmond at its base. While McClellan herded his divisions toward the Alexandria wharves to embark for the Peninsula, the Radicals stepped up their campaign to remove him.

For, while Lincoln had alienated McClellan by removing him as General-in-Chief, he had still failed to satisfy the Radicals. After the humiliation of the wooden guns and empty camps at Manassas, a majority of the Committee on the Conduct of the War, according to one, "strongly suspected that McClellan was a traitor" and begged the President to sack him. When Lincoln would not, the Radicals attacked Lincoln. "It is no longer doubtful that General McClellan is utterly unfit for his position. . . . And yet the President will keep him in command," wrote Senator Fessenden in a froth. "We went in for a railsplitter, and we have got one."

The Radicals changed their tactics. Now that the headquarters of the combined armies was in the War Department telegraph office and not in McClellan's tent, they could organize the general's failure from Washington. Lincoln's secretary John Hay heard the whisperings from his desk. He wrote in his diary, "Gen. McC. is in danger. Not in front but in rear."

The Radicals plotted to kill McClellan's campaign by a thousand cuts. Wade and Chandler started in immediately. They met with Lincoln and demanded that he subtract Blenker's division from McClellan's army and march it across Virginia to join their man, John C. Frémont, newly in charge of the Mountain Department in western Virginia. Blenker's division, a "foreign legion" of 10,000 European veterans, was McClellan's favorite. "So far as 'the pride, pomp, and circumstance of glorious war' were concerned," he wrote, "it certainly outshone all the others." Lincoln met with McClellan and told him that "he was most strongly pressed" to remove Blenker's men, but assured the general he would not deprive him of his choice unit. "[Lincoln] suggested several reasons against the proposed removal of the division," according to

McClellan. "He assured me he knew this thing to be wrong." Days later, however, McClellan received the following letter, a few hours before sailing:

> MY DEAR SIR: This morning I felt constrained to order Blenker's Division to Frémont; and I write this to assure you that I did so with great pain, understanding that you would wish it otherwise. If you could know the full pressure of the case, I am confident you would justify it——even beyond a mere acknowledgment that the Commander-in-chief, may order what he pleases.

> Yours very truly, A. Lincoln

Thus, as McClellan embarked his army for the decisive battle, his force was missing 10,000 men that he had counted on to spearhead the end of the rebellion. The general protested to Lincoln, dismayed that politics had been allowed to interfere with the crucial military campaign of the war. "[Lincoln] then assured me," McClellan wrote, "that he would allow no other troops to be withdrawn from my command."

Lincoln's assurances, however, proved worthless. Only three days later, on April 3, the day after McClellan arrived on the Peninsula, he received a telegram withdrawing the Fort Monroe garrison, another 10,000 men, from his force. And this was only prelude, for the very next day, just as he was first bringing rebel troops under fire at Yorktown, another telegram informed McClellan of the deepest cut: "By direction of the president," it said, "General McDowell's army corps has been detached from the forces under your immediate command, and is ordered to report to the Secretary of War." With this, McClellan learned that McDowell's corps—his largest, 35,000 men strong— had been suddenly subtracted from his army. A week earlier, he had counted on 156,000 men for the campaign that would decide the war; now he would have to fight that fight with 100,000. This, for McClellan, was the bitter fruit of Lincoln's first three weeks in command.

Lincoln, the lawyer-in-chief, the one man in the country most terrified of a rebel capture of Washington, had subtracted McDowell to guard the capital. He did so out of ignorance of McClellan's provisions for its defense. Besides the 19,000-man garrison in the forts around the capital itself, the general had left 35,000 men in the Shenandoah Valley, 8,000 in Warrenton, and 10,000 at Manassas. This was "defense in depth"—that is, not all concentrated in one place, but thrown forward to expose a rebel attack and delay it long enough to marshal a counterstroke. But these soldiers were beyond Lincoln's view. Neither did Lincoln understand that McClellan's huge Union army on the outskirts of the rebel capital would itself make Washington safe. No rebel army could march toward the Potomac with disaster in its rear.

So little did Lincoln understand, in fact, that he and Stanton had sent for a military expert for advice. This was sixty-four-year-old philosopher-soldier General Ethan Allen Hitchcock. It was a strange choice. Hitchcock had been absorbed with his real love, which was writing books on alchemy and eccentric interpretations of the Gospels, since his retirement from the army seven years before. Stanton summoned Hitchcock from his home in St. Louis and on March 17 put him in charge of the newest of Lincoln's growing list of advising councils. This was the Army Board, made up of the generals at the head of the Bureaus of the War Department—ordnance, commissary, quartermaster, paymaster, chief engineer, surgeon general, and adjutant general—bureaus that McClellan had called "miserable nests of petty intrigues." Now, Hitchcock and the seven bureau chiefs of the Army Board would be added to the roster of Lincoln's advisors, already crowded with the Committee on the Conduct of the War, General McClellan, the council of corps commanders in the Army of the Potomac, and the three political appointees—novice Generals Frémont, Banks, and Wadsworth—who commanded the armies defending Washington.

General James Wadsworth was not only newly in charge of Washington's soldiers, he was newly a soldier himself—a white-haired, fifty-two-year-old gentleman farmer from New York who had left the plow to join McDowell's staff only the previous summer. He had been installed in command of Washington because he was an abolitionist with connections to the Radical Republicans and because he had said wonderfully harsh things about McClellan in recent weeks. According to McClellan, "[Stanton] had spoken to me on the subject some days before, whereupon I objected to [Wadsworth's] selection for the reason that Gen. Wadsworth was not a soldier by training. I said that one of the very best soldiers in the army was necessary for the command of Washington, which was next in importance to the command of the Army of the Potomac—an officer fully posted in all the details of the profession." Stanton replied that Wadsworth had been selected to conciliate the agricultural interests of New York, and that there was no point in discussing it anyway because it was a *fait accompli*. McClellan was appalled by the choice. Wadsworth, he said, "was no general; he was a man of bad character and a pseudo-fanatic," a "vile traitorous miscreant."

With such bad blood between the two generals, it is not surprising that Wadsworth knew nothing of McClellan's sophisticated design for Washington's defense. McClellan had been so anxious to flee Washington, "that sink of iniquity," that before he sailed to the Peninsula on April 1 he had not informed Wadsworth—or Lincoln, or Stanton—of his defensive arrangements. With a cavalier disregard for the President's gnawing concern for the safety of the capital, and as an insult to all three leaders, he had seen fit only to send a copy of his defensive scheme to Hitchcock.

Hitchcock, however, had declined to inspect McClellan's plans. According to McClellan, Hitchcock, "after glancing his eye over the list, observed that he was not the judge of what was required for defending the capital; that [my] position was such as to enable [me] to understand the subject much better than he did, and he presumed that if the force designated was in [my] judgment sufficient, nothing more would be required." As a result, once the steamer *Commodore* puffed away with McClellan on it, no one in Washington knew the specifics of McClellan's plans for the capital's defense—in particular, of the importance of the troops posted in the approaches from Virginia.

General Wadsworth, in charge of Washington's safety, knew only that he could count barely 19,000 poorly-equipped recruits in the camps around the capital, now that McClellan's army was almost all gone to sea. Wadsworth concluded that McClellan had left Washington undefended—just as his Radical friends had suspected he might!—and came hurrying round to Stanton with the news. Stanton, who was as in the dark about McClellan's arrangements as Wadsworth, hustled Wadsworth's warning over to Hitchcock. Hitchcock, who had only days before signed off on McClellan's troop count, now looked at it again and decided that McClellan had left Washington at risk. Wadsworth, meanwhile, rushed to the Committee for the Conduct of the War with the news that McClellan had not done his duty, and they were of course delighted. Stanton, Wadsworth, and the Committee converged on the White House to tell Lincoln that they—the lawyer, the farmer, and the congressmen, with their vast military expertise—had determined that Washington was in danger. Lincoln, who nursed a visceral fear for the safety of the capital and who already had grave doubts about the wisdom of McClellan's Peninsula adventure, was easily convinced.

Thus, Lincoln, in a spasm of doubt and indecision, held back the 35,000 men of McDowell's 1st Corps, who were just then preparing to board the transport ships to the Peninsula. And thus, McClellan, just as his guns were getting the range of the enemy on the Peninsula in what all expected to be the war's decisive campaign, learned that more than one-third of his army had been made to disappear—not killed or captured by enemies in his front, but subtracted by Lincoln in the telegraph office.

Convinced that he had been stabbed in the back in Washington and was hopelessly outnumbered on the Peninsula, McClellan was now a beaten man. Without 55,000 men he had counted on before he sailed, and without the support of Lincoln, his hope of success for his campaign evaporated. He stormed and sputtered. "It is the most infamous thing that history has recorded," he raged in a letter to his wife. He wrote to Lincoln, pleading, "I beg that you will reconsider the order detaching the first Corps from my command. In my deliberate judgment the success of our cause will be imperiled by so greatly reducing my force . . . ." But Lincoln was unmoved, and McClellan remained in shock over his smashed plans. "I know of no instance in military history where a general in the field has received such a discouraging blow," he wrote. He fumed that he "had now only too good reason to feel assured that the administration, and especially the Secretary of War, were inimical to me and did not desire my success . . . ." The amateurs had deranged his plans when he was "too deeply committed to withdraw," he said. He called Lincoln's decision "a fatal error." He wrote to his friend Samuel Barlow of the conspiracy in Washington and of "the stupidity and wickedness" of his enemies there, "a set of heartless villains." Almost a week later, his bitterness toward Lincoln, Stanton, and their Radical councils was still brimming when he wrote to Ellen, with a hint of revenge at some future poll:

> Don't worry about the wretches—they have done nearly their worst & can't do much more. I am sure that I will win in the end, in spite of all their rascality.
>
> History will present a sad record of these traitors who are willing to sacrifice the country & army for personal spite & personal aims. The people will soon understand the whole matter & then woe betide the guilty ones.

According to one soldier, Lincoln's popularity, already low with the Army of the Potomac, sank lower as the rumors spread from tent to tent:

> [I]t was whispered that . . . sundry mischievous politicians in Washington had so influenced [Lincoln and Stanton] against General McClellan that they were doing everything in their power to destroy his plans and damage

him in the eyes of the public. These reports had a very bad effect on the army, and more especially on its officers. They placed McClellan in the position of an injured man, with an army to fight in front of him and a worse enemy in his rear; and yet it did him no real good. Respect for the authorities at Washington was already too low in the Army of the Potomac, and reports like these were not calculated to promote that good understanding between the executive powers and our army so necessary to success.

In the eyes of the Democratic newspapers of the North, Lincoln had thrown off his conservative mask. He had wrecked McClellan's plans, and was under the influence of the Radicals, who were jealous of the Democratic general's success and eager to deal a death blow to his Peninsula campaign and his presidential hopes, no matter the cost to the Union. Even the moderate Republican *Harper's Weekly* printed a rebuke: "It is impossible to exaggerate the mischief which has been done by division of counsels and civilian interference with military movements," it said. General Heintzelman, certainly no friend of McClellan's, called Lincoln's withholding of McDowell's corps "a great outrage."

*   *   *

McClellan's only consolation was that, just at that moment, with the rebels huddled in their trenches at Yorktown, he was ready to make the kind of war his whole military life had prepared him for. So upset by the sudden loss of his 1st Corps that he was unable to believe he still outnumbered the rebels five to one, he settled down to demonstrate the lessons he had learned in 1855 as an official observer at the siege of Sepastopol. There, the huge, fortified port city of Russia had fallen to the sheer weight of metal assembled by the more technically advanced British and French. McClellan now itched to reprise that performance in the mud of Virginia, and in the early days of April he started digging his trenches and inching forward his giant siege artillery. Lincoln was impatient at what he feared was a repeat of McClellan's stall before Manassas, and he wrote to the general on April 6, "You now have over one hundred thousand troops. . . . I think you better break the enemy's lines . . . at once. They will probably use *time*, as advantageously as you can." After the betrayal of the last week, however, McClellan had broken charity with Lincoln, and he showed his spite in a letter to his wife: "The Presdt very coolly telegraphed me yesterday that he thought I had better break the enemy's lines at once! I was much tempted to reply that he had better come & do it himself."

McClellan's go-slow instincts hardened in the next few days, as the nation shrank in revulsion at the news of the horrible bloodbath at the Battle of Shiloh in Tennessee on April 6 and 7, where as many people died in one battle as had died in the Revolutionary War, the War of 1812, and the Mexican War combined. McClellan no doubt watched the newspapers with interest as General Ulysses Grant was pilloried for exposing his army and almost fired for his carelessness. It was an object lesson that confirmed McClellan in his cautious course. He was content to roll up his huge guns—13 inch seacoast mortars that weighed nine tons and lobbed 220-pound shells. Day after day, week after week during the soaking rains of April he hauled them forward. Old Man Blair was one Republican who broke ranks with Lincoln to applaud McClellan for his caution, writing the general, "If you can accomplish your object of reaching Richmond by a slower process than storming redoubts & batteries in earth works, the country will applaud the achievement which gives success to its arms, with greatest parsimony of the blood of its children." Those children, the common soldiers in the Army of the Potomac, were certainly grateful to McClellan for his pains.

By May 5, the guns were in place and ready to make a historic roar that would be heard round the world. But the orange light of the rising sun, creeping over the Union siege artillery with their barrels loaded and lanyards taut, fell on empty rebel trenches. The rebels had left Yorktown overnight. Only a sharp rearguard action at Williamsburg slowed, very temporarily, their withdrawal up the Peninsula to within the sound of Richmond's church bells. When the outskirts of the capital were reached the Confederate army, now in numbers nearly equal to McClellan's, turned to face the Army of the Potomac.

*   *   *

The next two months were the rosiest of the entire war in the North. Complaints about the prairie president's lack of ability were drowned by the flood tide of Union victories in the West in the spring of 1862. There, the Union armies and gunboat fleets had been winning battles since February, when the previously obscure General Grant captured Fort Henry and Fort Donelson. The forts were gateways to the Tennessee and Cumberland rivers, which flowed like major highways into the deep southern states; whole Union armies floated deep into the Confederacy. On the Mississippi River, New Orleans in the south was captured, then Memphis in the north. On the Atlantic coast, too, General Burnside had made a beachhead on the shores of North Carolina.

Northern editors outdid each other proclaiming an early victory to the war. The *New York Times* exclaimed "The End at Hand," and underneath gushed, "The highest military authorities of our Government believe the Confederate rebellion to be hopelessly overthrown." The *New York Herald* predicted the end of the war in a mere seventy-five days, the New York *Tribune* in sixty, the Brooklyn *Eagle* "within a month or two." So complacent had become the general mood, in fact, that the Secretary of War disbanded the recruiting offices and suspended enlistments.

Democrats were delighted. Their generals were winning everywhere. Democrat General Henry Halleck presided over the victories in the West won by Democrat General Grant. (Grant would famously convert to Republicanism in time for his presidential run in 1868.) General Burnside, too, was a Democrat. And now George McClellan, the idol of the Democratic Party, was about the deliver the *coup de grace* at Richmond, and he would do it his way, entirely according to scientific military principles. His popularity rose higher than it had been since his celebrated strut into Washington the summer before. The Young Napoleon's mighty army could now see the steeples of Richmond, and almost nobody had been killed. McClellan's bloodless victories at Manassas and Yorktown, which had so frustrated the impatient Lincoln, were trumpeted as triumphs of modern warfare in the Democratic press. *Harper's Weekly* praised McClellan, saying, "No General of modern times ever displayed more sagacity, courage, and, to use his own words, 'adaptation of means to ends,' than Major-General McClellan." His war in the East was clean and civilized, certainly better than the awful gore of Shiloh. Now that reports were filtering through the lines that the Confederate government was evacuating its capital at Richmond, Northern editorials about Reconstruction popped up like wildflowers, urging McClellan's Democratic policy that everything, including slavery, be returned to its pre-war condition. Meanwhile, McClellan was feeling his way up the Virginia peninsula toward Richmond, rolling forward his giant siege guns on railroad tracks.

Now was the time to bend every effort, strain every nerve to capture Richmond. Now, more than ever, unity of purpose was needed, directed by one controlling mind. In the first week of April, however, after Lincoln had held back McDowell's corps from joining McClellan's army, he had divided the Virginia theater into a confused patchwork of military departments with overlapping responsibilities, under six generals: Frémont in western Virginia,

Banks in the Shenandoah Valley, McDowell at Fredericksburg, Wool at Fort Monroe, McClellan on the Peninsula, and Burnside on the North Carolina coast.

In mid-May, as McClellan crept westward toward Richmond with the Army of the Potomac, Lincoln planned to march McDowell's 1st Corps, now 41,000 strong, south from Fredericksburg on the Rappahannock River to link up with McClellan's army on the outskirts of the rebel capital. There, combined, the two forces would launch a final assault. This was exactly what General Robert E. Lee and the military men in Richmond dreaded. They knew that if McDowell completed his march and accomplished his junction with McClellan's army in front of Richmond, the defenders would be overwhelmed and it would simply a matter of time before the capital fell. Lee, however, spotted an opportunity in Lincoln's fractured command. On April 21 he wrote to General Thomas "Stonewall" Jackson that, "in the present divided condition of the enemy's forces," if he could strike hard in the Shenandoah Valley, "it will prove a great relief to the pressure [from McDowell]." Commander-in-Chief Lincoln unwittingly helped Jackson on May 1 by ordering General Shields and his 10,000-man division, now in the Shenandoah Valley with Banks, to return to Fredericksburg—about 50 miles to the southeast—to join McDowell for the 40-mile march south to Richmond.

Jackson, who had collected an army of some 17,000 men, timed his plunge down the Valley (that is, north, toward the Potomac) to take advantage of Shields' departure, On May 21 he attacked Banks, who had divided his remaining 9,000 men into three isolated posts. Banks and his tiny army broke and ran down the Valley for safety, not stopping until they were on the north side of the Potomac.

Washington convulsed with terror over Jackson's approach. Out of a desire to cut off the enemy general, trap him, and remove him from the map once and for all, Lincoln now contrived the most unfortunate stroke in his unfortunate season as acting General-in-Chief. On May 24 he sent an order to McDowell halting his march south to Richmond—the second time he had prevented him from joining McClellan—and ordered McDowell instead to send Shields' division back to the Shenandoah Valley to form a pincers with Frémont, who would hurry over from the mountains in the west. Between them they would bag Jackson.

McDowell, who was just then contemplating winning the war with a triumphant promenade into Richmond, was heartsick at the sudden change in plans. He immediately telegraphed Lincoln, "This is a crushing blow to us," and later that day wired a more complete protest to the President, pointing out that "I am entirely beyond helping distance of General Banks," and that "by a glance at the map it will be seen that the line of retreat of the enemy's force up the valley is shorter than mine to go against him." It was his expert opinion that "I shall gain nothing for you there, and shall lose much for you here." McDowell knew that it was folly to use the telegraph office to maneuver forces separated by hundreds of miles and expect them to cover long distances over rocky, muddy, rutted roads in wind and rain, and meet like ballet dancers at center stage. His protests, however, were in vain, and Shields' footsore men were soon traversing again, in reverse, the same stony tracks they had just taken from the Valley.

The inevitable blunders and delays—"friction," in military parlance—started immediately. To the west, Frémont misunderstood his orders and started the wrong way, and his tardy approach to the rendezvous with Shields was ruined in the end by a roaring thunderstorm, mud, and the exhaustion of his men and horses. Jackson and his army, now fairly flying south along the one paved highway on the Valley floor to escape the trap, passed through at the last hour, just before the jaws closed. Stonewall then turned about and bloodied both Union commands in twin battles—one against Frémont at Cross Keys on June 8 and the other against Shields at Port Republic on June 9—before disappearing into the countryside.

In the wake of this crushing disappointment, Lincoln again ordered McDowell to march south and link up with McClellan in front of the rebel capital. But McDowell's third order to march on Richmond was doomed, just as the first two had been. Shields' exhausted division was blown, unable to move any farther. And on June 20, with Jackson's whereabouts unknown, Lincoln held back two more of McDowell's divisions to guard the empty scenery.

Lee and Jackson had measured Lincoln exactly. Jackson and his tiny Valley army had tied up four times their number, in three military departments, as Lincoln chased him across the landscape. As a result of Lincoln's weeks in command, tens of thousands of Union troops would never arrive in front of Richmond where they were needed and could have been used. When Lee and Davis had dreaded a march toward Richmond, Lincoln had marched McDowell away from it. He had shifted McDowell's men to strike first one way and then the other, with the result that, in the end, they struck nowhere.

McClellan had clearly seen Lee and Jackson's design. When he got Lincoln's message halting McDowell's move toward Richmond in the attempt to trap Jackson, he had exploded, incredulous. "Heaven save a country governed by such counsels!" he wrote to his wife. "It is perfectly sickening to deal with such people . . . . I get more sick of them every day—for every day brings with it only additional proofs of their hypocrisy, knavery & folly." Lincoln and the other amateurs in Washington were, he said, "a precious lot of fools." In vain he telegraphed Lincoln, "The object of enemy's movement is probably to prevent reinforcements being sent to me."

McClellan knew that the best defense of Washington was an all-out attack on Richmond. Disheartened by what he perceived as Lincoln's betrayals, however, he could not bring himself to make it. June on the Peninsula became a month of inaction, of constant pouring rain and of day-to-day promises from McClellan to make the final assault. His best chance was in mid-June, when the rain subsided. He had been reinforced to a strength of 150,000 men, the largest army ever gathered on the continent, and with Jackson detached the rebel defenders were weak. Even then, however, McClellan hesitated, writing to his friend Barlow on June 23, "I dare not risk this Army on which I feel the fate of the nation depends."

While he waited, Jackson and his men returned from the Valley to join Lee, who had learned that the right wing of McClellan's army was "in the air"— vulnerable—extending north in the vain hope of linking up with McDowell. Lee pushed Jackson beyond the exposed flank, turning and crushing it while the balance of his army north of the Chickahominy pounded the Federals from the front. Ever audacious, Lee left only a skeleton force opposite the Federal left to defend Richmond. If McClellan had been so inclined, he could have pushed aggressively and likely driven into the rebel capital itself. After two days of attacks by Lee and his lieutenant that collapsed his right flank and drove it toward the James River, McClellan's overwhelming impulse was to shift the blame to Lincoln's government. Just after midnight on June 28, he wired the War Department:

I know that a few thousand men more would have changed this battle from a defeat to a victory—as it is the Govt must not & cannot hold me responsible for the result.

I feel too earnestly tonight—I have seen too many dead & wounded comrades to feel otherwise than that the Govt has not sustained this Army. If you do not do so now the game is lost.

> If I save this Army now I tell you plainly that I owe no thanks to you or any other persons in Washington—you have done your best to sacrifice this Army.

The Confederate assaults—complex, confusing, and usually delivered in piecemeal fashion—spanned nearly a full week, during which the officers and men in the ranks of the Army of the Potomac improvised a masterful fighting retreat, inflicting heavy casualties on Lee's army. A final grand Confederate attack at Malvern Hill just above the James River on July 1 was beaten back in a magnificent defensive effort. McClellan's army was now protected at Harrison's Landing along the James about twenty-five miles from Richmond, supplied by sea and defensible on all sides against any additional attacks. There the soldiers, still unbowed, enjoyed their first full rest in many weeks.

*   *   *

At first, it was unclear whether Harrison's Landing was the end of the Peninsula campaign, or just a pause before another drive on Richmond. McClellan immediately wired, "I need 50,000 more men, and with them I will retrieve our fortunes." Then two days later he asked for 100,000. McClellan had hit on a viable strategy: he would use the James River as a supply artery, ferry his men to the south bank of the river, and move inland to capture lightly-defended Petersburg, cutting Richmond's supply lines from the south. This strategy would help win the war when applied by Grant two years later. But Grant had the killer instinct, the confidence of Lincoln, and an exhausted foe. McClellan had none of these.

McClellan, it was clear, would not move without heavy reinforcements. And, because of Stanton's monumental blunder of stopping recruiting three months earlier, there were no reinforcements to be had. Lincoln considered bringing men from elsewhere, but it made little sense to give up gains in the West to reinforce losses in the East. It became clear to Lincoln by the middle of July that, despite his army's bravura display of engineering and fighting skill, the Peninsula campaign was the most magnificent defeat in the nation's history. "It seems unreasonable that a series of successes [in the West], extending through half-a-year, and clearing more than a hundred thousand square miles of country, should help us so little, while a single half-defeat should hurt us so much," he moaned.

Asked later if he had ever despaired of the country, Lincoln said, "When the Peninsula campaign terminated at Harrison's Landing, I was as nearly inconsolable as I could be and live." Mary Lincoln told friends of his sleepless nights. Those who saw him were shocked by his careworn appearance. George Julian mentioned that he looked "thin and haggard." Illinois friend Henry C. Whitney remembered:

> On Saturday, July 12th, 1862, I reached Washington on some business, and was the guest of one of the White House secretaries. . . . Presently Mr. Lincoln came slowly down-stairs; but oh! How haggard and dejected he looked. I had not seen him for nine months; and the change was frightful to behold. He looked the picture of heart-felt anguish—from which every ray of hope had forever fled. . . . Lincoln spoke to me and shook hands quite mechanically—he was absent-minded: he did not know me at all—he was oblivious of my presence, or of any one's presence.

Another Illinois friend who saw him then, Senator Orville Browning, wrote in his diary:

> [Lincoln] was in his Library writing, with directions to deny him to every body. I went in a moment. He looked weary, care-worn and troubled. I shook hands with him, and asked how he was. He said "tolerably well." I remarked that I felt concerned about him—regretted that troubles crowded so heavily upon him, and feared his health was suffering. He held me by the hand, pressed it, and said in a very tender and touching tone—"Browning I must die sometime." I replied, "Your fortunes Mr. President are bound up with those of the Country, and disaster to one would be disaster to the other, and I hope you will do all you can to preserve your health and life." He looked very sad, and there was a cadence of deep sadness in his voice. We parted I believe both of us with tears in our eyes.

Lincoln had taken on himself the anguish of the entire country, which now slowly became aware that the most anticipated campaign in its history had failed. In the West, too, things had stalled. The peak of public optimism in May had been so recent and so lofty that the slough of despond in July seemed that much deeper. Criticism of the administration came from every side.

There was a panic on Wall Street. People hoarded gold and shunned government bonds out of a lack of confidence in the future of the nation. Count Gurowski wrote that the Fourth of July was "the gloomiest since the birth of this republic. Never was the country so low, and after such sacrifices of blood, of time, and of money."

The soldiers in the Army of the Potomac generally shared McClellan's conviction that they had lost because Lincoln and the selfish politicians in Washington had refused to reinforce them. Artillery officer Alexander Webb spoke for many when he wrote to his father on July 10 that McClellan "stands higher this moment than he ever did before. In him all credit & damn the authorities who withheld reinforcements. . . ." Outside the army, many saw things the same way. Historian George Bancroft wrote to his son that the public was becoming aware of Lincoln's "successive, hasty, & contradictory acts of interference."

Even Greeley's staunch Republican—and anti-McClellan—New York *Tribune* agreed. On July 3, its correspondent with the Army of the Potomac termed the army's plight a "crime against the nation. . . . This crime is the refusal to reenforce McClellan." He went on, "I say that the blackest crime that Power can commit is to stalk upon the field of peril and say, 'Soldiers, I have no faith in your commander! Let your martyrdom proceed!'"

Private citizens from every Northern state told their gloom to public men with influence. "Public sentiment is . . . deep and bitter . . . against Mr. Lincoln because he is looked upon as an obstacle in the way of closing up this war," an Ohioan warned Salmon Chase; "Men are losing all respect for him and . . . for the office he holds and in these days of revolution God only knows what may come forth if the people get grounded in the belief that the inertia . . . of the President is . . . sapping the life of the Government." Instead of "inspiring the people, he represses their ardor," complained a Wisconsin man to his senator. General Benjamin Butler received a post from a Massachusetts congressman who predicted that "Unless Richmond is occupied before winter by the federal Army, Mr. Lincoln cannot complete his term of office." George Templeton Strong reported in his diary, "Prevailing color of people's talk is blue. What's very bad, we begin to lose faith in Uncle Abe." People saw Lincoln, he wrote, as "most honest and true, thoroughly sensible but without the decision and the energy the country wants." Among the most strident was abolitionist Wendell Phillips, who told Senator Charles Sumner, "Lincoln is doing twice as much today to break this Union as Davis is. We are paying . . . [the] penalty for having a *timid & ignorant* President, all the more injurious because honest."

Writing at this time, the elite British correspondent Edward Dicey, who had spent the first six months of 1862 traveling in America for London's *The Spectator*, noted that,

> With regard to the President himself, everybody spoke with an almost brutal frankness. Politically, at that time, Lincoln was regarded as a failure. Why he, individually, was elected, or rather, selected [nominated], nobody, to this day, seems to know. . . . A shrewd, hard-headed, self-educated man, with sense enough to perceive his own deficiencies, but without the instinctive genius which supplies the place of learning, he is influenced by men whom he sees through, but yet cannot detect. . . . [W]hen you have called the President "Honest Abe Lincoln," according to the favorite phrase of the American press, you have said a great deal, doubtless, but you have also said all that can be said in his favor. He works hard, and does little; and unites a painful sense of responsibility to a still more painful sense, perhaps, that his work is too great for him to grapple with.

In the North, the opposition press was silent no longer. Democratic editors, just starting to look ahead to the mid-term elections in the fall of 1862, began to emerge after spending the past year hunkering down. McClellan's reverse in front of Richmond required that they come to his defense and resume their places as critics of Lincoln's government. On July 16, 1862, the Brooklyn *Eagle* sounded its displeasure and signaled the start of the election season:

> The treasure, the life of the nation, was unhesitatingly placed at the disposal of the authorities. . . . With means absolutely limitless, and with an army as large as any nation ever raised—what has been done? . . . Who can claim that those vast elements of power placed in the hands of the administration have secured all that was justly expected of them? . . . Surely the country had a right to expect, after an expenditure of five hundred million dollars, after a loss of over one hundred thousand men something more than this. . . . It is evident to the people, it is evident to the whole world, that we have secured nothing commensurate with the sacrifices we have made. . . . The nation is bleeding to death.
>
> What the nation wants is leading men; men fit to meet the crisis; men adequate to wield the great elements of power still intact.

After hearing the Democratic tom-toms in July, Republicans began to look with concern toward the approaching fall elections. Lincoln, however, was listening only to the click of the telegraph key in the War Office tapping out the fate of McClellan's army. On July 7, he clambered aboard the USS *Ariel* and steamed to Harrison's Landing on the James River to see the army's condition for himself. When he arrived, McClellan, still confident in his notion that Lincoln deferred to him—that Lincoln "was always much influenced by me when we were together," as he had told his wife—came aboard the *Ariel* and handed the President a letter dictating to him what should be the guiding principles of the war. It was Little Mac's most spectacular insubordination, reminiscent of Seward's "Thoughts for Your Consideration" at the height of the Sumter crisis.

As with Seward earlier, McClellan mistook himself to be the maker of national policy. In the letter, which became famous as the "Harrison's Landing Letter," McClellan instructed Lincoln that the war "should be conducted upon the highest principles known to Christian Civilization." It should not be a war of subjugation. The confiscation of Southern property or freeing Southern slaves or any other such "radical views" must not "be contemplated for a moment." Such views, especially for the emancipation of slaves, "will rapidly disintegrate our present Armies," he insisted. Lincoln read the letter in McClellan's presence and then put it in his pocket without a word. The next day he steamed back to Washington with a fuller knowledge of the political pretensions of his top general.

President Lincoln's cold reception to McClellan's exquisitely wrought manifesto was the subject of the general's letter to his wife the following day. It reeked of the old and now stale disdain for the President: "I do not know to what extent he has profited by his visit—not much I fear, for he really seems quite incapable of rising to the height of the merits of the question & the magnitude of the crisis." For the next few weeks, McClellan's letters were full of venom for Lincoln and the politicians in the capital, for "the stupidity & wickedness at Washington which have done their best to sacrifice as noble an Army as every marched to battle." "I have lost all regard & respect for the majority of the Administration," he wrote, "& doubt the propriety of my brave men's blood being spilled to further the designs of such a set of heartless villains."

*   *   *

Lincoln, meanwhile, had concluded that he needed better military advice. On July 11 he sent for General Henry Halleck to come to Washington to take the post of General-in-Chief of all the armies, the position he himself had filled since McClellan's demotion exactly four months earlier. He also combined McDowell, Banks, and Frémont into one army, named it the Army of Virginia, and put in under the command of another import from the West, General John Pope. The new scheme was Lincoln's first indication that he had thought better of trying his hand at playing general, and had broken his bad habit of dividing military command among promiscuous combinations of booted councils and braided panels. Naming Halleck to McClellan's old post as General-in-Chief, however, tore completely Lincoln's already-shredded relationship with McClellan, who wrote to his wife:

> [The President and I] never conversed on the subject [of Halleck's appointment]—I was never informed of his views or intentions, & even now have not been officially informed of the appt. I only know it through the newspapers. In all these things the Presdt & those around him have acted so as to make the matter as offensive as possible—he has not shown the slightest gentlemanly or friendly feeling & I cannot regard him as in any respect my friend—I am confident that he would relieve me tomorrow if he dared do so. His cowardice alone prevents it. I can never regard him with other feelings than those of thorough contempt—for his mind, heart & morality.

Lincoln's four months as acting General-in-Chief had crippled his relationship with McClellan and many of the officers of his main army in the Eastern Theater, and plunged the country into desolation deeper than after Bull Run a year before. But the most far-reaching result of the failed Peninsula campaign was Lincoln's realization that the rebellious states would not be subdued by a "kid glove" war. The illusion that Union feeling was still strong in the South was finally shattered; the fantasy that the regime of a few Southern firebrands could be collapsed by one sharp blow was dashed. The Seven Days' Battles destroyed once and for all the notion that the war would be settled by anything short of conquest. From now on, Lincoln saw, the conflict must be a "hard war."

And the war must be revolutionary. It could no longer be fought to restore the nation as it had been before the firing on Fort Sumter. It could no longer be fought to bring the states back into their old relations. That, Lincoln now saw clearly, was impossible. Instead, the war's purpose must be to destroy the sin that had brought on the war. Slavery itself must not—could not—survive. As Lincoln told the story later, "Things had gone on from bad to worse, until I felt that we had reached the end of our rope on the plan of operations we had been pursuing; that we had about played our last card, and must change our tactics, or lose the game!"

On July 13, less than one week after his meeting at Harrison's Landing in Virginia with McClellan, Lincoln pulled up to Gideon Welles' door in his carriage and invited his naval secretary to accompany him and Seward to the funeral of Stanton's infant son. As the carriage started to roll away, Lincoln spoke of emancipation. He had given it much thought, he told Seward and Welles. "We must free the slaves," he said emphatically, "or be ourselves subdued."

Nine days later, on July 22, 1862, Lincoln laid his draft for the Emancipation Proclamation in front of the Cabinet.

"The Overdue Bill"

Part Three

Lincoln's Proclamation

"A Monstrous Usurpation, a Criminal Wrong,
and an Act of National Suicide."

Chapter 22

Lincoln, Race, and the North

"He is a first-rate *second-rate man.*"

A braham Lincoln was not harkening to the voice of the people when he sat down to draft the Emancipation Proclamation. Just the opposite, in fact—to propose emancipation, Lincoln would have to ignore the overwhelming weight of Northern prejudice against black people and a widespread complacency about slavery. To lift blacks into equality under the law, Lincoln would have to assert a kind of moral leadership not seen since the Revolution.

* * *

Free black men were just as unwanted in the North as in the South, and prejudice in the North was just as violent, if not more so. In 1832, Alexis de Tocqueville had remarked on it. "The prejudice of race," he wrote, "appears to be stronger in the states that have abolished slavery than in those where it still exists; and nowhere is it so intolerant as in those states where servitude has never been known." According to de Tocqueville,

> in those parts of the Union in which Negroes are no longer slaves they have in no wise drawn nearer to the whites. . . . Thus the Negro is free, but he can share neither the rights, nor the pleasures, nor the labor, nor the afflictions, nor the tomb of him whose equal he has been declared to be . . . Among the Americans of the South, Nature sometimes reasserts her rights and restores a transient equality between the blacks and whites. . . . Thus it is in the United States that the prejudice which repels the Negroes seems to increase in proportion as they are emancipated. . . . In the South, where slavery still exists, less trouble is taken to keep the negro apart: they sometimes share the labors and the pleasures of the white men; people are prepared to mix with them to some extent; legislation is more harsh against them, but customs are more tolerant and gentle.

Lydia Child, a Bostonian writing at the same time as de Tocqueville, told her New England readers that even though slavery did not exist among them, "the very spirit of the hateful and mischievous thing is here in all its strength. . . . Our prejudice against colored people is even more inveterate than in the South. The planter is often attached to his negroes, and lavishes caresses and kind words upon them, as he would a favorite hound; but our cold-hearted ignoble prejudice admits of no exception—no intermission."

In the three decades between de Tocqueville and Lincoln, life only got meaner for the black man in the North. Prejudice hardened as the Revolutionary belief in equality faded. In 1859, Alexander Stephens of Georgia could say, "In my judgment there are more thinking men at the North now who look upon our system of slavery as right—socially, morally, and politically—than there were even at the South thirty years ago." Everywhere in the free states, blacks were made painfully and constantly aware that they lived in a society made for the white man and dedicated to keeping the black man in his place. Blacks were "free" only in the strictest legal sense. They were still shackled by prejudice, custom, and law in every area of their lives. So pitiful was their daily existence that Northerners saw it as proof of their inferiority. British-born diarist Fanny Kemble, living in Philadelphia, wrote that blacks in the North, while "not slaves indeed . . . are pariahs; debarred from all fellowships save with their own despised race—scorned by the lowest white ruffians in your streets, not tolerated as companions even by the foreign menials in your kitchen. They are certainly free but they are also degraded, rejected, the offscum and offscourings of the very dregs of your society; they are free from the chain, the whip, the enforced task and unpaid toil of slavery; but they are not less under a ban." As Susan B. Anthony put it, "While the cruel slave-driver lacerates the black man's mortal body, we, of the North, flay the spirit."

When Lincoln was elected, four million black slaves lived in the slave states. At the same time, fewer than 250,000 blacks lived in the free states, where they made up only about 1% of the population. Of those quarter million, fewer than 15,000 lived in New England, the only states where they were allowed to vote on the same terms as white men. They rarely dared vote, however. Even in forward-thinking New England, blacks were men apart, living in small communities of jumbled shacks, gathering several generations under one roof for safety, discouraged from taking any positions but bootblacks, waiters, barbers, servants, cooks, laborers, porters, and chimney sweeps. Their existence was grim even in Boston, the Puritan cradle of the abolition movement, where one black man reported, "the position of the people . . . is far from an enviable one. . . . While colored men have many rights, they have few privileges."

More than one-half the Northern black population lived in the mid-Atlantic states. There, in the state of New York, black men were prohibited from voting by a requirement that they prove they owned $250 in property before they could cast a ballot. This was not an antique law—it was reaffirmed in 1860, the same year New York voted for Lincoln for President. Black people were ghosts in New York City. British correspondent Edward Dicey wrote, "At the hotels, and in wealthy private houses, the servants are frequently black, but in the streets there are few Negroes visible. Here, as elsewhere, they form a race apart, never walking in company with white persons, except as servants." Writing in 1862, Dicey sketched the miserable plight of Northern blacks: "I never by any chance, in the Free States, saw a colored man dining at a public table, or occupying any position, however humble, in which he was placed in authority over white persons. . . . I hardly ever remember seeing a black employed as shopman, or placed in any post of responsibility." New York's Henry Ward Beecher protested that blacks there were "almost without education, . . . cannot even ride in the cars of our city railroads, . . . are snuffed at in the house of God, or tolerated with ill-disguised disgust." They were "crowded down, down, down, through the most menial callings to the bottom of society. We heap upon them moral obloquy more atrocious than that which the master heaps upon the slave." A black New Yorker noted that there, blacks had become the "objects of . . . marked abuse and insult. From many of the grocery corners, stones, potatoes, and pieces of coal would often be hurled, by idle young loafers, standing about."

In Philadelphia—where 25,000 free blacks lived, more than in any other city—it was the same. A black journal asked, "What have the colored people done that they should be thus treated? Even here, in the city of Philadelphia, in many places, it is almost impossible for a respectable colored person to walk the streets without being insulted by a set of blackguards and cowards." When Frederick Douglass visited Philadelphia in 1862, he remarked, "Colored persons, no matter how well dressed or well behaved, ladies and gentlemen, rich or poor, are not permitted to ride on any of the many railways through that Christian city. . . . The whole aspect of city usage at this point is mean, contemptible and barbarous."

The further west a black man went, the harsher he found it. With a large population of people of Southern origin, and with a fluid social structure where a black man would be more apt to challenge whites for jobs, the

Northwest—especially the states of Ohio, Indiana, and Illinois—nurtured intense racial prejudice. In Ohio, there was a color test: anyone with a "visible admixture of Negro blood" could not vote. Dicey related a conversation with an Ohioan who said, "There is but one thing, sir, that we want here, and that is to get rid of the niggers."

If they left Ohio, blacks could not go to Indiana or Lincoln's Illinois. Those states barred black immigrants by law. George Julian of Indiana noted, "Our people hate the Negro with a perfect if not supreme hatred." In Illinois, no black person from another state could remain for more than ten days; beyond ten days he or she was subject to arrest, confinement in jail, a $50 fine, and removal from the state. As late as June of 1862, citizens there voted overwhelmingly to keep the exclusion clause; in Lincoln's hometown of Springfield, the exclusion clause was approved twelve hundred to two hundred. Several Western states prohibited blacks from testifying in cases in which white men were involved. When one black Illinoisan in 1860 circulated a petition against the "Testimony Law" barring black witnesses, Abraham Lincoln would not sign it, prompting the man to charge, "if we [blacks] sent our children to school, Abraham Lincoln would kick them out, in the name of Republicanism and anti-slavery."

There was no distinct statement in the Constitution about who could be an American citizen, but according to the Supreme Court's 1857 Dred Scott decision, blacks not only could not be citizens, they were "so far unfit that they had no rights which the white man was bound to respect." A black person could not hold a government job, even as a mail carrier, a rule the new Republican congress upheld in 1861. The *Brooklyn Daily Eagle* summed up the feeling of much of the North: "There are laws which govern the actions of men stronger than any upon the statute book. It is not within the power of the law-maker to place negroes on terms of equality with white men. The never-varying edict of God has set a barrier between them, and only at the cost of the degradation of both races and the final annihilation of both, can this barrier be bridged over."

*   *   *

Prejudice against blacks found its most violent expression among Democrats, whose party had been dominated by slave-owners since Jefferson, but racial prejudice was strong also among Republicans. From the beginning, free-soilers had been opposed to the extension of slavery, not out of love for the black man, but because they wanted an all-white West. David Wilmot, who gave his name to the historic free-soil Wilmot Proviso of the 1840s, described it as the "White Man's Proviso," insisting, "I plead the cause and rights of the free white man." By barring slavery in the new lands in the West he intended to save it for "the sons of toil, of my own race and own color." Most Republicans saw the great issue of stopping the spread of slavery the same way as Wilmot, and advertised the Republican Party, especially in the West, as "the real white man's party." Horace Greeley, the editor of the arch-Republican New York *Tribune*, went on record as saying that black people would always occupy an inferior social position. William Seward saw black men as a "foreign and feeble" element of the population, and he predicted that they would eventually die out in the Northern states. "They are God's poor," he said, "they always have been and always will be everywhere." Frank Blair, Jr., leader of the Missouri Republican Party, announced that the party's object there was "Missouri for white men and white men for Missouri." Even Senator Ben Wade, Washington's most energetic champion of blacks' rights, complained about their "odor," grumbled about all the "nigger" cooks in the capital, and swore that he had eaten food "cooked by Niggers until I can smell and taste the Nigger . . . all over."

The most dyed-in-the-wool Republican journals, while they championed the black man's cause in the abstract, despised him in the flesh. The *Tribune* published its opinion that, "As a class, the Blacks are indolent, improvident, servile, and licentious." The free-soil journal *National Era* stated ruefully, "It is the real evil of the negro race that they are so fit for slavery as they are." Even those radical Republicans who felt that the Republican mission extended to destroying slavery where it existed recoiled at the idea of raising the black man to their own level. "It [does not] necessarily follow," wrote the Republican editor of the Chicago *Evening Journal*, "that we should fellowship with the Negroes because our policy shakes off their shackles."

Many black leaders disdained the Republican Party for its racism at its heart. In an Independence Day speech at an anti-slavery meeting in 1860, Frederick Douglass painted Democrats and Republicans with the same brush: "So far as the principles of freedom and the hopes of the black man are concerned," he charged, "all these parties are barren and unfruitful; neither of them seeks to lift the Negro out of his fetters and rescue this day from odium and disgrace. Take Abraham Lincoln. I want to know if any man can tell me the difference between the antislavery of Abraham Lincoln and the antislavery of [slave owner] Henry Clay? . . . No party, it seems to me, is entitled to the sympathy of antislavery men, unless that party is willing to extend to the black man all the rights of a citizen."

Lincoln was the Republican nominee, of course, largely because his heart beat in time with his party's. Certainly he was anchored in his belief that, "If slavery is not wrong, nothing is wrong," but he also knew that "a universal feeling, whether well or ill-founded, can not be safely disregarded," and in his 1858 debates with Stephen Douglas, although he never pandered to the racism of his audiences, he was careful to show solidarity with the mainstream prejudices of his fellow Republicans. When Douglas baited him on his "Black Republican" views, Lincoln countered,

> I am not, nor ever have been in favor of bringing about in any way the social and political equality of the white and black races,—I am not nor ever have been in favor of making voters or jurors of negroes, nor of qualifying them to hold office, nor to intermarry with white people; and I will say in addition to this that there is a physical difference between the white and black races which I believe will for ever forbid the two races living together on terms of social and political equality. And inasmuch as they cannot so live, while they do remain together there must be the position of superior and inferior, and I as much as any other man am in favor of having the superior position assigned to the white race.

Lincoln made exactly the same speech, almost word for word, two more times before he became President. The Republican New York *Times* summed up his position on "the Negro question" just after his election: "He declares his opposition to negro suffrage, and to everything looking towards placing negroes upon a footing of political and social equality with the whites;—but he asserts for them a perfect equality of civil and personal rights under the constitution."

There were men, especially in the East, who would go farther; and men, especially in the West, who would not go so far. But Lincoln walked a middle path that allowed Republicans at both extremes to vote him into office. The Homeric clash of arms that ensued between the North and South was the setting for Lincoln's struggle to balance his elected responsibility to do the will of a racist people with his moral responsibility to put the expression of that will—slavery—on the road to extinction. It was in the tension between these two seemingly irreconcilable ends that he demonstrated the consummate statesmanship, his mastery of the art of the possible, whose culminating act was the Emancipation Proclamation.

* * *

Once Lincoln was safely in office it was inevitable that the schisms within the Republican Party over the race problem would appear. The national emergency over Sumter and the early-war danger to the capital submerged the differences until after Bull Run, but secretary John Hay's diary entry of May 7, 1861, reveals that, only four weeks after the first cannon shot, some already expected the war "to result in the entire abolition of slavery," and that Lincoln's "daily correspondence was thickly interspersed by such suggestions." Lincoln's answer to this, as stated privately to Hay, was that the war's purpose was not the revolutionary one of ending slavery but the conservative one of "proving that popular government is not an absurdity. . . . whether in a free government the minority have the right to break up the government whenever they choose," and his July 4, 1861, Message to Congress reaffirmed that he had "no purpose, directly or indirectly, to interfere with slavery in the States where it exists." Only after Bull Run dispelled the notion of a quick end to the war did the emancipation debate in the North begin in earnest.

The first battle in this war of ideas came after Frémont's September 1861 emancipation proclamation, which Lincoln rescinded to keep the loyalty of the Border State men, the Democrats, and the conservative generals. While the Democratic newspaper editors were soothed by Lincoln's conservative response to Frémont, they still bared their teeth, warning that emancipation "would bring sure and irretrievable defeat from the day on which it was promulgated." "Two-thirds of the army," they said, "would refuse to march another step or serve another day in such a crusade." The Democratic Pennsylvania *Valley Spirit* argued that the best way to "turn the world topsy turvey" would be to permit the abolitionists to "go on in their plan of turning loose 4,000,000 indolent negroes." *The Crisis* quoted an officer in the Army of the Potomac who said "that if this war was to be converted into one of emancipation of the Negroes, there would be a general resignation of the officers, which would be virtually a disbandment of our Army."

The Democrats' blasts were merely cautionary, however. By mid-summer of 1862, Lincoln had not yet strayed from his stated intention to uphold "the Constitution as it is" and restore "the Union as it was." Radicals still cursed the President in frustration. According to one, Lincoln had "gone to the rescue of slavery, which had almost committed suicide." One Massachusetts Republican complained, "The key of the slave's chain is now kept in the White House." "There has never been an Administration so thoroughly devoted to slavery as the present," fumed another; "no other ever returned so many fugitive slaves, nor did so much to propitiate the Slave Power." Joseph Medill mailed the President a call to action: "Our nation is on the brink of ruin," it warned. "Mr. Lincoln, for God's sake and your Country's sake rise to the realization . . . that this is a Slave-holders rebellion."

Even as Lincoln's policy remained "hands off slavery" as required by the Constitution, however, the problem of what to do with the slaves freed by the friction along the army's front lines remained. Northerners feared that the trickle of slaves liberated by advancing Union soldiers might grow into a torrent, flooding the North with poor, illiterate, despised blacks. This went to the heart of the race problem as Northerners saw it: *What do we do with the black people among us?* They overwhelmingly agreed with Old Man Blair: "It is certainly the wish of every patriot that all within the limits of our Union should be homogeneous in race and of our own blood." His heir, Frank Blair, Jr., insisted publicly, "The idea of liberating the slaves and allowing them to remain in the country is one that never will be tolerated." *The Crisis* shook a warning finger at Lincoln: "Should the abolitionists . . . finally convert this war into one to abolish slavery, they must first find some place to put the freed negroes, as well as those who are now free amongst us, before entering upon such a doubtful and revolutionary experiment."

*   *   *

With this in mind, in an attempt to sweeten the pill of emancipation for the North, Lincoln early on embraced a solution—or, more properly, a fantasy— that already enjoyed wide acceptance among Northerners, a solution that went back through Henry Clay all the way to Thomas Jefferson: he would ship the blacks away. In October 1861, he asked Secretary of the Interior Caleb B. Smith to look into a proposal for colonizing blacks on the isthmus of Chiriqui, in present-day Panama, and in his December 1861 Message to Congress he announced the project publicly for the first time.

Colonization was only the first part of Lincoln's two-part solution to the race problem. It made palatable the second part of the solution, which was that black slaves would be freed gradually, state by state, with compensation of $300 or so for each freed slave. On March 6, 1862, Lincoln sent to Congress a recommendation that money be set aside to compensate any state that, at some time, of its own free will, might wish to gradually emancipate its slaves. It left the prerogative with the states, precisely where the prerogative had been since the Revolution. But even this weak gesture, although applauded by the Republican press, provoked tirades from Border State men. It was unconstitutional, they said. Senator Willard Saulsbury of Delaware warned, "Adopt these measures . . . and the war upon which you have just entered, instead of being speedily closed, will not be closed in your day or mine, sir. It is folly to suppose that the people of this country . . . are going to allow you to interfere with their domestic institutions, and . . . to destroy their constitutional rights." Kentucky congressman William H. Wadsworth was less fastidious: "I utterly spit at it and despise it," he said. "Emancipation in the cotton States is simply an absurdity. . . . There is not enough power in the world to compel it to be done."

Lincoln listened in the spring of 1862 as the Democratic press stirred for the first time since the previous summer. *The Crisis* prophesied a red dawn:

> Victories or defeats amount to but little, if the war is to be converted into a war merely of freeing 4,000,000 of negroes, to be turned loose on the North. Do this, and it will take both armies united to protect the white people from their robberies, assassinations, house-burnings, and all other acts which a starving, revengeful, half-civilized race can conceive of in their madness.

Lincoln's March 6 proposal also drew fire from the other extreme, abolitionists such as William Lloyd Garrison, who thought that Lincoln had offered a stone where bread was needed. He called the proposal a "'decoy duck' or a 'red herring,'" a "cowardly and criminal avoidance of the one great saving issue." Count Gurowski saw it as a "trick" to save slavery by throwing its enemies "small crumbs." Thaddeus Stevens derided it as "the most diluted milk-and-water-gruel proposition that was ever given to the American nation." In the end, Lincoln's proposal went for nothing. The Border States repudiated Lincoln's offer, obstinately refusing to emancipate their slaves. Lincoln's proposal proved only that the loyal slave states would cling to slavery just as tenaciously as the rebel ones.

Thus rebuffed, he passed the torch of anti-slavery to the Republican-dominated 37th Congress. The Radicals on Capitol Hill acted swiftly and with a will, passing measures that now-departed Southern leaders had blocked for years: the prohibition of slavery in the territories (the signal issue of the 1860 election), a law for more effective suppression of the slave sea-trade, and recognition of the new black nations of Liberia and Haiti.

And Congress freed slaves—not gradually, but all 3,128 of them at once—in the only place it had jurisdiction, the District of Columbia. Sumner had chided, "Do you know who is at this moment the largest slave-*holder* in the United States? Abraham Lincoln, for he holds all the three thousand slaves of the District of Columbia, which is more than any other person in the country holds." Lincoln gave credence to Sumner's jibe by balking at signing the bill, according to a friend of the senator, who reported that "[Sumner's] severest trial, during these days, was in, as he expressed it, 'screwing Old Abe up to the sticking point.' With considerable impatience [Sumner] broke out, 'How slow this child of Freedom is being born!'" Orville Browning also mentioned Lincoln's reluctance to sign the bill, writing in his diary on April 14, two days before Lincoln signed it:

> He told me . . . that it should have been for gradual emancipation—that now families would at once be deprived of cooks, stable boys &c and they of their protectors without any provision for them. He further told me that he would not sign the bill before Wednesday—That old Gov Wickliffe [of Kentucky] had two family servants with him who were sickly, and who would not be benefited by freedom, and wanted time to remove them, but could not get them out of the City until Wednesday, and that the Gov had come frankly to him and asked for time.

While Lincoln was taking care of the Kentuckians, Congress was out-emancipating the President, and it was obvious. John Hickman of Pennsylvania rose in the House to denounce "the refusal on the part of the President . . . to discharge . . . a plain duty" to weaken the enemy, and decried Lincoln's "irresponsibility and imbecility" and his "lack of traits of character necessary to the discharge of grave responsibilities." Count Gurowski grumbled into his diary,

> Mr. Lincoln is forced out again from one of his pro-slavery entrenchments; he was obliged to yield, and to sign the hard-fought bill for emancipation in the District of Columbia; but how reluctantly, with what bad grace he signed it! Good boy; he wished not to strike his *mammy* [slavery]; and to think that the friends of humanity in Europe will credit

this emancipation not where it is due, not to the noble pressure exercised by the high-minded Northern masses, but to this Kentucky ———.

At the same time, Lincoln could not ignore that waking giant, the Democratic press, which parried every blow against the status quo. The Brooklyn *Daily Eagle* was one that raged against the District of Columbia's Emancipation Bill in a series of editorials, arguing that it angered the South at the same time that it hurt the freedmen themselves, and predicting its sorrowful effects on the "poor creatures," saying, "Many an old 'Aunty' in Washington will, for the few remaining years of their lives regret, in their stupid way, the measure that only separated them from their children and friends, and transferred them from the care of their owners, upon whom they had a just claim, to the charity of the world."

This was in mid-April of 1862. There was a new sensation in May. General David Hunter had begged Stanton for a front-line military command with the object of forcing Lincoln's hand on emancipation. "Please let me have my own way on the subject of slavery," he had pleaded. Stanton gave Hunter his wish. The Union army had won lodgments on a few islands off South Carolina, and Hunter had been put in command of the tiny beachhead with the grand title of the Department of the South, comprising South Carolina, Georgia, and Florida. On May 9, Hunter bid to make his name immortal by decreeing, "The persons in these three States . . . heretofore held as slaves, are . . . declared forever free."

Lincoln issued an order declaring Hunter's decree "altogether void," moving even more quickly than he had the previous September after Frémont's emancipation proclamation. As before, Radicals cursed him: "Be sure that Lincoln is at heart with Slavery," Gurowski wrote to Governor Andrew. Gurowski called the President "an unavoidable evil, an original sin," and told his diary, "Of course Mr. Lincoln overrules General Hunter's proclamation. It is too human, too noble, too great, for the tall Kentuckian." A Springfield friend of Lincoln's warned Senator Trumbull, "Our people feel disheartened, discouraged & disgraced and are ready to curse the administration and all that belongs to it . . . ." Greeley demanded from the pulpit of the *Tribune* that Lincoln get himself a policy and quit appeasing the Democrats, wailing, "We shuffle and trifle on, and let the Union go to ruin." Wendell Phillips, at a Republican rally in Boston, drew applause when he cried, "President Lincoln with a senile lick-spittle haste runs before he is bidden to remove the Hunter proclamation. The president and the Cabinet are treasonable. The President and the Secretary of War should be impeached."

This radical spasm was more persistent than after the Frémont affair, drawing its staying power from a growing sense that this time victory was near. In the coming months, Lincoln was pelted with abolitionist petitions, and there grew a long line of visitors to the White House arguing almost daily for emancipation. Abolitionist speakers such as Frederick Douglass, Wendell Phillips, and William Lloyd Garrison were criss-crossing the East, drawing record crowds and enjoying new admiration from mainstream journals like the *New York Times*. Governor Andrew of Massachusetts was one of many who wrote to Lincoln of a new problem: without emancipation, badly-needed new recruits were staying home. They "feel it a heavy draft on their patriotism," he said, that they should be asked to fight without being allowed "to fire on the enemy's magazine."

Lincoln would be tormented throughout the summer by the hard riddle of freedom. As he turned the great issue over and over in his mind, he often revealed his perplexity to visitors, as on June 20, when a group of Quakers came to his office and urged a proclamation. "If a decree of emancipation could abolish slavery," he told them, "John Brown would have done the work effectually." He then grew thoughtful, saying he was "deeply sensible of his need of Divine assistance," and wondered if "perhaps he might be an instrument in God's hands of accomplishing a great work." In the end, however, he turned them away, saying, "Perhaps . . . God's way of accomplishing the end [of slavery] . . . may be different from [yours]."

In the next two weeks, McClellan's failure on the Peninsula withered the hope of ending the war quickly and of reuniting the nation as it had been. In the first days of July, as Lincoln sat for hours in the War Office and listened to the telegraph key tapping out its chronicle of disaster from McClellan, he wrote out the first draft of the Emancipation Proclamation on pieces of foolscap. He still resisted the thought of issuing it, however. On the Fourth of July, Charles Sumner twice called on Lincoln to issue an emancipation decree, encouraging him to "make the day more sacred and historic than ever." Lincoln refused, telling Sumner it was "too big a lick," explaining, "I would do it if I were not afraid that half the officers would fling down their arms and three more States [Kentucky, Maryland, and Missouri] would rise."

A week later, on July 12, Lincoln invited the congressmen from the Border States to the White House and made a last, passionate appeal for gradual emancipation, with compensation, followed by colonization. He had made a similar argument to these same men before, in a short address he had added to his May 19 revocation of General Hunter's order. In both messages, he reasoned that the Border States' embrace of emancipation would shorten the war by dashing Southern hopes that they would someday unite with the Confederacy, and that "friction and abrasion" caused by the war and political pressure in Congress would free the slaves anyway, without the generous terms he now offered. "The change [gradual emancipation] contemplates would come gently as the dews of Heaven, not rending or wrecking anything," he pleaded.

Again the Border State men refused to budge. These were property rights, after all. Their written reply to Lincoln's proposition was all business: they dismissed it as "nothing less than deportation from the country of sixteen hundred million dollars' worth of producing labor, and the substitution in its place of an interest-bearing debt of the same amount."

*   *   *

Perhaps when he looked into the Border State men's faces that day, Lincoln saw the fierce glint of their intransigence and sensed the futility of his conservative appeal. Because overnight—in his disappointment over their backwardness, in his despair over the failure of the Peninsula Campaign, and under heavy pressure from Radical Republicans—his conservatism yielded to a new, revolutionary purpose. It was the very next morning, in his buggy ride with Seward and Welles, that he told them of his conclusion that the emancipation proclamation was a "military necessity" and that "we must free the slaves or be ourselves subdued."

Lincoln waited, however, before committing himself to such extreme steps. First he had to confront the Radical clique at work in the Capitol, who were ready that same week to seize direction of the war by passing a new, harsher Confiscation Act, a bill which they had introduced on the first day of the congressional session in December and which they had pushed, vehemently and almost continuously, for eight months. Now, in mid-July, it had become clear that the Radicals had the votes to pass the bill, which would declare "forever free" the slaves of rebels fighting the Union and would enlist them as soldiers in the Union army. It was well known that Lincoln opposed the bill on the grounds that it was unconstitutional, since it freed slaves in states where slavery was legal. If slaves were to be freed by force in those states, Lincoln maintained, it must be by the "war powers" which only he, as Commander-in-Chief, possessed.

When the Radicals rammed the bill through despite his objections, Lincoln responded by signing the bill on the last day of Congress with one embellishment: he attached his veto message to the signed bill, to become part of the record as a signal that he did not intend to enforce it. The bill, his act implied, was a dead letter. Lincoln's veto message was read in the crowded chambers "amid the sneers and laughter of the abolitionists."

The sneers and laughter turned to rage after the closing gavel sounded. Lincoln's snub, wrote George Julian, was "inexpressibly provoking to a large majority of Congress." "No one at a distance," he said, "could have formed any adequate conception of the hostility of Republican members toward Mr. Lincoln at final adjournment. . . . Mr. Wade said the country was going to hell,

Vanity Fair, October 4, 1862

"What Will He Do with Them?" A.L.—"Darn these here blackbirds!—If nobody won't buy 'em I'll have to open the cages and let 'em fly."

and that the scenes witnessed in the French Revolution were nothing in comparison with what we should see here." Gurowski murmured darkly into his inkpot and scrawled in his diary, "Mr. Lincoln makes a new effort to save his *mammy*, and tries to neutralize the confiscation bill. Mr. Lincoln will not make a step beyond what is called the Border-States' policy; and it may prove too late when he will decide to honestly execute the law of Congress."

This was in mid-July, when the North was becoming aware that McClellan's Peninsula campaign had failed. The collapse of the entire year's efforts, both in Congress and on the battlefield, plunged Republicans into a deep despondency. The anxious managing editor of the Chicago *Tribune* forwarded to Lincoln a letter from one reader who wrote that "the President . . . hangs back, hesitates, and leaves the country to drift," and he warned, "I am receiving daily many similar letters from all parts of the country for the [news]paper, evincing a deep-seated anxiety on the part of the people. I do not publish them because I know they would exercise a most serious influence on the public mind."

Senator John Sherman of Ohio wrote to Secretary Chase, "Oh God, how I feel what a blessing it would be, if in this hour of peril we had a strong firm hand at the head of affairs—who would use boldly all the powers of his office to put down this rebellion . . . . I never knew apprehension & fear settle upon the great mass of our People before—If we fail my conviction is that history will rest the awful responsibility upon Mr Lincoln—[not] for want of patriotism but for want of nerve."

"We are in a deplorable condition," agreed Chase, "—armies inactive—councils uncertain—credit drooping."

Such was the mood when, on August 1, Wendell Phillips ascended the stage in Abington, Massachusetts, and delivered an attack on Lincoln that resounded worldwide, a speech that prompted the London *Times* to write, "Anything more violent is scarcely possible to imagine, and anything more daring in time of Civil War was never perpetrated in any country by any sane man who valued his life and liberty." Phillips' oration derived its persuasive power from the collapse of his abolitionist audience's faith in Lincoln. He began simply: "I think the present purpose of the government, so far as it has now a purpose, is to end the war and save slavery." Then he warmed to his subject:

> It may be said of Mr. Lincoln,—that if he had been a traitor, he could
> not have worked better to strengthen one side, and hazard the success of

the other. There is more danger today that Washington will be taken than Richmond.

Our present policy neither aims to annihilate that state of things we call "the South" . . . nor replace it with a substitute. Such an aimless war I call wasteful and murderous. Better that the South should go to-day, than that we should prolong such a war. Until this nation announces, in some form or other, that this is a war, not against Jefferson Davis, but against a system . . . until we do that, we shall have no prospect of peace.

I do not believe in the government. I do not believe this government has got either vigor or a purpose. It drifts with events. The President has not uttered a word which gives even a twilight glimpse of any antislavery purpose. He may be honest,—nobody cares whether the tortoise is honest or not; he has neither insight, nor prevision, nor decision. . . .

I will tell you what he is. He is a first-rate *second-rate man*. He is one of the best specimens of a second-rate man, and he is honestly waiting, like any other servant, for the people to come and send him on any errand they wish. In ordinary times, when the seas are calm, you can sail without a pilot . . . to-day the nation's bark scuds, under the tempest, lee-shore and maelstrom on each side, needing no holiday captain, but a pilot, to weather the storm.

Lincoln deepened the disappointment of the abolitionists when, on August 14, he invited a delegation of five local black men to the White House as part of an effort to convince twenty-five or fifty black families to volunteer for his pet project, the colony on the Chiriqui isthmus. His tack was unflattering. He began by emphasizing the breadth of the racial divide: "We have between us a broader difference than exists between almost any other two races." He proceeded by discouraging the delegates about any prospects for equality on American soil: "Even when you cease to be slaves, you are yet far removed from being placed on an equality with the white race. . . . On this broad continent, not a single man of your race is made the equal of a single man of ours. Go where you are treated the best, the ban is still upon you." Finally, he argued that they had indirectly caused the war, and should not live side by side with whites: "But for your race among us, there could not be war, although many men engaged on either side do not care for you one way or the other. . . . It is better for us both . . . to be separated."

After leaving the White House, the offended black delegation quickly sent back word—they weren't going anywhere. Frederick Douglass, outraged at

Lincoln, denounced him, charging, "In this address Mr. Lincoln [shows] all his inconsistencies, his pride of race and blood, his contempt for negroes and his canting hypocrisy." Douglass declared in his monthly magazine that Lincoln had become the "miserable tool of traitors and rebels," and had shown himself to be "a genuine representative of American prejudice and negro hatred." The *Pacific Appeal*, an influential black newspaper, said the words of the President made it "evident that he, his cabinet, and most of the people, care but little for justice to the negro. If necessary, he is to be crushed between the upper and nether millstone—the pride and prejudice of the North and South."

White antislavery leaders were just as disappointed. William Lloyd Garrison had been notable among abolitionists for his patience with Lincoln, but he exploded at this. "President of African Colonization" ran the headline of *The Liberator*. No more "humiliating . . . impertinent . . . untimely spectacle" could be found in all Christendom than this extraordinary meeting, Garrison roared. Lincoln had demonstrated that his "education (!) with and among 'the white trash' of Kentucky was most unfortunate for his moral development." He was just an old Henry Clay colonization man after all. Salmon Chase exclaimed in his diary, "How much better would be a manly protest against prejudice against color!—and a wise effort to give freemen homes in America!"

The most highly advertised disappointment, however, was Horace Greeley's. Greeley had signaled his opposition to Lincoln's backwardness at the beginning of the year, when he scolded him onstage at the Smithsonian lecture on January 2. Ever since, he had lectured Lincoln from the pages of the *Tribune*, where he blew the emancipation trumpet all through the spring and summer. Finally, as the August heat baked the streets of Gotham, he prepared a public letter, the "Prayer of Twenty Millions," whose title proclaimed Greeley's towering—and wildly incorrect—presumption that he spoke for the entire Northern population. Greeley's front page, nine-paragraph rebuke of the President appeared in the August, 20, 1862, issue of the *Tribune*:

To ABRAHAM LINCOLN,
President of the United States

DEAR SIR: I do not intrude to tell you—for you must know already—
that a great proportion of those who triumphed in your election, and of all
who desire the unqualified suppression of the Rebellion now desolating
our country, are sorely disappointed and deeply pained by the policy you
seem to be pursuing with regard to the slaves of the Rebels. I write only to

set succinctly and unmistakably before you what we require, what we think we have a right to expect, and of what we complain.

I. We require of you . . . that you EXECUTE THE LAWS. . . .

II. We think you are strangely and disastrously remiss . . . with regard to the emancipating provisions of the new Confiscation Act. . . .

III. We think you are unduly influenced by the counsels . . . of certain fossil politicians hailing from the Border Slave States. . . .

IV. We think timid counsels in such a crisis calculated to prove perilous, and probably disastrous. . . .

V. We complain that the Union cause has suffered . . . from mistaken deference to Rebel Slavery. . . .

VI. We complain that the Confiscation Act which you approved is habitually disregarded by your Generals. . . .

VIII. On the face of this wide earth, Mr. President, there is not one disinterested, determined, intelligent champion of the Union cause who does not feel that all attempts to put down the Rebellion and at the same time uphold its inciting cause are preposterous and futile. . . .

IX. I close as I began with the statement that what an immense majority of the Loyal Millions of your countrymen require of you is a frank, declared, unqualified, ungrudging execution of the laws of the land, more especially of the Confiscation Act. . . .

Yours,

Horace Greeley
New York, August 19, 1862

The *Tribune* was read by millions of Republicans. Lincoln knew he could not ignore Greeley, but he was restrained by the conventions of the time that deemed it improper for a president to plead his case directly to the people. Newspaper reporters were still regarded as a raffish gang, not entirely respectable, and not entitled to published conversations with presidents. Lincoln was naturally cautious, and made even more so by the dilemmas of a divisive war, in which any statement would anger somebody. Consequently, he had made no public speeches and written few proclamations.

But when Greeley, the idealist, flung down the gauntlet in August 1862, Lincoln, the pragmatist, picked it up. He did what no President had ever done.

He composed an open letter, to be published for every citizen to read and consider. He made his response to Greeley in the Washington *National Intelligencer*—a pro-slavery newspaper, chosen perhaps to chide the editor who presumed to speak for the entire North. It displayed Lincoln's growing rhetorical power, and reached every reader in the nation. It exposed all the ligaments of his resolve, and rendered it with a distinctive literary vigor. Addressed to "Hon. Horace Greely [sic]," it was dated August 22, 1862:

> As to the policy I "seem to be pursuing" as you say, I have not meant to leave any one in doubt.
>
> I would save the Union. I would save it the shortest way under the Constitution. The sooner the national authority can be restored; the nearer the Union will be "the Union as it was." If there be those who would not save the Union, unless they could at the same time *save* slavery, I do not agree with them. If there be those who would not save the Union unless they could at the same time *destroy* slavery, I do not agree with them. My paramount object in this struggle *is* to save the Union, and is *not* either to save or to destroy slavery. If I could save the Union without freeing *any* slave I would do it, and if I could save it by freeing *all* the slaves I would do it; and if I could save it by freeing some and leaving others alone I would also do that. What I do about slavery, and the colored race, I do because I believe it helps to save the Union; and what I forbear, I forbear because I do *not* believe it would help to save the Union. I shall do *less* whenever I shall believe what I am doing hurts the cause, and I shall do *more* whenever I shall believe doing more will help the cause. I shall try to correct errors when shown to be errors; and I shall adopt new views so fast as they shall appear to be true views.
>
> I have here stated my purpose according to my view of *official* duty; and I intend no modification of my oft-expressed *personal* wish that all men every where could be free.
>
> Yours,
> A. LINCOLN

Lincoln's reply to Greeley chimed the three a.m. of the Radical soul, when many anti-slavery men felt the death of hope. The message angered Republicans who saw in it the same indifference to the evil of slavery that Lincoln himself had once criticized in his old nemesis, Stephen Douglas.

General Wadsworth, who had talked long with Lincoln, was sure "the president is not with us; has no antislavery instincts." John Jay sadly concluded, "We are sold out at Washington." William Lloyd Garrison, his spirits at rock bottom, called Lincoln "as near lunacy as any one not a pronounced Bedlamite," and despaired, "I am growing more and more skeptical as to the 'honesty' of Lincoln. He is nothing better than a wet rag . . . ." "The truth," lamented Secretary Chase, was that the President "has yielded so much to the Border State and negrophobic counsels that he now finds it difficult to arrest his own descent towards the most fatal concessions." The dismay of the true believers was summed up by a Republican editor who wrote, "I . . . fear that the President is rapidly alienating his friends and will soon find himself without a party, if not without a country."

But if they had read Lincoln's reply to Greeley more closely, they would have seen that Lincoln had also hinted at a new sense of his own constitutional power. For he had seen, in the distance, the coming of a "second revolution." He saw it in the swelling of the anti-slavery movement and in the increasing numbers of slaves pouring into the Union lines. After the recent defeats on the battlefield, he also saw the urgent need for new manpower and a mighty weapon against the rebels. With these in mind, he had already committed himself to bringing about "a new birth of freedom."

In July, as Lincoln told it later, "I determined upon the adoption of the emancipation policy; and, without consultation with, or the knowledge of the Cabinet, I prepared the original draft of the [emancipation] proclamation, and, after much anxious thought, called a Cabinet meeting upon the subject." At the July 22 meeting, "I said to the Cabinet that I had resolved upon this step, and had not called them together to ask their advice, but to lay the subject-matter of a proclamation before them . . . . Various suggestions were offered. . . . Nothing, however, was offered that I had not already fully anticipated and settled in my own mind, until Secretary Seward spoke. He said . . . 'The depression of the public mind, consequent upon our repeated reverses, is so great that I fear the effect of so important a step. . . . It may be viewed as the last measure of an exhausted government . . . .' His idea was that it would be considered our last *shriek*, on the retreat. . . . 'Now,' continued Mr. Seward, 'I suggest, sir, that you postpone its issue, until you can give it to the country supported by military success, instead of issuing it, as would be the case now, upon the greatest disasters of the war.'"

Lincoln agreed. He put the draft of the proclamation aside. When he wrote his letter to Greeley, he was waiting for a general to give him a victory.

Chapter 23

Lincoln Awaits a Victory

"Mr Lincoln will be dangling at the end of a rope."

Major General Henry Wager Halleck, "Old Brains" to his admirers, was an intellectual soldier, considered America's foremost authority on the theory of war. He had written *Elements of Military Art and Science*, which Lincoln had read as part of his self-education as a wartime Commander-in-Chief. Halleck had been put in charge of the Western theater after Frémont's ouster the previous autumn, and the victories won by his subordinate, General Grant, had inflated his reputation. On July 11, 1862, Lincoln, anxious to find someone to relieve him from the agony of military decisions, summoned Halleck to Washington to be General-in-Chief.

Halleck was reluctant to come East. Comfortable in the West, he did not want to get caught up in the notorious political infighting that made a career-killer of military command in Washington. But an official summons from the President in wartime was impossible to refuse. Halleck arrived on July 23 to mend Lincoln's fractured military system, which had crippled the war in the East during the President's unfortunate four months in command.

A look at the war map showed General McClellan with 100,000 men at Harrison's Landing, and, seventy-five miles to the north, the newly-installed General John Pope with the 43,000 men of Frémont, Banks, and McDowell. With Lee's army between them, this struck General Halleck as a horrifying predicament. The first principles of military science were the concentration of force and the value of the interior position. Both now belonged to Lee, who could strike at either of the separated Union armies and destroy it before help could arrive. Halleck decided that one of the Union armies must move to join the other, and that it must be McClellan who must move to join Pope. This transfer would reunite the Union army between the rebel army and Washington, just as Lincoln had desired in early spring.

McClellan, who until four months ago had been giving orders to Halleck, scorned him as "a man whom I know by experience to be my inferior." McClellan was furious at the idea of receiving orders—from Halleck of all people—to quit the Peninsula and send his men to join Pope's army. He assumed the new General-in-Chief was conspiring with the Radicals. On July 30, he wrote to his friend, Democratic kingmaker Samuel L. M. Barlow of New York City, "I *know* that the rascals will get rid of me as soon as they dare—they all know my opinion of them. They are aware that I have seen through their villainous schemes, & that if I succeed my foot will be on their necks." When on August 3 he received Halleck's order to leave the Peninsula, sail north, and march overland to join Pope, McClellan predicted it would be "disastrous in the extreme," "a fatal blow." He wanted to resign, but was dissuaded by his powerful Democratic friends in New York, mindful that he must remain without blemish for an 1864 presidential run.

The Radicals were delighted by the prospect of John Pope commanding the combined armies in northern Virginia. Pope had courted them from the beginning of the war, and after hearing his exaggerated versions of his triumphs in the West they had urged him for a command in the East. Lincoln had called him to Washington, and Pope had arrived on June 24, just as the Peninsula Campaign was coming to its climax. Enjoying his stroll through the parlors of power during his stay in the capital, he thrilled the Radicals with wicked insults of McClellan. They saw a brilliant future for Pope.

Once in the field, Pope continued to impress those who favored a sterner, harder war. He believed in fighting, not strategy, he boasted, and his soldiers would live off the enemy countryside. He advocated emancipation for the blacks freed by the progress of his army, and harsh treatment for rebels. He issued grandiose proclamations to his new army promising that they would see the backs of their enemies. Invigorated by the assurances of his Radical friends in Washington, he was sure that Halleck, his old boss in the West, would soon give him command of McClellan's Army of the Potomac.

During August 1862 Halleck showed more energy than he ever would thereafter, laboring to get McClellan to transfer his large army off the Peninsula and into the camps of Pope's Army of Virginia "with all possible promptness." McClellan dragged his feet every inch of the way. Always on guard against the Radicals, he suspected that every soldier he succeeded in transferring to Pope was a soldier he would never again command. Thus, even with Halleck pleading, "I beg of you, general, to hurry along this movement," it was mid-August—two weeks after he received Halleck's order—before he started his army toward the transports at Fort Monroe.

In fact, McClellan's slowness worked against him. Halleck, a Democrat who abhorred abolitionists and detested the Radical Republicans, would probably have installed Little Mac over Pope at the head of their combined armies, especially since McClellan had more experience against Lee. But by late August, when McClellan's men finally reached their tardy rendezvous with Pope's men, the climax of the campaign was only hours away. Pope, the man on the spot, would remain in command for the fight touted by Halleck as "the greatest battle of the century," and whose stakes were, according to William Seward, "nothing less than this capital; and, as many think, the *cause also*."

*   *   *

That is because Lee, as soon as he saw McClellan's men leaving their camps on the Peninsula, had recognized an opportunity in the short period when McClellan would be in transit to the north, before the two Union armies' strength would be combined. The Confederate commander had immediately moved part of his army northward to confront Pope in the sprawling countryside between Richmond and Washington, where there was plenty of room to maneuver. Pope soon realized that the Confederate army in his front was bigger than his own, and he fell back toward Washington—away from Lee's army and nearer to McClellan's arriving reinforcements. As Lee hove menacingly in front of Pope, a frantic Halleck sent flurries of telegrams to McClellan to hurry him along.

On August 26, Halleck stationed McClellan on the wharves of Alexandria. From here, McClellan would act as a deputy, forwarding troops and supplies to Pope, who was now face-to-face with the enemy twenty-five miles away at the old battlefield of Bull Run. Disgusted at his supporting role, McClellan immediately began doing what he always did: he prepared for the worst. He decided that the safety of the capital was more important than the lives of his own men now cleaning their weapons for the imminent battle a few miles away. He determined, as he put it in a telegram to Lincoln, "To leave Pope to get out of his scrape & at once use all our means to make the Capital perfectly safe." For four days, from August 27 to August 30, McClellan refused Halleck's repeated orders to forward the last two corps of the Army of the Potomac—some 25,000 men—to help Pope fight Lee. He kept them instead in the Washington defenses.

In the climactic Battle of Second Bull Run on August 29 and 30, Lee's army crushed Pope's Army of Virginia and sent it limping back to the security of Washington. Never had Northern morale sunk so low as in the days following the disaster. Near the end of June, the Army of the Potomac had been within sight of the church spires of Richmond, and the war had seemed all but won. Now, two months later, the situation was reversed. The rebels were at the outskirts of Washington, readying the killing blow. Lincoln, waiting for a victory to proclaim emancipation, instead found himself presiding over his army's most spectacular failure.

In the desperate uncertainty after the battle, everyone thought Washington was as good as captured. McClellan wrote to his wife that if he could slip into the city, he would send their silver off. Stanton gathered the War Department papers into bundles, ready to be shipped away. The Washington arsenal was ordered emptied and its guns and ammunition floated to New York. There were rumors that demoralized soldiers were surrendering so that they would be paroled and sent home.

"The nation is rapidly sinking just now," wrote George Templeton Strong in New York City. "Disgust with our present government is certainly universal." As for Lincoln, he lamented, "Nobody believes in him any more." A published sermon by Henry Ward Beecher laid the blame for the late disaster at Second Bull Run on "central imbecility" in Washington: "Certainly neither Mr. Lincoln nor his Cabinet have proved leaders. . . . Not a spark of genius has [Lincoln], not an element for leadership. Not one particle of heroic enthusiasm." A friend of Secretary Chase reported from Brooklyn, "Many of our best citizens say the President should resign."

*   *   *

In this dark hour, Treasury Secretary Chase was, indeed, working out his own formula for regime change. Now that Congress had adjourned, it had fallen to him and Secretary Stanton, the two Radical ministers of the Cabinet, to carry on the Jacobin fight in the capital. In late August, the two plotted a coup against Lincoln in an attempt to oust McClellan. With the air full of rumors that McClellan was out to undo Pope and cause the defeat of the Union army, and knowing from experience that verbal arguments with Lincoln were, as Chase put it, "like throwing water on a duck's back," Stanton and Chase composed a blunt manifesto. It insisted that Lincoln remove McClellan, and told him that the undersigned Cabinet heads were "unwilling to be accessory to the waste of natural resources, the protraction of the war, the destruction of our armies, and the imperiling of the Union which we believe must result from the continuance of George B. McClellan in command." The document was an ultimatum: *Fire McClellan or find a new Cabinet.* It was him or them.

Stanton and Chase signed the protest themselves, and then set out to enlist the other Secretaries to add their signatures. Interior Secretary Smith signed willingly, but Navy Secretary Welles refused, seeing it for what it was—an attempt by the Radical ministers to wrest control of the administration away from the President.

Thus thwarted, Stanton and Chase retreated and enlisted Secretary Bates to compose another, gentler version of the manifesto. Stanton, Chase, Bates, and Smith signed the new paper, and Stanton went again to Welles, arguing hotly that "he [Stanton] knew of no obligation he was under to the President, who had called him to a difficult position and imposed upon him labors and responsibilities which no man could carry." Again, however, Welles refused to comply, still unwilling to put his signature to an attempt to topple the elected leader of the Republic and inaugurate a scramble for control. His principled stand brought the coup attempt to an end. Lincoln would never know of it.

*   *   *

On the morning of September 2, while the plot of the two Judases unraveled, at the height of the hysteria over the latest disaster at Bull Run, at a time when everyone in the capital expected a battle in front of the capital that would decide the fate of the nation, Lincoln held the tensest Cabinet meeting of the Civil War. There was a tempest even before Lincoln arrived. Stanton was at the highest pitch of fury, speaking "in a suppressed voice, trembling with excitement" with news that McClellan had been restored to command of the Army of the Potomac! Lincoln entered, and confirmed that he had just been to McClellan's house and had ordered him to take command of the demoralized army now streaming into the defenses of Washington. Under the glares of Stanton and Chase, Lincoln admitted that McClellan had the "slows," but maintained, "McClellan knows this whole ground," and "can be trusted to act on the defensive." There was "no better organizer."

Though most listened in stunned silence, Chase spoke up, protesting that he "could not but feel that giving the command to McClellan is equivalent to giving Washington to the rebels." Lincoln put an end to the discussion, in Chase's account, by saying "it distressed him exceedingly to find himself differing on such a point from the Secretary of War and Secretary of the Treasury," but that events would vindicate his judgment.

Welles recorded that "there was a more disturbed and desponding feeling than I have ever witnessed in council; the President was greatly distressed."

Montgomery Blair reported, "The bitterness of Stanton on the reinstatement of McClellan you can scarcely conceive." Of this, Lincoln was painfully aware. According to Bates, the President "seemed wrung by the bitterest anguish—said he felt almost ready to hang himself." The President himself had privately called McClellan's recent conduct "unpardonable," but he believed also that McClellan was the only general who could restore the morale of the defeated army.

It was from these depths that Lincoln penned his most desolate document, a private "Meditation on the Divine Will":

> The will of God prevails. In great contests each party claims to act in accordance with the will of God. Both *may* be, and one *must* be wrong. God can not be *for*, and *against* the same thing at the same time. In the present civil war it is quite possible that God's purpose is something different from the purpose of either party—and yet the human instrumentalities, working just as they do, are of the best adaptation to effect His purpose. I am almost ready to say this is probably true—that God wills this contest, and wills that it shall not end yet. By his mere quiet power, on the minds of the now contestants, He could have either *saved* or *destroyed* the Union without a human contest. Yet the contest began. And having begun He could give the final victory to either side any day. Yet the contest proceeds.

Lincoln's agony was shared by millions in the North, magnified, among Radicals, by resentment that McClellan was once again—*even after his rank treason!*—in charge of the army at Washington. Zack Chandler was frantic with indignation. "Are mutinous *traitorous* Generals *now* controlling our destiny?" he raved to Chase. "If so! What are we fighting for? . . . For God's sake let us save the Government. Treason is raising its hideous head all over the land." He wrote to Senator Trumbull in disgust, "Your president is as unstable as water, if he has as I suspect been bullied by those traitor generals. How long will it be before he will by them be set aside & a military dictatorship set up. . . . For God & country's sake, send someone to stay with the President who will controll [sic] & hold him."

In the national emergency, a thunderhead formed on the horizon—a gathering of governors. Rumor had it that the governors together might remove the President. Governor Andrew of Massachusetts told Count Gurowski that he was organizing a movement "to save the Prest. from the infamy of ruining his country." The *New York Herald* speculated that "a vast conspiracy has been set on foot by the radicals . . . to depose the present administration, and place Frémont at the head of a provisional government; in other words, to make him military dictator." The governors' purpose, reported the *Herald*, was "to request Lincoln to resign, to enable them to carry out their scheme."

The mails to Washington were clogged with screeds. One wondered, "What does it mean that at such a time of darkness . . . there comes not from Washington a stirring word or courageous utterance . . . ?" Senator John Sherman, too, asked, "Shall the country crumble into dissolution for the want of *one great man?*" Joseph Medill expressed the feeling of the country with a newspaperman's directness:

> The Union cause is in a dismal plight. It is enough to make the strongest men despair and weep tears of blood. . . . Unless a new leaf is turned over the Republic is gone forever, and Mr Lincoln . . . and every leading Republican, *before two years,* will be in exile, or dangling at the end of a rope.

In the overwrought atmosphere of the crisis, one observer wrote that the country seemed "trembling on the brink of the precipice."

*   *   *

As the country trembled, Lee's tattered soldiers crossed the Potomac River and McClellan marched his hastily re-formed divisions out from the Washington forts to confront them. Sped forward by a Providential gift—a found copy of Lee's plans, discovered in a Maryland field wrapped around three cigars—McClellan attacked Lee's under strength army along Antietam Creek on September 17, the bloodiest day in American history. By the time the sun fell, 3,650 were dead and 19,000 more were wounded or missing. The next day, like two stunned rams, both armies stood in their places. That night, Lee's men began crossing back into Virginia, leaving McClellan in possession of the field. The rebel invasion had been turned back. The Army of the Potomac claimed a triumph.

When Lee's army had stepped onto Maryland soil, Lincoln told his Cabinet later, he had made a promise to himself and his Maker that "as soon as it shall be driven out," he would issue the Proclamation of Emancipation. Now the moment had come to redeem the pledge.

Chapter 24

Emancipation Promised

"A Death Blow to the Hope of Union."

"In the Faul of 1856, I showed my show in Utiky, a trooly grate sitty in the State of New York.

"The people gave me a cordyal recepshun. The press was loud in her prases.

"1 day as I was givin a descripshun of my Beests and Snaiks in my usual flowry stile what was my skorn & disgust to see a big burly feller walk up to the cage containin my wax figgers of the Lord's Last Supper, and cease Judas Iscarrot by the feet and drag him out on the ground. He then commenced fur to pound him as hard as he cood.

" 'What under the son are you about?' cried I.

"Sez he, 'What did you bring this pussylanermus cuss here fur?' & he hit the wax figger another tremenjis blow on the hed.

"Sez I, 'You egrejus ass, that air's a wax figger—a representashun of the false 'Postle.'

"Sez he, 'That's all very well fur you to say, but I tell you, old man, that Judas Iscarrot can't show hisself in Utiky with impunerty by a darn site!' with which observashun he kaved in Judassis hed. The young man belonged to 1 of the first famerlies in Utiky. I sood him, and the Joory brawt in a verdict of Arson in the 3d degree."

Cabinet members had arrived at the meeting of September 22, 1862, with a full sense of its weighty portent. Lincoln, who was allergic to weighty portent, broke the ice by reading the above, humorist Artemus Ward's "High-Handed Outrage at Utica," and laughing tremendously. He then grew solemn. He told them he had thought much "about the relation of this war to slavery," and made an admission:

I know very well that others might, in this matter, as in others, do better than I can; and if I were satisfied that the public confidence was more fully possessed by any one of them than by me, and knew of any Constitutional way in which he could be put in my place, he should have it. I would gladly yield it to him. But though I believe that I have not so much of the confidence of the people as I had some time since, I do not know that . . . any other person has more; and, however this may be, there is no way in which I can have any other man put where I am. I am here. I must do the best I can, and bear the responsibility of taking the course which I feel I ought to take.

For the past year, Radicals had tried to paint him as a slavery apologist, and Lincoln had sat still for the portrait. During that time, however, he had thought so deeply and so long about emancipation that his conclusions had come with a sense of Divine purpose. His mind was made up.

"I have got you together," he told his Cabinet, "to hear what I have written down. I do not wish your advice about the main matter—for that I have determined for myself." He then read his preliminary Emancipation Proclamation. The third paragraph contained its essence:

That on [January 1, 1863], all persons held as slaves within any State, or designated part of a State, the people whereof shall then be in rebellion against the United States, shall be then, thenceforward, and forever free; and the executive government of the United States, including the military and naval authority thereof, will recognize and maintain the freedom of such persons, and will do no act or acts to repress such persons, or any of them, in any efforts they may make for their actual freedom.

*   *   *

The preliminary Emancipation Proclamation is a document more admired than read. The popular image of Abraham Lincoln, the Great Emancipator, striking the shackles from the limbs of four million black slaves by a stroke of his pen is false. The document did not deliver emancipation, but the promise of emancipation; not then, but in one hundred days; not in the loyal states (where slaves would remain bound), but in rebellious states where Union armies had not yet gone. The proclamation drew its authority not from an appeal to human liberty, but from the Commander-in-Chief's war powers. It stated that the object of the war was not freedom for all, but reunion. It spoke not with high phrases to future generations, but with cold legality to a present enemy. And there were hedges: Lincoln recommended that ex-slaves not be made soldiers, and preferred that they be shipped abroad. The proclamation was not eloquent, nor did it say anything about the moral wrong of slavery. "The proclamation is written in the meanest and the most dry routine style," Count Gurowski wrote with deep regret in his diary. He continued:

> Not a word to evoke a generous thrill, not a word reflecting the warm and lofty . . . feelings of . . . the people. Nothing for humanity; nothing to humanity. . . . [I]t is clear that the writer was not in it either with his heart or with his soul; it is clear that it was done under moral duress, under the throttling pressure of events.
>
> General Wadsworth truly says, that never a noble subject was more belittled by the form in which it was uttered.

Frederick Douglass likewise deplored the proclamation's brittle tone:

> [Its words] kindled no enthusiasm. They touched neither justice nor mercy. Had there been one expression of sound moral feeling against Slavery, one word of regret and shame that this accursed system had remained so long the disgrace and scandal of the Republic, one word of satisfaction in the hope of burying slavery and the rebellion in one common grave, a thrill of joy would have run around the world, but no such word was said, and no such joy was kindled.

Karl Marx said the document reminded him of "ordinary summonses sent from one lawyer to another."

Massachusetts Governor Andrew was more generous, calling it "a poor document, but a mighty act." It was, in fact, the mightiest act of Lincoln's or any other Presidency, one that would trigger an explosion of feeling from all points of the compass.

The very first hearers of the Proclamation, Lincoln's own Cabinet members, were perplexed. War Secretary Edwin Stanton was the most enthusiastic; he recognized its usefulness as a weapon in removing the strong prop of slave labor from the Southern war effort. Stodgy old slave state native Edward Bates was a surprising supporter, but he especially liked the paragraph that recommended that the ex-slaves be deported. Navy Secretary Gideon Welles was initially silent, worried by the proclamation's doubtful constitutionality; it seemed to him "an arbitrary and despotic measure in the cause of freedom." Montgomery Blair was against it on political grounds, warning that it would put a club into the hands of the Democrats in the next election. Caleb Smith of Indiana was harshest, telling his Assistant Secretary that if Lincoln issued it, "I will resign and go home and attack the administration."

Salmon Chase's response was the most conflicted. He could not cheer it. He would rather the generals organize and arm the slaves. As the Radical champion, he had to give his blessing, but his support was tinged with resentment that the unwilling Lincoln would be seen as the champion of freedom, and not he, the true abolitionist.

William Seward also remained skeptical. His advice to postpone the proclamation in July had probably been an attempt to accomplish its defeat. He feared it might ignite a race war that would halt cotton production and bring worried European powers in on the side of the South. Also, he thought the measure too divisive; it went against his policy of settling the war by compromise. Finally, Seward saw no need for the proclamation as long as the Union armies advanced. "It is mournful," he said, "to see that a great nation shrinks from a war it has accepted and insists on adopting proclamations, when it is asked for force."

When the preliminary Emancipation Proclamation was released to the public the next day, the Cabinet's rainbow of opinion was reproduced across the whole nation.

Antislavery men leaped up in jubilation. Horace Greeley's New York *Tribune* proclaimed, "It is the beginning of the end of the rebellion, is the beginning of the new life of the nation. . . . GOD BLESS ABRAHAM LINCOLN." "The President may be a fool," wrote George William Curtis to a fellow Lincoln critic. "But see what he has done. He may not have a policy. But he has given us one." All the great New England men of letters—Whittier, Bryant, Lowell—sang praises. Most fulsome was Emerson, who published a rhapsody in the *Atlantic Monthly* whose pages scanned like poetry.

Lincoln himself did not share the euphoria of the bards of New England. From the first, he was doubtful about the success of the act. Unsurpassed as a reader of the public mind, Lincoln feared that he lacked enough personal popularity to enlist the nation in a crusade that a majority of Americans, even a majority of Northerners, disapproved. On the evening of September 24, the day after the proclamation was published, Lincoln broke his rule against impromptu remarks and spoke five sentences to the jubilant serenaders who gathered on the lawn of the White House. "I can only trust in God I have made no mistake," he began. "I shall make no attempt on this occasion to sustain what I have done or said by any comment. It is now for the country and the world to pass judgment on it, and, may be, take action upon it. I will say no more upon this subject. In my position I am environed with difficulties."

Four days later, he told his worry in a reply to the congratulations of Vice President Hannibal Hamlin:

> My Dear Sir: Your kind letter of the 25th is just received. It is known to some that while I hope something from the proclamation, my expectations are not as sanguine as are those of some friends. The time for its effect southward has not come; but northward the effect should be instantaneous.
>
> It is six days old, and while commendation in newspapers and by distinguished individuals is all that a vain man could wish, the stocks have declined, and troops come forward more slowly than ever. This, looked soberly in the face, is not very satisfactory. We have fewer troops in the field at the end of six days than we had at the beginning——the attrition among the old outnumbering the addition by the new. The North responds to the proclamation sufficiently in breath; but breath alone kills no rebels.
>
> I wish I could write more cheerfully; nor do I thank you the less for the kindness of your letter. Yours very truly,

> A. Lincoln

It appeared to the skeptical Gideon Welles that the proclamation "had imparted no vigor but rather depression and weakness to the North."

Lincoln had certainly not solved his political problems by issuing the proclamation. Rather, he had multiplied them. It shattered the coalition of War Democrats, Border State Unionists, and conservative Republicans that he had patiently built and carefully cemented since the beginning of the war. After the proclamation's release, conservative fury was signaled by the sullen silence of the governors of New Jersey, Delaware, Maryland, Kentucky, and Missouri. Dark mutterings were also heard from Illinois, Indiana, Ohio, and Pennsylvania.

Even as he cast off from the conservatives, Lincoln knew he could never depend on the support of the Radicals. They had never embraced him. Even now, many of them, unhappy with the proclamation's lack of whole-souled anti-slavery rhetoric, did not recognize Lincoln's proclamation as the blow at slavery that they had sought.

They must have taken some delight, however, in the shrieking of the angry editors in the Southern press. There, Lincoln's proclamation was seen as a wicked effort to incite the rampant bloodshed and chaos of slave revolt—a "reign of hell on earth," in the superheated prose of the Richmond *Enquirer*. The *Enquirer* expected the return, on a massive scale, of scenes from the Nat Turner massacre in 1831. "What shall we call him?" it asked: "Coward, assassin, savage, murderer of women and babies? Or shall we consider them all as embodied in the word fiend, and call him Lincoln, the Fiend?" The Staunton (Va.) *Spectator* roared that the proclamation would "strengthen the South and weaken the North, and bring down upon the Lincoln Administration the condemnation of the whole civilized world," who would surely see that "the Lincoln Government is now the most tyrannical military despotism which has ever existed upon the earth."

The fury from the South, of course, was predictable. But the cynics prevailed even in the European press. The anti-slavery papers regretted the proclamation's halfway measures. The London *Spectator*, for example, sneered that its principle "is not that a human being cannot justly own another but that he cannot own him unless he is loyal to the United States." A London *Punch* cartoonist drew Lincoln as a Satanic gambler attempting to trump the Confederacy with the ace of spades. The London *Times*, the British newspaper most widely regarded in America and Europe, forecast a lurid holocaust:

> Mr. Lincoln will, on the 1st of next January, do his best to excite a servile war in the States which he cannot occupy with his arms. . . . He will appeal to the black blood of the African; he will whisper of the pleasures of spoil and of the gratification of yet fiercer instincts; and when blood begins to flow and shrieks come piercing through the darkness, Mr. Lincoln will wait till the rising flames tell that all is consummated, and then he will rub his hands and think that revenge is sweet.

Two weeks later, the *Times* damned Lincoln with this prophesy:

> Lincoln . . . will be known to posterity and . . . ultimately be classed among the catalogue of monsters, the wholesale assassins and butchers of their kind. [The Emancipation Proclamation] will not deprive Mr. Lincoln of the distinctive affix which he will share with many, for the most part

foolish and incompetent, kings and emperors, caliphs and doges, that of being Lincoln—"The Last."

Closer and more dangerous to Lincoln were the Democratic editors in the North. They had smoldered while Lincoln had conserved slavery; now they ignited. The Chicago *Times* branded the Emancipation Proclamation "a

MASKS AND FACES.

Southern Illustrated News, November 8, 1862

"Masks and Faces"

London Punch, October 18, 1862

"Abe Lincoln's Last Card"

monstrous usurpation, a criminal wrong, and an act of national suicide." Over its copy of the proclamation, *The Crisis* flew the banner, "The 'Irrepressible Conflict' upon Us—President Lincoln Succumbs to the Radical Abolitionists—Four Millions of Blacks Turned Loose upon the Country." Another *Crisis* editorial asked, "Is not this a Death Blow to the Hope of Union?" and declared, "We have no doubt that this Proclamation seals the fate of this Union as it was and the Constitution as it is. . . . The time is brief when we shall have a DICTATOR PROCLAIMED, for the Proclamation can never be carried out except under the iron rule of the worst kind of despotism." The New York *World* shouted that "Lincoln has swung loose from . . . constitutional moorings" and was "fully adrift on the current of radical fanaticism." The New York *Evening Express* called it an "act of Revolution" that would render "the restoration of the Old Constitution and Union impossible." Border State opinion was especially outraged at Lincoln's betrayal. The *Louisville Journal* was defiant:

Privately distributed, September 1862

"Under the Veil"

The measure is wholly unauthorized and wholly pernicious. Though it cannot be executed in fact, and though its execution probably will never be seriously attempted, its moral influence will be decided, and purely hurtful. . . . It is a gigantic usurpation, . . . aggravated by the menace of great and unmixed evil.

Kentucky cannot and will not acquiesce in this measure. Never!

Lincoln was not blown off course by the gale of criticism. John Hay spoke to Lincoln on September 26 about the editorials in the leading papers. "He said he had studied the matter so long that he knew more about it than they did," Hay wrote in his diary. According to a correspondent of the *Springfield Republican*, Lincoln had good-naturedly mentioned the wrathful newspapers to a friend, telling him, "Having an hour to spare on Sunday I read this batch of editorials and when I was through reading I asked myself, 'Abraham Lincoln, are you a man or a dog?'"

While the press howled, angry letters piled up on Lincoln's desk and spilled onto the floor. William O. Stoddard, the secretary in charge of reading Lincoln's mail, wrote:

Dictator is what the Opposition press and orators of all sizes are calling him. Witness, also, the litter on the floor and the heaped-up wastebaskets. There is no telling how many editors and how many other penmen within these past few days have undertaken to assure him that this is a war for the Union only, and that they never gave him any authority to run it as an Abolition war. They never, never told him that he might set the negroes free, and, now that he has done so, or futilely pretended to do so, he is a more unconstitutional tyrant and a more odious dictator than ever he was before. They tell him, however, that his . . . venomous blow at the sacred liberty of white men to own black men is mere *brutum fulmen* [empty threat], and a dead letter and a poison which will not work. They tell him many other things, and, among them, they tell him that the army will fight no more, and that the hosts of the Union will indignantly disband rather than be sacrificed upon the bloody altar of fanatical Abolitionism.

*   *   *

This last was true: General McClellan was considering revolt. He wrote to his wife on September 25, "The Presdt's late Proclamation, the continuation of

Stanton & Halleck in office render it almost impossible for me to retain my commission & self respect at the same time. I cannot make up my mind to fight for such an accursed doctrine as that of a servile insurrection—it is too infamous." In the coming weeks, he would return to an old, bitter theme on the subject of his Commander-in-Chief: "[T]he good of the country requires me to submit to . . . men whom I know to be greatly my inferiors socially, intellectually, & morally! There never was a truer epithet applied to a certain individual than that of the 'Gorilla.'"

McClellan's top officers naturally adopted his views. One of his pet generals, Fitz-John Porter, in a letter to the editor of the New York *World*, called the emancipation edict the "absurd proclamation of a political coward," and reported:

> The Proclamation was ridiculed in the army—causing disgust, discontent, and expressions of disloyalty to the views of the administration, amounting I have heard, to insubordination, and for this reason—All such bulletins tend only to prolong the war by rousing the bitter feelings of the South—and causing unity of action among them—while the reverse with us. Those who fight the battles of the country are tired of the war and wish to see it ended soon and honorably—by a restoration of the union—not merely a suppression of the rebellion.

The other Democratic officers in Porter's tent shared his feelings. According to a New York *Tribune* reporter, McClellan's staff was mutinous, and plotted to "countermarch [the army] to Washington and intimidate the president." Another reporter added that the officers regarded Lincoln with contempt, believed the war futile, and that they were fighting for a boundary line and not to restore the Union. Rumors drifted back to Washington that McClellan would march his army on the capital and put "his sword across the government's policy." McClellan's quartermaster-general Montgomery Meigs spoke of "officers of rank" in the Army of the Potomac who openly threatened "a march on Washington to 'clear out those fellows.'" General Pope, too, reported a "Potomac Army clique," among whom there was open talk "of Lincoln's weakness and the necessity of replacing him by some stronger man."

There were enough angry letters home from McClellan's soldiers to give color to the rumors of a military coup. A large conservative element among the enlisted men felt, with Lt. George Breck of the 1st New York Light Artillery, that the proclamation was "an ill-timed, mischief making instrument . . .

uncalled for, except by a crazy lot of abolitionists, who are bent on destroying slavery, [even] if it costs the life of the nation, and sheds oceans of blood." The *Wayne County* (Ohio) *Democrat*, under the headline "The Death-Blow of the Nation," published three letters from soldiers that it said represented the feeling in the army. All were against emancipation. "I did not enlist to free the infernal niggers," said the first. The second predicted, "If the president makes this a war to carry out his Emancipation proclamation and it gets to be so understood by the army he will have to get a new set of soldiers." The third warned, "Those men of the South who have had no reason to fight, now have a reason to protect their slaves; and they say that we may kill them all but we can never whip them. They further say that if we succeed in whipping them they will teach their children to fight us." A *New York Herald* correspondent attached to the Army of the Potomac felt its temper and feared for the Republic:

> The army is dissatisfied and the air is thick with revolution. . . . God knows what will be the consequence, but at present matters look dark indeed, and there is large promise of a fearful revolution which will sweep before it not only the administration but popular government.

When Lincoln visited the army's camps in early October after the Battle of Antietam, some of the regiments sulked as he passed. "His proclamation, issued last month, has caused considerable discontent among the regiments of Maryland, Virginia, Pennsylvania, New York, and the West," according to one army surgeon. An aristocratic colonel, New Yorker Charles Wainwright, wrote his disgust at seeing the President of the United States ride up in "a common ambulance, with his long legs doubled up so that his knees almost struck his chin, and grinning out of the windows like a baboon." "Mr. Lincoln," he concluded, "not only is the ugliest man I ever saw, but the most uncouth and gawky in his manners and appearance." These soldiers showed an antagonism to Lincoln shared by masses of betrayed conservatives across the North. As they saw it, Lincoln had cast off his mask and shown his true nature—the meddling Puritan fanatic.

* * *

Then, on the day after the Emancipation Proclamation, Lincoln issued a second proclamation, suspending the writ of *habeas corpus* across the entire country.

Lincoln suspended *habeas corpus* to prevent resistance to another unpopular measure signed into law two months before. This was the Federal Militia Act, which had authorized the first military draft in the history of the United States. The draft was the realization of a great American fear. It ran counter to the Minuteman tradition that said that conscription was tyranny and that volunteer armies were the only true defense of a democracy. By early August, the Detroit *Free Press* was rejoicing at the exodus of hundreds of men leaving for Canada to flee the draft. Hundreds of citizens of Chicago and Rochester, too, were reported escaping across the border. Draft officials met organized resistance from Wisconsin to Maryland, particularly among the Irish and Germans. Mothers threw pots of scalding water at recruiters going house to house. Self-mutilations—cutting off fingers, knocking out teeth—were spotted by examining surgeons in recruitment offices. Rioters in Indiana destroyed the enrollment lists and the draft ballot box at one office, requiring 300 infantry to restore the peace. The most serious disturbances were in the Pennsylvania coal country, where thousands of armed protesters prevented trains loaded with draftees from leaving for Washington.

Lincoln's September 24 nationwide suspension of *habeas corpus*, in response to the rolling thunder of anti-draft violence across the North, was a shock to every patriot. Even Republicans condemned it. Senator William Fessenden of Maine called it "an exercise of despotic power." Orville Browning, until now one of Lincoln's few friends in Washington, turned away from the President forever after the twin proclamations, writing in his diary that the "useless and . . . . mischievous proclamations" served only "to unite and exasperate . . . the South, and divide and distract us in the North."

Democrats not only wrote their resentment into their diaries, they shouted it from the rooftops. On September 29, James Brooks told a packed house at the Democratic Union Association meeting in New York City, "The proclamation [suspending *habeas corpus*] is a corollary of Proclamation No. 1. It substantially says to the free white people of the North, if you discuss and agitate this subject of emancipation, if you make war against the Administration upon this subject, you shall be incarcerated in Fort Lafayette." The crowd roared its defiance. Lincoln's hometown *Illinois State Register* cried that he was "seeking to inaugurate a reign of terror in the loyal states by military arrests . . . without a trial, to browbeat all opposition by villainous and false charges of disloyalty against whole classes of patriotic citizens, to destroy all constitutional guaranties [sic] of free speech, a free press, and the writ of 'habeas corpus.'" One St. Louis merchant wrote to former Postmaster General Joseph Holt in

Washington, pleading, "Stop him! Hold him!—is all I can say by way of advice to you, as the friend of the President. Beg him . . . never to publish a proclamation. . . . His proclamations have paralized [sic] our armies." Lincoln, he said, would "drive the ship of state on the shoals of *proclamations* or the snags of '*Habeas Corpus*.'"

From a safe distance, the smug Richmond *Dispatch*, under the headline "The Twin Proclamations," etched its remarks with acid:

> The people of Yankeedom are . . . as absolutely the slaves of a military despotism as the Russians or Austrians. For them there is no law but the law military. They are learning, in its full force, the meaning of Julius Caesar's terrible saying, "*inter arma silent leges*" ("in time of war the laws are silent"). The law, indeed, has no more voice in Yankeedom at this moment than it had in Rome when the whole republic was writhing under the iron grasp of the great Dictator. The courts had as well be closed, if they are not already, for the voice of its victims cannot be heard beyond the walls of the military prison. Lincoln has effected a complete triumph over the Yankee nation. He has set aside its laws and trampled its boasted Constitution under foot. Those who were once his fellow citizens, are now his timid and abject slaves. They scarcely dare whisper opposition to their nearest and dearest friends. . . . Security to life, security to limb, security to property, the freedom of speech, the liberty of the press—all that renders life worth preserving—all that the fathers of the Revolution thought they had guaranteed by the Constitution—all, all, are swept into nonentity by the mere dash of his pen. History does not record a usurpation so bold, so open, so thoroughly successful. Caesar, Cromwell, or Bonaparte never attempted a revolution so astounding. Yet Caesar, Cromwell and Bonaparte were among the greatest men that ever lived, and Lincoln is one of the smallest.

Chapter 25

Emancipation Rebuked

"All the Blame on Mr. Lincoln"

Democrats in the North immediately recognized Lincoln's unpopular proclamations as a two-headed club they could wield against the Republicans in the coming midterm elections. With Election Day only weeks away, Republicans trembled at warnings by men such as elder statesman Thomas Ewing, who said that the twin proclamations had "ruined the Republican party in Ohio." One Lincoln man running in southern Ohio wailed that the Emancipation Proclamation "will defeat me and every other Union candidate for Congress along the border." There on the north bank of the Ohio River, where white voters feared an inundation of freed blacks, a new, amended Democratic slogan caught the ear of the masses: "The Constitution as it is, the Union as it was, and the Niggers where they are." Crowds cheered speeches by Democrats who scorched the Emancipation Proclamation as "another advance in the Robespierrian highway of tyranny and anarchy," and vowed "no more bloodshed to gratify a religious fanaticism." An Ohio editor cried that if "the *despot* Lincoln" thought white men "should be shot for the benefit of niggers and Abolitionists . . . he would meet with the fates he deserves: hung, shot or burned." In October, *Leslie's Newspaper* reported, "Party feeling runs high in Ohio, and political meetings seem like half-battles. Men go to them armed as to a fray, and bloodshed often occurs."

Voters in Illinois, Indiana, and Pennsylvania shared Ohioans' dread of a rush of freed slaves across their borders. Pennsylvania's *Valley Spirit* printed one of many cautionary tales that became popular: "Three big, ugly, black female niggers came to a farm house in his neighborhood and asked to stay all night. But they were told they could not stay." At this denial, "there came a second lot, consisting of four big, ugly, black male niggers." The white family, which until now had been fully in favor of Lincoln's emancipation policy, "became still more frightened . . . said they could give them their supper, but could not possibly accommodate them through the night." To this, the black people answered with an accusation of hypocrisy: "'O yes, dat's de way we am served;

you white people in de Norf told us to run away from our masters, an' would treat us like brudders an' dis am the way we am treated.'" According to the story, the former slaves took the meal and spent the night anyway, without "so much as even 'thanky.'" The *Valley Spirit* used the example to make a dire forecast: "This is only the beginning. Before a great while these runaway blacks will be among us as thick as five in a bed."

In Illinois, where Negrophobia was codified into a state law to keep blacks out, Secretary of War Stanton committed a blunder that resulted in a windfall for Democratic candidates. On September 18, he ordered thousands of "contraband" blacks, freed slaves temporarily being housed on the levees around Cairo, onto northbound trains to be resettled throughout Illinois. The move created an uproar. Democratic editors accused Lincoln of an unconstitutional attempt to "Africanize" their lily-white Prairie State.

Republican Senator Orville Browning was so dismayed by Lincoln's September proclamations that he refused to campaign; he urged his fellow Illinoisans to go to the polls, but would not tell them how to vote. In central Illinois, Democrat John Stuart Todd got attention by refusing to debate Lincoln's friend Leonard Swett, claiming that if he expressed his views freely, he might be thrown in prison.

A tight governor's race made the New York election the most sensational in the North. Horatio Seymour, the Democratic candidate for governor, made Lincoln's trampling of civil liberties his main issue, stirring voters with the pledge that he would fight arbitrary arrests "even if the streets be made to run red with blood." The New York *World* blew the battle trumpet for an electoral revolt against Lincoln. It was the apocalypse: "This election decides whether we are to have free speech, a free press, free political gatherings, and free elections." It told its readers that a Republican victory would mean that "a swarthy inundation of negro laborers and paupers shall flood the North, accumulating new burdens on taxpayers, cheapening the labor by black competition . . . and raising dangerous questions of political and social equality."

In New York City, Democratic crowds cheered Seymour when he called the Emancipation Proclamation "a proposal for the butchery of women and children, for scenes of lust and rapine, and of arson and murder."

Increasingly, as the war dragged on and bitterness deepened, Lincoln's own middle course was losing support across the North as extremists on both sides—those who hated him for going too far, and others who despised him for not going far enough—gained strength. The popular flight from moderation grieved him. As the 1862 fall elections drew near, observers noticed a deepening of his natural melancholy. He seemed "literally bending under the weight of his burdens," said one who saw him then. "His introverted look and his half-staggering gait were those of a man walking in his sleep."

A nervous John Hay wrote from Illinois, "Things look badly around here politically." Even the optimistic Seward shivered at an "ill wind" of discontent. Lincoln's party, split into warring factions and hamstrung by the lack of any good news, campaigned listlessly.

It surprised nobody, then, that when the Northern voters went to the polls in October and November, they returned a thumping Republican defeat—what the *New York Times* called "a vote of want of confidence" in Abraham Lincoln. The middle states that had swept the Railsplitter into the presidency in 1860— Illinois, Indiana, Ohio, Pennsylvania, and New York—deserted him. All of them sent new Democratic majorities to Congress. Illinois, Indiana, Ohio, and Pennsylvania also elected Democratic state legislatures. New Jersey was a Republican donnybrook—Democrats carried the state legislature, four of its five seats in the House, and delivered a new Democratic governor. The worst blow of all was in New York, where the victory of Horatio Seymour gave the Democrats a new national leader to oppose Lincoln. Perhaps the most embarrassing defeat was in Lincoln's own Springfield district, where Leonard Swett lost.

In all, the number of Democrats in the House almost doubled, from 44 to 75, cutting the Republican majority from 70 to 55 percent. The President and his party were saved an even worse beating only by the fact that the Republican governors of the Midwestern states were not up for election. Heartsick at the Republicans' ruin, Alexander McClure of Pennsylvania wrote, "I could not conceive it possible for Lincoln to successfully administer the government and prosecute the war with the six most important loyal States declaring against him at the polls."

*   *   *

Everybody had a theory to explain the disaster. Many blamed "that unwise, ill-timed and seditious" Emancipation Proclamation. The newspaper headlines were succinct in their appraisals: "No Emancipation" was the verdict of the Dubuque *Herald*; "Abolition Slaughtered" was the view of the Indianapolis *State Sentinel*. The *Illinois State Register* reported the Springfield results as "The Home of Lincoln Condemns the Proclamation." "Fanaticism, Abolitionism and Niggerism Repudiated" was the thoughtful analysis of the *Valley Spirit*. Voters, it said, had decided "against the unconstitutional proclamation of the President, proclaiming freedom to 3,000,000 negroes in the South, to be turned loose upon the country, to enter into competition with white men and eat out their substance, and against fanaticism, bigotry, tyranny and despotism in all their different phases and forms."

Others blamed the defeat on arbitrary arrests, a source of outrage ever since the Merryman case in the summer of 1861. Earnest judicial reformer David Dudley Field was horrified by Lincoln's *habeas corpus* edict, and wrote to him after the election debacle that "unless there is an immediate & continued change in the conduct of the war, and the practice of arresting citizens without legal process is abandoned, there is every reason to fear that you will be unable, successfully, to carry on the government."

Still others blamed Lincoln's oldest foe, the failure of the war. "The New York and other elections are simply a reproof of the inactivity of the Government," declared Boston lawyer John Chipman Ropes. "They have nothing to do with the nigger question. With the administration military success is everything—it is the verdict which cures all errors." William Cullen Bryant's comment in the New York *Evening Post* catalogued Lincoln's military impotence:

> The people after their gigantic preparations and sacrifices have looked for an adequate return, and looked in vain. They have seen armies unused in the field perish in pestilential swamps. They have seen their money wasted in long winter encampments, or frittered away on fruitless expeditions along the coast. They have seen a huge debt roll up, yet no prospect of greater military results.

Some Democrats glorified the election as the rising up of an oppressed people, throwing off their chains. The southern Illinois *Salem Advocate* gushed:

> We saw the President of the United States stretching forth his hand and seizing the reins of government with almost absolute power, and yet the people submitted. On the 4th day of November, 1862, the people arose in their might, they uttered their voice, like the sound of many waters, and tyranny, corruption and maladministration trembled.

Most, however, saw an accumulation of ruin. Politician-general John Cochrane of New York wrote to Lincoln his impression of the Waterloo there:

I do not think that the majorities have spoken designedly upon any one subject in hostility to your administration—Some have been adverse to the proclamation— others have been impelled by some uncertain indefinite sense that all was not right: and the greatest numbers have greedily visited their disappointment that the war is not finished & was not finished in 60 days upon the first responsible party they could discover— They have been aching for a head to smash— They thought they saw one, and they smashed Wadsworth's [the Republican candidate for governor of New York]—The restlessness of men when suffering and their usual conclusion that a change, no matter for what, will benefit them, have been fully asserted in the result of the election— I have toiled hard, but I confess with a bruised spirit & a desponding heart for the principles & conduct of your administration.

The day after the election, diarist George Templeton Strong attempted to read the mind of the multitude:

Probably two-thirds of those who voted for Seymour meant to say by their votes, "Messrs. Lincoln, Seward, Stanton & Co., you have done your work badly, so far. You are humbugs. My business is stopped, I have got taxes to pay, my wife's third cousin was killed on the Chickahominy, and the war is no nearer an end than it was a year ago. I am disgusted with you and your party and shall vote for the governor or the congressman you disapprove, just to spite you.

Another angry New Yorker admonished the President as the returns came in:

This great nation has given to you almost absolute authority. The people have, for nineteen months, poured out, at your call, sons, brothers, husbands & money.— What is the result?— Do you ever realize that the desolation, sorrow, grief, that pervades this country is owing to you? — that the young men who have been maimed, crippled, murdered, & made invalids for life, owe it to your weakness, irresolution, & want of moral courage?

Lincoln bowed his head against a storm of recriminations from resentful Republicans everywhere. "I deplore the result in New York," wrote Charles

Sumner; "It is worse for our country than the bloodiest disaster on any field of battle." William W. Orme of Illinois desponded, "I think the country is ruined." Pittsburgh Congressman J.K. Moorhead, returning to Washington from his district, scolded Lincoln, "it was not your fault we were not all beaten." He brought word from Pennsylvania state leaders, one-time Lincoln supporters who now said they "would be glad to hear some morning that you had been found hanging from the post of a lamp at the door of the White House." Historian George Bancroft lamented to fellow liberal Francis Lieber:

> [Lincoln] is ignorant, self-willed, and is surrounded by men some of whom are almost as ignorant as himself. So we have the dilemma put to us, What to do, when his power must continue two years longer and when the existence of our country may be endangered before he can be replaced by a man of sense. How hard, in order to save the country, to sustain a man who is incompetent.

In a column headlined "All the Blame on Mr. Lincoln," the Democratic *Crisis* gloated over the misery in Lincoln's party, reprinting an article from the Republican Cincinnati *Commercial* that was a litany of complaints:

> The result . . . is attributable to the mismanagement that has characterized the conduct of the war; the want of a sound policy, vigorously pursued; the manifold corruptions and extravagances in contracts; the failure of military plans through the untimely interference of civilians, who thought they knew all about it; a rather blind belief in the efficacy of proclamations over powder effectively used; and the desire of a patient and patriotic people for some change which may better the situation, and which, at most, cannot make matters much worse, and all of which is charged to the account of the Administration, though it be ever so innocent.

Lincoln deluded himself about the reasons for his party's election losses, preferring to believe, "The democrats were left in a majority by [Republican men] going to the war," as he explained to Carl Schurz in a letter. This was wrongheaded. Just as many Democrats had joined the army as Republicans, and Schurz, who had spent months as a general, knew it. He lectured the President in his reply:

I fear you entertain too favorable a view of the causes of our defeat in the elections. . . . Let us indulge in no delusions as to the true causes . . . . The people had sown confidence and reaped disaster and disappointment. They wanted a change, and . . . they sought it in the wrong direction. I entreat you, do not attribute to small incidents . . . what is a great historical event. It is best that you . . . should see the fact in its true light and appreciate its significance: *the result of the elections was a most serious and severe reproof administered to the administration.* . . ."

* * *

Lincoln did agree with those who complained that the war was not being fought aggressively enough, and he sought a quick cure. As early as October 6 he had directed McClellan to follow up his victory at Antietam by crossing the Potomac and forcing a battle with Lee. Four weeks later, the tardy Young Napoleon had still killed no rebels, so Lincoln sacked him on November 5, the day he received the election returns from New York.

Here was a defining moment for Lincoln at mid-term. He could have cemented the faith of the Radicals by doing what they had been demanding for a full year and installing a Republican in McClellan's place. Instead, he named a Democrat, an army favorite, McClellan's friend and right-hand man General Ambrose Burnside. By making the change of commanders seem like a legitimate military succession rather than a political purge, Lincoln tried to limit the damage to the morale of the Army of the Potomac.

Even so, soldiers bristled at Lincoln's beheading of their idol. According to McClellan, "Many were in favor of my refusing to obey the order, and of marching upon Washington to take possession of the government." There was campfire talk of mass resignations. "Officers and men unite in denouncing [McClellan's removal] as an outrage upon the army," one soldier wrote home. It was unfair, protested another: "Upon every occasion when General McClellan was upon the eve of a decisive battle . . . he has been prevented from striking the blow by the interference of the government." New York aristocrat Colonel Wainwright reported that regret among the officers was universal, "and a few even going so far as to beg him to resist the order, and saying that the army would support him." General Thomas Meagher of New York's famous Irish Brigade blasted Lincoln's action as notorious and criminal, "which the Army of the Union will never forgive." Scholar-soldier Francis A. Walker lamented,

"When the chief had passed out of sight, the romance of war was over for the Second Corps."

While McClellan's devotees were furious at his ouster, it was not equally true that his enemies were delighted. Rather, they were incensed that Lincoln missed another opportunity to put one of their own—Frémont, for instance, or "Fighting Joe" Hooker—in his place. After the repudiation of Lincoln in the elections, the Radicals now began to fear that he would swerve from his September promises. To them, his appointment of the Democrat Burnside was a first sign of retreat. The old doubts about Lincoln's timidity and vacillation returned. Boston intellectual Charles Eliot Norton summoned a metaphor: "I am much afraid that a domestic cat will not answer when one wants a Bengal tiger." Count Gurowski wrote his lack of confidence to Governor Andrew: "You can not change Lincoln's head, you can not fill his small but empty skull with brains." As political leaders gathered in Washington for the December session of Congress, there were grumblings by powerful men who maintained that Lincoln was but a "tow-string of a President" who had to be bound up "with strong, sturdy rods in the shape of Cabinet ministers."

Radicals squinting for signs of an about-face by Lincoln on emancipation thought their worst fears confirmed when his Annual Message to Congress was read on the floor of the House on December 1, 1862. In his Message, Lincoln recommended three constitutional amendments that offered compensation to any state that produced a gradual plan to abolish slavery by the year 1900, and included a new plea for colonization of freed blacks in some "place or places in a climate congenial to them." After page upon page of close argument for his elaborate proposal, he closed with phrases that reached new heights of rhetorical power: "The dogmas of the quiet past are inadequate to the stormy present.... In giving freedom to the slave, we assure freedom to the free.... We shall nobly save, or meanly lose, the last, best hope of earth." While those lines will be remembered forever, what has been forgotten is that when he wrote them, Lincoln was arguing for a plan that would have delayed the blessings of freedom to black slaves for two more generations.

That Lincoln included the "gradual—by 1900—compensated—with colonization" emancipation amendments in his Annual Message on December 1 reveals the deep doubts that still plagued him about the Proclamation scheduled for January 1. His Illinois friend, Judge Davis, who visited the President while he was preparing the Message, wrote that "Mr. Lincoln's whole soul is absorbed in his plan of remunerative emancipation and he thinks if Congress don't fail him, that the problem is solved." If so, Lincoln was laboring under an illusion. The idea of adding these amendments to the Constitution was a will-o'-the-wisp. One of Lincoln's bedrock tenets had been that secession was unconstitutional and that the rebel states were still in the Union, so all three amendments would have to be ratified by unanimous consent of the free states plus six slave states in order to have the three-fourths approval required by the Constitution.

The anti-slavery men wept bitterly when they heard Lincoln's amendments. They feared that the new proposal meant that he was reneging on his promise to issue the Emancipation Proclamation on New Years Day. "May the Lord hold to rigid account the fool that is set over us," one abolitionist wrote to William Lloyd Garrison; "What suicide the Administration is guilty of! What a weak pattern of Old Pharoah! What a goose!" In the columns of *The Liberator*, Garrison ranted, "The President is demented—or else a veritable Rip Van Winkle," adding that the Message's proposal "borders upon hopeless lunacy" and offered grounds for impeachment. "A man so manifestly without moral vision, so unsettled in his policy, so incompetent to lead, so destitute of hearty abhorrence of slavery," he told his readers, "cannot be safely relied on in any emergency."

*   *   *

Then, an emergency. On December 14 came awful news that the Army of the Potomac had suffered a crushing defeat at Fredericksburg. General Burnside, in his inaugural battle as army commander, had hurled his divisions first against the Confederate right without success, and then against the left atop well-defended Marye's Heights. A succession of attacks followed, each a bloody failure. Burnside retreated, leaving thousands of dead and dying in piles on the frozen Virginia ground. After hearing a full account of the disaster, Lincoln groaned to a friend, "If there is a worse place than Hell, I am in it."

As word of the massacre spread across the North, grief and wrath settled upon the people. Burnside was largely spared; the blame was heaped at Lincoln's door. Citizens were anguished by this newest, bloodiest evidence of Lincoln's ineptitude. "How long is such intolerable and wicked blundering to continue?" demanded the New York *Evening Post*. "The War is a failure!" cried the Albany *Atlas and Argus*. Joseph Medill of the Chicago *Tribune* recorded:

> The feeling of utter hopelessness is stronger than at any time since the war
> began. The terrible bloody defeat of our brave army . . . leaves us almost

without hope. . . . The public discontent waxes greater daily. . . . By a common instinct everybody feels that the war is drawing towards a disastrous and disgraceful termination. . . . Sometimes I think nothing is left now but "to fight for a boundary."

Even the moderate *Harper's Weekly* ran a cartoon that pictured an angry Spirit of Columbia pointing an accusing finger at Lincoln. *Harper's* spoke of a nationwide collapse of trust in Lincoln's government, and predicted ruin:

We are indulging in no hyperbole when we say that these events are rapidly filling the heart of the loyal North with sickness, disgust, and despair. Party lines are becoming effaced by such unequivocal evidences of administrative imbecility; it is the men who have given and trusted the most, who now feel most keenly that the Government is unfit for its office, and that the most gallant efforts ever made by a cruelly tried people are being neutralized by the obstinacy and incapacity of their leaders. Where this will all end no one can see. But it must end soon. The people have shown a patience, during the past year, quite unexampled in history. They have borne, silently and grimly, imbecility, treachery, failure, privation, loss of friends and means, almost every suffering which can

Harper's Weekly, January 3, 1863

"Columbia Confronts the President." Columbia: "Where are my 15,000 sons—murdered at Fredericksburg?" Lincoln: "This reminds me of a little joke." Columbia: "Go tell your joke at SPRINGFIELD."

afflict a brave people. But they can not be expected to suffer that such massacres as this at Fredericksburg shall be repeated. Matters are rapidly ripening for a military dictatorship.

The best men of the North wrote letters to their friends in Washington, or scribbled wretched entries in their diaries. "A year ago we laughed at the Honest Old Abe's grotesque genial Western jocosities, but they nauseate us now," wrote George Templeton Strong, predicting that Lincoln would have to "resign and make way for Hamlin," and that it would be "a change for the better, none for the worse being conceivable." One Pennsylvania constituent of Congressman Edward McPherson informed him that back home, "almost everybody is dissatisfied with the administration. President Lincoln is denounced by many of his most devoted friends in former times." Another Pennsylvanian reported that the locals were "utterly disgusted," believing "that the present administration is utterly incompetent," and a third that "if things are not more successfully managed the President will be generally deserted." From the Republican stronghold of Massachusetts, Charles Sumner was hearing much the same. "I am losing confidence in the executive capacity of Mr. Lincoln's administration," wrote one leader from Worcester; "I see plainly that doubt and discouragement are spreading among the people," he said, reporting "a fixed belief that the managers . . . at Washington are incompetent . . . ." A Boston man told Sumner that Lincoln's resignation "would be received with *great satisfaction*" and might "avert what . . . will otherwise come—viz., *a violent and bloody revolution at the North*." Southern poetasters minted jeering rhymes:

> *The days are growing shorter,*
> *The sun has crossed the line,*
> *And the people are all asking,*
> *"Will Abraham resign?"*

Republican senators were frantic, worried that Democrats would seize on the wave of hopelessness in the North and start a movement that would settle for peace on terms dictated by Richmond. "Folly, folly folly reigns supreme," moaned Zack Chandler to his wife. "The President is a weak man, too weak for the occasion. . . . The country is done for unless something is done at once."

*   *   *

Seeing Lincoln so universally reproached, the senators resolved that they, and not the President, must direct the war. They would start by deciding who should and who should not be in the Cabinet. A successful raid by the Republican senators on the Cabinet would establish the senators' authority over the man they saw as the overmatched rude boy in the Executive chair. Much more, it would signal the return of the legislature's control over American government.

Burnside's Fredericksburg fiasco had precipitated nothing less than a war between Congress and the President. "Reorganization" of the Cabinet would be the watchword of the coup attempt, and Seward would be the target. The Radicals had always distrusted Seward as a sinister influence on the simple Lincoln; now they feared he might sway the President from issuing the Emancipation Proclamation or make him sign a disgraceful peace with the Confederacy. They agreed with Joseph Medill: "Seward must be got out of the Cabinet. He is Lincoln's evil genius. He has been the President *de facto*, and has kept a sponge saturated with chloroform to Uncle Abe's nose all the while." Lincoln remarked to a friend, "They seemed to think that when I had in me any good purposes, Mr. Seward contrived to suck them out of me unperceived!" Conservative Republican senators went along, believing that Seward was an enemy of the legislature—*Wasn't it he who had convinced Lincoln to put off calling a special Congress after Sumter, and to schedule his important acts for times when Congress was not in session?*

For months, Secretary Chase had filled the ears of the senators with anti-Seward mutterings, calling him "a back stairs and malign influence which controlled the President." Chase had complained that the other Cabinet members had no say on policy, that under Lincoln's lax administration they only met "now and then for talk on whatever happens to come uppermost, not for grave consultation on matters concerning the salvation of the country." Angered by Chase's stories, alarmed by the collapse of hope after Fredericksburg, and betting that Lincoln, wounded by recent defeats at the polls and on the battlefield, would cave in and reshuffle his Cabinet to include more men like their ally Chase, the Republican senators met behind closed doors on December 16 and 17. According to Orville Browning, who attended, "Many speeches were made denouncing the President and expressing a willingness to vote for a resolution asking him to resign." In the end, it was determined to appoint a Committee of Nine to meet with Lincoln and demand that he remake the Cabinet to exclude anybody not in harmony with their demand for a "vigorous & successful prosecution of the war" (that is, William

Seward), and that he be bound in his policies by the "result of [the] combined wisdom and deliberation" of the reorganized "Cabinet council."

That evening, Seward, having heard about the caucuses and unwilling to be a burden on the President, gave his resignation to Lincoln and started packing his bags to leave Washington. Alerted to the senators' plot by the surprise appearance of Seward's resignation, Lincoln sent for his friend Orville Browning, and questioned him about the secret meetings. Browning admitted that they were "exceedingly violent towards the administration." Hearing this, Lincoln snapped, "They wish to get rid of me, and I am sometimes half disposed to gratify them." He then gave way to melancholy. "We are now on the brink of destruction," he said. "It appears to me the Almighty is against us, and I can hardly see a ray of hope. . . . Since I heard last night of the proceedings of the caucus I have been more distressed than by any event of my life."

An Illinois friend who saw him at this time described Lincoln as "perplexed to death nearly." Joshua Speed, Lincoln's dear friend from Kentucky, saw him that week and reported "the president looked haggard and care-worn beyond what [I] expected." Lincoln's old friend Noah Brooks, newly arrived in the capital, recalled, "His eyes were almost deathly in their gloomy depths, and on his visage was an air of profound sadness. His face was colorless and drawn."

Lincoln was showing the strain of the *coup* attempt. Nothing less than the survival of his government—in fact, of the American system of government—was at stake. If he surrendered cabinet choices to the senators, and his policy to the "Cabinet council," he would lose control of the government; if he refused, he would lose the support of the Senate at the height of a terrible civil war.

At seven p.m. on the evening of December 18, he met with the hostile Senate Committee of Nine for three hours, during which they hammered him with their resolutions. Lincoln listened calmly while the senators launched their indictments and pressed their demands, then he adjourned the meeting until the following evening. By the time Lincoln politely ushered them out of the White House with the promise that he would think it over, the senators felt confident that they had ousted Seward and insured a unified, right-thinking Cabinet that would dominate Lincoln's policies thereafter.

Lincoln, however, had other ideas. The next morning he convened five Cabinet members—Blair, Smith, Stanton, Chase, and Welles—and asked them to attend his meeting with the angry senators. That night, when the senators crowded into the room with the unexpected Cabinet members, Lincoln produced an inspired bit of political theater. He began with a solemn, careful review of his major decisions, which demonstrated that there was already unity in the Cabinet—here the Illinois lawyer stretched things a bit—and that, even if some members only acquiesced after a decision was made, the Secretaries generally agreed.

"Did they not?" he asked the Cabinet members. All eyes went to Chase. Everyone in the room knew it was he who had spent months whispering to the senators, engineering the loss of confidence in the Cabinet's performance in general and William Seward in particular. Now he would have to take his place with the accusers or with the President.

With everyone present leaning forward, Chase faltered. His lips fluttered; he protested; he dodged; he went silent.

Lincoln's embarrassment of Chase deftly demonstrated that no Cabinet member could afford to side with an attack by hostile senators—*if that became the fashion, how long could any of them expect to last?* When the fiery discussion over Seward had burnt itself out, Lincoln asked for a roll call vote. Discouraged by Chase's desertion, only four senators voted to remove the Secretary of State. Seward was saved, and the meeting broke up, said Welles, "in milder spirit than it met." Senator Trumbull turned to Lincoln and growled a parting shot: "Secretary Chase had a very different tone the last time I spoke with him!"

The next day Washington buzzed with rumors: *the whole Cabinet would resign! new slates were being proposed!* Lincoln was still in a bind, since a refusal to accept Seward's resignation would be a slap in the face to the senators. The answer to the problem, ironically, was provided by Chase, who delivered one of the truly Providential gifts of Lincoln's presidency. That morning, December 20, he appeared at the White House. According to Welles, who was there with Stanton, Chase said he "had been painfully affected by the meeting" the night before and had prepared his resignation.

Lincoln lit up. "Where is it?" he asked quickly.

"I brought it with me," Chase said, and pulled it from his pocket.

The President leaped at him. "Let me have it," he said, and reached for it with his long arms and fingers. There was a short tug of war, and then Lincoln had it away from Chase, who seemed reluctant to part with it, objecting that there was something further he wished to say. But Lincoln would not hear him. He hastily opened the letter, read it, and, as an air of satisfaction spread over his face, said, "This cuts the Gordian knot. I can dispose of this subject now without difficulty."

Stanton offered to submit his resignation as well. "I don't want yours," said Lincoln. "This is all I want—this relieves me—my way is clear—the trouble is ended. I will detain neither of you any longer."

Chase's resignation, neatly balancing that of Seward, offered a solution to the crisis that Lincoln happily summed up in a prairie metaphor: "I can ride on now. I've got a pumpkin in each end of my bag!" He addressed identical notes to Seward and Chase declining to accept their resignations. Both men would remain, and the Cabinet would continue as before. Just as important, all Republican factions now understood that there would be no tampering with the Departments. If they insisted on one man's ouster, his opposite would go also.

*   *   *

Lincoln's private triumph, however, gained no public confidence. As the year 1862 dwindled, he suffered from a wave of defeatism that swelled across the North. On New Year's Eve, a Wisconsin Democrat scribbled a final curse in his diary, writing, "The President of the United States is responsible for the miserable state of things, and for this and many special and arbitrary acts which he committed and authorized to be committed, I solemnly believe that [he] ought to be impeached and legally and constitutionally deposed from the high office of President of the United States." Samuel Medary of *The Crisis* also wanted Lincoln impeached, and published his inky reflections in a year-end editorial: "The year 1862 has been a year of blood and plunder, of carnage and conflagration, . . . of falsehood and corruption, . . . of bastilles, persecutions and tears, . . . of despotism, desolation and death."

The Radicals, meanwhile, gnashed their teeth at the failure of their latest scheme to force the awkward, disheveled, ungrammatical Westerner to bow to their program. Lincoln's masterful defense of his conservative Secretary of State renewed their doubts about his intention to issue the emancipation announcement. Panicky letters poured in to Charles Sumner from Boston anti-slavery men. "We feel no reliance that [Lincoln] will [carry out the proclamation] while we see him guided by the baleful councils of Seward & the Border State men," fretted one. Railroad tycoon J. M. Forbes desponded, "The first of January is near at hand, and we see no signs of any measures for carrying into effect the Proclamation." Another of Sumner's friends complained, "Old Abe will do nothing decent till driven to it by a force which would save all the devils in hell."

Sumner calmed these men with the assurance that, "The President says he would not stop the Proclamation if he could, and he could not if he would," which had the ring of genuine Lincoln. Literary lion Orestes Brownson would not be cheered, however. He wrote to Sumner as the New Year approached,

I do not believe Mr. Lincoln at all.... He is thick-headed; he is ignorant; he is tricky, somewhat astute in a small way, and obstinate as a mule. My opinion . . . is that nothing can be done with him . . . . He would damp the ardor of the bravest . . . & neutralize the efforts of the ablest . . . . He is wrong-headed, . . . the petty politician not the statesman, & . . . ill-deserving the *sobriquet* of Honest. I am out of all patience with him.

On December 27, even the moderate, pro-Lincoln *New York Times* reported a "general air of doubt" about Lincoln's resolve to issue the Proclamation, given the discouragements at the polls and on the battlefield since his September promise.

As the hours dwindled before proclamation day, George Templeton Strong jotted down in his diary: "Will Lincoln's backbone carry him through? Nobody knows."

London Fun, December 27, 1862

"Abe's Last"

Chapter 26

Emancipation Proclaimed

"The lack of respect for the President in all parties is unconcealed."

Lincoln, mindful of Chase's complaint that he never consulted his advisors, dutifully convened the Cabinet on December 29 to give a copy of the final Emancipation Proclamation to each Secretary and ask for suggestions. Their comments touched on two things.

The first was Lincoln's determination to exempt from freedom not only the slaves in the loyal Border States, but also the slaves in the parts of rebellious states that were already behind Union army lines. The exemptions were crucial, Lincoln thought, since his entire argument for the legality of the proclamation depended on the President's "war power" granted by the Constitution in times of rebellion. The emancipation decree, he reasoned, could therefore legally affect only the parts of the country still at war with the Union. Chase argued that the slaves should be emancipated in entire rebellious states to avoid confusion. Blair and Seward agreed. Lincoln, however, out of concern for the proclamation's constitutionality, overruled them—the rebellious states and counties that were already occupied would remain exempted, and the slaves there would remain bound.

The second issue was Lincoln's statement that the government "will do no act . . . to repress said persons . . . in suitable efforts they may make for their actual freedom." It was this sentence that since September had triggered the outrage of those who thought the proclamation encouraged a bloody slave revolt. Bates, Blair, and even Chase asked that it be struck out entirely, and Seward offered a rewriting. In the end, Lincoln agreed and rewrote the clause himself, calling upon the freed slaves to "abstain from all violence, unless in necessary self-defense" and to "labor faithfully for reasonable wages."

Lincoln had already made other critical changes. No longer were compensation and colonization recommended. Also, he had added a call for former slaves to take up arms and join the Union army. Since by long tradition military service was linked to citizenship, this was a signal that the Proclamation would ultimately bestow all the benefits of citizenship over and above freedom.

When the Cabinet met again on December 31, Secretary Chase suggested one more change. This was a felicitous closing sentence, one that invoked not only the constitutional requirement of military necessity, but also justice, the judgment of mankind (an echo of the Declaration of Independence), and God's favor. This was exactly the kind of thing Lincoln had purposely kept out of the Emancipation Proclamation. The reason he had maintained a dry, lawyerly tone so scrupulously throughout the document was his fear that it would not stand up in court, and that the intrusion of any moral note would cause racists in the North—still repulsed by abolitionist sentiment—to reject it. Lincoln, however, surrendered to Chase, the man whose resentments had almost brought down the administration only a week earlier, and added the Secretary's final sentence: "And upon this act, sincerely believed to be an act of justice, warranted by the Constitution, upon military necessity, I invoke the considerate judgment of mankind, and the gracious favor of Almighty God."

Lincoln wrote the sentence into his final version of the Emancipation Proclamation on New Year's Day morning. When he was finished, Lincoln summoned a clerk to take the draft to the State Department to be copied and engrossed. While he waited for the official copy to be returned for his signature, Lincoln received his first heckling about the Proclamation from his Kentuckian wife Mary, who was very much opposed to it. "Well, what do you intend doing?" she asked sharply. Lincoln looked heavenward and replied, "I am a man under orders, I cannot do otherwise."

When the official copy returned from the State Department, however, there was a snag. Lincoln, with his lawyer's eye, noticed that the copyist had inserted a wrong word in the State Department's closing subscription, and the botched document had to be sent back for recopying. Meanwhile, he was due at the traditional New Year's reception downstairs—open, in those days, to anyone who cared to shake hands with the President—and the signing would have to wait until afterwards. He went down to the reception room, and the raucous, teeming visitors entered, pushing and shoving, through the front double doors, which were opened at intervals to admit the mob that pressed noisily against the front of the building. The visitors were then funneled into a line to shake hands with the First Family, after which they were herded onto a ramp of wooden planks that led out through an open bay window. This lasted from noon to two o'clock, and required that Lincoln shake hands in his pump-handle style for two solid hours.

After the last of the guests had been shooed up the ramp and out the window, Seward returned with the corrected copy of the Emancipation

Proclamation. Lincoln took it upstairs, and—without ceremony, with fewer than a dozen witnesses on hand, and with a right hand still unsteady from the exhaustion of two hours of handshaking—affixed his name to the greatest document of the century.

No text of the decree had been sent out in advance for the nation's morning papers. New Year's Day dawned on Northern cities and towns in suspense— *would emancipation be proclaimed?* At the Music Hall in Boston the intelligentsia were gathered, including Henry Wadsworth Longfellow, John Greenleaf Whittier, William Lloyd Garrison, Ralph Waldo Emerson, Harriet Beecher Stowe, and Oliver Wendell Holmes, Sr., with the expectation that the blessed announcement would sing across the wires at noon. Noon, however, came and went; then the afternoon; then the evening, and still no word. Onstage, poems were recited and music played. Meanwhile, the audience watched the clock. Doubts increased. Anxiety became agony. Finally, at ten o'clock at night, Josiah Quincy burst through the doors and rushed to the platform with the joyous news: *Abraham Lincoln has signed the Emancipation Proclamation!* The Music Hall erupted, and there was pandemonium as the nation's most dignified ladies and gentlemen screamed, cried, jumped up and down, threw their hands in the air, and waved their silk handkerchiefs.

A few blocks away at the Tremont Temple, Frederick Douglass and the elite of black abolitionism heard the news at the same time, and there too the whole crowd leaped up, stomped their feet, shouted at the tops of their lungs, and shed tears of joy as they took up the hymn, "Sound the loud timbrel of Egypt's dark sea/ Jehovah hath triumphed, his people are free!"

The next morning the headline of *The Liberator* covered most of the page:

THE PROCLAMATION.
THREE MILLION OF SLAVES SET FREE!
GLORY HALLELUJAH!

Everywhere among those who had faithfully awaited such a consummation there was a free flowing ecstasy. "All trials were swallowed up in the great deep joy"; they had come from "midnight darkness to the bright noon of day"; there was "a bewilderment of joy," "a perfect furor of acclamation"—these were all notes in the symphony of enthusiasm from radicals and blacks.

* * *

Unfortunately for Abraham Lincoln, the wildly cheering friends of William Lloyd Garrison and Frederick Douglass were the most despised set in the Northern heartland, especially among the Democratic masses who had so recently reclaimed the electoral majority from Illinois to New York. The jubilation in Boston was soon drowned out by the same angry jangle of condemnation that had followed the earlier promise of emancipation in September.

The press was particularly hostile in the Northwest. The Chicago *Times* called the Emancipation Proclamation "a wicked, atrocious and revolting deed," which had perverted the war's purpose from a constitutional one into a struggle "for the liberation of three million negro barbarians and their enfranchisement as citizens." The Dubuque *Herald* called the proclamation the "crowning act of Lincoln's folly" and Lincoln "a brainless tyrant," "a perjured public servant," "a blundering partisan," "a buffoon President." The Chatfield (Minn.) *Democrat* dismissed it as "the most foolish joke ever got off by the six-foot-four Commander-in-Chief." In Ohio, editor Samuel Medary of *The Crisis* whipped himself into a three-column froth in which he called Lincoln "a half-witted Usurper, who, in an evil hour, was elected . . . under the whip and spur of a set of fanatical and sectional politicians." He declared that the proclamation created "a Dictatorship at Washington," and denounced it as a "monstrous, impudent and heinous Abolition proceeding . . . impudent and insulting to God as to man, for it declares those 'equal' whom god created unequal." *The Crisis* published a "Political Alphabet" whose twenty-six astringent stanzas began with this barbed rhyme:

> *"A" stands for Old Abe, who has made up his mind*
> *To yield to the pressure that crowds him behind;*
> *And to aid the malignants in splitting the nation,*
> *Has issued his mandate of Emancipation.*

The pro-slavery New York journals were also cruel. The *New York Herald* flayed Lincoln's act as "a dead letter," "unwise and ill-timed, impracticable, and outside of the constitution." The New York *World* called the Emancipation Proclamation "miserable balderdash," "not merely futile, but ridiculous." The *New York Evening Express* suggested its own modest proposal: "The best thing that can be done is for Mr. Lincoln to resign, and go home to Springfield, with Mr. Hamlin to follow him. These resignations would be worth twenty victories, and would reestablish public confidence."

The Catholic Church, representing the swelling Irish American contingent, was particularly critical of Lincoln's act. Bishop Hughes of New York City, through his organ the *Metropolitan Record*, raged against the perversion of the war from an attempt to restore the Union into an emancipation crusade. The "vile and infamous" Proclamation, it warned, would bring "massacre and rapine and outrage into the homes on Southern plantations, sprinkling their hearths with the blood of gentle women, helpless age, and innocent childhood.... Never was a blacker crime sought to be committed against nature, against humanity, against the holy precepts of Christianity." The Harrisburg *Patriot and Union*, too, branded it a "cold-blooded invitation to insurrection and butchery."

The newly-elected Democratic leaders across the loyal states climbed onto platforms and turned their inaugurals into anti-Proclamation circuses. On January 7, all eyes were on New York's Horatio Seymour as he mounted the dais. Seymour, aware of his instant eminence as a Democratic spokesman, issued a stinging condemnation of Lincoln's Emancipation Proclamation, calling it a "bloody, barbarous, revolutionary, and unconstitutional scheme." Democratic newspapers across the continent enthusiastically reprinted Seymour's speech, and it blew new wind into the sails of Lincoln's opponents.

Lincoln looked uneasily toward Kentucky. The *Louisville Daily Democrat* summed up the sentiment there: "We scarcely know how to express our indignation at this flagrant outrage of all constitutional law, all human justice, all Christian feeling." Governor James F. Robinson denounced the Proclamation in a message to the Kentucky legislature, and the legislature responded with its own denunciation of Lincoln's decree. There was talk in the state of recalling Kentucky troops from the Union army. In February, Kentucky Democrats held a state convention for the purpose of "preparing the Kentucky Mind for revolt against the Union," which had to be dispersed by Federal troops.

Conservative Republicans, opposed to the Proclamation from the beginning and dismayed by the brawny Democratic giant the document had awakened, drooped in discouragement. Illinois Senator Orville Browning had been permanently disaffected—"I am despondent, and have but little hope left for the Republic," he wrote in his diary as he prepared to leave office at the end of January. Browning met with Seward, who agreed that the Proclamation was "useless" and "mischievous." It was merely symbolic, Seward said. In one of his world-weary musings, he told reporter Donn Piatt that it was "a puff of wind over an accomplished fact," that "The Emancipation Proclamation was uttered in the first gun fired at Sumter and we have been the last to hear it. As it is, we show our sympathy with slavery by emancipating slaves where we cannot reach them and holding them in bondage where we can set them free." Browning's and Seward's discontent was shared by Senator Doolittle of Wisconsin and old Thomas Ewing of Ohio, who met with Browning on January 12. "We all agreed that we were upon the brink of ruin," Browning wrote, "and could see no hope of an amendment in affairs unless the President would change his policy, and withdraw or greatly modify his proclamation."

That same week, Judge Davis of Illinois, after seeing the intense anti-Proclamation feeling at home, begged Lincoln to alter his policy "as the only means of saving the Country." Seward's conservative crony, New York party boss Thurlow Weed, complained bitterly in a letter to the U.S. consul in Paris that "there was a strong attachment to the Constitution in many of the seceded states. . . . But [it] was entirely dispelled by the Proclamation of Emancipation." A few frantic conservatives revived talk of "sloughing off the secession sympathizers from the Dem[ocratic] party, of the ultras from the Rep[ublican party], and [forming] a new organization for 1864," headed by Seward. It came to nothing, however. Seward had become too loyal to Lincoln to lead a breakaway conservative faction now.

Other thoughtful Republicans swerved from Lincoln out of doubt about the Emancipation Proclamation's constitutionality. Benjamin R. Curtis, the former Supreme Court Justice who had written the dissenting opinion in the Dred Scott decision, now dissented from the Proclamation. "I know of no man of sense here," he wrote from Washington on New Year's Day, "who has any hope for the restoration of the union. I have seen a good many prominent men today . . . & I have not seen one who does not say the country is ruined & that its ruin is attributable largely to the utter incompetence of the Prest. . . . He is shattered, dazed, & utterly foolish." Curtis published a pamphlet titled *Executive Power*, in which he damned the Emancipation Proclamation as an executive decree that illegally proposed to "repeal and annul valid State laws which regulate the domestic relations of their people." Curtis rejected the idea that the President had any "war powers" over and above his rank as Commander-in-Chief of the army and navy. As an executive, asserted Curtis, "He cannot make a law. He cannot repeal one." The powers Lincoln claimed in the Proclamation, Curtis continued, were only those of a "usurper." If it stood, what would keep him from using the war power "to disregard each and every provision of the Constitution?"

Other former friends of Lincoln fell in behind Curtis. Massachusetts Republican Judge Joel Parker wrote that the power to issue the Emancipation Proclamation was tantamount to "a power to change Constitutional rights . . . at

Privately distributed, October 1862

"Writing the Emancipation Proclamation." Lincoln writes the
Emancipation Proclamation in a demonic setting, with his
foot on the Constitution.

the pleasure of the President in time of war." Robert Winthrop, Boston royalty
and former Senator from Massachusetts, condemned the Proclamation as
"undoubtedly one of the most startling exercises of the one-man
power—which the history of human government, free or despotic, has ever
witnessed." If it persisted, he warned, "we shall find ourselves plunged
irretrievably into the fearful and fathomless abyss."

As for the Radicals, some had never shared in the New Year's Day rapture.
Horace Greeley, for example, scolded Lincoln in the New York *Tribune* for not
liberating all slaves in Tennessee and Louisiana—two states, he pointed out,
which "have more than One Hundred Thousand of their citizens in arms to
destroy the Union." Radical anti-Lincoln grumblings reached the ears of the
Democratic newspapers, who delighted in publishing them, such as the *New
York Journal of Commerce*—"The proclamation of the President is not acceptable
to the Radicals. They argue that it is not universal, and is therefore not up to the
mark"—and the *Illinois State Register*—"[He] has made no friends among [the
Radicals], for the reason that he has not done everything in their particular way,
and at their designated moment."

Many anti-slavery men had grown so comfortable with their contempt for Lincoln that they simply could not break the habit. One was future President James Garfield, who looked down his nose at the Proclamation's author. "Strange phenomenon in the world's history," he sniffed, "when a second-rate Illinois lawyer is the instrument to utter words which shall form an epoch memorable in all future ages." Other Radicals who applauded the Proclamation doubted that Lincoln had the sand to see it through. Congressman William P. Cutler of southern Ohio wrote, "The feeling prevails that Lincoln allows the policy of the war to be dictated by Seward, Weed, and the border state men. To human vision all is dark . . . . All is confusion and doubt. . . . How striking the want of a leader! The nation is without a head. . . . The earnest men are brought to a dead-lock by the President."

Within a month, as conservative Republicans who had been Lincoln's closest supporters peeled away, even Radicals who had thrown their hats in the air on January 1 began to leave the celebration. John P. Hale of New Hampshire was one who became convinced before February that "we had made a great mistake upon the slavery question, and that it would have been better for the cause of the Country, and of emancipation if nothing had been said in regard to the negro since the war commenced." Joseph Medill, editor of the Chicago *Tribune* and anti-slavery champion, wrote to Illinois congressman Washburne on January 14 to propose an armistice. He listed his reasons for throwing in the towel—all, he said, stemming from what he called the "central imbecility" of Lincoln. He concluded,

> I can understand the awful reluctance with which you can be brought to contemplate a divided union. But there is no help for it. The war has assumed such proportions—the situation is so desperate and stubborn, our finances are so deranged and exhausted, the democratic party is so hostile and threatening that complete success has become a moral impossibility. . . . Lincoln is only half awake, and never will do much better than he has done. He will do the right thing always too late, and just when it does no good.

Friends of freedom across the North feared that the army, instead of delivering the slaves from bondage, would instead go home. Morale in the Army of the Potomac was already perilously low after the Battle of Fredericksburg. "The army is tired with its hard and terrible experience," wrote twenty-one-year-old Captain Oliver Wendell Holmes, Jr., "I've pretty much made up my mind that the South have achieved their independence." When the Emancipation Proclamation came on the heels of that slaughter, fighting spirit in the army went into free fall. Thomas Ewing confided to Browning his worry that "many of our officers would resign, and a 100,000 of our men lay down their arms." Other friends told Browning they had visited the army, and had "conversed with a great many soldiers, all of whom expressed the greatest dissatisfaction, saying they had been deceived—that they volunteered to fight for the Country, and had they known it was to be converted into a war for the negro they would not have enlisted. They think that scarcely one of the 200,000 whose term of service is soon to expire will re enlist."

Correspondents traveling with the army claimed that hardly one soldier in ten approved of the Emancipation Proclamation. The Philadelphians of the 106th Pennsylvania regiment were hostile, "with many . . . boldly stating that they would not have entered the army had they thought such would be the action of the Government." In the 51st Pennsylvania regiment, made up of veterans who had bravely stormed across Burnside's Bridge in a hail of bullets at Antietam, "officers and men swore that they would neither draw a sword or fire a shot in support of such a proclamation." Henry Abbot, a major in Boston's highly-educated "Harvard Regiment," huffed, "The president's proclamation is of course received with universal disgust, particularly the part which enjoins officers to see that it is carried out. You may be sure that we shan't see to any thing of the kind, having decidedly too much reverence for the constitution." Mailbags left the army bulging with letters like the following:

> I . . . would like to see the North win, but as to any interest in freeing the Negroes or in supporting the Emancipation Proclamation I in common with every other officer & soldier in the Army wash my hands of it. . . . I came out to fight for the restoration of the Union and to keep slavery as it is without going into the territories & not to free the niggers."

Every day during the month of January hundreds of deserters from the Army of the Potomac protested the Proclamation by skulking home along the back roads. One Vermont soldier reported on January 25 that his mates were "getting disgusted . . . and it is nothing uncommon for a Capt. to get up in the morning and find half his company gone." Senator John Sherman wrote to his brother General William Sherman, serving with the western army: "Military affairs look dark here in the Army of the Potomac. . . . The entire army seems demoralized."

Here was darkness at war's noon. With Northern political factions more bitterly divided than ever by the Emancipation Proclamation, with the army disintegrating from defeat and in full revolt against Lincoln's shifting of war aims, even the Emancipation Proclamation's supporters concluded that it was a dead letter, and dropped the subject.

Lincoln, in contrast, showed a growing steeliness, a hardening of his belief that the Proclamation would ultimately prove to be the bold stroke that would cut the hard knot of the slavery argument. On January 25, when a group of

London Fun, November 15, 1862

"Daring American Acrobat." Watched by the rulers of Europe, Lincoln prepares to advance from "Emancipation" to "Utter ruin."

Boston abolitionists journeyed to the White House to complain that the Proclamation had not accomplished its purpose, he conceded that it had accomplished little, and told them, according to one, that "he had not expected much from it at first and consequently had not been disappointed. He had hoped, and still hoped, that something would come of it after a while." Wendell Phillips, who was in the Boston delegation, quoted Lincoln as saying that "he doubted whether the proclamation had not done more harm than good." Lincoln used the same phrase when he told Senator George Julian, "My proclamation was to stir the country; but it has done about as much harm as good." Only an unquenchable confidence could have conceded so much so readily.

Others, however, had neither the patience nor farsightedness of Lincoln. Wendell Phillips told an audience that the President's "stumbling, faithless, uncertain" steps were to blame for a hopeless situation where "matters of vexed dispute"—that is, emancipation—had "passed into dead issues."

*   *   *

Defending the rightness of the Emancipation Proclamation against such widespread opposition was a huge drain on Lincoln, who had never cocooned himself with yes-men, but instead talked to and contended with men of every political hue all day, every day. Many people attested that his appearance during this period was shocking. Benjamin Brown French, the man responsible for the upkeep of the White House and a familiar figure in the halls of the Executive Mansion, wrote on February 22 that the President was "growing feeble. He wrote a note while I was present, and his hand trembled as I never saw it before, and he looked worn & haggard." A naval lieutenant who saw Lincoln then observed the strain: "Lincoln looks completely worn out," he wrote, "almost haggard, and seems very much depressed." Perhaps most shocking of all, Admiral John Dahlgren noted in his diary, "I observe that the President never tells a joke now."

Mary Lincoln could not console her husband, for she herself was inconsolable. Dressed in black every day, she was still consumed in mourning over Willie's death, and now that its anniversary approached, she was overcome with a new wave of grief. Neither could the President spend a carefree hour with his one friend in Congress, Orville Browning. The new Illinois legislature had replaced him with a Democrat, and Browning had left Washington on January 30. Nor was there any comfort in the familiar rituals of Washington society. The Emancipation Proclamation had been a stone upon which the conservatives and the radicals had sharpened their hatred for each other; all now carried daggers in their teeth.

As the cold hard rains of winter announced the approach of the third year of the war's unimaginable sorrow, Lincoln found himself largely isolated and alone. Congressman A. G. Riddle of Ohio wrote that, in late February 1863, the "criticism, reflection, reproach, and condemnation" of Lincoln in Congress was so complete that there were only two men in the House who defended him: Isaac Arnold of Illinois and Riddle himself. Author and lawyer Richard Henry Dana, after a visit to Washington in February, reported that "The lack of respect for the President in all parties is unconcealed." Two weeks later, he made the same observation in a letter to Charles Francis Adams. "As to the politics of Washington," he wrote, "the most striking thing is the absence of personal loyalty to the President. It does not exist. He has no admirers, no enthusiastic supporters, none to bet on his head. If a Republican convention were to be held to-morrow, he would not get the vote of a State." Dana listed Lincoln's crimes:

> He does not act, or talk, or feel like the ruler of a great empire in a great crisis. This is felt by all, and has got down through all the layers of society. It has a disastrous effect on all departments and classes of officials, as well as on the public. He seems to me to be fonder of details than of principles, . . . of patronage, and personal questions, than of the weightier matters of empire. He likes rather to talk and tell stories with all sorts of persons who come to him for all sorts of purposes than to give his mind to the noble and manly duties of his great post. It is not difficult to detect that this is the feeling of his cabinet. He has a kind of shrewdness and common sense, mother wit, and slipshod, low-levelled honesty, that made him a good Western jury lawyer. But he is an unutterable calamity to us where he is.

With no friends in Washington, with his armies shivering in their winter quarters, and with the Emancipation Proclamation null and void until the campaigns of spring, Lincoln suddenly heard warnings of a new threat to the nation as menacing as the rebel armies. He now told Charles Sumner he feared "the fire in the rear"—that is, the Democrats in the Northwest—more than the enemies at the front. Tales of treason were coming from Ohio, Indiana, and Illinois.

Chapter 27

The Rise of the Copperheads

"Jefferson Davis rules New York today."

In the first week of January, only days after the Emancipation Proclamation, Lincoln received a letter from the Republican governor of Indiana, Oliver P. Morton. Morton enclosed this clipping, the last paragraph of an editorial in the January 1 *Indiana State Sentinel*:

> Where, then does ABRAHAM LINCOLN derive his authority to issue a general emancipation proclamation? He has none. If he issues such a document, it is the act of an usurper; it is the exercise of despotic power. It is infamous. It means servile war—the butchery of white men not in arms, of helpless white women and children, by a race of semi-barbarians. Are the people willing that the American nation shall become the reproach of the whole civilized world by such acts of infamy? No, never. It cannot be. It must not be. If such a proclamation is issued to day, the people should rise in their might and repudiate it and its author. They have the power to do it, and they will be unworthy of the name of men and of Christians, if they do not.

This call for Hoosiers to "rise in their might" and throw off the Emancipation Proclamation's author sounded much like the Southern calls for secession two years earlier. Governor Morton's attached message to Lincoln was chilling: "We are on the eve of civil war in Indiana, and you need not be surprised to hear of a collision here at any time."

In the weeks after the Emancipation Proclamation, a secessionist convulsion in the Old Northwest—the states of Ohio, Indiana, and Illinois—threatened to take those states out of the Union just as Northern morale reached its lowest ebb of the war. Discontent in those states was deeper and more dangerous than anyplace else in the North. Their alliance with New England had always been uneasy. Westerners had never been rooted in the Yankee tradition. Below a line running through Columbus, Indianapolis, and

Springfield, the people of Ohio, Indiana, and Illinois were largely immigrants from Virginia and Kentucky, and had an affinity for the culture, people, and agricultural traditions of the South, strengthened by the ties of commerce on the Mississippi. Their natural friends were downriver. They were pro-slavery, and they looked with distrust on the commercial, industrial East.

This was especially true in early 1863, as the people of the Northwest chafed under new economic hardships brought on by the war. With the Mississippi River blocked by the Confederacy, river trade collapsed. Farm surpluses intended for Southern and foreign markets rotted in granaries. The prices of crops plummeted. With the Mississippi closed to commerce, Northwestern farmers were forced to use canals and railroads to get their products to markets in the East, and Yankee railroad barons gouged them with doubled and tripled freight rates. Jobs disappeared and banks failed: of the 112 Illinois banks doing business before the war, only seventeen had survived even 1861. As they struggled through mean times, Westerners watched New England manufacturers get fat from war contracts.

Economic pain translated into political poison. Democrats capitalized on Northwesterners' hardships and blamed Lincoln and the Republicans for their woes. The Democratic Party, historically controlled by Southerners, had always dominated the Northwest. The fall elections of 1862 had reestablished the Democratic ascendancy that had only recently been interrupted by the Republicans. As Ohio's Senator John Sherman put it, "They will fight for the flag & the country, but they hate niggers, and [are] easily influenced by a party cry." Now, when Lincoln proclaimed emancipation on New Year's Day, the resurgent Democrats interpreted it to mean that he had surrendered to abolitionist pressure and thrown in with the New Englanders. Anti-Lincoln and anti-Eastern feeling in the Northwest reached a level of intensity reminiscent of the Cotton States in the Secession Winter.

With this as background, a second alarm came from Governor Morton on the heels of the first: "I am advised that it is contemplated when the Legislature meets in this State to pass a joint resolution acknowledging the Southern Confederacy, and urging the States of the Northwest to dissolve all constitutional relations with the New England States. The same thing is on foot in Illinois." Thus alerted, Lincoln looked anxiously toward the opening of the heavily Democratic Illinois and Indiana legislatures.

The Hoosier legislature, as it turned out, lacked the will to secede from the Union as Morton feared. Instead, it passed a resolution demanding that Lincoln withdraw his Emancipation Proclamation. The Illinois legislature, opening at the same time as the Indiana legislature and working in tandem with the Indiana Democrats, likewise protested the Proclamation in purple prose:

> Resolved: That the emancipation proclamation of the President of the United States is as unwarranted in military as in civil law; a gigantic usurpation, at once converting the war, professedly commenced by the administration for the vindication of the authority of the constitution, into the crusade for the sudden, unconditional, and violent liberation of 3,000,000 negro slaves; a result which would not only be a total subversion of the Federal Union, but a revolution in the social organization of the Southern States, . . . the present and far-reaching consequences of which to both races cannot be contemplated without the most dismal foreboding of horror and dismay. The proclamation invites servile insurrection as an element in this emancipation crusade – a means of warfare, the inhumanity and diabolism of which are without example in civilized warfare, and which we denounce, and which the civilized world will denounce, as an uneffaceable disgrace to the American people.

Loyal onlookers were horrified at the noisy session: "All the [D]emocratic members of the legislature are open secessionists," one wrote. "They talked about going to Washington, hurling Mr Lincoln from the presidential chair, and inaugurating civil war north."

Appalled at the mischief of the Illinois lawmakers, Republican Governor Richard Yates used an obscure technicality to permanently adjourn the session before it could do further harm. For the next two years, Yates would rule his state like a prince, without legislative authority. There was a similar abrupt ending to the Indiana session. When a bill was introduced giving a Democratic committee the power to fund (or, more likely, to de-fund) the war, the Republican congressmen bolted. Without a quorum, the legislature adjourned, and for the next two years Governor Morton refused to call it back into session. He, like Yates in Illinois, would govern from 1863 to 1865 without a legislature, depending for money on handouts from Washington.

The anti-Lincoln voices inside the state capitols were restrained, as always, by eyes to re-election. On the street, there was no such restraint. As one Illinoisan wrote to Congressman Washburne, "Treason is everywhere bold, defiant—& active, *with impunity*!" After the Emancipation Proclamation, the Peace Democrats, known as "Copperheads"—named after the poisonous snake, but now openly wearing shiny copper Liberty head pennies in their lapels as badges of pride—lost all inhibition in the press. Wilbur F. Storey of the Chicago *Times*, Samuel Medary of the Columbus *Crisis*, Henry N. Walker of the *Detroit Free Press*, Charles H. Lanphier of the Springfield *Illinois State Register*, and more from a host of smaller cities all now bitterly attacked Lincoln and came out for peace without delay. They declared that there was not the remotest possibility that the rebellious Southern states could be subdued, and reprinted clippings from defiant Southern papers and letters from discouraged Union soldiers to prove it.

Some Copperhead journals called for violent resistance to the government, as in the *Indiana State Sentinel* paragraph Morton sent to Lincoln. A Dubuque *Herald* editorial told its readers, "There is but one way to deal with arbitrary power, and that is to treat it precisely as one would do . . . with a highwayman who might undertake to rob him of his money." Copperhead editors incited desertion, telling Union soldiers that, since Lincoln's proclamation had changed the character of the war, they were no longer under any obligation to fight. "You perceive that it is to emancipate slaves . . . that you are used as soldiers," hissed the *Herald*. "Are you, as soldiers, bound by patriotism, duty or loyalty to fight in such a cause?"

Taking advantage of the political ferment in early 1863, the Copperhead press organized and advertised anti-Lincoln "county meetings" all over the Northwest. These mass gatherings typically started with denunciations of the Emancipation Proclamation and then, as each speaker tried to draw an angrier response from the crowd than the man before him, escalated into resolutions to stop the war, vows to resist the draft, and out-and-out demands that the Northwestern states break away to form a new confederacy:

• Van Buren County, Michigan: "Since the war has been converted from its original purpose of a restoration of the Union under the Constitution, we are opposed to furnishing means or men."

• Wapello County, Iowa: "[We] deliberately and firmly pledge ourselves, one to another, that we will not render support to the present Administration in carrying on its wicked abolition crusade against the South; that we will resist to the death all attempts to draft any of our citizens into the army."

• Brown County, Indiana: "Our interests and our inclinations will demand of us a withdrawal from political association in a common government with the New England States."

• Douglas County, Illinois: "We regard the emancipation proclamation . . . as the entering wedge which will ultimately divide the middle and northwestern

States from our mischiefmaking, puritanical, fanatical New England brethren, and finally culminate in the formation of a Democratic republic out of the middle, northwestern and southern States. And for this we are thankful."

Suddenly warnings were everywhere that, just as Lincoln's election had sparked the secession of the South out of fear that he would abolish slavery, the Emancipation Proclamation would spark the secession of the Northwest now that the fear had been made real. On January 1, the very day of the Proclamation, former Supreme Court justice Benjamin R. Curtis wrote, "It is quite certain that a very unfriendly feeling towards [Massachusetts] now exists in the West & N. West, & a western member of the cabinet [probably Caleb Smith of Indiana] told me decidedly that if a division of the country should take place, it would not be an East & West line. He evidently had little hope." On January 13, Ohio Congressman Samuel "Sunset" Cox appeared before a large gathering of Democrats in New York City, and, in a speech that branded Lincoln's Proclamation as "Puritanism in Politics," made the same terrible augury as Curtis:

> My apprehension is, that before the people can thoroughly reform the conduct of their government, another civil strife may be raging; not the South against the North; not slave against free States; but the North against itself. . . . Abolition has made the Union, for the present, impossible. An aroused people may strike blindly and madly, and the result may be the formation of new alliances among the States and fresh conflicts among the people. . . . The erection of the States watered by the Mississippi and its tributaries into an independent Republic . . . is becoming more than a dream. It is the talk of every other western man. They do not intend to be ruled by the Constitution-breaking, law-defying negro-loving Phariseeism of New England!

On January 21, Lincoln's confidant Orville Browning was informed firsthand of the alarming developments in Illinois. He recorded in his diary:

> At night called to see Mr & Mrs Corning, and had a talk with him on the State of the Country. He is very despondent and thinks the radical and extreme policy of the administration has made the restoration of the Union impossible in any other way than by the North Western States forming an alliance with the States of the lower Mississippi. If this were

done he thinks Pennsylvania, New York, New Jersey &c would soon join, and ultimately the remaining states, and that thus we might become again one people.

Murat Halstead, from his vantage point as editor of the *Cincinnati Gazette*, warned his senator, John Sherman, about the public mood after emancipation:

There is a change in the current of public sentiment out West . . . . If Lincoln was not a damn fool, we could get along yet. He is an awful, woeful ass, and therefore all the enemies of the government look to him to give them all the capital that is necessary . . . . But what we want is not any more niggers—not any if you please.

On January 31, a panicked Governor Morton wired Lincoln, "It is important that I should see you a few hours but I cannot leave long enough to go to Washington. Can you meet me at Harrisburg?" Lincoln declined and suggested that Morton write a letter instead, explaining that at such a troubled time the absence of both leaders from their capitals would be "misconstrued a thousand ways." On February 9, Lincoln received Morton's letter divulging what he had hoped to reveal to the President face-to-face:

The Democratic scheme may be briefly stated thus; End the war by any means whatever at the earliest moment.

This of course lets the Rebel States go, and acknowledges the Southern Confederacy. They will then propose to the Rebels a re-union and re-construction upon the condition of leaving out the New England States; this they believe the Rebel leaders will accept and so do I. . . .

Every democratic paper in Indiana is teeming with abuse of New England and it is the theme of every speech . . . . These views are already entertained by the mass of the Democratic party, and there is great danger of their spreading until they are embraced by a large majority of our people, unless means are promptly used to counteract them. They are using every means in their power to corrupt and debauch the public mind.

Secret societies, which are but another type of the Knights of the Golden Circle, are being established in every County and Township in the State of Indiana, Speeches, Pamphlets and Newspapers are distributed in vast numbers and at great expense, and every man who can or will read is bountifully supplied, with the most treasonable and poisonous literature.

This last paragraph of Governor Morton's letter signaled other, murkier threats in the Northwest than those being proclaimed publicly in the legislatures, newspapers, and county meetings. Secret societies were engaged in treason, and they were spreading and strengthening in the southern parts of Ohio, Indiana, and Illinois. Chief among them were the Knights of the Golden Circle, named for the dreamed-of slave empire encircling the Gulf of Mexico. Lincoln had heard them mentioned with frightening frequency lately. Morton's excitable intelligence chief, Henry B. Carrington, included an alarm in a letter to Lincoln in mid-January "respecting the existance [sic] and character of the Secret societies existing in Indiana and having for their direct object our national ruin." It told him:

> Their oaths, signs, grips, &c, have direct relation to the following avowed objects.
>
> 1st The desertion of soldiers.
>
> 2d The inducement of officers to surrender, when attacked.
>
> 3d To oppose the further prosecution of the war and to compel peace; or, to break up the Union and consolidate the South and North-west.
>
> 4th To embarass the General and State Governments in all their efforts to promote genuine loyalty; and throw state policy, and state rights, into seeming antagonism with Federal policy and Federal authority. Not only do these societies avow these objects distinctly; but quite a number of newspapers avow similar purpose and policy, under a thin veil of subterfuge. Public meetings are full of it.

Letters to Illinois Congressman Washburne and Senator Trumbull were rife with warnings that bands of men were arming and drilling, openly singing Confederate songs, and threatening to murder or "burn out" Union men. Increasingly, Northwesterners were terrified by visions of their countryside turned red with neighbors' blood. One man, W. Holmes of southern Illinois, wrote to Lincoln describing nightly drunken "orgies" by Knights of the Golden Circle at a local saloon, where public cheers for Jeff Davis were loud. "The few union men of [Williamson County] live in great fear as to their property and persons," he reported. "At this present time there are union men who dare not return to their homes for fear of being dragged forth into the woods some night and cruelly maltreated." He said that the entire 128th Illinois regiment, recruited from the region, were southern sympathizers. Holmes ended by telling the President, "The fierce and bloody Spirit of opposition to you Sir, and to the

Govt of the Union, that exists in our midst, is I think more to be dreaded than an army of Rebels in the fields."

Another loyal correspondent wrote to Lincoln's secretary John Nicolay to warn of an impending Illinois revolution set for Washington's Birthday:

> It has now Become a Settled fact that we are to have a Blooddy Revolution in old [P]ike [County] & through the central & Southern portions of the State . . ., the disloyal . . . outnumber us two to one and have been largely ReEnforced by Sevearl Hundred from Missouri Bushwhackers & Bridge Burners that ware Driven from that State & took Refuge here they together with the coperhead Democrats have many Lodges of the K. G. C.s [Knights of the Golden Circle] with a membership of over 2000, well armed and have Resolved to resist the Government, disarm Union men & Claim the right to appropriate the property of Union men, and are now discussing in their secrit meeting the pallicy of Rising in mass at an Early day, Say (Feb 22d).

A nervous letter arrived on Lincoln's desk from Governor Yates, requesting "at least 4 regiments of well armed men in Illinois" to prevent an insurrection. Yates expected that the loyal regiments would soon be fighting pitched battles against thousands of armed deserters from the army who were sneaking home. Told by the Copperhead press and politicians that they had no obligation to fight a war to free slaves, soldiers were further encouraged to desert by disaffected relatives at home, who wrote letters such as this one, from a father to his son:

> I am sorry that you are engaged in this war, which has no other purpose but to free the negroes and enslave the whites; to overrun the free States with a negro population and place us all, who labor for a living, on an equality with d—d negroes sent on us by abolitionists, who alone are in favor of prosecuting this unholy, unconstitutional and hellish war.

Another father told his son to "come home, if you have to desert, you will be protected—the people are so enraged that you need not be alarmed if you hear of the whole of our Northwest killing off the abolitionists."

Discontented men in the ranks wrote back, such as this Hoosier private:

> As soon as I get my money . . . I am coming home let it be deserting or not, but if they don't quit freeing the niggers and putting them in the north I won't go back any more . . . it is very wrong to live with the niggers in freedom.

. . . and this Hoosier captain:

> I have just read the presidents proclamation. I don't like it. I don't want to fight to free the Darkeys. If any body else wants to do so, They are welcome to come & do so. I am not willing to stay in the army much longer, unless a different policy is inaugurated.

Desertions in the Union army averaged 5,000 per month in the hope-starved days of early 1863. In January the 109th Illinois regiment at Holly Springs, Mississippi, became so mutinous—some men deserting and others vowing they would never fight for emancipation—that the whole regiment was disbanded. By March the 128th Illinois regiment, with a nominal strength of 1,000, was reduced by desertions to 35 men. As they straggled home, deserters formed bands for self-protection and raiding. Once they reached the sanctuary of their old neighborhoods, they joined up with secret societies operating after dark. Armed, desperate, and accustomed to bloodshed, the deserters gave those societies a new, deadlier character. Authorities received reports of fresh activity in guns and ammunition. Loyal citizens were forced to keep their weapons always within reach as the vicious returnees started attacking them and their property. Guerrilla warfare seized the southern counties of the Northwest. One press item reported that, "A party of soldiers sent to Rush County, Indiana, captured six deserters. On their way to the cars the deserters were rescued by 'Southern sympathizers' armed with rifles. Two companies of infantry were then sent from Indianapolis, and the deserters again taken into custody." In another incident, seventeen deserters made a fortress of a log cabin, and defied arrest with the help of locals who smuggled in food.

* * *

The treasonous stirrings in the rural southern counties of the Northwest brought recruiting in the region to a full stop. On February 1, Governor David Tod of Ohio wired the War Department that volunteering was about played out in the Buckeye State. Faced with a rapidly developing manpower shortage in the

Union armies, and with war-weariness gripping the country, Congress reacted by pushing through a new Conscription Act on March 3, 1863.

Not only was the draft resented as un-American and incompatible with freedom, the Conscription Act took recruitment out of the hands of the states—where tradition had it and where the Militia Act of the previous summer had let it remain—and made it the responsibility of the federal government for the first time in American history. The new draft law was hated, moreover, because of an ill-considered clause that allowed any able-bodied draftee to avoid service by sending a substitute in his place or by paying $300. The practice of hiring substitutes was a traditional practice borrowed from France, where conscription had a long history. The $300 clause was meant to put a limit on the amount negotiated by a substitute, so that a man of moderate means could afford to buy his way out. Even so, there was explosive protest that the inequities in the Conscription Act made the war "a rich man's war and a poor man's fight." Immediately after the passage of the Conscription Act, Lincoln received a warning from Joseph Medill of Chicago: "Since I have lived in Illinois I never witnessed greater hostility to any public measure than that existing against . . . the new conscript law. . . . The attempt to draft under it will surely be the signal for general and bloody resistance." Governor Morton, too, alerted Lincoln, "I can assure you that [the $300 exemption] feature in the Bill is creating much excitement and ill feeling towards the Government among the poorer classes generally, . . . and may . . . lead to a popular storm."

A clash was inevitable. Congress created the elaborate machinery of the Provost Marshals Bureau, which sent federal officials into the hinterlands to enroll the more than three million male citizens between the ages of twenty and forty-five. To many, here was visible proof that the tentacles of Lincoln's government were curling around every American. Before now, only the humble mailman had been a visible presence of the federal government in daily life. Now, the appearance of United States enrollers going house to house provoked fears that the federal power had slipped the familiar bonds of the Constitution. The Chatfield (Minnesota) *Democrat* predicted that the small army of provost marshals fanning out into every congressional district would "obliterate state lines," and snarled, "No despot in the world today wields a greater power over the persons of his subjects than does King Abraham the First." Congressman Clifton White of Ohio saw the federal draft as "part and parcel of a grand scheme for the overthrow of the Union. . . . Arm the Chief magistrate with this power—and what becomes of the State Legislatures? . . . What becomes of State constitutions and State laws?" *Frank Leslie's Illustrated Newspaper* declared that "this law converts the Republic into one grand Military dictatorship."

There was violent resistance to the draft in every Northwestern state. Enrollment sheets were stolen. Draft enrollers were assaulted, some murdered. Cautious enrollers were forced to go one district at a time, with Union troops handy to crush pockets of resistance, as in Holmes County, Ohio, where about a thousand protesters built a makeshift fort and prepared to defend it with squirrel rifles, revolvers, and four artillery pieces. As the machinery of the draft rumbled across the Northwest, hostility against Lincoln—blasted by the Copperhead press, cursed in public meetings, and threatened in saloons after dark by oath-bound gangs—threatened to boil over into a second civil war.

At this worst possible time, the earnest, inept General Ambrose Burnside came onto the scene. After the fallout over the tragedy at Fredericksburg and a subsequent fiasco called the "Mud March," Lincoln had relieved Burnside of command of the Army of the Potomac and reassigned him to command the Department of the Ohio, a huge area that included the volatile Northwestern states. Arriving at his new headquarters in Cincinnati on March 23, he was treated to tales of vast conspiracies dished up by Henry B. Carrington and Governor Morton of Indiana, who told him that the Knights of the Golden Circle were 90,000 strong and that they were being armed by guns smuggled up through Kentucky. Burnside meanwhile read orders from General-in-Chief Halleck urging "more rigid treatment of all disloyal persons."

Burnside was not a nimble-minded man. He did not comprehend subtleties. He saw criticism of the government as treason, and believed in force as a cure. Halleck's orders were just the sort of thing he could understand. On April 13, 1863, Burnside wired his own instructions to his entire department. Titled "General Order No. 38," they stated:

> The habit of declaring sympathy for the enemy will not be allowed in this department. Persons committing such offenses will be at once arrested with a view of being tried . . . or sent beyond our lines into the lines of their friends. It must be understood that treason, expressed or implied, will not be tolerated in this department.

Burnside declared that those who committed "acts for the benefit of the enemies of our country" would be "tried as spies or traitors," punishable by death.

*   *   *

The person most interested in Burnside's Order Number 38 was his new neighbor, Clement L. Vallandigham of Dayton, Ohio. Vallandigham was a handsome forty-two-year-old Democratic congressman who aspired to be the next governor of Ohio. He had achieved notoriety as the leader of the Peace Democrats in the House of Representatives, and had been the darling of the Copperhead press since the first summer of the war. His motto, "Not a man or a dollar for the war," had guided his every vote since Sumter. Now, in the spring of 1863, he and the Peace Democrats were more popular than ever, lifted up by disgust with Lincoln, the Emancipation Proclamation, and the recent Union military defeats.

Vallandigham had blown the ram's horn for the Copperhead movement most recently on January 14, when he had risen in the House to repeat his favorite themes: that the South could never be defeated, and that the war had only produced "defeat, debt, taxation, sepulchres . . . the suspension of *habeas corpus*, the violation . . . of freedom of the press and of speech . . . which have made this country one of the worst despotisms on earth." As for emancipation, he saw "more of barbarism and sin . . . in the continuance of the war . . . and the enslavement of the white race by debt and taxes and arbitrary power" than in black slavery. His answer? "Stop fighting. Make an armistice." Democrats who wanted an immediate end to the war had leaped up and cheered, especially in his native Ohio and the Northwest.

Home from Congress in April, Vallandigham learned of Burnside's order and saw an opportunity to be lifted into the governor's office as a martyr to freedom. With enough advance publicity to make sure that Burnside's agents were present, Vallandigham on May 1 made an appearance at a Democratic rally in Mt. Vernon, Ohio. With three of Burnside's agents in the crowd taking notes, Vallandigham gave a defiant two-hour Copperhead harangue, exhorting the crowd of 20,000—many wearing their copper Liberty-head badges—to come together at the ballot box and throw off the despotism of "King Lincoln."

On pads of paper, Burnside's scribbling secret agents caught every verbal bomb Vallandigham threw, and three days later a squad of soldiers arrived at his home in the middle of the night, beat down the door with axes and dragged him off to the screams of his hysterical wife. They hustled him to a train, took him to Cincinnati, and pushed him into a cell in a military prison. Two days later, a military tribunal convicted him of violating Order No. 38 and sentenced him to spend the rest of the war in a stone casemate in Fort Warren, Boston Harbor.

Burnside's kangaroo court was the last thing Lincoln needed. In mid-afternoon on May 6, 1863, the same day he got word of Vallandigham's arrest,

Lincoln received a telegram informing him that the Army of the Potomac, now under General Joseph Hooker, had been defeated at the Battle of Chancellorsville by Lee with an army half its size. Reporter Noah Brooks was in Lincoln's office talking with a friend when the President came into the room. "I shall never forget that picture of despair," Brooks wrote. "He held a telegram in his hand, and as he closed the door and came toward us I mechanically noticed that his face, usually sallow, was ashen in hue. . . . The appearance of the President . . . was piteous. Never, as long as I knew him, did he seem to be so broken, so dispirited, and so ghostlike. Clasping his hands behind his back, he walked up and down the room, saying, 'My God! My God! What will the country say! What will the country say!'"

The catastrophe at Chancellorsville plunged the nation yet again into deep gloom over the war effort, coming on top of bad news from stalled armies everywhere along the front—at Vicksburg, in middle Tennessee, and at Charleston. There were renewed cries against Lincoln's futile butchery. The *Bangor* (Maine) *Democrat* published a doggerel verse that lampooned an earlier war poem, "We Are Coming, Father Abraham":

You saw those mighty legions, Abe,
And heard their manly tread;
You counted hosts of living men—
Pray—can you count the dead?
Look o'er the proud Potomac, Abe,
Virginia's hill along;
Their wakeful ghosts are beck'ning you,
Two hundred thousand strong.

Coming on the heels of the news from Chancellorsville, news of Vallandigham's arrest stoked Lincoln's dreaded "fire in the rear" to a white heat. Hundreds of angry partisans in Vallandigham's hometown of Dayton rioted, burning down a city block. Democrats everywhere were appalled. *Martial law enforced hundreds of miles from the nearest front line? A political candidate with years of service in Congress locked up for making a campaign speech?* It was a caricature of tyranny, the most paranoid nightmare of the most wild-eyed editor. Coming at the climax of the unrest in the Northwest, the case dominated the national political news.

Lincoln's secretaries wrote later that no act of the government was so strongly criticized as the Vallandigham arrest. The *New York Atlas* typified the temper of the Democratic press, declaring that "the tyranny of military despotism" shown in the arrest demonstrated "the weakness, folly, oppression, mismanagement and general wickedness of the administration." The *New York Herald* rued the arrest as only the first of "a series of fatal steps which must terminate at last in bloody anarchy." At a May 15 rally in New York City, the cradle of anti-Lincolnism in the East, speaker after speaker condemned the Lincoln government, one roaring, "the man who occupied the Presidential chair in Washington was tenfold a greater traitor to the country than was any Southern rebel." On May 16, New York's Governor Horatio Seymour listed Lincoln's latest outrages in a letter to a meeting of Albany Democrats who were then considering their own protest:

> [Vallandigham's arrest] interfered with the freedom of speech; it violated our rights to be secure in our homes against unreasonable searches and seizures; it pronounced sentence without a trial, save one which was a mockery.... [I]t is not merely a step towards revolution—it is revolution; it will not only lead to military despotism—it established military despotism. If it is upheld, our liberties are overthrown... The action of the Administration will determine, in the minds of more than one-half of the people of the loyal States, whether this war is waged to put down rebellion at the South, or to destroy free institutions at the North.

Even Republican editors condemned the "lost rights" demonstrated by Vallandigham's arrest, and their pain was reprinted in such anti-Lincoln journals as *The Crisis*, which told its readers exultantly, "every Republican paper in the city of New York opposes the arrest of Mr. Vallandigham except the *Times*. This speaks volumes." The Democratic *Louisville Journal* published a long list of protesting Republican papers, "the ablest and most influential champions of the Republican party, backed ... by at least three-fourths of the Republican party itself." The Cabinet, too, regretted the arrest. Gideon Welles considered it "arbitrary and injudicious. Good men who wish to support the administration, find it difficult to defend these acts."

The nation waited for some decision from Lincoln on Vallandigham's fate. To do nothing—to have the spokesman for the Copperheads scribbling tracts from a stone cell in an American Bastille in Boston Harbor—would be to invite a lasting catastrophe.

Rather than thus abetting Vallandigham's martyrdom, Lincoln reached for a kingly solution reminiscent of James I's expulsion of the Puritans: he banished him. Vallandigham was led through the lines to a rebel outpost in Tennessee and handed over to Southern leaders, who greeted him reluctantly.

When they convened for their state convention, the Ohio Democrats, caught up in the excitement of the moment, unanimously chose Vallandigham for their candidate for governor. They expected that a Vallandigham campaign would call attention to the dictatorship of Lincoln. Vallandigham's name would crystallize the voters' choice in the fall election to one between peace and war. His exile would be powerful, ongoing proof that Lincoln was a tyrant trampling on basic rights.

*   *   *

With much of the North like dry tinder to the lit match of Vallandigham's arrest, there was new urgency to a tip Lincoln received from a Philadelphia customs house official, dated April 7:

> I enclose herewith an exact copy of an Anonymous letter received by me this morning. I have recd several of somewhat similar import, and have also information from individual members of the "Southern League" alias "K. G. C." sufficient to convince me that a devilish and deep laid scheme is already concocted throughout the North to seize all the Arms at a favorable moment, and use them against the Government.
>
> The time supposed to be best suited for this rally of northern traitors is when the Government shall attempt the execution of the Conscript Act.

The informer recommended that the loyal people of the North be organized into regiments to combat the Copperheads.

It appeared increasingly likely that loyal regiments might be needed. The mid-May Copperhead rally-goers in New York City heard J.A. McMasters, the editor of *Freeman's Journal*, call on opponents of Lincoln to prepare to battle for states' rights, "not by street fighting, not by disorganized opposition. They should organize by tens and hundreds, by companies and regiments, and they should send to their Governor and ask him for commissions as soon as they had their regiments formed. They should keep their arms, and if they had not them, they should get them, and be ready, under their gallant Governor, to defend the liberties of their State."

This sounded eerily like the calls to arms in the South that had preceded the war. On June 3 in New York City, another huge Copperhead mass meeting was held at the Cooper Union that overflowed the building and spilled out into the street. Addresses were interrupted by groans and hisses for President Lincoln, and loud cheers for Vallandigham and peace. The gathering made a solemn declaration:

> Now, if, as is thus proven, the States, as such are sovereign, and that the Federal Government is simply a compact between the parties, with authority exceedingly restricted and definitely limited, can this feeble authority make war upon the States? . . .
>
> Therefore, this war of the General Government against the South is illegal, being unconstitutional, and should not be sustained if we are to regard the Constitution as still binding and in force.

The New York Democrats were making the same states' rights claims that the Confederate states had made to justify secession in 1861, and soon there were unsettling rumors that there would be pitched battle on the streets of New York. On June 29, Governor Seymour was privately informed that a small army of 1,800 deserters had banded together in New York City with a large body of Copperheads to oppose the draft. The plot was set to explode when the draft began in July, just as the customs house official had warned Lincoln. The governor went through the motions of protecting public property by putting guards in front of the city's armories and arsenals, but the blue lines were thin: thousands of Union soldiers had recently left to confront Lee at Gettysburg, and the city was empty of troops.

Then, with the draft lottery only a few days away, Governor Seymour recklessly loosed the Furies in the nation's largest city. He beckoned Democrats to a mammoth Fourth of July rally with a circular that began: "Freemen, awake! In everything, and in most stupendous proportion, is this Administration abominable!" When the crowds gathered on Independence Day, Seymour treated them to a public demonizing of Lincoln. Liberty itself was suspended, he shouted, "men deprived of the right of trial by jury, men torn from their homes by midnight intruders." The country was on "the very verge of destruction," not because of rebels—they were not mentioned—but because of government coercion, "seizing our persons, infringing upon our rights, insulting our homes, depriving us of those cherished principles for which our fathers fought." He issued a bold threat to the President: "Do you not create revolution when you say that our persons may be . . . seized, our property confiscated, our homes entered? The bloody, and treasonable, and revolutionary, doctrine of public necessity can be proclaimed by a mob as well as by a government."

Sober men regretted the governor's tirade as an incitement to riot. There were editors, however, who were happy for it. On July 13, the first Monday morning of the draft lottery in New York, the city's Democratic newspapers blasted Lincoln. The *World* protested the draft as "profoundly repugnant to the American mind," "thrust into the statute-book . . . almost by force." The *Daily News* saw a plot: "The miscreants at the head of the Government are bending all their powers . . . to securing a perpetuation of their ascendancy for another four years; and their triple method of accomplishing this purpose is, to kill off Democrats, stuff the ballot-box with bogus soldier votes, and deluge . . . districts with negro suffrages." "One out of about two and a half of our citizens," it wailed, "are destined to be brought off into Messrs. Lincoln & Company's charnel-house. God forbid!" It ended with the mutinous hope "that instant measures will be taken to prevent the outrage."

As if by a signal, "instant measures" came that morning: a pistol shot rang out in front of the draft office at Third Avenue and Forty-sixth Street, where the lottery drawing had just begun. At the crack of the revolver, the large crowd that had assembled in the street hurled a shower of missiles at the building, then rushed in, smashed furniture and windows, and set it ablaze. Police Superintendent Kennedy was seized and beaten nearly to death. The most deadly riot in American history had begun.

Another mob descended on the Second Avenue Armory. Finding it defended by militia with cannon, they drifted uptown, setting fires and sacking large homes. A limping detachment of loyal veterans from the Invalid Corps, brought in to grapple with the burly mob of stevedores, porters, factory hands, and longshoremen, were overwhelmed and scattered. The angry masses, largely Irishmen, sought out blacks, and where they found them they beat them to death or hanged them, sometimes burning their bodies. The Colored Orphan Asylum at Lexington and Forty-third Street was gutted and burned to the ground while the children escaped out the back. At the end of the day, the moon rose in a sky bright with fires raging all over the city. George Templeton Strong transcribed the street talk into his diary: "If a quarter one hears be true, this is an organized insurrection in the interest of the rebellion and Jefferson Davis rules New York today."

The next day, July 14, dawned on an entire city shuttered in dread. The mob attacked the mayor's house, and roamed the city setting more fires, plundering more houses, and catching and murdering more black men, women, and children. A police station on Twenty-second Street went up in a blaze. The Brooks Brothers clothing store, a symbol of the well-heeled upper class, was reduced to ashes.

Governor Seymour was hurried in to calm the roiling sea of rioters. Addressing them as "my friends," he expressed sympathy with men carried away by "an apprehension of injustice," but promised the riot would be quenched. At the end of the day, troops fresh from the battlefield of Gettysburg arrived, and grimly sent a ripping, deadly hail into reeling masses of rioters. Herman Melville, from a distant apartment, heard "fitfully from far breaks a mixed surf of muffled sound, the Atheist roar of riot," and saw "Red Arson glaring balefully." George Templeton Strong in his brownstone turret, recognizing the tearing sound of the soldiers' disciplined volleys and the sudden crack of cannon, scribbled more hopefully: "The people are waking up, and by tomorrow there will be adequate organization to protect property and life."

The next day, however, terror was undiminished among black citizens, who fled across the Hudson River into New Jersey, and across the East River into Brooklyn. Behind them, the beams and boards of their tenements crashed to the ground in flames, and unlucky blacks who remained were beaten, burned, hanged, and mutilated. The *New York Herald*, which after the second day had estimated that 150 blacks had been killed and wounded, reported that on the third, "Everywhere throughout the city they are driven about like sheep, and numbers are killed of whom no account will ever be learned."

Finally, at the end of the fourth day, with more bodies littering the cobblestones after a final bloody encounter with the Union soldiers, the riots guttered out and the mobs melted back into the squalid neighborhoods of the East Side.

This ugliest spasm of protest against the draft and detestation of the war, which claimed hundreds of victims and millions of dollars in destroyed property, now gave way to solemn weeks of funerals and columns of bitter recriminations in the partisan New York newspapers. On July 14, the New York *World* published its malediction on Lincoln, blaming him for the death and destruction:

> The law-abiding citizen hangs his head with shame that a government can
> so mismanage a struggle for the life of the nation, so wantonly put itself
> out of harmony and sympathy with the people, so deny itself the support
> of those whom it represents and serves . . . .

London Punch, August 8, 1863

"'Rowdy' Notion of Emancipation."

Will the insensate men at Washington now at length listen to our voice? . . . Will they now believe that Defiance of Law in the rulers breeds Defiance of Law in the people? . . . Will they continue to stop their ears and shut their eyes to the voice and will of a loyal people, which for three long years has told them by every act and every word that this war must be nothing but a war for the Union and the Constitution?

Does Mr. Lincoln now perceive what alienation he has put between himself and the men who three years ago thundered out with one voice in Union square—"The Union, it must and shall be preserved"? . . . Did the President and his cabinet imagine that their lawlessness could conquer, or their folly seduce, a free people?

*   *   *

Though nobody could know it yet, however, the clouds of black smoke that towered over Manhattan in July formed the exclamation point at the climax of the Copperhead struggle against Lincoln. The tears of loyal citizens were the lifeblood of the Copperhead movement. Despair over Union military failure was its hope; only by constant defeat were the Copperheads sustained.

And in the first week of July 1863, the war tide turned. On July 3, word came that, after three days of the bloodiest fighting of the war, the Army of the Potomac, under the command of General George Gordon Meade, had beaten Lee's Army of Northern Virginia at Gettysburg in Pennsylvania. The next day, Independence Day, Grant captured Vicksburg on the Mississippi River and with it, 30,000 enemy soldiers. When Navy Secretary Welles rushed to the White House and gave Lincoln the news that the citadel on the Mississippi had finally fallen, the President threw his arms around him and exclaimed, "I cannot, in words, tell you my joy over this result. It is great, Mr. Welles, it is great!"

Chapter 28

Lincoln Addresses the Nation

"Silly, flat, and dish-watery utterances."

T he elation over the Union victories at Gettysburg and Vicksburg ended a year of dejection over Union defeats. With Lee's wounded army streaming back into Virginia and with the Confederate grip on the Mississippi River broken, the feeling rose that the war might soon be over. Across the North, ceremonial cannon boomed and bands tootled down avenues lined with cheering crowds. Grudgingly, it seemed, confidence in Lincoln's leadership swelled. Republican congressmen received letters from their districts like the endorsement written to Senator Trumbull, "[I]f [Lincoln] don't go forward as *fast* as some of us like, *he never goes backwards.*"

Lincoln was aided in the last half of 1863, however, not only by the Union's sudden good fortune on the battlefield, but also by his willingness to break with precedent and speak directly to the American people. The season saw three dramatic displays of the literary gifts he brought to that task. The first was in June, after Lincoln received a letter protesting Vallandigham's arrest from a committee of New York Democrats chaired by railroad president Erastus Corning. The letter blasted Lincoln's whole system of arbitrary arrests and the suspension of the writ of *habeas corpus.*

Lincoln responded to the committee in the same "unpresidential" way he had responded to Horace Greeley's "Prayer of Twenty Millions" in August of 1862—with a public letter. Over the previous months, Lincoln had written down his thoughts about the restriction of civil liberties as they occurred to him, scribbling them on slips of paper and then storing them away in a drawer in his desk. When he received the bitter petition from the Corning Democrats, he laid out the little scraps of paper on his desk and from them crafted his defense of his policy on *habeas corpus*, military arrests, and his war powers.

Lincoln's reply to Corning lucidly, systematically, and gently argued his point: "that the constitution is not in it's [sic] application in all respects the same, in cases of Rebellion or invasion, . . . as it is in times of profound peace and public security." Printed in the New York *Tribune*, his public letter was reprinted as a pamphlet, and ten million people read it. Citizens across the North felt an emotional tug when they read his defense of political arrests: "Must I shoot a simple-minded soldier boy who deserts, while I must not touch a hair of a wiley agitator who induces him to desert?" They liked Lincoln's homely reassurance that he could no more believe Americans would permanently lose their cherished rights "than I am able to believe that a man could contract so strong an appetite for emetics during temporary illness as to persist in feeding upon them during the remainder of his healthful life."

Lincoln's Corning Letter was seen as a forceful vindication of his policy on the civil liberties in general and Vallandigham case in particular. Readers began to acknowledge the quality of his writing—so contrary to the fussy, elaborate style that was called fine writing at the time—for its clarity, its immediacy, its supple logic, and its humanity.

In August, Lincoln built on the success of the Corning Letter when James C. Conkling, chairman of the Illinois Republicans, invited him to speak at a rally in Springfield. Lincoln declined to appear personally but used the occasion to write a letter defending the Emancipation Proclamation and the recruitment of black soldiers. The letter, which Conkling read to the gathering of 50,000 ("very slowly," according to Lincoln's explicit instructions), defended emancipation in a bold, direct tone. "There are those who are dissatisfied with me," he began. "To such I would say: You desire peace; and you blame me that we do not have it. But how can we attain it? There are but three conceivable ways." He listed the ways, showed the folly of the first two— surrender and compromise—and ended with a direct appeal to his critics' desire to accomplish the third: military victory. "[T]he emancipation policy, and the use of colored troops, constitute the heaviest blow yet dealt to the rebellion," he answered his critics now.

The Conkling Letter showed a different Lincoln than the tentative, conflicted emancipator of January. By the time he wrote it, the President was convinced of the rightness of the Emancipation Proclamation and was resolved never to retract any part of it. Lincoln's Democratic enemies raged against the Conkling Letter. But it was as the New York *Times* said: the President had spoken so well, argued so cogently, and hit the nail so squarely on the head that "Even the Copperhead gnaws upon it as vainly as a viper upon a file."

Parts of the Conkling Letter indulged in colorful rhetoric. The President spoke poetically of the Vicksburg triumph—"the Father of Waters again goes unvexed to the sea"—and mentioned the navy as "Uncle Sam's Web-feet." Here, Lincoln's style, calculated to appeal to the "plain man," seemed like clowning to serious critics. The more whimsical parts of the letter led the London *Times* to the conclusion that Lincoln was drunk when he wrote it.

London's stuffy *Evening Standard*, too, registered once again the now-familiar complaints of the old guard against Lincoln's literary style:

> [Lincoln,] like many of his countrymen [possesses] . . . a very uncertain notion of grammar, and very loose ideas of the structure of English sentences. This might be forgiven, if through the haze of his clumsy diction we could discern a gleam of common sense or political sagacity or a sign of the dignity which befits his high office . . . . Whenever we read the effusions of that miserable buffoon who fills the seat of Washington, and Adams, and Madison, we are forced to pity the nation which is doomed to atone for its crimes and follies by doing penance before all the world in an attitude of such utter and abject humiliation.

Even in America there were those who still clung to the old, ornate, literary "high culture," and could not see that Lincoln was creating a simpler, more direct, more American style of writing. The nation's foremost man of letters, the high priest of the Boston intelligentsia, Ralph Waldo Emerson, was one of those. Tone-deaf to Lincoln's new music, Emerson sighed mournfully:

> You cannot refine Mr. Lincoln's taste, or extend his horizon; he will not walk dignifiedly through the traditional part of the President of America, but will pop out his head at each railroad station and make a little speech, and get into an argument with Squire A. and Judge B. He will write letters to Horace Greeley, and any editor or reporter or saucy party committee that writes to him, and cheapen himself.

Some classically trained scholars who had criticized Lincoln's utterances since the beginning of the war, however, were listening with new ears. Radical Charles Sumner, for example, showed a new-found appreciation for Lincoln's prose after the publication of the Conkling epistle: "Thanks for your true and noble letter. It is a historical document. The case is admirably stated, so that all but the wicked must confess its force. It cannot be answered." Harriet Beecher Stowe, the author of *Uncle Tom's Cabin*, made this confession:

> Sooth to say, our own politicians were somewhat shocked with his state-papers at first. Why not let make them a little more conventional,

and file them to a classical pattern? 'No,' was his reply. 'I shall write them myself. *The people will understand them.*' 'But this or that form of expression is not elegant, not classical.' '*The people will understand it,*' has been his invariable reply.

Stowe now admitted a need for a revision of the critics' view. "There are passages in the state-papers," she wrote, "that could not be better put; they are absolutely perfect. They are brief, condensed, intense, and with a power of insight and expression which make them worthy to be inscribed in letters of gold." She saw that, most importantly, "the state-papers of no President have more controlled the public mind."

The late summer of 1863 was golden for Lincoln. Not only had the war taken a sharp upturn for the Union side, but his public writing was adding momentum to the war effort. Still radiating the aura of the victories of July, and with no session of Congress to torture him, Lincoln spent quiet August days at the Soldiers' Home north of Washington, away from the heat, the flies, the stink, and the pestilence of the White House. Here he was briefly delivered from care. "The Tycoon is in fine whack," wrote John Hay on August 7. "I have rarely seen him more serene and busy."

* * *

Lincoln's idyll was brought short by worry over the coming fall elections. Rebel leaders had helped the banished Clement Vallandigham make his way to Windsor, Canada, and from there he was dictating a new strategy to the Copperheads, emphasizing the Democrats' superiority for the task of reconciliation of North and South. Copperhead leaders in the northern cities, however, still gripped the weapons that felt familiar in their hands. They harped on the old issues of lost rights and the popular dread of waves of freed blacks swarming into northern towns and cities. They cried for an immediate peace, pointing to the immense reserves of will and might in the rebellious states. They framed the 1863 fall campaign—as they did every electoral campaign during the Civil War—as a referendum on Lincoln's abuses and failures.

In the Northwest, campaign rallies drew tens of thousands of people. Republican governors and senators criss-crossed the contested states giving stump speeches. In Ohio, the sensational race between martyr-in-exile Vallandigham and Union Party candidate John Brough brought the Copperheads' views and Lincoln's into sharp contrast. From Columbus, *The*

Crisis waved Vallandigham's banner. On August 7, it huffed and puffed in a long column which unfurled the anti-Lincoln manifesto:

> It is now no longer a question whether Mr. Lincoln . . . will establish a military despotism, for such a despotism is already established: the only question involved is whether he can make that despotism permanent. . . . The elective franchise will . . . constitute our sole remaining hope of resisting his tyranny.
>
> Any advantages or victories obtained over the rebels is of small import to us as compared with the preservation of our own freedom. At what avail is the subjugation of the South to military rule, when, at the same time, our own constitutional rights are taken from us? The president is ostensibly conducting two wars: one against the South and the other against freedom in the North. The white race seems to be the especial object of hate. His acts, and especially his enlistment of black soldiers, indicate his object to rule the whites in the South through the blacks; and to rule the whites in the North through the soldiery and a corrupt judiciary. . . .
>
> We read history to little purpose, if we indulge the hope that a military usurper, when he has once firmly set his heels upon the necks of a subject people, will voluntarily relinquish the advantages of his position. . . .
>
> [Lincoln and the Republicans] are using their best endeavors to set up a Government outside of the Constitution. . . . This they call restoring the Union, when, in truth, it is destroying the Union, and all engaged in the treasonable undertaking are as disloyal as Jeff Davis and his followers. . . . Jeff Davis has as much right to set up a new Government, as has Mr. Lincoln to change, by force, the old one. Both are treasonable, and the only true Union men are those who oppose them both.

These complaints at least had the virtue of being sincere. One week before Election Day, however, in a last-ditch effort to steal the election, the Copperhead press smeared Lincoln with an out-and-out lie, accusing him of plotting the cancellation of the next presidential election—the ultimate betrayal of democracy. *The Crisis,* under the banner "Lincoln to Be Declared Perpetual President," announced, "It is now stated that a bill has been prepared and will be placed before the next Congress declaring Lincoln President while the war lasts." The *Cincinnati Enquirer* printed the story at the same time, crying, "Thus the mad fanatics are plotting against our liberties, and if we do not speak right soon through the ballot-box, the last vestige of our republican government will have been swept away."

It didn't work. On October 13, John Brough, representing Lincoln's views, beat Clement Vallandigham by 100,000 votes, a huge margin. When he heard the news, Lincoln, like a herald angel, wired Brough: "Glory to God in the highest. Ohio has saved the Nation." Almost everywhere across the North it was the same. Even in the Border States, the Union Party, standing for Lincoln, swept the fall elections. The battlefield victories of July, the strength of Lincoln's public letters, and the growing sense that emancipation and black soldiers were speeding the end of the war were irresistible.

Lincoln told Gideon Welles that he had been more worried about the results of this election than he had been about his own in 1860. For good measure, he had arranged furloughs for swarms of soldiers and government

Southern Punch, November 14, 1863

"Abduction of the Yankee Goddess of Liberty." "THE PRINCE OF DARKNESS (ABRAHAM LINCOLN) BEARS HER AWAY TO HIS INFERNAL REGIONS"

clerks to return home to vote—"This state has really been carried by fraud, but we have control of the State which is very important," one Ohio Republican conceded. Another was sure that Pennsylvania would have been lost "if it had not been for the soldiers we got at the last."

Democratic newspapers reported their defeats with curled lip. The day after the election, the *Brooklyn Daily Eagle* sneered, "The Democracy fail in [Ohio], but they fail contending for free speech, for a free press, for trial by jury, as opposed to drumhead court martial. Contending for such principles, victory would be glorious,—defeat brings no dishonor."

*   *   *

Just as the hostile editors were printing their barbed epitaphs of the 1863 elections, Lincoln received an invitation to attend the dedication of a soldiers' cemetery at the Gettysburg battlefield in Pennsylvania. The dead soldiers were being interred by state, with emphasis on each state's sacrifices. Lincoln's attendance was not especially coveted; the event's Board of Commissioners had sent out similar invitations to scores of prominent men. The Honorable Edward Everett, regarded as the greatest living American orator, had been enlisted to give a speech. According to Clark E. Carr, the Illinois committee man who sent Lincoln his invitation, asking the President to take part in the ceremony was an afterthought. Only when Lincoln sent a message that he would attend did the idea occur to anyone that he should be asked to speak.

For one thing, admitted Carr, "it did not seem to occur to any one that he *could* speak upon such an occasion." Since his inauguration, Lincoln had given no speeches except a few embarrassed, desultory remarks to serenaders at the White House. No member of the Gettysburg committee except Carr had ever heard him address a crowd. "While all expressed high appreciation of his great abilities as a political speaker, as shown in his debates with Senator Douglas, and in his Cooper Institute address," wrote Carr, "the question was raised as to his ability to speak upon such a grave and solemn occasion as that of the memorial services." Lincoln's image as an amiable, uncouth jokester was so deeply etched that it disqualified him from making properly sober remarks even now, three years after his election. The committee feared he might stand up and give a stump speech or, worse, tell a funny story. They were aware of a rumor that the year before, during a grim tour of the battlefield at Antietam in an ambulance, with bodies yet piled high all around and the field still wet with blood, Lincoln had thoughtlessly desecrated the ground and dishonored the dead by calling for a ribald minstrel song from his banjo-playing companion, Ward Lamon. (Lincoln had in fact been miles from the battlefield when he asked Lamon to sing a sad melody called "Twenty Years Ago," but the story would not die.)

Despite its misgivings, the committee, in the end, cautiously decided to invite Lincoln to say a few words after Everett's oration. To assure that Lincoln would take his duties seriously, however, David Wills, a prosperous Gettysburg banker who was the organizer of the event, included strict instructions in his invitation. He emphasized that the occasion would be "imposing and solemnly impressive," and asked Lincoln to make "a few appropriate remarks"—that is, to be dignified and brief. Wills ended the letter by once more reminding Lincoln that his part would be the "last solemn act to the Soldier dead."

Lincoln used the next two weeks to cobble together 272 words that started with a rhyme ("Four score") and whose sound and rhythm, whose simplicity of expression and delicate structure, carried it, rising and falling, through two minutes of sublime grace to a conclusion powerful enough to ennoble three days of butchery, rededicate the struggle for the Union, and reaffirm the nation's ideals. His theme—the central idea that gave rise to the Emancipation Proclamation and provided moral purpose to the nation's struggle—was the idea that was closest to his heart: the self-evident truth proclaimed in the Declaration of Independence "that all men are created equal." For the nation's first eighty-seven years, until the moment Lincoln delivered the Gettysburg Address, America's central document had been the Constitution, with its knotty *in*equalities and legal compromises. Lincoln, in his two minutes on the Gettysburg hillside, replaced the Constitution with the Declaration as the guiding American article of faith. He not only consecrated the cemetery, he announced a revolution rededicating America to Jefferson's first principle.

This went unnoticed by most of its hearers. Even John Hay, a poet with a fine ear, disposed of the affair in one sentence, writing "the President in a fine, free way, with more grace than is his wont, said his half dozen words of consecration, and the music wailed and we went home through the crowded and cheering streets." The rest of the listeners were also caught by surprise by the brevity of the President's address. It created an awkward moment at the end. When Lincoln finished, the crowd was silent for a time, not realizing that the thing was over. The only sound was laughter—by people watching a photographer who had not been quick enough to get a picture of the President giving his speech. Clark Carr, who was on the platform, stated, "So short a time was Mr. Lincoln before them that the people could scarcely believe their eyes when he disappeared from their view. They were almost dazed. They could not possibly, in so short a time, mentally grasp the ideas that were conveyed, nor even their substance. Time and again expressions of disappointment were made to me. Many persons said to me that they would have supposed that on such a great occasion the President would have made a speech."

Lincoln, veteran of a thousand stump speeches, knew when he wrote it that his Gettysburg Address was too brief to have much of an impact on the listening crowd. But he was aiming at bigger game. By limiting his address to so few words, he was insuring that it would be printed, in full, on the front page of every newspaper in the land. The readers of his speech in those thousands of city, town, and rural sheets would have time to reflect on the ideas it proposed.

The Gettysburg Address' first readers were the newspaper editors. Copperhead Wilbur Storey of the Chicago *Times* scanned it closely and perceived Lincoln's subversion of the Constitution and the audacity in his suggestion that the Founding Fathers' guiding principle had been equality. Storey, in his editorial, quoted the Constitution, noted its lack of equality in paragraphs on taxation and slavery, and raged indignantly:

> Mr. Lincoln occupies his present position by virtue of the constitution, and is sworn to the maintenance and enforcement of these provisions. It was to uphold this constitution, and the Union created by it, that our officers and soldiers gave their lives at Gettysburg. How dare he, then, standing on their graves, misstate the cause for which they died, and libel the statesmen who founded the government: They were men possessing too much self-respect to declare that negroes were their equals, or were entitled to equal privileges.

The *Times* accused Lincoln of pushing the abolition doctrine, denounced him for his "boorishness and vulgarity" and for being "less refined than a savage." "The cheek of every American must tingle with shame," it concluded, "as he reads the silly, flat, and dish-watery utterances of the man who has to be pointed out to intelligent foreigners as the President of the United States."

The Harrisburg *Patriot and Union* dismissed the Gettysburg Address: "We pass over the silly remarks of the President; for the credit of the nation, we are willing that the veil of oblivion shall be dropped over them and that they shall no more be repeated or thought of." The London *Times* scoffed, "the ceremony was rendered ludicrous by some of the sallies of that poor President Lincoln. . . . Anything more dull and commonplace it would not be easy to produce."

By late 1863, however, no one looked for anything but petty poison from the Copperhead press in America or the mouthpiece of the aristocracy in

England. The few nay-sayers were at odds with the general opinion of the Gettysburg Address. The *Springfield Republican* was one of many that conceded its ability to kindle strong emotion, calling the Address "a perfect gem," and admitting, "We had grown so accustomed to homely and imperfect phrase in his productions that we had come to think it was the law of his utterance. But this shows he can talk handsomely as well as act sensibly."

The Gettysburg Address was the last and finest of Lincoln's epic triad of literary compositions in the last six months of 1863, all written in an attempt to soften the hearts of Northerners and dedicate this racist, stiff-necked people to the great work begun by the Emancipation Proclamation.

The Gettysburg speech is even more impressive in view of the fact that Lincoln had to carve out time to write it during the first three weeks of November, a period when he was hard at work composing his Annual Message to Congress. One question that demanded an official answer from Lincoln was, since it was not a law but a war measure, whether the Emancipation Proclamation would be rescinded when the war ended. On December 9, Lincoln put all such questions to rest, announcing in his Annual Message that "while I remain in my present position I shall not attempt to retract or modify the emancipation proclamation; nor shall I return to slavery any person who is free by the terms of that proclamation, or by any of the acts of Congress." John Hay told his diary, "the effect of this paper is something wonderful. I never have seen such an effect produced by a public document. Men acted as if the millennium had come. Chandler was delighted. Sumner was beaming."

Lincoln's Annual Message was fortunate in its timing, coming during a period of good feeling after Grant's spectacular victory at the Battle of Chattanooga two weeks earlier. When Hay recorded the rosy glow after the Annual Message, he was intoxicated by talk that the war would soon come to a glorious end and that Lincoln would be reelected by a grateful nation.

The people in the farms and cities of the North refused to celebrate before they saw the results of the spring campaigns. They knew from three bitter years of experience that war was the most capricious of human endeavors. Anything could happen, any number of political flags might be flaunted, any number of careers might come in and go out with the ebb and flow of combat. The nineteen-foot statue of "Armed Liberty" had been hoisted to the top of the brand-new Capitol dome only the week before the opening of Congress. There would be battles under it that would be just as crucial for the country as the coming battles in the field. It soon became clear that Hay had been mistaken about the Radicals. Chandler was not delighted, and Sumner was not beaming.

Part Four

Lincoln's Reelection

"The Most Extraordinary Change in
Publick Opinion Ever Known."

Chapter 29

The 1864 Republican Nomination

"The politicians have again chosen this presidential
pigmy as their nominee."

W hen, at the end of the Annual Message to Congress, he first heard
Lincoln's Proclamation of Amnesty and Reconstruction, Charles
Sumner slammed his books and papers down on his desk and scattered them on
the floor in a fit of temper amid members of both Houses and beneath a packed
public gallery. As everyone rose to leave, he complained hotly to his friends:
*Why had Lincoln said nothing about whether the rebel states were in or out of the Union?
Was this the justice to be meted out to traitors? Were South Carolina and the rest going to get
away with trying to destroy the Union and lose nothing but their slaves?*

Sumner's tantrum was the public's first peek at a rupture in the Republican
Party over the Reconstruction of the nation. It was a split that not only
threatened Lincoln's nomination as the party's presidential candidate in 1864,
but also endangered his chances in the election itself. Indeed, the
Reconstruction argument would prove a calamity to the nation for a century.

Sumner's tirade had to do with the legal status of the rebellious states. As
early as February 11, 1862, Sumner had put into the Congressional Record the
lengthy theory that underlay the Radical plan for Reconstruction. More
recently, in October of 1863, he had argued it again, elaborately, in a fifty-page
article in the *Atlantic Monthly*. Known as the "State Suicide" theory, it said that if
any state declared its intention to destroy the United States government by
seceding, it was itself destroyed. Rebellious states, by this theory, had already
lost their statehood and had become United States territories—that is, land
owned by the United States—and therefore, like all territories, were under the
jurisdiction of Congress. To be admitted to the Union again, Sumner and the
Radicals would insist that each rebellious state not only frame a new
constitution that outlawed slavery, but also obliterate its aristocracy and divide
its land among Union soldiers, poor whites, and former slaves. Only when the
old order was in ashes could the South be embraced again by the Union, and its
representatives apply to Congress.

Lincoln, on the other hand, had always denied that any state could go out of the Union. He had always stressed national healing. He saw that hearts and minds were better won with lovingkindness. And, instead of constructing a fifty-page theory, he had acted. Not wanting to leave the seceded states to the harsh measures of the Radicals, Lincoln had made it his business to begin the work of Reconstruction under the war powers. At the time the Annual Message was read in December 1863, he had already started Reconstruction in the rebel states of Louisiana, Arkansas, and Tennessee.

The features of Lincoln's Proclamation of Amnesty and Reconstruction were simple: All rebels would be given full amnesty who took an oath of future loyalty to the United States and pledged to obey its laws and proclamations, including the one that freed the slaves. When one-tenth of the voters in a seceded state had taken the oath, they could establish a state government that could once again take its place in the Union. To make sure that the old secessionist troublemakers were not soon back in their seats in Washington and to placate the Radicals, Lincoln would let Congress determine whether representatives sent by the new states would be seated.

The Radicals could not fathom that Lincoln's purpose was to speed the end of the war. Senator William Fessenden called Lincoln's Amnesty and Reconstruction proclamation "a silly performance." "Think of telling all the rebels they may fight as long as they can," he sputtered, "and take a pardon when they have had enough of it." He and the other Radical leaders fervently believed that the generous, simple-minded Lincoln was not the man to handle the bitter business of Reconstruction. They still feared that he might listen to the serpent-tongued Seward and compromise on slavery at the moment of victory. Even if he didn't cave in and renounce emancipation, they were afraid that slave owners would be back in power in the South unbowed and unpunished, and freed slaves would remain poor and powerless.

* * *

The Radicals' main motive in holding sway on Reconstruction, however, was not love for the black man—it was power. They realized that the officials of rebel states who were reorganized under Lincoln's plan were likely to be Lincoln supporters, adding pro-Lincoln delegates to next summer's Republican convention. This would not do, for by the end of 1863, they had decided that the best way to force a Radical Reconstruction was to ditch Lincoln as the party candidate in 1864. They would throw him over for someone less independent.

For months, there had been signs that the Radicals had dismissed Lincoln as the next Republican candidate. The *Harper's Weekly* Washington correspondent, "The Lounger," noticed in late August that Lincoln had no home among any faction:

> At this moment, he stands a little outside of all parties even among loyal men. The rebels, and their tools the Copperheads, of course, hate him. The War Democrats doubt some points of his policy. The Conservative Republicans think him too much in the hands of the radicals; while the Radical Republicans think him too slow, yielding, and half-hearted.

In September there was an ill omen for Lincoln in Henry Ward Beecher's newspaper, *The Independent*, when it gave him a back-handed compliment for "a comprehensive policy and a wisdom in its execution which promise to broaden his sun at its setting." Mention of Lincoln's "setting sun" was Beecher's promise that the Radicals would look for a new candidate for the coming presidential election.

As they gathered for the start of Congress, Radical leaders spoke more frequently of the "one-term rule" that had applied since Andrew Jackson's time. For the last thirty-two years, over the span of eight presidencies, there had been no second terms, they pointed out.

Thaddeus Stevens provided another straw in the wind in November when, on the morning of the Gettysburg Cemetery Dedication, a man asked him where Lincoln and Seward were. "Gettysburg," he said sourly. "Let the dead bury the dead."

That same week, Zachary Chandler schooled Lincoln on right thinking. He informed Lincoln in writing that his recent election triumph was owed to bold radicalism, and he should let that be a lesson to him. "Conservatives & traitors are buried together," Chandler snarled, "for Gods sake dont exhume their remains in Your Message. They will smell worse than Lazarus did after he had been buried three days." Lincoln's answer to Chandler was characteristic—funny, flinty, and wise at the same time:

> I am very glad the elections this autumn have gone favorably, and that I have not, by native depravity, or under evil influences, done anything bad enough to prevent the good result.
>
> I hope to "stand firm" enough to not go backward, and yet not go forward fast enough to wreck the country's cause.

Yours truly

A. LINCOLN

Though Lincoln made light of it, it was clear to everyone by the end of 1863 that Radicals were already girding for battle with Lincoln over the Republican nomination, and that the main issue would be Reconstruction.

The Radicals were not alone in their distaste for the sitting President. The masses may have admired Lincoln's public letters of the previous months, but Washington men, who saw him at short range, were appalled by Lincoln's off-color stories and other grotesqueries. Also, "There is a strong feeling among those who have seen Mr. Lincoln, in the way of business, that he lacks practical talent for his important place," Sumner grumbled to a correspondent, adding that Chase "did not think him competent." Count Gurowski muttered into his diary about the "infatuation" of the people, "taken in" by the "great shifter" in the White House while their elected leaders groaned at his offenses. "The best men in both the Houses observe Lincoln and his workings," he wrote. "They know his length, his breadth, his mind, his nerve, and his cerebellum. The people at large does not know Mr. Lincoln, but judge him by his nickname, and by what greedy politicians and newspapers write and spread about him." He lamented the masses who willfully ignored their leaders on the Hill:

> The people sends to Congress a man in whose brains and integrity it seemingly has confidence, and nevertheless, in such a grave, mighty question as a Presidential election the people . . . pays no attention to the opinion of its Congressmen, [who] are better acquainted with [Lincoln's] good and bad qualities, his capacities and incapacities, his peculiarities, his character and the want of it.

As for Lincoln's re-election, Gurowski pointed out, "The majority in Congress is against it."

The earnest men in Washington could not comprehend a man who, they said, had joked his way through three years of national tragedy. One solemn Massachusetts man remarked to strait-laced Governor Andrew, "It is only just to say, that the reports from Washington in 1863 did impute a frivolity of language and demeanor in the President, which could not but offend many earnest men." He related an incident when an envoy from the Massachusetts

State House traveled to the White House to present President Lincoln with a parchment copy of the state's latest grave resolve on slavery:

> "The Chief Magistrate of the nation sat in an armchair, with one leg over the elbow, while the emissary of Massachusetts presented the parchment with a long speech.
>
> "The President took the document, slowly unrolled it, and remarked in a quaint way, 'Well, it isn't long enough to scare a fellow!'
>
> "The Massachusetts envoy said as he left the room, 'That is certainly an extraordinary person to be President of the United States!'"

Tales like these contributed to widespread doubt of Lincoln's fitness to be President. Even Lincoln's old Illinois friend Orville Browning wrote in 1864, "I am personally attached to the President, and have . . . tried to . . . make him respectable; tho' I never have been able to persuade myself that he was big enough for his position. Still, I thought he might get through, as many a boy has got through college, without disgrace, and without knowledge, but I fear he is a failure." George Wilkes of New York, the abolitionist editor of the *Spirit of the Times*, publicly predicted ruin: "The nation cannot live with Abraham Lincoln and Seward at its head during the next terrible four years," he cried. "Even if honest, they are unequal to the task."

As the election year opened, Lincoln had almost no friends in Congress to counter the hostile moves of the Radicals against him. Many remarked on Lincoln's almost total lack of popularity in Washington. Carl Schurz reported, "Mr. Lincoln had only one fast friend in the lower House of Congress, and few more in the Senate." That one fast friend was Isaac Arnold of Chicago. Arnold told the story of how one day Thaddeus Stevens appeared at his desk with a visitor to the House chamber and told him, "Here is a man who wants to find a Lincoln member of Congress. You are the only one I know, and I have come over to introduce my friend to you."

According to Indiana Radical George Julian, "The opposition to Mr. Lincoln was secretly cherished by many of the ablest and most patriotic men of the day. . . . Of the more earnest and thorough-going Republicans in both Houses of Congress, probably not one in ten really favored [his nomination]." Springfield Republican Shelby Collum visited Washington in early 1864, and reported, "I talked with numerous Representatives and Senators, and it really seemed to me as if there was hardly any one in favor of the renomination of Mr. Lincoln." Count Gurowski, likewise, after mixing daily with men in lobbies, clubs, and department offices, wrote on February 4, "I have not yet met one single earnest and clear-sighted man, from whatever State he may come, that avows his preference for Lincoln." The *Detroit Free Press* correspondent at Washington agreed: "Not a single Senator can be named as favorable to Lincoln's renomination as President."

This widespread opposition came despite reports that Lincoln was riding a swell of affection from the people. But public opinion in those days was hard to gauge. The first public opinion polls were still seventy years in the future, and no one could know for sure which way the winds were blowing, least of all the people themselves, who depended for their news on the partisan press. The confusion about public opinion helped keep power in the back rooms of the party bosses, away from the voters.

Too, public opinion was fickle, a will-o-the wisp, a vapor that trailed the slightest breeze. It could change with the next military defeat, or the next draft. One Ohioan judged that the common people went for Lincoln only because "everybody thinks that everybody else goes for Lincoln." This shallowness was the subject of Senator Trumbull's letter to a friend in early 1864:

> The feeling for Mr. Lincoln's reelection *seems* to be general, but much of it I discover is only on the surface. You would be surprised in talking with public men we meet here, to find how few when you come to get at their real sentiments are for Mr. Lincoln's reelection. There is a distrust & fear that he is too undecided & inefficient ever to put down the rebellion. You need not be surprised if a reaction sets in before the nomination in favor of some man supposed to possess more energy & less inclination to trust our brave boys in the hands, & under the leadership of Generals who have no heart in the war.

*   *   *

The problem among Lincoln's opponents was agreeing on a rival, someone who was a through-and-through Radical and who would enforce a harsh Reconstruction applied by Congress. Hopes clustered around four men. Some were for General Grant. Others looked toward General Benjamin Butler. Many were still convinced that Frémont was the guiding star. But the first, biggest boom was for Treasury Secretary Salmon P. Chase.

Two things were constant in Salmon P. Chase's political life: his opposition to slavery and his desire to be President. He had always considered himself a better man than Abraham Lincoln. In the 1840s in Ohio, he had been a leader of the anti-slavery Liberty and Free Soil parties. He had been elected Senator from Ohio in 1849, had organized the Republican Party in that state, and had been elected governor in 1855 and 1857—all while Lincoln was still drafting wills and vetting deeds in the backwoods. Once in the Cabinet, Chase had shown ability and energy.

He had never been comfortable inside Lincoln's sloppily-run administration, however. He was the source of a steady stream of letters to those outside, bemoaning the lack of direction and energy from the President. To Horace Greeley, he wrote, "I have seen a great deal in the shape of irregularity, assumptions beyond law, extravagance, and deference to generals and reactionists which I could not approve." To Murat Halstead, "The whole state of things is very far from satisfactory to me. But I am unable to do much outside of my own department." To Zack Chandler, "There is no cabinet except in name. The Heads of Departments come together now and then . . . but no reports are made; no regular discussions held; no ascertained conclusions reached." Recently he had called Cabinet meetings "useless."

Chase had never lacked self-esteem. Bluff Ben Wade had remarked on it: "Chase is a good man, but his theology is unsound. He thinks there is a fourth person in the Trinity." And now, at the head of an army of 15,000 Treasury Department agents who owed their jobs to him, there was a quickening of his ambition. While he burned for the high post, however, the pompous Secretary remained fastidious about holding to the high road, careful to maintain a seeming disinterest. On October 3, a friend of Horace Greeley called on Chase to propose plans for a campaign. Chase was careful to answer, "I could take no part—people must do as they please."

In the peculiar code of nineteenth century politics, that meant he was off and running. The comet streak of the Chase boom can be traced by a chronicle:

- October 15, 1863: A month after it marked Lincoln's "sun at its setting," Henry Ward Beecher's New York *Independent* touts Chase to its 50,000 subscribers as "the greatest, the strongest, the boldest" leader in the party.
- October 17, 1863: Chase's candidacy becomes obvious enough that Attorney General Edward Bates remarks in his diary, "I'm afraid Mr. Chase's head is turned by his eagerness in pursuit of the presidency."
- November 9, 1863: The *New York Herald* comments, "There is nothing fixed on either side, except what the Rev. Henry Ward Beecher would

call 'the great central facts'—that President Lincoln is prepared to serve another term, and that Mr. Secretary Chase expects to supersede him."

- December 9, 1863: The same day that Lincoln's Annual Message is read in Congress, a conference of Chase's supporters calling itself the "Organization to Make S P Chase President" is held in Washington to draft a list of prominent men who would support an organized Chase movement.

- December 28, 1863: Navy Secretary Gideon Welles notes that "there is an active, zealous, and somewhat formidable movement for Chase," and that "Chase clubs are being organized in all the cities to control the nominating convention." Chase's long months of plying pen to paper from morning to night lining up friends in support is now paying off. By the end of December, Chase's desk is piled with letters that gush, "You are head and shoulders above any other statesman in America," and, "My opinion is that you ought to be our next President. . . . The country demands that our best and only our best, men should be placed in nomination."

- January, 1864: Senator Samuel Pomeroy of Kansas heads an expanded Chase campaign committee, renamed the "Republican National Executive Committee."

- January 18, 1864: Chase, in a private letter to a friend, announces his candidacy.

- Early February: Chase's campaign committee circulates 100,000 copies of a pamphlet titled "The Next Presidential Election," which states that people "have lost all confidence" in Lincoln's ability to suppress the rebellion. The "vascillation [sic] and indecision of the president," it says, "has been the real cause why our well-appointed armies have not succeeded in the destruction of the rebellion. . . . the cant about 'Honest Old Abe' was at first amusing, it then became ridiculous, but now it is absolutely criminal." The pamphlet says that Lincoln is letting the war drag on to keep himself in office, warning, "With an army of more than half a million citizen soldiers under his command and an annual patronage of a thousand million in money, he can . . . have himself elected from term to term during his natural life." Lincoln betrayed the party, it says, and the party now needs "a statesman professionally versed in political and economic science, one who fully comprehends the spirit of the age in which we live."

- February 20, 1864: The *Washington Constitution Union* publishes the "Pomeroy Circular," signed by Chase's campaign manager, Senator Pomeroy. It calls for the "hearty cooperation" of all who wish the elevation of Chase to the presidency, and gives five reasons:

First, that even were the reelection of Mr. Lincoln desirable, it is practically impossible.

Second, that should he be reelected, his manifest tendency towards compromises and temporary expedients of policy will become stronger . . . and the cause of human liberty, and the dignity and honor of the nation, suffer proportionately, while the war may continue to languish . . . till the public debt shall become a burden too great to be borne.

Third, that [under Lincoln] the patronage . . . has been so rapidly increased . . . as to render . . . the "one-term principle" absolutely essential.

Fourth, that we find united in Hon. Salmon P. Chase more of the qualities needed in a president . . . than are combined in any other available candidate.

Fifth, . . . the discussion of the Presidential question . . . has developed a popularity and strength in Mr. Chase unexpected even in his warmest admirers.

Lincoln had been intensely interested in the progress of Chase's candidacy since it had lifted off in the fall of 1863. Outwardly, he professed little concern—John Hay, who was in close contact with the President every day, recorded his impression on October 28 that Lincoln "seems much amused at Chase's mad hunt after the Presidency." The President's insouciance toward the Chase boom puzzled many of his followers. But his casual behavior was a tactic. Proper handling of Chase was a delicate matter, one that could not stand lightning and thunder. Dismissing Chase would split the party in two—the Radicals would regard removing him from the Cabinet as a declaration of war and insure a defeat in November. Lincoln knew that Chase, cut loose from the Cabinet, unrestrained, would be twice as dangerous as Chase in the fold.

Navy Secretary Gideon Welles' keen eye saw that Lincoln was gnawed by the tooth of worry. "The President fears Chase, and he respects him," Welles told his diary. "Almost daily we have some indication of Presidential aspirations and incipient operations for the campaign. The President does not conceal the interest he takes." Alexander McClure also noticed, writing that Lincoln "carefully veiled his keen and sometimes bitter resentment against Chase, and waited the fullness of time when he could by some fortuitous circumstance remove Chase as a competitor." Lincoln avoided a stormy confrontation in the Cabinet chamber. Instead, he fought Chase's quiet challenge with quiet weapons: he stoked the party machinery and prepared to do battle with Chase in the state party conventions.

The rules of bare-fisted party politics as practiced since Jackson still applied in 1864, and Lincoln knew the ropes better than anyone. He had not spent countless hours in his office listening to the pleas of thousands of office seekers for nothing. His enormous investment in personal attention to patronage since the moment of his election—so thoroughly distasteful to friends and foes alike, privately and in the press—paid off at precisely this moment. Party bosses such as Thurlow Weed in New York and Simon Cameron in Pennsylvania, men to whom Lincoln had devoted hours, days, weeks in conference, were now solidly in Lincoln's pocket. In addition, all the paymasters, postmasters, assessors, clerks, customs house officials, marshals, deputies, district attorneys, and Indian agents who Lincoln had personally placed in the last three years were now the "party regulars" on the committees of the Republican state conventions and caucuses, men who could block an enemy and advance their favorite in a thousand ways. As one upstate New York editor observed, "A glance at the list of delegates to the Republican state convention will satisfy anyone that the people have had nothing to do with their selection, and that they represent only the great army of office-holders in our state."

The first Republican state convention was in New Hampshire on January 6. The only item on the agenda was to re-nominate Governor Joseph A. Gilmore, but a young state representative named William E. Chandler took the rostrum and, with the help of a loud chorus of Lincoln men, successfully hijacked the proceedings and rushed through a resolution declaring Lincoln "the people's choice for re-election to the Presidency in 1864." (Lincoln was ready with a reward. A few months later, he would appoint Chandler, not yet thirty years old, solicitor and judge advocate general of the Navy Department.)

Another trick was played in Indiana. Dissatisfaction was high among Hoosiers, and Governor Morgan, the favorite, was no fan of Lincoln. If left alone, the delegation would have been sent to the Republican convention uninstructed. At the opening of the state party convention, however, in the first burst of enthusiasm, while delegates were still taking their seats and the crowd was cheering every phrase, a friend of Lincoln mounted the stage and read a resolution that praised Lincoln and instructed the delegates to vote for Lincoln at the national convention, and then, in the same breath, read a second resolution that declared Oliver Morton—the unanimous choice—the candidate for re-election as governor. A single terrific hurrah from the hall was taken as a signal that both resolutions were passed. Thus, without any discussion, the Indiana Republicans were committed to Lincoln before all the delegates had even unfolded their chairs. The Chase men threw down their hats and swore in disgust.

Lincoln's brawling tactics in the state conventions did not go unnoticed by the press. George Wilkes of New York's *Spirit of the Times* decried "the fact that the patronage of the government is . . . being squandered at this moment to debauch the legislators into an illicit nomination of Mr. Lincoln," and put it down to "the corrupting temptations of a double term." Charles Mackay, the New York correspondent for the London *Times*, also noticed Lincoln's wire-pulling and cried foul. "Even his honesty," Mackay told his London readers, "appears to have succumbed to the veiled influences which surround him. Three years' possession of power has familiarized him with baseness. . . . He has learnt to play with principles as other men play with dice, and desiring to be renominated to the Presidency, he is determined to win the game unfairly if he cannot win it otherwise."

The Lincoln juggernaut had been put in motion, however, and it rumbled through February. The President's soldiers in the Republican caucuses of New Jersey, Maryland, Colorado, and California all pushed through instructions for their delegations to cast their votes for him. On February 22, the "Union National Committee," as the Republican leadership now called itself—stacked with men who owed their jobs to Abraham Lincoln and had a personal interest in continuing him in office—voted to hold the national nominating convention in Baltimore on June 7, as soon as possible, before any unfortunate events could prick his balloon.

It was at this point that Chase's infamous Pomeroy Circular surfaced. Soon it became obvious that the Chase campaign pamphlet was, as Secretary Welles had predicted when he read it, "more dangerous in its recoil than its projectile"—that is, damaging mainly to Chase himself. Pretending to be surprised and mortified by the appearance of his own campaign emerging into print, Chase immediately wrote a letter to Lincoln denying any knowledge of the pamphlet, and offering to resign.

Chase's candidacy was presently undone in his own state. Three days after the Pomeroy Circular appeared in the press, Chase's misbegotten run for president ended at the caucus of Republican legislators in Ohio. In the fallout over the Circular, Chase's agents proved to be no match for Lincoln's: Ohio, too, declared for the President. Mortally wounded by this unkindest cut of all, Chase, in a public letter to a friend, resigned his campaign for the nomination.

*   *   *

With the wreck of the *S.S. Chase* at the beginning of March, the Radicals on board swam for any floating spar. While they searched for another rival to Lincoln, a movement grew to postpone the convention from June 7 to a later date, on the pretext that the candidate should not be chosen until there was decisive news from the battlefront.

The erratic Horace Greeley, who shared the widespread suspicion that Lincoln was not the man to win a hard war, spearheaded the movement for delay. In the February 23 *Tribune*, Greeley broadcast his wish that all thoughts of a nominee be "banished from every loyal mind" until after July 4, "while every energy, every effort should be devoted to the one paramount object of suppressing the Rebellion and restoring Peace to our distracted country." In the same column, he pooh-poohed the masses' affection for Lincoln. In view of the national ordeal, he contended, they would love any president who "has not proved an utter disappointment and failure." He reaffirmed "the salutary One Term principle," and asked finally, "Has Mr. Lincoln proved so transcendently able and admirable a President that all consideration of the merits, abilities, and services of others should be postponed or forborne in favor of his reelection? We answer it in the negative. Heartily agreeing that Mr. Lincoln has done well, we do not regard it as at all demonstrated that Governor Chase, General Frémont, General Butler or General Grant cannot do as well."

In an editorial issued the same day, William Cullen Bryant of the New York *Evening Post* joined Greeley's anti-Lincoln bid. On March 25, other eminent New Yorkers joined with Bryant in publishing a statement that urged awaiting the developments of the spring and summer. In Chicago, Joseph Medill of the *Tribune* declared, "Lincoln has some very weak and foolish traits of character," and placed himself under Greeley's banner, writing, "I don't care much if the Convention is put off till August. . . . If Lincoln loses the nomination thereby he will have nobody but himself to blame." Massachusetts' powerful *Springfield Republican* also supported a delay. Even Charles Sumner, a constant visitor at the White House, held aloof: "I regret very much that the Baltimore convention is to be at so early a day," he said. "I see nothing but disaster from mixing our politics with battle and blood." Greeley confided his strategy to a friend, insisting Lincoln was "not out of the woods. I shall keep up a quiet but steady opposition and, if we should meantime have bad luck in war, I guess we shall back [Lincoln's supporters] out."

The wailing by the Radicals after Chase's withdrawal was overtopped by the coloratura soprano of New England intellectual Orestes Brownson. From his tireless pen came a 5,500-word pamphlet entitled "The Next President," a long-winded, scholarly slur of Lincoln. For sheer volume of pointy-headed disdain for the untutored President, it is unsurpassed. Here is the merest forkful of Brownson's seven-course meal:

> Mr. Lincoln evidently knows nothing of the philosophy of history, or of the higher elements of human nature. He imagines that men act only from low and interested motives, and does not suspect, because he does not feel, the presence of a heroic element, the element, Carlyle would call it, of Hero-worship, that makes men admire and cling to, and uphold a bold, daring policy, energetically proclaimed, firmly adhered to, and consistently acted on, though in the face and eyes of their interest. His soul seems made of leather, and incapable of any grand or noble emotion. Compared with the mass of men, he is a line of flat prose in a beautiful and spirited lyric. He lowers, he never elevates you. You leave his presence with your enthusiasm damped, your better feelings crushed, and your hopes cast to the winds. You ask not, can this man carry the nation through its terrible struggles? but, can the nation carry this man through them, and not perish in the attempt? He never adopts a clean policy. When he hits upon a policy, substantially good in itself, he contrives to belittle it, besmear it, or in some way to render it mean, contemptible, and useless. Even wisdom from him seems but folly. It is not his fault, but his misfortune. He is a good sort of man, with much natural shrewdness and respectable native abilities; but he is misplaced in the Presidential Chair. He lives and moves in an order of thought, in a world many degrees below that in which a great man lives and moves. We blame him not because he is mole-eyed and not eagle-eyed, and that he has no suspicion of that higher region of thought and action in which lie the great interests and questions he is called upon to deal with as President of the United States. He has done as much as was in his power to make himself, and should be respected for what he has made himself, and the fault that he is not fit for his position is the fault of us who put him there. His only fault is, the misfortune of being unconscious of his own unfitness for his place.

Brownson and others like him saw their savior in "The Pathfinder," General John Charles Frémont, who in late spring announced himself as the Radical candidate for the nomination. Frémont had been sulking in New York City for two years, nursing his grudge over the earlier quarrel with Lincoln in Missouri. Both New York City and Missouri had always been hotbeds of disaffection with the President, and Frémont was the perfect tool for plotters eager to destroy Lincoln's chances in the fall.

On March 18, 1864, Frémont devotees rallied at the Cooper Union building in New York. Horace Greeley dropped by to give encouragement, and the group issued a circular, calling all like-minded citizens to meet with them in convention in Cleveland on May 31. In it they denounced "the imbecile and vacillating policy of the present Administration in the conduct of the war, . . . its treachery to justice, freedom, and genuine democratic principles in its plan of reconstruction, whereby the honor and dignity of the nation have been sacrificed to conciliate the still existing and arrogant slave power, and to further the ends of unscrupulous ambition." A new pro-Frémont newspaper, *New Nation*, was launched. Its inaugural editions featured editorials like the following:

> We propose before ostracizing honest Abe from the White House to consider his right to the name of "Honest." . . . Mr. Lincoln's honesty is of a strange description. It consists in nearly ruining his country and in disregarding its interest in order to make sure of power for four years longer. . . . Even if President Lincoln were the honest man that his paid organs represent him to be, how dangerous would his reelection prove to the liberties of the people, under existing circumstances, surrounded as he is with the military influences that he has at his back!

Wendell Phillips, always alert for a chance to torture Lincoln, gave his benediction to Frémont's upcoming Cleveland gathering. An unlikely ally, the Democratic press, contributed countless columns of publicity, touting the coming assembly as a summit of the utmost gravity.

The event, however, was a fizzle. The hall was hired only at the last minute, and proved to be too big for the small crowd—composed largely of St. Louis longhairs with thick German accents—that never counted above four hundred. None of the big names showed. The Cleveland Convention adopted the Radical reconstruction platform, nominated John C. Frémont by acclamation, and placed John Cochrane on the ticket as Vice-president, all in one day. The conventioneers christened their party the "Radical Democracy" as a beacon to Lincoln-haters of every stripe, Democrats as well as Republicans.

Frémont hurried his acceptance speech into print before it could be drowned out in the hubbub of the approaching Baltimore Convention. In it, he sketched an apocalyptic clash with an unprincipled tyrant:

> This is not an ordinary election. It is a contest for the right even to have
> candidates, and not merely, as usual, for the choice among them. . . . The
> ordinary rights secured under the Constitution and the laws of the country
> have been violated, and extraordinary powers have been usurped by the
> Executive. . . . To-day we have in the country the abuses of a military
> dictation without its unity of action and vigor of execution—an
> Administration marked at home by disregard of constitutional rights, by
> its violation of personal liberty and the liberty of the press, and, as a
> crowning shame, by its abandonment of the right of asylum [for Border
> State slaves]. . . .
>
> If Mr. Lincoln should be nominated . . . there will remain no other
> alternative but to organize against him every element of conscientious
> opposition with the view to prevent the misfortune of his reelection.

The Democratic press hailed the Frémont men's courage and wisdom, but
few paid his candidacy much attention. As meager as the Cleveland Four
Hundred seemed to most observers, however, when Lincoln received a
telegram with news that the Radical convention had numbered four hundred
men, he immediately opened a Bible, found I Samuel 22:2, and read it aloud to
everyone present in the telegraph office: "And every one that was in distress,
and every one that was in debt, and every one that was discontented, gathered
themselves unto him; and he became a captain over them; and there were with
him about four hundred men."

Lincoln's Bible reading probably revealed his deep misgivings about his
own political future. He knew that the Biblical four hundred had gathered
around the future King David, and that David and his four hundred had
ultimately brought down the powerful King Saul.

Lincoln had pored over the primer on leadership contained in the Biblical
account of Israel's great kings—Saul, David, and Solomon. He had always been
uneasy that the Radicals had led the fight against slavery that had ennobled the
war. And he was quick to perceive omens. Lincoln likely thought he had found
one in Samuel's account of David's four hundred malcontents, and thought he
himself too much resembled King Saul—no longer God's man.

For Lincoln knew that Frémont's candidacy, even if the public at large
ignored it, still had the power to deny him another term. The hopeless candidate
of a splinter party had cost his hero, "The Great Compromiser" Henry Clay, the
presidency in 1844, when abolitionist James Birney polled only 62,000

votes—less than 3% of votes cast. Pro-slavery Democrat James K. Polk beat Clay by 38,000 votes.

* * *

In the countdown to the Republican convention, the voices of the Democratic editors became a continuous howl. They were joined—or rather rejoined—by James Gordon Bennett's mighty *New York Herald*. In late fall, Bennett, with his ear always to the ground, had heard the rumble of Lincoln's Republican enemies gathering and sensed that Lincoln was vulnerable. On December 16, 1863, the *Herald* abruptly announced that he had "proved a failure." From that moment, the *Herald*'s published opinion of the President plummeted. On February 19, 1864, it carried a smear entitled "Lincoln the Joker":

> President Lincoln is a joke incarnated. His election was a very sorry joke. The idea that such a man as he should be the President of such a country as this is a very ridiculous joke. The manner in which he first entered Washington—after having fled from Harrisburg in a Scotch cap, a long military cloak and a special night train—was a practical joke. His debut in Washington society was a joke; for he introduced himself and Mrs. Lincoln as "the long and short of the Presidency." His inaugural address was a joke, since it was full of promises which he has never performed. His Cabinet is and always has been a standing joke. All his State papers are jokes. His letters to our generals, beginning with those to General McClellan, are very cruel jokes. His plan for abolishing slavery in 1900 was a broad joke. His emancipation proclamation was a solemn joke. His recent proclamation of abolition and amnesty is another joke. His conversation is full of jokes . . . . His title of "Honest" is a satirical joke. The style in which he winks at frauds in the War Department, frauds in the Navy Department, frauds in the Treasury Department, and frauds in every department, is a costly joke. His intrigues to secure a re-nomination and the hopes he appears to entertain of a re-election are, however, the most laughable jokes of all.

The Chicago *Times* reprinted an anti-Lincoln editorial from the *South Carolinian* to quicken the pulses of its readers:

Better cringe under the sternest despotism of Europe—better the dominion of the fiend himself, even though he should come to us . . . with the hoof, horns, and tail of the old legends—better, a thousand times better extermination from the very face of the earth, than to own as a master, for the faintest shadow of a second, this mean, wily, illiterate, brutal, unprincipled, and utterly vulgar creature—in a word, this Yankee of Yankees!

In April, the New York *World* spread the rumor that Lincoln no longer bothered to call Cabinet meetings—he now ran the government single-handed, in his own vulgar style:

In the knots of two or three which sometimes gather, Mr. Lincoln's stories quite as often occupy the time as the momentous interests of a great nation, divided by traitors, ridden by fanatics and cursed with an imbecility in administration only less criminal than treason.

On May 18, the New York *Daily News* insisted, "No influence except compulsion can induce any respectable proportion of the people to cast their votes for that compound of cunning, heartlessness, and folly that they now execrate in the person of their chief magistrate."

But Lincoln's grip on the levers of the Republican Party machinery was unbreakable. On June 7, when the Republican Party met in convention in Baltimore, Lincoln's victory was so certain, the lack of suspense about the result so complete, that Democratic editors dismissed the whole affair. The Chicago *Times* sneered that Lincoln could lay his hand on the shoulder of any one of the "wire-pullers and bottle-washers" in the convention hall and say, "This man is the creature of my will." The *New York Herald* cited the empty spectacle as evidence that what was needed was to do away with conventions altogether—hadn't they delivered one political hack after another for twenty-eight years, and brought on a civil war? Why depend on "that self-constituted and irresponsible gathering of vagrant politicians known as the National Party Convention?" it asked, proposing instead a caucus of the members of both Houses (where it knew Lincoln had few friends) to decide a nominee.

As everyone had predicted, Lincoln's appointees delivered an easy victory in Baltimore. The Radicals bit their tongues and sat sullenly. Their scribe, Count Gurowski, hinted darkly, "What a chill runs through the best men! Many, many have not yet made up their minds to go for him." Attorney General Edward

Bates noted in his diary, "The Baltimore Convention . . . has surprised and mortified me greatly. It did indeed nominate Mr. Lincoln, but . . . as if the object were to defeat their own nomination. They were all (nearly) instructed to vote for Mr. Lincoln, but many of them hated to do it . . . ."

The Democratic journals all thumbed their noses. The Chicago *Times'* jaundiced version of the convention's results was, "I, A. Lincoln, hereby nominate myself as a candidate for reelection." Joseph Bennett, in the columns of the *New York Herald*, declared, "The politicians have again chosen this Presidential pigmy as their nominee." The New York *World* fell into a swoon:

> The age of statesmen is gone; the age of rail-splitters and tailors, of buffoons, boors, and fanatics, has succeeded. . . . In a crisis of the most appalling magnitude, requiring statesmanship of the highest order, the country is asked to consider the claims of two ignorant, boorish, third-rate backwoods lawyers [Lincoln and Vice Presidential nominee Andrew Johnson], for the highest stations in government. Such nominations, in such a conjuncture, are an insult to the common-sense of the people. God save the Republic!

The *Cincinatti Gazette* phrased its displeasure in the rhythms of the familiar "We Are Coming, Father Abraham":

> *We're coming Father Abraham, to make you doubly great,*
> *Another child of Destiny—conserver of the State—*
> *Be what you've been—do as you've done—tax, banish and proclaim;*
> *Joke, draft, arrest and shake your mane; you play no losing game.*
> *From your supreme prerogative no right can be reserved,*
> *Of rights make trifles, Father Abe, and the nation is preserved.*

The Republicans' most radical New York bugle, the *Tribune*, carried Horace Greeley's reluctant bow to the party's decision. He wrote regretfully:

> We cannot but feel that it would have been wiser and safer to spike the most serviceable guns of our adversaries by nominating another for President, and thus dispelling all motive, save that of naked disloyalty, for further warfare upon this Administration. We believe that the Rebellion would have lost something of its cohesion and venom from the hour in which it was known . . . that the President, having no more to expect or

hope, could henceforth be impelled by no conceivable motive but a desire to serve and save his country, and thus win for himself an enviable and enduring fame.

The bitterness of Greeley's disappointment was half-hid among his high-sounding phrases. To more plainly speak the editor's heart, the *Tribune* also printed Wendell Phillips' flaming reaction to Lincoln's nomination: "The Baltimore Convention was largely a mob of speculators and contractors willing to leave to their friend, Mr. Lincoln, his usurped power of reconstruction," Phillips said. He trusted that the radical Cleveland Conventioners might still "prevent the disaster of Mr. Lincoln's reelection." If not, he saw calamity: "As long as you keep the present turtle at the head of the Government you make a pit with one hand and fill it with the other."

*   *   *

Lincoln did not hear them, however. They were, suddenly, the least of his problems. For, on June 3, while the Republican delegates gathered in Baltimore to wave banners, General Grant—after a solid month of horrifying combat in the tangled woods of northern Virginia—launched an attack at Cold Harbor that, in fewer than sixty minutes, slaughtered 7,000 of his own men in a hopeless assault against Lee's entrenched army. A new, implacable swell of war-weariness settled over the North, and public disgust with the war effort and Lincoln's leadership entered its most hostile phase.

Chapter 30

The Fall and the Temptation

"The obscene ape of Illinois is about to be deposed."

The abyss of grief in June was so deep because hopes in May had been so high. Many people of the North were confident they had finally gotten the right general in the right place. After Ulysses S. Grant's capture of Vicksburg the previous 4th of July and his rout of the rebel army at Chattanooga in November, Congress offered him the rank of lieutenant general, whose three stars had previously been worn in the field only by George Washington. When he arrived in the nation's capital to take command, Grant was embarrassed by all the hoopla; he shunned the spotlight as fiercely as McClellan had sought it. Rather than attend adoring receptions in the parlors of the powerful, he headed straight for the front, with the remark that he was tired of the "show business."

On May 4, 1864, Grant's new-model Army of the Potomac began crossing the Rapidan River on its overland trek toward Richmond. Lee's Army of Northern Virginia pitched headlong into it the next day inside the depths of the Wilderness, a nearly impenetrable area of second growth timber, heavy brush, and soggy terrain. Predictions of certain victory crackled along the wires from the ocean to the prairies. All of Washington, announced correspondent Noah Brooks, "is pervaded with a feeling which can scarcely be called excitement, it is too intense. . . . People go about the streets with their hands full of 'extras' from the newspaper offices. . . . Every loyal heart is full of joy at the glorious tidings which continue to come up from the front, and citizens everywhere are congratulating each other upon the near prospect of an end of this wasteful and wicked war."

Within days the rhythm of Brooks' dispatches had changed to a slow drumbeat of sorrow: "All Washington is a great hospital. . . . Boatloads of unfortunate and maimed men are continually arriving. . . . The town is full of strangers from the North who have come in quest of friends and relatives who are in the hospitals or lying dead upon the battlefield. . . ." Union casualties were overwhelming: 18,000 in just the two days of havoc in the clotted undergrowth of the Wilderness, and another 18,000 in front of the strong rebel breastworks at Spotsylvania. On May 25, Brooks was on hand as 3,000 maimed soldiers were put ashore at the Sixth Street wharf: "The long, ghastly procession of shattered wrecks; the groups of tearful, sympathetic spectators, the rigid shapes of those who are bulletined as 'since dead'; the smoothly flowing river and the solemn hush in foreground and on distant evening shores—all form a picture which must some day perpetuate for the nation the saddest sight of all this war."

Well into May, as the fighting mounted and the casualties increased, Grant had written Lincoln, "I will fight it out on this line if it takes all summer," and the phrase had become famous. After meeting the hard reality of Lee's dug-in defenders, however, Grant changed his line often, sliding to his left over and over in an effort to slip around his enemy's flank and place his army between his enemy and Richmond. Then came the shocking slaughter of Cold Harbor, where thousands fell in less than an hour. After that grisly lesson, Grant changed his line yet again.

Continuing to move by his left, Grant skirted Richmond on its eastern side and took the same step McClellan had proposed at the end of the Peninsula Campaign two years earlier: he crossed the Army of the Potomac to the south side of the James River and, threatening Richmond from the southeast, advanced against the vital rail hub of Petersburg. Lee, however, traveled the chord of Grant's arc and reached Petersburg before him. In late June, at the end of Grant's long march, the rebel army defied the Union army from the safety of trenches throw up around the city. Grant's grinding campaign had cost some 60,000 men in just six gruesome weeks, and in the end his army was about where McClellan's had been two years earlier. The Overland Campaign had ended in a siege. Sherman's Western armies, moving south from Chattanooga, covered large swaths of territory but in the end were stymied outside Atlanta by overturned earth, sharpened logs, and a determined rebel army under General Joe Johnston.

Morale in the North plummeted. As fresh gouts of blood spattered the nation's psyche, all the old familiar disgust with Lincoln returned. Mailboxes in Washington overflowed with letters from prominent men in their gloom: "It makes me sick to think what we have lost & the prospect of having nearly five years more of this thing"; "I pray god we may have a change, as anything positive can hardly be worse"; "Mr. Lincoln may mean well, but he has far greater faculty for perpetuating evil than good, he is a politician never a statesman, he lives, breathes, and has his being in the brief hour that fortune—

ever blind—has allotted to him. Vacillating in policy, undecided in action, weak in intellectual grasp, he writhes in contortions of dissimulation."

With Northern discouragement watered by the rivers of coffins flowing north from the stalemates in front of Petersburg and Atlanta, Lincoln in Washington suffered one crisis after another. The first was a patronage battle with Secretary Chase over a Treasury Department appointment. Chase did what he always did when he felt himself slighted: he handed in his resignation. Now that his nomination was won, Lincoln surprised the Secretary by accepting it, writing, "You and I have reached a point of mutual embarrassment in our official relations which it seems can not be overcome, or longer sustained, consistently with the public service." On the heels of the news, of course, a delegation of Radicals stormed the White House to protest. Lincoln kept the peace by replacing Chase with one of them—William Fessenden, the chairman of the Senate Finance Committee—the next day.

* * *

A few days later, however, there came a crisis not to be patched over: the passage by Congress of the Wade-Davis Bill, the Radicals' challenge to Lincoln's Reconstruction policy.

Lincoln had a dangerous enemy in Maryland Rep. Henry Winter Davis. Davis was young, good-looking, and aristocratic, blessed with eloquence and a voice that was "clear and cold, like starlight." Davis was a protégé of Thaddeus Stevens, and he spoke in the scriptural cadences of Wendell Phillips. He was also, according to Noah Brooks, "a singularly violent politician," "mischievous in his schemes, and hollow-hearted and cold-blooded." He had hoped for a Cabinet appointment, and after Lincoln had appointed his Maryland rival Montgomery Blair Postmaster General instead, Davis had been insatiable in his hatred of the President, antagonistic to his every act.

In response to Lincoln's Amnesty and Reconstruction Proclamation in December of 1863, then, Davis introduced a hostile bill in the House that reserved Reconstruction to Congress. Davis' scheme demanded that in every Southern state a majority of voters—rather than Lincoln's one-tenth—take the loyalty oath before the state could form a government and be allowed to send representatives to Congress. In addition, the Radical loyalty oath would be stronger: the swearer must vow he had never been disloyal to the government, rather than that he merely would be loyal in the future. It thus disqualified almost every experienced Southern leader from a place in the new order.

Further, the bill included the unconstitutional demand that slavery be abolished in every reconstructed state.

Henry Winter Davis' bill was a censure of Lincoln's lack of firmness, a rebuke of Lincoln's unwillingness to give the fatal blow to the Slave Power, a corrective to Lincoln's attempt to reconstruct the nation without consulting Congress. Davis accused the President of low motives for his lenient plan, insisting that Lincoln was merely making Reconstruction a spoils system, with every officer of each newly-reconstructed state beholden to him. Davis' cry was a repetition of the Southern cry in 1860 that Lincoln was an illegitimate usurper. This time, however, Lincoln was skewing the electoral system to enslave Northern radicals. Better by far to fling aside the President's governments in Louisiana and Arkansas, Davis argued.

Debate on the bill in the House seemed to require that every Lincoln-hater take the podium. One was Garrett Davis of Kentucky, who called Lincoln a usurper equal to Caesar, Cromwell, and Bonaparte. "He is no statesman," he told the House, "but a mere political charlatan. He has inordinate vanity and conceit. He is a consummate dissembler, and an adroit and sagacious demagogue. He has the illusion of making a great historical name for himself in connection with the total abolition of slavery in the United States." Louisiana and Arkansas, he said, were "lawless and daring political enterprises" for the purpose of producing electoral votes for Lincoln in November.

With the help of such men, Davis' bill passed the House in May. Ben Wade pressed it in the Senate, and it passed there on July 2, with only two days left in the session. In the furious last minutes before Congress adjourned at noon on July 4, 1864, Lincoln sat in the frescoed and chandeliered President's Room just off the Senate chamber, signing eleventh-hour bills. On the floor of the House, as the clock ticked toward twelve, anxious members tilted toward Lincoln's door, straining for word on whether he had signed the Wade-Davis Bill. Charles Sumner stood over Lincoln's shoulder, fretting over its fate. Zack Chandler entered the President's Room and threatened Lincoln with the loss of Ohio and Michigan in the coming election if he didn't sign. "The important point," he chafed, "is that one prohibiting slavery in the reconstructed states."

"That is the point on which I doubt the authority of Congress to act," replied Lincoln. After Chandler left, he turned to those in the room and said, "I do not see how any of us now can deny and contradict all we have always said, that Congress has no constitutional power over slavery in the states." He said further, "This bill . . . seems to make the fatal admission that States whenever they please may of their own motion dissolve their connection with the union [under the "State Suicide" theory]. Now we cannot survive that admission, I am convinced. If that be true, I am not President, these gentlemen are not Congress." Lincoln "pocketed" the bill, declining to sign it into law.

The clock struck twelve, the Speaker sounded the gavel, and the doors of the chamber were thrown open. "In the disorder which followed," wrote Noah Brooks, "Davis standing at his desk, pale with wrath, his bushy hair tousled, and wildly brandishing his arms, denounced the President in good set terms. . . . I certainly was astonished to hear the bitter denunciations heaped upon the head of President Lincoln by some of the radical Senators and Representatives. Malcontents poured out of the doors of the Capitol on all sides . . . and the first session of the Thirty-eighth Congress ended in a curious condition of unrest and dissatisfaction." The Radicals returned to their homes plotting schemes of revenge. Lincoln admitted to Hay as they left the Capitol building, "If [the Radicals] choose to make a point upon this I do not doubt that they can do harm. They have never been friendly to me & I do not know that this will make any special difference as to that. At all events, I must keep some consciousness of being somewhere near right: I must keep some standard of principle fixed within myself."

*   *   *

The matter, however, was dropped for the moment in a panic over the sudden appearance of the rebel army moving toward the outskirts of Washington. From the Capitol dome, Confederates could be seen massing to the north. Jubal Early, at the head of 12,000 men detached from General Lee's army in Richmond, had sped down the Shenandoah Valley, crossed the Potomac River near Harpers Ferry, and laid waste to the Maryland countryside in his approach to the capital. Washington's communication with the rest of the loyal states was cut off. Nobody could know the size of the enemy army, and terrified guesses rose as high as 45,000 men.

Washington was more vulnerable than at any time since the days after Fort Sumter. There were no quality troops available—they had all gone to fill the gaping holes in Grant's lines on his drive to Richmond. The heavy artillerists, the men who knew how to work the big guns in the forts surrounding the capital, were gone, too, crouching in the steaming trenches outside Petersburg with rifled-muskets in their hands. What remained in the capital were government clerks, local militiamen commanded by a neighborhood grocer, and invalids from the Veteran Reserve Corps. "Washington was in a ferment," wrote Noah Brooks from the scene. While rebel cannon boomed in the distance, "men were marching to and fro; able-bodied citizens were swept up and put into the District militia; and squads of department clerks were set to drilling in the parks." Even the locals could not be coordinated, however. Organization in Washington was nearing collapse. Halleck and Stanton worked at cross-purposes with each other. Each had his favorite generals, who proliferated until Halleck wrote a dispatch to New York: "We have five times as many generals here as we want, but are greatly in need of privates. Anyone volunteering in that capacity will be thankfully received."

As smoke mushroomed above burning buildings just outside the city, Maryland refugees streamed into Washington in wild disorder with their household goods stacked crazily on their wagons. They were jostled by Washington secessionists pouring into the streets shouting with joy. Stanton, seized with dread, had his secretary take his bonds and gold from the War Department safe and hide them in his mattress at home. On the night of July 10, Stanton sent a carriage to snatch the Lincolns, who were staying at the Soldiers' Home north of town. The President irritably got into the coach and returned to the White House, where he was soon further embarrassed to learn that a gunboat was waiting at a Potomac wharf to speed his escape if the rebels should overrun the forts and enter the city.

The next afternoon Lincoln rode back to the north edge of town and mounted the parapet of Fort Stevens to witness the developing battle. The bullets whizzed by him as he stood upright in his black suit and stovepipe hat until a soldier—legend has it that it was future Supreme Court Justice Oliver Wendell Holmes, Jr.—shouted, "Get down, you damn fool, or you'll get your head knocked off!" Amused at the soldier's presumption, he did, quickly.

That day, the veteran Sixth Corps of the Army of the Potomac arrived, sent from Grant by steamer. Blocked by Washington's defenses and the recent reinforcements, Early slipped safely back into Virginia. Noah Brooks regretted the ability of the rebel host to withdraw unscathed: "Grant's distance from the scene, Halleck's disinclination to take the responsibility of pursuit, and Lincoln's firm refusal to decide any military question of detail, resulted in the safe departure of Early and his forces."

Immediately there were critics. Stanton's aide Charles Dana called it an "egregious blunder." Gideon Welles noted in his diary that in the eyes of the entire country, the administration appeared "contemptible" in this, "our national humiliation." Correspondent Brooks reported the deepening of defeatism caused by this latest rebel "invasion." "In the country at large," he wrote, "the effect . . . was somewhat depressing. The capital had been threatened; the President's safety had been imperiled; only a miracle had saved treasures, records, and archives from the fate that overtook them when Cockburn seized the city during the War of 1812." The Washington *Chronicle* and *National Intelligencer* told the nation that such a narrow escape so late in the war was more evidence of the impotence of the President and his generals. The *New York Herald* agreed, blaming "the great noodles who mismanage our military and all other matters at Washington."

With the national pride still stinging from the Early raid, Lincoln brought the country still lower when, on July 18, he sent out a proclamation, bare of rhetoric, calling for a new draft of half a million men to take place September 5. The call staggered the nation, and the Democratic press reacted in a wild spasm. Editorials like the following from the Newark *Evening Journal* burst into print:

> It will be seen that Mr. Lincoln has called for another half million of men. Those who wish to be butchered will please step forward. All others will please stay at home and defy Old Abe and his minions to drag them from their families. We hope that the people of New Jersey will at once put their feet down and insist that not a man shall be forced out of the state to engage in the Abolition butchery, and swear to die at their own doors rather than march one step to fulfill the dictates of the mad, revolutionary fanaticism which has destroyed the best government the world ever saw, and now would butcher its remaining inhabitants to carry out a more fanatical sentiment. This has gone far enough and must be stopped. Let the people rise as one man and demand that this wholesale murder shall cease.

The New York *Daily News* cast Lincoln in a grisly fantasy, "The Walpurgis Dance At Washington":

> *One, tall, and bony and lank, stood forward from the rest,*
> *And told a ribald story with a leer to give it zest,*
> *And said: "Our fire burns feebly, we must pile it up anew;*
> *Tell me the fuel to feed it with ye friends and comrades true!"*
> *And they shouted with mad rejoicing:*
> *BLOOD! BLOOD! BLOOD! Let the witches' cauldron boil with a nation's tears for*
> *water!*

BLOOD! BLOOD! BLOOD! Slabby and thick as mud, to sprinkle the hungry soil for the carnival of slaughter.

Many called the new draft political suicide. *The Crisis* editor Samuel Medary announced, "Lincoln is *deader* than dead."

With bleak news everywhere, the nation's finances went into a tumble. Union defeats sent the price of gold up. Financial confidence in the nation sank as speculators began to bet against a Union victory. The value of the new paper money was at so low an ebb—$2.60 in greenbacks to buy $1.00 in gold—that Greeley panicked in print: "Gold goes up like a balloon . . . . The business of the country is all but fatally deranged. . . . There is a danger of Social Convulsion . . . . Every necessity of life grows hourly dearer." A friend wrote to Greeley a letter from Buffalo confirming his fears. "Among the masses of the people," it warned, "a strong reaction is setting in favor of the Democrats and against the war. I have been among the mechanics, and the high prices of provisions are driving them to wish a change. . . . I write mainly today to say that I am alarmed."

*   *   *

With confidence in Lincoln now in free fall, Frémont's backers in New York grew bold. They issued a new handbill, a call to arms titled "Ten Reasons Why Abraham Lincoln Should Not Be Elected President of the United States a Second Term." Radicals in Washington now openly advertised their disenchantment with Lincoln as the party candidate. A reinvigorated Salmon Chase spread word that there was "great and almost universal dissatisfaction with Mr. Lincoln among all earnest men." Charles Sumner, who spoke guardedly when in Washington, was more candid in his opinion of Lincoln when he was among his friends in Boston. On July 23, 1864, abolitionist Amos Lawrence wrote in his diary, "Took tea at Mr. Longfellow's with Charles Sumner. The latter wishes to see a president with brains; one who can make a plan and carry it out." Sumner's opinion of Lincoln was "not higher than it was three years ago," according to another friend who saw him then. Senator Grimes of Iowa confessed to editor C. H. Ray of the Chicago *Tribune*, "This entire administration has been a disgrace from the very beginning to every one who had any thing to do with bringing it into power. I take my full share of the . . . shame to myself. I can atone for what I have done no otherwise than in refusing to be instrumental in continuing it."

Seeing Lincoln wounded, the Radicals went in for the kill. On August 5, Greeley devoted two columns in the New York *Tribune* to a sensational declaration by Ben Wade and Henry Winter Davis. It became famous as the Wade-Davis Manifesto, the fiercest, most public challenge to Lincoln's—or, for that matter, any President's—authority ever issued by members of his own party. It charged Lincoln with "grave Executive usurpation" and "a studied outrage on the legislative authority." It accused him of "personal ambition" and "sinister motives" in installing his "shadows of governments" in Arkansas and Louisiana in order to pile up electoral votes. It called his pocket veto of the Wade-Davis bill a "rash and fatal act," a strike at the "rights of humanity" and "the principles of Republican Government." It exhorted citizens to "consider the remedy of these usurpations and, having found it, fearlessly to execute it." Such a remedy could only be impeachment—or, what would be quicker, casting Lincoln off as the party's candidate.

James Gordon Bennett leaped up and applauded from beneath the banner of the *New York Herald*. He exulted, "the dissatisfaction which had long been felt by the great body of American citizens has spread even to [Lincoln's] own supporters." This "remarkable document," he reported, charged the President with "arrogance, ignorance, usurpation, knavery and a host of other deadly sins . . . . Nothing that Vallandigham or the most venomous of the copperhead tribe of politicians have uttered in derogation of Mr. Lincoln has approached in bitterness and force the denunciations which Messrs. Wade and Davis, shining lights of the Republican party, have piled up in this manifesto." Bennett then presumed to hold the mirror up to the ruined chief: "As President of the United States he must have sense enough to see and acknowledge he has been an egregious failure. One thing must be self-evident to him, and that is that under no circumstances can he hope to be the next President of the United States." Bennett gave Lincoln the same public advice he always gave him: *quit now*.

The Wade-Davis Manifesto, said the New York *World*, was "a blow between the eyes which will daze the President." It certainly dazed everyone around him. Lincoln's friend Noah Brooks wrote that the manifesto, "coming as it did . . . like a thunderbolt out of a clear sky, threw politicians of every stamp into the wildest confusion." "Its appearance," he said, "created something like a panic in the ranks of the President's supporters." J.K. Herbert, after a visit to the State Department on August 6, testified, "No such bomb has been thrown into Washington before. . . . The trepidation of the White House is worse to-day than ever it was when poor Old Jim B. [President Buchanan] sat up there & trembled."

The first reaction of Washington insiders was that Lincoln was a beaten man. "Union men were quite unanimous in sustaining Mr. Wade and Mr. Davis, as was the majority of both Houses of Congress," reported A. G. Riddle from the Capitol. Thaddeus Stevens was heard to say, "If the Republican party desires to succeed, they must get Lincoln off the track and nominate a new man." Herbert, the day after the Manifesto appeared in the *Tribune*, heard kingmaker Thurlow Weed say, "Lincoln is gone. I suppose you know as well as I." Weed, in fact, told Lincoln so to his face: "I told Mr Lincoln that his re-election was an impossibility," Weed wrote to Seward. "At any rate, nobody here doubts it; nor do I see any body from other States who authorises the slightest hope of success."

The flight from Lincoln sped outward from Washington. Correspondent Whitelaw Reid, listening to the people as he traveled from Cincinnati to Maine during July and August, became convinced that Lincoln's reelection was hopeless. Another prominent man confirmed Reid's pessimism in a letter to Elihu Washburne: "Things in a political way do not look so favorable as they did some time ago," he warned. "Pennsylvania, New York, and all the New England States are getting down on *Old Abe* as they call him." John Hay wrote to Nicolay from rural Illinois, telling him, "everywhere in the towns, the Copperheads are exultant and our own people either growling & despondent or sneakingly apologetic." Edgar Conkling of Cincinnati believed that in late July most Republicans were for Lincoln only "from pure necessity" and eager to "get a competent, loyal President, in the place of our present imbecile incumbent." General John H. Martindale reported from Rochester, New York, "The present condition of public sentiment is most unfavorable to the President. . . . [I]n this region the President has lost amazingly within a few weeks, and if the public sentiment here affords a fair indication of the public sentiment throughout the country, the popular suffrage to-day would be 'for a change.'" From New York City, a friend of General Butler confided, "I have seen and talked with nearly all the leading men in the city, and they all are of one opinion in regard to Lincoln. They considered him defeated." Another prominent New Yorker wrote to Montgomery Blair:

> Political affairs in this state are assuming a very unfavorable aspect for the Republican party, and unless some prompt action is taken, we will be unable to carry the state for Mr Lincoln. . . . [S]o great a change has taken place that if the Convention was again held, Mr Lincoln would not be re-nominated.

According to Lincoln's good friend Carl Schurz, "The people seemed to be utterly spiritless. . . . The administration party could not have been in a more lethargic and spiritless condition. Its atmosphere was thoroughly depressing." Gideon Welles confided to his diary a "feeling of despondency . . . . Wide discouragement prevails." A. K. McClure wrote later, "Distrust and disintegration were common throughout the entire Republican organization and nearly all of the sincere supporters of Lincoln were in next to utter despair of political success." Leonard Swett sketched the mood in a letter to his wife, writing, "I found the most alarming depression possessing the minds of all the Republicans, Greeley, Beecher, Raymond, Weed; and all the small politicians without exception utterly gave up in despair." "Unless material changes can be wrought," Swett wrote, "Lincoln's election is beyond any possible hope. It is probably clean gone now." The men closest to Lincoln used the most desperate terms. John Nicolay called it "disastrous panic—a sort of political Bull Run."

Newspapers across the North were quick to take up the story of Lincoln's fall from grace. The *New York Herald* declared, "The feeling against Old Abe is daily increasing." Richard Smith, Republican editor of the Cincinnati *Gazette*, told his readers,

> The people regard Mr. Lincoln's candidacy as a misfortune. His apparent strength when nominated was fictitious, and now the fiction has disappeared, and instead of confidence there is distrust. I do not know a Lincoln man, and in all our correspondence, which is large and varied, I have seen few letters from Lincoln men. . . . [T]he nomination of a man that would inspire confidence and infuse a life into our ranks would be hailed with general delight.

Joseph Medill of the Chicago *Tribune* wrote to John Hay a letter that the young secretary described as "inconceivably impudent, in which he informs me that on the fourth of next March, thanks to Mr. Lincoln's blunders & follies, we will be kicked out of the White House." Horace Greeley, whose trembling finger he himself always considered to be on the American pulse, declared:

> I know that nine-tenths of the whole American people, North and South, are anxious for peace—peace on almost any terms—and utterly sick of human slaughter and devastation. . . . I firmly believe that, were the election to take place to-morrow, the Democratic majority in this State

and Pennsylvania would amount to 100,000, and that we should lose Connecticut also.

Many newspapers, moving with the tide, cast off completely from the President, such as George Wilkes' New York *Spirit of the Times*, whose parting shot read:

> Under the figure of a jester, he is essentially a despot, and we may as well resign ourselves either to anarchy, or submit to imperialism at once. . . . He should gracefully resign. . . . It would be better than the fight of one hundred thousand troops, and would entitle him to the lasting respect and gratitude of the entire nation.

Others to quit Lincoln were the *New London* (CT.) *Chronicle*, the *New Yorker Democrat*, and the *Suffolk* (NY.) *Herald*, which announced its defection tersely: "[W]e determine him a man not calculated for the times—too easy, forbearing, and of short sight. We need a man of sterner stuff, and possessed of deeper penetration." Another was the *Boston Pioneer*, a German paper, which left the Lincoln camp sneering that he "has brought even honesty into disrepute." Another German sheet, Indiana's *Westliche Post*, likewise deserted the President, writing, "the only way to redeem the State for the Republican party would be to throw Lincoln overboard."

The Democratic New York *World* savored the spectacle of the President's demise, reprinting an editorial from the Richmond *Examiner*: "The fact . . . begins to shine out clear," it announced, "that Abraham Lincoln is lost; that he will never be President again. . . . The obscene ape of Illinois is about to be deposed from the Washington purple, and the White House will echo to his little jokes no more."

Greeley privately concurred with the *Examiner*. "Mr. Lincoln is already beaten," he spat. "He cannot be elected. And we must have another ticket to save us from utter overthrow." That Greeley and his bitterest Republican enemy, Thurlow Weed, who opposed each other in everything else, agreed in this gloomy prediction testified to the breadth of the feeling against Lincoln.

Earnest letters sped from every point on the compass to men whose blood quickened with the desire to replace the faltering President as the nominee. There were calls for a new convention to name a new man, someone who could win in the fall. As early as August 6 discontented groups in Ohio met to consider how to prevail on Lincoln to drop out of the race in order to hold a new Union caucus. They were answered on August 14 by a powerful circle of over twenty party leaders in New York City, including Greeley and Henry Winter Davis, who met secretly at the home of jurist David Dudley Field. They agreed to form a committee to urge Lincoln to withdraw, and meanwhile to privately circulate a call for a new convention to meet in late September "to concentrate the union strength on some one candidate who commands the confidence of the country, even by a new nomination if necessary." Three days later a friend of one of the hopefuls, General Ben Butler, wrote to inform him of another meeting, to be held at New York Mayor George Opdyke's:

> Chase will be there, many prominent men are invited. . . . I had an interview with Weed to-day of two hours, and it was very satisfactory. He says he thinks Lincoln can be prevailed upon to draw off. [Lincoln's friend Leonard] Swett . . . is of the same opinion. Weed says Lincoln told him substantially that he would not be in the way of success. Swett goes to Washington to-morrow night to tell Lincoln that it is the judgment of all the best politicians in this city and elsewhere, that he can't carry three states, and ask him to be prepared to draw off immediately after the Chicago [Democratic] Convention. Nearly all agree that the Baltimore Platform is a mistake, that we have reached that point where we simply want to make one condition. That is, the restoration of the Union. . . . [Lincoln's campaign manager, *New York Times* editor Henry] Raymond says Lincoln has gone up . . . . I understand from good authority that he has no hope of election.

The malcontents met at Opdyke's house the next evening. Among them were newspaper editors Greeley, Parke Godwin, George Wilkes of *Spirit of the Times*, Theodore Tilton of *The Independent*, Senators Benjamin Wade and Charles Sumner, Representative Henry Winter Davis, Governor Andrew, and David Dudley Field. They decided to call for a convention on September 28 in Cincinnati (Salmon Chase's home town). Each of the two dozen men in attendance were given a stack of letters to deliver to prominent men of like mind across the country, inviting them to participate as delegates to the new convention. They promised to meet again on August 30, then they adjourned to go and spread their mischief.

Lincoln was painfully aware of the plans to unseat him. Seward had read Lincoln the Wade-Davis Manifesto on the evening it was published, and Lincoln immediately perceived the threat to his candidacy, saying, "I would like to know whether these men intend openly to oppose my election.—The document looks that way." Carl Schurz, who talked with Lincoln during these days, described the President as profoundly saddened by this latest, surely fatal, betrayal. "He spoke," wrote Schurz later, "as if he felt a pressing need to ease his heart by giving voice to the sorrowful thoughts distressing him. 'They urge me with almost violent language,' he said, 'to withdraw from the contest, although I have been unanimously nominated, in order to make room for a better man. I wish I could. Perhaps some other man might do this business better than I. That is possible. I do not deny it. But I am here, and that better man is not here. And if I should step aside to make room for him, it is not at all sure—perhaps not even probable—that he would get here [the presidency]. . . . My withdrawal . . . might, and probably would, bring on a confusion worse confounded.'" Lincoln spoke, Schurz said, with "his sad eyes moist and his rugged features working strangely, as if under a very strong and painful emotion."

Another friend, A. K. McClure, who also saw Lincoln in mid-August, said, "I spent an hour with him in the Executive Chamber, and I never saw him more dejected in my life. His face, always sad in repose, was then saddened until it became a picture of despair, and he spoke of the want of sincere and earnest support from the Republican leaders with unusual freedom." Lincoln told his friend Noah Brooks mournfully, "To be wounded in the house of one's friends is perhaps the most grievous affliction that can befall a man." In plain talk with General Schuyler Hamilton he admitted, "You think I don't know I am going to be beaten, *but I do* and unless some great change takes place *badly* beaten."

Noah Brooks wrote, "In the memory of men who lived in Washington during the months of July and August, 1864, those days will appear to be the darkest of the many dark days through which passed the friends and lovers of the Federal Union." Henry Raymond described the political extremes that crushed Lincoln between upper and nether millstones:

> One denounces Mr. Lincoln because he did not abolish Slavery soon enough, another because he assumed to touch it at all. One refuses to vote for him because he keeps Mr. Blair in the Cabinet—another because he keeps somebody or anybody else. Frémont runs against him because he disregards the Constitution, and Wendell Phillips speaks against him because he recognizes that instrument at all. Some censure his lenient method of treating the people of the Southern States—others his barbarous and inhuman mode of carrying out the war. One set of politicians vilify him for not admitting the Southern States at once into the

Union, and Wade and Davis with equal malignity, brand him as a usurper for proposing to admit them at all.

On August 23, Lincoln wrote out a written pledge at the lowest moment of his term. In it, he promised to work to sustain what he was sure would be a new incoming administration. He folded it, then passed it around and had each of his Cabinet members sign it on the outside, sight unseen. Inside, the bizarre document read:

> This morning, as for some days past, it seems exceedingly probable that this Administration will not be re-elected. Then it will be my duty to so co-operate with the President elect, as to save the Union between the election and the inauguration; as he will have secured his election on such ground that he can not possibly save it afterwards. A. LINCOLN

* * *

London Punch, September 24, 1864

"Mrs. North and Her Attorney." Widow: "You see, Mr. Lincoln, we have failed utterly in our course of action. I want peace, and so, if you cannot effect an amicable arrangement I must put the case in other hands."

With Lincoln brought to rock bottom by the terrible events of the summer, his friends looked wretchedly about for the thinnest of straws to grasp at. In that desperate search for a stratagem that would turn the tables and win the election, a serpent—in the form of his campaign manager, Henry Raymond—whispered a seduction into Lincoln's ear. On August 22, Thurlow Weed foreshadowed the crisis in a letter to Seward from New York:

> Mr. Raymond, who has just left me, says that unless some prompt and bold step be now taken, all is lost.
>
> The People are wild for Peace. They are told that the President will only listen to terms of Peace on condition Slavery be "abandoned."
>
> . . . Mr Raymond thinks commissioners should be immediately sent to Richmond, offering to treat for Peace on the basis of Union. That something should be done and promptly done, to give the Administration a chance for its life, is certain.

That same day Henry Raymond sat down and wrote to Lincoln, holding out the shiny apple of temptation hinted at by Weed. He began with a plainspoken appraisal of the President's broken-down prospects for reelection:

> I feel compelled to drop you a line concerning the political condition of the Country as it strikes me. I am in active correspondence with your staunchest friends in every State and from them all I hear but one report. The tide is strongly against us. Hon. E. B. Washburne writes that "were an election to be held now in Illinois we should be beaten". Mr. Cameron writes that Pennsylvania is against us. Gov. Morton writes that nothing but the most strenuous efforts can carry Indiana. [New York], according to the best information I can get, would go 50,000 against us to-morrow. And so of the rest.

Raymond pointed at the two causes of the President's unpopularity: lack of military success, and "the impression in some minds, the fear and suspicion in others, that we are not to have peace in any event under this Administration until Slavery is abandoned. In some way or other the suspicion is widely diffused that we can have peace with Union if we would."

Raymond suggested a shrewd counterstroke, a gambit that would silence the critics and pave the way for an impossible-seeming Republican triumph in November. The President, he said, should "make distinct proffers of peace to

Davis . . . on the sole condition of acknowledging the supremacy of the Constitution, — all other questions to be settled in convention of the people of all the States." That is, Lincoln should drop the slavery condition. This offer, Raymond pointed out, would put the onus squarely on the Confederate President. If Davis accepted, which he almost certainly would not, the Union would be restored without further loss of life. If he refused the offer, which he almost certainly would,

> it would plant seeds of disaffection in the South, dispel all the delusions about peace that prevail in the North, silence the clamorous & damaging falsehoods of the opposition, take the wind completely out of the sails of the [Democrats], reconcile public sentiment to the War, the draft, & the tax as inevitable necessities, and unite the North as nothing since firing on Fort Sumter has hitherto done.

Such an offer could be done with "no abandonment of positions, no sacrifice of consistency," Raymond said.

But this was shamefully untrue. What about the promise of freedom to millions of slaves still behind enemy lines? Raymond failed to mention that his plan would mean reneging on the Emancipation Proclamation, backsliding on the greatest moral step forward in American history, repudiating everything to which Lincoln had pledged his presidency since January 1, 1863, almost twenty months before, and undoing what was most holy about the Northern cause.

The pressure to yield to necessity was tremendous. The warring factions in Lincoln's own party threatened to throw the election to the Democratic nominee, who was likely to call a halt to the struggle on inauguration day. If Lincoln did nothing and lost the election, he would also lose the ability to secure a lasting freedom for the slaves. Would his pragmatism in the service of the Union—always his guiding rule—now argue for renouncing his emancipation pledge, as Raymond's scheme demanded?

The next day, Lincoln okayed the deal in a letter to Raymond. It read:

> Executive Mansion,
> Sir: Washington, August 24. 1864.
>   You will proceed forthwith and obtain, if possible, a conference for peace with Hon. Jefferson Davis, or any person by him authorized for that purpose.

You will address him in entirely respectful terms, at all events, and in any that may be indispensable to secure the conference.

At said conference you will propose, on behalf this government, that upon the restoration of the Union and the national authority, the war shall cease at once, all remaining questions to be left for adjustment by peaceful modes.

Thus he put in writing his renunciation of the Emancipation Proclamation, his surrender of any claim of faithfulness to his slavery policy. It was Lincoln's habit to look the Tempter square in the face, and as Lincoln wrote the letter, he saw him eye to eye.

Lincoln may have assured himself of a victory in November if he had followed Raymond's advice. Davis would almost certainly have rejected peace with reunion as its condition, even as its only condition. But if Lincoln had sent the letter, if he had offered peace without freedom for all, he would have discarded the liberation of millions as just another political ploy that had outlived its usefulness. He would have reduced the greatest promise ever tendered by an American President to something like one of the broken treaties with the Native Americans. The war's ennobling proclamation would have been thrown onto the ashheap of history, a victim of political expediency.

But if he had recanted his pledge of liberty to the slave, he would not have been Lincoln, the man who never acted until he was sure, and then never retreated once he had acted. Just the week before, in the midst of all the darkness and doubt and discouragement described by everyone around him, he had defended his slavery policy at length in a conversation with a visitor to his office, saying, "There have been men who have proposed to me to return to slavery the black warriors . . . to their masters to conciliate the South. I should be damned in time & in eternity for so doing. The world shall know that I will keep my faith to friends & enemies, come what will." The one witness to this conversation wrote in his diary:

The President appeared to be not the pleasant joker I had expected to see, but a man of deep convictions & an unutterable yearning for the success of the Union cause. . . . As I heard a vindication of his policy from his own lips, I could not but feel that his mind grew in stature like his body, & that I stood in the presence of the great guiding intellect of the age, & that those huge Atlantian shoulders were fit to bear the weight of mightiest monarchies. His transparent honesty, his republican simplicity, his gushing sympathy for those who offered their lives for their country, his utter forgetfulness of self in his concern for his country, could not but inspire me with confidence, that he was Heavens instrument to conduct his people thro this red sea of blood to a Canaan of peace & freedom.

Thus, on August 25, when Henry Raymond and his party arrived at the White House to urge the mission to Davis, Lincoln rejected the proposal. He told Raymond that to follow his plan "would be worse than losing the Presidential contest—it would be ignominiously surrendering it in advance." He scuttled Raymond's scheme and accepted the almost certain fall of his presidency. Raymond returned to New York, and Lincoln's undelivered letter remained in its envelope, unseen for the next twenty-five years.

*   *   *

While Lincoln wrestled with the devils in Raymond's plan, the Radicals in New York were scurrying from meeting to meeting, pushing their project to hold a new convention and run a new man. On August 30 a meeting was held at the home of David Dudley Field. In attendance were the Gotham princes of the liberal press, along with other Radical leaders, such as Henry Winter Davis and Francis Lieber. On September 1, Count Gurowski distilled the purpose of the meeting into one malignant shriek: "Out Lincoln . . . is to be the war cry."

The Democrats were, of course, delighted by the stormy spectacle of the Republican house dividing. Even now Democratic delegates and thousands of onlookers were rolling and tumbling in the delirium of their own national convention. The hurrahs for their man of the hour, George McClellan, were amplified under the curved wooden dome of the same Chicago Wigwam that had four years earlier vibrated with shouts for Lincoln. Rich old Chicago Democrat Cyrus McCormick pronounced a smiling benediction over the scene: "Old Abe is quite in trouble just now. . . . I think he is already pretty well played out."

"Abraham's Dream." Lincoln sees McClellan ascend to the White House.

Chapter 31

The Election of 1864

"The doom of Lincoln and Black Republicanism is sealed."

T he delegates gathered in Chicago for the Democratic National Convention represented a huge following, one that anticipated a return to the dominance they had enjoyed before the Republicans' rude interruption of 1860. In late summer 1864, Democrats everywhere were optimistic. Lincoln received a warning on August 24 from a friend in Kansas:

> Dear Lincoln
> There is an evident sign of confidence among the Democrats all over the Country of success, they feel confident that the nominee at Chicago will be elected. . . . I confess to you I have some fear of our success— I am not easily discouraged in politics and never come to conclusions hurriedly.
> . . .
> Very Truly Your friend
>
> M W Delahay

The Democrats drew confidence from the fact that they, unlike the Republicans, were united on their nominee. George Brinton McClellan was that rare animal: a failed general still wildly popular with the soldiers and the people. He had been courted for two years by the chairman of the Democratic National Committee, New York financier August Belmont, who saw in McClellan the solution to the Democrats' problem of how to run against the Republicans without seeming to oppose the war and without being labeled traitors. McClellan, the war hero, the man shorn of power by vindictive politicians, was the one Democrat who could attack Lincoln without having his loyalty questioned or bringing his party's patriotism into doubt.

Almost two years before, in November of 1862, the day after being fired by Lincoln, the "Young Napoleon" had received a hero's welcome in Trenton, New Jersey. Within a week, he had moved into the Fifth Avenue Hotel in New

York City, the hotbed of Democratic politics in the North. A tumult greeted his arrival there, with bands blaring, artillery booming, and the people shouting alleluias. Whenever he emerged from his hotel, a large crowd cheered him and followed him wherever he went. In the following weeks, New York newspapers carried regular features headed "McClellan's Movements," reporting all his comings and goings—to theaters, to operas, to dinner parties and galas. He was surrounded by Democratic friends from his own set, the "best people," aristocrats of the most conservative stripe, including Belmont; "Prince" John Van Buren, the President's son; and captains of commerce Samuel L.M. Barlow, William Aspinwall, and John Jacob Astor. Belmont and Barlow had recently bought the New York *World* and had installed their young friend Manton Marble as its editor, and the World was soon singing the praises of New York's newly arrived celebrity-general.

Pleas to run for office followed. In May of 1863, he declined an offer to run for governor of Ohio. McClellan carefully maintained his show of disinterest in politics until the Pennsylvania state election of October of 1863, when he publicly endorsed the Democratic candidate for governor. This was McClellan's signal to Democratic Party bosses that he would play ball, and Manton Marble privately signaled their pleasure in return, writing to him, "the people's eyes are turned all one way in their search for the candidate who will win in 1864."

In early 1864, McClellan's presidential campaign unofficially opened with the publication of his book-length "Report of Maj. Gen. George B. McClellan, U. S. Army, Commanding the Army of the Potomac." It was written for twin purposes: to defend his generalship during the 1862 Peninsula and Antietam campaigns, and to expose the perfidy of Lincoln and the Radical Republicans. Included in the Report was McClellan's Harrison's Landing Letter of July 7, 1862, now published for the first time, which had dictated to Lincoln the conservative ideals that should guide the government's war policy. Here was the document that McClellan had always intended to be his own platform for the presidency. The New York *World* published a series of articles that praised the Report and singled out the Harrison's Landing Letter, which, it said, set down "with a statesman's vision the sound political as well as the sound military policy upon which the war should have been conducted." To rank-and-file Democrats, the Report lifted McClellan above all others as the man to beat Lincoln, who had so evidently caused the general's failure by neglecting to reinforce him, and who had intended to destroy him according to his own fanatical abolitionist designs.

On the strength of the surge caused by the Report, McClellan's backers on March 17 decked out the Cooper Union in New York for a huge rally that would announce him as a candidate for President. When a curtain at the back of the hall was dropped to reveal a gigantic portrait of their hero, superimposed over a vast Union flag, the standing-room-only crowd exploded. On one side hung a banner with the motto, "McClellan and Liberty"; on the opposite side was another banner emblazoned with weighty quotes from the Harrison's Landing Letter. Billowed up by thunderous applause, speaker after speaker plunged the hall into bedlam with hurrahs for McClellan and groans for the tyrant in the White House.

On June 15, McClellan, who had remained fashionably mute through all of the hoopla, broke his silence at the dedication of a battle monument at West Point, where he delivered an oration that lauded the Constitution and damned "extremists." McClellan's handlers made thousands of copies of the West Point Address together with his Harrison's Landing Letter and titled it "McClellan's Platform." Every delegate at the Democratic National Convention would get one.

Later that month, a military vindication came when General Grant, after the staggering price in blood paid for his Overland Campaign, adopted McClellan's original strategy of crossing the James River and striking at Petersburg.

Finally, as a prelude to the national convention in Chicago, the McClellan men on August 10 launched one of the most massive political rallies in the history of New York. Advertised on page one of the World under the headline "THE MCCLELLAN FURORE," the mass meeting's razzle-dazzle roared full-throated through Union Square from four stages, including bands, booming cannons, fireworks, sing-alongs, and speeches. That day, Manton Marble wrote to McClellan confidently that the next few days before his nomination in Chicago would be "your only fortnight of peace & quietness for four years." Samuel Barlow, too, was sure of success, writing Marble, "I have no doubt of our ability to elect McClellan and to restore the Union."

With the Republicans in disarray and the war effort stalled, victory seemed a safe prediction. On the eve of the convention, Ben Butler's wife Sarah wrote to her husband, "politically the chances are for McClellan, a strange thing when it was so clearly decided that his career was finished. Lincoln's hopes are less every day." The Republican malcontents conspiring in New York at the home of David Dudley Field concluded it was "useless and inexpedient" to run

Lincoln "against the blind infatuation of the masses in favor of McClellan." The
London *Morning Post* published an epitaph on Lincoln's political career:

> Mr. Lincoln will go down to posterity as the man who could not read the
> signs of the times, nor understand the circumstances and interests of his
> country; . . . who had no political aptitude; who plunged his country into a
> great war without a plan; who failed without excuse, and fell without a
> friend.

As soon as the Democrats convened, however, their own problems came
into view. As James Gordon Bennett put it, "They have a peace leg and a war
leg, but, like a stork by a frog pond, they are as yet undecided which to rest
upon." McClellan and his handlers were War Democrats, whose headquarters
were in New York. The Democratic National Convention, however, was in
Chicago, in the heartland of the Peace Democrats, the Copperheads. The Peace
men were led at the convention by none other than their banished leader
Clement Vallandigham, whom the savvy Lincoln had allowed back into the
country, sensing that he was, by now, more a danger to the Democratic Party
than to himself.

Over the next few days, the Copperheads hammered out a compromise
with the War Democrats that gave the nomination for President to McClellan,
but got a Copperhead as the Vice Presidential nominee, and a Peace platform,
whose most important plank was distilled into the slogan, "The War is a
Failure—Peace Now!"

*   *   *

The Democratic Convention had an astounding effect on dissident
Republicans. It was as if a switch had been thrown, and an electric current had
surged through a central pole and made a thousand scattered iron filings
instantly align. For, as bad as Lincoln may have seemed, he could never be as
bad as the treasonous products of the meeting in Chicago. The Democrats had
chosen George B. McClellan, the man who had battled the Republicans more
fiercely than he ever had the rebels, on a platform written by Clement
Vallandigham, the traitor who peddled peace at any price. From Iowa, Senator
Grimes wrote to Count Gurowski of the change: "One week before the
Chicago convention more than one half of the republicans in the northwest
wanted Lincoln defeated; one week after the convention none of them wanted

him defeated by McClellan." Even Gurowski, the most unrepentant Lincoln-hater in all of Washington, admitted that the Democratic choice "makes Lincoln an anchor of salvation to escape the curse of such a lee shore as McClellan."

And then, on September 3, only three days after the Chicago convention adjourned, a second, even more amazing deliverance arrived at the White House in the form of a telegram from General Sherman in Georgia: "Atlanta is ours and fairly won."

Its six simple words translated a military victory in Georgia into a political miracle unequalled in American history. As the news rang across the country, a reeling Zachary Chandler wrote to his wife, "There has been the most extraordinary change in publick opinion here that ever was known within a week." That same day, Leonard Swett, who had so recently been drafted to ask Lincoln to step aside and make way for a better man, marveled to his wife, "There has never been an instance in which Providence has kindly interposed in our behalf in our national struggles in so marked and essential manner as in the recent Union victories." He explained, "The first gleam of hope was in the Chicago convention. The evident depression of the public caused the peace men to control that convention, and then, just as the public began to shrink from accepting it, God gave us the victory at Atlanta, which made the ship right itself, as a ship in a storm does after a great wave has nearly capsized it." Lincoln's friend A.K. McClure sketched the election year in a stroke, writing, "There was no time between January of 1864 and September 3 of the same year when McClellan would not have defeated Lincoln for President." On September 4, the tide was, incredibly, reversed.

On September 5, the New York Republican malcontents struck their tent, conceding that recent events had made it "the duty of all Unionists to present a united front." A few days later, Thurlow Weed wrote to Seward: "The conspiracy against Mr. Lincoln collapsed on Monday last."

Greeley's skedaddle was the hastiest. On August 30, he told John Nicolay in New York, "I shall fight like a savage in this campaign. I hate McClellan." A week later, a go-between from Lincoln arrived in Greeley's office with an offer of a plum appointment to postmaster general, and the next day the *Tribune* heralded its new allegiance, crying, "Henceforth we fly the banner of ABRAHAM LINCOLN for the next Presidency." By the following week, the Republican ticket was emblazoned on the *Tribune* masthead, where it stayed until the election.

Another recent conspirator, political theorist Francis Lieber, wrote to Sumner that he wished Lincoln could know that people were going to vote against McClellan rather than for him, but then went to work at the Loyal Publication Society in New York, printing and mailing out more than half a million Republican pamphlets with titles like *No Party Now But All for Our Country*.

Meanwhile, Zachary Chandler grudgingly set his teeth and went out to heal party wounds and marshal support behind Lincoln. As he met with other Jacobins ranged against the President, he wrote of his determination—and his reluctance—to his wife:

> I may accomplish nothing, but I would certainly prefer the traitor Jeff Davis to the equal traitor McClelland [sic] for President. . . . I am disgusted beyond the power of language to express & yet here I am. . . . If it was only Abe Lincoln I would say, go to _____ in your own way, I will not stop a second to save you[,] but it is this great nation with all its hopes for the present & future[.] I cannot abandon the effort now.

Ben Wade and Winter Davis still refused to support Lincoln unless he removed conservative Montgomery Blair from the Cabinet. In early September, then, Chandler went to the White House and promised the support of the Radicals, including Frémont, if Lincoln would get rid of Blair. Lincoln agreed. Montgomery Blair, in fact, had seen this coming and had already immolated himself. He had given the President his resignation in June. Lincoln had refused it then, but Blair had told him that he could reconsider any time the political situation demanded it. After Chandler's visit in late September, Lincoln sent a grateful letter to Blair, telling him, "You very well know that this proceeds from no dissatisfaction of mine with you personally or officially. Your uniform kindness has been unsurpassed by that of any friend." But, "The time has come." The dutiful Blair wrote his final resignation that day.

With Blair gone, Wade would stump for Lincoln, though he grumbled to Chandler, "I only wish we could do as well for a better man. . . . Were it not for the country there would be a poetical justice in his being beaten by that stupid ass McClellan, who he persisted in keeping in the service. . . . When I think of those things, I wish the d——l had Old Abe. But the issue is now made up." Winter Davis also promised to speak for Lincoln, but he, too, had to swallow hard. J.K. Herbert wrote in late September, "He says sometimes he feels so disgusted that he cannot talk, and therefore has not said positively that he will speak, yet they expect he will & so do I." Both Wade and Davis campaigned—but they blasted the Democrats rather than glorify Lincoln.

The last man standing among Lincoln's Republican foes was the rival candidate, John Charles Frémont. Finally, under heavy pressure by Chandler and other friends, Frémont wrote a letter grudgingly bowing out of the race. Even as he withdrew, however, he fired a graceless parting shot, writing that he resigned,

> not to aid in the triumph of Mr. Lincoln, but to do my part towards preventing the election of the Democratic candidate.
>
> In respect to Mr. Lincoln, . . . I consider that his administration has been politically, militarily, and financially a failure, and that its necessary continuance is a cause of regret to the country.

Abolitionist Wendell Phillips would never come around. On September 27 he wrote to Elizabeth Cady Stanton in fiery epigrams: "I would cut off both hands before doing anything to aid Abraham Lincoln's election. I wholly distrust his fitness to settle this thing, and indeed his purpose. Lincoln wishes the end; won't consent to the means. I still reject Lincoln's quarter loaf. Justice is still more to me than Union."

Just as the Republicans were cobbling together a united front, an announcement came of another Union victory. On September 19, General Phil Sheridan met General Early's small motley command at Winchester and sent it flying back up the Shenandoah in the largest battle of the war in the Valley, a stunning victory that marked a turning point in the struggle for that strategically important region. As the political stars—party unity, military success, and Election Day—came into alignment, the Republican prospects grew bright. Without a failed war to condemn, Democrat stump speakers spread across the North to attack emancipation and black equality. They hammered the loss of civil liberties, arbitrary arrest, usurpation of unconstitutional powers, an inflated economy—and, as always, they abused the vulgar tyrant, Abraham Lincoln. As one New York Republican elector noted, the campaign "soon became one of great acrimony."

* * *

Democratic editors swung hard at the President. The New York *World* stooped to a malicious lie. It printed a new version of an already well-worn piece of propaganda that, according to his friend Ward Lamon, grieved Lincoln more than any slur ever published about him. This was the "Antietam song-singing" episode, which appeared in the *World* on June 20 and again the next day under the headline, "Lincoln Upon the Battlefield":

> Soon after one of the most desperate and sanguinary battles, Mr. Lincoln visited [George McClellan] and the army.—While on his visit the Commanding General with his staff took him over the field in a carriage and explained to him the plan of the battle, and the particular places where the fight was most fierce. At one point [McClellan] said, "here on this side of this road five hundred of our brave fellows were killed, and just on the other side of the road four hundred more were slain, and right on the other side of that wall five hundred rebels were destroyed. We have buried them where they fell." "I declare," said the President, "this is getting gloomy. Let us drive away." After driving a few rods the President said, "This makes a feller feel gloomy." "Jack," (speaking to a companion) "can't you give us something to cheer us up?" "Give us a song, and give us a lively one." Thereupon Jack [Ward Lamon] struck up, as loud as he could bawl, a comic negro song, which he continued to sing while they were riding off from the battle ground . . . .
>
> We know that this story is incredible, that it is impossible that a man who could be elected President of the United States could so conduct himself over the fresh made graves of the heroic dead.—When this story was told us we said that it was incredible, impossible, but the story is told on such authority that we know it to be true. We tell the story that the people may have some idea of this man, Abraham Lincoln, who is a candidate for four years more of such rule. If any Republican holds up his hands in horror, and says this story can't be true, we sympathize with him from the bottom of our soul; the story can't be true of any man fit for any office of trust, or even for decent society; but the story is every whit true of Abraham Lincoln, incredible and impossible as it may seem.

A doggerel verse was struck up to garnish the tale:

> *Abe may crack his jolly jokes*
> *O'er bloody fields of stricken battle,*
> *While yet the ebbing life-tide smokes*
> *From men that die like butchered cattle*

"Lincoln on the Battlefield" flooded the North in reprints by malignant Democratic journals. Though deeply hurt, Lincoln made no rebuttal to the fable. When Ward Lamon begged him to do so, Lincoln told him, "No, there has already been too much said about this falsehood. Let the thing alone. If I have not established character enough to give the lie to this charge, I can only say that I am mistaken in my own estimate of myself. In politics, every man must skin his own skunk. These fellows are welcome to the hide of this one. Its body has already given forth its unsavory odor."

As Election Day neared, the *World* was joined by the rest of the Democratic hireling press, who savaged Lincoln with a ferocity that drew its strength from desperation.

"If the loyal people of the Union do not set the seal of their condemnation upon Abraham Lincoln at the ballot-box, they will become speedily not only the most wretched, but the most despised people in history," warned the *Louisville Journal*.

"The most powerful monarchy in Europe would not dare commit the outrages which have been put upon us by the Lincoln administration," cried the *Illinois State Register*. "The doom of Lincoln and black republicanism is sealed. Corruption and the bayonet are impotent to save them. . . . The would be despots at Washington must succumb to their fate. Long live the republic!"

"We have no honeyed words for such a ruler as Abraham Lincoln who is a perjured traitor, who has betrayed his country and caused the butchery of hundreds of thousands of the people of the United States in order to accomplish either his own selfish purpose, or to put in force a fanatical, impracticable idea," cried the Newark *Evening Journal*.

"There is some excuse for those who were deceived in 1860; in view of the past four years, there will be no excuse in November next for a repetition of the most supreme blunder ever committed by any people," announced the *Brooklyn Daily Eagle*.

Lincoln "has swapped the Goddess of Liberty for the pate and wool of a nigger," said the *Ohio Statesman*. "He has swapped a land of peace for a desert of graves. . . . He has swapped all these as he once swapped jokes in an old saloon in Illinois."

"May Almighty God forbid that we are to have two terms of the rottenest, most stinking ruinworking small pox ever conceived by friends or mortals," wrote the *Lacrosse* (Wisconsin) *Democrat*, adding that a vote for Lincoln was a vote "for taxes—for Fort Lafayette—for the draft—for usurped power—for suspension of sacred writs—for a nigger millennium—for worthless

"The Commander-in-Chief Conciliates the Soldiers' Vote on the Battlefield." *Carrier and Ives*, October 1864

currency—for a ruined nation—for desolate cities." They suggested an epitaph for Lincoln: "Beneath this turf the Widow Maker lies/Little in everything, except for size."

"The Lincoln Catechism" was reprinted in Democratic screeds across the North. It read in part:

London Fun, November 7, 1863

"The Yankee Guy Fawkes"

Question: What is the Constitution?

Answer: A compact with hell—now obsolete.

Question: What is a President?

Answer: A General agent for negroes.

Question: What is the meaning of the word "liberty"?

Answer: Incarceration in a bastile.

Question: What is the meaning of the word "patriot"?

Answer: A man who loves his country less and the negro more.

Question: What is the meaning of the word "law"?

Answer: The will of the President.

Aristocratic British editors vied with the Democrats in piling up adjectives against Lincoln. The London *Evening Standard* called him a "foul-tongued and ribald punster" who was also the "most despicable tyrant of modern days." The Leeds *Intelligencer* abused him as "that concentrated quintescence [sic] of evil, that Nero in the most shrunken and detestable form of idolatry, that flatulent and indecent jester."

After reading a steady diet of such attacks at home and abroad, an exasperated *Harper's Weekly* published a list, noting, "These are the terms applied by the friends of General McClellan to the President:

Filthy Story-Teller, Ignoramus Abe, Despot, Old Scoundrel, Big Secessionist, Perjurer, Liar, Robber, Thief, Swindler, Braggart, Tyrant, Buffoon, Fiend, Usurper, Butcher, Monster, Land-Pirate, A Long, Lean, Lank, Lantern-Jawed, High-Cheek-Boned, Spavined, Rail-Splitting Stallion.

* * *

All the name-calling would avail the Democrats nothing. Lincoln was acutely aware of the stakes of the election for the country's future, and that he himself embodied the main issues of the campaign. With a sense of purpose sharpened by that understanding, he made himself, by fall, his own campaign manager. Lincoln could not, of course, make public appearances. He still observed the strong taboo against active campaigning by a candidate, and declined to so much as write a general letter to a political meeting. Instead, he labored mightily behind the scenes. As Fessenden commented in early autumn, "The President is too busy looking after the election to think of any thing else."

Little escaped Lincoln's eye, even small details far afield. He managed the speakers' bureau, taking a hand in getting General "Black Jack" Logan away from his command in Georgia so he could stump in Illinois and Indiana, and planning a tour for Gustave Koerner among the Germans of the Midwest. He interfered when he had to, as when he removed Pennsylvania party boss Simon Cameron and replaced him with A. K. McClure after disappointing returns in an October election. Lincoln used his powers of patronage and the purse, both made mighty by the massive scale of the war, and insisted that each of his thousands of appointees act as loyal party workers. They did countless lowly chores, from hiring halls to hanging signs to mailing out literature to swelling crowds at rallies. Government workers—all the way up to Cabinet members—were expected to contribute ten percent of their pay to the Republican Party war chest. If they hesitated, enough were fired to ensure discipline in the rest. People and companies doing business with the government were expected to contribute as well. This produced a tremendous advantage in campaign funding. In the October Pennsylvania election, for instance, the Republicans spent more than half a million dollars to the Democrats' $32,475.

With the size of the army approaching a million men—fully one quarter of the number expected to cast ballots in the election—politicians on both sides knew the soldier vote would be decisive. Sherman and Grant would not endorse their Commander-in-Chief, but Lincoln's decision to go ahead with the draft on September 5 was a huge boost to his popularity in the army, while the Democrats' peace platform hurt them badly among the soldiers. Regiments' straw polls showed an overwhelming preference for Lincoln. He did not take the soldier vote for granted, however. Wagonloads of Republican campaign literature—a million pieces—were dumped into army mailbags.

With such a large part of the population in uniform for the first time in a national election, fights broke out in state legislatures over proposed amendments to their constitutions that would allow soldiers to vote from the field. When states controlled by Democrats—Indiana, Illinois, and New Jersey—would not pass such an amendment, Lincoln prevailed on Generals Sherman and Rosecrans in the West to furlough soldiers from these states to go home to vote, especially in districts where races were close. In the East, too, Lincoln ordered Generals Sheridan and Meade to send home five thousand men each to vote and show themselves at the polls in Pennsylvania, which was still in doubt. Assistant Secretary of War Charles Dana marveled, "All the power and influence of the War Department, then something enormous from the vast expenditure and extensive relations of the war, was employed to secure the re-election of Mr. Lincoln." The interest taken in the political struggle, both in the White House and the War Department, he wrote, "was almost painful."

The October state elections were uncomfortably close, and as late as October 13, only one month before the national election, Lincoln did a tally of the numbers that showed himself barely ahead, with 117 electoral votes to McClellan's 114.

*   *   *

Then, with only three weeks left until the November 8 election day, Lincoln received his third gift in the election season from the fighting front. On October 19 in the Shenandoah Valley Sheridan crushed Early's army in the seesaw Battle of Cedar Creek, where "Little Phil" galloped twenty miles from Winchester to personally direct a turn of the tide in late afternoon. A poet penned an ode called "Sheridan's Ride" that was immediately added to the gospel of Lincoln's campaign, and in the two weeks before election day, it was read to thrilled gatherings across the country.

As the election approached, Lincoln became nervous about rumors of terrorism at the polls. Stanton had been warned that more than five thousand armed Confederates were roaming Illinois, intending to vote there and prevent thousands of loyal citizens from voting. From New York City, too, the War Secretary heard reports that rebel agents intended to start a riot and jam the polls with enemies. Stanton sent General Butler there with an entire regiment to keep the peace.

On Election Day, an anxious Lincoln watched the rain from a White House window, alone. When Noah Brooks arrived at noon, Lincoln fretted, "I am just enough of a politician to know that there was not much doubt about the results of the Baltimore convention, but about this thing I am very far from being certain." As the afternoon wore on, the waiting became unbearable—it was "one of the most solemn days of his life," according to his secretaries—and Brooks wrote that Lincoln "found it difficult to put his mind on any of the routine work of his office, and entreated me to stay with him." As Lincoln waited for results from the polls, he grew melancholy. Nicolay and Hay reported that he "seemed to have a keen and surprised regret that he should be an object in so many quarters of so bitter and vindictive an opposition." Hay heard Lincoln muse sadly, "It is a little singular that I, who am not a vindictive man, should have always been before the people for election in canvasses marked for their bitterness. . . . The contests in which I have been prominent have been marked with great rancor."

That evening at seven o'clock, Lincoln splashed over to the War Office with Hay and Brooks to get the returns with Seward, Stanton, and Charles Dana. While they drummed their fingers in the hush of expectancy for the click of the telegraph key, Lincoln brought a booklet out of his breast pocket and broke the suspense by reading out loud funny stories by Petroleum V. Nasby. Stanton, incensed at Lincoln's antics at such a moment, motioned Dana into the next room, and, Dana said, "I shall never forget the fire of his indignation at what seemed to him to be mere nonsense. The idea that when the safety of the republic was thus at issue . . . the man most deeply concerned . . . could turn aside to read such balderdash and to laugh at such frivolous jests was, to his mind, repugnant, even damnable."

The wires worked badly that evening on account of the storm, but the telegraph finally started to chatter. By midnight Lincoln's victory was secure. He declined to make merry at the assurance of a second term, however, and instead, according to Hay, "went awkwardly and hospitably to work shoveling out the fried oysters." At two o'clock in the morning he opened the War Office door to leave, and was met by a group of cheering serenaders, singing "The Battle Cry of Freedom," accompanied by a brass band. He treated them to an impromptu speech, gave thanks to the Almighty, then waded back to the White House and went to sleep.

Ward Lamon sat all night on a blanket outside the reelected President's door, surrounded by his pistols and bowie knives.

Chapter 32

The War at the End of the War

"Now we see the dregs of his backwardness."

Lincoln won the electoral vote overwhelmingly, 212 to 21, but he did not beat McClellan nearly so sweepingly in the popular vote—"The size of his majority did not come up to the expectation of Lincoln's friends," conceded Carl Schurz. After four years in the presidency, even in the spread-eagle patriotism of a civil war, Lincoln had only barely improved his popular showing in the North, from the 54% who voted for the unknown Railsplitter in 1860, when he had run against three opponents, to the 55% who voted for the Great Emancipator in 1864. In nine states—Maine, New Hampshire, Michigan, Wisconsin, Connecticut, Minnesota, New York, Pennsylvania, and Vermont—his percentage of the vote actually went down. The forty-five percent who voted for McClellan still considered Lincoln and the war a failure, and they lived mainly in cities, where they had proximity to the press. Lincoln lost in all the big cities, including a trouncing of 78,746 to 36,673 in New York. In the key states of New York, Pennsylvania, and Ohio, with their eighty electoral votes, only half a percentage point separated Lincoln and McClellan. A shift of 38,111 votes in a few selected states, less than one percent of the total, would have elected McClellan.

Lincoln had been fortunate in the fact that the army had been only just successful enough to elect him. If it had been more successful, any of a number of ambitious generals could have unseated him. If it had been less successful—failing, for instance, the last-minute victories of September and October—McClellan would have triumphed.

He had been fortunate, too, in the miserable campaign run by the opposition. "I am here by the blunders of the Democrats," Lincoln admitted to Hugh McCulloch early the next year. They had hamstrung themselves with foolish cries for peace in their platform, and supplied ammunition to the Republicans with their treasonous secret societies in the Northwest.

After Sherman's capture of Atlanta in September, a New York Republican had predicted, "No man ever was elected to an important office who will get so

many unwilling and indifferent votes as L. The cause takes the man along."
Now, plenty of Republicans were skeptical of Lincoln's contribution to the
victory. According to Ohio Congressman Lewis D. Campbell, "Nothing but
the undying attachment of our people to the Union has saved us from terrible
disaster. Mr. Lincoln's popularity had nothing to do with it." Count Gurowski
sniffed, "Mr. Lincoln . . . is re-consecrated only as the incidental standard-bearer
of the people's sacred creed. Nothing more." Henry Winter Davis insisted that
people had voted for Lincoln only "to keep out worse people—keeping their
hands on the pit of the stomach the while!" He called Lincoln's reelection "the
subordination of disgust to the necessities of a crisis." George Julian
proclaimed in the House that the people had voted "not that Abraham Lincoln
can save the country, but that they can save it, with him as their servant." Of the
seven presidential elections he had participated in, Julian said, "I remember
none in which the element of personal enthusiasm had a smaller share."
Bostonian Lydia Maria Child expressed the grudging tribute felt by many
Radical Republicans:

> There was no enthusiasm for honest old Abe. There is no beauty in him,
> that men should desire him; there is no insinuating, polished manner, to
> beguile the senses of the people; there is no dazzling military renown; no
> silver flow of rhetoric; in fact, no glittering prestige of any kind surrounds
> him; yet the people triumphantly elected him, in spite of all manner of
> machinations, and notwithstanding the long, long drag upon their
> patience and their resources which this war has produced.

Lincoln's hometown enemy, the *Illinois State Register*, called Lincoln's
reelection "the heaviest calamity that ever befell the nation . . . the farewell to
civil liberty, to a republican form of government, and to the unity of these
states." This, however, was a noisy exception in a generally quiet Democratic
press, which had used up all its rancor in the campaign and was dazed by defeat.

Only the British press had the heart to roast Lincoln with any heat after the
results were in. The London *Punch* published a John Tenniel caricature of
Lincoln as "The Federal Phoenix"—hard, proud, and rising above a fire that
consumed "commerce," "United States Constitution," "free press," "credit,"
"habeas corpus," and "state rights," over the caption:

As the bird of Arabia wrought resurrection
By a flame all whose virtues grew out of what fed it

So the Federal Phoenix has earned re-election
By a holocaust huge of rights, commerce, and credit.

The London *Herald* dismissed his reelection as due "to the strength of his party and to his own lawless abuse of executive power, not to the belief of the people that no better man could have been chosen. . . . Mr. Lincoln is a vulgar,

"The Federal Phoenix"

brutal boor, wholly ignorant of political science, of military affairs, of everything else which a statesman should know." The London *Standard* predicted, "The renewal of Mr. Lincoln's term is the inauguration of a reign of terror. . . . never were issues so momentous placed in so feeble a hand; never was so great a place in history filled by a figure so mean." The aristocratic London *Times*, as usual, arched its brow higher than all the others, proclaiming:

> We can regard the reappointment of Mr. Lincoln as little less than an abdication by the American people of the right of self-government, as an avowed step towards the foundation of a military despotism.
>
> Future historians will probably date from the second presidency of Mr. Lincoln the period when the American Constitution was thoroughly abrogated, and had entered on that transition stage, so well known to the students of history, through which Republics pass on their way from democracy to tyranny.

The response from Richmond was muted. A few journals sounded what even they now realized were the opening notes of their death song. One example will suffice, printed in the *Richmond Dispatch* the day after the election. It has the tired rhythm of a rote recital:

> Yesterday . . . the freest people on earth . . . made a formal surrender of their liberties . . . to a vulgar tyrant . . . whose personal qualities are those of a low buffoon, and whose most noteworthy conversation is a medley of profane jests and obscene anecdotes—a creature who has squandered the lives of millions without remorse and without even the decency of pretending to feel for their misfortunes; who still cries for blood and for money in the pursuit of his atrocious designs.

*   *   *

Most Northerners cared only that Lincoln's war was being won, and, in the weeks after his reelection, his star continued the ascent begun in September with the capture of Atlanta. In December, Sherman's armies cut their communications and disappeared into the *terra incognita* of Georgia, slashing and burning their way toward Savannah on their historic March to the Sea. Grant, meanwhile, held Lee largely immobile around Richmond and Petersburg. The Confederacy was counting its last months of existence.

Strengthened by his reelection and the progress of the armies, Lincoln sought a new harmony with Radicals in Congress over Reconstruction. On December 6, in his Annual Message, he closed with a warning to Southerners: the door to the amnesty he had extended a year earlier was still open, but "the time may come—probably will come—when public duty shall demand that it be closed . . . and more rigorous measures than heretofore shall be adopted." Moreover, he cautioned them, the end of the war would end his war powers, and the people of the South would be thrown on the mercies of the Jacobins in Congress. In his conclusion, he stated blunt terms for peace: "The war will cease on the part of the government, whenever it shall have ceased on the part of those who began it." This was a sterner Lincoln, not the Lincoln who had summoned "the better angels of our nature."

Many saw in it only blood. The Richmond *Sentinel* warned any would-be peacemakers in the South that the Message promised "absolute, unqualified submission, to be followed by spoliation of our property and the Africanization of our country." From Paris, *La France* viewed the Message as a signal of the "maintenance of the destructive policy of which Mr. Lincoln is the . . . instrument," that is, "implacable war, having no parallel for hatred and ferocity, except in the remote ages of barbarism—millions of men slaughtered and thousands of millions of money swallowed up, all to gratify an inflexible pride."

Seeing the Radicals appeased, the Democratic press in the North called the Message ludicrous. "Ridicule would seem to be the first and only weapon to be used against a production so full of nonsense," said *The Crisis*; "Lincoln is a famous joker, and he may have intended his message for a colossal joke." It depicted the country as a charnel-house: "Although the nation is filled with mourning, and the land is fertilized with the blood and bones of our citizens, butchered in a useless war, the chief ruler of the country congratulates the world that there are plenty more to be led to the slaughter." And it heard tyranny in the Message where Lincoln vowed that he would never allow any man to be returned to slavery, calling it "the ultimatum of the despot flung in the faces of the people, at once a threat and a defiance."

The Radicals, too, held aloof. Henry Winter Davis demanded a test of strength on December 15, when he ordered a House vote on his resolution that Congress should make foreign policy, and that it was the President's duty to obey. John Farnsworth, a Lincoln ally, moved to table the resolution, and Farnsworth's suppression passed 69 to 63 with 50 abstaining, in what may be taken as an indication of Lincoln's support in the House: 69 with him, 63 against him, and 50 wavering. For the Radicals, even this lukewarm backing for

Lincoln was bitter news. Elizabeth Cady Stanton wrote to Susan B. Anthony on December 29, "[Wendell] Phillips has just returned from Washington. He says the radical men feel that they are powerless and checkmated. Winter Davis told him the game was up—'Lincoln with his immense patronage can do what he pleases; the only hope is an appeal to the people.' They turn to such men as Phillips to say what politicians dare not say."

Phillips, Davis, and the other Radical Republicans still doubted Lincoln's desire to end slavery. They remembered his letter of the previous April to *Frankfort* (Kentucky) *Commonwealth* editor Albert G. Hodges, written to soothe Kentuckians who resented losing their slaves to enlistment in the Union army. In his letter, he had defended the Emancipation Proclamation with the plea, "I claim not to have controlled events, but confess plainly that events have controlled me." Radicals read the disclaimer as a sign of weakness, and pointed to the fact that even now, in December of 1864, Lincoln's promise of freedom was still just a promise. The great majority of those who had been slaves in 1861 were still in bondage, and the legal status of those who had been freed was still in question. The war was winding down, and the war powers on which the Emancipation Proclamation was based would soon disappear. Would Lincoln allow emancipation to end with the war? they wondered.

Lincoln answered by throwing all his influence behind the passage of the Thirteenth Amendment, which prohibited slavery in any part of the United States. With Lincoln recommending it as a "king's cure" for the evils of slavery, the landmark amendment passed the Senate. On January 31, 1865, after a close vote against Democratic opposition in the House, the Speaker, with trembling voice, announced the Amendment's fate: "The Joint Resolution has passed," he cried, and, in the account of Noah Brooks:

> For a moment there was a pause of utter silence, as if the voices of the dense mass of spectators were choked by strong emotion. Then there was an explosion, a storm of cheers, the like of which probably no Congress of the United States ever heard before. Strong men embraced each other with tears. The galleries and aisles were bristling with standing, cheering crowds. The air was stirred with a cloud of women's handkerchiefs waving and floating; hands were shaking; men threw their arms about each other's neck, and cheer after cheer, and burst after burst followed. Full ten minutes elapsed before silence returned.

The boom of a hundred cannon with heavy charges announced the great moment from Capitol Hill.

Radicals, however, still feared that, now that he was elected, now that the war was almost won, and now that the arrow of the Thirteenth Amendment was speeding toward the heart of slavery, Lincoln would return to his first friends—the War Democrats and the conservative Republicans—to give him ballast in the coming collision over Reconstruction. They pointed to Louisiana as proof that, while Lincoln had given slaves their civil rights, he would still deny their political rights out of tenderness for the feelings of Southern whites. Radical men deplored the President's instructions, the previous February, to hold new Louisiana elections according to the 1860 laws that barred blacks from voting, and saw a chance to foil Lincoln now that his new Louisiana government was seeking admission into the Union.

Charles Sumner fought it hotly in the Senate; he was violently opposed to the admission of any state where ex-slaves were still denied ballots. In addition, he recognized that Louisiana's readmission would be a benchmark for Reconstruction of the entire South according to Lincoln's lax policies, and dreaded a system where all the returning governments would be beholden to the President. Sumner charged that the Louisiana government was gotten up by voters "drummed up from the riff-raff of New Orleans," and called it "a mere seven months abortion, begotten by the bayonet, in criminal conjunction with the spirit of caste, and born before its time, rickety, unformed, unfinished, whose continued existence will be a burden, a reproach, and a wrong." Benjamin Wade, too, denounced Lincoln's ten percent principle as "the most absurd and impracticable that ever haunted the imagination of a statesman." Faced with the hostility of Sumner, Wade, and their fellow Radical senators, Lincoln withdrew Louisiana's bid for readmission, meaning to take it up again in December, when Congress reconvened.

Immediately after the Louisiana defeat, on February 2, Lincoln slipped out of Washington—and out from under the fierce scrutiny of earnest men from all sides—and steamed for Hampton Roads, Virginia, to meet privately with three Confederate commissioners to discuss terms for peace. At this, "The perturbation in Washington was something which cannot readily be described," according to Brooks. "The radicals were in a fury of rage; the excitement in and around the Capitol rose to a fever heat." *This is exactly what President McClellan would have done!* they cried. Rumors floated back that Lincoln had offered to block emancipation if the South would return; one had it that Lincoln had written the word "Union" at the top of a piece of paper and shoved it across the table to the rebels, saying, "Let me have that one condition and you can write below it whatever peace terms you choose." Thaddeus Stevens bellowed in the House that if the country were to vote over again for President, Benjamin Butler, not Abraham Lincoln, would be their choice. In a ten-thousand-word speech, George Julian summed up the war as a series of blunders by a faltering administration, hinting at impeachment and trial. Even in the Cabinet there was muttering. Diarist Gideon Welles complained, "None of the Cabinet were advised of this move, and without exception, I think it struck them unfavorably that the Chief Magistrate should have gone on such a mission."

The Hampton Roads Conference failed to produce peace—"Fools meet and separate" was Zack Chandler's epitaph of the episode—and when Lincoln returned and his report was read in the House on February 10, the reading began amid stony silence, with every listener motionless in the packed chamber. When the President's message reached the part that listed his three indispensable terms for peace—that national authority be restored throughout the states, that there would be no going back on the slavery question, and that there would be no peace short of the disbanding of the rebel armies—heads nodded as Lincoln's iron-backed stance became clear. Smiles came with the recognition that the conference had achieved Lincoln's purpose of showing that the South was not yet willing to return on any terms acceptable to the North, and that the war effort must continue. The listeners' scorn turned to praise for the "noble course" which the President had taken.

The stony silence resumed when Lincoln revealed privately to his Cabinet the generous terms he had tendered to the peace commissioners, which included payment of $400 million to slaveowners for the loss of their property. If his offer brought peace, the Union would save that much in war costs, he argued, and it would save soldiers' lives. But his advisers were appalled. Lincoln, ready to urge his plan in Congress if he could find even one Cabinet supporter, was disappointed. "It did not meet with favor, but was dropped," Welles curtly recorded in his diary.

*   *   *

Fortunately for Lincoln, his enemies in Congress failed also to agree on a Reconstruction plan, and with no hostile bills to torment him, he could devote his attention to his Second Inaugural Address. He had been pondering the meaning of the war at least since his "Meditation on the Divine Will," seeking to discover how God was working in the agony of the national trial. Increasingly, in the weeks and months before his second inaugural, his conversations with visitors turned to theology. In the last days of his first term, he developed his conclusions in private and set them to the cadences of the King James Bible.

Lincoln thought and wrote while visitors from all over the North filled Washington hotel rooms by the tens of thousands. Thousands of Confederate deserters, too, lurked in the streets and alleys, and Secretary of War Stanton, vigilant to the danger while the Confederacy was in its last desperate hours, marshaled an army for Lincoln's safekeeping much larger than the paltry guard Winfield Scott had assembled four years earlier. All roads leading to Washington were patrolled. The bridges over the Potomac were clogged with sentries. Sharpshooters once more looked down from housetops, and every knot of onlookers was leavened with plainclothes detectives.

It had rained for days leading up to the ceremony, and by Inauguration Day the unpaved streets were rivers of mud and standing water ten inches deep. March 4 dawned wind-whipped and drizzling, with bursts of rain. As the crowds gathered in the ooze, Brooks wrote, "Flocks of women streamed around the Capitol, in most wretched, wretched plight; crinoline was smashed, skirts bedaubed, and moiré antique, velvet, laces and such dry goods were streaked with mud from end to end." The inaugural ritual, too, was a chaotic mess. Lincoln was not in the parade on the way to the Capitol; he had ignored it and gone there earlier that morning to sign bills. On the procession down Pennsylvania Avenue, horses and carriages got in a tangle that took twenty minutes to unsnarl. Gideon Welles wrote disgustedly, "There was great want of arrangement and completeness in the ceremonies. All was confusion and without order—a jumble."

Even standing in mud up to their ankles, however, everyone was buoyed by the expectation of a triumphal address from the President, full of personal vindication and the imminent victory of the Union armies. Instead, they heard Lincoln hurl a lightning bolt, one of the briefest Inaugural Addresses ever spoken, with no place for cheering.

After he rose and took his place before the multitude, Lincoln passed over his reelection in one sentence, saying merely, "In this second appearing, . . . there is less occasion for an extended address than there was at the first." He mentioned nothing he had said or done during his term, and dismissed the war news with another single sentence: "The progress of our arms, upon which all else chiefly depends, is as well known to the public as to myself; and it is, I trust, reasonably satisfactory and encouraging to all." After shrugging off the causes for jubilation that forty thousand people had journeyed to hear, Lincoln paused. The crowd stood silent.

When Lincoln continued, he did not indulge in vindication, but instead drew parallels between the North and the South on the war: "All dreaded it—all sought to avert it. . . . Both parties deprecated war." He then drew his only distinction between the warring sides: "But one of them would make war rather than let the nation survive; and the other would accept war rather than let it perish." It was here that the crowd cheered for the only time. Lincoln waited for the clamor to die down, then finished his second paragraph with four simple words: "And the war came."

He passed on to four sentences on slavery. When he said, "All knew that this interest was, somehow, the cause of the war," there was some applause. But the crowd would be still for the rest of the speech.

Lincoln sustained the note of parity: "Neither side expected for the war, the magnitude, or the duration, which it has already attained. Neither anticipated that the cause of the conflict might cease with, or even before, the conflict itself should cease. Each looked for an easier triumph, and a result less fundamental and astounding. Both read the same Bible, and pray to the same God; and each invokes His aid against the other. . . . The prayers of both could not be answered; that of neither has been answered fully." Lincoln then ventured one lone Northern criticism of the South—"It may seem strange that any men should dare to ask a just God's assistance in wringing their bread from the sweat of other men's faces"—then carefully balanced it by reminding his listeners of Jesus' injunction from the Sermon on the Mount, "but let us judge not that we be not judged."

Lincoln now warmed to the heart of his message, and passed from the justice of men to the justice of God. "The Almighty has His own purposes," he began, and went again to the Gospel of Matthew: "'Woe unto the world because of offences! for it must needs be that offences come; but woe to that man by whom the offence cometh!'" He then made the crucial connection: "If we shall suppose that American Slavery is one of those offences which, in the providence of God, must needs come, but which, having continued through His appointed time, He now wills to remove, and that He gives to both North and South, this terrible war, as the woe due to those by whom the offence came, shall we discern therein any departure from those divine attributes which the believers in a Living God always ascribe to Him?"

He then made a short appeal—"Fondly do we hope, fervently do we pray, that this mighty scourge of war may speedily pass away"—and after this soft note, plunged on with a terrible power, invoking the Old Testament doctrine of exact retribution, saying, "Yet, if God wills that it continue, until all the wealth piled by the bond-man's two hundred and fifty years of unrequited toil shall be sunk, and until every drop of blood drawn with the lash, shall be paid by another drawn with the sword, as was said three thousand years ago, so still it must be said 'the judgments of the Lord, are true and righteous altogether.'" This was an austere and awesome creed, but also a forgiving one. It would rather worship a just God than punish a defeated enemy.

Lincoln closed with a reminder of the humble tasks remaining to men, in a benediction that was like a laying-on of hands: "With malice toward none; with charity for all; with firmness in the right, as God gives us to see the right, let us strive on to finish the work we are in; to bind up the nation's wounds; to care for him who shall have borne the battle, and for his widow, and his orphan—to do all which may achieve and cherish a just, and a lasting peace, among ourselves, and with all nations."

Lincoln then took the oath of office with his right hand on an open Bible, and, when he was done, leaned over and kissed it. The crowd cheered, the guns exploded, and Lincoln rode back in his carriage to the White House.

As at Gettysburg, his Address was over before many knew it had begun. It had been only six or seven minutes long, and people were still arriving when it ended. Frederick Douglass remarked on the solemnity of the few moments Lincoln spoke. "There was a leaden stillness about the crowd," he wrote. "The address sounded more like a sermon than a state paper." Douglass said he had clapped his hands in gladness at the words, but when he looked around, he "saw in the faces of many about me expressions of widely different emotion."

Lincoln's Address, one of the rare eruptions of pure religion in the history of American politics, bewildered many. The early reaction was mixed. On March 15, in a letter to Thurlow Weed, Lincoln was downbeat about its immediate reception:

> I believe it is not immediately popular. Men are not flattered by being shown that there has been a difference of purpose between the Almighty and them. To deny it, however, in this case, is to deny that there is a God governing the world. It is a truth which I thought needed to be told; and as whatever of humiliation there is in it, falls most directly on myself, I thought others might afford for me to tell it. Yours truly

A. Lincoln

Certainly the address was not immediately popular with the Chicago *Times*, which announced, "We did not conceive it possible that even Mr. Lincoln could produce a paper so slip shod, so loose-jointed, so puerile, not alone in literary construction, but in its ideas, its sentiments, its grasp." The *Times* was joined in the East by the savage New York *World*, which scorned the inaugural address "with a blush of shame and wounded pride," and deplored, "The pity of it, that a divided nation should neither be sustained in this crisis of agony by words of wisdom nor cheered with words of hope." The *World* condemned Lincoln's "substitution of religion for statesmanship" and his taking "refuge in piety." "The President's theology," it scoffed, "smacks as strong of the dark ages as does Pope Pius IX's policies."

Lincoln was no doubt aware that the powerful *New York Herald* and New York *Evening Post* had both been disappointed. They complained that he had said nothing about the issues of the day. The *Herald* was particularly unkind, calling the Second Inaugural "an effort to avoid any commitment regarding our domestic or foreign affairs," "a little speech of 'glittering generalities' used only to fill in the program." Lincoln had surely read, too, the comments of his one constant friend among the titans of the press, the *New York Times*, which was displeased that, "He makes no boasts of what he has done, or promises of what he will do. He does not reexpound the principles of the war; does not redeclare the worth of the Union; does not reproclaim that absolute submission to the Constitution is the only peace." And Lincoln must have been disappointed that Horace Greeley's New York *Tribune* declined to write any comment on the Second Inaugural whatsoever, printing it with only the bland kiss-off, "Thus in a day we retire and elevate our citizens [referring to the old and new Vice Presidents], but the Government is the same; founded not on the rulers but on the integrity of the people." Greeley published a more frank appraisal of Lincoln a few days later:

> We are not, it is known, among the idolators, not even the adulators, of . . . Lincoln. He was not our first choice for president in 1860, nor yet in 1864. We are among those who hold that the rescue of our country . . . will justly redound to the lasting honor of her Loyal Millions, not to that of any particular man, whether general or civilian. If Mr. Lincoln had never been born, or had never played a part in public affairs, . . . the net result would have been nearly the same.

* * *

After thus dismissing Lincoln's contribution to the Union almost entirely, Greeley in the same editorial feared for his health. Lincoln had lost thirty pounds in the last few months. Always lanky, he was now shockingly gaunt and sunken-cheeked. "His face was ragged with care," Greeley remarked later, "and seamed with thought and trouble. It looked care-plowed, tempest-tossed, and weather-beaten, as if he were some tough old mariner, who had for years been beating up against wind and tide, unable to make his port or find safe anchorage." Joshua Speed, visiting Lincoln about the same time, said, "He looked jaded and weary," "worn down in health & spirits." The President admitted to Speed, "I am very unwell, my feet & hands are always cold—I suppose I ought to be in bed." Mary Lincoln told her dresser, Elizabeth Keckley, "Poor Mr. Lincoln is looking so broken-hearted, so completely worn out, I fear he will not get through the next four years." Ms. Keckley noticed, "In their private chamber, away from the curious eyes of the world, the President and his wife wore sad, anxious faces."

After an exhausting triple ritual—the Inaugural, the evening reception (where he shook six thousand hands), and the Inaugural Ball two evenings later—Lincoln dreaded the prospect of a flood of office-seekers, remembering the chaos at the beginning of his first term. He told a friend that it seemed as if every visitor "darted at him, and with thumb and finger carried off a portion of his vitality." He told Senator Clark of New Hampshire, "It seems as though the bare thought of going through again what I did the first year here, would crush me." Ten days after the inauguration, he was sick in bed, "worn down," according to Noah Brooks, "by the constant pressure of office-seekers and legitimate business, so that for a few days he was obliged to deny himself to all comers."

When, on the morning of March 20, he received an invitation from General Grant—"Can you not visit City Point for a day or two? I would like very much to see you and I think the rest would do you good"—he leaped at the opportunity. By March 23, he was on board the *River Queen* with Mary and Tad, steaming away from Washington toward the comparative calm of the battlefront. Welles explained in his diary:

> The President has gone to the front, partly to get rid of the throng that is pressing upon him, though there are speculations of a different character. He makes his office much more laborious than he should. Does not generalize and takes upon himself questions that properly belong to the Departments, often causing derangement and irregularity. The more he

yields, the greater the pressure upon him. It has now become such that he is compelled to flee. There is no doubt he is much worn down.

Lincoln lived aboard the *River Queen*, tied up at City Point on the James River near Richmond, for two full weeks, far longer than he had ever been away from Washington. From there, he could hear the thunder of the Union artillery at Petersburg and see the cannon flashes reflected against the clouds at night.

At City Point, Lincoln took full advantage of the fact that the Radicals were a hundred miles away. On March 28 he met privately with Generals Sherman and Grant and gave confidential instructions for the generous terms he wanted extended to the defeated Confederate armies. Here he was fortunate in the conservative politics of his top generals—if they had been Radicals like Frémont and Butler, his instructions would have been flatly rejected.

*   *   *

After the meeting, Sherman and Grant returned to their commands. Within the next two weeks the heavy fruit of the Army of the Potomac's four years of bloody toil suddenly fell from the branch.

On April 2, the defenses around the rebel capital collapsed, and Lee and his embattled Army of Northern Virginia evacuated Richmond and Petersburg and fled west. At 11:15 a.m. on April 3, 1865, fifteen-year-old telegraph operator Willie Kettles bent over the receiver at the War Office in Washington as it clicked out a message "From Richmond." It was Grant. Richmond was captured. Within minutes, the news was sped to all the bureaus. Men leaned out the windows of the public buildings bellowing, "Richmond has fallen!" while others ran out into the streets crying the news to unbelieving passersby. Newspaper offices were instantly at work stamping out extras with breathless headlines: "Glory!!! Hail Columbia!!! Hallelujah!!! Richmond Ours!!!"

Noah Brooks chronicled the carnival that spread within minutes to all parts of the ecstatic capital:

> In a moment of time the city was ablaze with excitement the like of which was never seen before; and everybody who had a piece of bunting spread it to the breeze; from one end of Pennsylvania Avenue to the other the air seemed to burn with the bright hues of the flag. The sky was shaken by a grand salute of eight hundred guns, fired by order of the Secretary of War—three hundred for Petersburg and five hundred for Richmond.

Almost by magic the streets were crowded with hosts of people, talking, laughing, hurrahing, and shouting in the fullness of their joy. Men embraced one another, "treated" one another, made up old quarrels, renewed old friendships, marched through the streets arm in arm, singing and chatting in that happy sort of abandon which characterizes our people when under the influence of a great and universal happiness. The atmosphere was full of the intoxication of joy. . . . Bands of music, apparently without any special direction or formal call, paraded the streets, and boomed and blared from every public place, until the air was resonant with the expression of the popular jubilation in all the national airs, not forgetting "Dixie."

Rejoicing crowds clamored for speeches, and dozens of public men, suddenly silver-tongued in the euphoria, improvised jubilant speeches on every corner. In jammed saloons, champagne corks popped and glasses overflowed while outside church bells clanged, flags waved, and fire engines rushed through the streets behind galloping teams, blowing off blasts of steam.

Lincoln, meanwhile, was shambling through the rubble-strewn streets of Richmond in his awkward, flat-footed gait, with twelve wary Union sailors going before and behind, carrying carbines. Tumbling, shouting freedmen, wild with delight, surrounded the man they recognized as the Great Emancipator. But Lincoln's was no parade of personal triumph. His mission in Richmond was to prevent a bloody, drawn-out guerrilla war fought by rebel armies that might melt away into the countryside within days. He met with rebel Assistant Secretary of War John Campbell, now the only Confederate official remaining in Richmond, and asked him to convene the Virginia Legislature to send Lee's soldiers back to their homes.

Lincoln's plans were swiftly overtaken by events. During the week that followed Grant ran Lee's starving army to ground near Appomattox Court House, sixty miles west of Richmond. On the evening of April 9, when Lincoln returned to Washington, a boy ran up to him with a telegram: Lee had surrendered.

In the rainy dark of Washington the next morning, 500 cannon boomed the news of Lee's defeat, sending shock waves that broke the windows along Lafayette Square. The news came on the heels of an entire week of celebration in the capital. Ever since the seizure of Richmond, Washington had been a constant whirl of parties, bonfires, and parades. At night, the whole city was one grand, shimmering lake of light. Lamps, lanterns, candles, gas jets, and fireworks illuminated all the public buildings and most of the residences. The new Capitol dome burned like a floating beacon. Six thousand candles shone in the windows of the Patent Office, and 3,500 lit the Government Post office. The War Department and the Treasury were swathed in colored flame. Fireworks made a comet trail of Pennsylvania Avenue, from the White House to Capitol Hill. Robert E. Lee's Arlington mansion glowed in candlelight on its hill across the Potomac, and rockets and colored lights blazed from its lawn.

With Lee's army conquered and Lincoln returned from City Point, a throng of three thousand made their way up Pennsylvania Avenue in the mud and rain. They gathered under the front portico of the White House to sing "The Star Spangled Banner" while brass bands blew and howitzers thundered, and they cried out for a victory speech from the President himself. Lincoln appeared at his second story window, but declined to make any remarks, telling them he was planning a speech for the following evening and didn't want to "dribble it all out" before he gave it some thought.

That afternoon, the Radicals had held an informal meeting on the steps of Willard's Hotel. They rehearsed their vision of a South scorched, with no stone left upon a stone, where the last would be first and the first would be last. They blasted the "bribe of unconditional forgiveness" Grant had just extended to Lee at Appomattox and blamed Lincoln for Grant's leniency. They stacked their ammunition for the war at the end of the war, the struggle with Lincoln over Reconstruction. The fast-approaching showdown was the subject of Noah Brooks' next dispatch to the Sacramento *Union*:

> Those who are ready to fight the President on Reconstruction . . . are only waiting for the occasion to pounce upon the President's expected clemency toward the offending rebel leaders. . . . The extremists are thirsting for a general hanging, and if the president fails to gratify their desires in this direction, they will be glad, for it will afford them more pretexts for the formation of a party which shall be pledged to "a more vigorous policy."

The next night, a crowd gathered in a shrouding mist on the White House lawn as bands played patriotic songs and fireworks crackled and lit up the misty darkness with bouquets of color. "There was something terrible in the enthusiasm" of the people who waited for Lincoln to appear, wrote Noah Brooks. The multitude, in their moment of triumph, were ready to be swept away at a word from their leader. When Lincoln appeared at his second story window, an ocean of cheers crashed against the walls of the White House, and he waited long minutes for it to subside.

When he spoke, however, he spoke not to spark a celebration, but to deliver a closely argued proposal on Reconstruction, read intently from sheets of paper to avoid any misstatements. "The speech was longer than most people had expected, and of a different character," noted Brooks. The jubilant crowd was soon silent, its elation punctured by Lincoln's attention to the serious business of making governments from nothing.

Much of the speech was given to a defense of Louisiana. He used a folksy metaphor to make his point: "Concede that the new government of Louisiana is only to what it should be as the egg is to the fowl, we shall sooner have the fowl by hatching the egg than smashing it." He continued to hope that the South would grant the vote to intelligent blacks and those who had been soldiers, but he would not insist. Here was his challenge to the Radicals—if they wanted to push him to extremes, he would fight them from the middle ground.

According to Brooks, "it was a silent, intent, perhaps surprised multitude" that heard Lincoln's speech. By the end, many of his listeners had drifted off out of disappointment or boredom. There was no ovation at the end as there had been at the beginning. What was left of the crowd wandered off quietly, puzzled.

The New York *Tribune* said the speech "fell dead, wholly without effect on the audience," and that it "caused a great disappointment and left a painful impression." A friend of Charles Sumner, Edward L. Pierce, came away with the sense that, "The speech was not in keeping with what was in men's minds. The people had gathered, from an instinctive impulse, to rejoice over a great and final victory; and they listened with respect, but with no expression of enthusiasm, except that the quaint simile of 'the egg' drew applause. The more serious among them felt that the president's utterances on the subject were untimely, and that his insistence at such an hour on his favorite plan was not the harbinger of peace among the loyal supporters of the government."

"Sumner," Pierce said, "was thoughtful and sad when the speech was reported to him; for he saw at hand another painful controversy." Sumner had not attended the celebration, even declining an invitation from Mary Lincoln to watch the celebration from a window adjacent to the President out of fear that it would signal his approval of Lincoln's message. Now, to his friend and confidant Franz Lieber, he wrote: "The President's speech and other things augur confusion and uncertainty in the future, with hot controversy. Alas! Alas!"

Sumner rose to publicly challenge Lincoln's analogy of the eggs and the fowls. "The eggs of crocodiles can produce only crocodiles," he contended, "and it is not easy to see how eggs laid by military power can be hatched into an American State." He was encouraged in his opposition by baskets full of letters condemning the President's charity. "Magnanimity is the great word with the disloyal who think to tickle the president's ear with it," wrote one New Yorker. "Magnanimity is one thing and weakness is another. I know you are near the throne and you must guard its honor. . . . The Blacks are entitled to all the rights that white men are bound to Respect. . . . A universal amnesty must not be granted. Never were men more guilty. The honor of the country requires a sacrifice and it cannot be dispensed with." R.F. Fuller of Boston wrote to Sumner that Lincoln's Louisiana plan was "wicked and blasphemous," betraying blacks with easy compromises. "No power but God ever has or could have forced him up to the work he has been instrumental of; and now we see the dregs of his backwardness."

Neither did the Democrats applaud Lincoln's gentle, conservative plans. The New York *World* printed its view that he was rudderless: "Mr. Lincoln gropes, in his speech, like a traveler in an unknown country without a map," it said, calling attention to "the vagueness, indecision, and emptiness of the speech," and charging that he had "said nothing, or what comes so near to nothing that he might as well have not broken silence at all." The *World* did rejoice, however, in the heat Lincoln was receiving from Radicals over the speech, informing its readers, "The Washington telegrams to the *Tribune* foam over with rage." The *New York Herald*, too, reported "the more radical of the Republicans much chagrined at the indications of a disposition to heal up existing difficulties." Noah Brooks' dispatch to the Sacramento *Union* said, "The radicals . . . are as virulent and bitter as ever, and they have gladly seized upon this occasion to attempt to reorganize the faction which fought against Lincoln's nomination. These men were the bitter opponents of new Louisiana in the last Congress, and they are enraged that the President should dare to utter his sentiments as antagonistic to theirs."

* * *

While the Radicals anguished over Lincoln's leniency toward the rebels and regretted that he had not gone far enough in demanding black suffrage, there were others listening to Lincoln's Reconstruction speech who were outraged that he had gone so far. When he uttered the words, "I would myself prefer that [voting rights] were now conferred on the very intelligent [blacks], and on those who serve our cause as soldiers," it was the first time any President had publicly advocated giving blacks the vote.

"That means nigger citizenship," muttered an angry man in the crowd that evening. He turned to one of his companions and urged him to shoot Lincoln on the spot. When his friend refused, the man turned to his other companion and growled, "Now, by God, I'll put him through. That is the last speech he will ever make." The man was John Wilkes Booth.

Threats of assassination had blighted Lincoln's presidency since before he took office—the Baltimore threat on his approach to Washington had been a spectacular example. In his desk he kept an envelope labeled "Assassination" which bulged with more than eighty death threats, from all sides. His secretary estimated that he received about one a day, observing that, "Not all of these letters, by any means, came from professed rebels; there was no want of variety in the avowed causes for hatred." The times were so violent that assassination was threatened not only in the private mails, but also in the public print. During the previous election campaign, Wisconsin's *LaCrosse Democrat* told its readers, "If Abraham Lincoln should be reelected for another term of four years of such wretched administration, we hope that a bold hand will be found to plunge the dagger into the tyrant's heart for the public welfare."

With so much danger, when so much was at risk, what was most remarkable about Lincoln's security was that it was so lax. Political assassinations were alien to America. In the Old World, it was thought, such extreme measures were necessary to remove tyrants, but never in a republic whose leaders could be removed at the next election day. Lincoln's closest advisor, William Seward, had said, "Assassination is not an American practice or habit, and one so vicious and so desperate cannot be engrafted into our political system. This conviction of mine has steadily gained strength since the Civil War began. Every day's experience confirms it." Lincoln was of the same opinion. When one evening General Butler rode with him four miles to the Soldiers' Home, Butler was appalled that there was no guard, and protested, "I think you peril too much. We have passed a half dozen places where a well-directed bullet might have taken you off." Lincoln reassured him, "Oh, assassination of public officers is not an American crime."

Besides, being accessible was part of Lincoln's job. The White House belonged to the public, and it was part of the republican tradition that anybody could meet with his President face to face. Lincoln, in fact, was irritated by arrangements for his personal safety. John Nicolay wrote that the President "had himself so sane a mind, and a heart so kindly, even to his enemies, that it was hard for him to believe in political hatred so deadly as to lead to murder." William Crook, Lincoln's guard, testified, "He hated being on his guard, and the fact that it was necessary to distrust his fellow-Americans saddened him. . . . Both from his own feelings and as a matter of policy, he did not want it blazoned over the country that it had been found necessary to guard the life of the President of the United States from assassination. It was not wise—especially at this critical time—to admit so great a lack of confidence in the people. He was sensitive about it, too. It hurt him to admit it." As Lincoln told Stanton, "It is important that the people know I come among them without fear."

Lincoln, in fact, had developed a curious indifference to his own safety. His lack of concern sprang from a profound fatalism. He had come to see a grand design in his election as President at a time of such grave danger to the Union, and was convinced that his fate was not in his own hands. Noah Brooks reported that one night, after walking with Lincoln, "I could not help saying that I thought his going to and fro in the darkness of the night, as it was usually his custom, often alone and unattended, was dangerous recklessness. That night, in deference to his wife's anxious appeal, he had provided himself with a thick oaken stick. He laughed as he showed me this slight weapon, and said, but with some seriousness: 'I long ago made up my mind that if anybody wants to kill me, he will do it. If I wore a shirt of mail, and kept myself surrounded by a body-guard, it would be all the same. There are a thousand ways of getting at a man if it is desired that he should be killed.'"

For much of the war, Lincoln was alone in his room in the evenings with no guards at the entrances to the White House. His secretaries stayed up late, remembered one, working "with a sharp eye and ear open for the footstep in the hall," feeling that "in some vague and unaccountable way we were 'on guard.'" A horrified visitor remarked on "the utterly unprotected condition of the president's person, and the fact that any assassin or maniac, seeking his life, could enter his presence without the interference of a single armed man to hold him back. The entrance-doors, and all doors on the official side of the building, were open at all hours of the day, and very late into the evening; and I many times entered the mansion, and walked up to the rooms of the two private secretaries, as late as nine or ten o'clock at night, without seeing or being challenged by a single soul." Lincoln explained to him, "It would never do for a President to have drawn sabres at his door, as if he were an emperor."

Stanton placed a cavalry guard at the gates of the White House for a while, but, as Lincoln chuckled privately to a friend, he "worried until he got rid of it." When Stanton provided a cavalry detachment to accompany him to and from the Soldiers' Home, Lincoln complained that they were too noisy—"he and Mrs. Lincoln couldn't hear themselves talk for the clatter of their sabres and spurs," he told a guard, and, "as many of them appeared new hands and very awkward, he was more afraid of being shot by the accidental discharge of one of their carbines or revolvers, than of any attempt on his life." Furthermore, he thought it futile: "He said it seemed to him like putting up the gap in only one place when the fence was down all along." When he could, he escaped his protectors, with chilling results. One evening in August of 1864, when Lincoln was riding to the Soldiers' Home alone on horseback, someone fired a shot at him, sending a bullet through the crown of his stovepipe hat.

To those most vexed about his safety, he was a constant worry, walking at night through the streets of Washington alone or with a single companion, or strolling unguarded through the wooded White House grounds to the War Department to read the day's dispatches. His habit of attending the theater accompanied only by Mary and one or two friends was particularly exasperating to U.S. Marshal Ward Lamon, who offered to resign after one such episode in late 1864, writing:

> Tonight, as you have done on several previous occasions, you went unattended to the theatre. When I say unattended, I mean that you went alone with Charles Sumner and a foreign minister, neither of whom could defend himself against an assault from any able-bodied woman in this city. And you know, or ought to know, that your life is sought after, and will be taken unless you and your friends are cautious; for you have many enemies within our lines.

Lamon's last sentence alluded to the sharp spike of malice toward Lincoln in the months after his reelection, as dissenting Northerners and ground-under-heel Southerners woke to the awful dawn of four more years of Lincoln's "abuses." Now that his enemies saw there would be no quick end to his term, a new swell of hostility threatened. There was an ugly temper in Washington as soldiers in blue began to be outnumbered by men in tattered gray. Knots of aimless, hard-looking men, the deserters of Lee's army, drifted steadily into the capital in the last months of the war—more than a thousand in

February, almost three thousand more in March. Nervous citizens were constantly on the alert for the ragged bands roaming the streets.

*   *   *

All caution was forgotten, however, in the euphoria after the capture of Richmond and Lee's surrender. And in the days around Lincoln's Reconstruction speech, "Washington was a little delirious. Everybody was celebrating," according to William Crook:

> The city became disorderly with the men who were celebrating too hilariously. Those about the President lost somewhat of the feeling, usually present, that his life was not safe. It did not seem possible that, now that the war was over and the government . . . had been so magnanimous in its treatment of General Lee, after President Lincoln had offered himself a target for Southern bullets in the streets of Richmond and had come out unscathed, there could be danger. For my part, I had drawn a full breath of relief after we got out of Richmond, and had forgotten to be anxious since.

On April 14, Good Friday, Lincoln was himself buoyant, breathing deeply of Washington's ongoing jubilee. The war was all but won. Sherman was expected hourly to telegraph an announcement of the surrender of the last large rebel army. It was the fourth anniversary of Sumter, and that day in Charleston, the festivities called for a speech by the Reverend Henry Ward Beecher and a raising of the Stars and Stripes over the fort to the roar of massed cannon.

At the Cabinet meeting that morning, newly appointed Attorney General James Speed thought he had never seen Lincoln in better spirits. Frederick Seward, sitting in for his injured father, wrote that "visible relief and content" showed on Lincoln's face. Stanton described him as "grander, graver, more thoroughly up to the occasion than he had ever seen him." As his busy, pleasant day wound down, Noah Brooks and two old Illinois friends met with Lincoln for some light reminiscences. "He was unusually cheerful that evening, and never was more hopeful and buoyant," remembered Brooks. "His conversation was full of fun and anecdotes, feeling especially jubilant at the prospect before us."

A few minutes later, he stepped into the carriage with Mary for his short journey to Ford's Theater.

The Sudden Saint

"The murderer's bullet opens to him immortality."

No living man was ever charged with political crimes of such multiplicity and such enormity as Abraham Lincoln. He has been denounced without end as a perjurer, a usurper, a tyrant, a subverter of the Constitution, a destroyer of the liberties of his country, a reckless desperado, a heartless trifler over the last agonies of an expiring nation. Had that which has been said of him been true there is no circle in Dante's Inferno full enough of torment to expiate his iniquities.

So editorialized the *New York Times* the previous May. Now, in April of 1865, the war was won and Lincoln was murdered. Elation at the war's end gave way to shock over the assassination, and so closely did one follow on the other that the red, white, and blue bunting of victory had to be torn down to put up the black crepe of mourning.

Lincoln had been shot on Good Friday, and the next day, April 15, the slow toll of church bells went on hour after hour, knelling not just a death, but a martyrdom. Pastors across America rewrote their Easter sermons to include a new, exalted view of Lincoln as an American Moses, a leader out of slavery, a national savior who was not allowed to cross over into the Promised Land. The sermons were read the next day to overflow congregations dressed in black. The people in the pews were the first to hear the mournful reappraisal of Lincoln after his murder. In the next few weeks, almost every prominent man in America would take up the new gospel. Suddenly, it had become to every man's advantage to hallow the memory of the slain Lincoln.

Although many Northern pastors had criticized Lincoln's policies while he was alive, they sang only praises on "Black Easter," as people called it. The President had been dead only twenty-four hours, and even the breath of a rebuke of Lincoln in the Easter sermon would have caused a furor. Ministers weighed their words carefully in front of crowded, overwrought congregations. One who was not careful declared, "If Johnson pursues the same course as Lincoln, he will meet the same fate!" and was arrested for it. On this day, preachers could accuse Father Abraham of only one sin: of being too gentle, too lenient with Southern traitors who deserved a harsh justice. Some preached that this was why God had taken him just now. Out of the human instinct that demands that great events must have great causes, it seemed clear to everyone that the South must have been involved in the assassination, and that slavery was somehow responsible for Lincoln's murder. Many proclaimed, like the Reverend Albert G. Palmer, "It was treason, it was the Rebellion, it was the internal wickedness of slavery that sped the ball . . . for the life of Abraham Lincoln."

Even men who loathed Lincoln knew they must yield to his sudden sainthood. "This murder, this oozing blood, almost sanctify Lincoln," wrote Count Gurowski on the day he died. "His end atones for all the short-comings for which he was blamed and condemned by earnest and unyielding patriots. . . . [W]hatever sacrifices his vacillations may have cost the people, those vacillations will now be forgiven. . . . The murderer's bullet opens to him immortality." Radical Senator James W. Grimes of Iowa, who had regarded Lincoln as "a disgrace," glumly predicted on the day after the assassination, "Mr. Lincoln is to be hereafter regarded as a saint. All his foibles, and faults, and shortcomings, will be forgotten, and he will be looked upon as the Moses who led the nation through a four years' bloody war, and died in sight of peace." A journalist lamented, "It has made it impossible to speak the truth of Abraham Lincoln hereafter."

Radical Lincoln-haters wasted no time in convening. On the afternoon of April 15, as shock mixed with grief in the North, they gathered in Washington only hours after Lincoln's death. There, they rejoiced. "While everybody was shocked at his murder, the feeling was universal that [it] would prove a godsend to the country," wrote George Julian, who was there. "I . . . have not in a long time heard so much profanity," he wrote. "It became intolerably disgusting. Their hostility towards Lincoln's policy of conciliation and contempt for his weakness were undisguised."

Zachary Chandler, who was also there, wrote to his wife, "I believe that the Almighty continued Mr. Lincoln in office as long as he was useful and then substituted a better man [Andrew Johnson] to finish the work." Ben Wade, Henry Winter Davis, and the others present agreed, of course, as did Radicals everywhere. Oliver Wendell Holmes, when he heard the news in Boston, judged that "more than likely Lincoln was not the best man for the work of reconstruction." Wendell Phillips assured his listeners in a memorial speech at Tremont Temple the next week, "God has graciously withheld from him any fatal misstep in the great advance, and withdrawn him at the moment when his star touched its zenith, and the nation needed a sterner hand for the work God gives it to do."

Even in the first few days after Lincoln's murder, however, Lincoln's Radical enemies saw that his death was a propaganda windfall—Lincoln could be made to stand for the North, for freedom, and his murderer for the South, for slavery.

*   *   *

Secretary of War Edwin Stanton was the first to use the assassination as a weapon. When Mary Lincoln asked that her husband's funeral be in Springfield, Stanton made it the business of his own War Department, and made the martyr's corpse a traveling exhibit of Southern wickedness. He announced a funeral procession for Lincoln's body that would traverse the North by slow train, retracing the same 1,600-mile route Lincoln had used when he came to Washington. The sight of Lincoln visible in his casket, surrounded by mute soldiers in blue, would fuse the sacrifice of Lincoln and the Union soldiers in the memories of millions who would witness the spectacle first-hand, and help cement Republican dominance for two generations.

Stanton sharpened the image by forbidding anyone to obscure the damage caused by the assassin's bullet. The *New York Herald*'s Washington correspondent reported:

> The eyes and upper part of the cheeks are still discolored by the effects of the cruel shot which caused his death. It was proposed to remove the discoloration from the face by chemical processes, but the Secretary of War insisted that it was a part of the history of the event, and it should be allowed to remain as an evidence to the thousands who would view the body, when it shall be laid in state, of the death which this martyr to his ideas of justice and right suffered.

Stanton set Lincoln's funeral train in motion across the North on April 21, at the same time telling the press that Lincoln's murder was the work of a vast conspiracy, "planned and set on foot by rebels under pretense of avenging the rebel cause." A proclamation was released that offered a one hundred thousand dollar reward for Jefferson Davis, whose "unscrupulous hand has guided the assassin's trigger and dagger." Even so even-tempered a Radical as William Pitt Fessenden swore, "We will hang Jeff Davis!"

Just as the cry for an old-fashioned smiting of the Southern leaders rose in pitch across the North, the funeral train left Washington. It labored through the countryside at a stately twenty miles per hour, slowing down where men took off their hats and families waved miniature flags along the track, sometimes in the thousands. Women covered the rails with flowers. Memorial arches were built over the tracks for the train to pass under, and the nearby hills were dotted with tableaus, signs, and mock graves. As evening came on, bonfires lit the dark and torches flared along the roadbed. Cannon boomed constantly as the train passed along the route.

The funeral train made its way through Baltimore, through Harrisburg, through Philadelphia, with adorations and tributes heaped up in eulogies given by the most prominent men in each city. On Monday, April 24, it reached New York City, the headquarters of the Democratic Party, where in November Lincoln had been crushed more than two to one at the polls. These same New Yorkers now gave the greatest show in the city's long history—a carnival of sorrow, a two-day Mardi Gras of grief. Estimates of the crowd that poured into the streets ranged up to one million. The fronts of all the great buildings had been draped in black, solemn quotations swayed over arches and doorways, all flags hung at half-mast. A parade of 160,000 mourners accompanied the hearse, drawn by six gray horses draped in black, to City Hall. Most of the slow marchers were in organized groups carrying banners bearing mottoes, each group vying with the next to be the best in its woe. As the *New York Herald* reported, "New York never before saw such a day. Rome in the palmiest days of its power never witnessed such a triumphal march as New York yesterday formed and looked upon."

From noon on Monday until noon the next day, Lincoln's body lay in City Hall, and hundreds of thousands of New Yorkers, many of whom had looted and burned the city in a riot of rebellion less than two years before, waited long hours for the few seconds when they could file past the coffin and gaze at the famous face. The next day, the hearse was drawn from the City Hall to the train station by sixteen black horses, accompanied by twenty thousand soldiers and hundreds of thousands of bedazzled onlookers.

In Brooklyn, the greatest preacher of the age, Henry Ward Beecher, preached his Sunday sermon to intent listeners who crammed into Plymouth church and spilled out onto the lawn. The famous abolitionist had attacked the President through the previous four years—it was he who had said, "Not a spark of genius has he; not an element of leadership; not one particle of heroic enthusiasm." Only days earlier, in fact, when the assassination was reported, Beecher had told a man that Andrew Johnson's "little finger was stronger than Lincoln's loins." From the pulpit, however, Beecher heaped only praise on Lincoln. He was a "simple, truthful, noble soul, our faithful and sainted Lincoln." "Not thine the sorrow, but ours, sainted soul!" he wailed. Halfway through his tribute, Beecher switched to the pointed end of the new Radical creed, and laid the blame for the assassination on the South. Booth's act was "the venomous hatred of liberty wielded by an avowed advocate of slavery," he declared. "This blow was but the expiring rebellion. . . . [E]pitomized in this foul act, we find the whole nature and disposition of slavery. It begins in a wanton destruction of all human rights, . . . and it is the universal enemy of mankind, and of God, who made man."

* * *

Beecher and the Radicals soon saw that all their enemies would fall before the sword that Lincoln's death had put in their hands, and they widened its swath to wound the Democratic press. Gurowski put it in his diary: "All over the rebel region, the press for years incited to Lincoln's murder. For years a part of the Northern press, which was and is the gospel of the Northern Copperheads, slavers, and traitors, pointed to Lincoln as a tyrant, and to Seward as his henchman. Murder and slaughter by infuriated wretches are now the fruits of those stimulating teachings." The *New York Herald*, which had reviled Lincoln as "the great ghoul at Washington" during the war, did not want to be on the wrong side now, and on Black Easter it, too, found murderers in the Democratic press:

> The blow has fallen, and whence did it come? From Richmond, no one doubts; yet wherever the idea was conceived, or the plan framed, it is as clear as day that the real origin of this dreadful act is to be found in the fiendish and malignant spirit developed and fostered by the rebel press North and South. That press has, in the most devilish manner, urged men to the commission of this very deed.

Even the moderate *Harper's Weekly* indicted the Democratic press, saying:

He has been denounced as a despot, as a usurper, as a man who arbitrarily annulled the Constitution, as a magistrate under whose administration all the securities of liberty, property, and even life, were deliberately disregarded and imperiled. Political hostility has been inflamed into hate by the assertion that he was responsible for the war, and that he had opened all the yawning graves and tumbled the bloody victims in. . . . If there were a military despotism in the country, as was declared, he was the despot. If there were a tyranny, he was the tyrant. Is it surprising that somebody should have believed all this, that somebody should have said, if there is a tyranny it can not be very criminal to slay the tyrant, and that working himself up to the due frenzy he should strike the blow?

The Democratic papers quickly realized that if they didn't repent their opposition to Lincoln, they risked ruin by mobs like the ones that had gutted their offices in the first summer of the war. Herman Melville caught the vengeful mood in his poem "The Martyr":

> *He lieth in his blood—*
> *The Father in his face;*
> *They have killed him, the Forgiver—*
> *The Avenger takes his place.*
> *There is sobbing of the strong,*
> *And a pall upon the land;*
> *But the people in their weeping*
> *Bare the iron hand:*
> *Beware the People weeping*
> *When they bare the iron hand.*

Lincoln's body was still warm when "the People weeping" took their first victim. As they carried Lincoln away from the house where he had just died, one onlooker foolishly sent up a cheer for Jefferson Davis. He was set upon by mourners and nearly torn to pieces. As the news of the assassination spread across the country, violence was widespread against anyone who spoke lightly of the tragedy. Melville Stone, the general manager of the Associated Press, was in the lounge of a Chicago hotel when, he reported, "I heard the crack of a revolver, and a man fell in the centre of the room. His assailant stood perfectly composed with a smoking revolver in his hand, and justified his action by saying: 'He said it served Lincoln right.' There was no arrest, no one would have dared arrest the man. He walked out a hero. I never knew who he was." George Templeton Strong said three or four men on Wall Street made light of Lincoln's murder "and were instantly set upon by the bystanders and pummeled. One of them narrowly escaped death." The doors of local jails rattled shut behind men in every city who were heard exulting in the news of Lincoln's death, some of them rescued from murderous mobs and put behind bars for their own safety.

Nervous newspapermen paid particular attention to a California wire that told of a mob that traveled from one "copperhead organ" to another and "emptied their contents into the street amid the applause of an immense crowd," warning that "other Democratic newspaper offices are threatened." Soon there came news that the editor of a Democratic newspaper in Maryland, Joseph Shaw, had been killed by a mob after he had published criticism of Lincoln on Black Sunday.

Democratic editors everywhere knew what was good for them and rushed their protestations of patriotic grief into print. They even tried to claim Lincoln as their own. His arch-enemy in his home state, the Chicago *Times*, now said:

> There are not on this day mourners more sincere than the democracy of the Northern States. Widely as they have differed with Mr. Lincoln—greatly as their confidence in him had been shaken—they saw in the indications of the last few days of his life that he might command their support in the close of the war, as he did in the beginning. These indications inspired them with hope, and confidence, and joy, which are now dashed to the ground. The democracy may well mourn the death of Abraham Lincoln.

Lincoln's relentless abuser, the New York *World*, likewise beat its breast—"Today every loyal heart must suffer the terrible shock, and swell with overburdening grief at the calamity which has been permitted to befall us in the assassination of the Chief Magistrate"—as did its Lincoln-hating twin, the *New York Daily News*, which vowed, "We are stunned, shocked, horrified beyond measure at this fearful announcement." The leader of Copperhead opinion in Boston, the *Evening Courier*, now wailed, "No language of which we are capable could half express the horror and dismay with which the dreadful event of the day has affected us." The *Dayton Daily Empire*, Vallandigham's Copperhead mouthpiece, solemnly swore, "We had opposed Mr. Lincoln in his lifetime. Yet just at this juncture we had the expectation of lending him our support." Many Copperhead journals pleaded, like the Milwaukee *See-Bote*, "We have voted against Lincoln's election, written against it, spoken against it—that we have done, and as we believe with pure conscience. But we may say with an equally pure conscience that there are no more sincere mourners today—none who deplore the death of the President more than the Democracy of the Northern States." Lincoln's nemesis in Ohio, *The Crisis*, anxious to deflect the charges against the Democratic press, argued, "Since the assassination of President Lincoln, we have examined nearly two hundred Democratic journals, from every State and district in the Northern States, and we have not been able to find in one of them an expression in the remotest degree justifying that horrible crime."

Republicans were skeptical of the Democrats' sudden alleluias for Old Abe, and resented them dodging the punishment for their years of wickedness merely by singing in the choir for one Sunday. The Chicago *Tribune* sneered that "the men who had misrepresented, abused and vilified the President while he lived, should at least stop praising him now that he is dead. It's all of mercy these men have a right to expect, that they are allowed to live . . . . They have not the decency to go out and hang themselves, like Judas."

* * *

With Lincoln's enemies in the North now prostrate, wrath over his murder was focused mainly on his murderer's "accomplices" in the South. Here, for four years, Southern papers had regularly carried private advertisements offering rewards for Lincoln's head. Indeed, pent-up hatred among Southerners briefly gave way to raptures over Lincoln's death. The thousands of rebel prisoners in Fort Delaware sent up a cheer and threw their hats in the air when they heard the news. One rebel soldier from Lee's army wrote later that "Lincoln's death seemed . . . like a gleam of sunshine on a winter's day." Southern women thrilled to the romantic derring-do of John Wilkes Booth, like the Georgia woman for whom the news of the assassination came as "one sweet drop among so much that is painful." Young Emily LeConte of Columbia, South Carolina, confessed that she quivered with joy at the news of Lincoln's fate, and asked, "Could there have been a fitter death for such a man?" Kay Stone of Texas wrote in her diary, "All honor to J. Wilkes Booth, who has rid the world of a tyrant and made himself famous for generations."

Texas, the only rebel state without Union troops on its soil and thus the least inhibited, was the noisiest in its celebrations. The *Dallas Herald* called Booth "a Divine instrument sent to remove a bloody despot." The Marshall

Texas Republican proclaimed, "the world is happily rid of a monster that disgraced the form of humanity." Men will thrill to Lincoln's killing, shouted the Houston *Telegraph*, "from now until God's judgment day." The *Galveston News* exulted in a similar vein: "It does look to us . . . as if an avenging Nemesis had brought swift and inevitable retribution upon a man stained with so many bloody crimes."

Outside of Texas, however, Southern cities were occupied by Union armies, and citizens there had to be much more circumspect about their reaction to Lincoln's murder. Union soldiers were wild with grief when they heard that their Commander-in-Chief had been slain, and were keen for bloody reprisals. When the news was read to Sherman's army in North Carolina, for example, many soldiers swore "eternal vengeance against the whole Southern race," according to one. "Few men will stop from committing any outrage of crime they may wish to," wrote another in the wake of the news; "I would like to see [General Sherman] turn his army loose over what is left." A Wisconsin soldier reported that his messmates proposed burning Raleigh down and killing every rebel in it.

Thus, when a proclamation came to observe a day of mourning, the people in the occupied South quietly did as they were told, adjusting to whatever was required of them. Ministers delivered the mandatory sermons, and Southern newspapers issued the compulsory regrets. Where the Union army was strongest, Southern protestations of sorrow for Lincoln's death were loudest. In Richmond, for instance, the *Richmond Whig* dressed its borders in black and cried, "The heaviest blow which has ever fallen upon the people of the South has descended." Its editor made sure to wave aside the rumors of Southern conspiracy, insisting that Booth's secrecy "indicates that there were but few accomplices in this inhuman crime," and added a plea for mercy, saying, "The abhorrence with which it is regarded on all sides will, it is hoped, deter insane and malignant men from the emulation of the infamy which attaches to this infernal deed." Other journals in the South, many with new editors installed by Union armies, followed suit. Witnessing these faux laments in New Orleans, one observer wrote, "The more violently 'secesh' the inmates, [and] the more thankful they are for Lincoln's death, the more profusely the houses are decked with emblems of woe. . . . Men who have hated Lincoln with all their souls, under terror of confiscation and imprisonment which they understand is the alternative, tie black crape from every practicable knob and point to save their homes." In their private scribblings, Southerners regretted Lincoln's death only because they knew they would suffer harsher punishments under President Andrew Johnson, the turncoat Tennessean.

*   *   *

If the sudden proclamations of Lincoln's nobility in the black-bordered columns of the Democratic and Southern press were mere show, drafted with an eye to survival, the sorrowful response to his murder in British journals showed a genuine change of heart. There were still dissenters, like London's *Evening Standard*, who maintained, "He was not a hero while he lived, and therefore his cruel murder does not make him a martyr." But most British editors dreaded the ferocity of the spirit of vengeance in the North, and realized belatedly that a living Lincoln had been the surest guarantee of a peaceful Reconstruction.

The *Times* of London, the pre-eminent opinion-maker not only of Britain but of all Europe, which had printed hostility to Lincoln's every act during his term and which had recently viewed Lincoln's re-election as "an avowed step towards the foundation of a military despotism," was the most conspicuous penitent, saying now, "Abraham Lincoln was as little of a tyrant as any man who ever lived. He could have been a tyrant had he pleased, but he never uttered so much as an ill-natured speech."

The conversion of the London *Punch* was nearly as dramatic. The magazine's renowned illustrator, John Tenniel, had caricatured Lincoln throughout the war as a bearded ruffian—malicious, vulgar, and arrogant. Now, *Punch* blazoned its May 6, 1865 issue with Tenniel's sentimental illustration of a tearful Britannia mourning at the deathbed of the slain American President. *Punch's* editor, Tom Taylor, composed an eloquent *mea culpa* of nineteen stanzas that read in part:

> *Yes, he had lived to shame me from my sneer,*
> *To lame my pencil, and confute my pen—*
> *To make me own this hind of princes peer,*
> *This rail-splitter a true-born king of men.*

The London *Morning Star* spoke for the vast majority in the British press when it confessed to a long list of injustices in the four years past:

London Punch, May 6, 1865

"Britannia Lays a Wreath on Lincoln's Bier"

English writers degraded themselves to the level of the coarsest caricaturists when they had to tell of Abraham Lincoln. They stooped to criticize a foreign patriot as a menial might comment on the bearing of a hero. They sneered at his manners, . . . they made coarse pleasantry of his figure, . . . they were facetious about his dress, . . . they were indignant about his jokes . . . . History will proclaim, to the eternal humiliation of our country, how an influential section of the British press outbade the journalists of the South in their slander and invective against the great man who has been so cruelly slain; how his every action was twisted and tortured into a wrong, his every noble aspiration spoken of as a desire for blood, his personal appearance caricatured, his lowly origin made the theme for scorn by men as base-born as he, but without the nobleness of soul which made Lincoln a prince among princes; how even that proclamation which conferred liberty upon four millions of down-trodden slaves was reviled as a base effort to incite the negroes to servile war.

*   *   *

In all the world, there was one editor conspicuously absent from the ranks of the converts to the revised, glorified view of Lincoln. This was Horace Greeley, Lincoln's most dependable tormenter, the erratic sachem of the Radical press. On the day the President was shot, in fact, Greeley had written a scathing anti-Lincoln rant. The next day, as bells tolled the martyr's death in every town and hamlet in the North, the *Tribune's* managing editor blanched at what he called Greeley's "brutal, bitter, sarcastic, personal attack" and prudently declined to print it. Greeley burst into his office, roaring, "They tell me you ordered my leader out of this morning's paper. Is it your paper or mine?" The manager replied, "The paper is yours, Mr. Greeley. The article is in type upstairs and you can use it when you choose, but if you run that editorial there will not be one brick left standing in the *Tribune* building."

By Monday, April 17, Greeley had recovered himself enough to write an official requiem, but it remembered Lincoln as a tardy student who was "among the last to perceive . . . that Slavery had challenged the Union to mortal encounter and that the gage must be taken up as it was thrown down." Two days later, Greeley still could not bring himself to write a proper eulogy. Beginning defiantly that he was, "Without the least desire to join in the race of heaping extravagant and preposterous laudations on our dead President as the wisest and greatest man who ever lived," Greeley admitted that "Mr. Lincoln's reputation will stand higher with posterity than with the mass of his contemporaries," and that "future generations will . . . be puzzled by the bitter fierceness of the personal assaults by which his temper was tested." He closed his admission, however, with a sly cut: "Mr. Lincoln has suffered in the judgment of his immediate contemporaries from the fact that, of all things that he might have been required to do, the conduct of a great war was that for which he was least fitted." Lincoln was "pretty certain to be right in the end," Greeley continued, "but in War to be right a little too late is equivalent to being wrong altogether." Greeley concluded that Lincoln was "not the man of transcendent genius, of rare insight, of resistless force of character."

Greeley's conflicted feelings about Abraham Lincoln continued to war in him for the seven remaining years of his life. In Greeley's 1868 autobiography, he began his chapter on Lincoln with a cruel slur—"There were those who say that Mr. Lincoln was fortunate in his death as in his life"—and then added a curious rebuttal: "I judge otherwise. I hold him most inapt for the leadership of a people involved in desperate, agonizing war; while I deem few men better fitted to guide a nation's destinies in time of peace." Since Lincoln was never permitted to guide the nation in time of peace, this was Greeley's own version of the Democrats' suspect claim, *We opposed him while he lived; we were about to support him when he died.* Greeley's appraisal tottered toward its finish with a frank reproach—"I didn't favor his re-nomination as President; for I wanted the War driven onward with vehemence, and this was not in his nature." Finally, his essay praised, not Lincoln, but God's mysterious ways: "We have had chieftains who would have crushed out the Rebellion in six months, and restored 'the Union as it was,'" he wrote, "but God gave us the one leader whose control secured not only the downfall the Rebellion, but the eternal overthrow of Human Slavery under the flag of the Great Republic."

Almost to the end, Greeley could never manage a tribute for Lincoln that did not also include a curse. While he still trailed the smoke of the battles they had fought, he could not see him clearly. The passing of years, however, improved his vision. Shortly before he died in 1872, Greeley penned a summation that went unpublished for nearly two decades. "Looking back through the lifting mists of seven eventful, tragic, trying, glorious years," wrote Greeley,

> I clearly discern that the one providential leader, the indispensable hero of the great drama, faithfully reflecting even in his hesitations and seeming vacillations the sentiment of the masses—fitted by his very defects and shortcomings for the burden laid upon him, the good to be wrought out through him—was Abraham Lincoln.

Sources and Notes

Part One: Lincoln's Entrance

Chapter 1: Lincoln Comes to Washington

Page 1   "Plums arrived here with Nuts": Douglas L.Wilson and Rodney O. Davis, eds., *Herndon's Informants: Letters, Interviews, and Statements about Abraham Lincoln*, (Urbana and Chicago: University of Illinois Press, 1998), p. 291.

2   "What would the nation think": A. K. McClure, *Abraham Lincoln and Men of War-Times* (Lincoln: University of Nebraska Press, 1996), p. 52.

2   "a dog fight now": Carl Sandburg, *The War Years*, 4 vols. (NY: Harcourt, Brace & World, 1939), p. I: 4.

3   "as soon as the train stopped": Baltimore *Sun*, reprinted in February 27, 1861, New York *World*, from Robert S. Harper, *Lincoln and the Press* (NY: McGraw-Hill, 1951), p. 88.

3   "the moment the train arrived": L.K. Bowen to Howell Cobb, from Sandburg, *The War Years*, p. I: 77.

3   "skulked off himself": New York *Journal of Commerce*, reprinted in February 25, 1861, Brooklyn *Daily Eagle*

3   "Had we any respect for Mr. Lincoln": February 25, 1861, Baltimore *Sun*, Harper, p. 89.

4   "a Scotch plaid cap": February 25, 1861, *New York Times*, from *ibid.*

4   *"Abe Lincoln tore through Baltimore"*: Melvin L. Hayes, *Mr. Lincoln Runs for President* (NY: Citadel Press, 1960), p. 295.

6   *"They went and got a special train"*: Reprinted in March 7, 1861, *The Crisis*, from Harper, p. 91.

6   "[Lincoln] ran": March 2, 1861, *Louisville Courier*, from William H. Townsend, *Lincoln and the Bluegrass* (Lexington: The University of Kentucky Press, 1955), p. 268.

7   "Lo, the Conquering Hero Comes!": February 26, 1861, New Orleans *Daily Delta*, from Dwight Lowell Dumond, ed., *Southern Editorials on Secession* (Gloucester, MA: Peter Smith, 1964), p. 469.

7   "What brought him here": February 26, 1861, Chicago *Tribune*, from J.G. Randall, *Lincoln the President: Springfield to Gettysburg* (NY: Dodd, Mead & Co., 1945), p. I: 293.

7   "Flight of the Imagination": Hayes, p. 294.

7   "By the advice of weak men": Sandburg, *The War Years*, p. I: 84.

8   "Mr. Lincoln's Flight": February 25, 1861, Brooklyn *Daily Eagle*.

8   "How unwisely": New York *World*, reprinted in February 25, 1861, Brooklyn *Daily Eagle*.

8   "Mr. Lincoln may live": February 25, 1861, New York *Tribune*, from Harper, p. 90.

8   "What a misfortune": February 26, 1861, *New York Herald*, from *ibid.*

8   "Never idol fell so suddenly": Ernest B. Furgurson, *Freedom Rising: Washington in the Civil War* (NY: Alfred Knopf, 2004), p. 47.

8   "His friends reproached him": Ward Hill Lamon, *The Life of Abraham Lincoln From His Birth to His Inauguration as President* (Lincoln: University of Nebraska Press, 1999), p. 526-7.

8   "was convinced": Ward Hill Lamon, *Recollections of Abraham Lincoln* (Lincoln: University of Nebraska Press, 1994), p. 46-7.

Chapter 2: The Presidency

Page 11   "Life, hitherto": Edward Dicey, *Spectator of America,* ed. Herbert Mitgang (Athens: The University of Georgia Press, 1989), p. 131.

11   "a happy-go-lucky style": James Russell Lowell, *Letters of James Russell Lowell,* ed. Charles Eliot Norton, 3 vols. (Boston: Houghton, Mifflin Company, 1904), p. II: 55.

12   "Did you ever see": Carl Sandburg, *The Prairie Years,* 2 vols. (NY: Harcourt, Brace & World, 1926), p. II: 376.

12   "In the nineteenth century": Theodore Lowi, *The Personal President* (Ithaca: Cornell University Press, 1985), p. 40.

14   Modern White House staff figures: Bradley Patterson, *The White House Staff: Inside the West Wing and Beyond* (NY: Brookings Institution Press, 2001).

15   "One great blemish": Charles Dickens, *American Notes* (NY: D. Appleton and Co., 1868), p. 100-101.

Chapter 3: The Rise of Party Politics

16   An apocryphal story: Harper, p. 62.

16   "an accidental instrument": Abraham Lincoln, *The Collected Works of Abraham Lincoln,* ed. Roy P. Basler (New Brunswick, NJ: Rutgers University Press), p. IV: 193-4.

16   "the unknown man": James Russell Lowell, "Abraham Lincoln," *Political Essays* (Boston: Houghton, Mifflin and Company, 1871), p. 283

20   "General Jackson's power": Alexis de Tocqueville, *Democracy in America, Vol. II* (NY: D. Appleton and Co., 1904), p. 454-5.

21   "I contributed": Leonard Lurie, *Party Politics: Why We Have Poor Presidents* (NY: Scarborough, 1982), p. 69.

21   "That national conventions": Allan Nevins, *Ordeal of the Union: Fruits of Manifest Destiny, 1847-1852* (NY: Charles Scribner's Sons, 1947), p.187.

23   "the political activity": Alexis de Tocqueville, *Democracy in America, Vol. I,* (NY: The Century Company, 1898), p. 253-4.

23   "It engrosses every conversation": Frances Trollope, *Domestic Manners of Americans* (NY: Dodd, Mead and Co., 1901), p. 65.

24   "I yet hope": Dickens, p. 296.

24   "Some new most paltry exhibition": Page Smith, *The Nation Comes of Age: A People's History of the Ante-Bellum Years* (NY: McGraw-Hill, 1981), p. 256.

24   "How quiet the streets are": *ibid.,* p. 769-70.

24   "Healthful amusements": Dickens, p. 294, 296.

25   "The New York publications": Smith, *The Nation Comes of Age,* p. 904.

26   "While the newspaper press": Dickens, p. 295-6.

26   "the *Sewer*" etc.: Brayton Harris, *Blue & Gray in Black & White: Newspapers in the Civil War* (Washington: Brassey's, 1999), p. 17.

27   "horse-whipped": Smith, *The Nation Comes of Age,* p. 904.

27   "to attend exclusively to the fighting part": *ibid.,* p. 906.

28   "was impregnable": *ibid.,* p. 1058.

28   "Nobody knows much of Franklin Pierce" and "a galvanized cypher": Entry of June 7, 1852, from Brayton Harris, p. 96.

28   "blasts where it is excited": Kenneth S. Greenburg, *Masters and Statesmen: The Political Culture of American Slavery* (Baltimore: Johns Hopkins University Press, 1985), p. 126.

28   "The Dignity Departing": *ibid.*

Page 29   "no one was safe": Leonard D. White, *The Jacksonians* (NY: Macmillan and Co., 1954), p. 26, 15.

29   "deformed, mediocre": Sandburg, *The War Years,* p. I: 22.

29   "feeble-minded": *ibid.*

Chapter 4: The Spoils System

31   "When they are contending": M. Ostragorski, *Democracy and the Organization of Political Parties* (New York, Macmillan, 1908), p. 50.

31   "could not fail to degrade any Administration": Marcus Cunliffe, *The Presidency* (Boston: Houghton Mifflin, 1987), p. 104.

31   "Such a system would corrupt a nation of angels": Jesse Macy, *Our Nation: How it Grew, What It Does, and How It Does It* (Boston: Ginn and Co., 1897), p. 137.

32   "The election ceases": Leonard D. White, p. 325-6.

32   "both have degenerated": Mark W. Summers, *The Plundering Generation: Corruption and the Crisis of the Union 1849-1861* (NY: Oxford University Press, 1987), p. 185.

32   "has converted almost the whole body of young men": Nevins, *1847-1852,* p. 178

32   "the treasury doors": Summers, p. 5.

32   "demoralization is rapidly spreading": *ibid.,* p. 6.

33   "and the actual sum of money": *ibid.,* p. 29.

33   "The evil which he began remains": James Parton, *Life of Andrew Jackson* (NY: Mason Brothers, 1860), p. III:694.

33   "the public affairs of the United States": *ibid.,* p. 700.

33   "Corruption is . . . perhaps more prevalent": Sandburg, *The Prairie Years,* p. II: 324-326.

34   "one might despair of the Republic": Summers, p. 18.

34   "When official corruption": *ibid.*

34   "Our foundations are crumbling": *ibid.*

34   "The patronage of government": Greenburg, p. 131.

34   "we shall be betrayed": *ibid.,* p.132.

34   "We cannot coalesce": *ibid.,* p.137.

Chapter 5: The Slavery Debate

38   "related to an imaginary Negro": George H. Haynes, *Charles Sumner* (Philadelphia: George W. Jacobs and Co., 1909), p. 278.

39   "in the insult they conveyed to the South": George Harmon Knoles, *The Crisis of the Union, 1860-1861* (Baton Rouge: Louisiana State University Press, 1865), p. 89

39   "to sever himself": Tocqueville, p. II: 119.

40   "When were the good": William Lee Miller, *Lincoln's Virtues: An Ethical Biography* (NY: Vintage Book, 2003), p. 447.

40   "One, on God's side, is a majority": *ibid.*

40   "Let me admonish you": David Donald, *Lincoln Reconsidered* (NY: Vintage Books, 2001), p. 56.

40   "The citizen of the Southern states": Tocqueville, p. I: 507.

40   "The people worship themselves": Smith, *The Nation Comes of Age,* p. 263-4

41   "The steadily augmenting power": Donald, *Lincoln Reconsidered,* p. 58.

41   "One might enumerate the items": Henry James, Jr., *Hawthorne* (NY: Harper and Brothers, 1901), p. 42-3.

42   "I go first for Greenville": Donald, *Lincoln Reconsidered,* p. 60.

Page 42   "every person of good moral character": Stanley Elkins, *Slavery* (Chicago: The University of Chicago Press, 1976), p. 30.

43   "no methodical system": Smith, *The Nation Comes of Age*, p. 150.

43   "We are so young a people": *ibid.,* p. 913-914.

44   "I *will be* as harsh as truth": Henry Mayer, *All on Fire: William Lloyd Garrison and the Abolition of Slavery* (NY: St. Martin's Press, 1998), p. 112.

45   "a dark cloud" and "Many in the South": Arnold Whitridge, *No Compromise! The Story of the Fanatics Who Paved the Way to the Civil War* (NY: Farrar, Straus and Cuday, 1960), p. 29-30.

45   "The Negro slaves": George Fitzhugh, *Cannibals All! or Slaves Without Masters* (Richmond: A. Morris, 1857), p. 29.

45   "No fact is plainer": Albert Taylor Bledsoe, "Essay on Liberty and Slavery," 1856, Henry S. Commager, ed., *American Destiny, Vol. 6: A House Dividing* (NY: Grolier Publishing, 1976), p. 57.

45   "*Instructed thus*": William J. Grayson, "The Hireling and the Slave," *The Hireling and the Slave, Chicora, and Other Poems* (Charleston: McCarter & Co., 1856), p. 34.

45   "criminal agitators": This was the phrase used by future president James K. Polk. Russel B. Nye, *Fettered Freedom: Civil Liberties and the Slavery Controversy, 1830-1860* (East Lansing: Michigan State University Press, 1963), p. 23-24.

46   "Freedom of speech": September 28, 1837, *The Western Presbyterian Herald, ibid.,* p. 181.

46   "truth and sound philosophy": Macy, p. 292.

46   State "slavery speech" laws: Nye, p. 174-5.

46   "no more a mob": *ibid.,* p. 177.

47   "The free labor of the states": November 10, 1847, *New York Evening Post*, from James McPherson, *Battle Cry of Freedom,* (NY: Oxford University Press, 1988), p. 55.

48   "secure to the South": November 10, 1846, *Milledgeville Federal Union, ibid.,* p. 52.

48   "You could not look upon the table": James Loewen, *Lies My Teacher Told Me* (NY: Simon and Schuster, 1995), p. 141.

48   "pretends to an insulting superiority": Greenburg, p. 132.

48   "I would rather my state": *ibid.,* p. 86.

48   "not half so humiliating": *ibid.,* p. 87.

48   "It is clear": McPherson, *Battle Cry of Freedom,* p. 68.

49   "Southerners must refuse": Greenburg, p. 132.

49   "naked submission or secession": *ibid.,* p. 140.

49   "We are either slaves": *ibid.,* p. 141.

49   "Modern free society is wrong," "Free society is impracticable," "the whole hireling class are slaves," "make the laboring man the slave of one man," and "The South now maintains": Nye, p. 304-309.

50   "In Southern states": *ibid.,* p. 289.

Chapter 6: Lincoln's Nomination

52   "a considerable notion": Benjamin Thomas, *Abraham Lincoln: A Biography* (NY: Alfred A. Knopf, 1952), p. 178

52   "if the [New York] Tribune continues": Lincoln, *Works,* II: 430.

52   "Twenty-two years ago": *ibid.,* p. II: 383.

53   "Lincoln must do something": Sandburg, *The Prairie Years,* p. II: 137.

53   "Though I now sink out of view": Lincoln, *Works,* p. III: 339.

54   "Without Douglas Lincoln would be nothing": September 20, 1859, Cincinnati *Enquirer*, Herbert Mitgang, ed., *Abraham Lincoln: A Press Portrait* (Athens, The University of Georgia Press, 1989), p. 141-142.

54   "I must, in candor, say": Lincoln, *Works,* p. III: 377.

Page 54   "For my single self": *ibid.,* p. III: 491.

55   "Let us have faith": *ibid.,* p. III: 550

55   "It is not probable": February 27, 1860, New York *Tribune,* from Randall, *Springfield to Gettysburg,* p. I: 135-6.

56   "If you don't nominate Seward": Charles C. Nourse, "A Delegate's Memories of the Chicago Convention of 1860," *Annals of Iowa, Vol. 12, 3rd Series* (Des Moines: Historical Department of Iowa, 1921), p. 463

59   "I am not in a position": Lincoln, *Works,* p. III: 517

60   "Abraham Lincoln. The Rail Candidate": David Donald, *Lincoln* (NY: Simon & Schuster, 1996), p. 245.

62   "My name is new": Lincoln, *Works,* p. IV: 34.

62   "I am for the man": James S. Pike, *First Blows of the Civil War* (NY: American News Company, 1879), p. 484.

62   "The Bates movement": Murat Halstead, *Three Against Lincoln: Murat Halstead Reports the Caucuses of 1860,* ed. William Hesseltine (Baton Rouge: LSU Press, 1960), p. 165-172.

63   Train votes: Webb Garrison, *The Lincoln No One Knows* (Nashville: Rutledge Hill Press, 1993), p. 69.

63   First-day motion vote: Emerson David Fite, *The Presidential Campaign of 1860* (NY: MacMillan, 1911), p. 127.

63   "intense enthusiasm": Halstead, p. 165-172.

63   "My conclusion": James Trietsch, *The Printer and the Prince* (NY: Exposition Press, 1955), p. 93.

64   Details and quotes on the night before the nomination vote: Sandburg, *The Prairie Years,* p. II: 342; and Trietsch, p. 95.

66   "made soft vesper breathings": Thomas, p. 212.

66   "The uproar was beyond description": Halstead, p. 165-172.

66   "It was perfectly amazing": Hayes, p. 62-3.

66   New England first ballot votes: Miller, p. 402.

67   "And the roar": Halstead, p. 165-172.

67   "It is a damned shame": George Milton, *The Eve of Conflict* (NY: Houghton Mifflin, 1934), p. 458.

68   "The fact of the Convention": Halstead, p. 176-7.

68   "The main work of the Chicago Convention": May 22, 1860, *New York Times,* Harper, p. 59.

68   "the triumph of politically available mediocrity": *Springfield Republican, ibid.,* p. 192.

68   "The nomination . . . will disappoint the country": *Troy Whig,* reprinted in May 21, 1860, New York *Tribune,* ibid., p. 58.

68   "[C]urses both loud and deep": Hayes, p. 74.

68   "Mr. Lincoln is a very respectable lawyer": Reprinted in May 21, 1860, New York *Tribune,* from Harper, p. 58.

68   "The Republicans of Illinois": May 24, 1860, *Springfield Register,* from William Baringer, *Lincoln's Rise to Power* (Boston: Little, Brown, and Co., 1937), p. 309.

68   "What has Mr. Lincoln ever done": June 2, 1860, Belleville *Democrat, ibid.,* p. 310.

68   "That Wm. H. Seward": May 24, 1860, Cairo City *Gazette, ibid.*

69   "The conduct of the Republican Party": *New York Herald,* reprinted in May 21, 1860, New York *Tribune,* from Harper, p. 56.

69   "He is not known": Albany *Atlas and Argus,* reprinted in May 21, 1860, New York *Tribune, ibid.,* p. 57.

69   "The laboring mountains": Hayes, p. 77.

69   "A disgraceful burlesque": *ibid.,* p. 78.

Page 69   "third rate district politician": *Baltimore American*, May 19. 1860, from Harper, p. 154.

69   "By what process": Trenton *True American*, reprinted in May 21, 1860, New York *Tribune, ibid.*, p. 57.

69   "Why Should Lincoln Be President": *Philadelphia Journal*, reprinted in May 24, 1860, New York *Tribune*, Mitgang, p. 181-2.

70   "The Chicago Republican Convention is over": Edward Bates, *The Diary of Edward Bates*, Ed. Howard K. Beale (Washington: U.S. Gov't. Printing Office, 1933), p. 128.

70   "Mr. Lincoln personally, is unexceptionable.": *ibid.*, p. 131.

70   "Few men believed": Lamon, *The Life of Abraham Lincoln*, p. 468

70   "referred deprecatingly to the nominee": Nourse, p. 464

71   "that the nomination of Lincoln": Baringer, p. 313.

71   "I had never heard of him": Smith, *The Nation Comes of Age*, p. 1166

71   "a Western 'screamer'": *ibid.*

71   "I remember": Ida Tarbell, *The Life of Abraham Lincoln* (NY: Lincoln History Society, 1902), p. I: 159.

71   "we heard the result": Doris Kearns Goodwin, *Team of Rivals* (NY: Simon and Schuster, 2005), p. *xvi*.

71   "He is unknown here": Entry of May 19, 1960, George Templeton Strong, *The Diary of George Templeton Strong*, Allan Nevins and Milton H. Thomas, eds. (NY: Macmillan, 1952), p. III: 28.

73   "a relentless ruffian": October 15, 1860, Charleston *Mercury*, from Robert W. Johannsen, *Lincoln, the South, and Slavery* (Baton Rouge: Louisiana State University Press, 1991), p. 104

73   "A horrid looking wretch": Fite, p. 210.

73   "enough to scare one": Johannsen, p. 112.

73   "most subtle and dangerous form": May 26, 1860, Louisville *Courier*, Dumond, p. 115.

73   "determined hostility": May 21, 1860, Richmond *Enquirer*, from Johannsen, p. 104.

73   "revolutionary and destructive theories": May 19, 1860, *New York Herald, ibid.*

74   "Who is this huckster in politics?": Oscar Sherwin, *Prophet of Liberty: The Life and Times of Wendell Phillips* (NY: Bookman Associates, 1958), p. 413.

Chapter 7: The 1860 Presidential Campaign

75   "Nobody believes": October 20, 1855, Albany *Argus*, from Gabot Boritt, ed., *Why the Civil War Came* (NY: Oxford University Press, 1996), p. 102

78   "the minds of the people": November 2, 1860, Natchez *Daily Free Trader*, from Randall, *Springfield to Gettysburg*, p. I: 192.

79   "the procession moved along": Entry of September 13, 1860, Strong, p. III: 41.

79   "I know the country is not Anti-Slavery": Letter of January 6, 1860, to Margaret Allen, from Jeter Allen Isely, *Horace Greeley and the Republican Party, 1863-1861: A Study of the New York Tribune* (Princeton: Princeton University Press, 1947), p. 166.

80   "Let Lincoln be President": Allan Nevins, *The Emergence of Lincoln: Prologue to the Civil War, 1859-1861* (NY: Charles Scribner's Sons, New York, 1950), p. 290.

Chapter 8: Lincoln's Election

83   "five to six trillion dollars": Senator James A. Bayard of Delaware, in a letter written on December 12, 1860, put aggregate slave value at "more than $2 billion dollars..." (Nevin,

1859-1861, p. 331) Robert Toombs of Georgia put the loss of the value of slaves at $4 billion, and asked, "Is that not a cause of war?" (Sandburg, *Prairie Years*, p. II: 377) Recently, James L. Huston, in *Calculating the Value of the Union* (Chapel Hill: University of North Carolina Press, 2003), put slave value in 1860 at $3 billion. Ward Hill Lamon, Lincoln's friend, put the average value of a slave in 1860 at $600, which would make the aggregate value at $2.4 billion. In trying to give a modern perspective to that number, I have used the GDP (Gross Domestic Product). Although GDP was not computed before 1869, *The Reader's Companion to American History* puts the 1860 GDP at $6 billion. In 1869, the GDP was calculated at $6.1 billion. So the GDP for 1860 may be put somewhere around $6 billion dollars, and the value of slaves to be somewhere around $3 billion, or in the neighborhood of half of the 1860 GDP. Since the GDP of 2004 is more than $11 trillion dollars, the value of the slaves can be viewed, in modern terms, as approximately $5-6 trillion dollars.

Page 83   "Secret conspiracy": October 11, 1860, Charleston *Mercury*, from Smith, *The Nation Comes of Age*, p. 1169-70.

84   "If you are tame enough": McPherson, *Battle Cry of Freedom*, p. 243.

84   "Submit to have our wives and daughters": *ibid.*

84   "I shudder to contemplate it!": Issue of December 12, 1860, *Southern Advocate*.

85   "The South will never permit": Atlanta *Southern Confederacy*, reprinted in August 7, 1860, New York *Times*.

85   "Did you think the people of the South": Greenburg, p. 130-131.

85   "senseless fulminations": Henry Villard, *Lincoln on the Eve of '61: A Journalist's Story*, ed. Harold and Oswald Villard (NY: Knopf, 1941), p. 28

85   "He showed me": Henry Clay Whitney, *Life on the Circuit with Lincoln* (Boston: Estes and Lauriat, 1892), p. 432.

86   "Old Abe Lincoln": Letter of November 8, 1860, Harold Holzer, ed., *Dear Mr. Lincoln: Letters to the President* (Reading, MA: Addison-Wesley, 1993), p. 340.

Chapter 9: Lincoln in the Secession Winter

87   "were suspended . . . across various streets": Mary Chesnut, *The Private Mary Chesnut: The Unpublished Civil War Diaries*, C. Vann Woodward and Elisabeth Muhlenfeld, eds. (NY: Oxford University Press, 1984), p. 4.

87   "The tea has been thrown overboard.": November 8, 1860, Charleston *Mercury*, from David M. Potter and Don E. Fehrenbacher, *The Impending Crisis, 1848-1861* (NY: Harper Collins, 1976), p. 485.

88   "All this talk": Lincoln, *Works*, p. II: 355.

88   "this controversy will soon be settled": *ibid.*, p. III: 316.

89   "in no probable event": *ibid.*, p. IV: 95.

89   "does not believe": November 12, 1860, Chicago *Tribune*, from Randall, *Springfield to Gettysburg*, p. I: 247.

89   "[His] low estimate of humanity": Paul M. Angle, ed., *The Lincoln Reader* (New Brunswick: Rutgers University Press, 1947), p. 299.

89   "I think, from all I can learn": Stephen B. Oates, *With Malice Toward None* (NY: Harper & Row, 1977), p. 198.

90   "Stubborn facts": Villard, *Lincoln on the Eve of '61*, p. 23

90   "would do no good": Letter of October 23, 1860, to William S. Speer, Lincoln, *Works*, p. IV: 130

90   "the country was in a condition" and "a strange and bewildering chaos": Adams, *The Great Secession Winter*, p. 3.

Page 90   "There is only one man": December 15, 1860, *New York Herald*

91   "Form Reply to Requests": Lincoln, *Works*, p. IV: 60.

91   "By the lessons of the past": Letter of June 19, 1860, to Samuel Galloway, *ibid.*, p. IV: 80.

92   "impressing your readers": Letter of Oct. 29. 1860, to George D. Prentice, *ibid.*, p. IV: 134.

92   "There are no such men": Angle, p. 289.

92   "bold bad men": Letter of October 27, 1860, to George T.M. Davis, Lincoln, *Works*, p. IV: 133.

93   "To expose Mr. Lincoln": Harper, p. 57.

93   "A house divided": Lincoln, *Works*, p. IV: 491.

94   "If the Cotton States": November 9, 1860, New York *Tribune*, from McPherson, *The Battle Cry of Freedom*, p. 251-2

95: *I'm not stopping you!:* This analysis is taken from McPherson, who credits David M. Potter's writing on the subject as an influence on his interpretation of the "go in peace" strategy.

95   "Disunion sentiment": November 13, 1860, New York *Times*, from David M. Potter, *Lincoln and His Party in the Secession Crisis* (New Haven: Yale University Press, 1942), p. 63

95   "a spirit of compromise": November 14, New York *Times*, *ibid.*

95   "If he persists": Sandburg, *The War Years*, p. I: 12.

95   "All of the States": Lincoln, *Works*, p. IV: 141-2.

Chapter 10: The Flight Toward Compromise

98   "it is the end of us": Letter of January 11, 1861, to James T. Hale, Lincoln, *Works*, p. IV:172.

98   "Let there be no compromise": Letter of December 10, 1860, to Lyman Trumbull, *ibid.*, p. IV: 149-150.

99   "Entertain no proposition": Letter of December 11, 1860, to William Kellogg, *ibid.*, p. IV: 150.

99   "immediately filibustering": Letter of December 13, 1860, to Elihu Washburne, *ibid.*, p. IV: 151.

99   "Should the . . . Governors": December 17, 1860, *ibid.*, p. IV: 154.

99   "trouble holding them steady": Potter, *Lincoln and His Party*, p. 191.

99   "many of our Republican friends": *ibid.*

99   "who confess the error": Sandburg, *The War Years*, p. I: 32.

99   "better things will occur": December 9, 1860, *New York Herald*, from Potter, *Lincoln and His Party*, p. 128-9.

101   "very fishy and weak-kneed": *ibid.*, p. 179.

101   "prepare yourself": *ibid.*, p. 131.

101   "three fourths of the people" etc.: All Crittenden Compromise quotes, *ibid.*, p. 191-200.

102   "25% approval rating": *ibid.*, p. 113-114. The *Herald* again published its "less than one-fourth" estimate of Lincoln's minority on inauguration day—March 4, 1861. The Massachusetts returns are from Potter, *Lincoln and His Party*, p. 190.

103   "On the territorial question": Lincoln, *Works*, p. IV: 152.

103   "You think slavery is right": *ibid.*, p. 160.

104   "I have seen Mr. Lincoln": Thomas, p. 231.

104   "Not only was the old-time zest lacking": Tarbell, p. I: 406.

Chapter 11: The Journey to Washington

Page 105   "Some thought the cars": Lamon, *The Life of Abraham Lincoln*, p. 465.

105   "Our adversaries have us": Letter of January 3, 1861, to William Seward, Lincoln, *Works*, p. IV: 170.

106   "So we shall have an 'ovation'": February 7, 1861, *The Crisis*, from Harper, p. 77.

106   "Let us believe": Lincoln, *Works*, p. IV: 191.

106   "as a family relation": *ibid.,* p. IV: 195.

106   "Who would have supposed": February 21, 1861, *New Orleans Daily Crescent*, Dumond, p. 466-7.

107   "It is a war proposition": February 13, 1861, *Louisville Courier, ibid.*

107   "Whatever may have been": February 15, 1861, Nashville *Patriot, ibid.*

107   "should my administration": Lincoln, *Works*, p. IV: 197.

107   "the humblest of all individuals": *ibid.,* p. IV: 226.

107   "without a name": *ibid.,* p. IV: 204.

107   "I fear that the great confidence": *ibid.,* p. IV: 207.

108   "by a mere accident": *ibid.,* p. IV: 208.

108   "a mere instrument": *ibid.,* p. IV: 193.

108   "there is nothing going wrong": *ibid.,* p. IV: 204.

108   "In plain words": *ibid.,* p. IV: 211.

108   "I think that there is no occasion": *ibid.,* p. IV: 216.

108   "Have not our forts and vessels been seized": Sandburg, *The War Years*, p. I: 47.

108   "At Columbus, Ohio": February 15, 1861, Saint Louis *Daily Missouri Republican,* Dumond, p. 460-61.

109   "no capacity to grapple manfully": Sandburg, *The War Years*, p. I: 48.

109   "thoroughly matured judgment": Lincoln, *Works*, p. IV: 215.

109   "crude, ignorant twaddle": Villard, *Memoirs*, p. 152.

109   "absolutely unknown": Randall, *Springfield to Gettysburg*, p. I: 292.

110   "Lincoln is a 'Simple Susan.'": G.S. Merriam, *Life and Times of Samuel Bowles* (NY: The Century Co.,1885), p. I: 318.

110   "These speeches thus far": Sandburg, *The War Years,* p. I: 48.

110   "His speeches have fallen": Entry of February 18, 1861, from Nevins, *1859-1861*, p. 438.

110   "Abe is becoming more grave": Sandburg, *The War Years*, p. I: 61.

110   "The illustrious Honest Old Abe": *Salem Advocate*, from Carl Sandburg, *The Lincoln Collector* (NY: Harcourt, Brace, 1950), p. 23.

111   "The lack of good taste": February 21, 1861, Harrisburg *Daily Patriot and Union*, Perkins, II: p. 1004

"There is that about his speechification": Sandburg, *The War Years*, p. I: 48.

111   "His speeches on his tour": Donald E. Reynolds, ed., *Editors Make War* (Nashville: Vanderbilt University Press, 1970), p. 187.

111   "a beastly figure" and "No American of any section": *ibid.*

111   "fiddle-faddle": Harold Holzer, "The Legacy of Lincoln's Impromptu Oratory," James McPherson, ed.,*"We Cannot Escape History": Lincoln and the Last Best Hope of Earth* (Urbana and Chicago, University of Illinois Press, 1995)

111   "If any one can read the speeches": February 21, 1861, *New Orleans Daily Crescent*, Dumond, p. 465.

112   "His silly speeches": February 26, 1861, New Orleans *Daily Delta, ibid.,* p. 469-70.

112   "Mr. Lincoln": February 15, 1861, Albany *Atlas and Argus*, from Randall, *Springfield to Gettysburg*, p. I: 292.

Chapter 12: Lincoln and the Merchants

Page 113   "While he thus satisfied the public curiosity": Villard, *Memoirs*, p. 93, 151-2.

113   "Old Abe Lincoln was here": Townsend, p. 66.

113   "Awfully ugly": Sandburg, *The War Years*, p. I: 49.

114   "He is distressingly homely": Maury Klein, *Days of Defiance: Sumter, Secession, and the Coming of the Civil War* (New York, Alfred Knopf, 1997), p. 265.

"the masses of people did not turn out": Sandburg, *The War Years*, p. I: 58.

114   "crowd which cheered": Sandburg, *The Lincoln Collector*, p. 241.

114   "possessed no personal popularity": Walter Lowenfels, *Walt Whitman's Civil War* (Da Capo Press, 1989) p. 269-270.

115   "a prolongation of the South": Potter, *Lincoln and His Party*, p. 117.

115   "The mercantile world is in a ferment": *ibid.*, p. 127.

115   "I am not insensible": Letter of November 10, 1860, to Truman Smith, in Lincoln, *Works*, p. IV: 138.

116   "It annoyed me": John G. Nicolay, and John Hay, *Abraham Lincoln: A History* (NY: The Century Co., 1890), p. III: 281.

116   "it is easy to perceive": Smith, *The Nation Comes of Age*, p. 148-9.

116   "the upper world of millionaire merchants": William Howard Russell, *My Diary North and South* (NY: Harper & Brothers, 1863), p. 16.

116   "Oh, indeed, is that so?": Anonymous, *The Diary of a Public Man* (New Brunswick: Rutgers University Press, 1946), p. 49.

Conversation with William L. Dodge: Angle, p. 325

117   "sorely afflicted": Sandburg, *The War Years*, p. I: 59.

117   "I think we ought to send some flowers": Anonymous, p. 51-2.

118   "if you don't Resign": Holzer, *Dear Mr. Lincoln*, p. 341.

Part Two: Lincoln's First Eighteen Months

Chapter 13: Lincoln's First Impression

121   "A person who met Mr. Lincoln": Russell, p. 22.

122   "the majority of the people": *ibid.*, p. 14.

122   "I was astonished": *ibid.*, p. 15.

122   "Deformed Sir": Sandburg, *The Prairie Years*, p. II: 381-2.

"Mr. Lincoln was the homeliest man": Angle, p. 298.

122   "To say that he is ugly is nothing": Dicey, p. 91.

122   "homeliest and the awkwardest": Garrison, p. 51.

122   "as far as all external conditions": Villard, *Memoirs*, p. 92-3.

122   "his phiz is truly awful": J.G. Randall, *Mr. Lincoln*, ed. Richard Current (NY: Dodd, Mead, and Co., 1957), p. 27.

122   "Slouchy, ungraceful": Letter of November 15, 1860, Thomas Webster to John Sherman, from Oates, p. 181.

122   "I was somewhat startled by his appearance": Harold Holzer, ed., *Lincoln As I Knew Him* (Chapel Hill: Algonquin Books of Chapel Hill, 1999), p. 54.

123   "He is lank and hard-featured": Strong, p. III: 188.

123   "I doubt whether I wholly concealed my disappointment": McClure, p. 48.

123   "coconut shaped and somewhat too small": Dicey, p. 91.

Page 123　"long, sallow, and cadaverous": Lamon, *The Life of Abraham Lincoln*, p. 469.

123　"His complexion was very dark": *ibid.*

123　"nose and ears": Dicey, p. 91.

123　"flapping and wide-projecting" and "a prominent organ": Russell, p. 45.

123　"thatch of wild republican hair": *ibid.*, p. 44.

123　"had apparently been acquainted with neither brush": Holzer, *Lincoln As I Knew Him*, p. 167.

123　"dark, almost black": Randall, *Mr. Lincoln*, p. 30.

123　"rough, uncombed and uncombable": Dicey, p. 91.

123　"bristling and compact": Russell, p. 44.

123　"lean, lank, and indescribably gawky figure": Villard, *Memoirs*, p. 93.

123　"a thin . . . raw-boned man": Lamon, *The Life of Abraham Lincoln*, p. 469.

123　"Always cadaverous": Holzer, *Lincoln As I Knew Him*, 90-91.

123　"Fancy a man six-foot": Dicey, p. 91.

124　"a huge skeleton in clothes": Angle, p. 299.

124　"awkwardness that was uncommon in men of intelligence": McClure, p. 49.

124　"loose-jointed" and "There is no describing": Holzer, *Lincoln As I Knew Him*, p. 166, 167.

124　"His posture was awkward": *ibid.*, p. 117.

124　"with a shambling . . . unsteady gait": Russell, p. 44.

124　"thin through the breast": John Fort Newton, *Lincoln and Herndon* (Cedar Rapids: The Torch Press, 1910), p. 324.

124　"He was very awkward in all the little common-places of life": Whitney, p. 538.

124　"when standing Straight": Wilson and Davis, p. 201.

124　"the length of his legs" and "When he sat down on a chair": Lamon, *Lincoln As I Knew Him*, p. 468-9.

125　Description of Lincoln's walk: *ibid.*, p. 470.

125　"Lincoln stands six feet twelve in his socks": Harry J. Maihafer, *War of Words* (Washington: Brassey's, 2003), p. 218.

125　"Abraham Lincoln is a man": September 13, 1864, *Kentucky Statesman*, from Townsend, p. 296.

126　"If he aint a long wun an a narrow wun, I'm durned": Michael Davis, *The Image of Lincoln in the South* (Knoxville: University of Tennessee Press, 1971), p. 33.

126　"He probably had as little taste": Holzer, *Lincoln As I Knew Him*, p. 60.

126　"an ungainly back woodsman": Donald, *Lincoln* p. 186-7.

126　"more or less careless": Wilson and Davis, p. 728.

126　"wearing a dirty linen duster": Sandburg, *The War Years,* p. I: 442.

127　"On his head he wore": Holzer, *Lincoln As I Knew Him*, p. 55.

127　"dressed in an ill-fitting, wrinkled suit of black": Russell, p. 44.

127　"in a long, tight, badly fitting suit of black": Dicey, p. 91.

127　"He was dressed in a rusty black frock-coat": Holzer, *Lincoln As I Knew Him*, p. 167.

127　"Abraham Lincoln looks very awkward": February 26, 1861, *Springfield Republican*, from Harper, p. 94.

127　"He had very defective taste": Lamon, *Recollections of Abraham Lincoln*, p. 96-100.

128　"He was, apparently, the tallest": Francis Adams Donaldson, *Inside the Army of the Potomac: The Civil War Experience of Captain Francis Adams Donaldson,* Ed. J. Gregory Acken (Mechanicsburg, PA: Stackpole, 1998), p. 433-4.

128　"His grammar is weak": Entry of October 23, 1861, Strong, p. III:188.

Page 128   "words in a manner that puzzles": September 18, 1859, Cincinnati *Enquirer*, Harper, p. 40.

128   *keer fer sich idees* and *unly way he would ra-ally yearn respect*: These are not direct quotes, but collections of Lincoln's mispronunciations I have gleaned from many first person accounts of his speech, including those in Paludan, *The Presidency of Abraham Lincoln*, p. 95; Sandburg, *The Prairie Years*, p. II: 137; Garrison, *The Lincoln No One Knows*, p. 51; *The Diary of George Templeton Strong*, p. III: 204; and P.M. Zall, "Abe Lincoln Laughing" in Gabor Boritt, ed., *The Historian's Lincoln* (Urbana: University of Illinois Press, 1996), p. 24. His mispronunciation of "inauguration" and "inaugural" were well known, and his misspellings of those words can be found in his letter to Trumbull, April 29, 1860 and his letter to A.G. Curtin, Dec. 21, 1860. That he mispronounced "picture" I infer from the misspelling in his letter to Henry Raymond, Dec. 18, 1860.

129   "Wa-al that reminds me": Entry of January 29, 1862, Strong, p. III: 204-5.

129   "Here was an heir of poverty": Holzer, *Lincoln As I Knew Him*, p. 111.

129   "the Magician asked the Presdt": Letter of November 21, 1861, George B. McClellan, *The Civil War Papers of George B. McClellan: Selected Correspondence 1860-1865*, Ed. Stephen Sears (NY: Ticknor and Fields, 1989), p. 137.

129   "far from musical": Holzer, *Lincoln As I Knew Him*, p. 117.

129   "His voice was naturally good": Villard, "Recollections of Lincoln," *Atlantic Monthly* (February 1904).

129   "a thin tenor": Garrison, p. 51-2.

129   "a homeliness of manner": McClure, p. 48.

130   "I don't believe first class people": Reprinted in September 12, 1861, *The Crisis*, from Harper, p. 93.

130   "Neither was Lincoln a good listener.": William Herndon and Jesse Weik, *Herndon's Lincoln, Vol. I*, (Springfield: The Herndon's Lincoln Publishing Co., 1888), p. 333.

130   "He is an overgrown nature-child": Letter of October 12, 1864, Schurz to Theodore Petrasch, Carl Schurz, *Intimate Letters of Carl Schurz* (Kessinger Publishing, 2005), 308-309.

130   "a barbarian, a Scythian, a yahoo": Entry for January 29, 1862, Strong, p. III: 204.

130   "rarely read": According to his friend and law partner William Herndon, "The truth about Mr. Lincoln is, that he read *less* and thought *more* than any man in his sphere in America. No man can put his finger on any great book written in the last or present century that he read." (Herndon and Weik, p. 593) His secretary John Hay wrote, "He read very little. Scarcely ever looked into a newspaper unless I called his attention to an article on some special subject. He frequently said, 'I know more about that than any of them.'" (Wilson and Davis, p. 332) Lincoln told artist Francis Carpenter, "It may seem somewhat strange to say, but I never read an entire novel in my life! . . . I once commenced 'Ivanhoe,' but never finished it." (Francis B. Carpenter, *The Inner Life of Abraham Lincoln: Six Months at the White House* (Lincoln: University of Nebraska Press, 1995), p. 114-115.)

130   "read out loud": William Herndon wrote that Lincoln "never read any other way but aloud. This habit used to annoy me almost beyond the point of endurance. I once asked him why he did so. This was his explanation: 'When I read aloud two senses catch the idea: first, I see what I read; second, I hear it, and therefore can remember it better.'" (Herndon and Weik, p. 332.) Lincoln's sister-in-law, Mrs. Wallace, also testified, "He would read, generally aloud (couldn't read otherwise)." (Lamon, *The Life of Abraham Lincoln*, p. 472.)

130   "*abandon* of President Lincoln": June 17, 1861, New York *Times*, from Goodwin, p. 386.

130   "like a man pumping for life": Randall, *Mr. Lincoln*, p. 173.

131   "As he advanced through the room": Russell, p. 22.

131   "It is impossible to be more bitter": Anonymous, p. 55-6.

Page 131   "His conversation consists of vulgar anecdotes": Donald, *Lincoln,* p. 186-7.

131   "his laugh was the laugh of a yahoo": Entry of October 23, 1861, Strong, p. III: 188.

132   "the 'neigh' of a wild horse": Carpenter, p. 150.

132   "When he told": George Julian, from Allen Thorndike Rice, ed., *Reminiscences of Abraham Lincoln by Distinguished Men of His Time* (NY: Harper & Bros., 1909), p. 234.

132   "His body shook all over": Holzer, *Lincoln As I Knew Him*, p. 93-95.

132   "Such a book would stink like a thousand privies.": Don E. Fehrenbacher and Virginia E. Fehrenbacher, eds., *Recollected Words of Abraham Lincoln* (Stanford University Press, 1996), p. 146. However, both Thurlow Weed and Francis Carpenter both testified to the contrary—that in their presence, Lincoln did not tell dirty stories.

132   "the *riskiest* of story tellers": William E. Gienapp, *Abraham Lincoln and Civil War America: A Biography* (NY: Oxford University Press, 2002), p. 185-6.

132   "I do wish Abraham": Entry of February 24, 1864, from Strong, p. III: 408.

132   "Although Mr. Lincoln's walk": Lamon, *The Life of Abraham Lincoln*, p. 480.

133   "Well, there was a party once": P.M. Zall, ed., *Abe Lincoln Laughing* (Berkeley: University of California Press, 1982), p. 100-101.

134   "We had gatherings": Angle, p. 300.

134   "He interspersed our conversation": Holzer, *Lincoln As I Knew Him*, p. 56.

134   "What a disgusting Scene": Sandburg, *The War Years*, p. I: 116.

134   "a man of no intelligence": Letter of February 22, 1861, Doniphan to "My dear Jno," from William Marvel, *Mr. Lincoln Goes to War* (Boston: Houghton Mifflin, 2006), p. 10.

134   "a cross between a sandhill crane" Sandburg, *The War Years,* p. I: 115.

135   "Superficially vulgar": Entry of October 23, 1861, Strong, p. III: 188.

135   "sense of superiority possessed President Lincoln": Don Piatt, from Rice, p. 359.

135   "Lincoln's intellectual self-confidence": Miller, p. 64

136   "[Charles Francis Adams] had been summoned": Charles Francis Adams, Jr., *Charles Francis Adams*, (Boston: Houghton, Mifflin, & Co., 1900), p. 145-146.

137   "Few, very few, of the Republican leaders": McClure, p. 59.

137   "Few men believed": Lamon, *The Life of Abraham Lincoln,* p. 468.

137   "Mr. Lincoln has not hitherto given proof": Jay Monoghan, *Diplomat in Carpet Slippers* (Indianapolis: Charter Books, 1945), p. 36.

137   "honest simplicity": Klein, p. 276.

137   "He is not a great man": Burton J. Hendrick, *Lincoln's War Cabinet* (Boston: Little, Brown, and Company, 1946), p. 117.

137   "I doubt Mr. Lincoln's capacity": Holzer, *Lincoln As I Knew Him*, p. 93.

137   "He is unequal to the crisis": Allan Nevins, *The War for the Union: The Improvised War, 1861-1862* (NY: Charles Scribner's Sons, 1959), p. 4.

137   "great ability in affairs": *ibid.*, p. 437.

138   "Old Abe is honest": *ibid.*, p. 452.

138   "simply, we believe, an honest man": Sandburg, *The War Years*, p. I: 115.

138   "no man living": Henry Adams, *The Education of Henry Adams* (Boston: Houghton Mifflin, 1918), p. 172.

Chapter 14: The First Inaugural

139   "Caesar had his Brutus": Furgurson, p. 59.

141   "The 4th of March": Leech, Margaret, *Reveille in Washington* (NY: Harper & Brothers, 1941), p. 46.

141   "for the first time": Michael Davis, p. 65.

141   "dissolve the Confederacy": Holzer, *Lincoln As I Knew Him*, p. 110.

Page 141: The First Inaugural Address: Lincoln, *Works*, p. IV: 265.

143   "We are receiving Lincoln's inaugural": Klein, p. 317.

143   "A tall, ungainly man": Furgurson, p. 60.

143   "Mr. Lincoln was pale": Anonymous, p. 85.

143   "The address has disappointed every one": *ibid.,* p. 86.

144   "was received with nothing like enthusiasm": Villard, *Memoirs*, p. 156.

144   "just what was expected": Klein, p. 317.

144   "tocsin of battle": March 6, 1861, Charleston *Mercury*, Mitgang, p. 243.

144   "It would have been almost as instructive": Sandburg, *The War Years*, p. I: 137.

144   "The Country No Wiser" and "weak, vacillating": Douglas Fermer, *James Gordon Bennett and the New York Herald: A Study of Editorial Opinion in the Civil War Era, 1854-1867* (NY: St. Martin's Press, 1986), p. 179.

144   "to terrify the heart": March 4, 1861, Philadelphia *Morning Pennsylvanian,* from Kenneth Stampp, *And the War Came: The North and the Secession Crisis, 1860-1861* (Baton Rouge: LSU Press, 1970), p. 197.

144   "a sad disappointment": Klein, p. 316.

144   "a wretchedly botched and unstatesmanlike paper": Hartford *Times*, reprinted in March 7, 1861, *New York Times,* from Goodwin, p. 330

144   "lost beyond hope": Randall, *Springfield to Gettysburg*, p. I: 306.

144   Wood refused to hoist the national flag: Sandburg, *The War Years*, p. I: 137.

144   "if it means what it says": *ibid.*

144   "If declaring the Union perpetual": E.B. Long, *The Civil War Day by Day* (NY: Doubleday & Co., 1971), p. 46.

145   "deceptive": Klein, p. 316.

145   "the cool, unimpassioned, deliberate language": Sandburg, *The War Years*, p. I: 137.

145   "involved, coarse, colloquial": Potter, *The Impending Crisis*, p. 568.

145   "a wishy-washy, unscholarly affair": Howard Cecil Perkins, ed., *Northern Editorials on Secession* (Gloucester, MA: Peter Smith, 1964), p. II:643.

145   "one of the most awkwardly constructed": Philip Shaw Paludan, *The Presidency of Abraham Lincoln* (Lawrence, University Press of Kansas, 1994), p. 57.

145   "a lame, unsatisfactory and discreditable production": Klein, p. 316.

145   "mean, involved, and inconclusive": Reynolds, p. 190.

145   "A loose, disjointed, rambling affair": Randall, *Springfield to Gettysburg,* p. I: 306.

145   "tawdry and corrupt schoolboy style": *ibid.,* p. 303.

145   "A schoolboy production": Reynolds, p. 190.

145   John Tyler's criticism: Sandburg, *The War Years*, p. I: 137.

145   "is generally attributed": Monoghan, p. 38.

145   "the New Yorker with his Illinois attachment": Nevins, *1859-1861*, p. 446.

Chapter 15: The Struggle with Seward, Then Sumter

146   "I am without schemes": Potter, *Lincoln and his Party*, p. 83.

146   "It has been my purpose": Lincoln, *Works*, p. IV: 148.

147   "some loud threats and much muttering": Thurlow Weed, *Autobiography of Thurlow Weed*, Ed. Harriet Weed (Boston: Houghton Mifflin, 1884), p. 604-5.

149   "that there was no great difference": Goodwin, p. 342.

150   "I will try to save freedom": Potter, *The Impending Crisis*, p. 562.

150   "I have assumed a sort of dictatorship" Letter of January 3, 1861, to his wife, from Potter, *The Impending Crisis,* p. 310.

Page 150   "If you will only give it time": *ibid.*, p. 243.

151   "All old party platforms": Klein, p. 325.

151   "Come forward promptly": Letter of February 6, 1861, Barbour to Seward, from Daniel W. Crofts, *Reluctant Confederates: Upper South Unionists in the Secession Crisis* (Chapel Hill: University of North Carolina Press, 1993), p. 261.

152: Seward looked to the Virginia elections in May: Henry Adams, *The Great Secession Winter of 1860-1861, and Other Essays* (NY: Sagamore Press, 1958), p. 27-8.

152   "Mr. Seward's real view": Nevins, *1859-1861*, p. 401.

152   "the two or three hundred thousand voices": Crofts, p. 269

154   "The quietest joint Assembly": Klein, p. 274.

155   "meet prejudice with conciliation": Julian, p. 185

155   "I listened to every word": Sandburg, *The War Years*, p. I: 19.

156   "is now . . . virtual ruler": Glyndon G. Van Deusen, *William Henry Seward* (NY: Oxford University Press, 1967), p. 246.

156   "Mad men North and mad men South": Hendrick, p. 129.

156   "It seems to me": Van Deusen, p. 246.

156   "Away with all parties": *ibid.,* p. 305.

156   "They have abandoned the doctrine": Douglas in United States Senate, March 3, 1861, from Randall, *Springfield to Gettysburg,* p. I: 230.

156   "Mr. Seward waived": James G. Blaine, *Twenty Years of Congress* (Norwich, CN: Henry Bill, 1884), p. I: 271.

156   "The Gulf Confederacy can count Virginia out": Potter, *The Impending Crisis,* p. 310.

156   "For more than two months": *ibid.*, p. 310.

157   "The ancient Seward is in high spirits": *ibid.*, p. 313.

157   "Those who saw and followed Mr. Seward": Adams, *The Great Secession Winter*, p. 22-23.

157   "Seward has had Old Abe": Klein, p. 277.

158   "A distracted country appeared" and "I did not dare to go home": Letter of March 8, 1861, to his wife, from Goodwin, p. 318.

159   "Only the soothing words": Nevins, *1861-1862*, p. 22.

159   "give such an advantage to the Disunionists": Hendrick, p. 152

159   "I am loath to close": Lincoln, *Works*, p. IV:271.

160   "It was this almost implicit trust": Gideon Welles, *The Diary of Gideon Welles*, Ed. Howard K., Beale (NY: W. W. Norton & Co., 1860), p. I: 33-3.

162   "It was bad enough in Springfield": Villard, *Memoirs*, p. 156.

162   "more scheming, plotting heads": Russell, p. 20

162   "two thousand and five hundred patriots": Sandburg, *The War Years*, p. I: 163.

162   "Solicitants for offices": *ibid.,* p. 164.

162   "I have been to see him": *ibid.*

162   "Mr. Lincoln I have not seen": Letter of April 3, from Anonymous, p. 117.

163   "he was entirely ignorant": Wilson and Davis, p. 207.

163   "Mr. Lincoln had no method": Holzer, *Lincoln As I Knew Him*, p. 63-4.

163   "much absorption in the details": Goodwin, p. 341.

163   "the difficulty with Mr Lincoln": Donald, *Lincoln*, p. 285.

163   "He is ignorant, and must have help": Goodwin, p. 335.

163   "Our poor President is having a hard time of it": Sandburg, *The War Years,* p. I: 164.

163   "unconciliatory," "ignorant," etc.: Fermer, p. 180

163   "owes a higher duty": April 4, 1861, *New York Times*, from Goodwin, p. 335.

163   "I am like a man": Sandburg, *The War Years,* p. I: 182.

Page 164: March, April Confederate Army strength: Albert Nofi, *A Civil War Treasury* (Da Capo Press, 1995), p. 42.

164   "I must have reached Washington": Paul M. Angle and Earl Schenk Miers, eds., *Tragic Years, 1860-1865: A Documentary History of the American Civil War* (NY: Simon & Schuster, 1960), 76-7.

165   "Through patronage and offices": Adam Gurowski, *Diary, from March 4, 1861 to November 12, 1862* (Boston: Lee and Shepard, 1862), p. 17-21.

166   "every day affords proof": Letter of March 16, 1861, Edwin Stanton to James Buchanan, from Hedrick, p. 258.

167   "with a familiarity": Welles, p. I: 135.

167   "There was very little concerted action": *ibid.*, p. 136.

168   "Erring Sisters, depart in Peace": Crofts, p. 271.

168   "I now see no alternative": Lincoln, *Works*, p. IV:279.

169   "in favor of withdrawing the Troops": *ibid.,* p. IV:288.

169   "the Hector or Atlas": Goodwin, p. 341.

169   "Unionists look only to yourself": *ibid.*

169   "the speedy adjustment": Hendrick, p. 154.

170   "a talk with Seward": Klein, p. 323.

170   "I am able to state": Nevins, *1861-1862,* p. 43.

170   "Anderson and his gallant band": Donald, *Lincoln*, p. 287.

171   "approved by the entire body": *ibid.*

171   "growing sentiment": *ibid.*

171   "acted like a charm": *ibid.*, p. 275.

171   "a burning sentiment": Perkins, p. II:652-3.

171   "stepping directly into the footsteps": *ibid.*, p. II: 665-6.

171   "Washington was full of indignant Northern men": Villard, *Memoirs*, p. 156.

171   "Is it possible Lincoln is getting scared?": Donald, *Lincoln*, p. 288.

171   "The President is drifting": Paludan, p. 61.

171   "The bird of our country": Entry of March 11, 1861, Strong, p. III: 109.

171   "submission to a band of traitors": Klein, p. 355.

171   "a blacker and more infamous name": *ibid.*

171   "the new administration is done forever": *ibid.*

172   "The South will proclaim [Lincoln] a Damned fool": Potter, *The Impending Crisis*, p. 359-60.

172   "Dear Sir I voted for you": Holzer, *Dear Mr. Lincoln*, p. 144.

172   "Thirty days more of '*Peace Policy*' at Washington": *ibid.*, p. 145.

172   "the true way": Nevins, *1861-1862*, p. 54.

173   "shut up every Southern port": March 22 and 23, 1861, New York *Times*, from Crofts, p. 284.

173   "A state of war": March 30, 1861, *New York Times, ibid.*

173   "if we are to fight, so be it": April 3, 1861, New York *Tribune*, from Gray, p. 49

173   "the disgraceful policy": April 8, 1861, New York *Evening Post*, from Kenneth Stampp, *The Imperiled Union: Essays on the Background of the Civil War* (NY: Oxford University Press, 1981), p. 298

173   "Wanted—A Policy": Perkins, p. II: 660.

173   "There is a general discontent": Letter of April 5, 1861, from Carl Schurz, Abraham Lincoln, *The Abraham Lincoln Papers at the Library of Congress,* http://memory. Loc.gov /ammem/alhtml/alser1_dates.html

Page 174   "because the evacuation of Sumter": Frederic Bancroft, *The Life of William H. Seward* (NY: Harper & Bros., 1900), p. II: 114.
174   Campbell-Seward conversation: Nevins, *1861-1862*, p. 50.
174   "In all political or administrative movements": McClure, p. 136.
174   "My policy is to have no policy": Sandburg, *The War Years*, p. I: 211.
175   "I am satisfied of the policy": Klein, p. 345.
175   "Unquestionably separate nationality" and "They expect a golden era": *ibid.*, p. 192.
175   "an unanimity," "no attachment," and "irrevocably gone": Nevins, *1861-1862*, p. 53-4.
175   "the evacuation of both forts": Hendrick, p. 170.
176   "Some Thoughts for the President's Consideration": Bancroft, p. 132.
176   "Whatever policy we adopt": Hendrick, p. 176.
177   "If this must be done": Bancroft, p. 138.
177   "I am afraid you have come too late": Nevins, *1861-1862*, p. 64.
177   Campbell-Seward conversation: *ibid.*, p. 59.
177   "the President is light": Klein, p. 370.
177   "Faith as to Sumter fully kept": Nevins, *1861-1862*, p. 59.
178   "a large military expedition": Crofts, p. 310.
178   "the Lincoln administration": Fermer, p. 183.
178   "vicious, imbecile, demoralized Administration": Brayton Harris, p. 43.
178   "our only hope": April 10, 1861, *New York Herald*, from Sandburg, *The War Years*, p. I: 352.
178   "The feeling of loyalty": Frank A. Flower, *Edwin McMasters Stanton* (Akron: The Saalfield Publishing Co, 1905), p. 106.
179   "more incumbent than ever": Crofts, p. 312.
179   "It would be treason": Nevins, *1861-1862,* p. 48.
179   "[Blair's] earnestness": Welles, p. I: 13-14.
179   "far less evil and bloodshed": Potter, *Lincoln and His Party*, p. 316.
179   "if you undertake to destroy the Union": Lincoln, p. III: 502 For insight into Lincoln's view of history with regard to wars, I am indebted to Gabor Boritt's essay, "Abraham Lincoln and the Question of Individual Responsibility", from Boritt, *Why the Civil War Came*, p. 11.
180   "I, Abraham Lincoln": Lincoln, *Works*, p. IV: 331-2.
180   "Lincoln prostrated us": Crofts, p. 336.
180   "The fight at Charleston": *ibid.*
180   "the conflict at Charleston": *ibid.*
180   "Union feeling was strong": *ibid.*
180   "in many respects the most unfortunate state paper": *ibid.*, p. 335.
180   "the President's extraordinary proclamation": *ibid.*, p. 334.
180   "If Mr. Lincoln had only insisted": *ibid.*, p. 335.
181   "We are struck": *ibid.*, p. 337.
181   "drive us all into rebellion": *ibid.*, p. 338.
181   "I think no candid man": Michael Davis, p. 55.
181   "allowed it to go forth": Crofts, p. 338.
181   "This, to our apprehension, is *rank usurpation*": *ibid.*
181   "It is against the friends of the Union": *ibid.*
181   "Union men feel": *ibid.*, p. 338-9.
"the disgusting baseness": April 18, 1861, *New Orleans Daily Delta*, from Michael Davis, p. 55.
182   "If Mr. Lincoln contemplated this policy": *Louisville Journal*, reprinted in April 17, 1861, *Cincinnati Enquirer*, from Harper, p. 211.
182   "deceived by false assurances": Crofts, p. 310.

Page 182   "cheated, imposed upon, and deceived": *ibid.*

182   "the god of battles": *ibid.*, p. 339.

182   "knocked away the props": *ibid.*

182   "I was opposed to secession": Michael Davis, p. 61.

182   Border State governors' replies: Angle and Miers, p. 65-6.

183   " *I told you last spring*": Edward L. Ayers, *In the Presence of Mine Enemies: The Civil War in the Heart of America* (NY: W.W. Norton & Company, 2003), p. 228.

184   "It appears, we confess, to complete the character": Sandburg, *The War Years*, p. I: 212.

Chapter 16: The Capital Surrounded

185   "Fort Sumter is temporarily lost": Brayton Harris, p. 47.

185   "On every corner": April 15, 1861, New York *Times*

185   "Secession, disunion, and even fault finding ": Letter of April 16, 1861, W.H. Hanna of Bloomington, Illinois, to Ward Lamon, from Lamon, *Recollections of Abraham Lincoln*, p. 320.

185   "The business community": Sandburg, *The War Years*, p. I: 217.

186   "local commotion": Garrison, p. 86-7.

186   "Illinois can whip the South": Donald, *Lincoln*, p. 295.

186   "Jeff. Davis & Co. will be swinging": *ibid.*

186   "if ABRAHAM LINCOLN is equal": May 4, 1861, *Harper's Weekly*

186   "Broadway crowded": Entry of April 20, 1861, Strong, p. III: 127-128.

187   "There is one wild shout": April 23, 1861, *Richmond Examiner*, from Sandburg, *The War Years*, p. I: 230.

187   "in readiness to dislodge": April 23, 1861, *Richmond Whig*, from Harper, p. 92.

188   "the removal of Lincoln": Sandburg, *The War Years,* p. I: 250.

188   "Lincoln is in a trap": Letter of April 20, 1861, H.D. Bird to Leroy P. Walker, from *The War of the Rebellion: A Compilation of the Official Records of the Union and Confederate Armies* (Washington: Government Printing Office, 1880), p. I: 2: 771-2.

188   "The impression here": Letter of April 12, 1861, from Anonymous, p. 118.

188   "starved, washed-out creatures": Russell, p. 61.

189   "no description": Letter of May 11, 1861, from Anonymous, p. 119.

189   "reliable information": April 20, 1861, *Richmond Whig*, from Frank Moore, ed., *The Rebellion Record, Vol. I, 1860-1861* (NY: G.P. Putnam, 1861), p. 54.

190   "A gentleman arrived here": *ibid.*

190   "Old Abe sleeps with a hundred men": *ibid.*, p. 55.

190   "He has not passed a night": May 4, 1861, *Petersburg Express*, from Davis, p. 65-6.

190   Iron cage story and "Jeff Davis is after me!": *ibid.*

190   "[The panic in Washington] was increased": Letter of May 11, 1861, from Anonymous, p. 119.

190   "The town is full": Entry of April 20, 1861, John Hay, *Lincoln and the Civil War in the Diaries and Letters of John Hay,* ed. Tyler Dennett (NY: Dodd, Mead and Co., 1939), p. 5.

191   Rumor of forty thousand Virginia volunteers: Frederick W. Seward, *Reminiscences of a War-Time Statesman and Diplomat, 1830-1915* (NY: G.P. Putnam, 1916), p. 157.

191   Other rumors: Leech, p. 63, and Dean Sprague, *Freedom Under Lincoln* (Boston: Houghton Mifflin, 1965), p. 114-115.

191   "'Mr. Brown, I am not a learned man!'": Geoffrey Perrett, *Lincoln's War* (NY: Random House, 2004), p. 37.

191   "Jumped up": Letter of May 12, 1861, William Faxon to Mark Howard, John Hay, *Inside Lincoln's White House: The Complete Civil War Diary of John Hay,* ed. Michael Burlingame and

John R. Turner Ettinger (Carbondale: Southern Illinois University Press, 1997), notes to pages 6-7, footnote 25.

Page 191   "They think and in fact find it perfectly safe": Entry of April 23, 1861, Bates, p. 185-6.

192   "merely the general notion of drifting": Sandburg, *The War Years,* p. I: 231.

192   "the disunionists have anticipated us": John G. Nicolay and John Hay, "The Border States," from *The Century,* Volume 36, Issue 1, May 1888, p. 58-9.

192   "If good Uncle Abe": April 22, 1961, New York *Tribune,* from Harper, p. 103.

192   "An indescribable gloom": Nicolay and Hay, "The Border States," p. 155.

192   "Business was at a standstill": Seward, p. 157.

193   "impatience, gloom, and depression" and "No one felt it more than the President": Hay, *Inside Lincoln's White House,* notes to pages 7-11, footnote 37.

193   "miserable traitorous head": Letter of April 20, 1861, Edmund J. McGarn and William Fairchild to Lincoln, from Oates, p. 89.

193   *"To Abe Lincon Esqr":* Letter of April 11, 1861, from Unknown, Lincoln, *Papers.*

193   "It does seem to me": McClure, p. 68-9.

193   "a feeling came over him": Schurz, *Reminiscences,* p. 227-8

194   "a day of gloom and doubt," and "I don't believe there is any North": Entry of April 24, 1861, Hay, *Lincoln and the Civil War,* p. 11.

194   "From the known assemblage": *Official Records,* p. I: 2: 602.

194   "The Seventh marched up Pennsylvania Avenue": Nicolay and Hay, *A History,* p. IV: 149-153, 155-157.

195   Three "villainous articles": April 25, 1861, *New York Times,* from Lincoln, *Papers.*

196   "For God's sake": Letter of April 26, 1861, J.H. Jordan of Cincinnati to Salmon P. Chase, from Wood Gray, *The Hidden Civil War: The Story of the Copperheads* (NY: Viking Press, 1942), p. 75.

196   "Neither pighead Lincoln": Leroy H. Fischer, *Lincoln's Gadfly: Adam Gurowski* (Norman: University of Oklahoma Press, 1969), p. 98.

196   "the undecided conduct": Entry for April 1861, Gurowski, *Diary, 1861-1862,* p. 32.

196   "become a vast consolidated despotism": Sandburg, *The War Years,* p. I: 365.

197   "From Mr. Lincoln nothing is to be hoped": Letter of April 23, 1861, R.F. Fuller to Salmon Chase, from Rhodes, p. 368.

Chapter 17: The Hundred Days to Bull Run

198   "The Maryland Disunionists": Entry of May 4, 1861, Hay, *Lincoln and the Civil War,* p. 18.

198   "History tells us": Sandburg, *The War Years,* p. I: 183.

199   "the powers of a dictator" sketched: *ibid.,* p. I: 231-2.

199   "put in force the war power": Entry of March 30, 1864, Welles, p. I: 549.

199   "One of the interesting features": Letter from Schleiden to Sumner, from James Rawley, *The Politics of Union: Northern Politics during the Civil War* (Lincoln: University of Nebraska Press, 1974), p. 27.

200   "judicial power also": Sprague, p. 42.

200   "more regal and absolute power": J.G. Randall, *Lincoln the President: Midstream* (NY: Dodd, Mead, & Co., 1953), p. 164.

200   "is an instrument whose powers": June 22, 1861, *Cincinnati Daily Enquirer,* from Gray, p. 64.

200   "Is he not a President": June 27, 1861, *The Crisis.*

Page 201   "the vicinity of any military line": Lincoln, *Works*, p. IV: 419.

201   "I am not disposed to say": Sprague, p. 119.

202   Lincoln swears off military concerns: Entry of April 21, 1861, Hay, *Lincoln and the Civil War*, p. 6.

202   "That's so": Klein, p. 361.

202   "All these failures": Entry of April 22, 1861, Hay, *Lincoln and the Civil War*, p. 7

202   "no one seemed to know": Michael C. C. Adams, *Fighting for Defeat: Union Failure in the East, 1861-1865* (Lincoln: University of Nebraska Press, 1982), p. 66.

203   "[T]he Government is weak": Wayne Mahood, *General Wadsworth: The Life and Times of Brevet Major General James Wadsworth* (Da Capo Press, 2003), p. 61.

"the first service": Lincoln, *Works*, p. IV:332.

203   "provide for the entire safety": Entry of April 25, 1861, Hay, *Lincoln and the Civil War*, p. 11.

203   "envelop the insurgent states": *Official Records*, p. I: 51: I: 369-370.

204   "hot for war": Letter of May, 1861, Sen. Morrill to Sen. Fessenden, from T. Harry Williams, *Lincoln and the Radicals* (Madison: University of Wisconsin Press, 1965), p. 24.

204   "Instead of boldly crushing": Entry of April 1861, Gurowski, *Diary, 1861-1862*, p. 33.

204   "not only unequal": Sandburg, *The War Years*, p. I: 288.

204   "*a certain lack of sovereignty*": *ibid.*

205   "the painful imbecility": Benjamin P. Thomas and Harold M. Hyman, *Stanton: The Life and Times of Lincoln's Secretary of War* (NY: Alfred A. Knopf, 1962), p. 124.

205   "disperse and retire peaceably": Lincoln, *Works*, p. IV: 332.

205   "public sentiment": McClure, p. 70.

205   "Already the murmurs": Nevins, *1861-1862*, p. 210-211.

205   "Something Wrong": June 15, 1861 and June 27, 1861, *New York Herald*.

205   "energy, vigor": Trietsch, p. 181.

205   "Our soldiers have been requested": June 21, 1861, New York *Tribune*, from Perret, p. 52.

206   "THE NATION'S WAR CRY": June 24, 1861, New York *Tribune*, from Harper, p. 103.

206   "By no government": June 30, 1861, New York *Times*, from Gienapp, p. 86.

206   "The whole administration": July 6 and 7, 1861, New York *Evening Post*, from Harper, p. 101

206   "the arrogant tone": Russell, p. 224.

206   "Strategy—strategy repeats now every imbecile": Entry for June 1861, Gurowski, *Diary, 1861-1862*, p. 56.

207   "The country could not understand": William Swinton, *The Army of the Potomac* (NY: Smithmark, 1995), p. 41.

207   "That is splendid": Russell, p. 265-266.

208   "Of these men": July 25, 1861, from Fehrenbacher, Don, "The Anti-Lincoln Tradition," *Journal of the Abraham Lincoln Association* (Vol. 4, 1982), p. 9.

208   "The imbecility of the Administration": Letter of July 26, 1861, from Edwin Stanton, George B. McClellan, *McClellan's Own Story* (NY: Charles L. Webster, 1887), p. 67n.

208   "I do not wonder that people desert": Entry of August 1861, Gurowski, *Diary, 1861-1862*, p. 90.

208   "not equal to the occasion": Letter of August 31, 1861, Trumbull to Judge Doolittle of Wisconsin, from Randall, *Springfield to Gettysburg*, p. I: 389.

208   "everything to his Cabinet": July 25, 1861, *New York Herald, ibid.*, p. I: 390.

208   "cease to be the politician": August 17, 1861, *New York Herald, ibid.*

Page 208   "I am the greatest coward" and "Your conversation": Thomas, p. 273.

209   "You are not considered a great man": Trietsch, p. 183.

210   "If this is to be a war": July 23, 1861, Chicago *Tribune,* from Gienapp, p. 86-7.

210   "There is no longer observable": Sprague, p. 129-130

210   "our defeat was the worst event": Letter of April 3, 1861, to Wendell Phillips, Charles Sumner, *The Selected Letters of Charles Sumner,* ed. Beverly Wilson Palmer (Boston: Northeastern University Press, 1990), p. II: 74.

Chapter 18: The Rise of the Radical Republicans

211   "Though I approve the war": Horatio Bridge, *Personal Recollections of Nathaniel Hawthorne* (NY: Harper & Brothers, 1893), p. 169.

212   "denounced the President": Letter of January 28, 1862, Giddings to George Julian, from J.G. Randall, *Lincoln the Liberal Statesman* (London: Eyre and Spottiswode, 1947), p. 70.

213   "Without a little blood-letting": Hendrick, p. 274.

213   "steeped and steamed in whisky": Entry for Dec. 5, 1866, from Welles, p. II: 633.

213   "despotic ruler of the House": Ben Perley Poore, *Perley's Reminiscences of Sixty Years in the National Metropolis* (Philadelphia: Hubbard Bros., 1886), p. 101.

213   "the stern demand for justice": Letter of April 30, 1861, Wade to Elisha Whittlesey, from Hans Trefousse, *The Radical Republicans: Lincoln's Vanguard for Racial Justice* (NY: Knopf, 1969), p. 171.

214   "Well that is a fact": Reprinted in July 8, 1867, *New York Herald,* from Richard N. Current, *Old Thad Stevens* (Westport, CT: Greenwood Press, 1980), p. 146-7.

214   "[It] embraces more": Lincoln, *Works,* p. IV: 426.

215   "Mr. Lincoln writes": Sandburg, *The War Years,* p. I: 299.

215   "We lay down the President's message": July 20, 1861, The London *Herald,* Reprinted in August 8, 1861, *The Crisis.*

215   "partisan tone, and sectional principles": July 11, 1861, *The Crisis.*

215   "wicked and most desperate cunning": Sandburg, *The War Years,* p. I: 299.

215   "There never was a king": *ibid.,* p. 300.

216   "obvious faults in style": July 7, 1861, *New York Times,* from Goodwin, p. 368.

216   "I can forgive the jokes": Gienapp, p. 85.

216   "Any one reading": August 1861, *Douglass' Monthly,* from Goodwin, p. 368.

216   "We have an honest President": *ibid.*

216   "Lincoln is under the t[h]umb of Seward": Letter of May 1, 1861, Gurowski to Charles Sumner, from Randall, *Springfield to Gettysburg,* p. I: 368.

216   "Mr. Lincoln in some way": Entry for August 1861, Gurowski, *Diary, 1861-1862,* p. 89.

217   "to preserve the Union": Edward McPherson, *The Political History of the United States of America During the Period of Reconstruction* (Washington: Solomons & Chapman, 1875), p. 100.

217   "A rebel has sacrificed all his rights": Nathaniel W. Stephenson, *Lincoln,* (Grosset & Dunlap, 1922), p. 193.

218   "I don't know anything about diplomacy": Norman B. Ferris, "Lincoln and Seward in Civil War Diplomacy: Their Relationship at the Outset Reexamined." For more information see http://www.historycooperative.org/journals/jala/12/ferris.html

218   "that if Kentucky made no demonstration": Nevins, *1861-1862,* p. 133.

219   "Little Bo-Peep Policy": *ibid.,* p. 136.

220   "I have given you *carte blanche*": John C. Fremont, "In Command in Missouri," *Battles and Leaders of the Civil War,* ed. Robert Underwood Johnson and Clarence Buel (NY: The Century Company, 1888), p. I:279.

Page 220   "the tide of rebellion": Nevins, *1861-1862,* p. 331.

221   "This letter is written in a spirit of caution": Lincoln, *Works,* p. IV: 506.

221   Three to one in favor of Fremont: Among the September 1861 letters to Lincoln, the total of letters to Lincoln supporting Fremont was 30; 12 supported Lincoln himself. Lincoln, *Papers.*

221   A Cincinnatian wrote Horace Greeley: Nevins, *1861-1862.,* p. 340.

221   "It would have been difficult": Letter of September 16, 1861, L.B. Moon to Lincoln, from Donald, *Lincoln,* p. 316-317.

221   "They unanimously condemn the President's letter": Letter of September 20, 1861, E.H. Owen to Welles, from Randall, *Springfield to Gettysburg,* p. II: 21.

221   "It is said that we must consult the border states": Letter of September 17, 1861, J.R. Hawley to Welles, *ibid.*

222   "My wife expressed the common feeling": Sandburg, *The War Years,* p. I: 347.

222   "Does [Lincoln] suppose he can crush": Donald, *Lincoln,* p. 317.

222   "Mr. Lincoln and his advisers": September 20, 1861, New York *Tribune,* from Brayton Harris, p. 197.

222   "My own indignation": September 14, 1861, White to David Davis, from Donald, *Lincoln,* p. 316-317.

222   "a mere scheme": Harper, p. 143.

222   "The President's letter to Gen. Fremont": Letter of September 15, 1861, Medill to Chase, from Trefousse, *The Radical Republicans,* p. 176.

"the unlooked-for assistant": October 19, 1861, Chicago *Times.*

223   "What do you think": Letter of September 23, 1861, Wade to Chandler, from Nevins, *1861-1862,* p. 340

224   "To me the Presdt's letter": Sumner, *The Selected Letters,* p. II: 79.

224   "He is not a genius": Sandburg, *The War Years,* p. I: 347-351.

224   "timid, depressing, suicidal," etc.: Mayer, p. 527.

224   "Mr. President": Letter of September 17, 1861, from Orville Browning, Lincoln, *Papers.*

225   "Coming from you": Lincoln, *Works,* p. IV: 531-2.

226   "The german people have talked": Letter of November 9, 1861, from Leonard Swett, Lincoln, *Papers.*

226   "smote the community like a loss in battle": Nevins, *1861-1862,* p. 383.

226   Citizens were pulling down portraits: *Cincinnati Gazette,* from Sandburg, *The War Years,* p. I: 350.

226   "I have never seen such excitement": Nevins, *1861-1862.,* p. 384.

226   "[The Republicans'] attitude towards [Lincoln]": November 27, 1861, Chicago *Times.*

Chapter 19: The Phony War of 1861

227   McClellan biographical items are from Nevins, *1861-1862,* p. 269-271; Sandburg, *The War Years,* p. I: 315-316.; Kenneth Williams, *Lincoln Finds a General* (Indiana University Press, 1985), p. I: 104 ff.; and Stephen W. Sears, *George McClellan: The Young Napoleon* (NY: Ticknor and Fields, 1988), p. 27 ff.

228   "one continuous ovation": Sears, *The Young Napoleon,* p. 95.

228   "I find myself": Letter of July 27, 1861, to his wife, McClellan, *Papers,* p. 70.

228   "For the first time": Entry of July 1861, Gurowski, *Diary, 1861-1862,* p. 76.

229   "Confidence Renewed": Sears, *The Young Napoleon,* p. 97.

Page 229   "His manner is self-possessed": Letter of September 12, 1861, H.W. Bellows to his wife, from Nevins, *1861-1862,* p. 269.

229   "A neck" and "muscular as a prize-fighter's": Sandburg, *The War Years*, p. I: 316.

229   "[I]n everyone" and "idol of Washington": Nicolay and Hay, *A History*, p. IV: 444.

230   "In almost every class" and "Some how or other": Sears, *The Young Napoleon,* p. 6.

231   "was not a man of very strong character": *ibid.,* p. 59.

231   "liked me personally": McClellan, *McClellan's Own Story*, p. 160.

231   "they would probably give more": Letter of November 17, 1861, to his wife, McClellan, *Papers,* p. 136.

231   "a tall man with a navvy's cap": Russell, p. 317

231   "A minute passes": Goodwin, p. 383.

232   August 16 to November 17, 1861 quotes from letters to Mrs. McClellan: Sears, *The Young Napoleon,* pp. 105, 106, 113-114, 135-6.

233   Heintzelman anecdote: Entry for November 11, 1861, Heintzelman Journal, from Gabor S. Boritt, ed., *Lincoln's Generals* (NY: Oxford University Press,1994), p. 12.

233   McClellan snub anecdote: Entry of November 13, 1861, Hay, *Lincoln and the Civil War,* p. 34-5.

233   "The Radicals had only the negro": Sears, *The Young Napoleon,* p. 117.

234   "that sink of iniquity": Letter of April 1, 1862, to his wife, McClellan, *Papers,* p. 223.

234   "Not one common soldier": Lincoln, *Works,* p. IV: 321.

235   "aristocratical" and "exclusive": Sister May Karl George, *Zachariah Chandler: A Political Biography* (East Lansing: Michigan State University Press, 1969), p. 59.

235   "We absolutely need": Entry of September 30, 1861, Bates, p. 194.

235   "They do it differently": Entry of May 1861, Gurowski, *Diary, 1861-1862*, p. 44

236   "commonly presumed the abler": December 4, 1861, New York *Tribune*, Mitgang, p. 276.

236   *"Jeff Davis rides"*: Harwell, Richard B., "Lincoln and the South," Ralph G. Newman, ed., *Lincoln for the Ages* (Garden City: Doubleday, 1960), p. 203.

236   "He seems to be devoting himself": Letter of October 12, 1861, Chandler to his wife, from Sears, *The Young Napoleon,* p. 119.

236   "I intend to be careful," and "You shall have your own way": Entry of October 10, Hay, *Lincoln and the Civil War*, p. 27.

237   "timid, vacil[l]ating and inefficient": Letter of October 27, 1861, Chandler to his wife, from Donald, *Lincoln,* p. 318.

237   "fool": Letter of October 25, 1861,Wade to his wife, from Hans Trefousse, *Benjamin Franklin Wade: Radical Republican from Ohio* (NY: Twayne Publishers, 1963), p. 154.

237   "You could not inspire Old Abe": Letter of October 8, 1861, Wade to Zachary Chandler, from George, p. 55.

237   "It is now evident": Entry of October 1, 1861, Bates, p. 196.

237   "What shall we do?": Entry of November, 1861, Gurowski, *Diary, 1861-1862*, p. 117.

237   "Give the President": Richard Wheeler, *Sword Over Richmond: An Eyewitness History of McClellan's Peninsula Campaign* (NY: Harper & Row, 1986), p. 50.

237   "This evening the Jacobin Club": Entry for October 26, 1861, Hay, *Lincoln and the Civil War*, p. 31.

237   "Lincoln means well": Letter of November 16, 1861, Chandler to Henry W. Lord, from Trefousse, *The Radical Republicans*, p. 180-1.

237   "You must not fight": Entry of October 26, 1861, Hay, *Lincoln and the Civil War*, p. 31.

237   "We have seen it" and "The most charitable": Furgurson, p. 142.

Page 237   "with that sort of indifference": Anthony Trollope, *North America* (NY: Alfred A. Knopf, 1951), p. 325-6.

238   "Old Abe is now unmasked": Garrison, p. 140.

239   "I reached Washington last night": Letter of November 6, 1861, Grimes to his wife, from Williams, *Lincoln and the Radicals*, p. 51.

"ill arranged": December 17, 1861, London *Times*, Mitgang, p. 279.

239   "It is not a great State paper": Reprinted in December 12, 1861, *The Crisis*.

240   "a fair picture": December 14, 1861, London *Saturday Review*, from Robert Bloom, "As the British Press Saw Lincoln," in *Topic 9: A Journal of the Liberal Arts* (Washington, PA: Washington and Jefferson College, Spring 1965), p. 46.

240: December 1861 Annual Message: Lincoln, *Works*, p. V: 49.

240   "reactionary and feeble": Trefousse, *The Radical Republicans*, p. 181.

240   "when the time comes": *ibid.*, p. 58.

240   "There is no greatness": Letter of December 8, 1861, Davis to his wife, from Perrett, p. 106.

240   "Not one single manly, bold, dignified position": Letter of December 5, 1861, S. York to Trumbull, from Randall, *Springfield to Gettysburg*, p. II: 27.

240   "No man": Letter of December 8, 1861, J.H. Bryant to Trumbull, from Randall, *Lincoln the Liberal Statesman*, p. 73.

240   "Let the administration continue": Letter of December 17, 1861, John Russell to Trumbull, *ibid.,* p. 72.

240   "Every one is disappointed": Letter of December 10, 1861, P.A. Allaire to Trumbull, *ibid.,* p. 67.

240   "lacks confidence": Sandburg, *The War Years,* p. I: 390-1.

240   "What a wishy-washy message": Letter of December 8, 1861, Garrison to Oliver Johnson, *ibid.*, p. 27.

241   "I demand of the government": Williams, *Lincoln and the Radicals*, p. 58.

241   "as a pint-pot may be full": Poore, p. 106.

241   "A sort of bland, respectable middle-man": *ibid.*, p. 383-4.

241   "For the last three months": Letter of Dec. 16, 1861, W.A. Baldwin to Trumbull, from Gray, p. 74-5.

241   "How many times": Nevins, *1861-1862,* p. 340.

242   "It is high time": December 10, 11, and 23, *New York Tribune*, from Williams, *Lincoln and the Radicals*, p. 54.

242   "We will strike them there": Swinton, p. 69.

242   "was in favor of sending for Jeff Davis": Letter of October 27, 1861, Zachary Chandler to his wife, from Donald, *Lincoln*, p. 320.

243   "an active war": January 13, 1862, Chicago *Tribune*, *ibid.*, p. 81.

243   "We want the President": Letter of January 23, 1862, G.S. Ward to W.P. Fessenden, *ibid.*

245   "I greatly fear": Letter of January 15, 1862, James W. Stone to Salmon Chase, from Bruce Tap, *Over Lincoln's Shoulder: The Committee on the Conduct of the War* (Lawrence: University Press of Kansas, 1998), p. 109.

245   "I find that nearly a majority": Letter of January 10, 1862, W.C. Dunning to Elihu Washburne, from Randall, *Lincoln the Liberal Statesman*, p. 76.

245   "nearly paralyzed": Letter of February 4, 1862, John Russell to Lyman Trumbull, *ibid.* p. 67-8.

245: The Greeley Smithsonian lecture: Furgurson, p. 152.

Page 245   "I am confident": Letter of January 31, 1862, J.W. Shaffer to Lyman Trumbull, *ibid.*, p. 114.

245   "blundering, cowardly, and inefficient": Letter of October 3, 1861, Benjamin Wade to Zachary Chandler, from George, p. 55.

245   "If the new year": Entry for January 1862, Gurowski, *Diary, 1861-1862*, p. 137.

245   "Many of the deficiencies": Entry for December 31, 1861, Bates, p. 218-220.

246   "For the first time": Gienapp, p. 98.

246   "General, what shall I do?": *ibid.*

Chapter 20: Democrats Disappear

247   "Mr. Lincoln is evidently a believer": April 18, 1862, *The New York Evening Day Book*, Mitgang, p. 261.

247   "The so-called 'peace policy'": April 12, 1862, Bedford *Gazette,* from Brayton Harris, p. 43.

247   "Abraham Lincoln, a Tory": April 18, 1862, Bangor *Democrat*, Mitgang, p. 257.

248   "there will now be but one party": Fermer, p. 189.

248   "for a man to express doubt" and "prudent": Stampp, *And the War Came*, p. 292.

248   "seize at once": Sprague, p. 50.

249   "against whom no charges have been preferred": August 1, 1861, Brooklyn *Eagle*.

249   "The Old Constitution has been superceded": *Cincinatti Enquirer,* reprinted in August 1, 1861, Brooklyn *Eagle*.

250   "attempt to muzzle the Democratic press": Jeffrey Manber and Neil Dahlstrom, *Lincoln's Wrath: Fierce Mobs, Brilliant Scoundrels and a President's Mission to Destroy the Press* (Napierville, IL: Sourcebooks, Inc., 2005), p. 112.

250: List of 154 "peace" papers: August 12, 1861, New York *Daily News, ibid.,* p. 121

250: Account of August anti-press riots: *ibid.,* p. 118-122

251   "AN ACCOUNTING": *ibid.*, p. 3.

251   "All who do not shout hosannas": *ibid,*, p. 130-131.

251   "disseminators of doctrines": Brayton Harris, p. 98.

251   "The course which a despotic": Manber and Dahlstrom, p. 171.

252   "This is not only": Toronto *Globe,* reprinted in August 19, 1861, *New York Times, ibid.*, p. 137-8.

252   "reign of terror," "journals are suppressed," "are gutted and destroyed," and "no Neapolitan despotism": September and October, 1861, *Staunton* (Va.) *Spectator* and *Richmond Whig,* from Ayers, p. 220.

252   "cross two columns over the Potomac": Sprague, p.184.

253   "separating the sheep from the goats": Seward, p. 177.

253   Maryland military arrests in September: *Official Records,* p. I: 5: 194-196.

253   "The action of the government": September 14, 1861, Chicago *Times.*

254   Chicago *Times*, November 22, 1861

254   14,400 arrests: Mark E. Neely, Jr., "The Lincoln Administration and Arbitrary Arrests: A Reconsideration," *Journal of the Abraham Lincoln Association*, Vol. 5, No. 1, p. 8.

Chapter 21: A Military House Divided

255   "It has been said": Lincoln, *Works,* p. V: 51.

255   "We were greatly surprised": George W. Julian, *Political Recollections: 1840 to 1872* (Chicago: Jansen, McClurg & Company, 1884), p. 201.

255   "remarkably bold and vigorous": *ibid.,* p. 202.

Page 256   "Mr. Lincoln took no part": Wheeler, p. 63.

256   "if General McClellan did not want to use the army": Henry J. Raymond, *Life and Public Service of Abraham Lincoln* (NY: Darby and Miller, 1865), p. 773.

257   Low opinion of Seward: Anthony Trollope, p. 240; also Dicey, p. 96.

257   "in any official matter": Sandburg, *The War Years*, p. I: 434.

257   "openly discourteous to the President": Notes for October 2, 1861, John G. Nicolay, *Lincoln's Secretary: A Biography of John G. Nicolay*, ed. Helen Nicolay (NY: Longman's, Green, and Co., 1949), p. 125.

257   "We want a great man": Sandburg, *The War Years*, p. I: 441.

258   "did his best" and "The most disagreeable thing": McClellan, *McClellan's Own Story*, p. 152.

258   "that damned long-armed Ape": Letter of January 6, 1887, William Herndon to Jesse Weik, from Randall, *Springfield to Gettysburg*, p. I: 39.

258   "If that giraffe appeared": Thomas and Hyman, p. 66.

258   "a withering sneer" and "[Stanton] loved antagonism": McClure, p. 170-171.

259   "My first inkling": McClellan, *McClellan's Own Story*, p. 155.

259   January 13 council account taken from Meigs's account in Angle, p. 381; McDowell's account in Swinton, p. 84-5; and McClellan's account in McClellan, *My Own Story*, p. 156-7, and Sears, *The Young Napoleon*, p. 141.

260   "weak and wicked": Williams, *Lincoln and the Radicals*, p. 108.

260   "And Lincoln is in their clutches": Entry for January 1862, Gurowski, *Diary, 1861-1862*, p. 148.

260   "the champagne and oysters on the Potomac must be stopped": Letter of January 24, 1862, Edwin Stanton to Charles Dana, from Russell H. Beatie, *Army of the Potomac: McClellan Takes Command* (Da Capo Press, 2004), p. 530.

261   "he was thinking of taking the field himself": Entry of January 12, 1862, Orville Hickman Browning, *The Diary of Orville Hickman Browning*, ed. Theodore Calvin Pease (Springfield: Illinois State Historical Library, 1925), p. I: 523.

261   "he must take these army matters": Donald, *Lincoln*, p. 331.

262   "Are the President and Mrs. Lincoln aware": Jerrold M. Packard, *The Lincolns in the White House: Four Years That Shattered a Family* (NY: St. Martin's Press, 2005), p. 113-14.

262   "Well, anybody!": Oates, p. 293.

263   "an ugly matter": McClellan, *McClellan's Own Story*, p. 195-6.

263   General War Order No. 2: Lincoln, *Works*, p. V: 149-150.

263   General War Order No. 3: *ibid.*, p. V: 151.

264   "He surprised and delighted the committee": Julian, p. 205.

265   "to tie my hands": McClellan, *McClellan's Own Story*, p. 225.

265   "The rascals are after me again": Letter of March 11, 1862, to his wife, McClellan, *Papers*, p. 202.

265   "strongly suspected": Julian, p. 205.

265   "It is no longer doubtful": Letter of March 15, 1862, William Fessenden to his family, from Goodwin, p. 428.

265   "Gen. McC. is in danger": Entry of April 3, 1862, Hay, *Lincoln and the Civil War*, p. 39.

265   "So far as 'the pride'": McClellan, *McClellan's Own Story*, p. 142.

265   "[Lincoln] suggested several reasons": *ibid.*, p. 164.

266   "He assured me": *ibid.*, p.165.

266   "MY DEAR SIR": Letter of March 31,1862, Lincoln, *Works*, p. V: 176.

266   "[Lincoln] then assured me": McCellan, *McClellan's Own Story*, p. 165.

266   "By direction of the president": McClellan, *Papers*, p. 229.

Page 266: Troops counts for the dispositions of McClellan's defense of Washington: *Official Records,* p. I: 5: 61.

267 "miserable nests of petty intrigues": Sears, *The Young Napoleon*, p. 127.

267 "[Stanton] had spoken to me": McClellan, *McClellan's Own Story*, p. 226.

267 "He was no general": Mahood, p. 80-81.

267 "vile, traitorous miscreant": *ibid.*, p. 111.

268 "that sink of iniquity": Letter of April 1, 1862, McClellan, *Papers*, p. 223.

268 "after glancing his eye": *Official Records,* p. I: 5: 63.

269 "It is the most infamous thing": Letter of April 6, 1862, McClellan, *Papers*, p. 240.

269 "I beg that you will reconsider": Letter of April 5, 1862, *ibid.*, p. 238-9.

269 "I know of no instance": Stephen W. Sears, *To the Gates of Richmond: The Peninsula Campaign* (Ticknor & Fields, New York, 1992), p. 40.

269 "had now only too good reason": McClellan, *McClellan's Own Story*, p. 242.

269 "too deeply committed" and "a fatal error": Randall, *Springfield to Gettysburg*, p. II: 88-90.

269 "the stupidity" and "a set of heartless villains": Sears, *To the Gates of Richmond*, p. 40.

269 "Don't worry about the wretches": Letter of April 11, 1862, McClellan, *Papers*, p. 235.

269 "[I]t was whispered": Wheeler, p. 140.

270 "It is impossible to exaggerate": August 9, 1862, *Harper's Weekly*.

270 "a great outrage": Williams, *Lincoln and the Radicals*, p. 131.

270 "You now have over one hundred thousand troops": Lincoln, *Works,* p. V: 182.

270 "The Presdt very coolly telegraphed me": Letter of April 8, 1862, to his wife, McClellan, *Papers,* p. 234.

271 "If you can accomplish your object": Letter of April 12, 1862, from Francis P. Blair, *ibid.*, p. 240.

272 "The End at Hand": Sears, *The Young Napoleon*, p. 154.

272: The *New York Herald* and New York *Tribune* predictions: Gary W. Gallagher, *The Richmond Campaign of 1862: The Peninsula & the Seven Days* (Chapel Hill: The University of North Carolina Press, 2000), p. 9.

272 "within a month or two": May 10, 1862, Brooklyn *Eagle*.

272 "No General of modern times": April 12, 1862, *Harper's Weekly*.

273 "in the present divided condition": Allan Nevins, *The War for the Union: War Becomes Revolution, 1862-1863* (NY: Charles Scribner's Sons), p. 124.

273 "it will prove a great relief": Sears, *To the Gates of Richmond*, p. 97.

273 "This is a crushing blow": *Official Records,* p. I: 12: III: 220.

275 "Heaven save a country": Letter of May 25, 1862, to his wife, McClellan, *Papers*, p. 275.

275 "a precious lot of fools": Letter of May 26, 1862, to his wife, *ibid.,* p. 278.

275 "The object of enemy's movement": Telegram of May 25, 1862, to Lincoln, *ibid.,* p. 276.

275 "I dare not risk this Army": Letter of June 23, 1862, to S.L.M. Barlow, *ibid.*, p. 306.

275 "I know that a few thousand men": Telegram of June 28, 1862, to Stanton, *ibid.*, p. 323.

276 "I need 50,000 more men": *Official Records,* p. I: 11: III: 281

276 "It seems unreasonable": Lincoln, *Works,* p. V: 355-6

277 "When the Peninsula campaign terminated": Carpenter, p. 219.

277 "thin and haggard": Julian, p. 218.

277 "On Saturday": Whitney, p. 491.

277 "[Lincoln] was in his Library": Entry of July 15, 1862, Browning, p. II: 559-560

278: Panic on Wall Street: Nevins, *1862-1863,* p. 168-9.

278 "the gloomiest": Entry for July 1862, Gurowski, *Diary, 1861-1862*, p. 235.

Page 278   "stands higher this moment": Letter of July 10, Alexander Webb to his father, from Sears, *The Young Napoleon*, p. 231.

278   "successive, hasty, & contradictory": Thomas and Hyman, p. 212.

278   "crime against the nation": July 3, 1862, New York *Tribune*, from Sears, *The Young Napoleon*, p. 230.

278   "Public sentiment is deep and bitter": Letter of July 26, 1862, J.H. Geiger to Salmon Chase, from Randall, *Lincoln the Liberal Statesman*, p. 73.

278   "inspiring the people": Letter, August 6, 1862, Israel Holmes to Sen. J. R. Doolittle, *ibid.*

278   "Unless Richmond is occupied": Letter of August 26, 1862, George B. Loring to Ben Butler, *ibid.*, p. 74.

278   "Prevailing color of people's talk": Page Smith, *Trial by Fire: A People's History of the Civil War and Reconstruction*, (NY: Penguin, 1990), p. 187.

278   "Lincoln is doing twice as much": Letter of June 29, 1862, Wendell Phillips to Charles Sumner, from Randall, *Lincoln the Liberal Statesman*, p. 67.

279   "With regard to the President": Dicey, p. 90-1.

279   "The treasure": July 16, 1862, Brooklyn *Eagle*.

280   Harrison's Landing letter: McClellan, *Papers*, p. 344-5.

280   "I do not know": Letter of July 10, 1862, to his wife, *ibid.*, p. 348.

280   "the stupidity and wickedness": Letter of July 15, 1862, to S.L.M. Barlow, *ibid.*, p. 361.

281   "[The President and I] never conversed": Letter of July 27, 1862, to his wife, *ibid.*, p. 374.

282   "Things had gone on": Carpenter, p. 20-21.

282   "We must free the slaves": Welles, p. I:70.

Part Three: Lincoln's Proclamation

Chapter 22: Lincoln, Race, and the North

285   "The prejudice of race": Tocqueville, Alexis de, p. I:343.

286   "the very spirit": Smith, *The Nation Comes of Age*, p. 655.

286   "In my judgment": May 3, 1862, *Harper's Weekly*.

286   "not slaves indeed": Smith, *The Nation Comes of Age*, p. 640.

286   "While the cruel slave-driver": Smith, *Trial by Fire*, p. 249.

287   "the position of the people": Rawley, p. 72.

287   "At the hotels": Dicey, p. 11.

287   "I never by any chance": *ibid.*, p. 46.

287   "almost without education": Ayers, p. 53.

287   "objects of marked abuse": Smith, *Trial by Fire*, p. 248.

287   "What have the colored people done": *ibid.*

287   "Colored persons, no matter how well dressed": *ibid.*, p. 241.

288   "visible admixture of Negro blood": Rawley, p. 72.

288   "There is but one thing, sir, that we want here": Dicey, p. 47-8.

288   "Our people hate the Negro": Rawley, p. 72.

288   "if we [blacks] sent our children to school": *ibid.*, p. 73.

288   "There are laws": August 5, 1862, Brooklyn *Daily Eagle*.

289   "I plead the cause": Commager, p. 90.

Page 289   "the sons of toil": Eric Foner, *Free Soil, Free Labor, Free Men: The Ideology of the Republican Party Before the Civil War* (NY: Oxford University Press, 1970), p. 267.

289   "the real white man's party": *ibid.*, p. 265.

289   "foreign and feeble": *ibid.*, p. 295.

289   Seward believed black people in the North would die out: Dicey, p. 99-100.

289   "They are God's poor": Foner, p. 300.

289   "Missouri for white men": *ibid.*, p. 270.

289   "cooked by Niggers": Trefousse, *The Radical Republicans*, p. 31.

289   "As a class, the Blacks are indolent": Foner, p. 297.

289   "It is the real evil of the negro race": *ibid.*, p. 298.

289   "It [does not] necessarily follow": *ibid.*, p. 265.

289   "So far as the principles": Smith, *The Nation Comes of Age*, p. 1169-70.

290   "If slavery is not wrong, nothing is wrong": Lincoln, *Works*, p. VII:281.

290   "a universal feeling": *ibid.*, p. II:256.

290   "I am not, nor ever have been in favor": *ibid.*, p. III:145-6.

290   "He declares his opposition": November 8, 1860, *New York Times*.

291   "to result in the entire abolition" and "daily correspondence": Entry for May 7, 1861, Hay, *Lincoln and the Civil War*, p. 19.

291   "proving that popular government is not an absurdity": *ibid.*

291   "no purpose, directly or indirectly": Lincoln, *Works*, p. IV: 263.

291   "would bring sure and irretrievable defeat" and "Two-thirds of the army": September 11, 1861, *Valley Spirit*, from Ayers, p. 216.

291   "turn the world topsy turvey": December 4, 1861, *Valley Spirit*, *ibid.*

291   "that if this war was to be converted": December 12, 1861, *The Crisis*.

291   "gone to the rescue" and "The key of the slave's chain": January 31, 1862, *The Liberator*, from Donald, *Lincoln*, p. 342.

292   "There has never been an Administration": Paludan, p. 124.

292   "Our nation is on the brink" and "Mr. Lincoln, for god's sake": Letter of February 9, 1862, from Joseph Medill, Lincoln, *Papers*.

292   "It is certainly the wish": Foner, p. 269.

292   "The idea of liberating the slaves": *ibid.*, p. 270.

292   "should the abolitionists": November 7, 1861, *The Crisis*.

293   "Adopt these measures": March 25, 1862, *Congressional Globe*, 37th Congress, 2nd session, p. 1333.

293   "I utterly spit at it": Smith, *Trial by Fire*, p. 257

293   "Victories or defeats amount to but little": March 19, 1862, *The Crisis*.

293   "'decoy duck' or a 'red herring'": Ralph Korngold, *Two Friends of Man: The Story of William Lloyd Garrison and Wendell Phillips and Their Relationship with Abraham Lincoln* (Boston: Little, Brown, 1950), p. 292.

293   "cowardly and criminal avoidance": Mayer, p. 533.

293   "trick" and "small crumbs": Entry for February 1862, Gurowski, *Diary, 1861-1862*, p. 159.

293   "the most diluted": Nevins, *1862-1863*, p. 32.

294   "Do you know": Sandburg, *The War Years*, p. I: 577.

294   "[Sumner's] severest trial": *ibid.*, p. I: 578.

294   "He told me": Entry of April 14, 1862, Browning, p. I: 541.

294   "the refusal on the part of the President": April 23, 1862, *Congressional Globe*, 37th Congress, 2nd session, p. 1801.

294   "Mr. Lincoln is forced out": Entry of April, 1862, Gurowski, *Diary, 1861-1862*, p. 192-3.

Page 295   "Many an old 'Aunty' in Washington": April 16, 1862, Brooklyn *Daily Eagle.*

295   "Please let me have my own way": Korngold, p. 294.

295   "The persons in these three States": Lincoln, *Works,* p. V: 222.

295   "altogether void": *ibid.*

295   "Be sure that Lincoln": Letter of May 7, 1862, Gurowski to John A. Andrew, from Randall, *Lincoln the Liberal Statesman,* p. 73.

295   "an unavoidable evil, an original sin": Fischer, p. 100.

295   "Of course Mr. Lincoln overrules": Entry of May 1862, Gurowski, *Diary, 1861-1862,* p. 210.

295   "Our people feel disheartened": Letter of May 31, 1862, James C. Conkling to Trumbull, from Randall, *Lincoln the Liberal Statesman,* p. 67.

295   "We shuffle and trifle on": Letter of April 28, 1862, Horace Greeley to William P. Cutler, from Williams, *Lincoln and the Radicals,* p. 159.

295   "President Lincoln with a senile lick-spittle haste": Korngold, p. 295.

296   "feel it a heavy draft on their patriotism": *ibid.*

296   Lincoln's reply to a group of Quakers: Lincoln, *Works,* p, V: 278-9.

296   "too big a lick": Louis Morris Starr, *Bohemian Brigade: Civil War Newsmen in Action* (NY: Knopf, 1954), p. 126.

296   "I would do it": Sandburg, *The War Years,* p. I: 566.

297   "The change it contemplates": Lincoln, *Works,* p. V: 222.

297   "friction and abrasion": *ibid.,* p. V: 318-19.

297   "nothing less than deportation": Korngold, p. 296.

298   "amid the sneers and laughter of the abolitionists": July 18, 1862, New York *Herald,* from Randall*, Springfield to Gettysburg,* p. II: 229.

298   "inexpressibly provoking": Rice, p. 237-8.

298   "No one at a distance": Julian, p. 220.

299   "Mr. Lincoln makes a new effort": Entry for July 1862, Gurowski, *Diary, 1861-1862*, p. 243.

299   "the President hangs back" Letter of July 28, 1862, "Enquirer" to Editor New York *Tribune,* Lincoln, *Papers.*

299   "I am receiving daily": Letter of July 30, 1862, from Sidney Howard Gay, Lincoln, *Papers.*

299   "Oh God, how I feel": Letter of August 3, 1862, from John Sherman, Salmon P. Chase, *The Correspondence of Salmon P. Chase,* Ed. John Niven (Kent, OH: Kent State University Press, 1996), p. III:241.

299   "We are in a deplorable condition": Letter of August 5, 1862, from Randall, *Lincoln the Liberal Statesman*, p. 68.

299   "Anything more violent": Korngold, p. 302.

299   "I think the present purpose": *ibid.,* p. 300-302.

300   August 14, 1862 address on colonization to blacks: Lincoln, *Works,* p. V: 371-2.

301   "In this address": Rawley, p. 83.

301   "miserable tool of traitors and rebels": August 1862, *Douglass' Monthly*, from Fehrenbacher, "The Anti-Lincoln Tradition," p. 13.

301   "evident that he": September 6, 1862, *Pacific Appeal*, from Donald, *Lincoln*, p. 368.

301   "humiliating . . . impertinent": Korngold, p. 538-9.

301   "How much better": Entry for August 15, 1862, Chase, *Diaries*, p. 112.

301   "The Prayer of Twenty Millions": Lincoln, *Works,* p. V: 389

303   "As to the policy I 'seem to be pursuing'": *ibid.*

304   "the president is not with us": Mahood, p. 106.

Page 304   "We are sold out": Letter of September 12, 1862, John Jay to Charles Sumner, from Randall, *Lincoln the Liberal Statesmen,* p. 67.

304   "as near lunacy": Letter of September 9, 1862, William Lloyd Garrison to Oliver Johnson, *ibid.,* p. 76.

304   "The truth": Entry for September 12, 1862, Chase, *Diaries,* p. 136.

304   "I fear that the President": Letter of September 12, 1862, from S. G. Arnold, *ibid.,* p. 67.

304   Lincoln's description of the July 22 Cabinet meeting: Carpenter, p. 21-22.

Chapter 23: Lincoln Awaits a Victory

305   "a man I know by experience": Letter of July 20, 1862, to his wife, McClellan, *Papers,* p. 368

306   "I know that the rascals will get rid of me": Letter of July 30, 1862, to S.L.M. Barlow, *ibid.,* p. 376-7

306   "disastrous" and "a fatal blow": Letter of August 4, 1862, to Henry Halleck, *ibid.,* p. 383

306   McClellan persuaded not to resign: T. Harry Williams, *Lincoln and His Generals* (NY: Alfred A. Knopf, 1952), p. 138

306   "with all possible promptness": Telegram of August 5, 1862, Halleck to McClellan, *Official Records,* p. I: 11: I: 82.

306   "I beg of you, general": Letter of August 7, 1862, Halleck to McClellan, *McClellan's Own Story,* p. 475

307   "the greatest battle of the century": Entry of September 1, 1862, Hay, *Lincoln and the Civil War,* p. 46

307   "nothing less than this capital": Goodwin, p. 474

307   "To leave Pope to get out of his scrape": August 29, 1862, to Abraham Lincoln, McClellan, *Papers,* p. 416

308: McClellan would send his wife's silver off: Letter of August 31, 1862, to his wife, *ibid.,* p. 423-4

308   Rumors of soldiers letting themselves be captured: Sandburg, *The War Years,* p. I: 538

308   "The nation is rapidly sinking": Entry of September 7, 1862, Strong, p. III: 253

308   "Disgust with our present government" and "Nobody believes in him": Entry of September 13, 1862, *ibid.,* p. III: 256

308   "central imbecility" and "Certainly neither Mr. Lincoln": Sandburg, *The War Years,* p. I: 555

308   "Many of our best citizens": Letter of September 13, 1862, H.C. Bowen to Salmon Chase, from Randall, *Lincoln the Liberal Statesman,* p. 68

308   "like throwing water on a duck's back": Entry of August 31, 1862, Welles, p. I:102

308   "unwilling to be accessory": Goodwin, p. 476

309   "he knew of no obligation he was under to the President": Entry of August 31, 1862, Welles, p. 98

309   "in a suppressed voice": Entry of September 2, 1862, *ibid.,* p. 104

309   "the slows," McClellan knows this whole ground," "can be trusted," and "no better organizer": *ibid.,* p. 105

309   "could not but feel": Entry of September, 2, 1862, Chase, *Diaries,* p. 119

309   "it distressed him exceedingly": *ibid.*

309   "there was a more disturbed and desponding feeling": Entry of September 2, 1862, Welles, p. 105

310   "The bitterness of Stanton": Tap, p. 131

Page 310   "seemed wrung by the bitterest anguish": Lincoln, *Works,* p. V: 404

310   "unpardonable": Entry of September 5, 1862, Hay, *Lincoln and the Civil War*, p. 47

310   "The will of God prevails": Lincoln, *Works,* p. V: 403-4

310   "Are mutinous *traitorous* Generals": Letter of September 13, 1862, Zachary Chandler to Salmon Chase, from Tap, p. 134

310   "Your president is as unstable as water": Letter of September 10, 1862, Zachary Chandler to Lyman Trumbull, from Williams, *Lincoln and the Radicals*, p. 179

310   "to save the Prest.": Letter of September 6, 1862, John A. Andrew to Adam Gurowski, from Nevins, *1862-1863*, p. 240

311   "a vast conspiracy": Randall, *Springfield to Gettysburg*, p. II: 230-231

311   "to request Lincoln to resign": *ibid.*, p. II: 231

311   "What does it mean": Letter of September 15, 1862, Francis Gillette to Charles Sumner, from Randall, *Lincoln the Liberal Statesman*, p. 68

311   "[S]hall the country crumble": Letter of September 10, 1862, from John Sherman, Chase, *Correspondence*, p. 264

311   "The Union cause is in a dismal plight": *ibid.,* p. 265

311   "trembling on the brink": Letter of September 15, 1862, Francis Gillette to Charles Sumner, from Randall, *Lincoln the Liberal Statesman,* p. 74

311   "as soon as it shall be driven out": Goodwin, p. 481

Chapter 24: Emancipation Promised

312   "I know very well": Chase, *Diaries*, p. 150-151.

313   "I have got you together": *ibid.,* p. 150.

313   "That on [January 1, 1863], all persons held as slaves": Lincoln, *Works,* p. V: 434.

314   "The proclamation is written": Entry for September 23, 1862, Gurowski, *Diary, 1861-1862*, p. 278.

314   "[Its words] kindled no enthusiasm"   "Emancipation Proclamation: Domestic Reaction," www.mrlincolnandfreedom.org

314   "ordinary summonses": Adam Gopnik, "Angels and Ages," *New Yorker* (May 28, 2007), p. 33.

314   "a poor document": Nevins, *1862-1863*, p. 234.

314   "an arbitrary and despotic measure": Hendrick, p. 359.

315   "I will resign": *ibid.,* p. 356.

315   "It is mournful": David Donald, *"We Are Lincoln Men"* (NY: Simon and Schuster, 2003), p. 164.

315   "It is the beginning of the end": Brayton Harris, p. 201.

315   "The President may be a fool": Nevins, *1862-1863,* p. 237.

315   "I can only trust in God": Lincoln, *Works,* p. V: 438.

316   "My Dear Sir:": *ibid.,* p. 444.

316   "had imparted no vigor": Allen C. Guelzo, *Abraham Lincoln: Redeemer President* (Grand Rapids: W. B. Eerdmans, 1999), p. 352.

317   "reign of hell on earth": October 1, 1862, Richmond *Enquirer*, from Brayton Harris, p. 201.

317   "What shall we call him?": Sandburg, *The War Years*, p. I: 588.

317   "strengthen the South": October 7, 1862, Staunton *Spectator*, from Ayers, p. 332.

317   "is not that a human being": Gienapp, p. 116.

317   "Mr. Lincoln will do his best": October 7, 1862, London *Times,* Hugh Brogan, ed., *The Times Reports the American Civil War* (London: Times Books, 1975), p. 86, 88.

Page 317   "Lincoln will be known": October 21, 1862, London *Times*, from Harper, p. 178.

318   "a monstrous usurpation": September 24, 1862, Chicago *Times*, Mitgang, p. 303.

319   "The 'Irrepressible Conflict' upon Us": September 24, 1862, *The Crisis.*

319   "Is not this a Death Blow" and "We have no doubt": October 1, 1862, *The Crisis.*

319   "Lincoln has swung loose": September 24, 1862, New York *World*, reprinted in October 1, 1862, *The Crisis.*

319   "act of Revolution" and "the restoration": September 23, 1862, New York *Evening Express*, from Donald, *Lincoln*, p. 380.

321   "The measure is wholly unauthorized": *Louisville Journal*, reprinted in October 8, 1862, *National Intelligencer*, Mitgang, p. 313.

321   "He said he had studied the matter": Entry of September 26, 1862, Hay, *Lincoln and the Civil War*, p. 50.

321   "Having an hour to spare": *Springfield Republican*, reprinted in November 29, 1862, *Cincinnati Gazette*, from Harper, p. 179.

321   "Dictator": William O. Stoddard, *Inside the White House in War Times* (Lincoln: University of Nebraska Press, 2000), p. 97.

321   "The Presdt's late Proclamation": Letter of September 25, 1862, to his wife, McClellan, *Papers*, p. 481.

322   "[T]he good of the country": Letter of October (c. 29), 1862, to his wife, *ibid.*, p. 515.

322   "absurd proclamation": McPherson, *Battle Cry of Freedom*, p. 559.

322   "The Proclamation was ridiculed": September 30, 1862, New York *World*, from Nevins, *1862-1863*, p. 238.

322   "countermarch [the army]" and "his sword across the government's policy": *ibid.*, p. 231n.

322   "officers of rank": Allen C. Guelzo, *Lincoln's Emancipation Proclamation: The End of Slavery in America* (NY: Simon and Schuster, 2004), p. 107

322   "Potomac Army clique": Donald, *Lincoln,* p. 385

322   "an ill-timed, mischief making instrument": Mahood, p. 114

323   "I did not enlist": Letter of February 19, 1863, from Brayton Harris, p. 201.

323   "If the president makes this a war": *ibid.*

323   "Those men of the South": *ibid.*

323   "The army is dissatisfied": Letter of September 24, 1862, L.A. Whiteley to James Gordon Bennett, from George Winston Smith and Charles Judah, eds., *Life in the North During the Civil War: A Source History* (Albuquerque: University of New Mexico Press, 1966), p. 91.

323   "His proclamation": William C. Davis, *Lincoln's Men* (NY: Touchstone, 1999), p. 93.

323   "a common ambulance": Donald, *Lincoln*, p. 387.

324   Instances of resistance to the draft   "Northern Draft of 1862," "The American Civil War", http://www.etymonline.com/cw/draft.htm

324   "an exercise of despotic power": Entry for November 28, 1862, Browning, p. I: 588.

324   "useless and . . . mischievous proclamations": Randall, *Springfield to Gettysburg*, p. II: 174.

324   "The proclamation": Mark E. Neely, *The Fate of Liberty* (NY: Oxford Press, 1991), p. 64.

324   "seeking to inaugurate a reign of terror": Donald, *Lincoln*, p. 382.

325   "Stop him! Hold him!": Letters of September 26, 1862 and November 15, 1862, Hugh Campbell to Joseph Holt, *ibid.*

325   "The people of Yankeedom": October 2, 1862, Richmond *Dispatch*, Mitgang, p. 315-316.

Chapter 25: Emancipation Rebuked

Page 326 "ruined the Republican party": Entry of December 5, 1862, Browning, p. I: 592.

326 "will defeat me": John C. Waugh, *Reelecting Lincoln: The Battle for the 1864 Presidency* (Da Capo Press, 1997), p. 13.

326 "The Constitution as it is": McPherson, *Battle Cry of Freedom*, p. 560.

326 "another advance": *ibid.*

326 "the *despot* Lincoln": Gray, p. 112.

326 "Party feeling runs high in Ohio": Sandburg, *The War Years,* p. I: 614.

326 Refugee cautionary tale: October 22, 1862, *Valley Spirit*, from Ayers, p. 329.

327 John Stuart Todd's refusal to debate: Donald, *Lincoln*, p. 382.

327 "even if the streets be made to run red with blood": *ibid.*

327 "This election decides": Joel H. Silbey, *A Respectable Minority: The Democratic Party in the Civil War Era, 1860-1868* (NY: W. W. Norton, 1977), p. 85-6n.

327 "a swarthy inundation": *ibid.*

327 "a proposal for the butchery": Nevins, *1862-1863,* p. 302.

328 "literally bending under the weight": Donald, *Lincoln*, p. 382

328 "Things look badly": Letter of October 28, 1862, to John Nicolay, Hay, *Lincoln and the Civil War*, p. 52.

328 "ill wind": Goodwin, p. 485.

328 "a vote of want of confidence": November 7, 1862, *New York Times*, from Donald, *Lincoln*, p. 383.

328 "I could not conceive it possible": McClure, p. 113.

328 "that unwise, ill-timed and seditious": V. Jacque Voegeli, *Free but Not Equal* (Chicago: University of Chicago Press, 1967), p. 64.

328 "No Emancipation": *ibid.*

328 "Abolition Slaughtered": *ibid.*

328 "The Home of Lincoln Condemns the Proclamation": *ibid.*

328 "Fanaticism, Abolitionism and Niggerism Repudiated": October 22, 1862, *Valley Spirit*, from Ayers, p. 327-8.

329 "unless there is an immediate & continued change": Letter of November 8, 1862, from David Dudley Field, Lincoln, *Papers.*

329 "The New York and other elections": Letter of November 9, 1862, John C. Ropes to John C. Gray, from Tap, p. 138.

329 "The people after their gigantic preparations": Sandburg, *The War Years,* p. I: 610-11.

329 "We saw the President of the United States": *ibid.*, p. 611.

330 "I do not think": Letter of November 5, 1862, from John Cochrane, Lincoln, *Papers.*

330 "Probably two-thirds": Entry of November 5, 1862, Strong, p. III: 271-272.

330 "This great nation": Letter of November 5, 1862, from S.W. Oakey, Lincoln, *Papers.*

330 "I deplore the result": Letter of November 8, 1862, from Charles Sumner, Lincoln, *Papers.*

331 "I think the country is ruined": Waugh, p. 12.

331 "it was not your fault": Sandburg, *The War Years,* p. I: 606-7.

331 "[Lincoln] is ignorant": Letter of October 29, 1862, George Bancroft to Francis Lieber, from Donald, *Lincoln Reconsidered*, p. 62.

331 "All the Blame on Mr. Lincoln": October 22, 1862, *The Crisis.*

331 "The democrats were left in a majority": Lincoln, *Works*, p. V: 494.

332 "I fear you entertain too favorable a view": Lincoln, *Works*, p. V: 510, 511.

332 "Many were in favor": McClellan, *McClellan's Own Story*, p. 652.

Page 332   "Officers and men unite" and "Upon every occasion": November 12, 1862, *Valley Spirit*, from Ayers, p. 329-330.

332   "and a few even going so far": Sears, *The Young Napoleon*, p. 342.

332   "which the Army of the Union will never forgive": *ibid.*, p. 342-3.

333   "When the chief had passed": Nevins, *1862-1863.*, p. 332.

333   "I am much afraid": John G. Nicolay and John Hay, *Abraham Lincoln: The Observations of John G. Nicolay and John Hay*, Ed. Michael Burlingame (Carbondale: S. Ill. Univ. Press, 2007), p. 117.

333   "You can not change Lincoln's head": Letter of October 27, 1862, Adam Gurowski to John A. Andrew, from Fischer, p. 100.

333   "tow-string of a President": Williams, *Lincoln and the Radicals*, p. 183.

333   "The dogmas of the quiet past": Lincoln, *Works*, p. V: 537.

333   "Mr. Lincoln's whole soul": Letter of November 26, 1862, David Davis to Leonard Swett, from Nevins, *1862-1863,* p. 235. The proposal in Lincoln's December 1862 Annual Message, and his signing of a contract for a colonization of 500 blacks on Vache Island, off the coast of Haiti on December 31, 1862, were Lincoln's last public attempts to advance colonization. The latter project met with disaster, so that on July 1, 1864, John Hay wrote in his diary that Lincoln had given up on the scheme   "I am glad the President has sloughed off that idea of colonization." For excellent discussions of the history and politics of Lincoln's colonization schemes, see Michael Vorenberg, "The Politics of Black Colonization," *The Journal of the Abraham Lincoln Association*, Vol. 14, No. 2, p. 23; and Philip Shaw Paludan, "Lincoln and Colonization: Policy or Propaganda?" *The Journal of the Abraham Lincoln Association,* Vol. 25, No. 1, p. 23.

334   "May the Lord": Letter of December 3, 1862, James Sloan Gibbons to Garrison, from Randall, *Springfield to Gettysburg*, p. II: 240-1.

334   "The President is demented" and "borders upon hopeless lunacy": December 5, 1862, *The Liberator*, from Mayer, p. 543-4.

334   "A man so manifestly": December 26, 1862, *The Liberator*, *ibid.*

334   "If there is a worse place than Hell": Nevins, *1862-1863*, p. 351-2.

334   "How long": Rawley, p. 99.

334   "The War is a failure!": December 18, 1862, Albany *Atlas and Argus*, from Gary Gallagher, ed., *The Fredericksburg Campaign* (Chapel Hill: University of North Carolina Press, 1995), p. 64.

334   "The feeling of utter hopelessness": Letter of December 1862, Joseph Medill to Schuyler Colfax, from Williams, *Lincoln and the Radicals*, p. 236.

335   "We are indulging in no hyperbole": December 27, 1862, *Harper's Weekly.*

336   "A year ago we laughed": Entry for December 18, 1862, Strong, p. III: 281-2.

336   "almost everybody is dissatisfied," "utterly disgusted" and if things are not more successfully managed": Letters of December 17, 19, 1862, from Nicolay and Hay, *Observations*, p. 117-18.

336   "I am losing confidence": Letter of December 30, 1862, John D. Baldwin to Charles Sumner, from Randall, *Springfield to Gettysburg*, p. II: 241.

336   "would be received with *great satisfaction*": Letter of December 17, 1862, George F. Williams to Sumner, from David Donald, *Charles Sumner and the Rights of Man* (NY: Alfred A. Knopf, 1970), p. 89.

336   "*The days are growing shorter*": Guelzo, *Redeemer President,* p. 354.

336   "Folly, folly folly reigns supreme": Letter of Dec. 18, 1862, Zachary Chandler to his wife, from Randall, *Midstream*, p. 134, and Nicolay and Hay, *Observations*, p. 118.

337   "Seward must be got out": Williams, *Lincoln and the Radicals,* p. 205.

Page 337   "They seemed to think": Entry of December 19, 1862, Bates, p. 269

337   "a back stairs and malign influence": Entry of December 16, 1862, Browning, p. I: 597-98.

337   "now and then for talk": Letter of September 20, 1862, Chase to John Sherman, Chase, *Correspondence,* p. III: 278.

337   "Many speeches were made": Entry of December 17, Browning, p. I: 598-9.

337   "vigorous & successful" and "result of [the] combined wisdom": December 17, 1862, Lincoln, *Papers.*

338   "exceedingly violent": Randall, *Springfield to Gettysburg,* p. II: 243.

338   "They wish to get rid of me" and "We are now on the brink": Entry of December 18, 1862, Browning, p. I: 600-601.

338   "perplexed to death": Letter of December 25, 1862, S. Noble to E.B. Washburne, from Randall, *Springfield to Gettysburg,* p. II: 243.

338   "the president looked haggard": Letter of December 22, 1862, T.S. Bell to Joseph Holt, *ibid.,* p. 243-4n.

338   "His eyes were almost deathly": Noah Brooks, *Washington, D.C., in Lincoln's Time,* Ed. Herbert Mitgang (Athens: University of Georgia Press, 1989), p. 15.

339   "in milder spirit than it met": Nicolay and Hay, *Observations,* p. 130.

339   "Secretary Chase had a very different tone": *ibid.,* p. 131.

339   Cabinet rumors in Washington: Entry for December 20, 1862, Bates, p. 270.

339   Chase resignation episode: Entry for December 20, 1862, Welles, p. I: 201-2.

340   "I can ride on now": Donald, *Lincoln,* p. 405.

340   "The President of the United States is responsible": Entry of December 31, 1862, George B. Smith Diary, from Frank Klement, *The Copperheads in the Middle West* (Chicago: University of Chicago Press, 1960), p. 39.

340   "The year 1862": December 31, 1862, *The Crisis, ibid.*

340   "We feel no reliance": Letter of December 19, 1862, G.F. Forbes to Charles Sumner, from Randall, *Springfield to Gettysburg,* p. II: 167.

340   "The first of January": Letter of December 18, 1862, J.M. Forbes to Charles Sumner, *ibid.*

340   "Old Abe will do nothing decent": Letter of December 24, 1862, from Donald, *Charles Sumner,* p. 89.

340   "The President says": Letter of December 28, 1862, to J. M. Forbes, Sumner, *Selected Letters,* p. 136.

341   "I do not believe Mr. Lincoln": Letter of December 26, 1862, Orestes Brownson to Charles Sumner, from Donald, *Charles Sumner,* p. 89, and Randall, *Springfield to Gettysburg,* p. II: 241.

341   "general air of doubt": December 27, 1862, *New York Times,* from Goodwin, p. 497.

341   "Will Lincoln's backbone carry him through?": Entry of December 30, 1862, Strong, p. III: 284.

Chapter 26: Emancipation Proclaimed

342   "will do no act": Lincoln, *Works,* p. V: 434.

342   "abstain from all violence": Lincoln, *Works,* p. VI: 30.

343   "And upon this act": *ibid.*

343   "Well, what do you intend doing?": Guelzo, *Emancipation Proclamation,* p. 181.

344   New Year's Day Music Hall and Tremont Temple meetings: Mayer, p. 545-7.

344   "THE PROCLAMATION": *ibid.,* p. 547.

344   "All trials are swallowed up": Randall, *Springfield to Gettysburg,* p. II: 169.

Page 344   "midnight darkness": Mayer, p. 547.

344   "a bewilderment of joy": Randall, *Springfield to Gettysburg*, p. II: 170.

344   "a perfect furor of acclamation": *ibid.*

345   "a wicked, atrocious and revolting deed": January 3, 1863, Chicago *Times*, from Voegeli, p. 76-7.

345   "crowning act of Lincoln's folly," etc.: Issues of January 1, 3, 6, 10, 18, 1863, Dubuque *Herald*, from Klement, p. 43.

345   "the most foolish joke": January 10, 1863, Chatfield *Democrat, ibid.*, p. 44.

345   "a half-witted Usurper": January 7, 1863, *The Crisis.*

345   "'A' stands for Old Abe": May 6, 1863, *The Crisis.*

345   "a dead letter": January 3, 1863, *New York Herald*, from Randall, *Springfield to Gettysburg*, p. II: 176.

"miserable balderdash": February 7, 1863, New York *World, ibid.*, p. 36-7.

345   "not merely futile, but ridiculous" and also "Lincoln and Emancipation," see http://www.civilwarhome.com/lincolnandproclamation.htm

345   "The best thing": January 19, 1863, *New York Evening Express*, from Hans Trefousse, *First Among Equals: Abraham Lincoln's Reputation During His Administration* (NY: Fordham University Press, 2005), p. 66.

346   "vile and infamous": March 28, 1863, *Metropolitan Record, ibid.*

346   "cold-blooded invitation to insurrection and butchery": Guelzo, *Emancipation Proclamation*, p. 189.

346   "bloody, barbarous, revolutionary": *ibid.*, p. 187.

346   "We scarcely know": January 3, 1863, *Louisville Daily Democrat*, from Trefousse, *First Among Equals*, p. 66.

346   Kentucky reaction: Letter of January 7, 1863, Lincoln to Green Adams, note 1, Lincoln, *Papers.*

346   "I am despondent": Entry of January 30, 1863, Browning, p. I: 621.

346   "useless" and "mischievous": Entry of January 2, 1863, *ibid.*, p. I: 609.

346   "a puff of wind" and "The Emancipation Proclamation": Guelzo, *Emancipation Proclamation*, p. 222.

347   "We all agreed": Browning, p. I: 613.

347   "as the only means": Entry of January 19, 1863, *ibid.*, p. I: 616.

347   "there was a strong attachment": Letter of April 16, 1863, Thurlow Weed to John Bigelow, from Silbey, p. 84.

347   "sloughing off the secessionist sympathizers": Letter of January 21, 1862, Abraham Oakey Hall to William H. Seward, from Donald, *Lincoln*, p. 422; see also Gray, p. 129.

347   "I know of no man of sense": Letter of January 1, 1863, Benjamin Curtis to Greenough, Gray, p. 130.

347   Benjamin R. Curtis's constitutional objections: Guelzo, *Emancipation Proclamation*, p. 190-1.

347   "a power to change Constitutional rights": *ibid.*, p. 191.

348   "undoubtedly one of the most startling exercises": *ibid.*, p. 191-2.

348   "have more than One Hundred Thousand": January 3, 1863, New York *Tribune*, from Nevins, *1862-1863*, p. 235.

348   "The proclamation of the President": New York Journal of Commerce, reprinted in January 7, 1863, *Detroit Free Press*, from Williams, *Lincoln and the Radicals*, p. 216.

348   "[He] has made no friends": January 13, 1863, *Illinois State Register, ibid.*

349   "Strange phenomenon": Letter of January 6, 1863, James Garfield to Burke Hinsdale, from Goodwin, p. 501.

Page 349 "The feeling prevails": James Ford Rhodes, *History of the United States from the Compromise of 1850* (NY: Macmillan, 1913), p. IV: 221.

349 "we had made a great mistake": Entry of January 10, 1863, Browning, I: 612.

349 "I can understand the awful reluctance": Gray, p. 128-9.

349 "The army is tired": Packard, p. 153.

350 "many of our officers": Entry for January 1, 1863, Browning, p. I: 609.

350 "conversed with a great many": Entry for January 29, 1863, *ibid.*, p. I: 621.

350: Only one soldier in ten: Bell Irvin Wiley, *The Life of Billy Yank* (Indianapolis: Bobbs-Merrill, 1952), p. 40-43.

350 "with many boldly stating": Guelzo, *Emancipation Proclamation,* p. 188.

350 "officers and men swore": *ibid.*

350 "The president's proclamation": Henry Livermore Abbott, *Fallen Leaves: The Civil War Letters of Major Henry Livermore Abbott*, Ed. Robert G. Scott (Kent, OH: Kent State University Press, 1991), p. 161.

350 "I would like to see": Letter of February 7, 1863, A. Norton to homefolks, from Wiley, p. 42.

350 Hundreds of deserters a day: Nevins, *1862-1863,* p. 367. The monthly desertion rate for 1863 averaged 4,650, and was greatest in January.

350 "getting disgusted": Letter of January 25, 1863, Joseph Miller to Pvt. William Wilmoth, from Guelzo, *Emancipation Proclamation,* p. 188.

350 "Military affairs look dark here": Rhodes, p. 221-2n.

352 "he had not expected much": Don E. and Virginia E. Fehrenbacher, p. 120.

352 "he doubted": *ibid.,* p. 356.

352 "My proclamation was to stir the country": Rice, p. 235-6.

352 "stumbling, faithless, uncertain": Sandburg, *The War Years,* p. II: 172.

352 "growing feeble": Benjamin Brown French, *Witness to the Young Republic: A Yankee's Journal,* 1828-1870, Ed. Donald B. Cole and John J. McDonough (Hanover and London: University Press of New England, 1989), p. 417.

352 "Lincoln looks completely worn out": Letter of January 20, 1863, Roswell Lamson to "Kate", Roswell H. Lamson, *Lamson of the Gettysburg: The Civil War Letter of lieutenant Roswell H. Lamson, U. S. Navy,* Ed. James M. McPherson and Patricia R. McPherson (NY: Oxford University Press, 1997), p. 76.

352 "I observe": Entry of February 6, 1863, from Donald, *Lincoln,* p. 426.

353 "criticism, reflection": Albert Gallatin Riddle, *Recollections of War Times: Reminiscences of Men and Events in Washington, 1860-1865* (NY: G. P. Putnam's Sons, 1895), p. 218.

353 "The lack of respect": Letter of February 23, 1863, Richard Henry Dana to Thornton K. Lothrop, from Rhodes, p. 210n.

353 "As to the politics of Washington": Letter of March 9, 1863, Richard Henry Dana to Charles Francis Adams, *ibid.,* p. 210-11n.

353 "the fire in the rear": Letter of January 17, 1863, Charles Sumner to Francis Lieber, from Donald, *Lincoln,* p. 419.

Chapter 27: The Rise of the Copperheads

354 "Where, then" and "We are on the eve of civil war": Letter of January 2, 1863, from Oliver P. Morton, Lincoln, *Papers.*

355 "They will fight for the flag": Letter of May 18, 1863, John Sherman to William Sherman, from Voegeli, p. 82.

355 "I am advised": Rawley, p.121-2.

Page 356　"Resolved": January 7, 1863, *Illinois State Register.*

356　"All the [D]emocratic members": Letter of January 11, 1863, Mercy Conkling to Clinton Conkling, from Guelzo, *Emancipation Proclamation*, p. 189.

356　"Treason is everywhere": Gray, p. 126.

357　"There is but one way": Dubuque *Herald*, reprinted in January 10, 1863, *Davenport Daily Gazette, ibid.,* p. 122.

357　"You perceive": Dubuque *Herald*, reprinted in February 4, 1863, *Davenport Daily Gazette, ibid.*

357　"Since the war" and all other quotes from county meetings: *ibid.,* p. 123, 125.

358　"It is quite certain": Letter of January 1, 1863, Benjamin Curtis to Greenough, *ibid.,* p. 130.

358　"My apprehension is": Samuel S. Cox, *Eight Years in Congress* (NY: D. Appleton and Company, 1865), p. 283.

358　"At night called to see Mr & Mrs corning": Entry of January 21, 1862, Browning, p. I: 617.

359　"There is a change": Letter of February 8, 1863, Murat Halstead to William Sherman, from Williams, *Lincoln and the Radicals*, p. 281.

359　"It is important": Telegram of January 31, 1863, from Oliver P. Morton, Lincoln, *Papers.*

359　"misconstrued a thousand ways": Lincoln, *Works,* p. VI: 87.

359　"The Democratic scheme": Letter of February 9, 1863, from Oliver P. Morton, Lincoln, *Papers.*

360　"respecting the existance [sic]": Letter of January 14, 1863, from Henry B. Carrington, *ibid.*

360　"The few union men": Letter of January 22, 1863, from W. Holmes, *ibid.*

361　"it has now Become a Settled fact": Letter of February 8, 1863, Daniel F. Coffey to John G. Nicolay, *ibid.*

361　"at least 4 regiments": Letter of January 30, 1863, from Richard Yates, *ibid.*

361　"I am sorry that you are engaged": Gray, p. 133.

361　"come home" *ibid.,* p. 133.

362　"As soon as I get my money": Letter of January 31, 1863, Stephen A. Miller to his sister, from Wiley, p. 112.

362　"I have just read": Alan D. Gaff, *On Many a Bloody Field: Four Years in the Iron Brigade* (Bloomington: Indiana University Press, 1996), p. 214.

362　5,000 desertions per month in 1863: Klement, p. 75.

362　"A party of soldiers sent to Rush County": Sandburg, *The War Years*, p. II: 156.

363　"Since I have lived in Illinois": Letter of March 5, 1863, from Joseph Medill, Lincoln, *Papers.*

363　"I can assure you": Letter of March 6, 1863, from Oliver Morton, *ibid.*

363　"obliterate state lines": March 7, 1863, Chatfield *Democrat*, from Klement, p. 77.

363　"part and parcel": Smith, *Trial by Fire*, p. 476.

364　"this law converts the Republic": *ibid.,* p. 476.

364　"more rigid treatment": Marvel, *Burnside*, p. 227.

364　"The habit of declaring sympathy"　　"General Order No. 38" found at http://www.ohiohistorycentral.org/entry.php?rec=1481

365　"Not a man or a dollar for the war": Joseph H. Barrett, *The Life of Abraham Lincoln* (Cincinnati: Moore, Wilstach & Baldwin, 1865), p. 451.

365　"defeat, death, taxation, sepulchres": Nicolay and Hay, *A History*, p. VII: 330.

366　"I shall never forget": Brooks, *Washington, D.C.*, p. 60-61.

Page 366   "*You saw those mighty legions, Abe*": Geoffrey Stone, *Perilous Times: Free Speech in Wartime from the Sedition Act of 1798 to the War on Terrorism* (NY: W.W. Norton & Co., 2004), p. 131.

367   "the tyranny of military despotism": Donald, *Lincoln*, p. 420.

367   "a series of fatal steps": *ibid.*, p. 421.

367   "the man who occupied the Presidential chair": *ibid.*, p. 420-1.

367   "[Vallandigham's arrest] interfered": Nicolay and Hay, *A History*, p. 342.

367   "every Republican paper": May 20, 1863, *The Crisis*, from Harper, p. 244.

367   "the ablest and most influential champions": *ibid.*, p. 245.

367   "arbitrary and injudicious": Garrison, p. 199.

368   "I enclose herewith": Letter of April 7, 1863, from William B. Thomas, Lincoln, *Papers*.

368   "not by street fighting": Sidney David Brummer, *Political History of New York State During the Period of the Civil War* (NY: AMS Press, 1967), p. 313.

369   "Now, if, as is thus proven": Gray, p. 147.

369   "Freemen, awake!": Stephenson, p. 310.

369   "men deprived of the right of trial by jury," etc.: Horace Greeley, *The American Conflict: Its Causes, Incidents, and Results* (Hartford: O.D. Case & Co., 1866), p. 500.

370   "profoundly repugnant": July 13, 1863, New York *World, ibid.*, p. 502.

370   "The miscreants at the head," etc.: July 13, 1863, New York *Daily News, ibid.*

370   "If a quarter one hears be true": Entry for July 13, 1863, Strong, p. III: 336.

371   "fitfully from far breaks" and "Red Arson": Allan Nevins, *The War for the Union: The Organized War, 1863-1864* (NY: Charles Scribner's Sons, 1971), p. 123.

371   "The people are waking up": Entry for July 14, 1863, Strong, p. III: 337.

371   "Everywhere throughout the city": Nevins, *1863-1864,* p. 123.

371   "The law-abiding citizen hangs his head": July 14, 1863, New York *World.*

373   "I cannot, in words, tell you my joy": Entry of July 7, 1863, Welles, p. I: 364.

Chapter 28: Lincoln Addresses the Nation

374   "[I]f [Lincoln] don't go forward": Letter of August 11, 1863, Jesse M. Fell to Lyman Trumbull, from Gray, p. 149.

374   "that the constitution is not in it's [sic] application": Lincoln, *Works,* p. VI: 267.

375   "Must I shoot a simple-minded soldier boy": *ibid.*, p. VI: 266.

375   "than I am able to believe": *ibid.,* p. VI: 267.

375   "There are those who are dissatisfied": *ibid.,* p. VI: 406.

375   "[T]he emancipation policy": *ibid.*, p. VI: 408-9.

375   "Even the Copperhead gnaws upon it": Sandburg, *The War Years,* p. II: 382.

375   "the Father of Waters" and "Uncle Sam's Web-feet": Lincoln, *Works,* p. VI: 409.

376   "[Lincoln,] like many of his countrymen": September 17, 1863, London *Evening Standard,* from Bloom, p. 46.

376   "You cannot refine Mr. Lincoln's taste": Douglas L. Wilson, *Lincoln's Sword: The Presidency and the Power of Words* (NY: Alfred A. Knopf, 2006), p. 197.

376   "Thanks for your true and noble letter": Sandburg, *The War Years,* p. II: 385.

376   "Sooth to say, our own politicians": Wilson, p. 195-6.

377   "The Tycoon is in fine whack": Entry of August 6, 1863, Hay, *Lincoln and the Civil War*, p. 76.

378   "It is now no longer a question": August 7, 1863, *The Crisis.*

378   "Lincoln to Be Declared Perpetual President": Sandburg, *The War Years,* p. II: 449.

378   "Thus the mad fanatics": *ibid.*

Page 379 "Glory to God": Waugh, p. 13.

380 "This state has really been carried": Letter of October 15, 1863, Alfred Denny to John Sherman, from Williams, *Lincoln and the Radicals*, p. 293.

380 "if it had not been": Letter of October 24, 1863, V.H. Painter to John Sherman, *ibid.*

380 "The Democracy fail": October 14, 1863, Brooklyn *Daily Eagle*.

380 "it did not seem to occur": Angle, p. 444.

381 "imposing and solemnly impressive": Letter of November 2, 1863, from David Wills, Lincoln, *Papers.*

381 "the President in a fine, free way": Entry of November 20, 1863, Hay, *Lincoln and the Civil War*, p. 121.

381 "So short a time": Wilson, p. 226-7.

382 "The President at Gettysburg": November 23, 1863, Chicago *Times*, Mitgang, p. 361.

382 "The cheek of every American": Wilson, p. 229.

382 "We pass over the silly remarks": Sandburg, *The War Years*, p. II: 472.

382 "the ceremony was rendered ludicrous": *ibid.*, p. 474.

383 "a perfect gem": *ibid.*

383 "while I remain": Lincoln, *Works*, p. VII: 51.

383 "the effect of this paper": Entry of December 9, 1863, Hay, *Lincoln and the Civil War*, p. 131.

Part Four: Lincoln's Reelection

Chapter 29: The 1864 Republican Nomination

385 Sumner's outburst on House floor: Brooks, *Washington, D.C.,* p. 151.

385 Sumner's "State Suicide" theory: October 1863, *Atlantic Monthly*, Charles Sumner, "Our Domestic Relations: Power of Congress over the Rebel States," *The Works of Charles Sumner*, 17 vols. (Boston: Lee and Shepard, 1900) p. VII:541.

386 "a silly performance": Letter of December 19, 1863, William Fessenden to his family, from Williams, *Lincoln and the Radicals*, p. 302.

387 "[A]t this moment": August 29, 1863, *Harper's Weekly.*

"a comprehensive policy": September 17, 1864, *The Independent*, from Williams, *Lincoln and the Radicals,* p. 292.

"Let the dead bury the dead": Carpenter, p. 38.

"Conservatives & traitors": Letter of November 15, 1863, from Zachary Chandler, Lincoln, *Works,* p. VII: 24.

387 "I am very glad": Lincoln, *Works,* p. VII: 24.

388 "There is a strong feeling": Letter of September 18, 1864, Sumner to Richard Cobden, Charles Sumner, *Memoirs and Letters of Charles Sumner,* Ed. Edward L. Pierce (NY: Oxford University Press, 1878), p. 199.

388 "infatuation": Entry of February 12, 1864, Adam Gurowski, *Diary, 1863, '64, '65* (Washington: WH & OH Morrison, 1866), p. 99-100.

388 "taken in" by the "great shifter": Entry of January 3, 1864, *ibid.*, p. 60.

388 "The best men": Entry of January 12, 1864, *ibid.*, p. 69.

388 "The people sends": Entry of April 4, 1864, *ibid.*, p. 159.

388 "It is only just to say": Sanburg, *The War Years*, p. II: 566

389 "I am personally attached": Letter of September 6, 1864, Orville Browning to Edgar Cowan, from Randall, *Lincoln the Liberal Statesman*, p. 81.

Page 389   "The nation cannot live": Reprinted in May 18, 1864, *The Crisis.*

389   "Mr. Lincoln had only one fast friend": William Frank Zornow, *Lincoln & the Party Divided,* (Norman: University of Oklahoma Press, 1954), p. 19

389   "Here is a man": Sandburg, *The War Years,* p. II: 561-2

389   "The opposition to Mr. Lincoln": *ibid.,* p. 564

389   "I talked with numerous Representatives": Shelby Collum, *Fifty Years of Public Service* (Chicago: A.C. McClurg & Co., 1911), p. 98

390   "I have not yet met one": Entry of February 4, 1864, Gurowski, *1863-1865,* p. 91.

390   "Not a single Senator": Sandburg, *The War Years,* p. II: 561.

390   "everybody thinks": Letter of March 16, 1864, Al Denny to John Sherman, from Donald, *Lincoln,* p. 494.

390   "The feeling for Mr. Lincoln's reelection": Letter of February 6, 1864, Trumbull to H.G. Pike, from Williams, *Lincoln and the Radicals,* p. 310.

391   "I have seen a great deal": Letter of May 21, 1862, Chase to Horace Greeley, from Chase, *Correspondence,* p. III: 203.

391   "The whole state of things": Letter of May 24, 1862, Chase to Murat Halstead, *ibid.,* p. 204.

391   "There is no cabinet": Letter of September 20, 1862, Chase to Zachariah Chandler, *ibid.,* p. 276.

391   "useless": Entry of September 29, 1863, Chase, *Diaries,* p. 207.

391   "Chase is a good man": Entry at beginning of 1863, Hay, *Lincoln and the Civil War,* p. 53.

391   "I could take no part": Entry for October 3, 1863, Chase, *Diaries,* p. 208.

391   "the greatest, the strongest, the boldest": October 15 and November 5, 1863, from Williams, *Lincoln and the Radicals,* p. 296.

391   "I'm afraid Mr. Chase's head": Entry for October 17, 1863, Bates, p. 310.

391   "There is nothing fixed": Maihafer, p. 170.

392   "there is an active movement": Entry of December 28, 1863, Welles, p. I: 498.

392   "You are head and shoulders": Letter of December 8, 1863, M.F. Conway to Chase, *ibid.,* p. 95.

392   "my opinion": Letter of December 18, 1863, J.R. Freese to Chase, *ibid.*

392   "The Next Presidential Election": Chase, *Diaries,* p. 24-5.

392   "With an army": Hedrick, p. 414.

393   "First, that even were the reelection": Nicolay & Hay, *A History,* p. VIII: 320.

393   "seems much amused": Entry of October 28, 1863, Hay, *Lincoln and the Civil War,* p. 110.

393   "The President fears Chase": Entry of February 15, 1864, Welles, p. I: 525.

393   "carefully veiled his keen and sometimes bitter resentment": McClure, p. 136.

394   "A glance at the list of delegates": May 27, 1864, *Albany Atlas and Argus,* from Maihafer, p. 210.

394   "the people's choice": Donald, *Lincoln,* p. 480.

394   Indiana state convention: J.G. Randall and Richard Current, *Lincoln the President: The Last Full Measure* (Urbana: University of Illinois Press, 1999), p. 122-3.

395   "the fact that the patronage": Reprinted in February 24, 1864, *The Crisis.*

395   "Even his honesty": March 17, 1864, London *Times,* from Bloom, p. 51.

395   "more dangerous in its recoil": Entry of February 22, 1864, Welles, p. I: 529.

396   "while every energy," etc.: February 24, 1864, New York *Tribune,* Mitgang, p. 381-384.

396   "Lincoln has some very weak and foolish traits": Waugh, p. 118.

396   "I regret very much": *ibid.,* p. 119.

Page 396   "not out of the woods": Letter of February 28, 1864, Greeley to Beman Brockway, from Williams, *Lincoln and the Radicals*, p. 312-313.

397   "The Next President": *Brownson's Quarterly Review* (April 1864). For more information, see http://orestesbrownson.com/index.php?id=361

398   "the imbecile and vacillating policy": Nicolay and Hay, *A History*, p. IX: 30.

398   "We propose before ostracizing honest Abe": Sandburg, *The War Years*, p. III: 71-2.

399   "This is not an ordinary election": Nicolay and Hay, *A History*, p. IX: 41-2.

400   "proved a failure": Randall & Current, p. 43.

400   "Mr. Lincoln is a joke incarnated": Randall, *Mr. Lincoln*, p. 303.

401   "Better cringe under the sternest despotism": Sandburg, *The War Years*, p. II: 579.

401   "In the knots of two or three": *ibid.*, p. 581.

401   "No influence except compulsion": May 18, 1864, New York *Daily News*, from Harper, p. 117.

401   "wire-pullers and bottle-washers": Sandburg, *The War Years*, p. II: 70.

401   "that self-constituted and irresponsible gathering": Waugh, p. 145.

401   "What a chill": Entry of June 9, 1864, Gurowski, *Diary, 1863-1865*, p. 251.

402   "The Baltimore Convention": Entry for June 10, 1864, Bates, p. 374-5.

402   "I, A. Lincoln": June 11, 1864, Chicago *Times*, from Sandburg, *The War Years*, p. II: 100.

402   "The politicians": June 10, 1864, from Maihafer, *War of Words*, p. 179.

402   "The age of statesmen is gone": *ibid.*, p. 183.

402   "*We're coming Father Abraham*": Reprinted in June 19, 1864, *The Crisis*.

402   "We cannot but feel": June 9, 1864, New York *Tribune*, Mitgang, p. 402.

403   "The Baltimore Convention was largely a mob": Sandburg, *The War Years*, p. II: 101.

Chapter 30: The Fall and the Temptation

404   "show business": Sandburg, *The War Years*, p. IV: 262.

404   "is pervaded with a feeling": Furgurson, p. 299.

404   "All Washington is a great hospital": *ibid.*

405   "The long, ghastly procession": *ibid.*, p. 299-300.

405   "It makes me sick": Letter of May 29, 1864, John A Hiestand to Thaddeus Stevens, from Randall and Current, p. 112.

405   "I pray god": Letter of February 6, 1864, A. Wattles to Horace Greeley, *ibid.*

405   "Mr. Lincoln may mean well": Letter of March 7, 1864, S. Wolf to Rev. Dr. McMurdy, *ibid.*

406   "You and I have reached a point": Lincoln, *Works*, p. VII: 419.

406   "clear and cold" and "a singularly violent politician": Brooks, *Washington, D.C.*, p. 152.

406   "mischievous in his schemes": July 1, 1864, from Allan Nevins, *The War for the Union: Organized War to Victory, 1864-1865* (NY: Charles Scribner's Sons, 1971), p. 88.

407   "He is no statesman" and "lawless and daring": Sandburg, *The War Years*, p. III: 131.

407   "The important point": Entry of July 4, 1864, Hay, *Lincoln and the Civil War*, p. 205

408   "In the disorder": Brooks, *Washington, D.C.*, p. 154-5.

408   "If [the Radicals] choose": Entry of July 4, 1864, Hay, *Lincoln and the Civil War*, p. 204-6

408   "Washington was in a ferment": Brooks, *Washington, D.C.*, p. 159.

409   "We have five times as many generals": Frank Vandiver, *Jubal's Raid* (NY: McGraw-Hill, 1960), p. 142.

409   "Get down, you damn fool": Entry of July 11, 1864, Hay, *Lincoln and the Civil War*, p. 208.

Page 409   "Grant's distance from the scene": Brooks, *Washington, D.C.*, p. 162.

409   "egregious blunder": Goodwin, p. 644.

409   "contemptible": Entry of July 13, 1864, Welles, p. II: 76

409   "our nation humiliation": Entry of July 15, 1864, *ibid.*, p. II: 77.

409   "In the country at large": Brooks, *Washington, D.C.*, p. 163-4.

410   "the great noodles": July 27, 1864, from Waugh, p. 244.

410   "It will be seen": Reprinted in July 30, 1864, *Illinois Daily State Journal*, from Harper, p. 126.

410   *"One tall, and bony and lank"*: Reprinted in July 27, 1864, *The Crisis*.

411   "Lincoln is *deader* than dead": Letter of July 20, 1864, Samuel Medary to Charles Medary, from David E. Long, *The Jewel of Liberty: Abraham Lincoln's Re-election and the End of Slavery* (Mechanicsburg, Pa.: Stackpole, 1994), p. 122.

411   "Gold goes up like a balloon": Nevins, *1864-1865*, p. 95.

411   "Among the masses": Sherwin, p. 496.

411   "great and almost universal dissatisfaction": Letter of July 11, 1864, Chase to William C. Noyes, from Donald, *Lincoln*, p. 524.

411   "Took tea at Mr. Longfellow's": Lawrence, William, *Life of Amos A. Lawrence*, (Boston: Houghton Mifflin, Boston, 1888), p. 195.

411   "not higher than it was": Donald, *Charles Sumner and the Rights of Man*, p. 186.

411   "This entire administration": Letter of August 3, 1864, James Grimes to C. H. Ray, from Donald, *Lincoln*, p. 524.

412:    Text   of   the   Wade-Davis   Manifesto: http://www.civilwarinteractive.com/DocsWadeDavisManifesto.htm

412   "the dissatisfaction": August 6, 1864, *New York Herald*, from Stephenson, p. 372.

412   "arrogance": August 6, 1864, *New York Herald*, from Maihafer, p. 194-5.

412   "As President": August 6, 1864, *New York Herald*, from Randall and Current, p. 209.

412   "a blow between the eyes": August 9, 1864, New York *World*, from Donald, *Lincoln*, p. 524.

412   "coming as it did": Brooks, *Washington, D. C.*, p. 156.

412   "Its appearance created something like a panic": *ibid.*, p. 155.

412   "No such bomb": Letter of August 6, 1864, from J. K. Herbert, Benjamin Butler, *Correspondence of Gen. Benjamin F. Butler during the Period of the Civil War, Ed. Jessie Ames Marshall, 5 vols* (The Plimpton Press, Norwood, Mass., 1917), p. V: 8, 9.

413   "Union men were quite unanimous": Riddle, p. 305.

413   "If the Republican party desires to succeed": Richard N. Current, *Old Thad Stevens: A Story of Ambition* (Westport CT: Greenwood Press, 1980), p. 202.

413   "Lincoln is gone": Letter of August 6, 1864, from J. K. Herbert, Butler, p. V: 9.

413   "I told Mr Lincoln": Lincoln, *Works*, p. VII: 514n.

413   Whitelaw Reid convinced Lincoln's reelection was hopeless: Letter of August, 22, 1864, from Reid, Chase, *Correspondence*, p. 423-4.

413   "Things in a political way": Letter of August 14, 1864, G. C. Rice to Washburne, from Randall and Current, p. 211.

413   "everywhere in the towns": Letter of August 25, 1864, Hay, *Lincoln and the Civil War*, p. 211-12.

413   "from pure necessity" and "get a competent, loyal President": Letter of July 18, 1864, Edgar Conkling to Benjamin Butler, from Zornow, p. 111.

413   "The present condition": Letter of August 16, 1864, from John H. Martindale, Butler, p. 54-5.

413   "I have seen and talked": Letter of August 17, 1864, from J. W. Shaffer, *ibid.*, p. 67.

Page 413   "Political affairs in this state": Letter of August 20, 1864, John A. Gray to Montgomery Blair, Lincoln, *Papers*.

414   "The people seemed to be utterly spiritless": Carl Schurz, *The Reminiscences of Carl Schurz* (NY: Doubleday, Page & Company, 1917), p. III:102.

414   "feeling of despondency": Entry for August 13, 1864, Welles, p. II: 103.

414   "Distrust and disintegration": McClure, p. 125.

414   "I found the most alarming depression": Letter of September 8, 1864, Leonard Swett to his wife, from David E. Long, p. 235.

414   "Unless material changes can be wrought": Waugh, p. 265.

414   "disastrous panic": Letter of August 28, 1864, *ibid.*, p. 264.

414   "The feeling against Old Abe is daily increasing": Sherwin, p. 496.

414   "The people regard Mr. Lincoln's candidacy as a misfortune": Rhodes, p. IV: 518-9.

414   "inconceivably impudent": Letter of August 25, 1864, to John Nicolay, Hay, *Lincoln and the Civil War*, p. 211-12.

414   "I know that nine-tenths": August 9, 1864, from Rhodes, p. IV: 517.

415   "Under the figure of a jester": Reprinted in August 18, 1864, *Brooklyn Daily Eagle*.

415   "[W]e determine him": Reprinted in August 1, 1864, Brooklyn *Daily Eagle*.

415   "has brought even honesty into disrepute": Entry for September 8, 1864, Bates, p. 404.

415   "the only way to redeem the State": *ibid.*

415   "The fact begins to shine out": August 12, 1864, Richmond *Examiner*, reprinted in August 16, 1864, New York *World*, from Waugh, p. 262.

415   "Mr. Lincoln is already beaten": Rhodes, p. 518.

416   "to concentrate the union strength": Williams, *Lincoln and the Radicals*, p. 326.

416   "Chase will be there": Letter of August 17, 1864, from J.W. Shaffer, Butler, p. 68.

417   "He spoke as if he felt a pressing need": Schurz, *Reminiscences*, p. III: 103-4.

417   "I spent an hour with him": McClure, p. 125.

417   "To be wounded": Brooks, *Washington, D.C.*, p., 156.

417   "You think I don't know": Letter of August 11, 1864, from J. K. Herbert, Butler, p. 35.

417   "In the memory of men": Brooks, *Washington D.C.*, p. 157.

417   "One denounces Mr. Lincoln": August 10, 1864, New York *Times*, from Waugh, p. 264.

418   "This morning": Lincoln, *Works*, p. VII: 514.

419   "Mr. Raymond, who has just left me": *ibid.*, p. VII: 514-5n.

419   "I feel compelled": Letter of August 22, 1864, from Henry Raymond, Lincoln, *Papers*.

420   "Executive Mansion": Lincoln, *Works*, p. VII: 517.

421   "There have been men": *ibid.*, p. VII: 507.

421   "The President appeared to be not the pleasant joker": *ibid.*

422   "to follow his plan": Nicolay and Hay, *A History*, p. IX: 221.

422   "Out Lincoln": Entry for September 1, 1864, Gurowski, *Diary, 1863-1865*, p. 329.

422   "Old Abe is quite in trouble": Letter of August 17, 1864, McCormick to Manton Marble, from Waugh, p. 272.

Chapter 31: The Election of 1864

424   "Dear Lincoln": Letter of August 24, 1864, from M. W. Delahay, Lincoln, *Papers*.

425   "the people's eyes": Letter of November 14, 1863, from Sears, *The Young Napoleon*, p. 358.

425   "with a statesman's vision": *ibid.*, p. 360.

426   "your only fortnight of peace": Letter of August 10, 1864, *ibid.*, p. 369

426   "I have no doubt": Letter of August 21, 1864, *ibid.*

Page 426   "politically the chances are for McClellan": Letter of August 13, 1864, from his wife, Butler, p. V: 47-48.

426   "useless and inexpedient": Letter of August 31, 1864, George Wilkes to E.B. Washburne, from Randall and Current, p. 224.

427   "Mr. Lincoln will go down to posterity": Reprint in October 5, 1864, *The Crisis*.

427   "They have a peace leg and a war leg": Waugh, p. 89.

427   "One week before the Chicago convention": *ibid.*, p. 307.

427   "makes Lincoln an anchor": Entry of October 2, 1864, Gurowski, *Diary, 1863-1865*, p. 366.

427   "Atlanta is our and fairly won": Raymond, p. 544.

427   "There has been the most extraordinary change": Letter of September 8, 1864, Zachary Chandler to his wife, from David E. Long, p. 235.

427   "There has never been an instance": Letter of September 8, 1864, Leonard Swett to his wife, *ibid.*

427   "There was no time": McClure, p. 124.

428   "the duty of all Unionists": Letter of September 5, 1864, from Theodore Tilton to Anna Dickinson, from Randall and Current, p. 226.

428   "The conspiracy against Mr. Lincoln": Letter of September 20, 1864, Thurlow Weed to William Seward, from David E. Long, p. 237.

428   "I shall fight like a savage": Letter of August 30, 1864 from John Nicolay, Lincoln, Papers.

428   "Henceforth we fly the banner": September 6, 1864, New York *Tribune*, from Maihafer, p. 204.

429: Lieber's letter to Sumner: Sumner, *Memoirs*, p. IV: 196.

429   "I may accomplish nothing": Letter of September 2, 1864, Zachary Chandler to his wife, from David E. Long, p. 240.

429   "You very well know": Letter of September 23, 1864, Lincoln, *Works*, p. VIII: 18.

429   "I only wish": Trefousse, *Benjamin Franklin Wade*, p. 231.

429   "He says sometimes he feels so disgusted": Letter of September 26, 1864, from J.K. Herbert, Butler, p. 167.

430   "trickster" and "truckler": Sandburg, *The War Years*, p. IV: 366.

430   "not to aid in the triumph of Mr. Lincoln": Letter of September 21, 1864, Fremont to "Messrs. George L. Stearns and others," from Edward McPherson, *The Political History of the United States of America, During the Great Rebellion* (Washington: James J. Chapman, 1882), p. 426-7.

430   "I would cut off both hands": Sandburg, *The War Years*, p. III: 246.

430   "soon became one of great acrimony": Waugh, p. 315.

431   "Lincoln Upon the Battlefield": Reprinted in August 3, 1864, *The Crisis*.

431   *"Abe may crack his jolly jokes"*: Lamon, *Recollections*, p. 146.

432   "No, there has already been too much said": *ibid.*, p. 145.

432   "If the loyal people": Reprinted in July 26, 1864, *Cincinnati Enquirer*, from Harper, p. 215.

432   "The most powerful monarchy": August 7, 1864, *Illinois State Register*, Mitgang, p. 406-7.

432   "We have no honeyed words": Reprinted in August 10, 1864, *The Crisis*.

432   "There is some excuse": August 26, 1864, Brooklyn *Daily Eagle*.

432   "has swapped the Goddess of Liberty": August 29, 1864, *Ohio Statesman*, from Harper, p. 229.

432   "May Almighty God forbid": William Hanchett, *The Lincoln Murder Conspiracies* (Urbana: University of Illinois Press, 1983), p. 18.

Page 434   "The Lincoln Catechism": April 15, 1863, *The Crisis.*

435   "foul-tongued and ribald punster": October 8, 1864, London *Evening Standard*, from Bloom, p. 48-9.

435   "that concentrated quintescence": November 5, 1864, Leeds *Intelligencer, ibid.,* p. 49.

435   "These are the terms": September 24, 1864, *Harper's Weekly.*

435   "The President is too busy": Donald, *Lincoln,* p. 538.

436   Lincoln's campaign moves: Randall, *Mr. Lincoln,* p. 329.

436   Political officials tithe to the party: Donald, *Lincoln Reconsidered,* p. 177.

436   Party finances: Randall and Current, p. 252.

436   "All the power and influence": Charles A. Dana, *Recollections of the Civil War* (NY: D. Appleton and Company, 1913), p. 261.

437   "I am just enough": Brooks, *Washington, D.C.,* p. 196.

437   "one of the most solemn days": Nicolay and Hay, *A History,* p. IX: 375.

437   "found it difficult": Brooks, *Washington D.C.,* p. 196.

437   "seemed to have a keen and surprised regret": Nicolay and Hay, *A History,* p. IX: 375.

437   "It is a little singular": Entry for November 8, 1864, Hay, *Lincoln and the Civil War,* p. 233.

438   "I shall never forget the fire": Dana, p. 262.

438   "went awkwardly and hospitably to work": Entry for November 8, 1864, Hay, *Lincoln and the Civil War,* p. 235.

Chapter 32: The War at the End of the War

439   "The size of his majority": Schurz, *Reminiscences,* p. 106

439   "I am here by the blunders": Hugh McCulloch, *Men and Measures of Half a Century* (NY: Charles Scribner's Sons, 1888), p. 162.

440   "No man was ever elected": Letter of September 5, 1864, from "Mr. Sedgwick," John Murray Forbes, *Letters and Recollections of John Murray Forbes,* ed. Sarah Forbes Hughes, 2 vols. (Boston: Houghton Mifflin, 1899), p. II:101.

440   "Nothing but the undying attachment": Donald, *Lincoln Reconsidered,* p. 169.

440   "Mr. Lincoln is re-consecrated": Entry for November 10, 1864, Gurowski *Diary, 1863-1865,* p. 394.

440   "to keep out worse people": Nevins, *1864-1865,* p. 142.

440   "not that Abraham Lincoln": Address of February 7, 1865, from Sandburg, *The War Years,* p. IV: 59.

440   "There was no enthusiasm": *ibid.,* p. III: 662.

440   "the heaviest calamity": Waugh, p. 357.

440   "*As the bird of Arabia*": December 3, 1863, London *Punch*, Mitgang, p. 423.

441   "to the strength of his party": Sandburg, *The War Years,* p. III: 582.

442   "The renewal of Mr. Lincoln's term": *ibid.,* p. III: 582-3.

442   "We can regard the reappointment of Mr. Lincoln": November 22, 1864, London *Times*, Brogan, p. 153-4.

442   "Yesterday": November 9, 1864, *Richmond Dispatch*, Mitgang, p. 417.

443   "the time may come": Lincoln, *Works,* p. VIII: 152.

443   "The war will cease": *ibid.*

443   "absolute, unqualified submission": Nevins, *1864-1865,* p. 210.

443   "maintenance of the destructive policy": Sandburg, *The War Years,* p. III: 652.

443   "Ridicule would seem to be the first and only weapon": December 14, 1864, *The Crisis.*

443   Davis demanded a test of strength in the House: *The Congressional Globe*, House of Representatives, 38th Congress, Second Session, p. 48.

Page 444   "[Wendell] Phillips has just returned": Sandburg, *The War Years*, p. III: 663.

444   "I claim not to have controlled events": Lincoln, *Works*, p. VII: 282.

444   "king's cure": *ibid.*, p. VIII: 254.

444   "For a moment": Brooks, *Washington, D.C.*, p. 187.

445   "drummed up from the riff-raff": Sumner, *Memoirs*, p. 226.

445   "the most absurd": Charles Hallan McCarthy, *Lincoln's Plan of Reconstruction* (NY: McClure, Phillips & Co., 1901), p. 333.

445   "The perturbation in Washington": Brooks, *Washington, D.C.*, p. 202.

446   "Let me have that one condition": Sandburg, *The War Years*, p. IV: 61.

446   "None of the Cabinet were advised": Entry of February 2, 1865, Welles, p. II: 235.

446   "Fools meet and separate": Letter of February 6, 1865, from Chandler to wife, from Williams, *Lincoln and the Radicals*, p. 355.

446   "It did not meet with favor": Entry of February 6, 1865, Welles, p. 251.

447   "Flocks of women": Dispatch of March 12, 1865, to the *Sacramento Union*, from Noah Brooks, *Lincoln Observed: The Civil War Dispatches of Noah Brooks*, Ed. Michael Burlingame (Baltimore: The Johns Hopkins University Press, 1998), p. 165.

447   "There was great want": Entry of March 4, 1865, Welles, p. II: 251.

447   Second Inaugural Address: Lincoln, *Works*, p. VIII: 332-3.

449   "There was a leaden stillness": Ronald C. White, *Lincoln's Greatest Speech: The Second Inaugural* (NY: Simon & Schuster, 2002), p. 184.

449   "I believe it is not immediately popular": Lincoln, *Works*, p. VIII: 356.

450   "We did not conceive": March 6, 1865, Chicago *Times*, from Ronald C. White, p. 191.

450   "with a blush of shame": March 6, 1865, New York *World*, *ibid.*, p. 190-191.

450   "substitution of religion": March 6, 1865, New York *World*, from Goodwin, p. 700.

450   "The President's theology": March 6, 1865, New York *World*, from Ronald C. White, p. 194.

450   "an effort to avoid any commitment": March 5, 1865, *New York Herald*, p. 190.

450   "He makes no boasts": March 6, 1865, *New York Times*, *ibid.*, p. 189.

450   "Thus in a day": March 6, 1865, New York *Tribune*.

450   "We are not": March 17, 1865, New York *Tribune*.

451   "His face was ragged with care": July, 1891, *Century Magazine*, from J. Seymour Currey, *Chicago: Its History and Its Builders: A Century of Marvelous Growth* (Chicago: S. J. Clarke, 1912), p. 157.

451   "He looked jaded": Letter of January 12, 1866, Speed to William Herndon, from Wilson and Davis, p. 156, 157; also Joshua Speed, *Reminiscences of Abraham Lincoln* (Louisville: John P. Morton and Company, Louisville, 1884), p. 26, 28.

451   "Poor Mr. Lincoln": Elizabeth Keckley, *Behind the Scenes: Or, Thirty Years a Slave and Four Years in the White House* (NY: Oxford University Press, 1988), p. 157

451   "In their private chamber": *ibid.*, p. 158.

451   "darted at him": Carpenter, p. 276.

451   "It seems as though the bare thought": *ibid.*

451   "worn down": Sandburg, *The War Years*, p. IV: 113.

451   "Can you not visit": Lincoln, *Works*, p. VIII: 367.

451   "The President has gone to the front": Entry for March 23, 1865, from Welles, p. II: 264.

452   "Glory!!! Hail Columbia!!!": Washington *Star*, from Leech, p. 378.

452   "In a moment of time": Brooks, *Washington, D.C.*, p. 219.

453   Descriptions of the celebrations in Washington, D.C.: Brooks, *Lincoln Observed*, p. 180; Brooks, *Washington, D.C.*, p. 222; Leech, p. 379; Jay Winik, *April 1865: The Month That Saved America* (NY: Harper Collins, 2001), p. 213-14.

454   "dribble it all out": Lincoln, *Works*, p. VIII: 393.

Page 454   "bribe of unconditional forgiveness": April 11, 1865, New York *Tribune*, from Williams, *Lincoln and the Radicals*, p. 371.

454   "Those who are ready to fight": Dispatch of April 12, 1865, Brooks, *Lincoln Observed*, p. 185.

454   "There was something terrible": Brooks, *Washington, D.C.*, p. 226.

455   "The speech was longer": *ibid.*

455   "Concede that the new government of Louisiana": Lincoln, *Works*, p. VIII: 404.

455   "it was a silent, intent, perhaps surprised multitude": Brooks, *Washington, D. C.*, p. 227.

455   "fell dead": Sandburg, *The War Years*, p. IV: 224.

455   "The speech was not in keeping": Sumner, *Memoirs*, p. 236.

455   "Sumner was thoughtful and sad": *ibid.*

455   "The President's speech": *ibid.*

456   "The eggs of crocodiles": From Sumner's tribute to Senator Collamer, December 14, 1865, *ibid.*

456   "Magnanimity is the great word": Sandburg, *The War Years*, p. IV: 225.

456   "wicked and blasphemous": Letter of April 13, 1865, R.F. Fuller to Charles Sumner, *ibid.*, p. IV: 225.

456   "Mr. Lincoln gropes": April 13, 1865, New York *World*, Mitgang, p. 456.

456   "the more radical of the Republicans": Sandburg, *The War Years*, p. IV: 256-7.

456   "The radicals are as virulent and bitter as ever": *ibid.*, p. IV: 256.

456   "I would myself prefer": Lincoln, *Works*, p. VIII: 403.

457   "That means nigger citizenship": Hanchett, p. 37.

457   "Not all of these letters": Stoddard, p. 168.

457   "If Abraham Lincoln should be reelected": Reprinted in November 5, 1864, Buffalo *Commercial Advertiser*, from Randall and Current, p. 368-9.

457   "Assassination is not an American practice": Letter of July 15, 1862, Seward to John Bigelow, from Bancroft, p. II: 418.

457   "I think you peril too much": Rice, p. 252.

458   "had himself so sane a mind": Nicolay, John G., *Abraham Lincoln* (NY: The Century Co., 1902), p. 533.

458   "He hated being on his guard": William H. Crook, *Through Five Administrations: Reminiscences of Colonel William H. Crook*, ed. Margarita Spalding Gerry, (NY: Harper & Brothers, 1910), p. 1-4.

458   "It is important": Winik, p. 252.

458   "I could not help saying": Brooks, *Washington D.C.*, p. 44.

458   "with a sharp eye and ear open": Stoddard, p. 168.

458   "the utterly unprotected condition": Carpenter, p. 65.

458   "It would never do": *ibid.*

459   "worried until he got rid of it": *ibid.*, p. 64.

459   "he and Mrs. Lincoln couldn't hear": *ibid.*, p. 67.

459   "He said it seemed to him": Letter of December 8, 1866, Joseph Gillespie to William Herndon, from Randall & Current, p. 370.

459   "Tonight": Lamon, *Recollections*, p. 275.

460   Ragged bands roaming the streets: Leech, p. 357.

460   "Washington was a little delirious": Crook, p. 65.

460   "visible relief and content": Seward, p. 254.

460   "grander, graver": Donald, *Lincoln*, p. 591.

460   "He was unusually cheerful": Dispatch of April 16, 1865, Brooks, *Lincoln Observed*, p. 188.

Epilogue: The Sudden Saint

Page 461   "No living man": May 28, 1864, *New York Times*, from Waugh, p. 261.

461   "If Johnson pursues the same course": David Chesebrough, *No Sorrow Like Our Sorrow* (Kent, OH: Kent State University Press, 1994), p. *xviii*.

462   "It was treason": *ibid.,* p. 42.

462   "This murder, this oozing blood": Entry of April 15, 1865, Gurowski, *Diary, 1863-1865*, p. 398-9.

462   "Mr. Lincoln is to be hereafter regarded as a saint": Letter of April 16, 1865, from James Grimes to his wife, from William C. Harris, *Lincoln's Last Months* (Cambridge, MA: Harvard University Press, 2004), p. 228.

462   "It has made it impossible": Thomas R. Turner, "The Creation of an American Myth," Charles M. Hubbard, ed., *Lincoln and his Contemporaries* (Macon, GA: Mercer University Press, 1999), p. 160.

462   "While everybody was shocked": Julian, p. 255.

462   "I believe that the Almighty": Letter of April 23, 1865, Zachary Chandler to his wife, from Trefousse, *Benjamin Franklin Wade*, p. 248.

462   "more than likely": Roy P. Basler, *The Lincoln Legend* (NY: Octagon Books, 1969), p. 74.

462   "God has graciously withheld": Speech of April 23, 1865, Wendell Phillips and Louis Filler, *Wendell Phillips on Civil Rights and Freedom* (NY: Hill and Wang, 1965), p. 187.

463   "The eyes and upper part of the cheeks": Lloyd Lewis, *Myths After Lincoln* (NY: Harcourt, Brace, and Co., 1929), p. 107.

463   "planned and set on foot": Thomas and Hyman, p. 400.

463   "unscrupulous hand": Leech, p. 405.

464   "We will hang Jeff Davis!": Sandburg, *The War Years*, p. IV: 339.

464   "New York never before saw such a day": *ibid.*

465   "little finger was stronger than Lincoln's loins": *ibid.*

465   "a simple, truthful, noble soul": Waldo W. Braden, *Building the Myth: Selected Speeches Memorializing Abraham Lincoln* (Urbana: University of Illinois Press, 1990), p. 35-46.

465   "All over the rebel region": Sandburg, *The War Years*, p. IV: 341-2.

465   "The blow has fallen": *ibid.*

466   "He has been denounced": April 29, 1865, *Harper's Weekly*.

466   "The Martyr": Hubbard, p. 150.

466   "I heard the crack" Melville Stone, *Fifty Years a Journalist* (Garden City: Doubleday, Page, & Company, 1921), p. 30.

467   "and were instantly set upon": Entry of April 15, 1865, Strong, p. III: 583-4.

467   "copperhead organ": Sandburg, *The War Years*, p. IV: 350.

467   "There are not on this day mourners more sincere": *ibid.*, p. IV: 409.

467   "Today every loyal heart": New York *World*, reprinted in April 17, 1865, *National Intelligencer*, from Harper, p. 353.

467   "We are stunned": New York *Daily News*, reprinted in April 17, 1865, *National Intelligencer, ibid.*

467   "No language of which we are capable": *Boston Courier*, Reprinted in April 19, 1865, *National Intelligencer, ibid.*

467   "We had opposed Mr. Lincoln": April 17, 1865, *Dayton Daily Empire, ibid.*, p. 357.

467   "We have voted against Lincoln's election": April 26, 1865, Milwaukee *See-Bote*, from Klement, p. 243-4.

468   "Since the assassination": April 26, 1865, *The Crisis*.

468   "the men who had misrepresented": Sandburg, *The War Years*, p. IV: 409.

468   "Lincoln's death seemed": Michael Davis, p. 99.

Page 468   "one sweet drop": Fehrenbacher, "The Anti-Lincoln Tradition," p. 8.

468   "Could there have been a fitter death": Michael Davis, p. 100.

468   "All honor to J. Wilkes Booth": Carolyn L. Harrell, *When the Bells Tolled for Lincoln: Southern Reaction to the Assassination* (Macon, GA: Mercer Press, 1997), p. 86.

469   "the world is happily rid of a monster": Fehrenbacher, "The Anti-Lincoln Tradition," p. 10

469   "from now until God's judgment day": April 25, 1865, Houston *Tri-Weekly Telegraph*, Mitgang, p. 476-7.

469   "It does look to us": Harrell, p. 85.

469   "eternal vengeance against the whole Southern race": *ibid.*, p. 40.

469   "Few men will stop from committing any outrage": *ibid.*, p. 43-4.

469   "The heaviest blow," etc.: April 17, 1865, reprinted in the April 27, 1865 *Louisville Journal*, Mitgang, p. 476.

469   "The more violently 'secesh'": Entry of April 22, 1865, in the diary of Sarah Dawson, from Davis, p. 101.

470   "He was not a hero": Sandburg, *The War Years*, p. IV: 372.

470   "Abraham Lincoln was as little of a tyrant": April 29, 1865, London *Times*, Brogan, p. 176.

470   *"Yes, he had lived"*: May 6, 1865, London *Punch*, Mitgang, p. 488.

471   "English writers": April 27, 1865, London *Morning Star*, from Harper, p. 488.

472   "brutal, bitter, sarcastic, personal attack": Trietsch, p. 297.

472   "They tell me" and "The paper is yours": Maihafer, p. 253.

472   "among the last" April 17, 1865, New York *Tribune*.

472   "Without the least desire": April 19, 1865, New York *Tribune*, Mitgang, p. 468-472.

472   "There were those who say": Horace Greeley, *Reflections of a Busy Life* (NY: J.B. Ford & Co., 1869), p. 404.

473   "I didn't favor his re-nomination": *ibid.*, p. 409.

473   "Looking back": July, 1891, *Century Magazine*, from Currey, p. 158.

Bibliography

Primary Sources

Abbott, Henry Livermore. *Fallen Leaves: The Civil War Letters of Major Henry Livermore Abbott.* Ed. Robert G. Scott. Kent, OH: Kent State University Press, 1991.

Adams, Charles Francis, Jr. *Charles Francis Adams.* Boston: Houghton, Mifflin, & Co., 1900.

Adams, Henry. *The Education of Henry Adams.* Boston: Houghton Mifflin, 1918.

———. *The Great Secession Winter of 1860-1861, and Other Essays.* NY: Sagamore Press, 1958.

Anonymous. *The Diary of a Public Man.* New Brunswick: Rutgers University Press, 1946.

Bates, Edward. *The Diary of Edward Bates, 1859-1866.* Ed. Howard K. Beale. Washington: United States Government Printing Office, 1933.

Blaine, James G. *Twenty Years of Congress.* Norwich, CT: Henry Bill, 1884.

Brogan, Hugh, ed. *The* Times *Reports the American Civil War.* London: Times Books, 1975.

Brooks, Noah. *Lincoln Observed: The Civil War Dispatches of Noah Brooks.* Ed. Michael Burlingame. Baltimore: The Johns Hopkins University Press, 1998.

———. *Washington, D.C., in Lincoln's Time.* Ed. Herbert Mitgang. Athens: University of Georgia Press, 1989.

Browning, Orville Hickman. *The Diary of Orville Hickman Browning.* Ed. Theodore Calvin Pease. 2 vols. Springfield: The Illinois State Historical Library, 1925.

Butler, Benjamin F. *Correspondence of Gen. Benjamin F. Butler during the Period of the Civil War.* Ed. Jessie Ames Marshall. Norwood, MA: The Plimpton Press, 1917.

Carpenter, Francis B. *The Inner Life of Abraham Lincoln: Six Months at the White House.* Lincoln: University of Nebraska Press, 1995.

Chase, Salmon P. *Inside Lincoln's Cabinet: The Civil War Diaries of Salmon P. Chase.* Ed. David Donald. NY: Longman's, Green, and Co., 1954.

———. *The Correspondence of Salmon P. Chase.* Ed. John Niven. 5 vols. Kent, OH: Kent State University Press, 1998.

Chesnut, Mary. *The Private Mary Chesnut: The Unpublished Civil War Diaries.* Ed. C. Vann Woodward and Elisabeth Muhlenfeld. NY: Oxford University Press, 1984.

Collum, Shelby. *Fifty Years of Public Service.* Chicago: A.C. McClurg & Co., 1911.

Congressional Globe, 37th Congress, 2nd Sess. (1862).

———, 38th Cong., 2nd Sess. (1864).

Cox, Samuel S. *Eight Years in Congress.* NY: D. Appleton and Company, 1865.

Crook, William H. *Through Five Administrations: Reminiscences of Colonel William H. Crook.* Ed. Margarita Spalding Gerry. NY: Harper & Brothers, 1910.

Dana, Charles A. *Recollections of the Civil War.* NY: D. Appleton and Company, 1913.

Dicey, Edward. *Spectator of America.* Ed. Herbert Mitgang. Athens: The University of Georgia Press, 1989.

Dickens, Charles. *American Notes.* NY: D. Appleton and Co., 1868.

Donaldson, Francis Adams. *Inside the Army of the Potomac: The Civil War Experience of Captain Francis Adams Donaldson.* Ed J. Gregory Acken. Mechanicsburg, PA: Stackpole, 1998.

Dumond, Dwight Lowell, ed. *Southern Editorials on Secession.* Gloucester, MA: Peter Smith, 1964.

Fehrenbacher, Don E. "The Anti-Lincoln Tradition." *Journal of the Abraham Lincoln Association,* Vol. 4, 1982.

———, and Virginia E. Fehrenbacher, eds. *Recollected Words of Abraham Lincoln.* Palo Alto: Stanford University Press, 1996.

Fitzhugh, George. *Cannibals All! or Slaves Without Masters*. Richmond: A. Morris, 1857.

Forbes, John Murray. *Letters and Recollections of John Murray Forbes*. Ed. Sarah Forbes Hughes. 2 vols. Boston: Houghton Mifflin, 1899.

French, Benjamin Brown. *Witness to the Young Republic: A Yankee's Journal, 1828-1870*. Ed. Donald B. Cole and John J. McDonough. Hanover and London:
University Press of New England, 1989.

Grayson, William J. "The Hireling and the Slave." *The Hireling and the Slave, Chicora, and Other Poems*. Charleston: McCarter & Co., 1856.

Greeley, Horace. *The American Conflict: Its Causes, Incidents, and Results*. Hartford: O.D. Case & Co., 1866.

———. *Reflections of a Busy Life*. NY: J.B. Ford & Co., 1869.

Gurowski, Adam. *Diary, from March 4, 1861, to November 12, 1862*. Boston: Lee and Shepard, 1862.

———. *Diary, 1863, '64, '65*. Washington: WH & OH Morrison, 1866.

Halstead, Murat. *Three Against Lincoln: Murat Halstead Reports the Caucuses of 1860*. Ed. William Hesseltine. Baton Rouge: LSU Press, 1960.

Hay, John. *Inside Lincoln's White House: The Complete Civil War Diary of John Hay*. Ed. Michael Burlingame and John R. Turner Ettinger. Carbondale: Southern Illinois University Press, 1997.

———. *Lincoln and the Civil War in the Diaries and Letters of John Hay*. Ed. Tyler Dennett. NY: Dodd, Mead and Co., 1939.

Herndon, William, and Jesse Weik. *Herndon's Lincoln*. Springfield: The Herndon's Lincoln Publishing Co., 1888.

Holzer, Harold, ed. *Dear Mr. Lincoln: Letters to the President*. Reading, MA: Addison-Wesley, 1993.

———, ed. *Lincoln As I Knew Him*. Chapel Hill: Algonquin Books of Chapel Hill, 1999.

James, Henry, Jr. *Hawthorne*. NY: Harper and Brothers, 1901.

Johnson, Robert Underwood, and Clarence Buel, eds. *Battles and Leaders of the Civil War*. 4 vols. NY: The Century Company, 1888.

Julian, George W. *Political Recollections: 1840 to 1872*. Chicago: Jansen, McClurg & Company, 1884.

Keckley, Elizabeth. *Behind the Scenes: Or, Thirty Years a Slave and Four Years in the White House*. NY: Oxford University Press, 1988.

Lamon, Ward Hill. *The Life of Abraham Lincoln From His Birth to His Inauguration as President*. Lincoln: University of Nebraska Press, 1999.

———. *Recollections of Abraham Lincoln*. Lincoln: University of Nebraska Press, 1994.

Lamson, Roswell H. *Lamson of the Gettysburg: The Civil War Letters of Lieutenant Roswell H. Lamson, U. S. Navy*. Ed. James M. McPherson and Patricia R. McPherson. NY: Oxford University Press, 1997.

Lincoln, Abraham. *The Collected Works of Abraham Lincoln*. Ed. Roy P. Basler. 8 vols. New Brunswick, NJ: Rutgers University Press, 1953.

———. *The Abraham Lincoln Papers at the Library of Congress*. http://memory.loc.gov/ammem/alhtml/malhome.html

Lowell, James Russell. "Abraham Lincoln." *Political Essays*. Boston: Houghton, Mifflin and Company, 1871.

———. *Letters of James Russell Lowell*. Ed. Charles Eliot Norton. 3 vols. Boston: Houghton, Mifflin Company, 1904.

McClellan, George B. *The Civil War Papers of George B. McClellan: Selected Correspondence 1860-1865*. Ed. Stephen Sears. NY: Ticknor and Fields, 1989.

———. *McClellan's Own Story*. NY: Charles L. Webster, 1887.

McClure, A.K. *Abraham Lincoln and Men of War-Times*. Lincoln: University of Nebraska Press, 1996.

McCulloch, Hugh. *Men and Measures of Half a Century*. NY: Charles Scribner's Sons, 1888.

Mitgang, Herbert, ed. *Abraham Lincoln: A Press Portrait*. Athens: The University of Georgia Press, 1989.

Moore, Frank, ed. *The Rebellion Record, Vol. I, 1860-1861*. NY: G.P. Putnam, 1861.

"The Next President." *Brownson's Quarterly Review* (April 1864). www.orestesbrownson.com/index.php?id=361

Nicolay, John G. *Abraham Lincoln*. NY: The Century Co., 1902.

———. *Lincoln's Secretary: A Biography of John G. Nicolay*. Ed. Helen Nicolay. NY: Longman's, Green, and Co., 1949.

———, and John Hay. *Abraham Lincoln: A History*. 10 vols. NY: The Century Co., 1890.

———. *Abraham Lincoln: The Observations of John G. Nicolay and John Hay*. Ed. Michael Burlingame. Carbondale: Southern Illinois University Press, 2007.

———. "The Border States." *The Century*, Volume 36, Issue 1 (May 1888), p. 58-9.

Nourse, Charles C. "A Delegate's Memories of the Chicago Convention of 1860." *Annals of Iowa*, Vol. 12, 3rd Series. Des Moines: Historical Department of Iowa, 1921.

Perkins, Howard Cecil, ed. *Northern Editorials on Secession*. 2 vols. Gloucester, MA: Peter Smith, 1964.

Phillips, Wendell, and Louis Filler. *Wendell Phillips on Civil Rights and Freedom*. NY: Hill and Wang, 1965.

Poore, Ben Perley. *Perley's Reminiscences of Sixty Years in the National Metropolis*. Philadelphia: Hubbard Bros., 1886.

Raymond, Henry J., ed. *Life and Public Service of Abraham Lincoln*. NY: Darby and Miller, 1865.

Reynolds, Donald E., ed. *Editors Make War*. Nashville: Vanderbilt University Press, 1970.

Rice, Allen Thorndike, ed. *Reminiscences of Abraham Lincoln by Distinguished Men of His Time*. NY: Harper & Bros., 1909.

Riddle, Albert Gallatin. *Recollections of War Times: Reminiscences of Men and Events in Washington, 1860-1865*. NY: G.P. Putnam's Sons, 1895.

Russell, William Howard. *My Diary North and South*. NY: Harper & Brothers, 1863.

Schurz, Carl. *Intimate Letters of Carl Schurz*. Whitefish, MT: Kessinger Publishing, 2005.

———. *The Reminiscences of Carl Schurz*. 3 vols. NY: Doubleday, Page & Company, 1917.

Seward, Frederick W. *Reminiscences of a War-Time Statesman and Diplomat, 1830-1915*. NY: G.P. Putnam, 1916.

Smith, George Winston, and Charles Judah, eds. *Life in the North During the Civil War: A Source History*. Albuquerque: University of New Mexico Press, 1966.

Speed, Joshua. *Reminiscences of Abraham Lincoln*. Louisville: John P. Morton and Company, 1884.

Stoddard, William O. *Inside the White House in War Times*. Lincoln: University of Nebraska Press, 2000.

Stone, Melville. *Fifty Years a Journalist*. Garden City: Doubleday, Page, & Company, 1921.

Strong, George Templeton. *The Diary of George Templeton Strong*. Ed. Allan Nevins and Milton H. Thomas. 3 vols. NY: Macmillan, 1952.

Sumner, Charles. *Memoirs and Letters of Charles Sumner*. Ed. Edward L. Pierce. NY: Oxford University Press, 1878.

———. *The Selected Letters of Charles Sumner*. Ed. Beverly Wilson Palmer. 2 vols. Boston: Northeastern University Press, 1990.

———. *The Works of Charles Sumner*. 17 vols. Boston: Lee and Shepard, 1900.

Swinton, William. *The Army of the Potomac*. NY: Smithmark, 1995.

Toqueville, Alexis de. *Democracy in America, Vol. I.* NY: The Century Company, 1898.
————. *Democracy in America, Vol. II.* NY: D. Appleton and Co., 1904.
Trollope, Anthony. *North America.* NY: Alfred A. Knopf, 1951.
Trollope, Frances. *Domestic Manners of Americans.* NY: Dodd, Mead and Co., 1901.
Villard, Henry. *Lincoln on the Eve of '61: A Journalist's Story.* Ed. Harold and Oswald Villard. NY: Knopf, 1941.
————. *Memoirs of Henry Villard.* Boston: Houghton Mifflin, 1904.
————. "Recollections of Lincoln." *Atlantic Monthly.* February 1904.
"Wade-DavisManifesto." www.civilwarinteractive.com/DocsWadeDavisManifesto.htm
The War of the Rebellion: A Compilation of the Official Records of the Union and Confederate Armies. 128 vols. Washington: Government Printing Office, 1880.
Weed, Thurlow. *Autobiography of Thurlow Weed.* Ed. Harriet Weed. Boston: Houghton Mifflin, 1884.
Welles, Gideon. *The Diary of Gideon Welles.* Ed. Howard K. Beale. 3 vols. NY: W.W. Norton & Co., 1960.
Whitney, Henry Clay. *Life on the Circuit with Lincoln.* Boston: Estes and Lauriat, 1892.
Wilson, Douglas L., and Rodney O. Davis, eds. *Herndon's Informants: Letters, Interviews, and Statements about Abraham Lincoln.* Urbana and Chicago: University of Illinois Press, 1998.

Secondary Sources

Adams, Michael C.C. *Fighting for Defeat: Union Failure in the East, 1861-1865.* Lincoln: University of Nebraska Press, 1982.
"The American Civil War." www.etymonline.com/cw/draft.htm.
Angle, Paul M., ed. *The Lincoln Reader.* New Brunswick: Rutgers University Press, 1947.
————, and Earl Schenk Miers, eds. *Tragic Years, 1860-1865: A Documentary History of the American Civil War.* NY: Simon & Schuster, 1960.
Ayers, Edward L. *In the Presence of Mine Enemies: The Civil War in the Heart of America.* NY: W.W. Norton & Company, 2003.
Bancroft, Frederic. *The Life of William H. Seward.* 2 vols. NY: Harper & Bros., 1900.
Baringer, William. *Lincoln's Rise to Power.* Boston: Little, Brown, and Co., 1937.
Barrett, Joseph H. *The Life of Abraham Lincoln.* Cincinnati: Moore, Wilstach & Baldwin, 1865.
Basler, Roy P. *The Lincoln Legend.* NY: Octagon Books, 1969.
Beatie, Russell H. *Army of the Potomac: McClellan Takes Command.* NY: Da Capo Press, 2004.
Bloom, Robert. "As the British Press Saw Lincoln." *Topic 9: A Journal of the Liberal Arts* (Spring 1965).
Boritt, Gabor S., ed. *The Historian's Lincoln.* Urbana: University of Illinois Press, 1996.
————, ed. *Lincoln's Generals.* NY: Oxford University Press, 1994.
————, ed. *Why the Civil War Came.* NY: Oxford University Press, 1996.
Braden, Waldo W. *Building the Myth: Selected Speeches Memorializing Abraham Lincoln.* Urbana: University of Illinois Press, 1990.
Bridge, Horatio. *Personal Recollections of Nathaniel Hawthorne.* NY: Harper & Brothers, 1893.
Brummer, Sidney David. *Political History of New York State During the Period of the Civil War.* NY: AMS Press, 1967.
Chesebrough, David. *No Sorrow Like Our Sorrow.* Kent, OH: Kent State University Press, 1994.
Commager, Henry S., ed. *American Destiny, Vol. 6: A House Dividing.* NY: Grolier Publishing, 1976.

Crofts, Daniel W. *Reluctant Confederates: Upper South Unionists in the Secession Crisis.* Chapel Hill: University of North Carolina Press, 1993.

Cunliffe, Marcus. *The Presidency.* Boston: Houghton Mifflin, 1987.

Current, Richard N. *Old Thad Stevens: A Story of Ambition.* Westport CT: Greenwood Press, 1980.

Currey, J. Seymour. *Chicago: Its History and Its Builders: A Century of Marvelous Growth.* Chicago: S. J. Clarke, 1912.

Davis, Michael. *The Image of Lincoln in the South.* Knoxville: University of Tennessee Press, 1971.

Davis, William C. *Lincoln's Men.* NY: Touchstone 1999.

Donald, David. *Charles Sumner and the Rights of Man.* NY: Alfred A. Knopf, 1970.

————. *Lincoln.* NY: Simon & Schuster, 1996.

————. *Lincoln Reconsidered.* NY: Vintage Books, 2001.

————. *"We Are Lincoln Men."* NY: Simon and Schuster, 2003.

Elkins, Stanley. *Slavery.* Chicago: The University of Chicago Press, 1976.

"Emancipation Proclamation: Domestic Reaction." See www.mrlincolnand freedom.org.

Fehrenbacher, Don. "The Anti-Lincoln Tradition." *Journal of the Abraham Lincoln Association,* Vol. 4 (1982).

Fermer, Douglas. *James Gordon Bennett and the New York Herald: A Study of Editorial Opinion in the Civil War Era, 1854-1867.* NY: St. Martin's Press, 1986.

Ferris, Norman B. "Lincoln and Seward in Civil War Diplomacy: Their Relationship at the Outset Reexamined." Http://www.historycooperative. org/journals/jala/12/ferris.html

Fischer, LeRoy H. *Lincoln's Gadfly: Adam Gurowski.* Norman: University of Oklahoma Press, 1969.

Fite, Emerson David. *The Presidential Campaign of 1860.* NY: MacMillan, 1911.

Flower, Frank A. *Edwin McMasters Stanton.* Akron: The Saalfield Publishing Co, 1905.

Foner, Eric. *Free Soil, Free Labor, Free Men: The Ideology of the Republican Party Before the Civil War.* NY: Oxford University Press, 1970.

Furgurson, Ernest B. *Freedom Rising: Washington in the Civil War.* NY: Alfred Knopf, 2004.

Gaff, Alan D. *On Many a Bloody Field: Four Years in the Iron Brigade.* Bloomington: Indiana University Press, 1996.

Gallagher, Gary, ed. *The Fredericksburg Campaign.* Chapel Hill: University of North Carolina Press, 1995.

————, ed. *The Richmond Campaign of 1862: The Peninsula & the Seven Days.* Chapel Hill: The University of North Carolina Press, 2000.

Garrison, Webb. *The Lincoln No One Knows.* Nashville: Rutledge Hill Press, 1993.

"General Order No. 38." www.ohiohistorycentral.org/ entry.php?rec=1481

George, Sister May Karl. *Zachariah Chandler: A Political Biography.* East Lansing: Michigan State University Press, 1969.

Gienapp, William E. *Abraham Lincoln and Civil War America: A Biography.* NY: Oxford University Press, 2002.

Goodwin, Doris Kearns. *A Team of Rivals.* NY: Simon and Schuster, 2005.

Gopnik, Adam. "Angels and Ages." *New Yorker.* May 28, 2007.

Gray, Wood. *The Hidden Civil War: The Story of the Copperheads.* NY: Viking Press, 1942.

Greenburg, Kenneth S. *Masters and Statesmen: The Political Culture of American Slavery.* Baltimore: Johns Hopkins University Press, 1985.

Guelzo, Allen C. *Lincoln's Emancipation Proclamation: The End of Slavery in America.* NY: Simon and Schuster, 2004.

————. *Abraham Lincoln: Redeemer President.* Grand Rapids: W. B. Eerdmans, 1999.

Hanchett, William. *The Lincoln Murder Conspiracies.* Urbana: University of Illinois Press, 1983.

Harper, Robert S. *Lincoln and the Press.* NY: McGraw-Hill, 1951.

Harrell, Carolyn L. *When the Bells Tolled for Lincoln: Southern Reaction to the Assassination.* Macon, GA: Mercer Press, 1997.

Harris, Brayton. *Blue & Gray in Black & White: Newspapers in the Civil War.* Washington: Brassey's, 1999.

Harris, William C. *Lincoln's Last Months.* Cambridge, MA: Harvard University Press, 2004.

Hayes, Melvin L. *Mr. Lincoln Runs for President.* NY: Citadel Press, 1960.

Haynes, George H. *Charles Sumner.* Philadelphia: George W. Jacobs and Co., 1909.

Hendrick, Burton J. *Lincoln's War Cabinet.* Boston: Little, Brown, and Company, 1946.

Hubbard, Charles M., ed. *Lincoln and his Contemporaries.* Macon, GA: Mercer University Press, 1999.

Isely, Jeter Allen. *Horace Greeley and the Republican Party, 1853-1861: A Study of the New York Tribune.* Princeton: Princeton University Press, 1947.

James, Henry, Jr. *Hawthorne.* NY: Harper and Brothers, 1901.

Johannsen, Robert W. *Lincoln, the South, and Slavery.* Baton Rouge: Louisiana State University Press, 1991.

Klein, Maury. *Days of Defiance: Sumter, Secession, and the Coming of the Civil War.* NY: Alfred Knopf, 1997.

Klement, Frank. *The Copperheads in the Middle West.* Chicago: University of Chicago Press, 1960.

Knoles, George Harmon. *The Crisis of the Union, 1860-1861.* Baton Rouge: Louisiana University Press, 1965.

Korngold, Ralph. *Two Friends of Man: The Story of William Lloyd Garrison and Wendell Phillips and Their Relationship with Abraham Lincoln.* Boston: Little, Brown, 1950.

Lawrence, William. *Life of Amos A. Lawrence.* Boston: Houghton Mifflin, 1888.

Leech, Margaret. *Reveille in Washington.* NY: Harper & Brothers, 1941.

Lewis, Lloyd. *Myths After Lincoln.* NY: Harcourt, Brace, and Co., 1929.

"Lincoln and Emancipation." www.civilwarhome.com/lincolnand proclamation.htm

Loewen, James. *Lies My Teacher Told Me.* NY: Simon and Schuster, 1995.

Long, David E. *The Jewel of Liberty: Abraham Lincoln's Re-election and the End of Slavery.* Mechanicsburg, Pa.: Stackpole, 1994.

Long, E.B. *The Civil War Day by Day.* NY: Doubleday & Co., 1971.

Lowenfels, Walter. *Walt Whitman's Civil War.* NY: Da Capo Press, 1989.

Lowi, Theodore. *The Personal President.* Ithaca: Cornell University Press, 1985.

Lurie, Leonard. *Party Politics: Why We Have Poor Presidents.* NY: Scarborough, 1982.

McCarthy, Charles Hallan. *Lincoln's Plan of Reconstruction.* NY: McClure, Phillips & Co., 1901.

McPherson, Edward. *The Political History of the United States of America, During the Great Rebellion.* Washington: James J. Chapman, 1882.

———. *The Political History of the United States of America During the Period of Reconstruction.* Washington: Solomons & Chapman, 1875.

McPherson, James. *Battle Cry of Freedom.* NY: Oxford University Press, 1988.

———, ed. *"We Cannot Escape History": Lincoln and the Last Best Hope of Earth.* Urbana and Chicago: University of Illinois Press, 1995.

Macy, Jesse. *Our Nation: How it Grew, What It Does, and How It Does It.* Boston: Ginn and Co., 1897.

Mahood, Wayne. *General Wadsworth: The Life and Times of Brevet Major General James Wadsworth.* NY: Da Capo Press, 2003.

Maihafer, Harry J. *War of Words.* Washington: Brassey's, 2003.

Manber, Jeffrey, and Neil Dahlstrom. *Lincoln's Wrath: Fierce Mobs, Brilliant Scoundrels and a President's Mission to Destroy the Press*. Napierville, IL: Sourcebooks, Inc., 2005.

Marvel, William. *Burnside*. Chapel Hill: University of North Carolina Press, 1988.

———. *Mr. Lincoln Goes to War*. Boston: Houghton Mifflin, 2006.

Mayer, Henry. *All on Fire: William Lloyd Garrison and the Abolition of Slavery*. NY: St. Martin's Press, 1998.

Merriam, G. S. *Life and Times of Samuel Bowles*. 2 vols. NY: The Century Co., 1885.

Miller, William Lee. *Lincoln's Virtues: An Ethical Biography*. NY: Vintage Books, 2003.

Milton, George. *The Eve of Conflict*. NY: Houghton Mifflin, 1934.

Monoghan, Jay. *Diplomat in Carpet Slippers*. Indianapolis: Charter Books, 1945.

Neely, Mark E., Jr. *The Fate of Liberty*. NY: Oxford Press, 1991.

———."The Lincoln Administration and Arbitrary Arrests: A Reconsideration." *Journal of the Abraham Lincoln Association*, Vol. 5, No. 1, p. 8.

Nevins, Allan. *The Emergence of Lincoln: Prologue to the Civil War, 1859-1861*. NY: Charles Scribner's Sons, 1950.

———. *Ordeal of the Union: Fruits of Manifest Destiny, 1847-1852*. NY: Charles Scribner's Sons, 1947.

———. *The War for the Union: The Improvised War, 1861-1862*. NY: Charles Scribner's Sons, 1959.

———. *The War for the Union: War Becomes Revolution, 1862-1863*. NY: Charles Scribner's Sons, 1960.

———. *The War for the Union: The Organized War, 1863-1864*. NY: Charles Scribner's Sons, 1971.

———. *The War for the Union: Organized War to Victory, 1864-1865*. NY: Charles Scribner's Sons, 1971.

Newman, Ralph G., ed. *Lincoln for the Ages*. Garden City: Doubleday, 1960.

Newton, John Fort. *Lincoln and Herndon*. Cedar Rapids: The Torch Press, 1910.

Nofi, Albert. *A Civil War Treasury*. NY: Da Capo Press, 1995.

"Northern Draft of 1862." www.etymonline.com/cw/draft.htm.

Nye, Russel B. *Fettered Freedom: Civil Liberties and the Slavery Controversy, 1830-1860*. East Lansing: Michigan State University Press, 1963.

Oates, Stephen B. *With Malice Toward None*. NY: Harper & Row, 1977.

Ostragorski, M. *Democracy and the Organization of Political Parties*. NY: Macmillan, 1908.

Packard, Jerrold M. *The Lincolns in the White House: Four Years That Shattered a Family*. NY: St. Martin's Press, 2005.

Paludan, Philip Shaw. *The Presidency of Abraham Lincoln*. Lawrence: University Press of Kansas, 1994.

Parton, James. *Life of Andrew Jackson*. 3 vols. NY: Mason Brothers, 1860.

Patterson, Bradley. *The White House Staff: Inside the West Wing and Beyond*. NY: Brookings Institution Press, 2001.

Perrett, Geoffrey. *Lincoln's War*. NY: Random House, 2004.

Pike, James S. *First Blows of the Civil War*. NY: American News Company, 1879.

Potter, David M. *Lincoln and His Party in the Secession Crisis*. New Haven: Yale University Press, 1942.

———, and Don E. Fehrenbacher. *The Impending Crisis, 1848-1861*. NY: Harper Collins, 1976.

Randall, J.G. *Lincoln the Liberal Statesman*. London: Eyre and Spottiswode, 1947.

———. *Lincoln the President: Midstream*. NY: Dodd, Mead & Co., 1953.

———. *Lincoln the President: Springfield to Gettysburg*. 2 vols. NY: Dodd, Mead & Co., 1945.

————. *Mr. Lincoln.* Ed. Richard Current. NY: Dodd, Mead & Co., 1957.

————, and Richard Current. *Lincoln the President: The Last Full Measure.* Urbana: University of Illinois Press, 1999.

Rawley, James. *The Politics of Union: Northern Politics during the Civil War.* Lincoln: University of Nebraska Press, 1974.

Rhodes, James Ford. *History of the United States from the Compromise of 1850.* NY: Macmillan, 1919.

Sandburg, Carl. *The Lincoln Collector.* NY: Harcourt, Brace, 1950.

————. *The Prairie Years.* 2 vols. NY: Harcourt, Brace & World, 1926.

————. *The War Years.* 4 vols. NY: Harcourt, Brace & World, 1939.

Sears, Stephen W. *George McClellan: The Young Napoleon.* NY: Ticknor and Fields, 1988.

————. *To the Gates of Richmond: The Peninsula Campaign.* NY: Ticknor & Fields, 1992.

Sherwin, Oscar. *Prophet of Liberty: The Life and Times of Wendell Phillips.* NY: Bookman Associates, 1958.

Silbey, Joel H. *A Respectable Minority: The Democratic Party in the Civil War Era, 1860-1868.* NY: W. W. Norton, 1977.

Smith, Page. *The Nation Comes of Age: A People's History of the Ante-Bellum Years.* NY: McGraw-Hill, 1981.

————. *Trial by Fire: A People's History of the Civil War and Reconstruction.* NY: Penguin, 1990.

Sprague, Dean. *Freedom Under Lincoln.* Boston: Houghton Mifflin, 1965.

Stampp, Kenneth. *And the War Came: The North and the Secession Crisis.* Baton Rouge: Louisiana State University Press, 1970.

————. *The Imperiled Union: Essays on the Background of the Civil War.* NY: Oxford University Press, 1981.

Starr, Louis Morris. *Bohemian Brigade: Civil War Newsmen in Action.* NY: Knopf, 1954.

Stephenson, Nathaniel W. *Lincoln.* NY: Grosset & Dunlap, 1922.

Stone, Geoffrey. *Perilous Times: Free Speech in Wartime from the Sedition Act of 1798 to the War on Terrorism.* NY: W.W. Norton & Co., 2004.

Summers, Mark W. *The Plundering Generation: Corruption and the Crisis of the Union 1849-1861.* NY: Oxford University Press, 1987.

Tap, Bruce. *Over Lincoln's Shoulder: The Committee on the Conduct of the War.* Lawrence: University Press of Kansas, 1998.

Tarbell, Ida. *The Life of Abraham Lincoln.* 3 vols. NY: Lincoln History Society, 1902.

Thomas, Benjamin. *Abraham Lincoln: A Biography.* NY: Alfred A. Knopf, 1952.

————, and Harold M. Hyman. *Stanton: The Life and Times of Lincoln's Secretary of War.* NY: Alfred A. Knopf, 1962.

Townsend, William H. *Lincoln and the Bluegrass.* Lexington: The University of Kentucky Press, 1955.

Trefousse, Hans. *Benjamin Franklin Wade: Radical Republican from Ohio.* NY: Twayne Publishers, 1963.

————. *First Among Equals: Abraham Lincoln's Reputation During His Administration.* NY: Fordham University Press, 2005.

————. *The Radical Republicans: Lincoln's Vanguard for Racial Justice.* NY: Knopf, 1969.

Trietsch, James. *The Printer and the Prince.* NY: Exposition Press, 1955.

Van Deusen, Glyndon G. *William Henry Seward.* NY: Oxford University Press, 1967.

Vandiver, Frank. *Jubal's Raid.* NY: McGraw-Hill, 1960.

Voegeli, V. Jacque. *Free but Not Equal.* Chicago: University of Chicago Press, 1967.

Waugh, John C. *Reelecting Lincoln: The Battle for the 1864 Presidency.* NY: Da Capo Press, 1997.

Wheeler, Richard. *Sword Over Richmond: An Eyewitness History of McClellan's Peninsula Campaign.* NY: Harper & Row, 1986.

White, Leonard D. *The Jacksonians.* NY: Macmillan and Co., 1954.

White, Ronald C. *Lincoln's Greatest Speech: The Second Inaugural.* NY: Simon & Schuster, 2002.

Whitridge, Arnold. *No Compromise! The Story of the Fanatics Who Paved the Way to the Civil War.* NY: Farrar, Straus and Cuday, 1960.

Wiley, Bell Irvin. *The Life of Billy Yank.* Indianapolis: Bobbs-Merrill, 1952.

Williams, Kenneth. *Lincoln Finds a General.* 5 vols. Bloomington: Indiana University Press, 1985.

Williams, T. Harry. *Lincoln and the Radicals.* Madison: University of Wisconsin Press, 1965.

———. *Lincoln and His Generals.* NY: Alfred A. Knopf, 1952.

Wilson, Douglas L. *Lincoln's Sword: The Presidency and the Power of Words.* NY: Alfred A. Knopf, 2006.

Winik, Jay. *April 1865: The Month That Saved America.* NY: Harper Collins, 2001.

Zornow, William Frank. *Lincoln & the Party Divided.* Norman: University of Oklahoma Press, 1954.

Index

An Interview with Larry Tagg, author of
The Battles That Made Abraham Lincoln

Larry Tagg's book is the first study of its kind to concentrate on what Lincoln's contemporaries actually thought of him during his lifetime.

Q: You were born in Lincoln, Illinois. Did that spark your interest in Lincoln?

LT: Not consciously, but perhaps something happens to a person growing up in the heart of Lincoln country, as I did until I was eight years old. My hometown was the only town in America named for Abraham Lincoln before he became president—in 1853, after he worked as counsel for the new railroad that led to the town's founding. And from Lincoln, Illinois, my family moved to Decatur, where we lived on the Sangamon River, a few miles from the Lincoln family's first Illinois home. People there still talked about Lincoln in a neighborly way, and I picked it up, even as a young kid.

Q: How did you come up with the idea to write this book?

LT: I initially began to gather material for a history of the Army of the Potomac. But early on in that project, I bumped into an amazing amount of anti-Lincoln references by its generals. The intensity and personal nature of their animosity was remarkable. I thought, "Now here's a story!" I had only glimpsed a tiny part of the story, as it turned out.

Q: I know you used a wide variety of primary source material. Tell our readers what some of those sources were and how you conducted your research.

LT: For a couple of years, I read everything I could get my hands on about Lincoln, focusing on his contemporaries' comments on his presidency. I spent lots and lots of time at the California State University at Sacramento library, which has an excellent Civil War section. Then I started sending away for complete archives of Democratic newspapers of the Civil War, especially the Chicago *Times,* the New York *World,* and The (Columbus, OH) *Crisis.* I read every Civil War issue of those papers on microfilm. (Laughing.) My eyeballs were rolling around like searchlights after a few hours of that, but it was worth it to have done the original research.

Whenever I spotted a book I had to have that wasn't at Sac State, I bought it online. I bought so many of the important primary sources that it finally got so that most of the time, if I saw an important reference that I had to check, I already had the book in my bookcase. In the latter stages of my research, I was helped tremendously by the fact that Civil War references and primary sources were coming online due to the Googlebooks digitization project. Increasingly, if I found a promising reference, no matter how obscure, I could read it online.

Q: What surprised you the most during your research?

LT: I was astonished at what a hole Lincoln was in even as he took up the presidency. So much of that was due to the low prestige of the presidency itself, as a result of the eccentricities of the Jacksonian Period: the weak central government, the weak president, the disrepute of government itself in the wake of years of rigged nominating conventions and the spoils system, the power of the partisan press, and, of course, the torsions of the slavery argument. For this reason, the context of Lincoln's appearance in 1860 dominates the first part of my book, and I think that it is crucial to understanding Lincoln's lack of popularity during his term.

Also, the level of animosity toward Lincoln is astounding. It appears to have been a country with a no-holds-barred brawler, a Rush Limbaugh or Keith Olbermann, at the editorial desk of every newspaper in the country. I found so many over-the-top disparagements of Lincoln—even out-and-out threats!—that I only needed include the most outrageous of them to fill up a book.

Q: Why do you think that Lincoln was so hated during his presidency?

LT: Americans were suspicious that they had been robbed of the government that the Founding Fathers intended, especially when Lincoln, an anonymous rustic, was produced as a candidate by a sectional party, and was assured of election by the suicide of the only national party, the Democrats.

That he was dedicated to re-defining property to exclude slaves was the most explosive issue in American history—to get something of the fury Lincoln's candidacy produced, it is necessary to imagine a modern-day candidate who would make one-third of the country fear losing the entire value of their homes. Then, once the war started, he presided over a centralization of power that was terrifying in a country so dedicated to the *de*centralization of power that a civil war had just broken out over it. Finally, he was a centrist in a country whose citizens had been driven to extremes in the heat of the national convulsion over slavery—whatever he did, citizens thought he had either gone too far, or failed to go far enough.

Q: Walk us through some of the high and low points of Lincoln's presidency.

LT: Lincoln's presidency started at a low point—his election by less than 40% of the voters, which was an electoral mandate *against* him—and proceeded to an even lower point—his secret entry by night train, which produced derision and laughter across the nation—even before he was sworn in. The whole while he appeared to be indecisive and drifting during the Secession Winter. His first "high point" in the North was produced by his Proclamation calling for 75,000 men to put down the rebellion after Fort Sumter, but at the same time it produced a disastrous "low point" in the Border States, four of which promptly seceded and doubled the size of the Confederacy, and made it a credible nation for the first time.

During the first eighteen months of the war, the success of his presidency sank with the misfortunes of the Union armies. There was failure after failure in the East: First Bull Run, Ball's Bluff, the Peninsula Campaign, and Second Bull Run. (He did, however, have one period, from February to May of 1862, where there was swift success in the West and the Northern mood was briefly buoyant.)

Q: How did the Northern victory at Antietam change things?

LT: It allowed Lincoln to issue the Emancipation Proclamation, which immediately prompted a strong Northern rebuke at the polls in the mid-term elections in the fall of 1862. That was certainly a low point, and things got worse and worse, with the Northwest threatening to secede and Copperheadism everywhere ascendant, until the double victory of Gettysburg and Vicksburg turned the tide at the beginning of July 1863.

That gave Lincoln another respite until the bloodbath of Grant's Overland Campaign in the spring of 1864. All that summer, Northern war-weariness almost sank Lincoln's reelection hopes, and only at the last minute did Sherman and Sheridan win victories that lifted Lincoln into another term. He was still not popular, however, and controversy plagued every month of his presidency until his assassination in April 1865. It was only after his death that he became "popular."

Q: Do you think readers will be surprised by what they discover in your book? If so, what do you think will surprise them the most?

LT: If they're anything like the people who have read it so far, they will be very surprised. Lincoln is not a figure you associate with loathing. Perhaps most surprising, to me at least, was the intensity of racism in the North and the Northern hostility toward the Emancipation Proclamation, which almost led to the secession of Illinois, Indiana, and Ohio, caused a large part of the army to desert, and culminated in the New York Draft Riots, which were the second-largest insurgency in American history, after the Civil War itself.

Q: There are hundreds of Lincoln books out there. What makes yours different?

LT: I continue to be amazed that nobody has written this book before. Every book about Lincoln makes occasional mention of opposition to this or that policy, but there has never been a full treatment of the length and breadth of that opposition, which was so vehement, so relentless, and so ubiquitous—coming from all sides, Republican as well as Democrat. My book goes directly against the grain of mainstream Lincoln literature, which almost invariably takes a reverential tone, and leaves out the rabid ravings of the opinion-makers of the time. This conventional treatment has left the false impression that Lincoln governed from strength, when the more interesting truth is that he accomplished so much in the teeth of violent dissent. To me, this adversity is a large part of what makes Lincoln great.

Q: That dovetails nicely to my final question: What do you think of Lincoln?

LT: I am in awe of the man. He is one of the few true originals. As a writer, I notice especially his writing. Every time he wrote anything, even the merest note to a clerk, he put a stamp on it that is recognizably his. There is an agile strength and a love of logic and clarity in his writing, wedded to the rhythms of the King James Bible, that is beautiful. There is greatness in it.

But even more importantly, his political acumen—so at odds with his awkward appearance, as many men testified—was a thing to wonder at. That a man who called himself "an accidental instrument," with very little prestige or popularity, could overmaster the centripetal force of an entire nation of thirty million people and pull it back together again, and at the same time achieve emancipation, which most of the nation, even the North, was against, is a miracle of politics, politics in its very best sense.

Q: Thank you for your time, Mr. Tagg.

LT: You are welcome, thank you.

Photo by *Amanda Wilson*

I was born in Lincoln, Illinois. After living in the Land of Lincoln for eight years, my family moved to Dallas, Texas, where, as a high school senior, I won the city-wide high school extemporaneous writing contest in 1969. (It was easy. The prompt was "Describe a concert," and just the week before I had seen Jimi Hendrix for the first time—just after "Are You Experienced" came out. Security was lax in the 1960s, and after the show I jumped onstage and walked back to Jimi's dressing room, where I talked to Mitch Mitchell, his drummer.)

I attended the University of North Texas, graduating cum laude in Philosophy in two years and was awarded a teaching assistantship at the University of Texas. After one semester of graduate school I knew academia was not for me. I was more a musician—a bass player, singer, and songwriter.

I moved to California in 1978 with the band Uncle Rainbow to record under the aegis of Michael Hossack, one of the Doobie Brothers. In 1985, Brent Bourgeois and my band Bourgeois Tagg, was signed to Island Records. We recorded two albums and had two hits—"Mutual Surrender" and "I Don't Mind at All." We toured with Robert Palmer, Heart, Belinda Carlisle, and others.

After Bourgeois Tagg broke up in 1989 during the making of our third album, I played as a bass player and singer with Todd Rundgren and Hall and Oates. (My audition gig with Hall & Oates was in front of a million people at the Great Meadow in Central Park on the 20th Anniversary of Earth Day.) During the 1990s I was signed as a staff songwriter by Warner Chappell Music. My songs were recorded by Eddie Money, Kim Carnes, Cliff Richard, and others. I released two solo albums—"With a Skeleton Crew" and "Rover"—in Europe and America.

By the mid-90s I had a family, and the road had lost much of its allure. I became an English and drama teacher and Lead Teacher of the Arts Academy at Hiram Johnson High School in Sacramento, California. While I taught I began writing in my spare time. My first book, *The Generals of Gettysburg*, was published in 1998 by Savas Publishing, and the paper edition appeared a couple years later by Da Capo. It is still in print today. Right now I am finishing a book about generalship and the Battle of Shiloh.

Lincoln has long held a fascination for me, and I found the spectacular animosity against Lincoln irresistible as a subject.